A MANUAL OF PLAINSONG

FOR DIVINE SERVICE

CONTAINING

THE CANTICLES NOTED

THE PSALTER NOTED

TO GREGORIAN TONES

TOGETHER WITH

THE LITANY AND RESPONSES

A NEW EDITION

PREPARED BY

H. B. BRIGGS AND W. H. FRERE

UNDER THE GENERAL SUPERINTENDENCE OF

JOHN STAINER

(LATE PRESIDENT OF THE PLAINSONG AND MEDIÆVAL MUSIC SOCIETY)

The Rev. H. W. vanCouenhoven
St. Matthew's Rectory
Hallowell, Maine

LONDON: NOVELLO AND COMPANY, LIMITED.
NEW YORK: THE H. W. GRAY CO., SOLE AGENTS FOR THE U.S.A.
1902.

MADE IN ENGLAND.

MUSIC
M
2136.7
.M29
1902

PREFACE.

THE first edition of *The Psalter Noted* was published in 1849 under the supervision of the late Rev. Thomas Helmore, and secured for the Gregorian Tones a general recognition of their appropriateness for Divine worship. Subsequently Mr. Helmore's scheme was enlarged by the issue of *The Canticles Noted*, of *A Brief Directory*, and of three *Appendixes to the Psalter;* and the whole collection was issued in one volume under the title of *A Manual of Plainsong*. The Manual had also two companion books, one of Words only containing *The Canticles and Psalter Accented*, the other a collection of *Accompanying Harmonies*. Thus complete provision was made for the musical performance of the regular services of the Prayer Book. Practical objections, however, to the monotony of the recitation of several Psalms to one Tone without the relief of Antiphons, added to certain difficulties in the pointing, led to the issue of other Psalters which have competed with *The Psalter Noted*, but without obtaining, any of them, a marked supremacy; and nothing has been issued which covers the whole field so completely as Mr. Helmore's *Manual*.

Study of the Art of Plainsong during the last half century has, however, undergone something like a revolution; on every branch of the question new light has been thrown, and not least upon the principles of pointing. In consequence of repeated demands for a new edition of the *Manual*, the work of revision was entrusted to the late Sir John Stainer. He readily undertook the task, and called into collaboration Mr. H. B. Briggs and the Rev. W. H. Frere, with the result that before his death he had passed for the press the greater part of the revised proofs prepared by them for the new edition. He had also devoted much time to the consideration, with Mr. Shebbeare, of the Organ Accompaniments, so that the complete work may be considered as his last contribution to the music of the English Church.

His was not the only loss that this book had to undergo in the course of revision, for on the eve of its completion, Mr. Briggs was suddenly called to his rest. So the foregoing words which he had written about Sir John Stainer have now become his own epitaph. Without competing with Sir John Stainer in the wider domain of Church Music he had, in the narrower department of Plainsong, an influence and a competence which were unrivalled; and whatever merits this book may have are due almost entirely to him.

The *Manual* thus appears in a New Edition, revised in accordance with modern standards of taste and science; it does not cover quite so large a field as formerly, for it contains no music for the Holy Communion; but it has the same counterparts as before in the shape of *The Canticles and Psalter Accented*, and *The Accompanying Harmonies* prepared by Mr. Shebbeare, which include accompaniments for the Responses, *Te Deum* and Litany, as well as for the Tones.

INTRODUCTION TO THE PSALTER.

I. PRACTICAL INSTRUCTIONS
FOR ALL WHO USE THIS PSALTER.

THE Gregorian Tones provide for the musical recitation of the Psalms in the simplest possible manner. They are eight in number, corresponding with the eight Modes of Mediæval music-theory, and each of them consists of three chief parts:—

1. A *reciting note*, on which the greater part of each verse is said. This is in each case the dominant of the Mode.

2. A short melodic inflection before the colon, termed the *mediation*.

3. Another inflection at the close of the verse, termed the *ending*.

To these there is added, in certain cases, an opening phrase, called the *intonation*.

The mediations proper to each of the Tones are invariable, as are also the intonations; but there are various endings, each designed to correspond with the opening notes of the Antiphons which, properly, are always associated with the Tone. It is the Antiphons, indeed, which, strictly speaking, should determine which Tone is to be sung, and complete the Tone (which of itself more often than not is incomplete), and should thus serve as a melodic cadence in the Mode, or what in modern music would be called a *Coda*.

The forms of the Tones used at Salisbury have been adopted in this revision of the Psalter, and the pointing is based on the principles followed in the palmy days of Plainsong, and preserved in the early manuscripts. The *rationale* of this system is explained in the recent works of the Benedictines of Solesmes. The application of it to an English text was first satisfactorily made by the Rev. G. H. Palmer in his *Sarum Psalter*, and the rules explained by him in the Introduction to that work mainly govern the pointing in this volume. Occasional divergences in detail are due partly to the exigencies of modern pronunciation, but, on the other hand, partly to a stricter adherence to mediæval principles, as this appeared to be more conducive to simplicity and congregational singing, than the use of modifications adopted with a view to extreme perfection in rendering.

To attain a correct method in chanting, a choir should first deliberately and naturally recite a psalm in monotone; then, setting it to a simple Tone—*e.g.*, Tone V.—they should add the inflections of the mediation and the ending in exactly the same style and rhythm as were used in the monotone, bearing in mind the following rules:—

1. Do not hurry the syllables sung on the reciting note, or drag those which fall to the inflections.
2. Give every syllable its proper rhythmical accent and a very distinct enunciation, with the full value of a syllable to those words which end in "ed,' such as "blessèd," "promisèd," &c.
3. Do not make any gap between the reciting note and the beginning of the inflection.
4. Take a good breath at the colon.
5. Recite the whole *mezza voce* rather than sing it.
6. Sing the last note of the mediation and of the ending, especially the latter quite softly.

The first half-verse should be precented, then the whole choir or the whole of the side of the choir should join in at the colon : the succeeding verses should be sung alternately either from side to side, or men's voices alternating with boys' voices, or Chanters with full choir. There is no authority for singing the verses of the *Gloria Patri* full.

The music is all diatonic except for the occasional use of the B♭: the C clef, 𝄡, and F clef, 𝄢, indicate the position of those notes upon the stave of four lines. The Tone is not necessarily sung at the normal pitch, and when it is transposed these clefs of course represent respectively the key-note or the fourth of any key in which it may be agreeable to sing the Tone. The forms of the notes indicate no time-value whatever, for this is entirely determined by the rhythm of the words. When two or more notes are combined in a group it is the first note of the group that is accented, but it is probable that the opposite accent is intended in the peculiar form of group ♫ which occurs in I. 8 and III. 5.

II. THE PRINCIPLES OF THE POINTING.

1. The Psalms were invariably chanted in former times from unpointed manuscripts, and the principle that governed the pointing was that the melodic inflection should be deferred to as near the close of the sentence as possible. The musical form of the endings is based on the ordinary accentuation of the close of a psalm-verse. In the great majority of cases, in English as well as in Latin, an accent will be found on either the penultimate or the antepenultimate syllable,—

e.g.: with holy wórship.
dwell together in únity.

The former, the trochaic ending, was taken as the model for the musical phrase, and consequently the last note (or note-group) but one of the ending is normally accented, because it falls to the accented syllable of the final trochee. If, however, the ending is dactylic, *i.e.*, if the accent occurs on the antepenultimate syllable, there is a redundant penultimate syllable which must be filled in on some convenient note. (*See* □ in the Tables.) Observe that this must not be done by splitting up the penultimate member of the ending should it consist of a group of two notes, for such groups are always kept intact; but the few three-note groups which occur may be split into two, so as to accommodate the redundant syllable

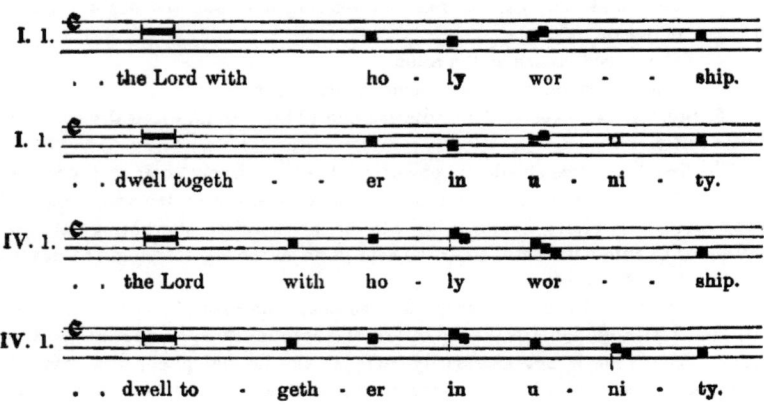

It is only in exceptional cases in English (about eight per cent. against half as many in the Latin) that the latest accent in the verse occurs so far back as the fourth syllable from the end, *e.g.*, *téstimonies, Náme of the Lord.* Then the difficulty has to be met as in parallel cases in the Latin, viz., by treating the accented penultimate note of the ending as *rallentando* rather than *accented*, and singing to it the penultimate syllable, even though that be unaccented, the effect of an accent being avoided by singing the weak syllable softly. The alternative of singing the last three syllables to the final note is impossible, as the over-weighting of this essentially weak note completely destroys the musical form of the Tone.

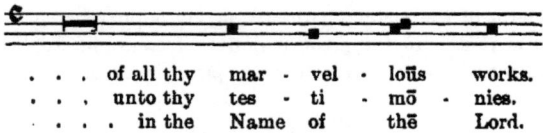

```
. . . of all thy    mar - vel - lous      works.
. . . unto thy     tes - ti - mō -       nies.
. . . in the      Name   of     thē      Lord.
```

The principle which forbids the splitting up of a note-group equally forbids the combination of two distinct members of an inflection by a slur. This rule is only subject to exception when the main accented syllable of the ending is preceded by another accented syllable following on two that have no accent, *e.g.*, *such as are trúe héarted*, where two notes of the inflection must be grouped on *true*. It is not necessary to apply this exceptional treatment to the sixth tone.

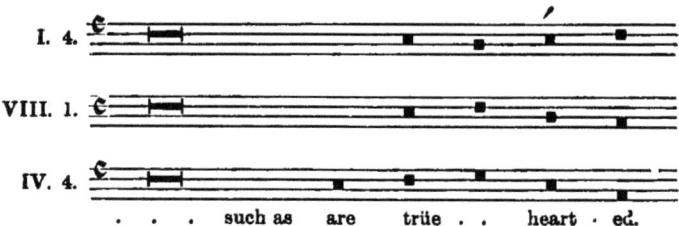

. . . such as are trúe . . heart · ed.

2. Beyond the accent on the penultimate note or member of the ending, which is common to all Tones, the Fifth and Seventh Tones have a second fixed musical accent in the endings. In these the inflection begins four places from the end on a rising note, and therefore demands an accented syllable, while in all the others the inflection begins on a note which is lower than the reciting note, and is consequently equally well suited either to an accented or unaccented syllable. In these latter the notes preceding the penultimate will naturally accommodate themselves to, and take the accentuation of, any syllables that happen to fall to them. But in the Fifth and Seventh Tones an accented syllable must be allotted to the first note of the ending, because it is higher than the reciting note. There is no difficulty in this if the rhythm at this point is trochaic—

e.g. : . . . Lord with | hóly | wórship. (Double trochaic.)

. . . midst a- | -móng thine | énemies. (Trochaic, dactylic.)

But if it is dactylic there will be, as before, a redundant syllable to be filled in :—

e.g. : . . . people im- | -ágine a | vaín thing. (Dactylic, trochaic.)

. . . dwell to- | -géther in | únity. (Double dactylic.)

This accent may thus be found as far back as the sixth syllable from the end in a double dactylic ending, but in no case can it be set farther back than that. Musical examples of this will be seen in the appended tables.

3. The mediations of the First and Sixth Tones consist of the fall of a tone on the penultimate syllable before the colon, whether accented or not, and a return to the reciting note on the last syllable. The pointing of these is therefore quite uniform, and presents no difficulty. The mediations of the Second, Fifth, and Eighth Tones rise a tone, and this rise must be set to the accented syllable nearest the colon, with a return to the reciting note on the unaccented syllables following, should there be any. The mediation of the Fourth Tone is somewhat similar; the accented note, however, is preceded by two notes, but since these do not rise above the reciting note, they have no special requirements, but accommodate themselves to any syllables which may fall to them.

The mediations of the Third and Seventh Tones contain four notes, and in each case the first of these requires an accented syllable, because it is higher than the reciting note. With regard to the other notes the treatment of the two Tones differs. In the Third Tone the penultimate note, being lower than the reciting note, is sung, as in the First and Sixth Tones, to the penultimate syllable, whatever its accentuation, and any redundant syllables, even if one be accented, are filled in on the preceding note, which is the same as the reciting note. In the Seventh Tone the penultimate note, which in this case is the same as the reciting note, requires an accented or quasi-accented syllable, so that the preceding note is only repeated in the case of a redundant unaccented syllable.

When the text does not admit of the use of the full form of these two mediations, the *abrupt* form is adopted, in which the non-essential notes are omitted (*see* ◊ in the Tables). In all the Tones, if the half-verse does not contain enough syllables, the mediation may be omitted entirely when the intonation is used. The same principle of omission also applies to the endings, only such notes being used as suffice for the syllables in the half-verse.

4. The notes of intonations in the Psalm-tones are never grouped on syllables; if there are not enough syllables the intonation may be shortened. In some cases the intonation is altogether omitted.

5. The florid forms of the Tones which belong to the Canticles consist of the same four parts as the simpler forms which are used for the Psalms. The intonations and mediations are extensions of the simple forms, and in the second half of the verse the endings are the same, but the reciting note has a slight decoration on an accented syllable if the text is of sufficient length

6. The *Tonus Peregrinus* is of a more elaborate character than the ordinary Tones, but is pointed on the same principle; except that, though the first note of the mediation is lower than the reciting note, it is always accented, because the next and final note is still lower. Where extreme simplicity of rendering is desired the second half of the verse may be begun at once on the G, the second intonation being omitted.

7. It may be well to remark that the accentuation of the ending of the Second Tone is different from that which, by some accident, is current in England. Also that *World withoút end, Amen*, is thus accented as the equivalent of *seculórun Amen*.

8. Only the simpler endings have been used in this book, but in case any should prove too ornate the same pointing can be applied to another form of the same ending.

III. THE METHOD OF CHANTING

The structure of the Tones shows that the Psalms are intended to be chanted to them almost exactly in the style in which they would be read in monotone, but as the same time it suggests certain musical refinements in the rendering. The trochaic close implies that there should be, as a rule, a *rallentando e diminuendo* at the end of every Psalm-verse, and the same rule will affect the mediation to the extent of making its final syllable more or less *piano*. This rule is specially to be observed where that syllable, though weak accentually, is, through being a monosyllable, allotted to the rising note of the abrupt mediations of the Second, Fourth, Fifth, and Eighth Tones—*e.g., and ever shall be*. Unless these final monosyllables are sung softly as compared with the preceding syllables the effect will be given of a false accent, but by care in this point the false effect may be avoided. The division of the Psalm-verse into two parts also suggests that a definite pause should be made at the colon long enough to cause a cessation of all vocal sound in the building, whatever its size. The antiphonal singing of the verses implies, on the other hand, that there need be no more interval between them than is necessary to make the alternation of voices clear, and to prevent the effect of overlapping, or the drowning of the *sostenuto* on the last note of one verse by the beginning of the next.

The recitation of a Psalm in monotone distinctly and deliberately, but yet naturally, will show that the words have a rhythm of their own, rather more regular than that which would be produced if they were read in a speaking voice, but quite distinct from the duple or triple time of modern measured music. When the Psalms are chanted, the music must therefore follow this rhythm, so that both recitation and inflection will be in the same *tempo*. To attain this, pains should be taken that the words on the reciting note are not sung too quickly, nor those on the inflection too slowly, and that there is no hesitation in beginning the inflection. If the recitation is taken too quickly there will be an unconscious effort to complete the rhythm by a pause before the inflection. But if it be deliberate and rhythmical it will flow easily into the inflection, the rhythm of which will be the same as that of the recitation; in other words, the inflection must be begun without the slightest gap immediately after the last note of the recitation. In order to assist this even flow of the words and obviate any pause at the end of the recitation, a few of the reciting notes are in this edition inserted *in extenso* before the mediations and endings.

When the Psalms are correctly chanted, it will be found that a regular rhythmical movement is created, which may be represented by a series of beats, which will coincide with many, though not all, of the accented syllables in the verse. Such beat, however, is distinct from a time-beat in measured music in being *indivisible*, insomuch that, though it may contain two or three syllables or notes, it cannot be divided into two, three, or four equal or proportionate parts. In the recitation, moreover, though a certain number of syllables may be covered by the duration of two beats, the second of these will not necessarily fall exactly on an accented syllable. In the inflections, however, if a simple syllabic Tone, such as Tone I. 4, be chosen, the last syllable of the mediation and the next preceding accented syllable will coincide with two of these beats. A space equivalent to two beats will then represent the pause signified by the colon, and the next beat will fall to the first accented syllable in the second half of the verse. The penultimate note of the ending will fall to one beat, the last note to another, and after a *sostenuto* of one beat, the next verse should be begun.

The pause of one beat at a semicolon is marked by a half-bar, and where a quick breath is necessary, an asterisk is inserted in the text. No pauses should be made at commas, as the effect intended by the punctuation should be obtained by slightly sustaining the preceding syllable.

All the Tones do not conform exactly to the above rules of rhythm, but when the chanting of a simple Tone has been perfected, it will be easy to apply the principles to the more elaborate Tones and endings. Good chanting is above all perfectly natural, and there should be nothing forced either about the pitch, the rhythm, or the *tempo*, which must vary according to the size of the building, the number of the singers, and similar conditions.

H. B. B.
W. H. F.

TABLES OF THE MEDIATIONS AND ENDINGS.

MEDIATIONS.

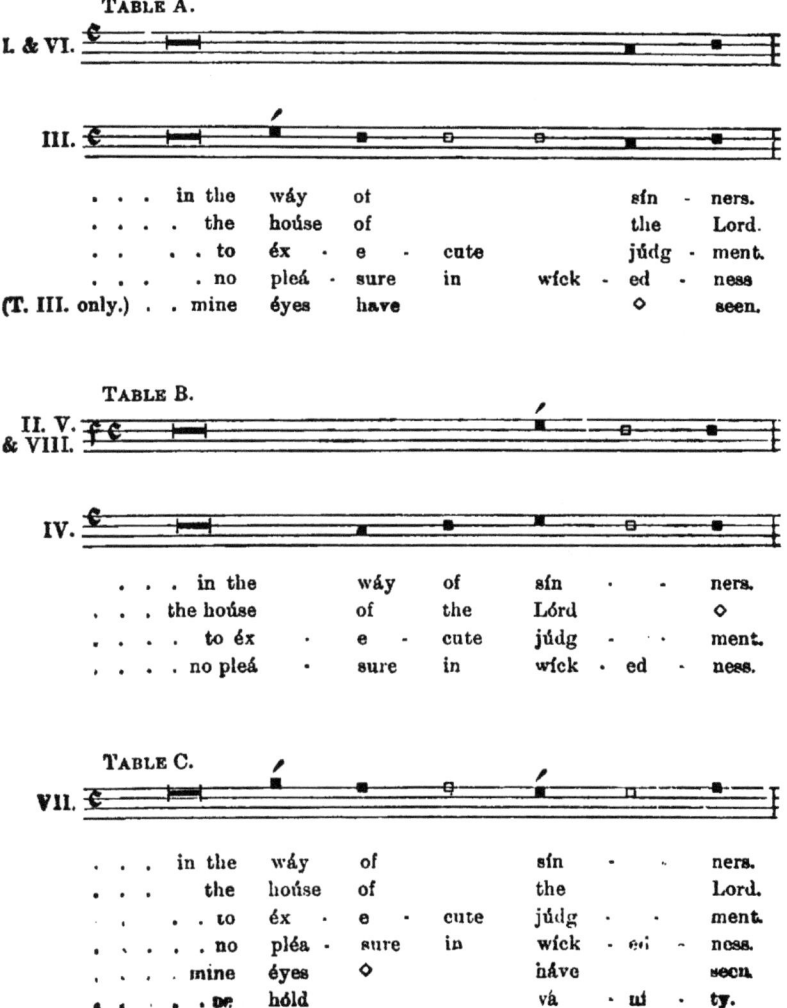

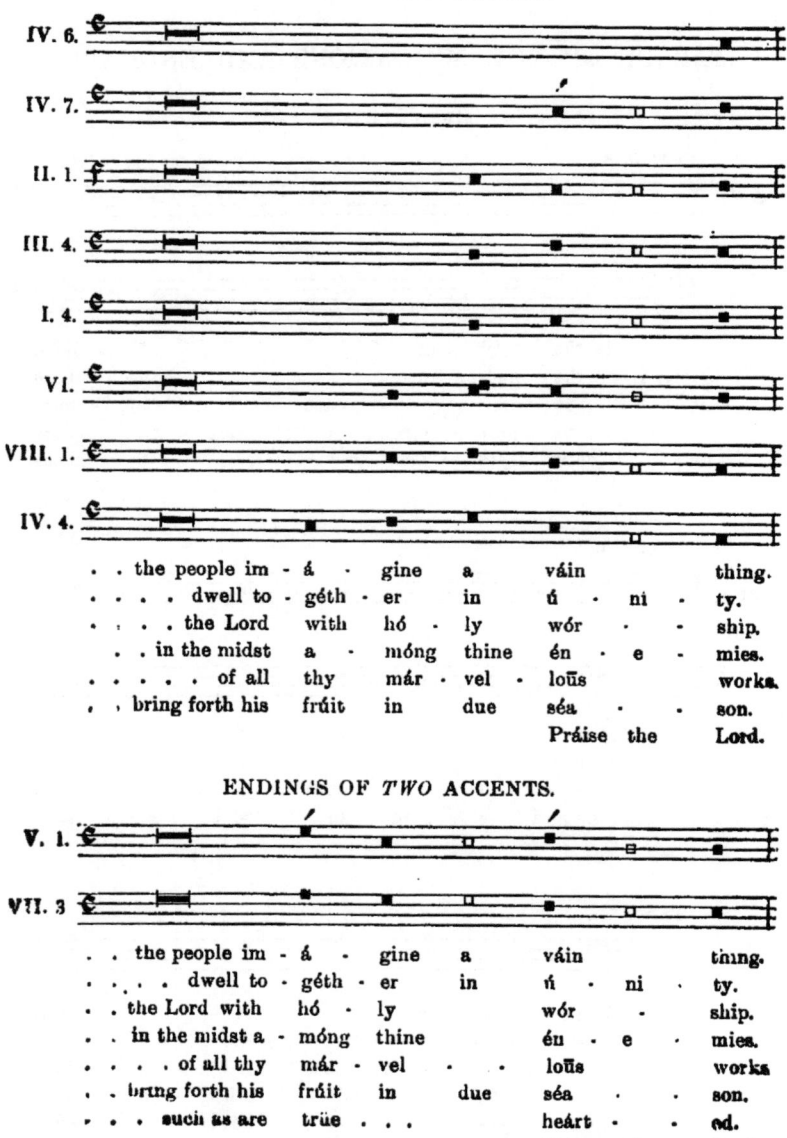

THE TONES OF THE PSALMS.

TONE I.

This is the in-to-na-tion of the First Tone,

and this is the me-di-a-tion: and this the first end-ing.

and this the sec-ond end-ing. and this the third end-ing.

and this the fourth end-ing. and this the fifth end-ing,

and this the sixth end-ing. and this the seventh end-ing.

and this the eighth end-ing. and this the ninth end-ing.

THE SOLEMN FORM FOR *BENEDICTUS* AND *MAGNIFICAT*.

Bless-ed be the Lord God of Is-ra-el: for he hath vis-it-ed, &c.
My soul — doth mag-ni-fy the Lord: and my spi-rit, &c.

TONE II.

This is the in-to-na-tion of the Sec-ond Tone,

and this is the me-di-a-tion: and this the first end-ing.

and this the sec-ond end-ing.

THE TONES OF THE PSALMS.

THE SOLEMN FORM FOR *BENEDICTUS* AND *MAGNIFICAT*.

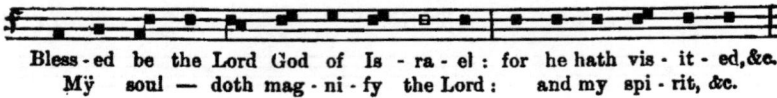

Bless-ed be the Lord God of Is-ra-el: for he hath vis-it-ed,&c.
My soul — doth mag-ni-fy the Lord: and my spi-rit, &c.

TONE III.

This is the in-to-na-tion of the Third Tone,
and this is the me-di-a-tion: and this the first end-ing.
and this the sec-ond end-ing. and this the third end-ing.
and this the fourth end-ing. and this the fifth end-ing.
and this the sixth end-ing.

THE SOLEMN FORM FOR *BENEDICTUS* AND *MAGNIFICAT*.

Bless-ed be, &c.
My soul doth, &c.

TONE IV.

This is the in-to-na-tion of the Fourth Tone,
and this is the me-di-a-tion: and this is the first end-ing.
and this is the sec-ond end-ing. and this is the third end-ing.
and this is the fourth end-ing. and this is the fifth end-ing.

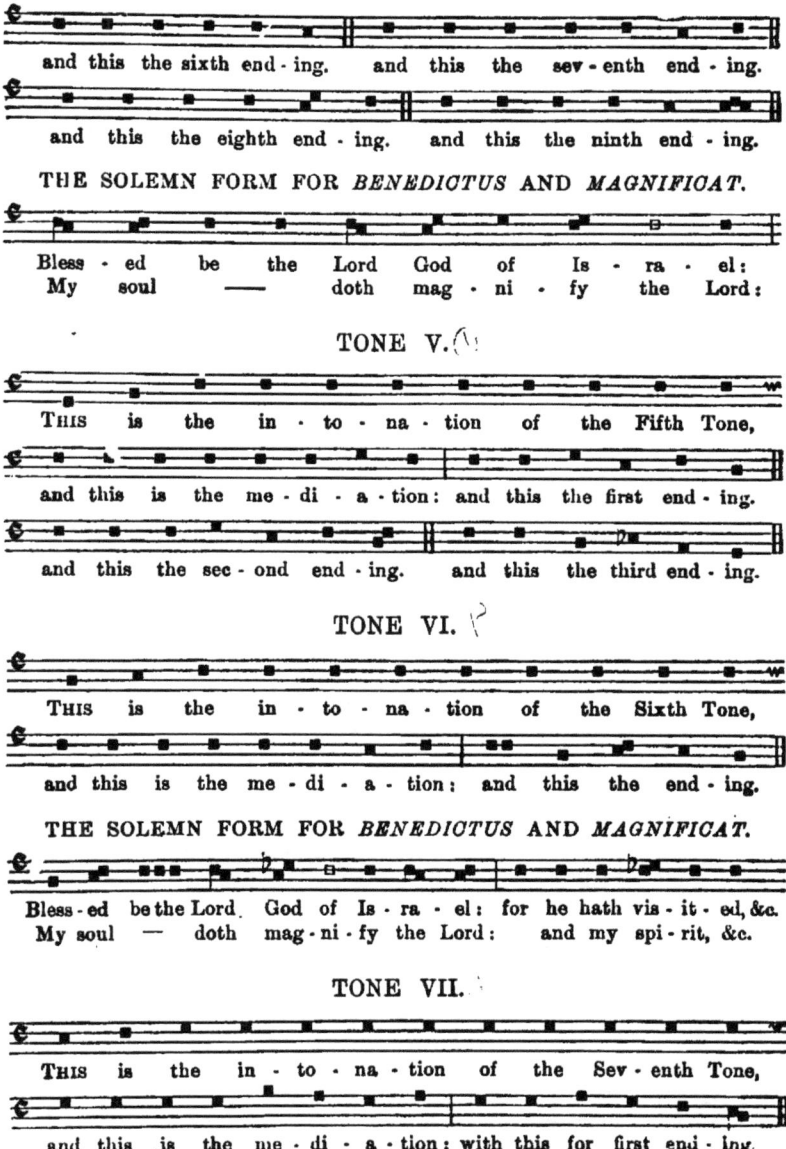

THE TONES OF THE PSALMS.

THE SOLEMN FORM FOR *BENEDICTUS* AND *MAGNIFICAT*.

TONE VIII.

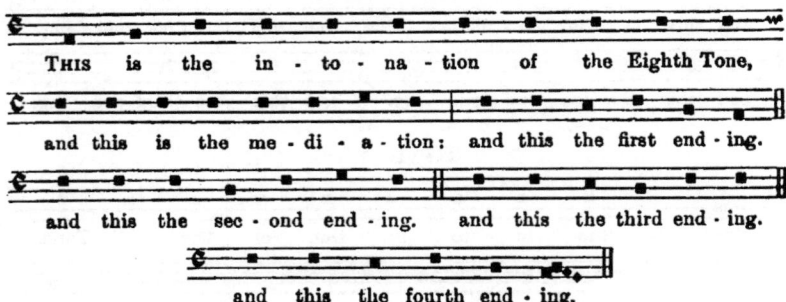

THE SOLEMN FORM FOR *BENEDICTUS* AND *MAGNIFICAT*.

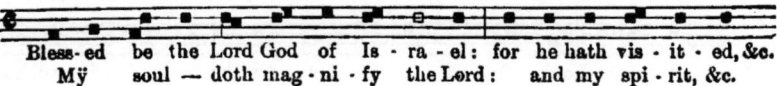

THE IRREGULAR OR *PEREGRINE* TONE.

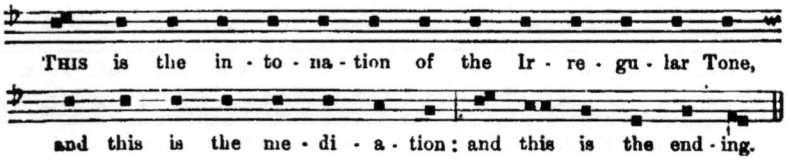

THE VERSICLES AND RESPONSES

AT MATTINS AND EVENSONG.

The introductory matter preceding the ℣. O Lord, open thou our lips, should be said in a low voice, without note

The opening Versicles are sung as follows and at any pitch which is convenient.

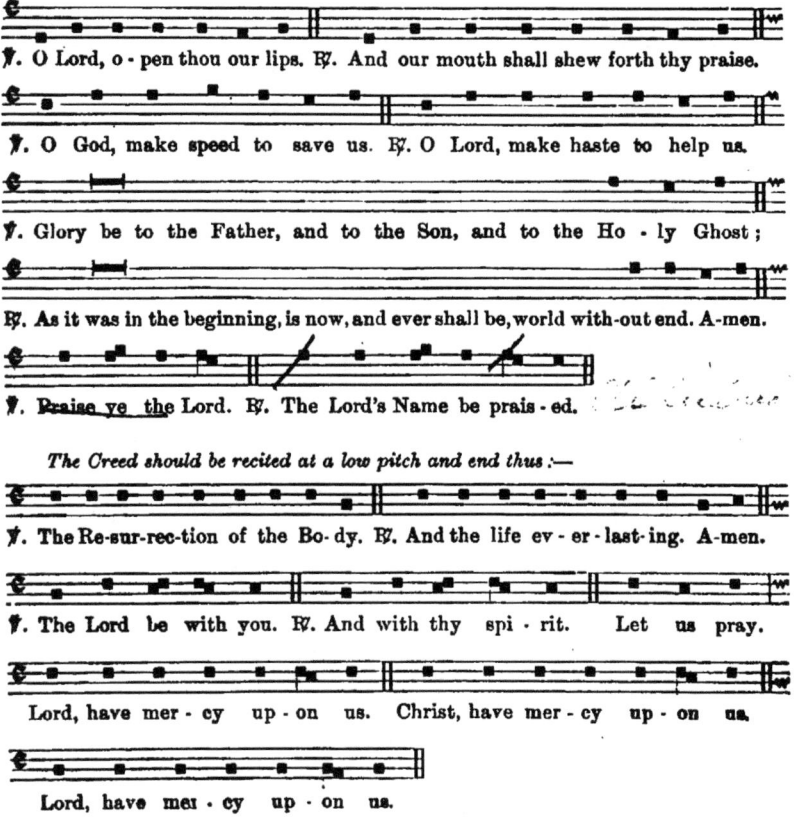

℣. O Lord, o-pen thou our lips. ℟. And our mouth shall shew forth thy praise.

℣. O God, make speed to save us. ℟. O Lord, make haste to help us.

℣. Glory be to the Father, and to the Son, and to the Ho-ly Ghost;

℟. As it was in the beginning, is now, and ever shall be, world with-out end. A-men.

℣. Praise ye the Lord. ℟. The Lord's Name be prais-ed.

The Creed should be recited at a low pitch and end thus:—

℣. The Re-sur-rec-tion of the Bo-dy. ℟. And the life ev-er-last-ing. A-men.

℣. The Lord be with you. ℟. And with thy spi-rit. Let us pray.

Lord, have mer-cy up-on us. Christ, have mer-cy up-on us.

Lord, have mer-cy up-on us.

(xvii)

VERSICLES AND RESPONSES.

The Lord's Prayer should be recited like the Creed and end thus:—

℣. And lead us not in-to temp-ta-tion, ℟. But de-liv-er us from e-vil. A-men.

℣. O Lord, shew thy mer-cy up-on us. ℟. And grant us thy sal-va-tion.

℣. O Lord, save the King. ℟. And mer-ci-ful-ly hear us when we call up-on thee.

℣. En-due thy ministers with righteousness. ℟. And make thy chosen people joyful.

℣. O Lord, save thy peo-ple. ℟. And bless thine in-he-ri-tance.

℣. Give peace in our time, O Lord. ℟. Be-cause there is none oth-er that fight-eth

for us, but on-ly thou, O God. ℣. O God, make clean our heart with-in us.

℟. And take not thy ho-ly Spi-rit from us.

At the Collect there is only one inflexion, at the close.

Collect of the Day.

Al-might-y God . . . now and ev-er. ℟. A-men.
world without end.

Other Collects have one of these two inflexions, with Amen as above.

Je-sus Christ our Lord.   Je-sus Christ, our Sa-viour.
Sa-viour, Je-sus Christ.

The Five Prayers should be said without note.

(xviii)

THE CANTICLES.

MORNING PRAYER

VENITE, EXULTEMUS DOMINO. —*Psalm* xcv.

1st Tone, 1st Ending.

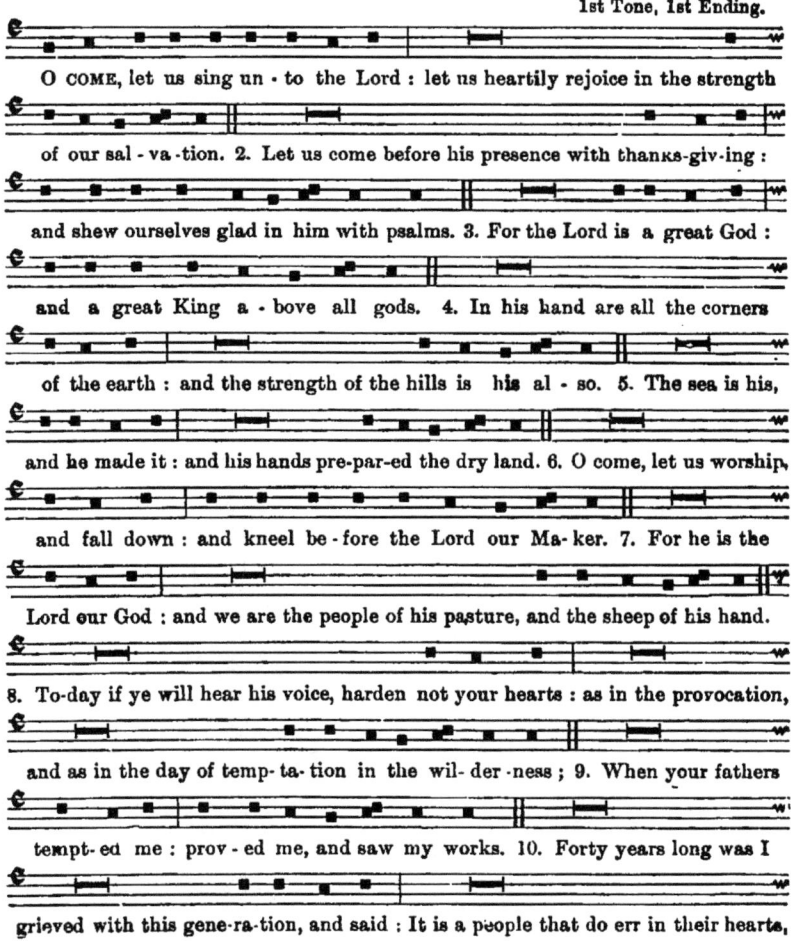

O COME, let us sing un-to the Lord : let us heartily rejoice in the strength of our sal-va-tion. 2. Let us come before his presence with thanks-giv-ing : and shew ourselves glad in him with psalms. 3. For the Lord is a great God : and a great King a-bove all gods. 4. In his hand are all the corners of the earth : and the strength of the hills is his al-so. 5. The sea is his, and he made it : and his hands pre-par-ed the dry land. 6. O come, let us worship, and fall down : and kneel be-fore the Lord our Ma-ker. 7. For he is the Lord our God : and we are the people of his pasture, and the sheep of his hand. 8. To-day if ye will hear his voice, harden not your hearts : as in the provocation, and as in the day of temp-ta-tion in the wil-der-ness ; 9. When your fathers tempt-ed me : prov-ed me, and saw my works. 10. Forty years long was I grieved with this gene-ra-tion, and said : It is a people that do err in their hearts,

MORNING PRAYER.

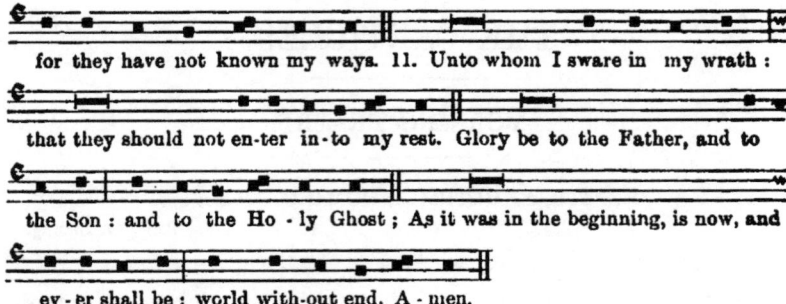

for they have not known my ways. 11. Unto whom I sware in my wrath :

that they should not en-ter in-to my rest. Glory be to the Father, and to

the Son : and to the Ho - ly Ghost ; As it was in the beginning, is now, and

ev - er shall be : world with-out end. A - men.

VENITE, EXULTEMUS DOMINO.—*Psalm* xcv.

5th Tone, 1st Ending.

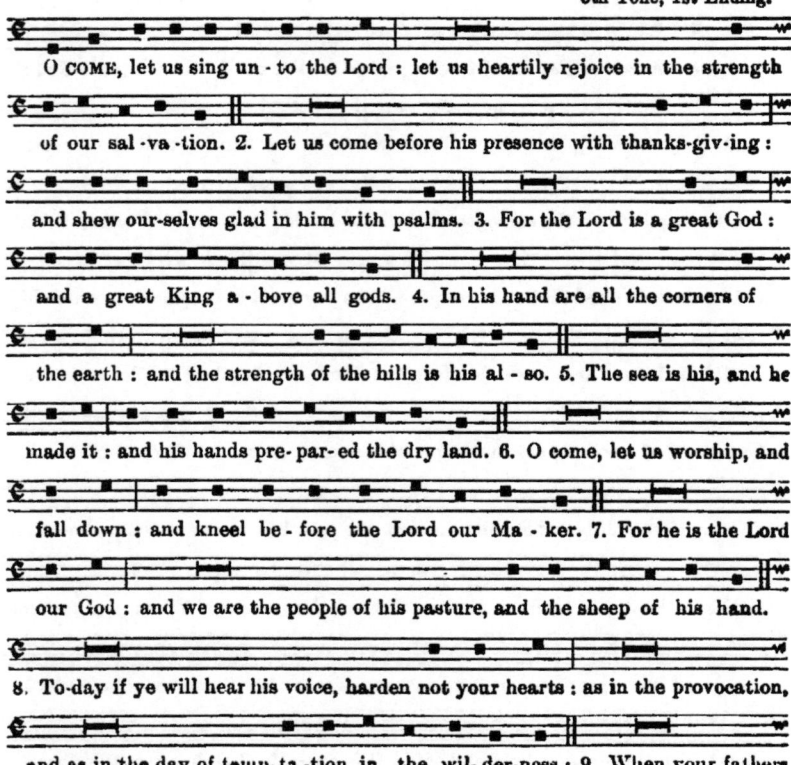

O COME, let us sing un - to the Lord : let us heartily rejoice in the strength

of our sal -va -tion. 2. Let us come before his presence with thanks-giv-ing :

and shew our-selves glad in him with psalms. 3. For the Lord is a great God :

and a great King a - bove all gods. 4. In his hand are all the corners of

the earth : and the strength of the hills is his al - so. 5. The sea is his, and he

made it : and his hands pre-par-ed the dry land. 6. O come, let us worship, and

fall down ; and kneel be - fore the Lord our Ma - ker. 7. For he is the Lord

our God : and we are the people of his pasture, and the sheep of his hand.

8. To-day if ye will hear his voice, harden not your hearts : as in the provocation,

and as in the day of temp-ta-tion in the wil-der-ness ; 9. When your fathers

(xx)

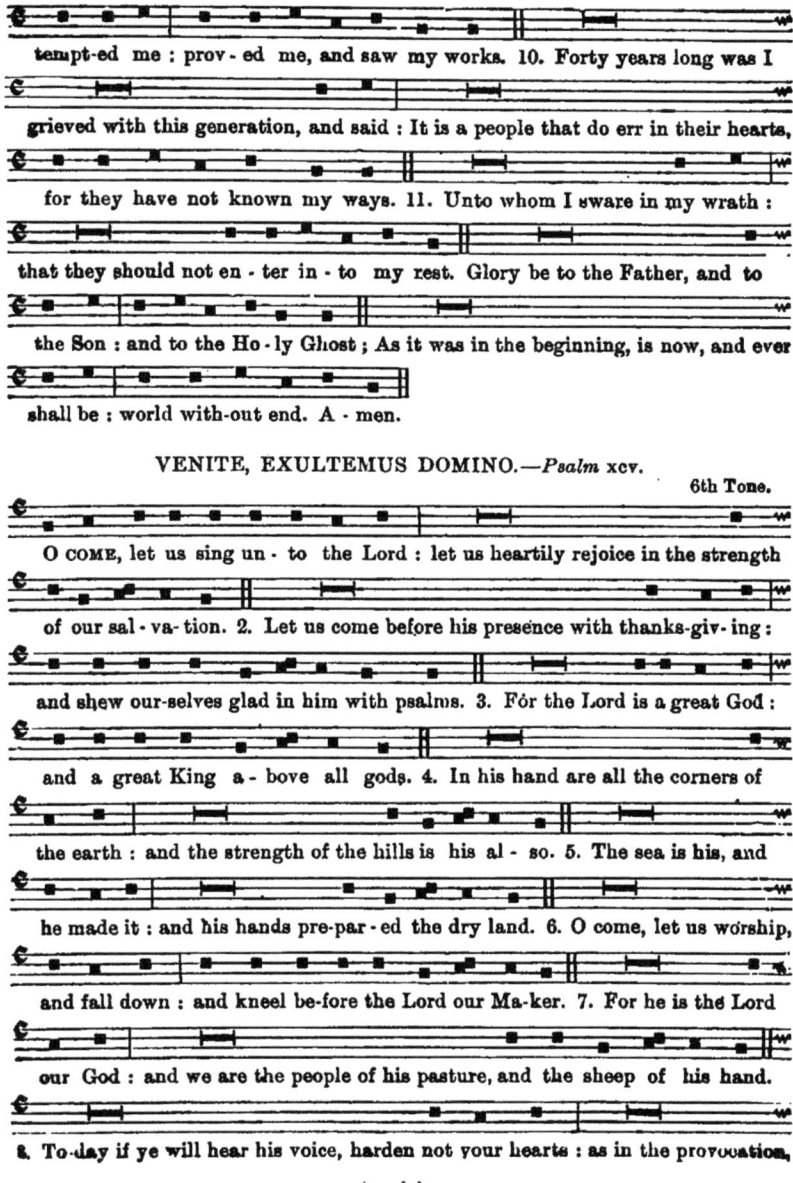

MORNING PRAYER.

tempt-ed me : prov-ed me, and saw my works. 10. Forty years long was I grieved with this generation, and said : It is a people that do err in their hearts, for they have not known my ways. 11. Unto whom I sware in my wrath : that they should not en-ter in-to my rest. Glory be to the Father, and to the Son : and to the Ho-ly Ghost ; As it was in the beginning, is now, and ever shall be : world with-out end. A-men.

VENITE, EXULTEMUS DOMINO.—*Psalm* xcv.

6th Tone.

O COME, let us sing un-to the Lord : let us heartily rejoice in the strength of our sal-va-tion. 2. Let us come before his presence with thanks-giv-ing : and shew our-selves glad in him with psalms. 3. For the Lord is a great God : and a great King a-bove all gods. 4. In his hand are all the corners of the earth : and the strength of the hills is his al-so. 5. The sea is his, and he made it : and his hands pre-par-ed the dry land. 6. O come, let us worship, and fall down : and kneel be-fore the Lord our Ma-ker. 7. For he is the Lord our God : and we are the people of his pasture, and the sheep of his hand. 8. To-day if ye will hear his voice, harden not your hearts : as in the provocation,

MORNING PRAYER.

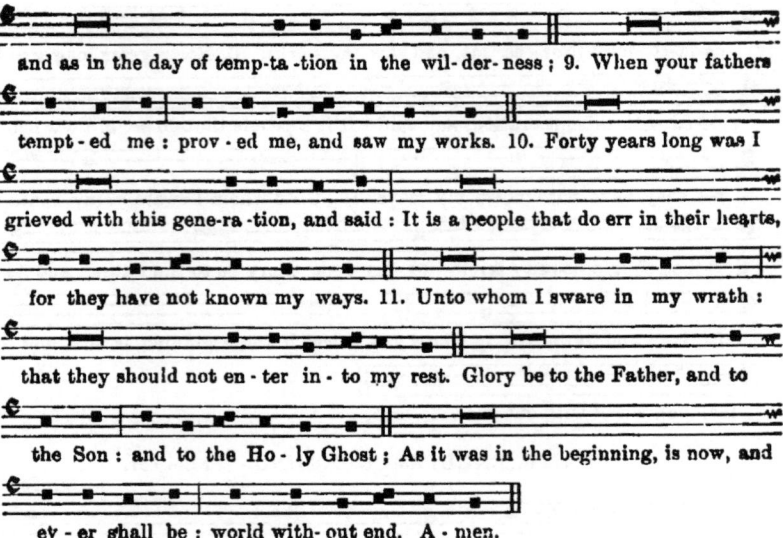

and as in the day of temp-ta-tion in the wil-der-ness; 9. When your fathers tempt-ed me : prov-ed me, and saw my works. 10. Forty years long was I grieved with this gene-ra-tion, and said : It is a people that do err in their hearts, for they have not known my ways. 11. Unto whom I sware in my wrath : that they should not en-ter in-to my rest. Glory be to the Father, and to the Son : and to the Ho-ly Ghost; As it was in the beginning, is now, and ev-er shall be : world with-out end. A-men.

VENITE, EXULTEMUS DOMINO.—*Psalm* xcv.

7th Tone, 1st Ending.

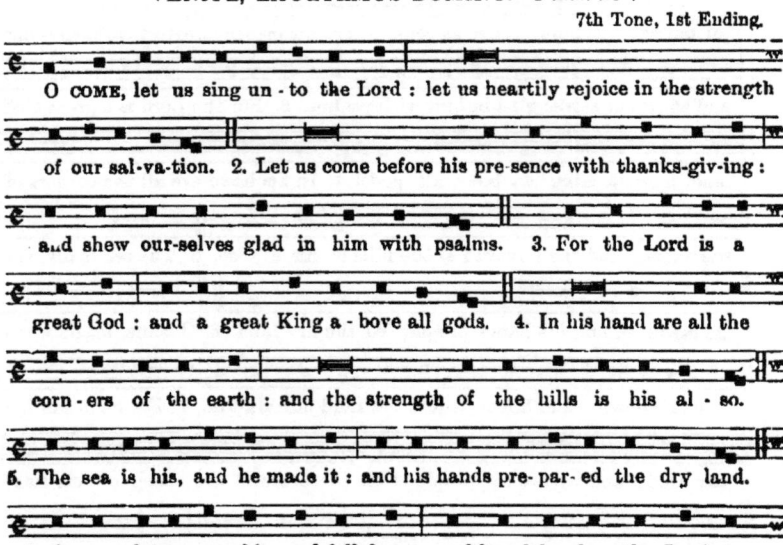

O COME, let us sing un-to the Lord : let us heartily rejoice in the strength of our sal-va-tion. 2. Let us come before his pre-sence with thanks-giv-ing : and shew our-selves glad in him with psalms. 3. For the Lord is a great God : and a great King a-bove all gods. 4. In his hand are all the corn-ers of the earth : and the strength of the hills is his al-so. 5. The sea is his, and he made it : and his hands pre-par-ed the dry land. 6. O come, let us wor-ship, and fall down : and kneel be-fore the Lord our

(xxii)

MORNING PRAYER.

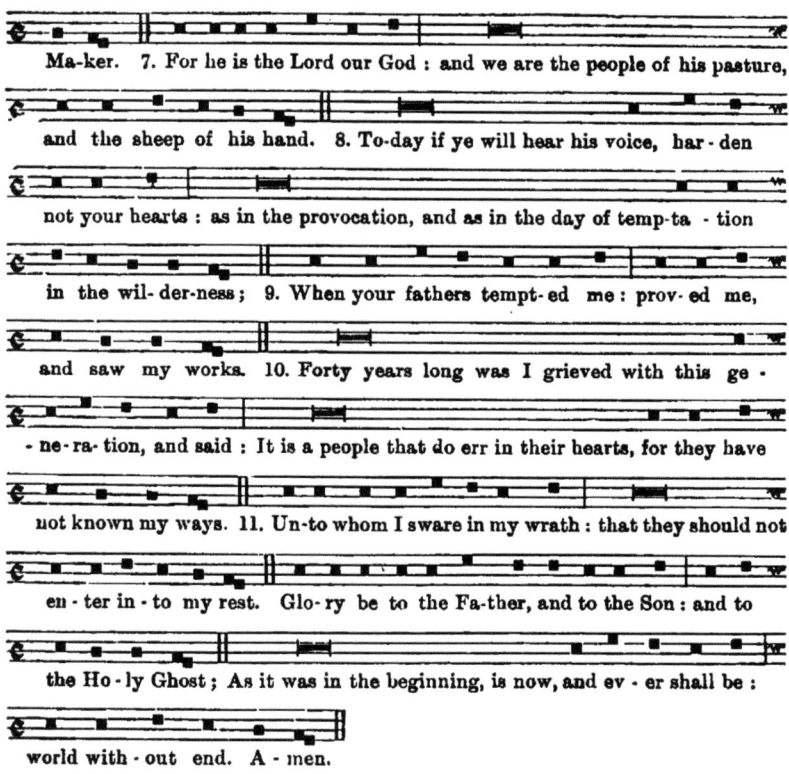

Ma-ker. 7. For he is the Lord our God : and we are the people of his pasture, and the sheep of his hand. 8. To-day if ye will hear his voice, har-den not your hearts : as in the provocation, and as in the day of temp-ta-tion in the wil-der-ness; 9. When your fathers tempt-ed me : prov-ed me, and saw my works. 10. Forty years long was I grieved with this ge- -ne-ra-tion, and said : It is a people that do err in their hearts, for they have not known my ways. 11. Un-to whom I sware in my wrath : that they should not en-ter in-to my rest. Glo-ry be to the Fa-ther, and to the Son : and to the Ho-ly Ghost; As it was in the beginning, is now, and ev-er shall be : world with-out end. A-men.

TE DEUM LAUDAMUS.

8th Tone, 1st Ending.

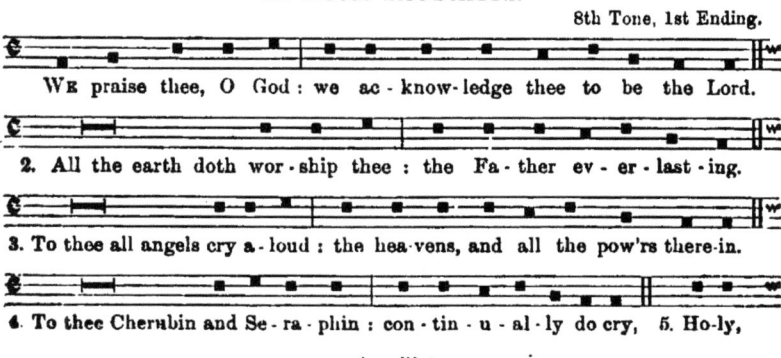

WE praise thee, O God : we ac-know-ledge thee to be the Lord.

2. All the earth doth wor-ship thee : the Fa-ther ev-er-last-ing.

3. To thee all angels cry a-loud : the hea-vens, and all the pow'rs there-in.

4. To thee Cherubin and Se-ra-phin : con-tin-u-al-ly do cry, 5. Ho-ly,

MORNING PRAYER.

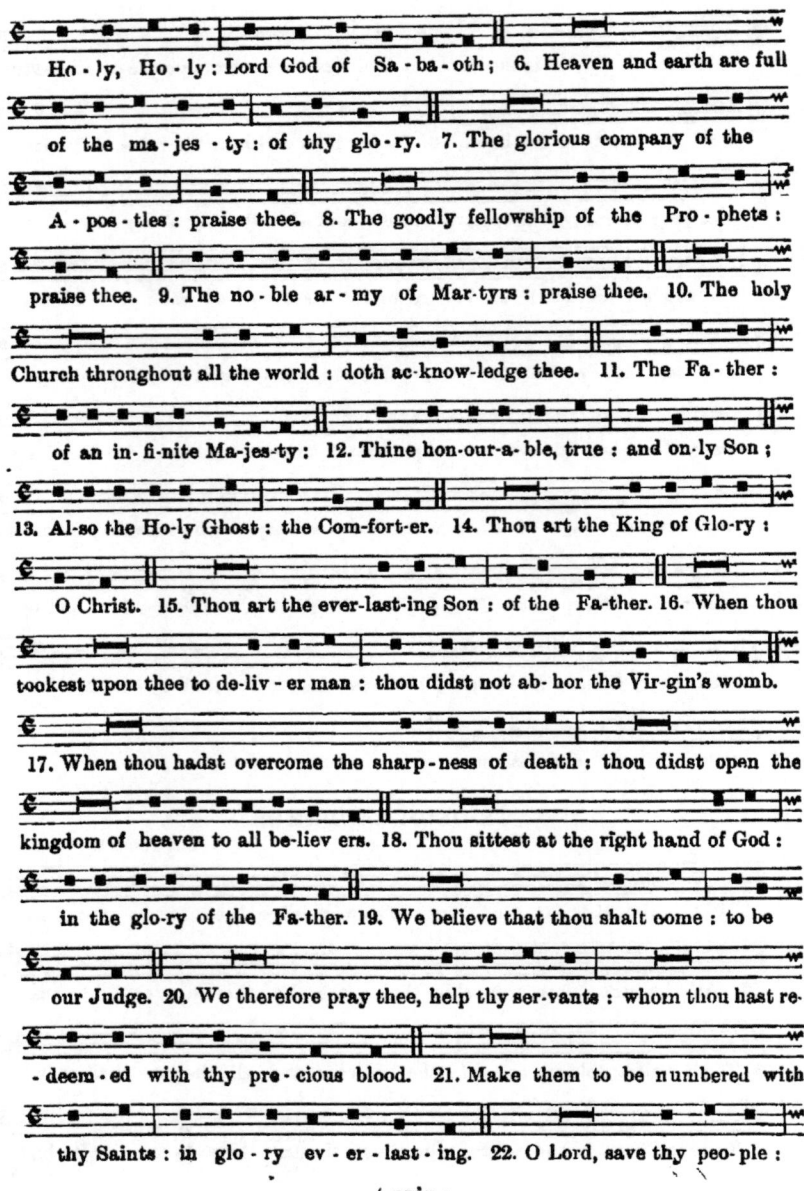

Ho-ly, Ho-ly: Lord God of Sa-ba-oth; 6. Heaven and earth are full of the ma-jes-ty: of thy glo-ry. 7. The glorious company of the A-pos-tles: praise thee. 8. The goodly fellowship of the Pro-phets: praise thee. 9. The no-ble ar-my of Mar-tyrs: praise thee. 10. The holy Church throughout all the world: doth ac-know-ledge thee. 11. The Fa-ther: of an in-fi-nite Ma-jes-ty: 12. Thine hon-our-a-ble, true: and on-ly Son; 13. Al-so the Ho-ly Ghost: the Com-fort-er. 14. Thou art the King of Glo-ry: O Christ. 15. Thou art the ever-last-ing Son: of the Fa-ther. 16. When thou tookest upon thee to de-liv-er man: thou didst not ab-hor the Vir-gin's womb. 17. When thou hadst overcome the sharp-ness of death: thou didst open the kingdom of heaven to all be-liev-ers. 18. Thou sittest at the right hand of God: in the glo-ry of the Fa-ther. 19. We believe that thou shalt come: to be our Judge. 20. We therefore pray thee, help thy ser-vants: whom thou hast re--deem-ed with thy pre-cious blood. 21. Make them to be numbered with thy Saints: in glo-ry ev-er-last-ing. 22. O Lord, save thy peo-ple:

MORNING PRAYER.

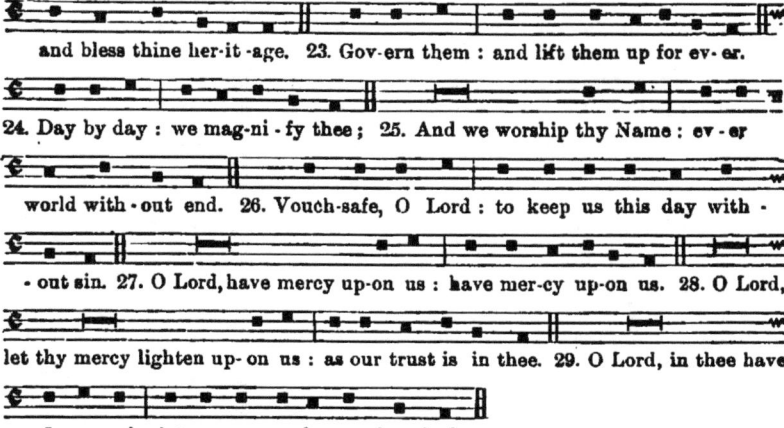

and bless thine her-it-age. 23. Gov-ern them : and lift them up for ev-er. 24. Day by day : we mag-ni-fy thee ; 25. And we worship thy Name : ev-er world with-out end. 26. Vouch-safe, O Lord : to keep us this day with--out sin. 27. O Lord, have mercy up-on us : have mer-cy up-on us. 28. O Lord, let thy mercy lighten up-on us : as our trust is in thee. 29. O Lord, in thee have I trust-ed : let me nev-er be con-found-ed.

TE DEUM LAUDAMUS.

Authentic Melody.

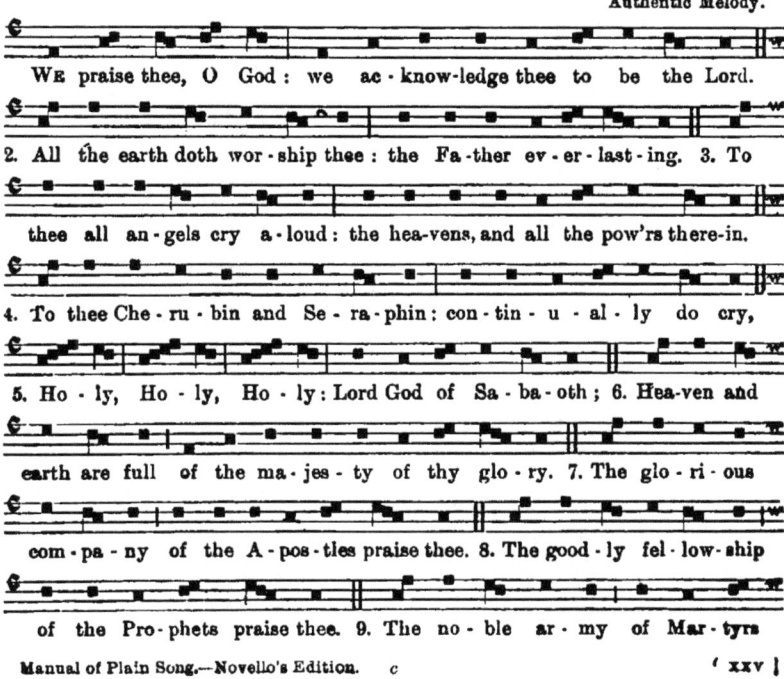

We praise thee, O God : we ac-know-ledge thee to be the Lord. 2. All the earth doth wor-ship thee : the Fa-ther ev-er-last-ing. 3. To thee all an-gels cry a-loud : the hea-vens, and all the pow'rs there-in. 4. To thee Che-ru-bin and Se-ra-phin : con-tin-u-al-ly do cry, 5. Ho-ly, Ho-ly, Ho-ly : Lord God of Sa-ba-oth ; 6. Hea-ven and earth are full of the ma-jes-ty of thy glo-ry. 7. The glo-ri-ous com-pa-ny of the A-pos-tles praise thee. 8. The good-ly fel-low-ship of the Pro-phets praise thee. 9. The no-ble ar-my of Mar-tyrs

Manual of Plain Song.—Novello's Edition.

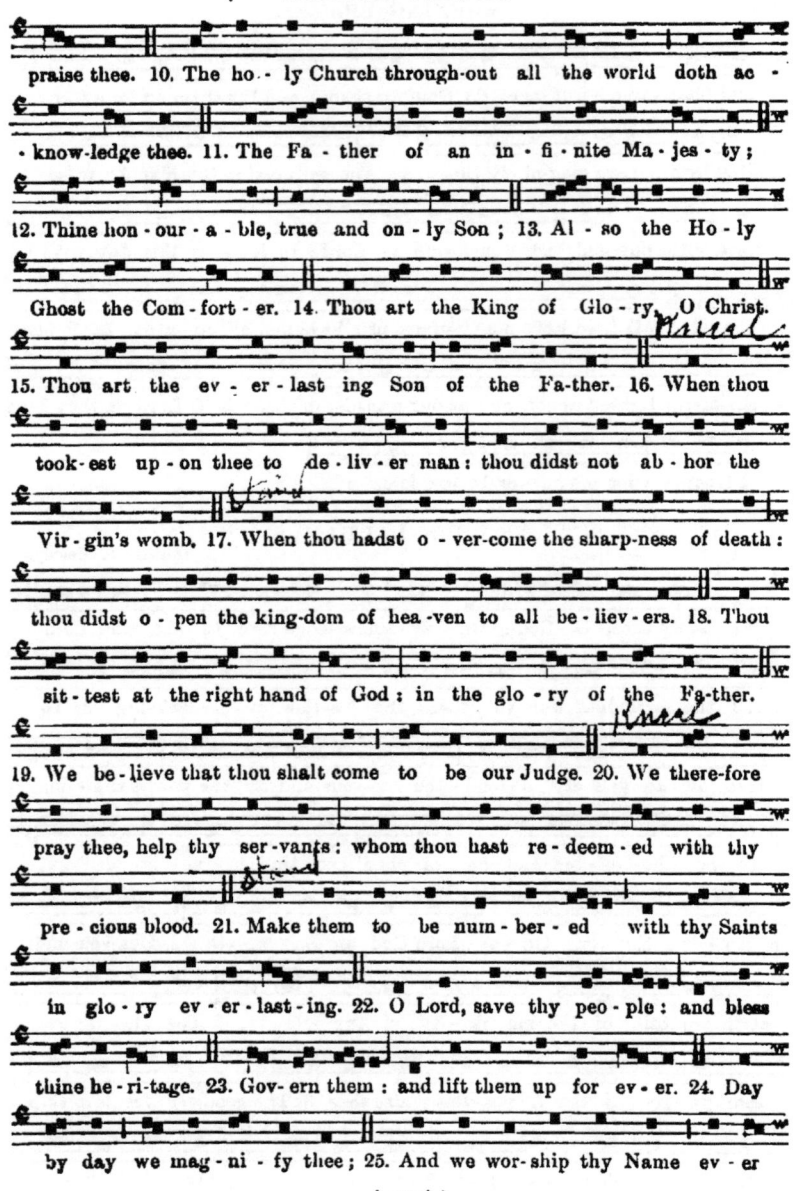

MORNING PRAYER.

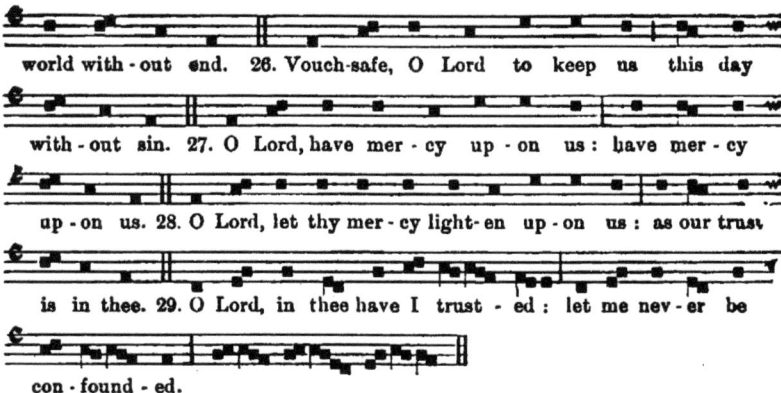

TE DEUM LAUDAMUS.   MERBECKE.

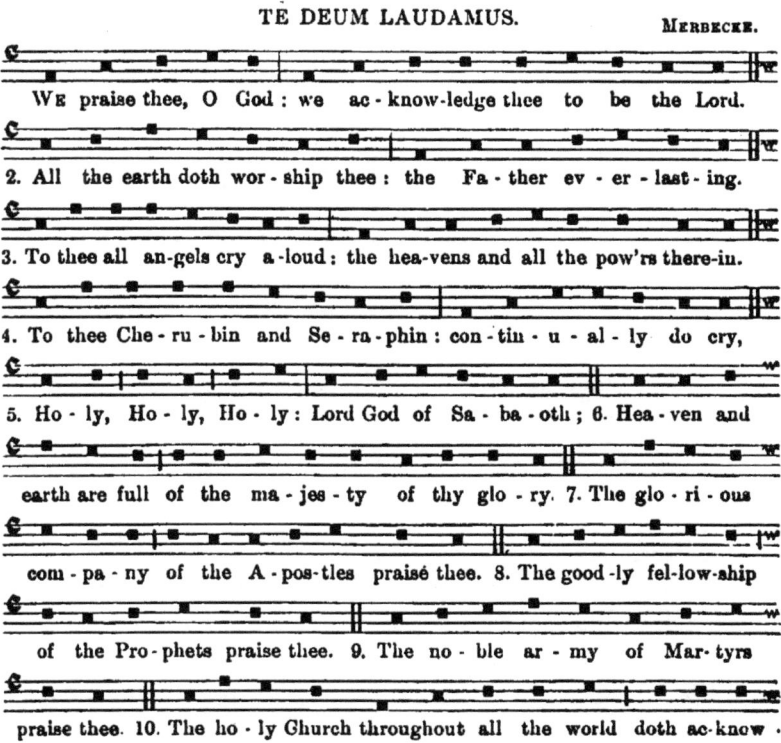

MORNING PRAYER.

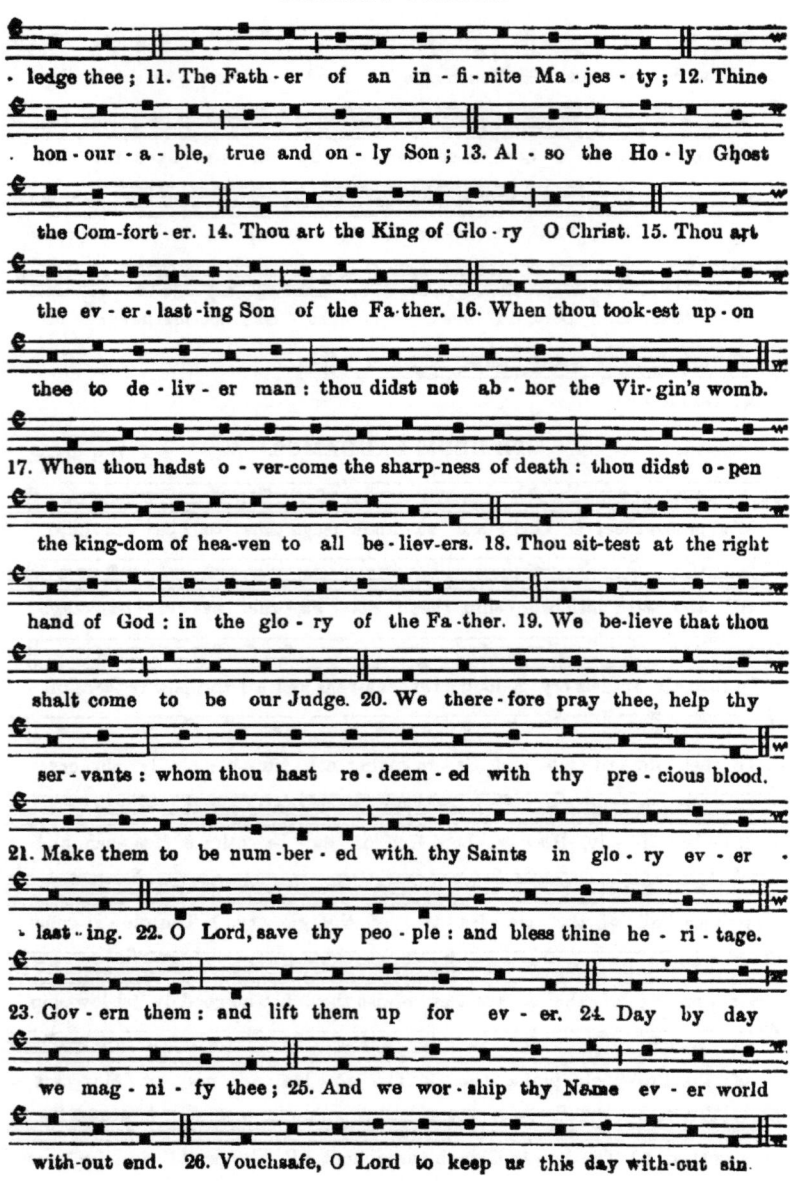

- ledge thee; 11. The Father of an in-fi-nite Ma-jes-ty; 12. Thine
. hon-our-a-ble, true and on-ly Son; 13. Al-so the Holy Ghost
the Com-fort-er. 14. Thou art the King of Glo-ry O Christ. 15. Thou art
the ev-er-last-ing Son of the Fa-ther. 16. When thou took-est up-on
thee to de-liv-er man: thou didst not ab-hor the Vir-gin's womb.
17. When thou hadst o-ver-come the sharp-ness of death: thou didst o-pen
the king-dom of hea-ven to all be-liev-ers. 18. Thou sit-test at the right
hand of God: in the glo-ry of the Fa-ther. 19. We be-lieve that thou
shalt come to be our Judge. 20. We there-fore pray thee, help thy
ser-vants: whom thou hast re-deem-ed with thy pre-cious blood.
21. Make them to be num-ber-ed with thy Saints in glo-ry ev-er-
last-ing. 22. O Lord, save thy peo-ple: and bless thine he-ri-tage.
23. Gov-ern them: and lift them up for ev-er. 24. Day by day
we mag-ni-fy thee; 25. And we wor-ship thy Name ev-er world
with-out end. 26. Vouchsafe, O Lord to keep us this day with-out sin.

(xxviii)

MORNING PRAYER.

27. O Lord, have mer-cy up-on us : have mer-cy up-on us. 28. O Lord, let thy mer-cy light-en up-on us : as our trust is in thee. 29. O Lord, in thee have I trust-ed : let me nev-er be con-found-ed.

BENEDICITE, OMNIA OPERA.

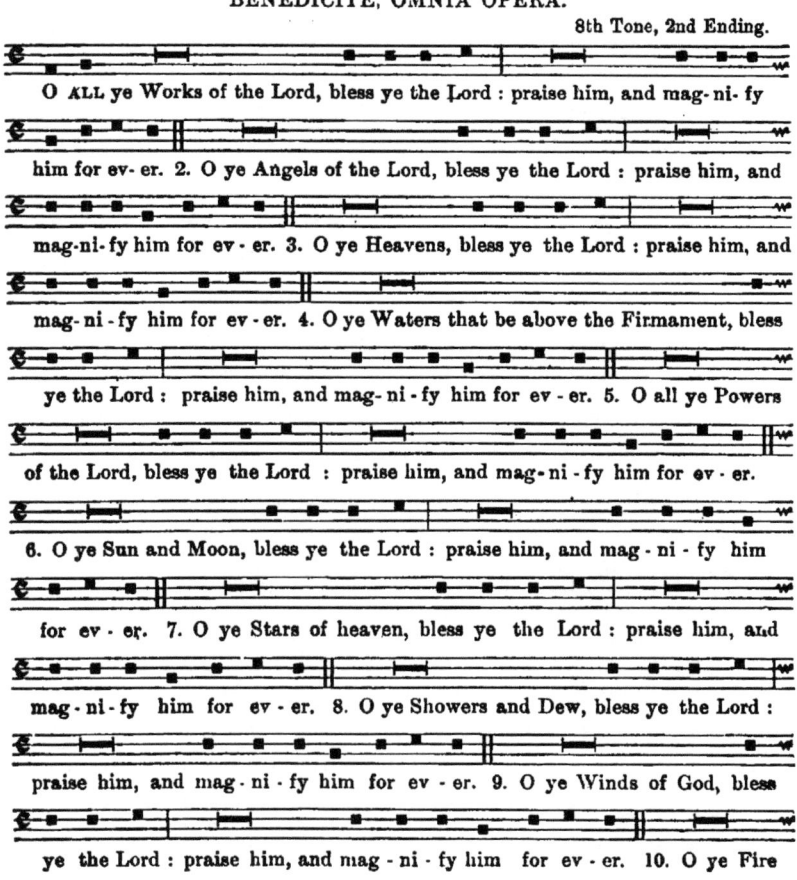

8th Tone, 2nd Ending.

O ALL ye Works of the Lord, bless ye the Lord : praise him, and mag-ni-fy him for ev-er. 2. O ye Angels of the Lord, bless ye the Lord : praise him, and mag-ni-fy him for ev-er. 3. O ye Heavens, bless ye the Lord : praise him, and mag-ni-fy him for ev-er. 4. O ye Waters that be above the Firmament, bless ye the Lord : praise him, and mag-ni-fy him for ev-er. 5. O all ye Powers of the Lord, bless ye the Lord : praise him, and mag-ni-fy him for ev-er. 6. O ye Sun and Moon, bless ye the Lord : praise him, and mag-ni-fy him for ev-er. 7. O ye Stars of heaven, bless ye the Lord : praise him, and mag-ni-fy him for ev-er. 8. O ye Showers and Dew, bless ye the Lord : praise him, and mag-ni-fy him for ev-er. 9. O ye Winds of God, bless ye the Lord : praise him, and mag-ni-fy him for ev-er. 10. O ye Fire

MORNING PRAYER.

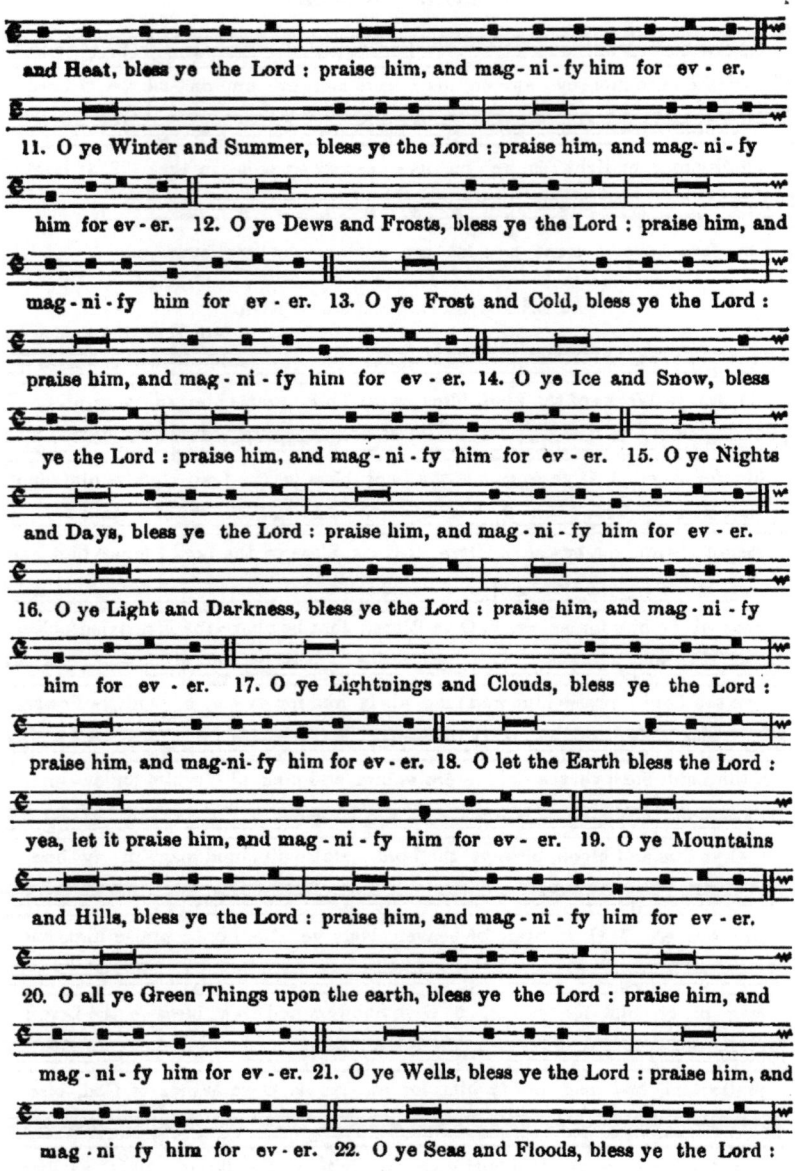

and Heat, bless ye the Lord : praise him, and mag-ni-fy him for ev-er.

11. O ye Winter and Summer, bless ye the Lord : praise him, and mag-ni-fy him for ev-er. 12. O ye Dews and Frosts, bless ye the Lord : praise him, and mag-ni-fy him for ev-er. 13. O ye Frost and Cold, bless ye the Lord : praise him, and mag-ni-fy him for ev-er. 14. O ye Ice and Snow, bless ye the Lord : praise him, and mag-ni-fy him for ev-er. 15. O ye Nights and Days, bless ye the Lord : praise him, and mag-ni-fy him for ev-er. 16. O ye Light and Darkness, bless ye the Lord : praise him, and mag-ni-fy him for ev-er. 17. O ye Lightnings and Clouds, bless ye the Lord : praise him, and mag-ni-fy him for ev-er. 18. O let the Earth bless the Lord : yea, let it praise him, and mag-ni-fy him for ev-er. 19. O ye Mountains and Hills, bless ye the Lord : praise him, and mag-ni-fy him for ev-er. 20. O all ye Green Things upon the earth, bless ye the Lord : praise him, and mag-ni-fy him for ev-er. 21. O ye Wells, bless ye the Lord : praise him, and mag-ni-fy him for ev-er. 22. O ye Seas and Floods, bless ye the Lord :

MORNING PRAYER.

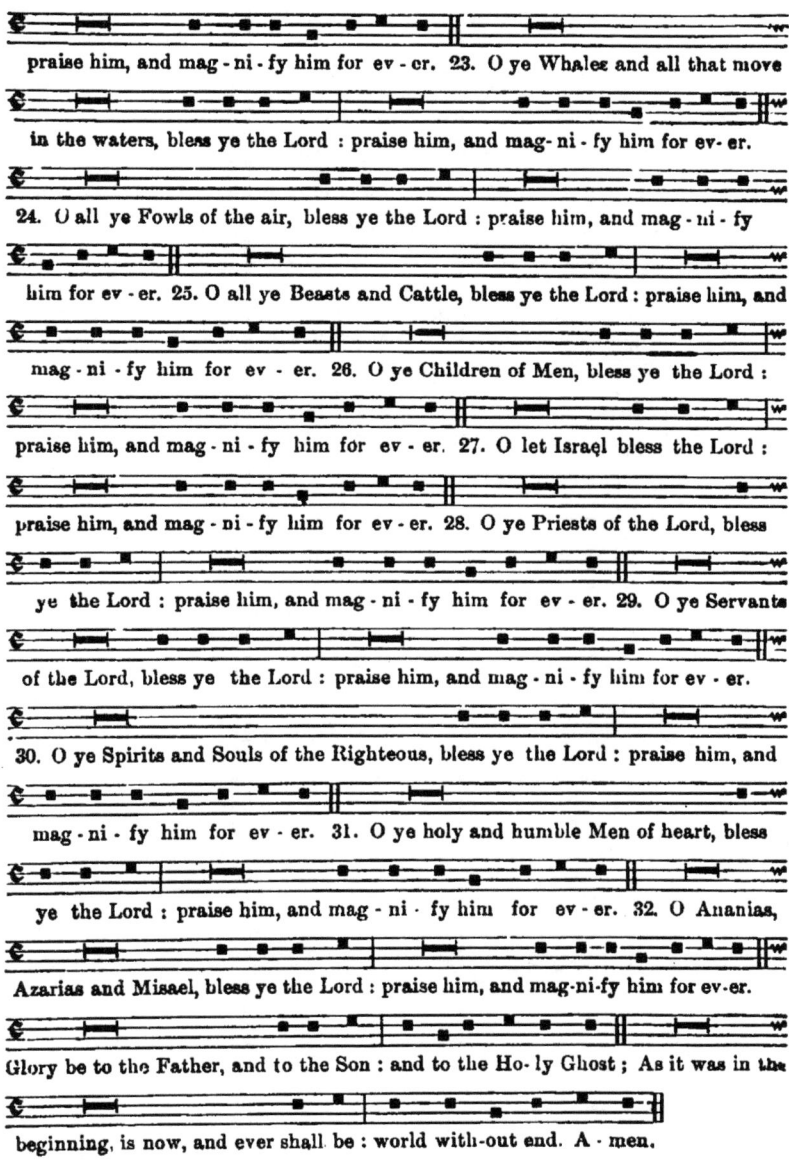

praise him, and mag-ni-fy him for ev-er. 23. O ye Whales and all that move in the waters, bless ye the Lord : praise him, and mag-ni-fy him for ev-er.

24. O all ye Fowls of the air, bless ye the Lord : praise him, and mag-ni-fy him for ev-er. 25. O all ye Beasts and Cattle, bless ye the Lord : praise him, and mag-ni-fy him for ev-er. 26. O ye Children of Men, bless ye the Lord : praise him, and mag-ni-fy him for ev-er. 27. O let Israel bless the Lord : praise him, and mag-ni-fy him for ev-er. 28. O ye Priests of the Lord, bless ye the Lord : praise him, and mag-ni-fy him for ev-er. 29. O ye Servants of the Lord, bless ye the Lord : praise him, and mag-ni-fy him for ev-er.

30. O ye Spirits and Souls of the Righteous, bless ye the Lord : praise him, and mag-ni-fy him for ev-er. 31. O ye holy and humble Men of heart, bless ye the Lord : praise him, and mag-ni-fy him for ev-er. 32. O Ananias, Azarias and Misael, bless ye the Lord : praise him, and mag-ni-fy him for ev-er.

Glory be to the Father, and to the Son : and to the Ho-ly Ghost ; As it was in the beginning, is now, and ever shall be : world with-out end. A-men.

MORNING PRAYER.

BENEDICITE, OMNIA OPERA.

Tonus Peregrinus

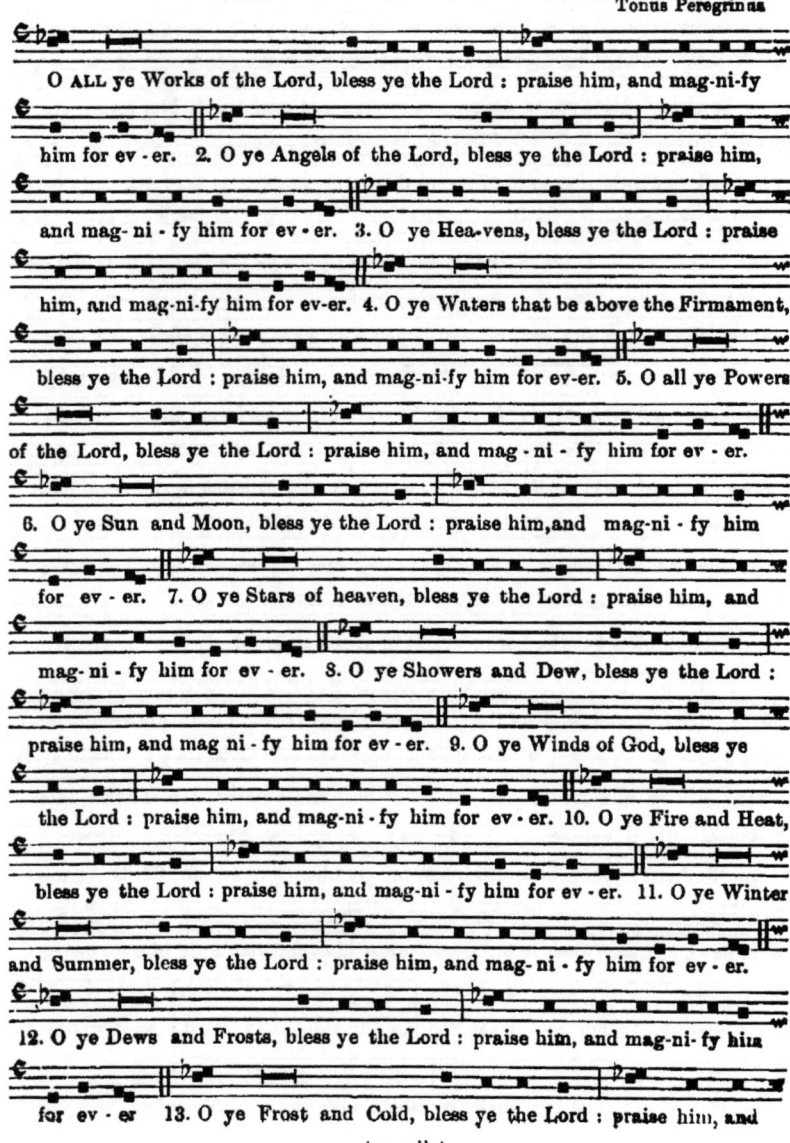

O ALL ye Works of the Lord, bless ye the Lord : praise him, and mag-ni-fy him for ev-er. 2. O ye Angels of the Lord, bless ye the Lord : praise him, and mag-ni-fy him for ev-er. 3. O ye Hea-vens, bless ye the Lord : praise him, and mag-ni-fy him for ev-er. 4. O ye Waters that be above the Firmament, bless ye the Lord : praise him, and mag-ni-fy him for ev-er. 5. O all ye Powers of the Lord, bless ye the Lord : praise him, and mag-ni-fy him for ev-er. 6. O ye Sun and Moon, bless ye the Lord : praise him, and mag-ni-fy him for ev-er. 7. O ye Stars of heaven, bless ye the Lord : praise him, and mag-ni-fy him for ev-er. 8. O ye Showers and Dew, bless ye the Lord : praise him, and mag ni-fy him for ev-er. 9. O ye Winds of God, bless ye the Lord : praise him, and mag-ni-fy him for ev-er. 10. O ye Fire and Heat, bless ye the Lord : praise him, and mag-ni-fy him for ev-er. 11. O ye Winter and Summer, bless ye the Lord : praise him, and mag-ni-fy him for ev-er. 12. O ye Dews and Frosts, bless ye the Lord : praise him, and mag-ni-fy him for ev-er 13. O ye Frost and Cold, bless ye the Lord : praise him, and

(xxxii)

MORNING PRAYER.

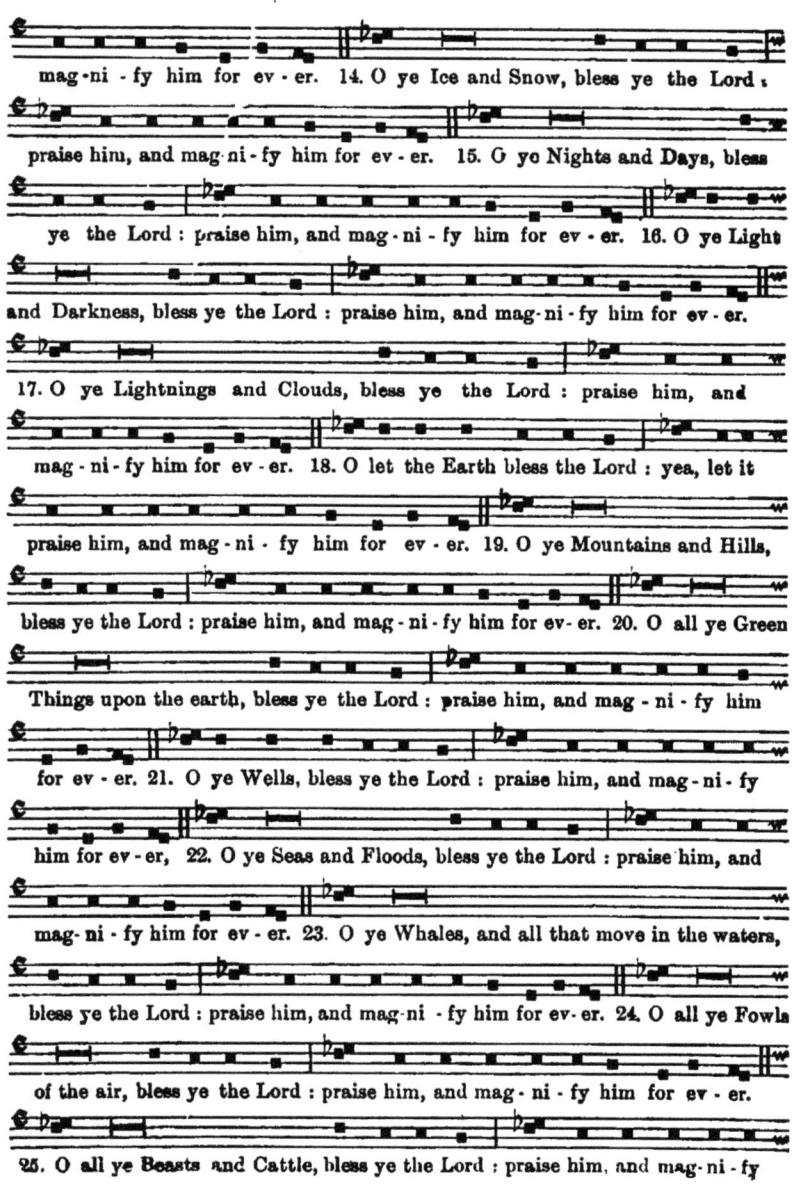

mag-ni-fy him for ev-er. 14. O ye Ice and Snow, bless ye the Lord: praise him, and mag-ni-fy him for ev-er. 15. O ye Nights and Days, bless ye the Lord: praise him, and mag-ni-fy him for ev-er. 16. O ye Light and Darkness, bless ye the Lord: praise him, and mag-ni-fy him for ev-er. 17. O ye Lightnings and Clouds, bless ye the Lord: praise him, and mag-ni-fy him for ev-er. 18. O let the Earth bless the Lord: yea, let it praise him, and mag-ni-fy him for ev-er. 19. O ye Mountains and Hills, bless ye the Lord: praise him, and mag-ni-fy him for ev-er. 20. O all ye Green Things upon the earth, bless ye the Lord: praise him, and mag-ni-fy him for ev-er. 21. O ye Wells, bless ye the Lord: praise him, and mag-ni-fy him for ev-er. 22. O ye Seas and Floods, bless ye the Lord: praise him, and mag-ni-fy him for ev-er. 23. O ye Whales, and all that move in the waters, bless ye the Lord: praise him, and mag-ni-fy him for ev-er. 24. O all ye Fowls of the air, bless ye the Lord: praise him, and mag-ni-fy him for ev-er. 25. O all ye Beasts and Cattle, bless ye the Lord: praise him, and mag-ni-fy

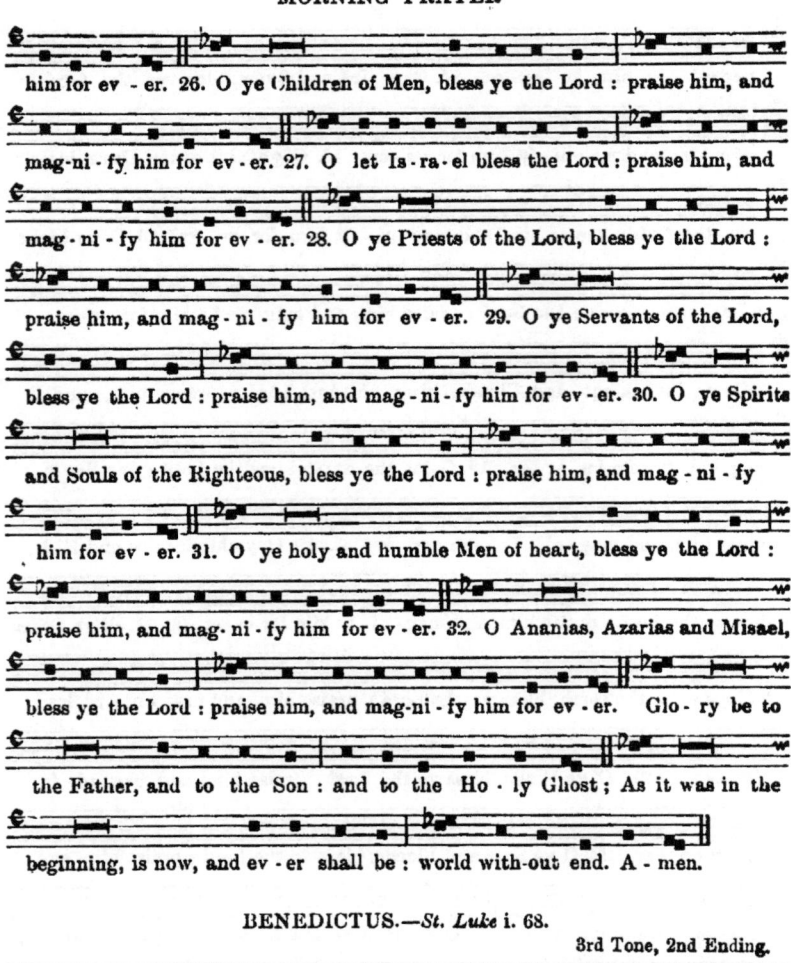

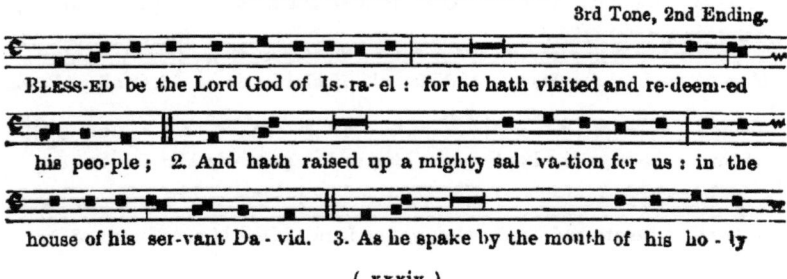

MORNING PRAYER

him for ev-er. 26. O ye Children of Men, bless ye the Lord : praise him, and mag-ni-fy him for ev-er. 27. O let Is-ra-el bless the Lord : praise him, and mag-ni-fy him for ev-er. 28. O ye Priests of the Lord, bless ye the Lord : praise him, and mag-ni-fy him for ev-er. 29. O ye Servants of the Lord, bless ye the Lord : praise him, and mag-ni-fy him for ev-er. 30. O ye Spirits and Souls of the Righteous, bless ye the Lord : praise him, and mag-ni-fy him for ev-er. 31. O ye holy and humble Men of heart, bless ye the Lord : praise him, and mag-ni-fy him for ev-er. 32. O Ananias, Azarias and Misael, bless ye the Lord : praise him, and mag-ni-fy him for ev-er.   Glo-ry be to the Father, and to the Son : and to the Ho-ly Ghost ; As it was in the beginning, is now, and ev-er shall be : world with-out end. A-men.

BENEDICTUS.—*St. Luke* i. 68.

3rd Tone, 2nd Ending.

BLESS-ED be the Lord God of Is-ra-el : for he hath visited and re-deem-ed his peo-ple ; 2. And hath raised up a mighty sal-va-tion for us : in the house of his ser-vant Da-vid. 3. As he spake by the mouth of his ho-ly

MORNING PRAYER.

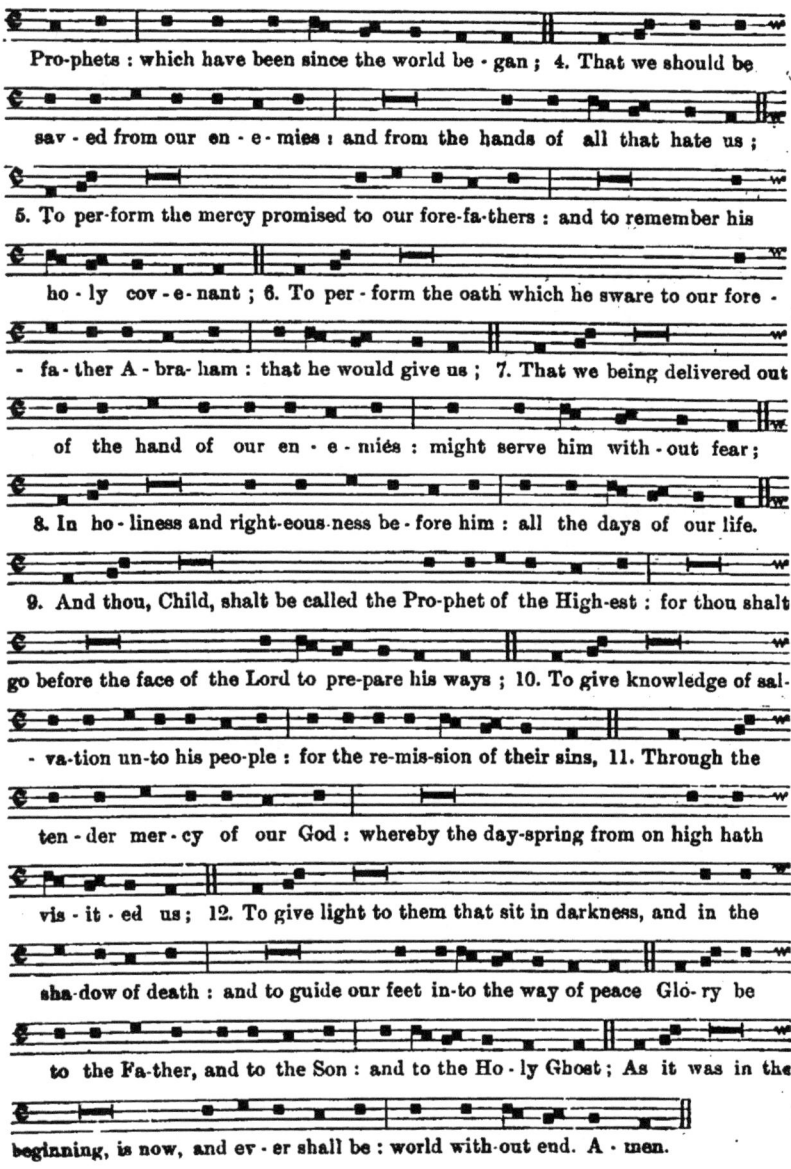

(xxxv)

MORNING PRAYER.

BENEDICTUS.—*St. Luke* i. 68.

5th Tone, 3rd Ending.

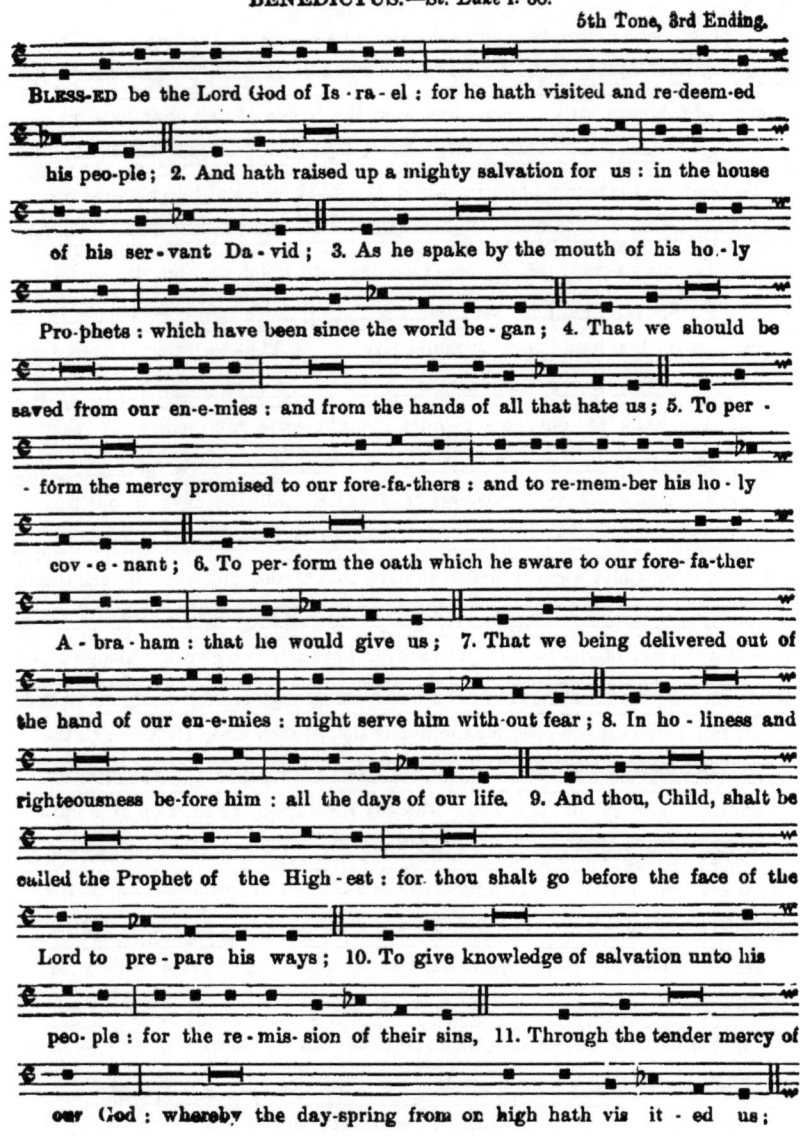

BLESS-ED be the Lord God of Is-ra-el : for he hath visited and re-deem-ed his peo-ple; 2. And hath raised up a mighty salvation for us : in the house of his ser-vant Da-vid ; 3. As he spake by the mouth of his ho-ly Pro-phets : which have been since the world be-gan ; 4. That we should be saved from our en-e-mies : and from the hands of all that hate us ; 5. To per-fórm the mercy promised to our fore-fa-thers : and to re-mem-ber his ho-ly cov-e-nant ; 6. To per-form the oath which he sware to our fore-fa-ther A-bra-ham : that he would give us ; 7. That we being delivered out of the hand of our en-e-mies : might serve him with-out fear ; 8. In ho-liness and righteousness be-fore him : all the days of our life. 9. And thou, Child, shalt be called the Prophet of the High-est : for thou shalt go before the face of the Lord to pre-pare his ways ; 10. To give knowledge of salvation unto his peo-ple : for the re-mis-sion of their sins, 11. Through the tender mercy of our God : whereby the day-spring from on high hath vis it-ed us ;

MORNING PRAYER.

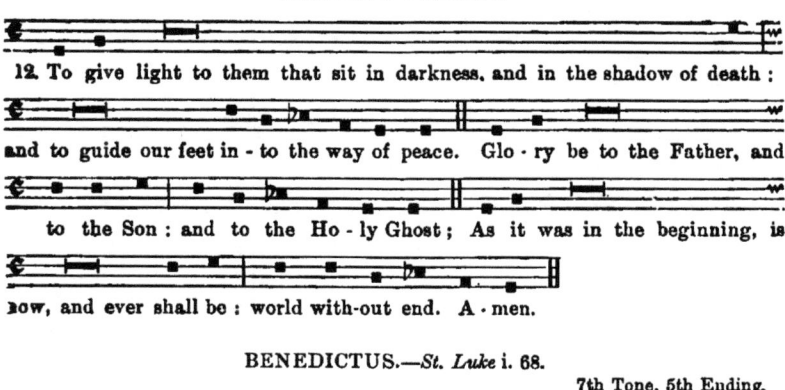

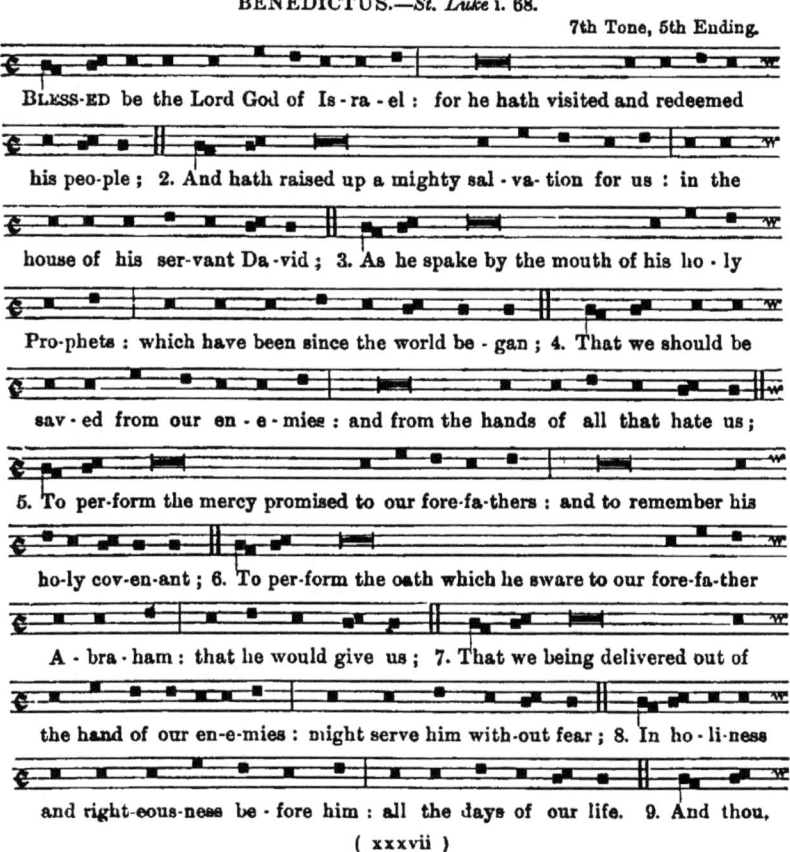

12. To give light to them that sit in darkness, and in the shadow of death :

and to guide our feet in - to the way of peace. Glo - ry be to the Father, and

to the Son : and to the Ho - ly Ghost ; As it was in the beginning, is

now, and ever shall be : world with-out end. A - men.

BENEDICTUS.—*St. Luke* i. 68.

7th Tone, 5th Ending.

BLESS-ED be the Lord God of Is - ra - el : for he hath visited and redeemed

his peo-ple ; 2. And hath raised up a mighty sal - va- tion for us : in the

house of his ser-vant Da-vid ; 3. As he spake by the mouth of his ho - ly

Pro-phets : which have been since the world be - gan ; 4. That we should be

sav - ed from our en - e - mies : and from the hands of all that hate us ;

5. To per-form the mercy promised to our fore-fa-thers : and to remember his

ho-ly cov-en-ant ; 6. To per-form the oath which he sware to our fore-fa-ther

A - bra - ham : that he would give us ; 7. That we being delivered out of

the hand of our en-e-mies : might serve him with-out fear ; 8. In ho - li-ness

and right-eous-ness be - fore him : all the days of our life. 9. And thou,

(xxxvii)

MORNING PRAYER.

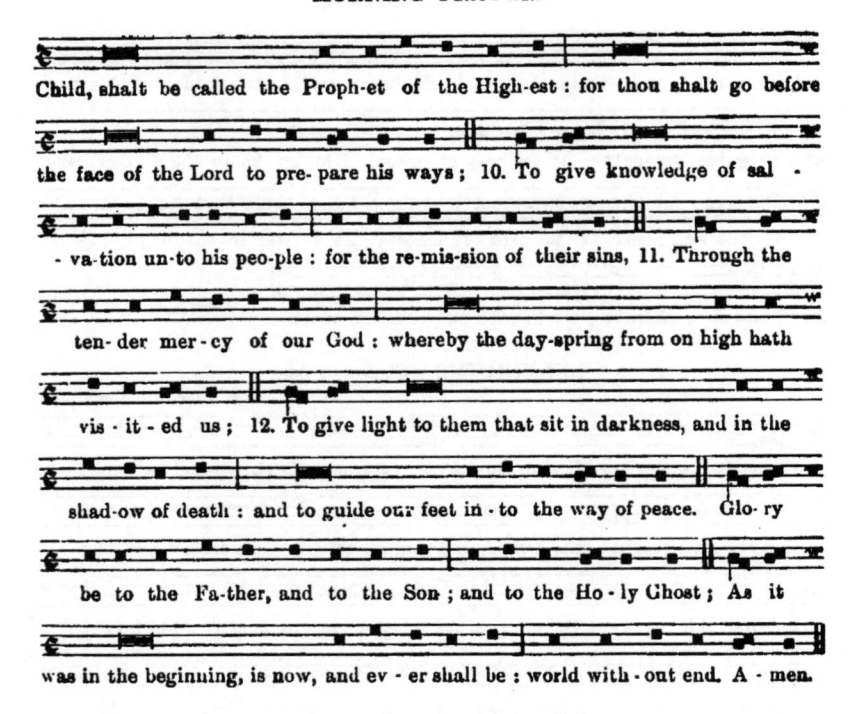

Child, shalt be called the Proph-et of the High-est : for thou shalt go before the face of the Lord to pre-pare his ways ; 10. To give knowledge of sal - va-tion un-to his peo-ple : for the re-mis-sion of their sins, 11. Through the ten-der mer-cy of our God : whereby the day-spring from on high hath vis-it-ed us ; 12. To give light to them that sit in darkness, and in the shad-ow of death : and to guide our feet in-to the way of peace. Glo-ry be to the Fa-ther, and to the Son ; and to the Ho-ly Ghost ; As it was in the beginning, is now, and ev-er shall be : world with-out end. A-men.

BENEDICTUS.—*St. Luke* i. 68.

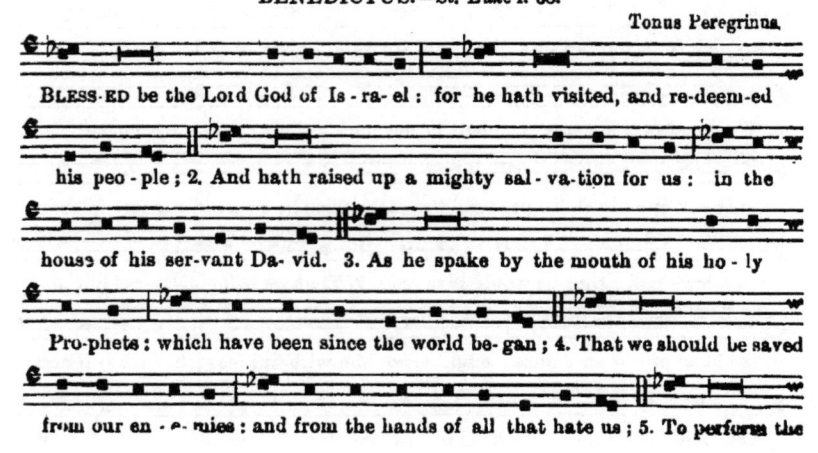

Tonus Peregrinus.

Bless-ed be the Lord God of Is-ra-el : for he hath visited, and re-deem-ed his peo-ple ; 2. And hath raised up a mighty sal-va-tion for us : in the house of his ser-vant Da-vid. 3. As he spake by the mouth of his ho-ly Pro-phets : which have been since the world be-gan ; 4. That we should be saved from our en-e-mies : and from the hands of all that hate us ; 5. To perform the

(xxxviii)

MORNING PRAYER.

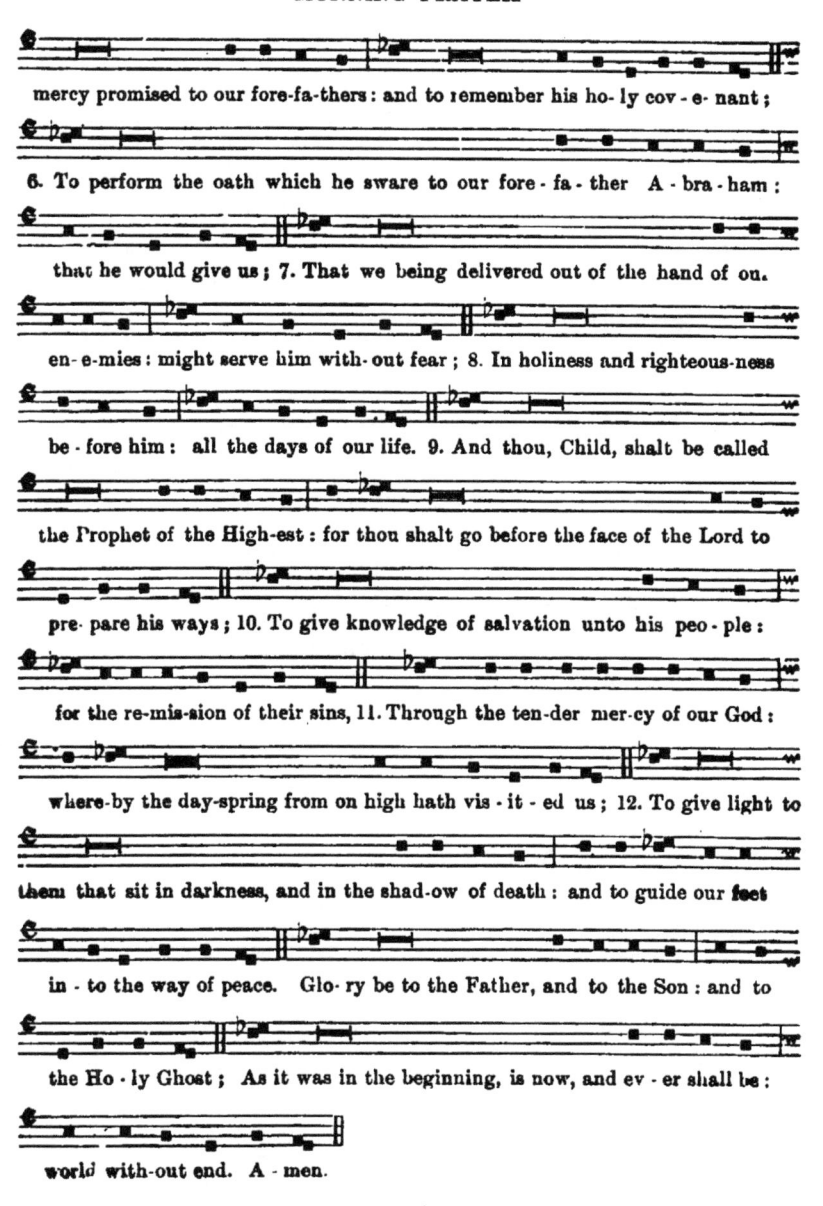

mercy promised to our fore-fa-thers: and to remember his ho- ly cov - e- nant;

6. To perform the oath which he sware to our fore - fa - ther A - bra - ham :

that he would give us ; 7. That we being delivered out of the hand of our

en- e-mies : might serve him with- out fear ; 8. In holiness and righteous-ness

be - fore him : all the days of our life. 9. And thou, Child, shalt be called

the Prophet of the High-est : for thou shalt go before the face of the Lord to

pre- pare his ways ; 10. To give knowledge of salvation unto his peo - ple :

for the re-mis-sion of their sins, 11. Through the ten-der mer-cy of our God :

where-by the day-spring from on high hath vis - it - ed us ; 12. To give light to

them that sit in darkness, and in the shad-ow of death : and to guide our feet

in - to the way of peace. Glo- ry be to the Father, and to the Son : and to

the Ho - ly Ghost ; As it was in the beginning, is now, and ev - er shall be :

world with-out end. A - men.

(xxxix)

EVENING PRAYER.

JUBILATE DEO.—*Psalm c.*

5th Tone, 3rd Ending.

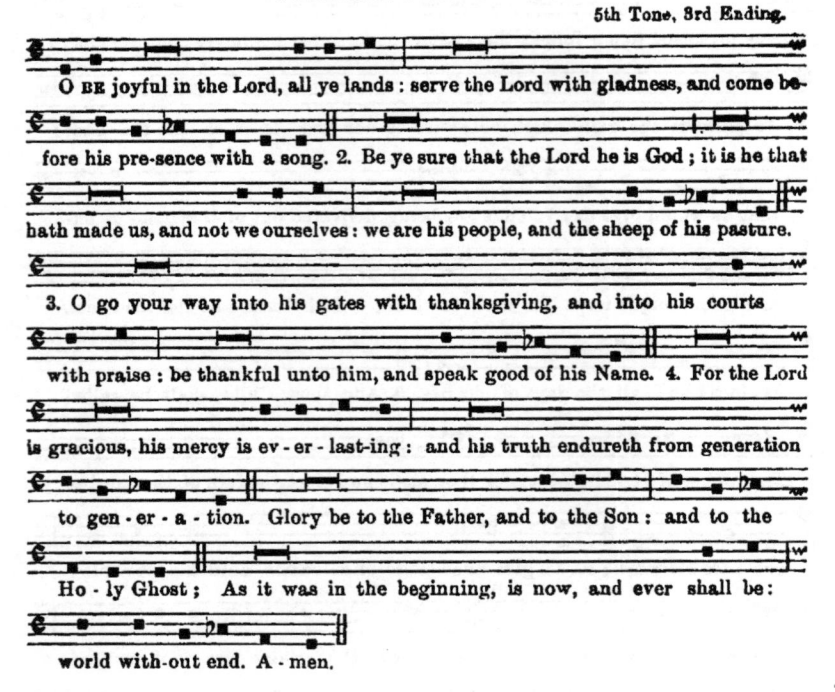

O be joyful in the Lord, all ye lands : serve the Lord with gladness, and come before his pre-sence with a song. 2. Be ye sure that the Lord he is God ; it is he that hath made us, and not we ourselves : we are his people, and the sheep of his pasture. 3. O go your way into his gates with thanksgiving, and into his courts with praise : be thankful unto him, and speak good of his Name. 4. For the Lord is gracious, his mercy is ev-er-last-ing : and his truth endureth from generation to gen-er-a-tion. Glory be to the Father, and to the Son : and to the Ho-ly Ghost ; As it was in the beginning, is now, and ever shall be : world with-out end. A-men.

EVENING PRAYER.

MAGNIFICAT.—*St. Luke i.*

1st Tone, 5th Ending.

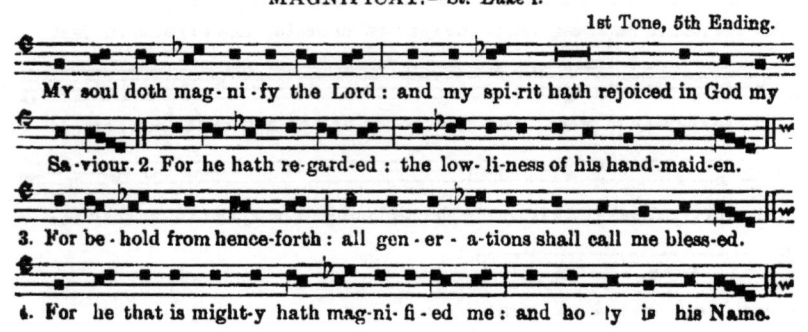

My soul doth mag-ni-fy the Lord : and my spi-rit hath rejoiced in God my Sa-viour. 2. For he hath re-gard-ed : the low-li-ness of his hand-maid-en. 3. For be-hold from hence-forth : all gen-er-a-tions shall call me bless-ed. 4. For he that is might-y hath mag-ni-fi-ed me : and ho-ly is his Name.

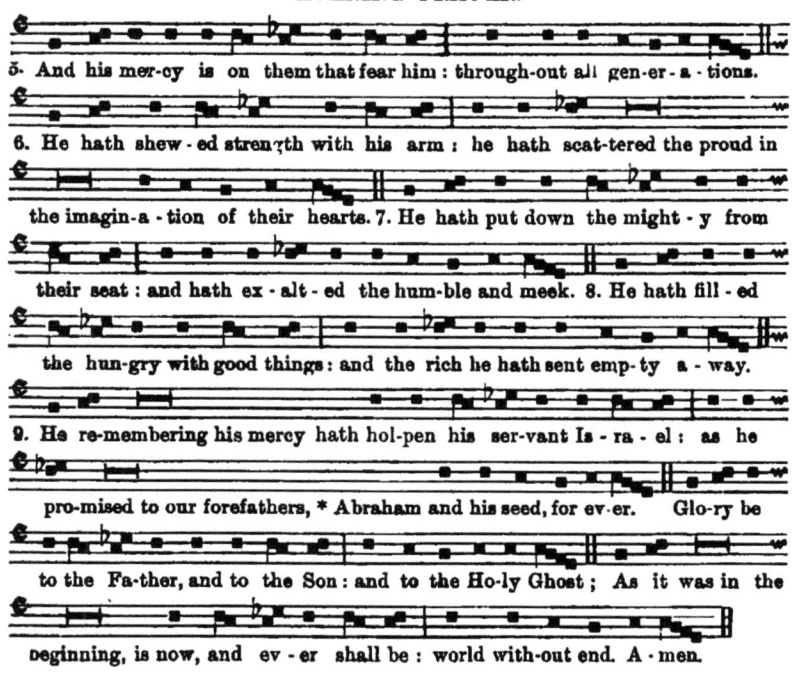

EVENING PRAYER.

5. And his mer-cy is on them that fear him : through-out all gen-er-a-tions.

6. He hath shew-ed strength with his arm : he hath scat-tered the proud in the imagin-a-tion of their hearts. 7. He hath put down the might-y from their seat : and hath ex-alt-ed the hum-ble and meek. 8. He hath fill-ed the hun-gry with good things : and the rich he hath sent emp-ty a-way.

9. He re-membering his mercy hath hol-pen his ser-vant Is-ra-el : as he pro-mised to our forefathers, * Abraham and his seed, for ev-er. Glo-ry be to the Fa-ther, and to the Son : and to the Ho-ly Ghost ; As it was in the beginning, is now, and ev-er shall be : world with-out end. A-men.

MAGNIFICAT.—*St. Luke* i.

1st Tone, 1st Ending.

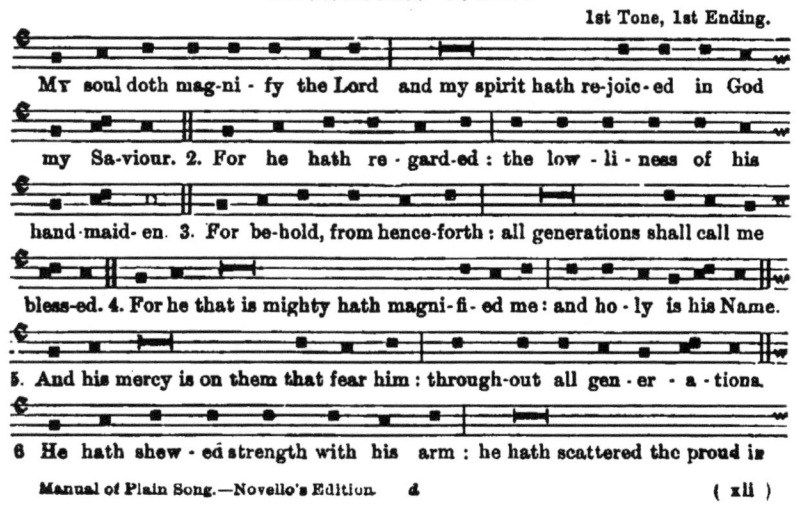

My soul doth mag-ni-fy the Lord and my spirit hath re-joic-ed in God my Sa-viour. 2. For he hath re-gard-ed : the low-li-ness of his hand-maid-en. 3. For be-hold, from hence-forth : all generations shall call me bless-ed. 4. For he that is mighty hath magni-fi-ed me : and ho-ly is his Name.

5. And his mercy is on them that fear him : through-out all gen-er-a-tions.

6 He hath shew-ed strength with his arm : he hath scattered the proud in

Manual of Plain Song.—Novello's Edition.

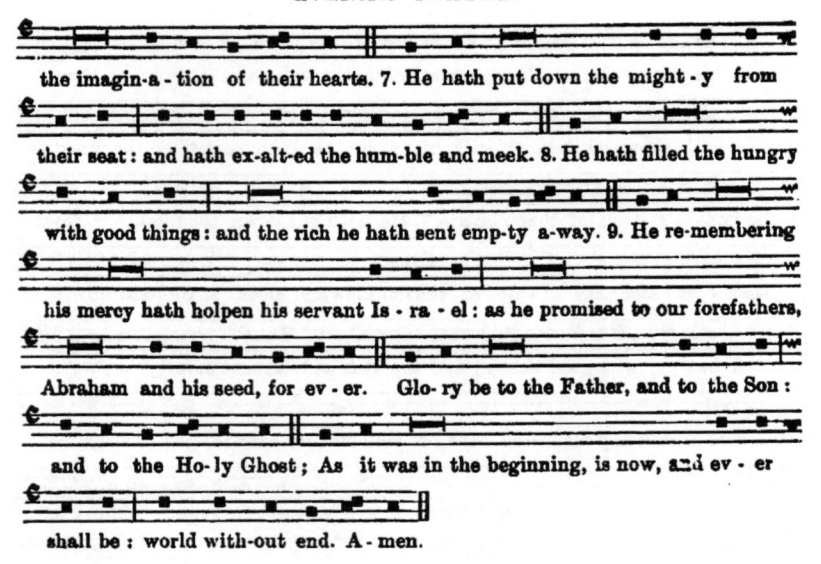

EVENING PRAYER.

the imagin-a-tion of their hearts. 7. He hath put down the might-y from their seat: and hath ex-alt-ed the hum-ble and meek. 8. He hath filled the hungry with good things: and the rich he hath sent emp-ty a-way. 9. He re-membering his mercy hath holpen his servant Is-ra-el: as he promised to our forefathers, Abraham and his seed, for ev-er. Glo-ry be to the Father, and to the Son: and to the Ho-ly Ghost; As it was in the beginning, is now, and ev-er shall be: world with-out end. A-men.

MAGNIFICAT.—*St. Luke i.*

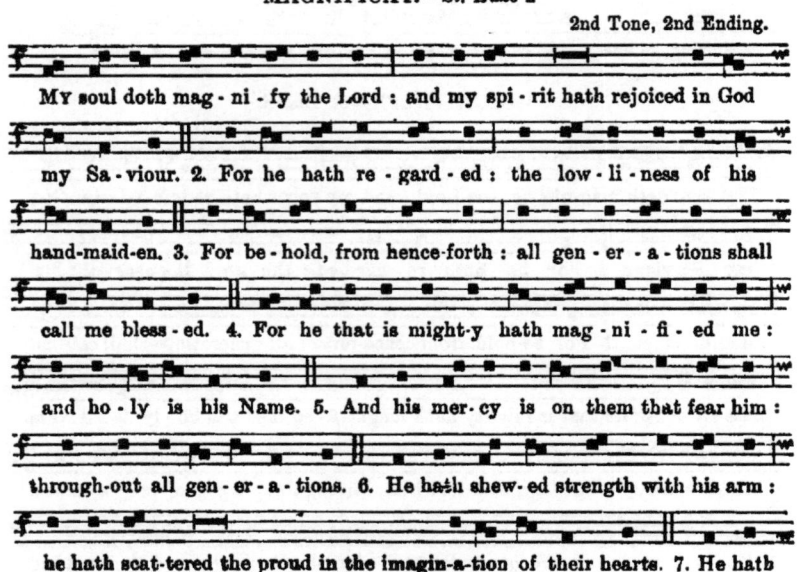

2nd Tone, 2nd Ending.

MY soul doth mag-ni-fy the Lord: and my spi-rit hath rejoiced in God my Sa-viour. 2. For he hath re-gard-ed: the low-li-ness of his hand-maid-en. 3. For be-hold, from hence-forth: all gen-er-a-tions shall call me bless-ed. 4. For he that is might-y hath mag-ni-fi-ed me: and ho-ly is his Name. 5. And his mer-cy is on them that fear him: through-out all gen-er-a-tions. 6. He hath shew-ed strength with his arm: he hath scat-tered the proud in the imagin-a-tion of their hearts. 7. He hath

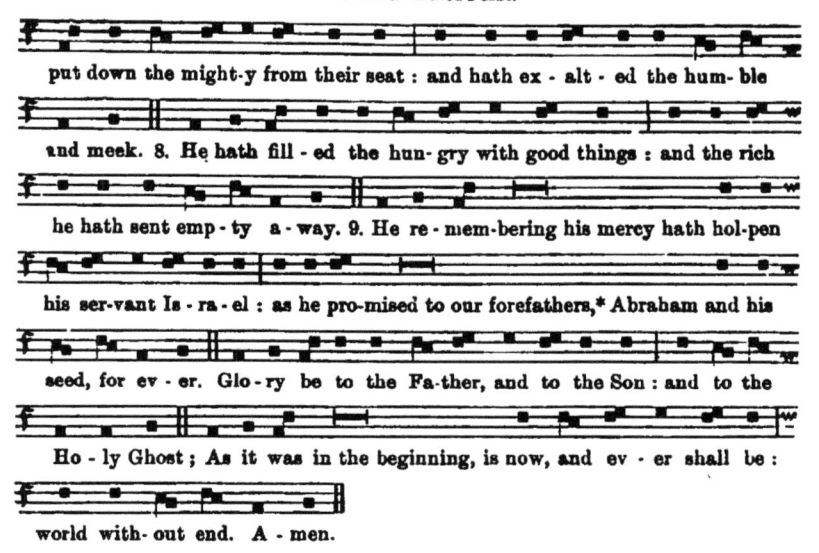

EVENING PRAYER.

put down the might-y from their seat : and hath ex - alt - ed the hum - ble

and meek. 8. He hath fill - ed the hun- gry with good things : and the rich

he hath sent emp - ty a - way. 9. He re - mem-bering his mercy hath hol-pen

his ser-vant Is - ra - el : as he pro-mised to our forefathers,* Abraham and his

seed, for ev - er. Glo - ry be to the Fa-ther, and to the Son : and to the

Ho - ly Ghost ; As it was in the beginning, is now, and ev - er shall be :

world with- out end. A - men.

MAGNIFICAT.—*St. Luke* i.

3rd Tone, 2nd Ending.

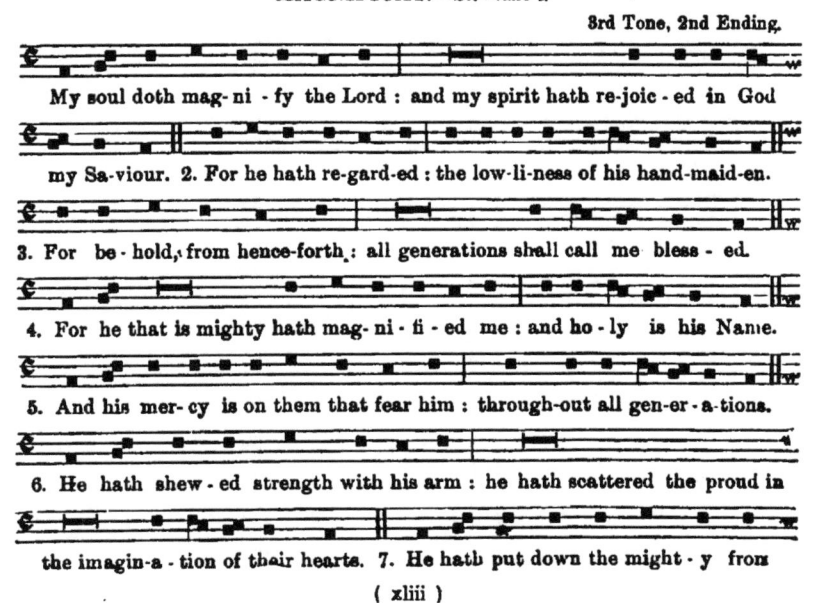

My soul doth mag-ni - fy the Lord : and my spirit hath re-joic - ed in God

my Sa-viour. 2. For he hath re-gard-ed : the low-li-ness of his hand-maid-en.

3. For be - hold, from hence-forth : all generations shall call me bless - ed.

4. For he that is mighty hath mag-ni - fi - ed me : and ho - ly is his Name.

5. And his mer- cy is on them that fear him : through-out all gen-er - a-tions.

6. He hath shew - ed strength with his arm : he hath scattered the proud in

the imagin-a - tion of their hearts. 7. He hath put down the might - y from

(xliii)

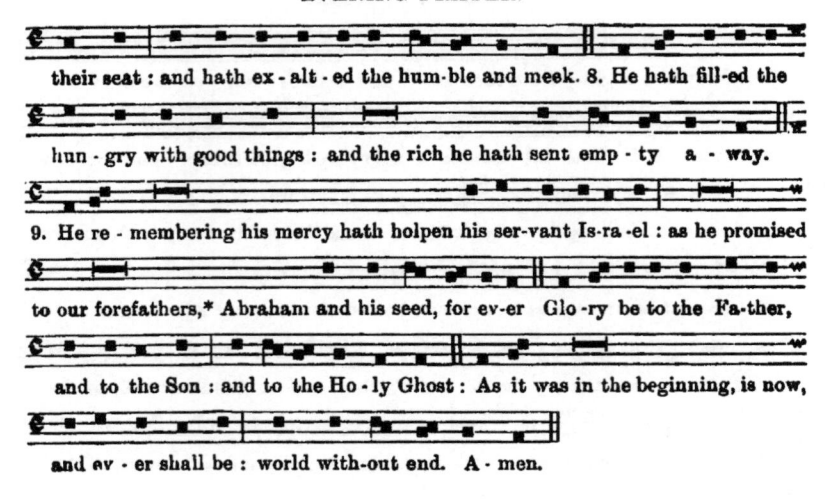

EVENING PRAYER.

their seat : and hath ex-alt-ed the hum-ble and meek. 8. He hath fill-ed the hun-gry with good things : and the rich he hath sent emp-ty a-way.

9. He re-membering his mercy hath holpen his ser-vant Is-ra-el : as he promised to our forefathers,* Abraham and his seed, for ev-er Glo-ry be to the Fa-ther, and to the Son : and to the Ho-ly Ghost : As it was in the beginning, is now, and ev-er shall be : world with-out end. A-men.

MAGNIFICAT.—*St. Luke* i.

4th Tone, 1st Ending.

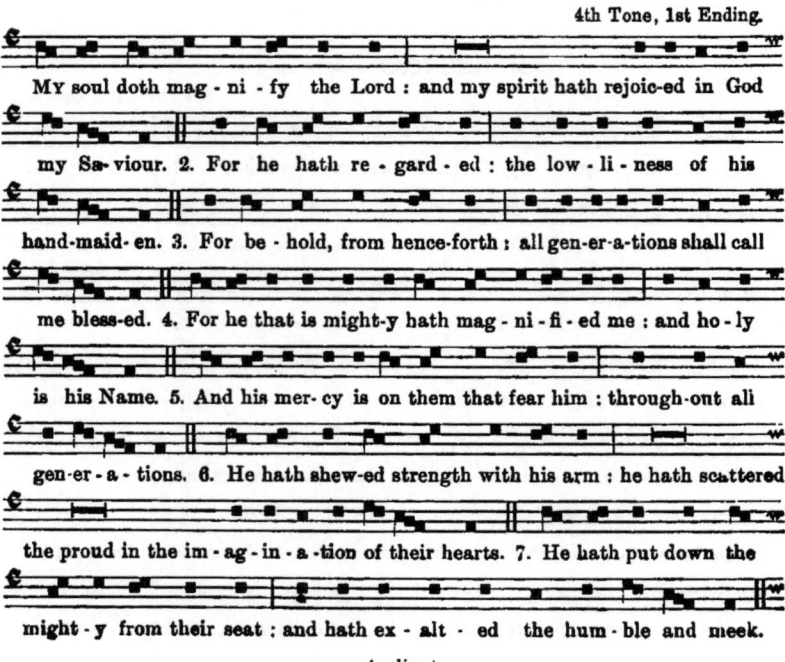

My soul doth mag-ni-fy the Lord : and my spirit hath rejoic-ed in God my Sa-viour. 2. For he hath re-gard-ed : the low-li-ness of his hand-maid-en. 3. For be-hold, from hence-forth : all gen-er-a-tions shall call me bless-ed. 4. For he that is might-y hath mag-ni-fi-ed me : and ho-ly is his Name. 5. And his mer-cy is on them that fear him : through-out all gen-er-a-tions. 6. He hath shew-ed strength with his arm : he hath scattered the proud in the im-ag-in-a-tion of their hearts. 7. He hath put down the might-y from their seat : and hath ex-alt-ed the hum-ble and meek.

(xliv)

EVENING PRAYER.

8. He hath fill-ed the hun-gry with good things : and the rich he hath sent empty a-way. 9. He re-membering his mercy hath hol-pen his ser-vant Is-ra-el : as he promised to our forefathers,* Abraham and his seed, for ev-er. Glo-ry be to the Fa-ther, and to the Son : and to the Ho-ly Ghost; As it was in the beginning, is now, and ev-er shall be : world with-out end. A-men.

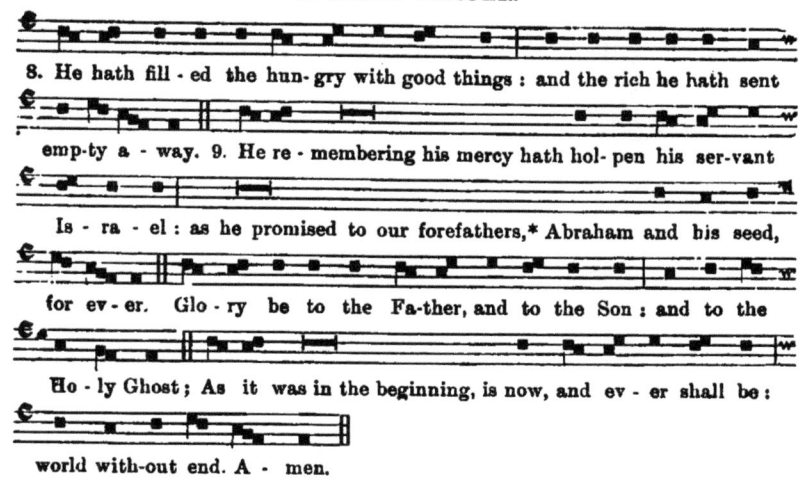

MAGNIFICAT.—*St. Luke i.*

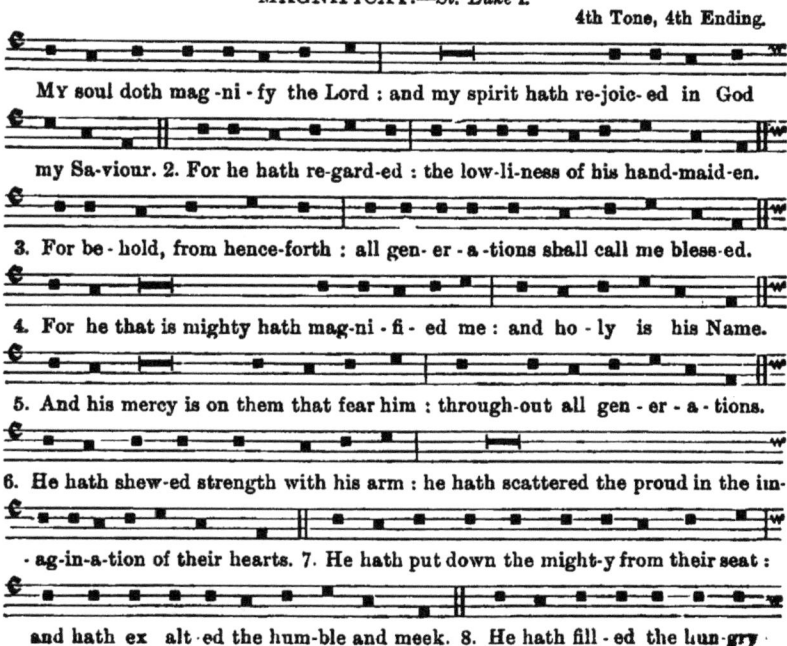

4th Tone, 4th Ending.

MY soul doth mag-ni-fy the Lord : and my spirit hath re-joic-ed in God my Sa-viour. 2. For he hath re-gard-ed : the low-li-ness of his hand-maid-en.

3. For be-hold, from hence-forth : all gen-er-a-tions shall call me bless-ed.

4. For he that is mighty hath mag-ni-fi-ed me : and ho-ly is his Name.

5. And his mercy is on them that fear him : through-out all gen-er-a-tions.

6. He hath shew-ed strength with his arm : he hath scattered the proud in the im- -ag-in-a-tion of their hearts. 7. He hath put down the might-y from their seat : and hath ex-alt-ed the hum-ble and meek. 8. He hath fill-ed the hun-gry

(xlv)

EVENING PRAYER.

with good things : and the rich he hath sent emp-ty a-way. 9. He re-

-membering his mercy hath holpen his ser-vant Is-ra-el : as he promised to

our forefathers,* Abraham and his seed, for ev-er. Glo-ry be to the Father,

and to the Son : and to the Ho-ly Ghost ; As it was in the beginning, is now, and

ev-er shall be : world with-out end. A-men.

MAGNIFICAT.—*St. Luke* i.

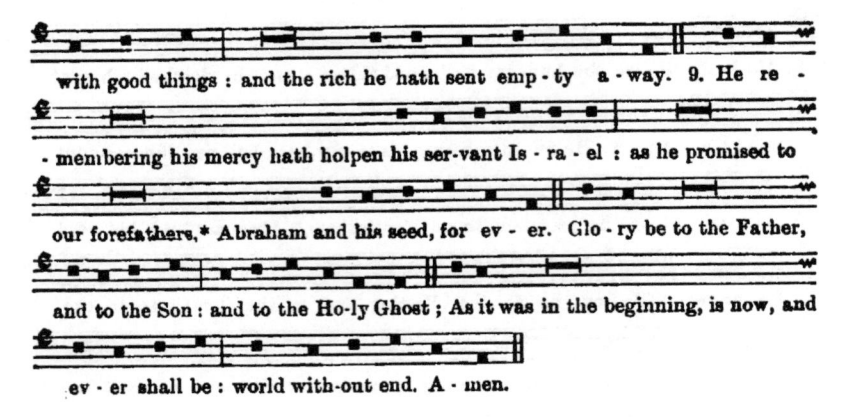

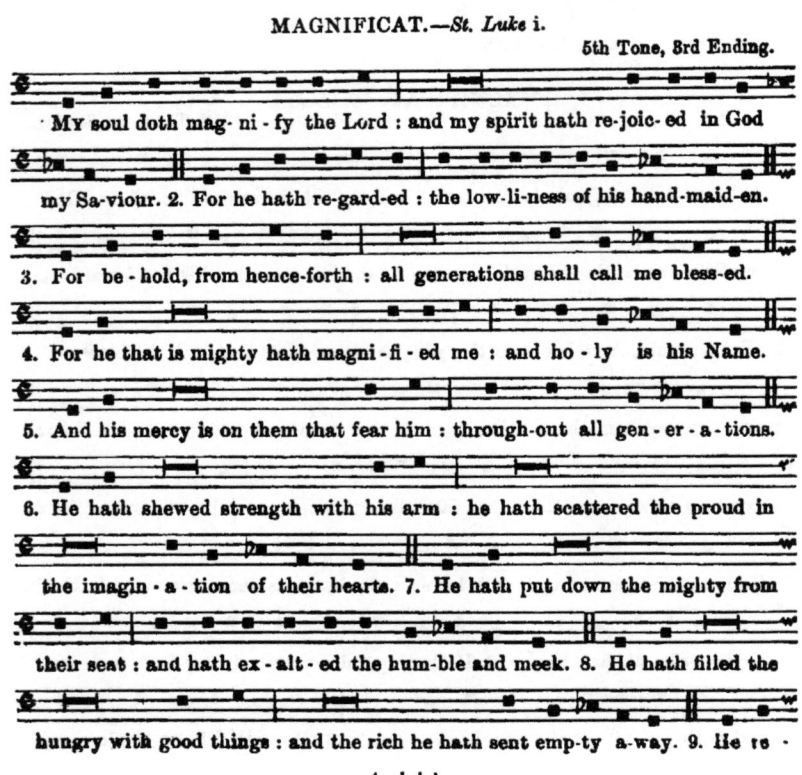

5th Tone, 3rd Ending.

My soul doth mag-ni-fy the Lord : and my spirit hath re-joic-ed in God

my Sa-viour. 2. For he hath re-gard-ed : the low-li-ness of his hand-maid-en.

3. For be-hold, from hence-forth : all generations shall call me bless-ed.

4. For he that is mighty hath magni-fi-ed me : and ho-ly is his Name.

5. And his mercy is on them that fear him : through-out all gen-er-a-tions.

6. He hath shewed strength with his arm : he hath scattered the proud in

the imagin-a-tion of their hearts. 7. He hath put down the mighty from

their seat : and hath ex-alt-ed the hum-ble and meek. 8. He hath filled the

hungry with good things : and the rich he hath sent emp-ty a-way. 9. He re-

EVENING PRAYER.

-membering his mercy hath holpen his ser-vant Is-ra-el : as he promised to our forefathers,* Abraham and his seed, for ev-er. Glo-ry be to the Father, and to the Son : and to the Ho-ly Ghost ; As it was in the beginning, is now, and ever shall be : world with-out end. A-men.

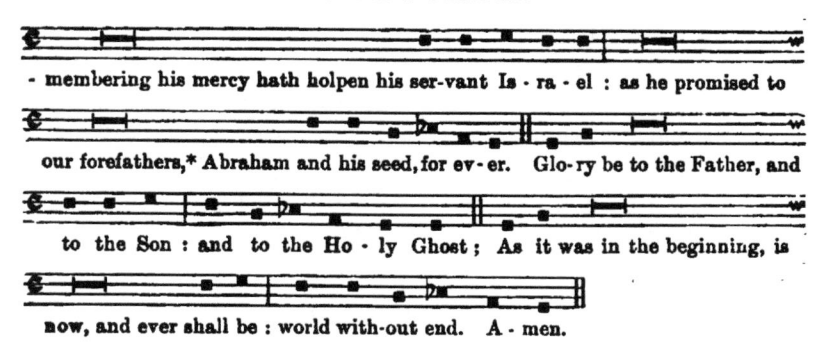

MAGNIFICAT.—*S. Luke* i.

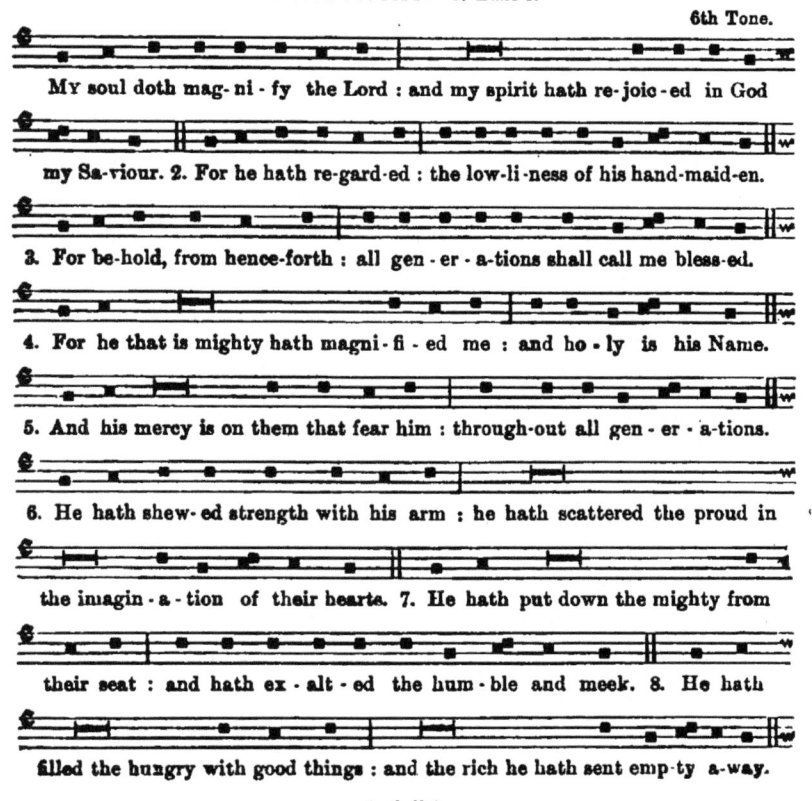

6th Tone.

My soul doth mag-ni-fy the Lord : and my spirit hath re-joic-ed in God my Sa-viour. 2. For he hath re-gard-ed : the low-li-ness of his hand-maid-en.

3. For be-hold, from hence-forth : all gen-er-a-tions shall call me bless-ed.

4. For he that is mighty hath magni-fi-ed me : and ho-ly is his Name.

5. And his mercy is on them that fear him : through-out all gen-er-a-tions.

6. He hath shew-ed strength with his arm : he hath scattered the proud in the imagin-a-tion of their hearts. 7. He hath put down the mighty from their seat : and hath ex-alt-ed the hum-ble and meek. 8. He hath filled the hungry with good things : and the rich he hath sent emp-ty a-way.

EVENING PRAYER.

9. He re-membering his mercy hath holpen his servant Is-ra-el : as he promised to our forefathers,* Abraham and his seed, for ev-er. Glo-ry be to the Father, and to the Son : and to the Ho-ly Ghost ; As it was in the beginning, is now, and ev-er shall be : world with-out end. A-men.

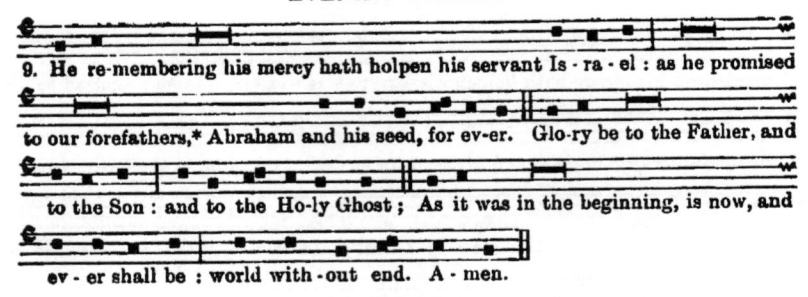

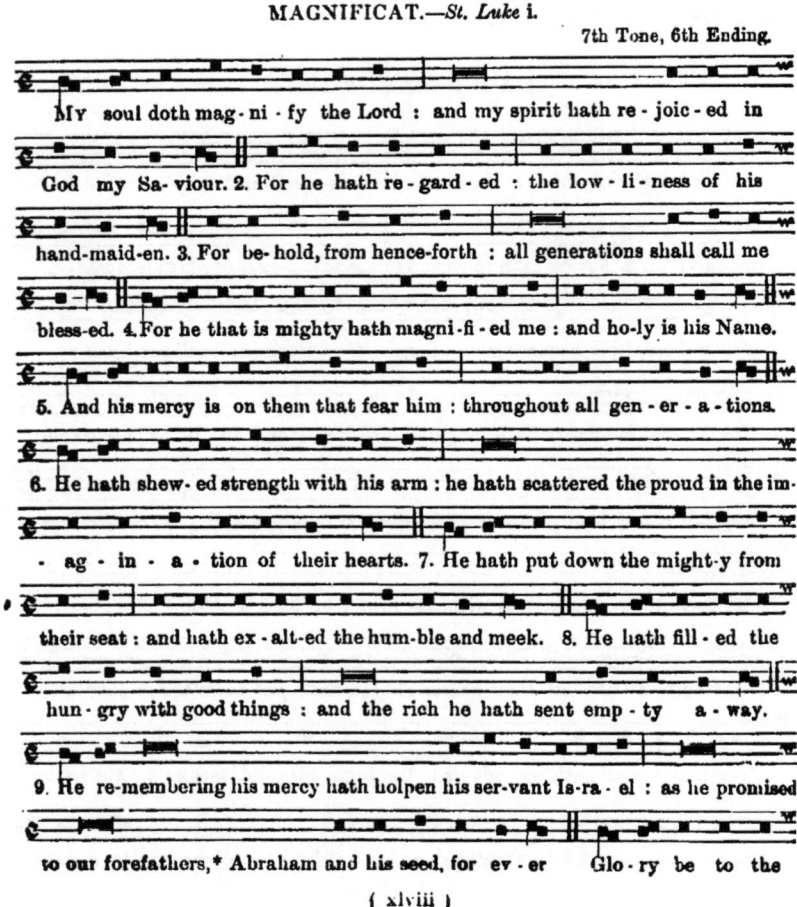

MAGNIFICAT.—*St. Luke* i.

7th Tone, 6th Ending.

My soul doth mag-ni-fy the Lord : and my spirit hath re-joic-ed in God my Sa-viour. 2. For he hath re-gard-ed : the low-li-ness of his hand-maid-en. 3. For be-hold, from hence-forth : all generations shall call me bless-ed. 4. For he that is mighty hath magni-fi-ed me : and ho-ly is his Name. 5. And his mercy is on them that fear him : throughout all gen-er-a-tions. 6. He hath shew-ed strength with his arm : he hath scattered the proud in the im--ag-in-a-tion of their hearts. 7. He hath put down the might-y from their seat : and hath ex-alt-ed the hum-ble and meek. 8. He hath fill-ed the hun-gry with good things : and the rich he hath sent emp-ty a-way. 9. He re-membering his mercy hath holpen his ser-vant Is-ra-el : as he promised to our forefathers,* Abraham and his seed, for ev-er Glo-ry be to the

(xlviii)

EVENING PRAYER.

Fa-ther, and to the Son : and to the Ho-ly Ghost: As it was in the beginning, is now, and ev-er shall be : world with-out end. A-men.

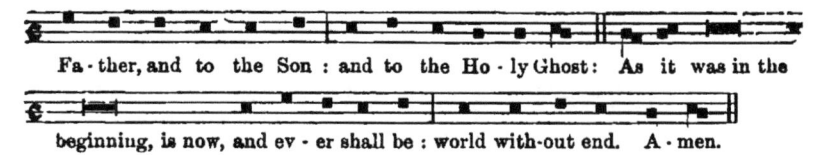

MAGNIFICAT.—*St. Luke i.*

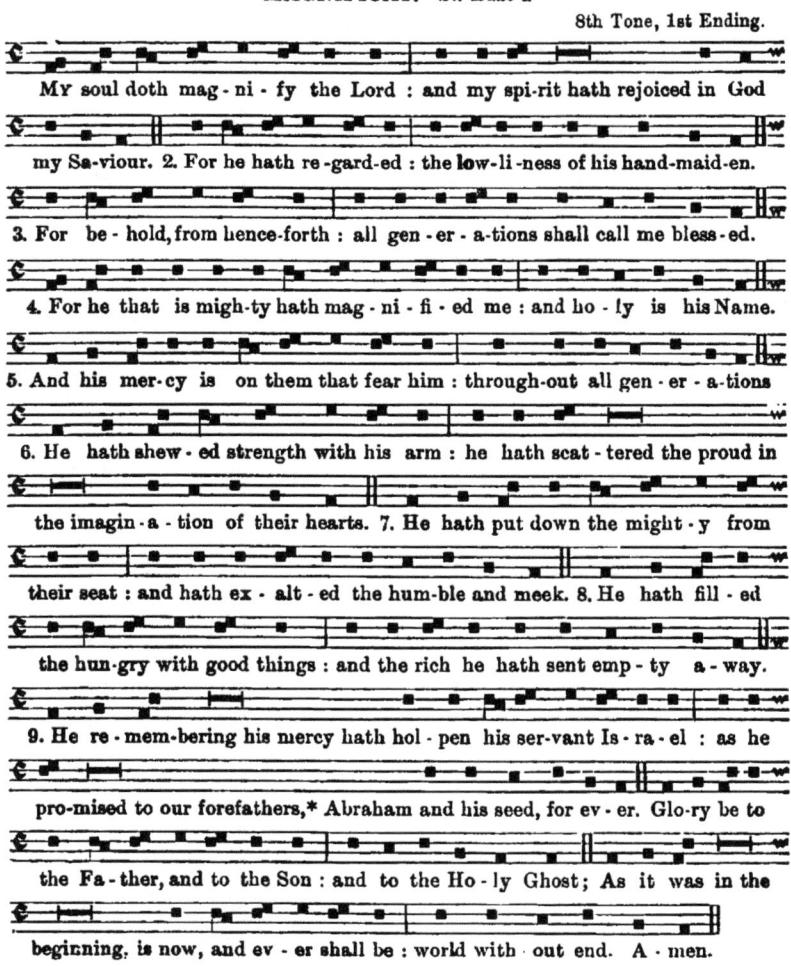

8th Tone, 1st Ending.

My soul doth mag-ni-fy the Lord : and my spi-rit hath rejoiced in God my Sa-viour. 2. For he hath re-gard-ed : the low-li-ness of his hand-maid-en. 3. For be-hold, from hence-forth : all gen-er-a-tions shall call me bless-ed. 4. For he that is migh-ty hath mag-ni-fi-ed me : and ho-ly is his Name. 5. And his mer-cy is on them that fear him : through-out all gen-er-a-tions 6. He hath shew-ed strength with his arm : he hath scat-tered the proud in the imagin-a-tion of their hearts. 7. He hath put down the might-y from their seat : and hath ex-alt-ed the hum-ble and meek. 8. He hath fill-ed the hun-gry with good things : and the rich he hath sent emp-ty a-way. 9. He re-mem-bering his mercy hath hol-pen his ser-vant Is-ra-el : as he pro-mised to our forefathers,* Abraham and his seed, for ev-er. Glo-ry be to the Fa-ther, and to the Son : and to the Ho-ly Ghost; As it was in the beginning, is now, and ev-er shall be : world with-out end. A-men.

EVENING PRAYER.

MAGNIFICAT.—*St. Luke* I.

8th Tone, 2nd Ending.

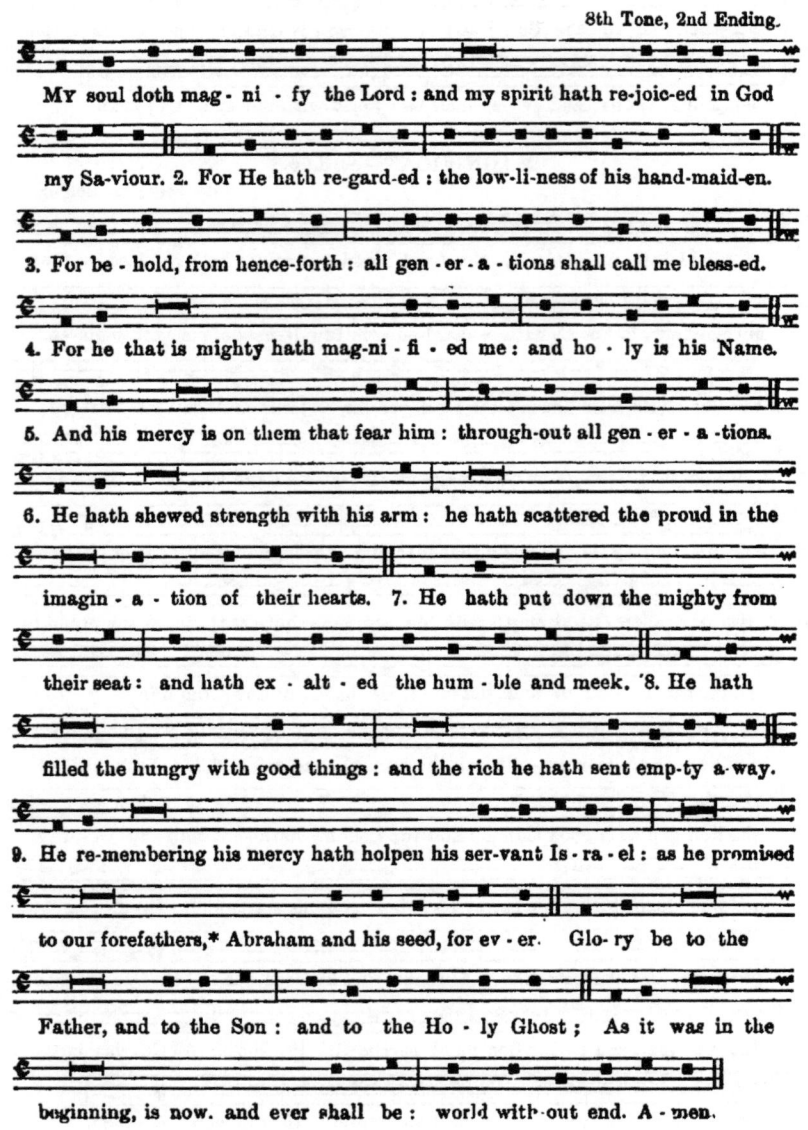

My soul doth mag-ni-fy the Lord : and my spirit hath re-joic-ed in God my Sa-viour. 2. For He hath re-gard-ed : the low-li-ness of his hand-maid-en.

3. For be-hold, from hence-forth : all gen-er-a-tions shall call me bless-ed.

4. For he that is mighty hath mag-ni-fi-ed me : and ho-ly is his Name.

5. And his mercy is on them that fear him : through-out all gen-er-a-tions.

6. He hath shewed strength with his arm : he hath scattered the proud in the imagin-a-tion of their hearts. 7. He hath put down the mighty from their seat : and hath ex-alt-ed the hum-ble and meek. 8. He hath filled the hungry with good things : and the rich he hath sent emp-ty a-way.

9. He re-membering his mercy hath holpen his ser-vant Is-ra-el : as he promised to our forefathers,* Abraham and his seed, for ev-er. Glo-ry be to the Father, and to the Son : and to the Ho-ly Ghost ; As it was in the beginning, is now, and ever shall be : world with-out end. A-men.

EVENING PRAYER.

MAGNIFICAT.—*St. Luke* i

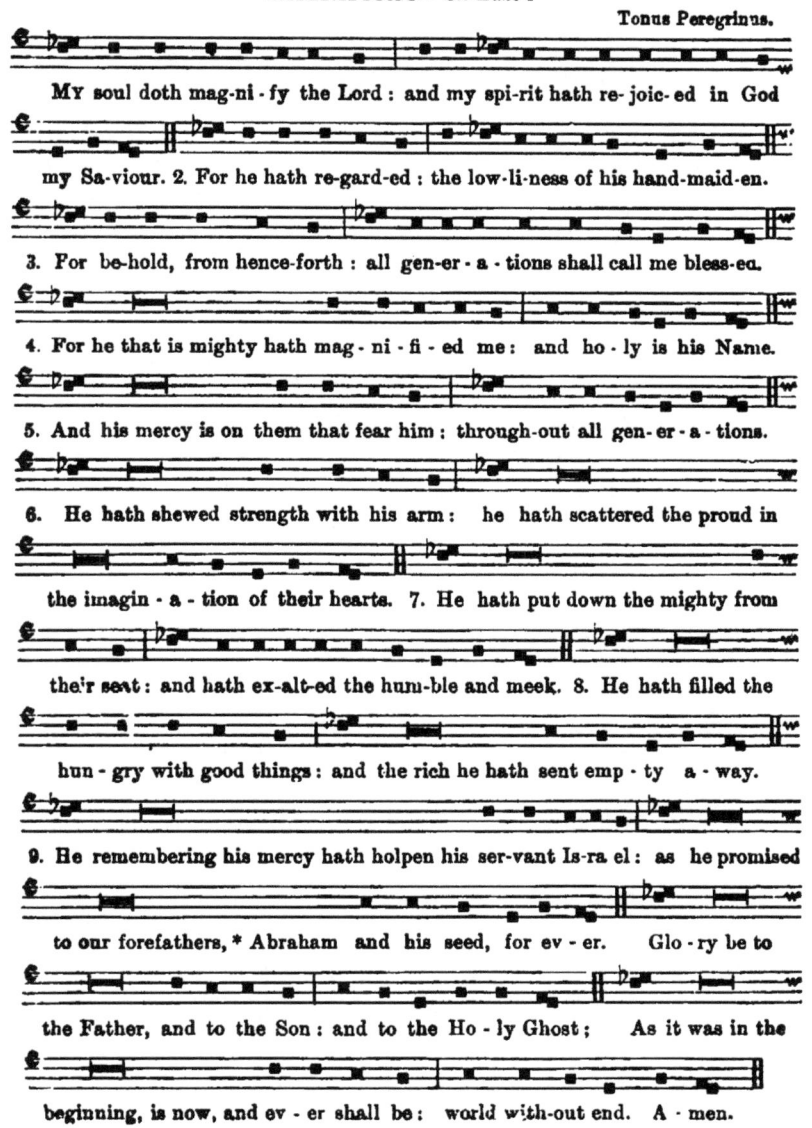

Tonus Peregrinus.

My soul doth mag-ni-fy the Lord : and my spi-rit hath re-joic-ed in God my Sa-viour. 2. For he hath re-gard-ed : the low-li-ness of his hand-maid-en.

3. For be-hold, from hence-forth : all gen-er-a-tions shall call me bless-ed.

4. For he that is mighty hath mag-ni-fi-ed me : and ho-ly is his Name.

5. And his mercy is on them that fear him : through-out all gen-er-a-tions.

6. He hath shewed strength with his arm : he hath scattered the proud in the imagin-a-tion of their hearts. 7. He hath put down the mighty from their seat : and hath ex-alt-ed the hum-ble and meek. 8. He hath filled the hun-gry with good things : and the rich he hath sent emp-ty a-way.

9. He remembering his mercy hath holpen his ser-vant Is-ra el : as he promised to our forefathers, * Abraham and his seed, for ev-er. Glo-ry be to the Father, and to the Son : and to the Ho-ly Ghost ; As it was in the beginning, is now, and ev-er shall be : world with-out end. A-men.

EVENING PRAYER.

CANTATE DOMINO.—*Psalm* xcviii.

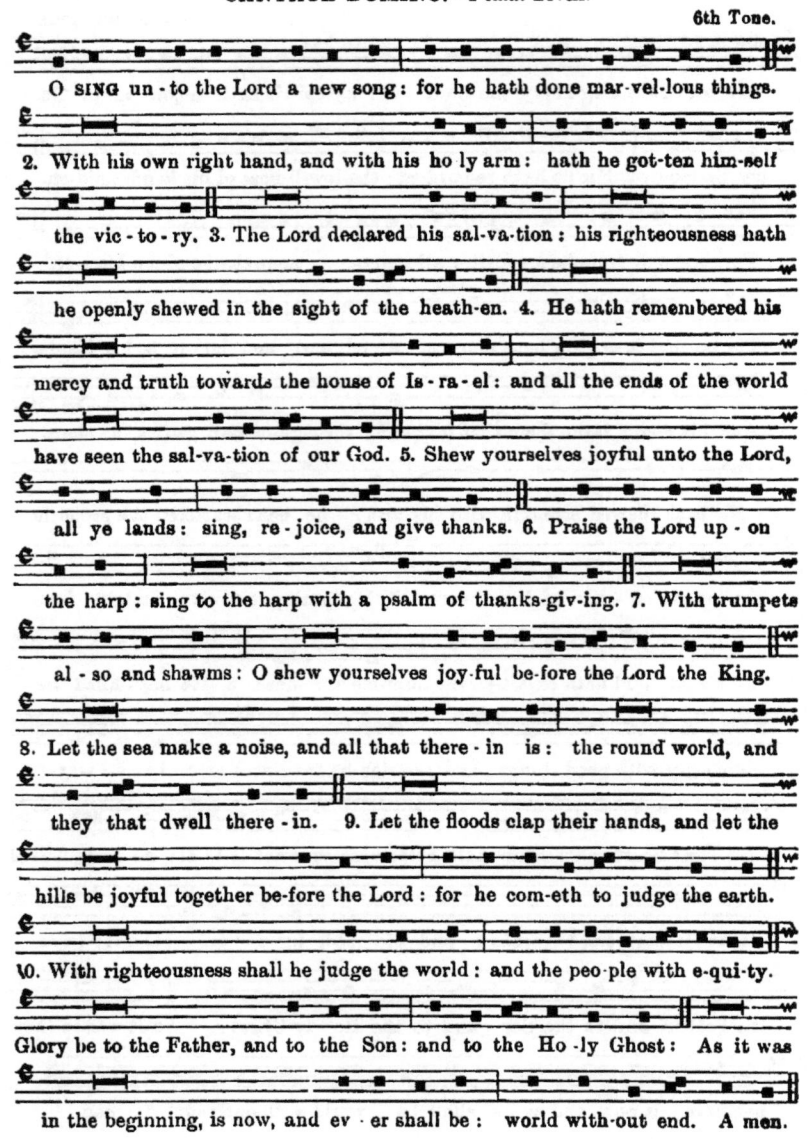

6th Tone.

O SING un-to the Lord a new song: for he hath done mar-vel-lous things.

2. With his own right hand, and with his ho-ly arm: hath he got-ten him-self the vic-to-ry. 3. The Lord declared his sal-va-tion: his righteousness hath he openly shewed in the sight of the heath-en. 4. He hath remembered his mercy and truth towards the house of Is-ra-el: and all the ends of the world have seen the sal-va-tion of our God. 5. Shew yourselves joyful unto the Lord, all ye lands: sing, re-joice, and give thanks. 6. Praise the Lord up-on the harp: sing to the harp with a psalm of thanks-giv-ing. 7. With trumpets al-so and shawms: O shew yourselves joy-ful be-fore the Lord the King. 8. Let the sea make a noise, and all that there-in is: the round world, and they that dwell there-in. 9. Let the floods clap their hands, and let the hills be joyful together be-fore the Lord: for he com-eth to judge the earth. 10. With righteousness shall he judge the world: and the peo-ple with e-qui-ty.

Glory be to the Father, and to the Son: and to the Ho-ly Ghost: As it was in the beginning, is now, and ev-er shall be: world with-out end. A-men.

EVENING PRAYER.

NUNC DIMITTIS.—*St. Luke* ii. 29.

1st Tone, 2nd Ending.

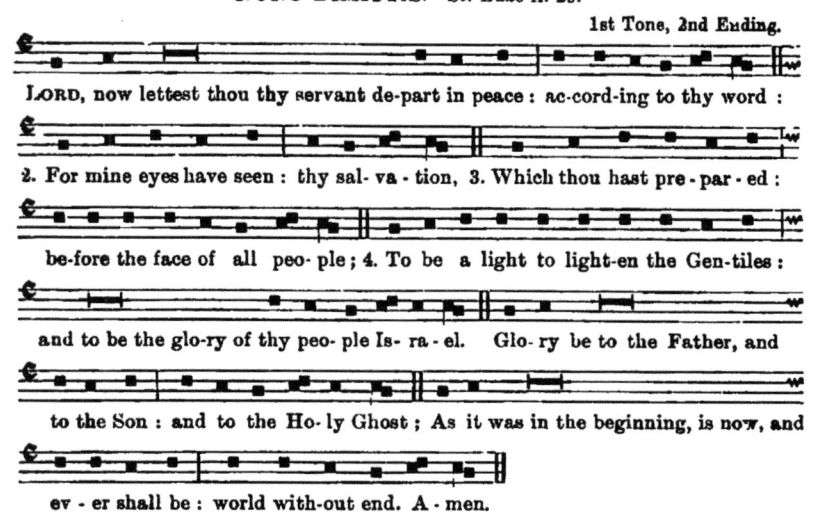

LORD, now lettest thou thy servant de-part in peace : ac-cord-ing to thy word :

2. For mine eyes have seen : thy sal- va - tion, 3. Which thou hast pre - par - ed :

be-fore the face of all peo- ple ; 4. To be a light to light-en the Gen-tiles :

and to be the glo-ry of thy peo- ple Is- ra - el. Glo- ry be to the Father, and

to the Son : and to the Ho- ly Ghost ; As it was in the beginning, is now, and

ev - er shall be : world with-out end. A - men.

NUNC DIMITTIS.—*St. Luke* ii. 29.

2nd Tone, 1st Ending.

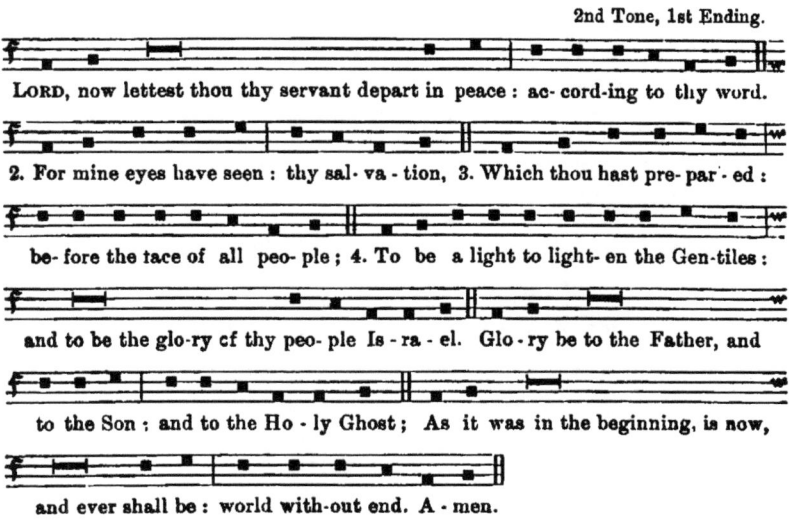

LORD, now lettest thou thy servant depart in peace : ac- cord-ing to thy word.

2. For mine eyes have seen : thy sal- va - tion, 3. Which thou hast pre- par - ed :

be- fore the face of all peo- ple ; 4. To be a light to light- en the Gen-tiles :

and to be the glo-ry cf thy peo- ple Is - ra - el. Glo - ry be to the Father, and

to the Son : and to the Ho - ly Ghost ; As it was in the beginning, is now,

and ever shall be : world with-out end. A - men.

EVENING PRAYER.

NUNC DIMITTIS.—*St. Luke* ii. 29.

3rd Tone, 2nd Ending.

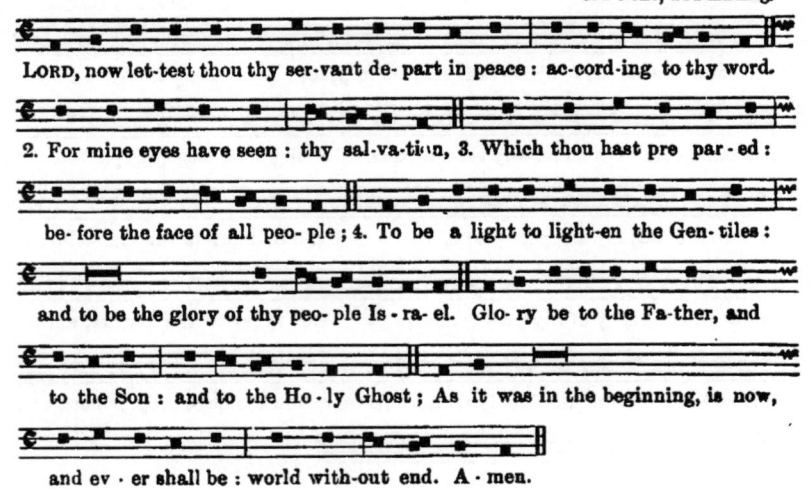

Lord, now let-test thou thy ser-vant de-part in peace : ac-cord-ing to thy word.

2. For mine eyes have seen : thy sal-va-tion, 3. Which thou hast pre par-ed :

be-fore the face of all peo-ple ; 4. To be a light to light-en the Gen-tiles :

and to be the glory of thy peo-ple Is-ra-el. Glo-ry be to the Fa-ther, and

to the Son : and to the Ho-ly Ghost ; As it was in the beginning, is now,

and ev-er shall be : world with-out end. A-men.

NUNC DIMITTIS.—*St. Luke* ii. 29.

4th Tone, 4th Ending.

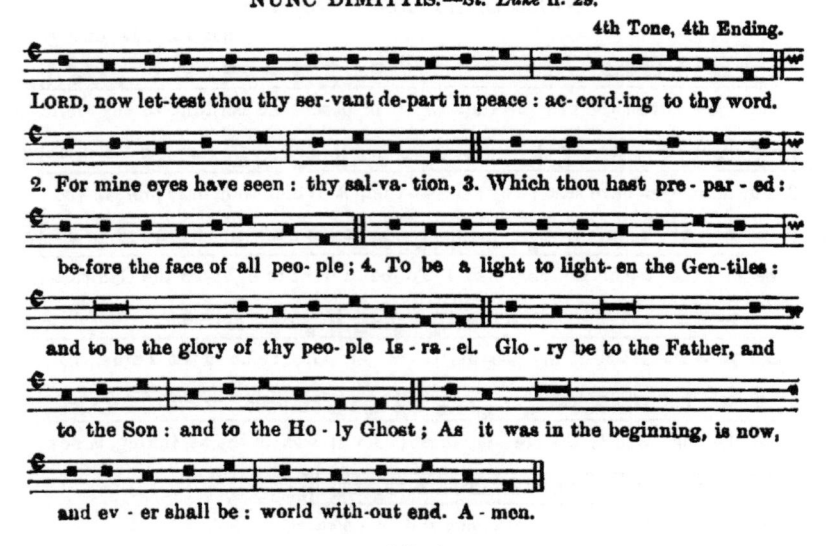

Lord, now let-test thou thy ser-vant de-part in peace : ac-cord-ing to thy word.

2. For mine eyes have seen : thy sal-va-tion, 3. Which thou hast pre-par-ed :

be-fore the face of all peo-ple ; 4. To be a light to light-en the Gen-tiles :

and to be the glory of thy peo-ple Is-ra-el. Glo-ry be to the Father, and

to the Son : and to the Ho-ly Ghost ; As it was in the beginning, is now,

and ev-er shall be : world with-out end. A-men.

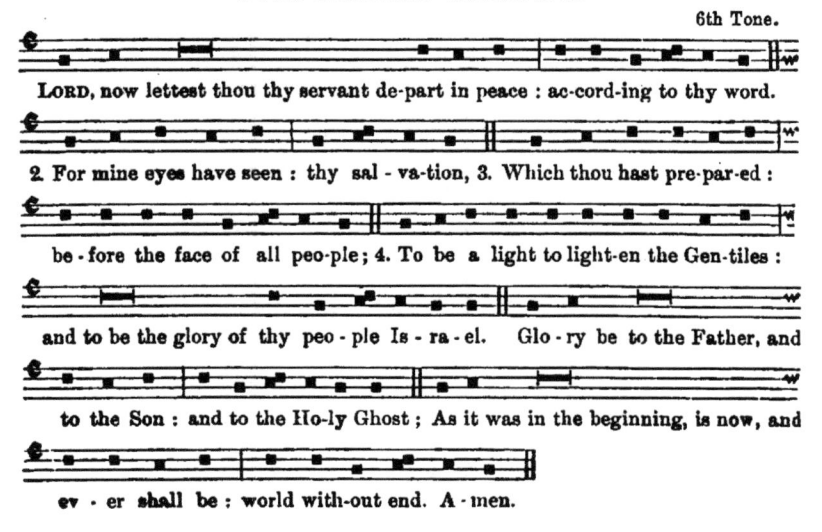

EVENING PRAYER.

NUNC DIMITTIS. —*St. Luke* ii. 29.

5th Tone, 1st Ending.

LORD, now lettest thou thy servant de-part in peace : ac-cord-ing to thy word.

2. For mine eyes have seen : thy sal-va-tion, 3. Which thou hast pre-par-ed :

be-fore the face of all peo-ple; 4. To be a light to light-en the Gen-tiles :

and to be the glory of thy peo-ple Is-ra-el. Glo-ry be to the Father, and

to the Son : and to the Ho-ly Ghost; As it was in the beginning, is now,

and ev-er shall be : world with-out end. A-men.

NUNC DIMITTIS. —*St. Luke* ii. 29.

6th Tone.

LORD, now lettest thou thy servant de-part in peace : ac-cord-ing to thy word.

2. For mine eyes have seen : thy sal-va-tion, 3. Which thou hast pre-par-ed :

be-fore the face of all peo-ple; 4. To be a light to light-en the Gen-tiles :

and to be the glory of thy peo-ple Is-ra-el. Glo-ry be to the Father, and

to the Son : and to the Ho-ly Ghost; As it was in the beginning, is now, and

ev-er shall be : world with-out end. A-men.

EVENING PRAYER.

NUNC DIMITTIS.—*St. Luke* ii. 29.

7th Tone, 6th Ending.

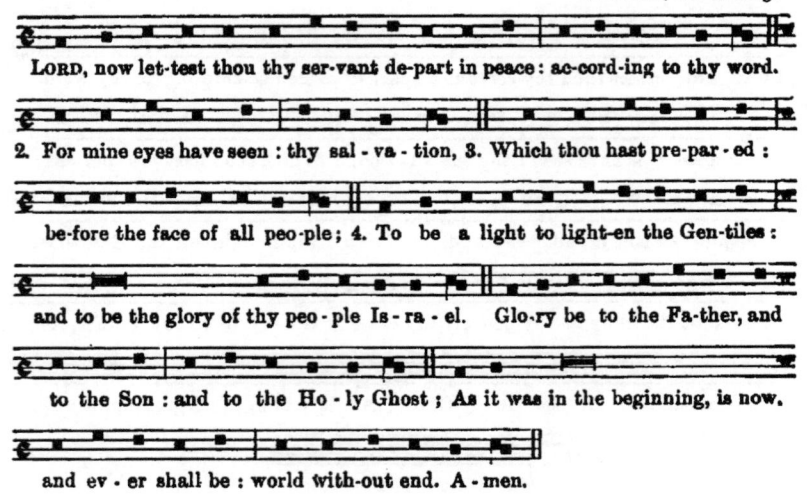

Lord, now let-test thou thy ser-vant de-part in peace : ac-cord-ing to thy word.

2. For mine eyes have seen : thy sal - va - tion, 3. Which thou hast pre-par - ed :

be-fore the face of all peo-ple; 4. To be a light to light-en the Gen-tiles :

and to be the glory of thy peo - ple Is - ra - el. Glo-ry be to the Fa-ther, and

to the Son : and to the Ho - ly Ghost ; As it was in the beginning, is now,

and ev - er shall be : world with-out end. A - men.

NUNC DIMITTIS.—*St. Luke* ii. 29.

8th Tone, 1st Ending.

Lord, now lettest thou thy servant depart in peace : ac-cord-ing to thy word.

2. For mine eyes have seen : thy sal - va - tion, 3. Which thou hast pre-par - ed :

be - fore the face of all peo-ple ; 4. To be a light to light-en the Gen-tiles :

and to be the glory of thy peo-ple Is - ra - el. Glo - ry be to the Father, and

to the Son : and to the Ho-ly Ghost : As it was in the beginning, is now, and ever

shall be : world with-out end. A - men.

EVENING PRAYER.

DEUS MISEREATUR.—*Psalm* lxvii.

1st Tone, 1st Ending.

GOD be merciful unto us, and bless us : and shew us the light of his countenance, and be mer - ci - ful un - to us; 2. That thy way may be known up - on earth : thy sa-ving health a-mong all na-tions. 3. Let the people praise thee, O God : yea, let all the peo-ple praise thee. 4. O let the na-tions re-joice and be glad : for thou shalt judge the folk righteously, and govern the na - tions up - on earth. 5. Let the people praise thee, O God : yea, let all the peo-ple praise thee. 6. Then shall the earth bring forth her in-crease : and God, even our own God, shall give us his bless-ing. 7. God shall bless us : and all the ends of the world shall fear him. Glory be to the Father, and to the Son : and to the Ho-ly Ghost : As it was in the beginning, is now, and ev - er shall be : world with-out end. A - men.

AT MORNING PRAYER.

QUICUNQUE VULT.

8th Tone, 1st Ending.

WHO-SO-EV-ER will be sa-ved : before all things it is necessary that he hold

the Cath-o-lick Faith. 2. Which Faith except every one do keep whole and

un-de-fi-led : without doubt he shall per-ish ev-er-last-ing-ly.

3. And the Catholick Faith is this : that we worship one God in Trinity, and

Trin-i-ty in U-ni-ty ; 4. Neither confounding the Per-sons : nor di-vi-ding

the Sub-stance. 5. For there is one Person of the Father, another of the Son :

and an-oth-er of the Ho-ly Ghost. 6. But the Godhead of the Father, of the

Son, and of the Holy Ghost, is all one : the Glory equal, the Ma-jes-ty

co-e-ter-nal. 7. Such as the Father is, such is the Son : and such is the

Ho-ly Ghost. 8. The Father uncreate, the Son un-cre-ate : and the

Ho-ly Ghost un-cre-ate. 9. The Father incomprehensible, the Son in-

-com-pre-hen-si-ble : and the Holy Ghost in-com-pre-hen-si-ble. 10. The Father

eternal, the Son e-ter-nal : and the Ho-ly Ghost e-ter-nal. 11. And yet they are not

(lviii)

QUICUNQUE VULT.

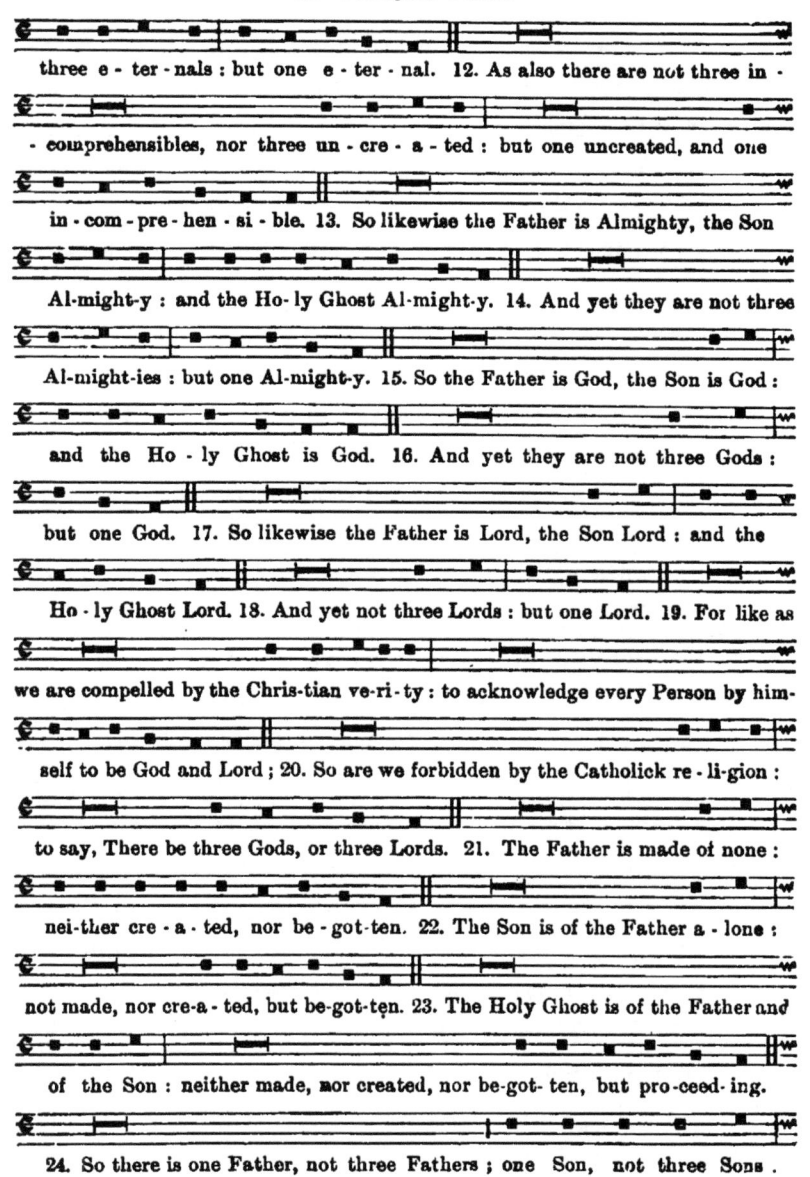

three e-ter-nals : but one e-ter-nal. 12. As also there are not three in-comprehensibles, nor three un-cre-a-ted : but one uncreated, and one in-com-pre-hen-si-ble. 13. So likewise the Father is Almighty, the Son Al-might-y : and the Ho-ly Ghost Al-might-y. 14. And yet they are not three Al-might-ies : but one Al-might-y. 15. So the Father is God, the Son is God : and the Ho-ly Ghost is God. 16. And yet they are not three Gods : but one God. 17. So likewise the Father is Lord, the Son Lord : and the Ho-ly Ghost Lord. 18. And yet not three Lords : but one Lord. 19. For like as we are compelled by the Chris-tian ve-ri-ty : to acknowledge every Person by him-self to be God and Lord ; 20. So are we forbidden by the Catholick re-li-gion : to say, There be three Gods, or three Lords. 21. The Father is made of none : nei-ther cre-a-ted, nor be-got-ten. 22. The Son is of the Father a-lone : not made, nor cre-a-ted, but be-got-ten. 23. The Holy Ghost is of the Father and of the Son : neither made, nor created, nor be-got-ten, but pro-ceed-ing. 24. So there is one Father, not three Fathers ; one Son, not three Sons.

(lix)

QUICUNQUE VULT.

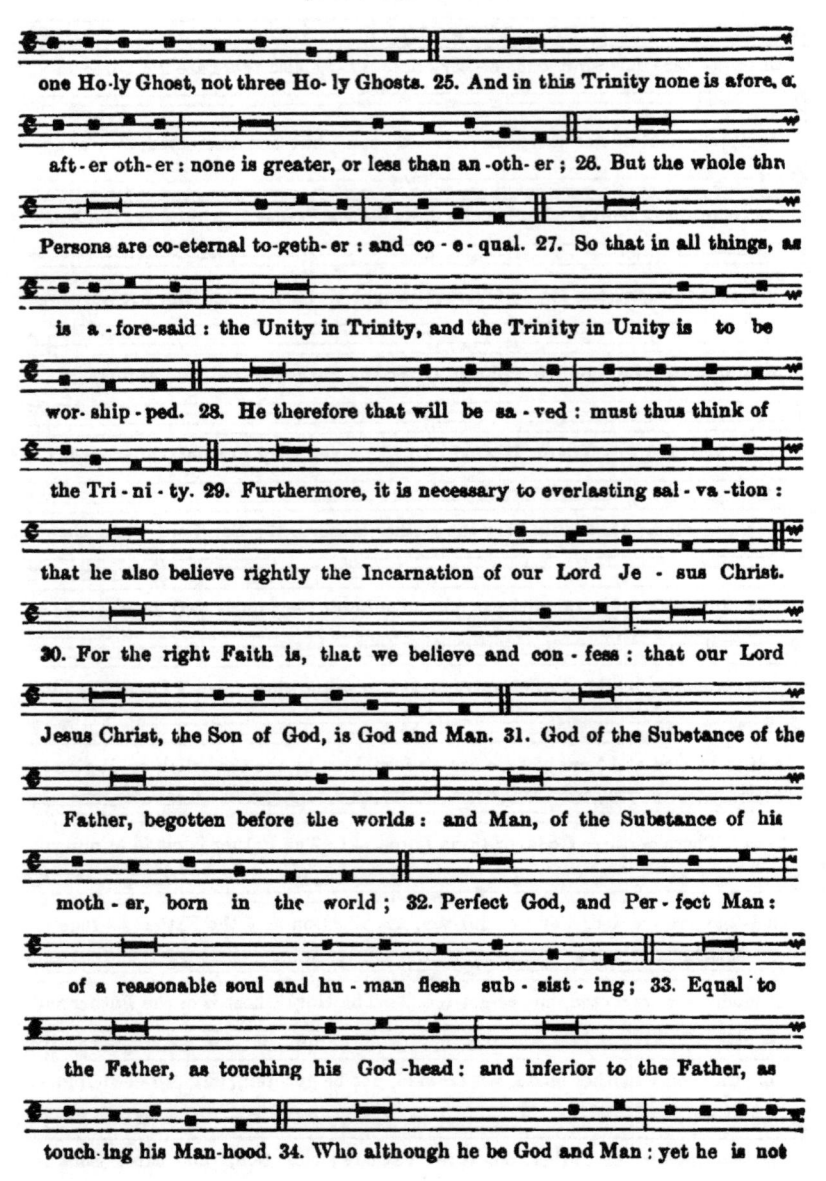

one Ho-ly Ghost, not three Ho-ly Ghosts. 25. And in this Trinity none is afore, α

aft-er oth-er: none is greater, or less than an-oth-er; 26. But the whole thn

Persons are co-eternal to-geth-er: and co-e-qual. 27. So that in all things, as

is a-fore-said: the Unity in Trinity, and the Trinity in Unity is to be

wor-ship-ped. 28. He therefore that will be sa-ved: must thus think of

the Tri-ni-ty. 29. Furthermore, it is necessary to everlasting sal-va-tion:

that he also believe rightly the Incarnation of our Lord Je-sus Christ.

30. For the right Faith is, that we believe and con-fess: that our Lord

Jesus Christ, the Son of God, is God and Man. 31. God of the Substance of the

Father, begotten before the worlds: and Man, of the Substance of his

moth-er, born in the world; 32. Perfect God, and Per-fect Man:

of a reasonable soul and hu-man flesh sub-sist-ing; 33. Equal to

the Father, as touching his God-head: and inferior to the Father, as

touch-ing his Man-hood. 34. Who although he be God and Man: yet he is not

(lx)

QUICUNQUE VULT.

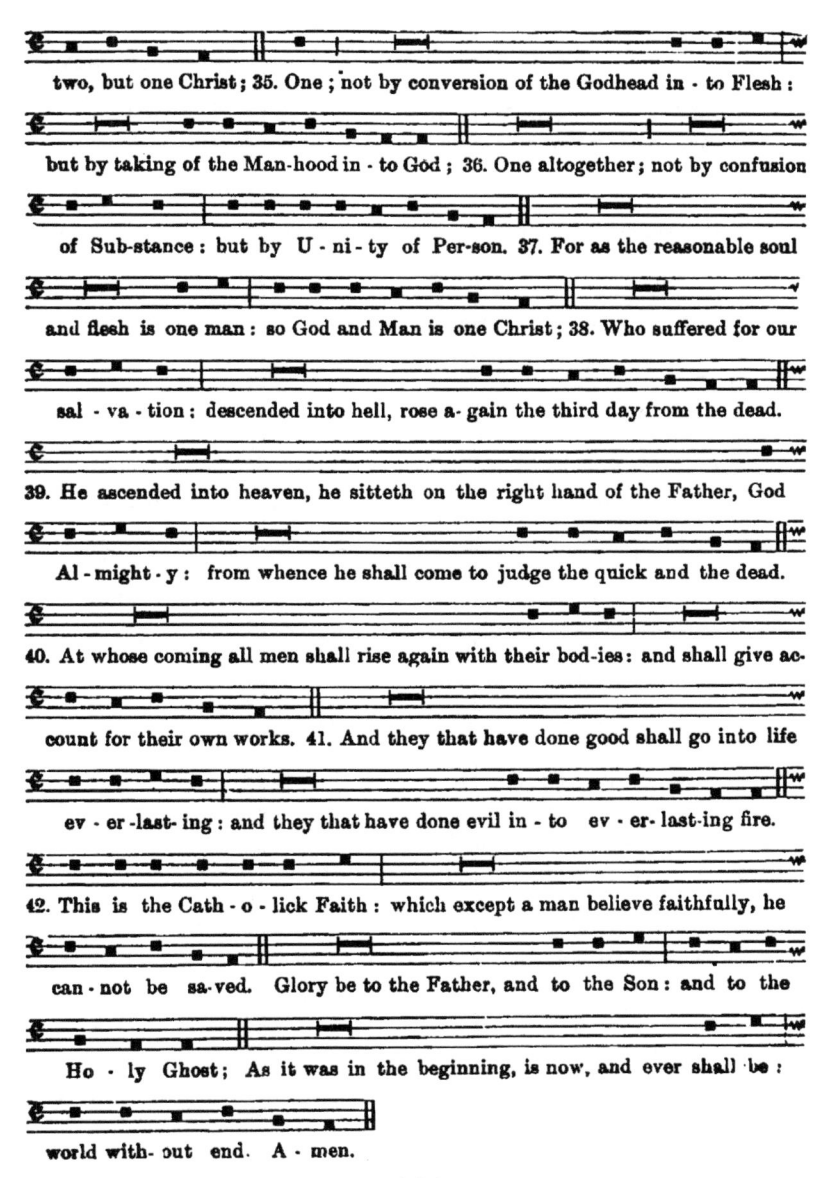

two, but one Christ; 35. One ; not by conversion of the Godhead in - to Flesh:
but by taking of the Man-hood in - to God ; 36. One altogether; not by confusion
of Sub-stance : but by U - ni - ty of Per-son. 37. For as the reasonable soul
and flesh is one man : so God and Man is one Christ; 38. Who suffered for our
sal - va - tion : descended into hell, rose a- gain the third day from the dead.
39. He ascended into heaven, he sitteth on the right hand of the Father, God
Al - might - y : from whence he shall come to judge the quick and the dead.
40. At whose coming all men shall rise again with their bod-ies : and shall give ac-
count for their own works. 41. And they that have done good shall go into life
ev - er -last- ing : and they that have done evil in - to ev - er- last-ing fire.
42. This is the Cath - o - lick Faith : which except a man believe faithfully, he
can - not be sa- ved. Glory be to the Father, and to the Son : and to the
Ho - ly Ghost; As it was in the beginning, is now, and ever shall be :
world with- out end. A - men.

(lxi)

AT MORNING PRAYER ON EASTER DAY.

Instead of the Psalm " O come let us sing," &c.

5th Tone, 1st Ending.

CHRIST our Passover is sacrificed for us : there-fore let us keep the feast :

Not with the old leaven, nor with the leaven of malice and wick - ed - ness :

but with the unleavened bread of sin - cer - i - ty and truth.
1 COR. v. 7.

CHRIST be-ing raised from the dead dieth no more : death hath no more do -

min-ion o - ver him. For in that he died, he died unto sin once : but in that

he liveth, he liv-eth un - to God. Like-wise reckon ye also yourselves to be

dead indeed un - to sin : but alive unto God through Je - sus Christ our Lord.
ROM. vi. 9.

CHRIST is ris - en from the dead : and be-come the first-fruits of them that slept.

For since by man came death : by man came also the re-sur-rec-tion of the dead.

For as in Ad - am all die : e - ven so in Christ shall all be made a-live.
1 COR. xv. 20.

Glo-ry be to the Father, and to the Son : and to the Ho - ly Ghost ; As it

was in the beginning, is now, and ever shall be : world with-out end. A - men.

THE LITANY.

FROM THE *SARUM PROCESSIONAL.*

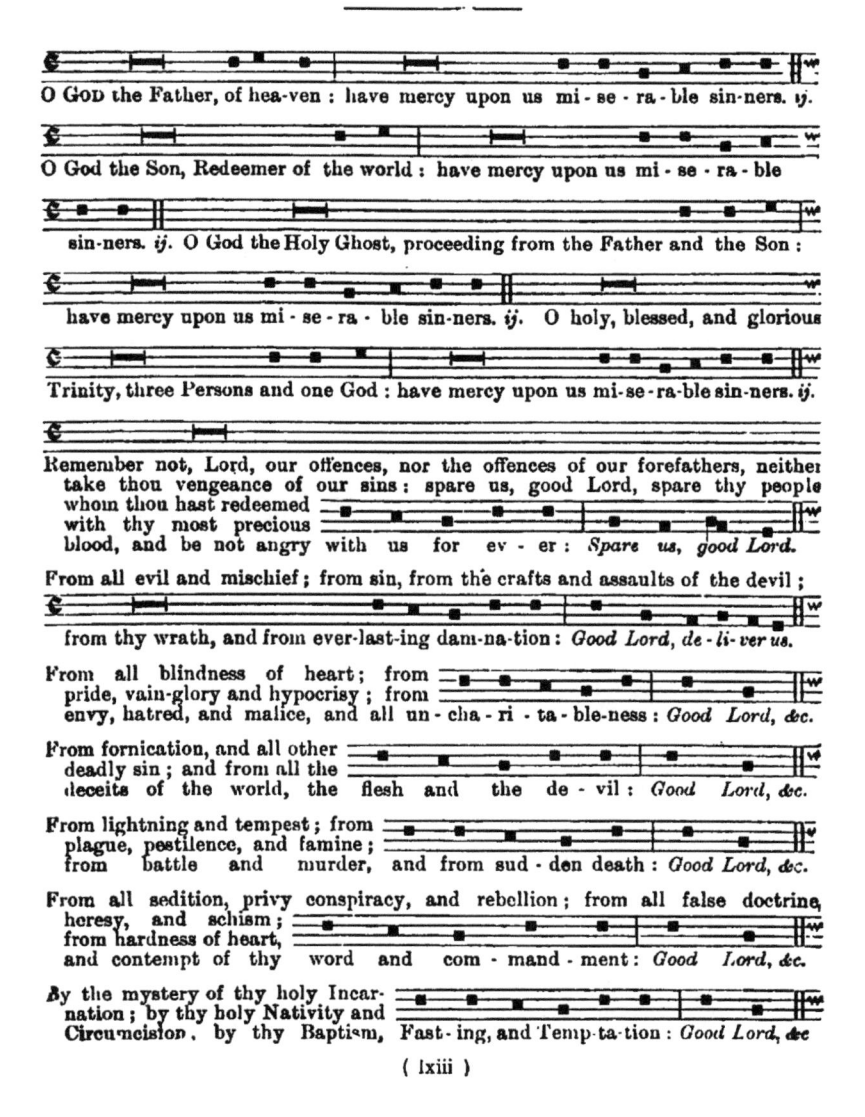

O GOD the Father, of hea-ven : have mercy upon us mi - se - ra - ble sin-ners. *ij.*

O God the Son, Redeemer of the world : have mercy upon us mi - se - ra - ble sin-ners. *ij.* O God the Holy Ghost, proceeding from the Father and the Son : have mercy upon us mi - se - ra - ble sin-ners. *ij.* O holy, blessed, and glorious Trinity, three Persons and one God : have mercy upon us mi-se-ra-ble sin-ners. *ij.*

Remember not, Lord, our offences, nor the offences of our forefathers, neither take thou vengeance of our sins : spare us, good Lord, spare thy people whom thou hast redeemed with thy most precious blood, and be not angry with us for ev - er : *Spare us, good Lord.*

From all evil and mischief ; from sin, from the crafts and assaults of the devil ; from thy wrath, and from ever-last-ing dam-na-tion : *Good Lord, de - li- ver us.*

From all blindness of heart ; from pride, vain-glory and hypocrisy ; from envy, hatred, and malice, and all un - cha - ri - ta - ble-ness : *Good Lord, &c.*

From fornication, and all other deadly sin ; and from all the deceits of the world, the flesh and the de - vil : *Good Lord, &c.*

From lightning and tempest ; from plague, pestilence, and famine ; from battle and murder, and from sud - den death : *Good Lord, &c.*

From all sedition, privy conspiracy, and rebellion ; from all false doctrine, heresy, and schism ; from hardness of heart, and contempt of thy word and com - mand - ment : *Good Lord, &c.*

By the mystery of thy holy Incar- nation ; by thy holy Nativity and Circumcision, by thy Baptism, Fast- ing, and Temp-ta-tion : *Good Lord, &c.*

(lxiii)

THE LITANY.

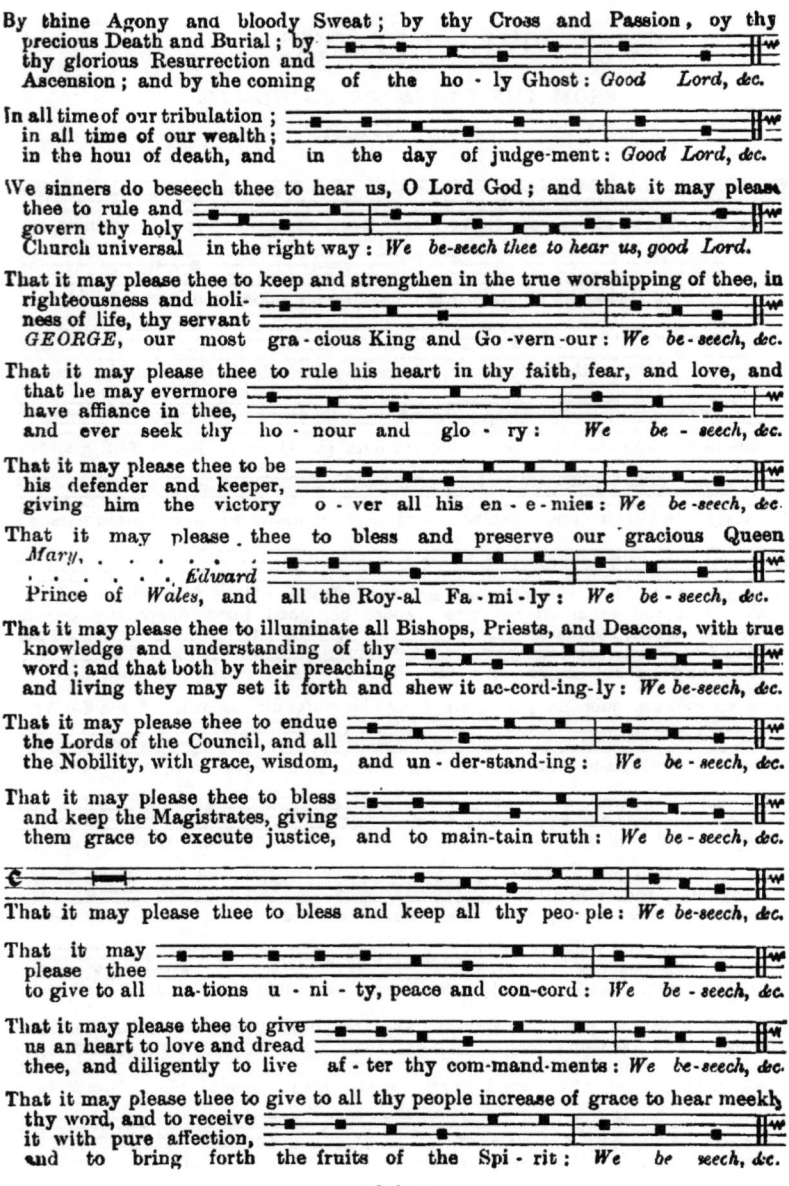

By thine Agony and bloody Sweat; by thy Cross and Passion, oy thy precious Death and Burial; by thy glorious Resurrection and Ascension; and by the coming of the ho-ly Ghost: *Good Lord, &c.*

In all time of our tribulation; in all time of our wealth; in the hour of death, and in the day of judge-ment: *Good Lord, &c.*

We sinners do beseech thee to hear us, O Lord God; and that it may please thee to rule and govern thy holy Church universal in the right way: *We be-seech thee to hear us, good Lord.*

That it may please thee to keep and strengthen in the true worshipping of thee, in righteousness and holiness of life, thy servant GEORGE, our most gra-cious King and Go-vern-our: *We be-seech, &c.*

That it may please thee to rule his heart in thy faith, fear, and love, and that he may evermore have affiance in thee, and ever seek thy ho-nour and glo-ry: *We be-seech, &c.*

That it may please thee to be his defender and keeper, giving him the victory o-ver all his en-e-mies: *We be-seech, &c.*

That it may please thee to bless and preserve our gracious Queen Mary, ... Edward Prince of Wales, and all the Roy-al Fa-mi-ly: *We be-seech, &c.*

That it may please thee to illuminate all Bishops, Priests, and Deacons, with true knowledge and understanding of thy word; and that both by their preaching and living they may set it forth and shew it ac-cord-ing-ly: *We be-seech, &c.*

That it may please thee to endue the Lords of the Council, and all the Nobility, with grace, wisdom, and un-der-stand-ing: *We be-seech, &c.*

That it may please thee to bless and keep the Magistrates, giving them grace to execute justice, and to main-tain truth: *We be-seech, &c.*

That it may please thee to bless and keep all thy peo-ple: *We be-seech, &c.*

That it may please thee to give to all na-tions u-ni-ty, peace and con-cord: *We be-seech, &c.*

That it may please thee to give us an heart to love and dread thee, and diligently to live af-ter thy com-mand-ments: *We be-seech, &c.*

That it may please thee to give to all thy people increase of grace to hear meekly thy word, and to receive it with pure affection, and to bring forth the fruits of the Spi-rit: *We be-seech, &c.*

(lxiv)

THE LITANY.

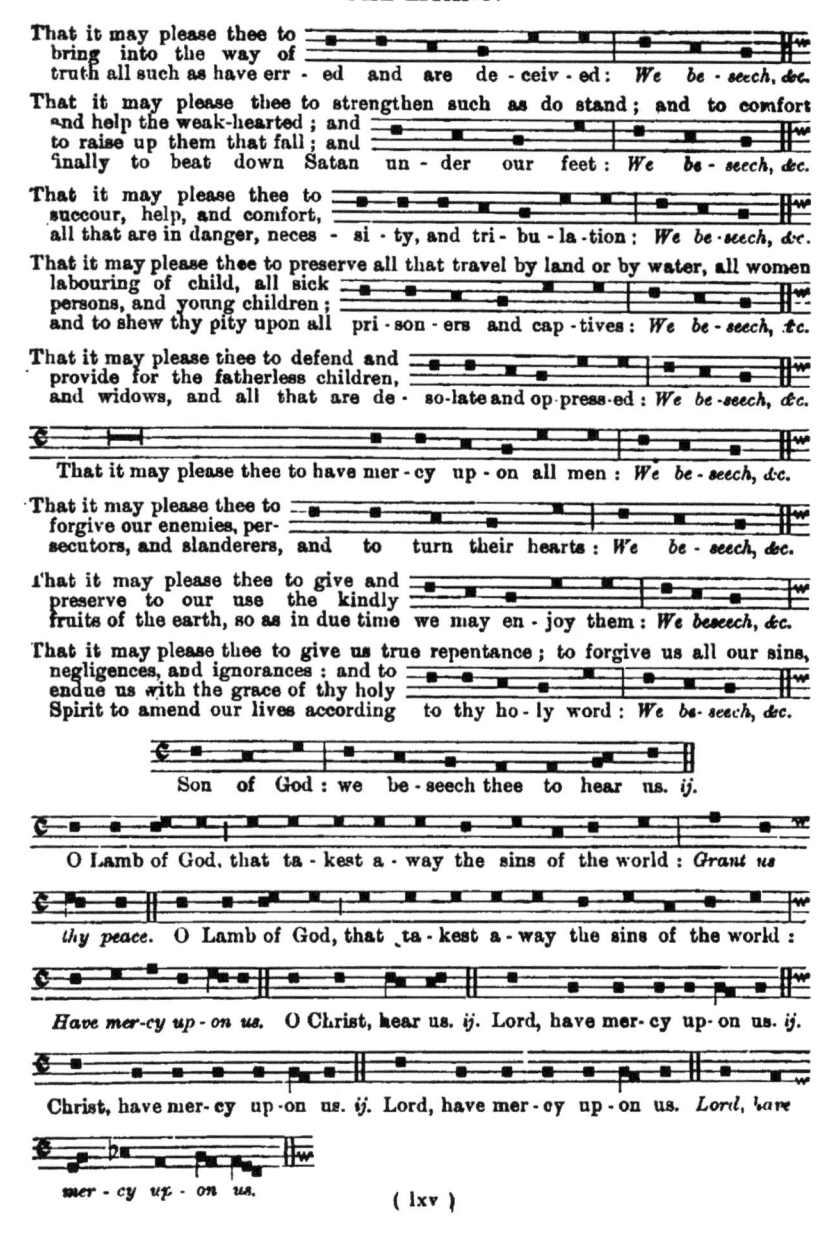

That it may please thee to bring into the way of truth all such as have err - ed and are de - ceiv - ed: *We be - seech, &c.*

That it may please thee to strengthen such as do stand; and to comfort and help the weak-hearted; and to raise up them that fall; and finally to beat down Satan un - der our feet: *We be - seech, &c.*

That it may please thee to succour, help, and comfort, all that are in danger, neces - si - ty, and tri - bu - la - tion: *We be - seech, &c.*

That it may please thee to preserve all that travel by land or by water, all women labouring of child, all sick persons, and young children; and to shew thy pity upon all pri - son - ers and cap - tives: *We be - seech, &c.*

That it may please thee to defend and provide for the fatherless children, and widows, and all that are de - so - late and op - press - ed: *We be - seech, &c.*

That it may please thee to have mer - cy up - on all men: *We be - seech, &c.*

That it may please thee to forgive our enemies, per - secutors, and slanderers, and to turn their hearts: *We be - seech, &c.*

That it may please thee to give and preserve to our use the kindly fruits of the earth, so as in due time we may en - joy them: *We beseech, &c.*

That it may please thee to give us true repentance; to forgive us all our sins, negligences, and ignorances: and to endue us with the grace of thy holy Spirit to amend our lives according to thy ho - ly word: *We be - seech, &c.*

Son of God: we be - seech thee to hear us. *ij.*

O Lamb of God, that ta - kest a - way the sins of the world: *Grant us thy peace.* O Lamb of God, that ta - kest a - way the sins of the world:

Have mer-cy up - on us. O Christ, hear us. *ij.* Lord, have mer - cy up - on us. *ij.*

Christ, have mer - cy up - on us. *ij.* Lord, have mer - cy up - on us. Lord, have mer - cy up - on us.

(lxv)

THE LITANY.

Then shall the Priest and the People with him say the Lord's Prayer.

OUR Father, which art in heaven, hallowed be thy Name : thy kingdom come ; thy will be done : in earth, as it is in heaven. Give us this day our daily bread : and forgive us our trespasses, as we forgive them that trespass against us :

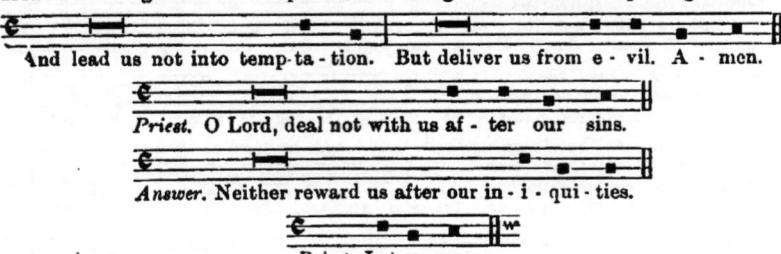

And lead us not into temp-ta-tion. But deliver us from e-vil. A-men.

Priest. O Lord, deal not with us af-ter our sins.

Answer. Neither reward us after our in-i-qui-ties.

Priest. Let us pray.

O GOD, merciful Father, that despisest not the sighing of a contrite heart, nor the desire of such as be sorrowful ; mercifully assist our prayers that we make before thee in all our troubles and adversities, whensoever they oppress us ; and graciously hear us, that those evils, which the craft and subtilty of the devil or man worketh against us be brought to nought, and by the providence of thy goodness they may be dispersed ; that we thy servants, being hurt by no persecutions, may evermore give thanks unto thee in thy holy Church ; through Jesus Christ our Lord. A-men.*

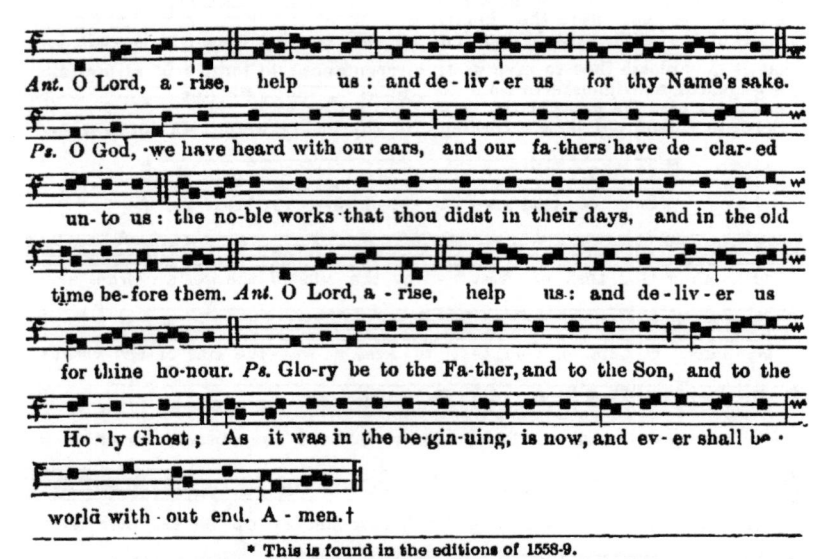

Ant. O Lord, a-rise, help us : and de-liv-er us for thy Name's sake.

Ps. O God, we have heard with our ears, and our fa-thers have de-clar-ed un-to us : the no-ble works that thou didst in their days, and in the old time be-fore them. *Ant.* O Lord, a-rise, help us : and de-liv-er us for thine ho-nour. *Ps.* Glo-ry be to the Fa-ther, and to the Son, and to the Ho-ly Ghost ; As it was in the be-gin-ning, is now, and ev-er shall be · world with-out end. A-men.†

---
* This is found in the editions of 1558-9.

† The Antiphon should be precented and the first half of each Psalm verse sung by Chanters, the whole may conclude with a repetition of the Antiphon. The Suffrages next following are sung by the Choir alternately

(lxvi)

THE LITANY.

From our enemies defend us, O Christ. Graciously look upon our afflictions. Pitifully behold the sorrows of our hearts. Mercifully forgive the sins of thy people. Favourably with mercy hear our prayers. O Son of David, have mercy upon us. Both now and ever vouchsafe to hear us, O Christ. Graciously hear us, O Christ, graciously hear us, O Lord Christ.

Priest. O Lord, let thy mercy be shewed upon us.

Answer. As we do put our trust in thee.

Priest. Let us pray.

WE humbly beseech thee, O Father, mercifully to look upon our infirmities; and for the glory of thy Name turn from us all those evils that we most righteously have deserved; and grant, that in all our troubles we may put our whole trust and confidence in thy mercy, and evermore serve thee in holiness and pureness of living, to thy honour and glory; through our only Mediator and Advocate, Jesus Christ our Lord. *A-men.*

A Prayer of S. Chrysostom.

ALMIGHTY God, who hast given us grace at this time with one accord to make our common supplications unto thee; and dost promise, that when two or three are gathered together in thy Name thou wilt grant their requests; fulfil now, O Lord, the desires and petitions of thy servants as may be most expedient for them; granting us in this world knowledge of thy truth, and in the world to come life ev-er-last-ing. *A-men.*

2 Cor. xiii.

THE grace of our Lord Jesus Christ, and the love of God, and the fellowship of the Holy Ghost, be with us all ev-er-more. *A-men.*

(lxvii)

THE LITANY.

FROM THE *FIRST ENGLISH LITANY*, OF 1544.

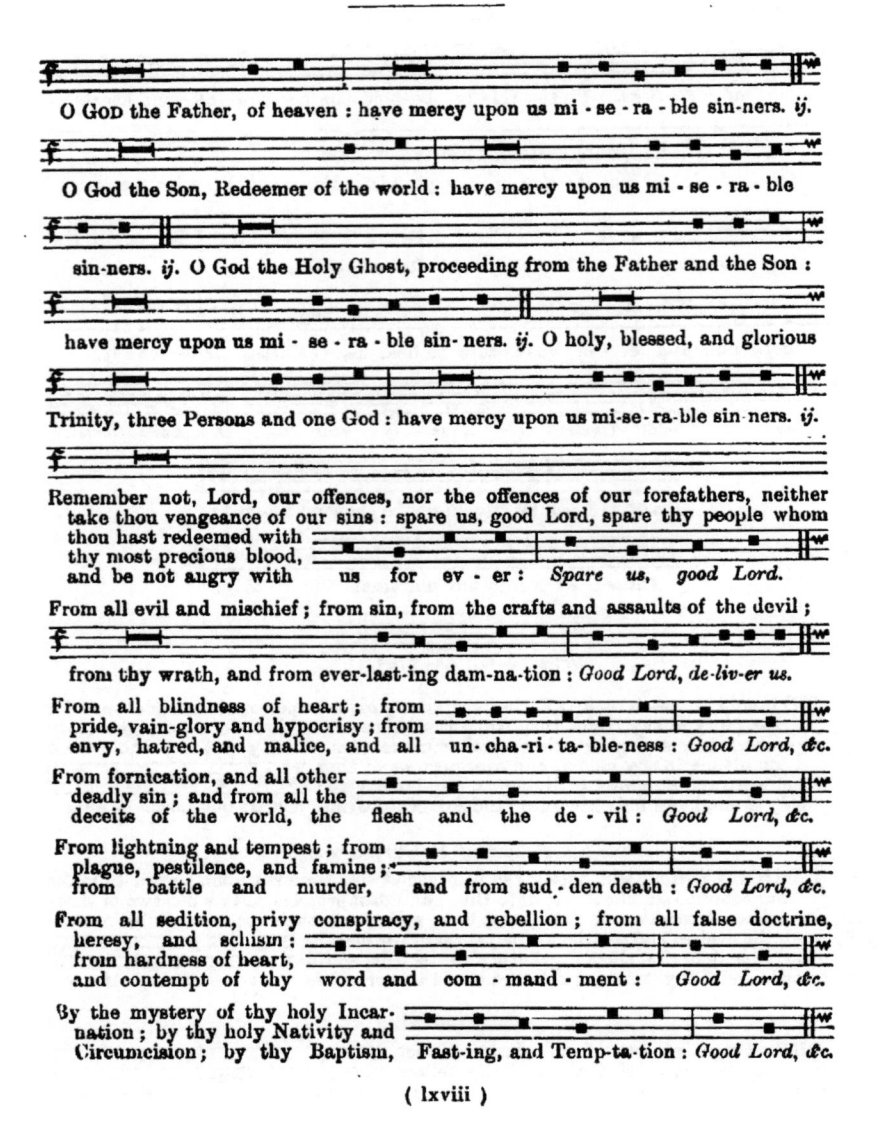

O GOD the Father, of heaven : have mercy upon us mi - se - ra - ble sin - ners. *ij.*

O God the Son, Redeemer of the world : have mercy upon us mi - se - ra - ble sin - ners. *ij.* O God the Holy Ghost, proceeding from the Father and the Son : have mercy upon us mi - se - ra - ble sin - ners. *ij.* O holy, blessed, and glorious Trinity, three Persons and one God : have mercy upon us mi-se-ra-ble sin-ners. *ij.*

Remember not, Lord, our offences, nor the offences of our forefathers, neither take thou vengeance of our sins : spare us, good Lord, spare thy people whom thou hast redeemed with thy most precious blood, and be not angry with us for ev - er : *Spare us, good Lord.*

From all evil and mischief; from sin, from the crafts and assaults of the devil; from thy wrath, and from ever-last-ing dam-na-tion : *Good Lord, de-liv-er us.*

From all blindness of heart; from pride, vain-glory and hypocrisy; from envy, hatred, and malice, and all un - cha - ri - ta - ble-ness : *Good Lord, &c.*

From fornication, and all other deadly sin ; and from all the deceits of the world, the flesh and the de - vil : *Good Lord, &c.*

From lightning and tempest; from plague, pestilence, and famine ; from battle and murder, and from sud - den death : *Good Lord, &c.*

From all sedition, privy conspiracy, and rebellion ; from all false doctrine, heresy, and schism : from hardness of heart, and contempt of thy word and com - mand - ment : *Good Lord, &c.*

By the mystery of thy holy Incar-nation ; by thy holy Nativity and Circumcision; by thy Baptism, Fast-ing, and Temp-ta-tion : *Good Lord, &c.*

(lxviii)

THE LITANY.

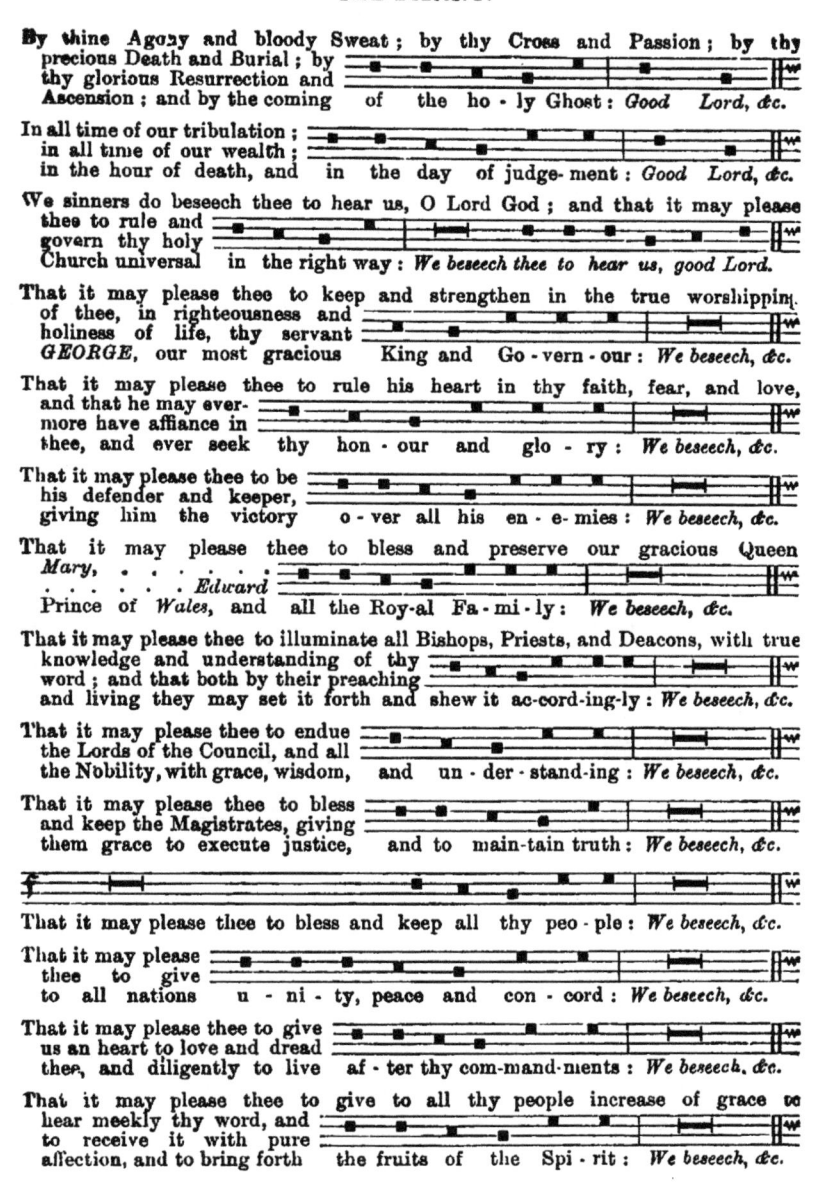

By thine Agony and bloody Sweat; by thy Cross and Passion; by thy precious Death and Burial; by thy glorious Resurrection and Ascension; and by the coming of the ho-ly Ghost: *Good Lord, &c.*

In all time of our tribulation; in all time of our wealth; in the hour of death, and in the day of judge-ment: *Good Lord, &c.*

We sinners do beseech thee to hear us, O Lord God; and that it may please thee to rule and govern thy holy Church universal in the right way: *We beseech thee to hear us, good Lord.*

That it may please thee to keep and strengthen in the true worshipping of thee, in righteousness and holiness of life, thy servant GEORGE, our most gracious King and Go-vern-our: *We beseech, &c.*

That it may please thee to rule his heart in thy faith, fear, and love, and that he may ever-more have affiance in thee, and ever seek thy hon-our and glo-ry: *We beseech, &c.*

That it may please thee to be his defender and keeper, giving him the victory o-ver all his en-e-mies: *We beseech, &c.*

That it may please thee to bless and preserve our gracious Queen Mary, ... Edward Prince of *Wales*, and all the Roy-al Fa-mi-ly: *We beseech, &c.*

That it may please thee to illuminate all Bishops, Priests, and Deacons, with true knowledge and understanding of thy word; and that both by their preaching and living they may set it forth and shew it ac-cord-ing-ly: *We beseech, &c.*

That it may please thee to endue the Lords of the Council, and all the Nobility, with grace, wisdom, and un-der-stand-ing: *We beseech, &c.*

That it may please thee to bless and keep the Magistrates, giving them grace to execute justice, and to main-tain truth: *We beseech, &c.*

That it may please thee to bless and keep all thy peo-ple: *We beseech, &c.*

That it may please thee to give to all nations u-ni-ty, peace and con-cord: *We beseech, &c.*

That it may please thee to give us an heart to love and dread thee, and diligently to live af-ter thy com-mand-ments: *We beseech, &c.*

That it may please thee to give to all thy people increase of grace to hear meekly thy word, and to receive it with pure affection, and to bring forth the fruits of the Spi-rit: *We beseech, &c.*

THE LITANY.

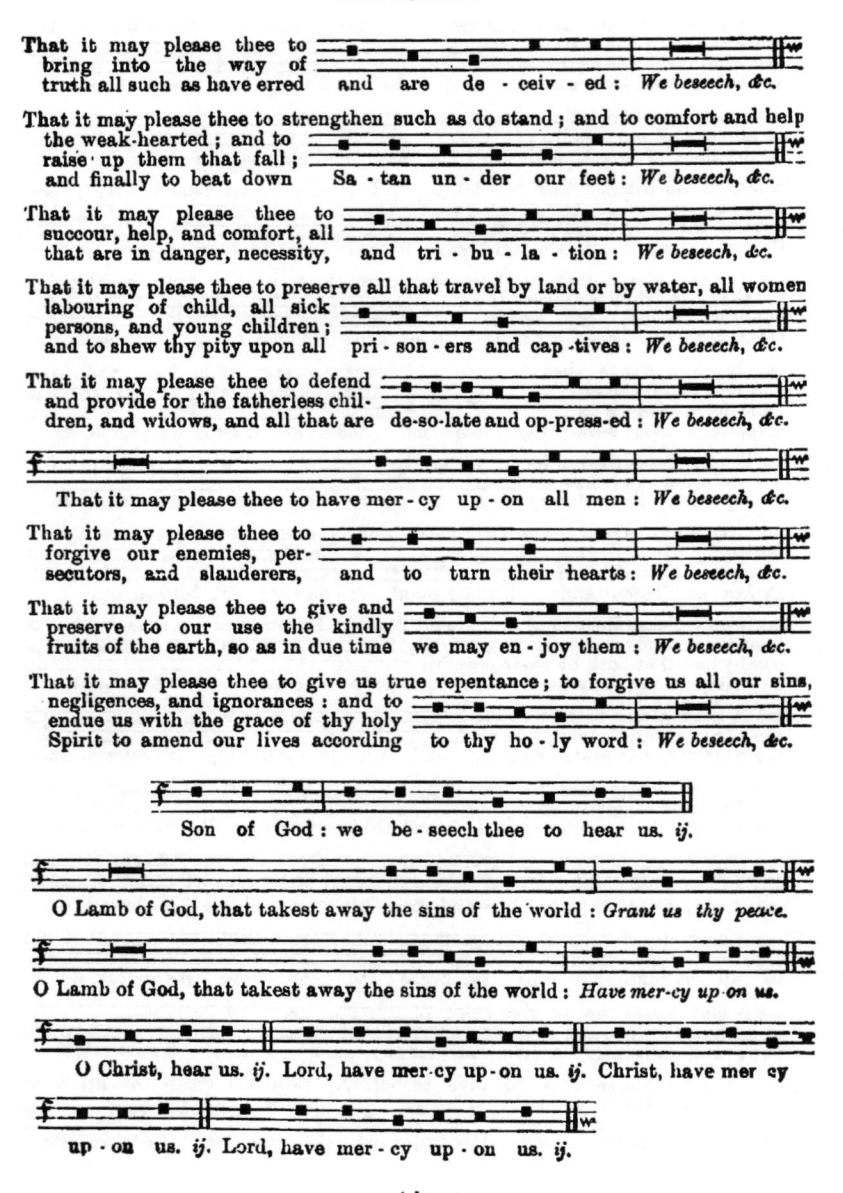

That it may please thee to bring into the way of truth all such as have erred and are de-ceiv-ed: *We beseech, &c.*

That it may please thee to strengthen such as do stand; and to comfort and help the weak-hearted; and to raise up them that fall; and finally to beat down Sa-tan un-der our feet: *We beseech, &c.*

That it may please thee to succour, help, and comfort, all that are in danger, necessity, and tri-bu-la-tion: *We beseech, &c.*

That it may please thee to preserve all that travel by land or by water, all women labouring of child, all sick persons, and young children; and to shew thy pity upon all pri-son-ers and cap-tives: *We beseech, &c.*

That it may please thee to defend and provide for the fatherless children, and widows, and all that are de-so-late and op-press-ed: *We beseech, &c.*

That it may please thee to have mer-cy up-on all men: *We beseech, &c.*

That it may please thee to forgive our enemies, persecutors, and slanderers, and to turn their hearts: *We beseech, &c.*

That it may please thee to give and preserve to our use the kindly fruits of the earth, so as in due time we may en-joy them: *We beseech, &c.*

That it may please thee to give us true repentance; to forgive us all our sins, negligences, and ignorances: and to endue us with the grace of thy holy Spirit to amend our lives according to thy ho-ly word: *We beseech, &c.*

Son of God: we be-seech thee to hear us. *ij.*

O Lamb of God, that takest away the sins of the world: *Grant us thy peace.*

O Lamb of God, that takest away the sins of the world: *Have mer-cy up-on us.*

O Christ, hear us. *ij.* Lord, have mer-cy up-on us. *ij.* Christ, have mer-cy up-on us. *ij.* Lord, have mer-cy up-on us. *ij.*

(lxx)

THE LITANY.

Then shall the Priest and the People with him say the Lord's Prayer.

OUR Father, which art in heaven, hallowed be thy Name: thy kingdom come; thy will be done in earth, as it is in heaven. Give us this day our daily bread: and forgive us our trespasses, as we forgive them that trespass against us:

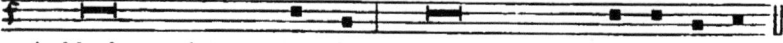

And lead us not into temp-ta - tion. But deliver us from e - vil. A-men.

Priest. O Lord, deal not with us af - ter our sins.

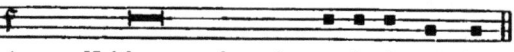

Answer. Neither reward us after our in - i - qui-ties.

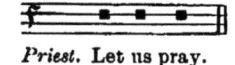

Priest. Let us pray.

O GOD, merciful Father, that despisest not the sighing of a contrite heart, nor the desire of such as be sorrowful; mercifully assist our prayers that we make before thee in all our troubles and adversities, whensoever they oppress us; and graciously hear us, that those evils, which the craft or subtilty of the devil or man worketh against us be brought to nought, and by the providence of thy goodness they may be dispersed; that we thy servants, being hurt by no persecutions, may evermore give thanks unto thee in thy holy Church; through Je - sus Christ our Lord.

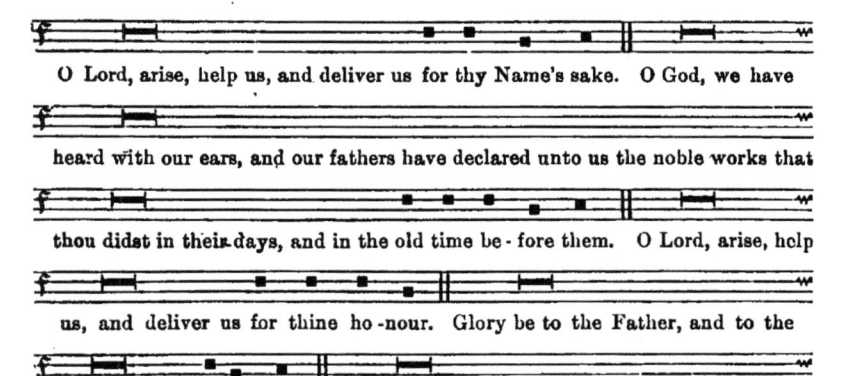

O Lord, arise, help us, and deliver us for thy Name's sake. O God, we have heard with our ears, and our fathers have declared unto us the noble works that thou didst in their days, and in the old time be - fore them. O Lord, arise, help us, and deliver us for thine ho - nour. Glory be to the Father, and to the Son, and to the Ho-ly Ghost; As it was in the beginning, is now, and ever shall be, world with-out end. A - men.

THE LITANY.

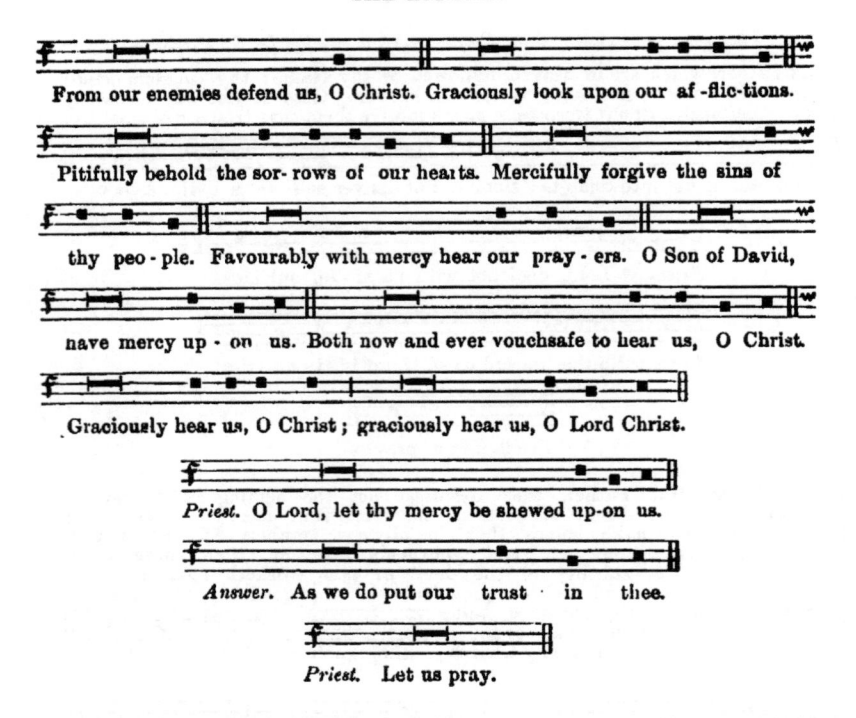

From our enemies defend us, O Christ. Graciously look upon our af-flic-tions.

Pitifully behold the sor-rows of our hearts. Mercifully forgive the sins of

thy peo-ple. Favourably with mercy hear our pray-ers. O Son of David,

have mercy up-on us. Both now and ever vouchsafe to hear us, O Christ.

Graciously hear us, O Christ; graciously hear us, O Lord Christ.

Priest. O Lord, let thy mercy be shewed up-on us.

Answer. As we do put our trust in thee.

Priest. Let us pray.

WE humbly beseech thee, O Father, mercifully to look upon our infirmities; and for the glory of thy Name turn from us all those evils that we most righteously have deserved; and grant, that in all our troubles we may put our whole trust and confidence in thy mercy, and evermore serve thee in holiness and pureness of living, to thy honour and glory; through our only Mediator and Advocate, Jesus Christ our Lord. A-men.

A Prayer of S. Chrysostom.

ALMIGHTY God, who hast given us grace at this time with one accord to make our common supplications unto thee; and dost promise, that when two or three are gathered together in thy Name thou wilt grant their requests; fulfil now, O Lord, the desires and petitions of thy servants as may be most expedient for them; granting us in this world knowledge of thy truth, and in the world to come life ev-er last-ing. A men.

2 Cor. xiii.

THE grace of our Lord Jesus Christ, and the love of God, and the fellow-ship of the Holy Ghost, be with us all ev - er - more. A - men.

(lxxii)

THE PSALTER NOTED.

MORNING PRAYER.   DAY 1

PSALM I.—*Beatus vir, qui non abiit, &c.*

1st Tone, 1st Ending.

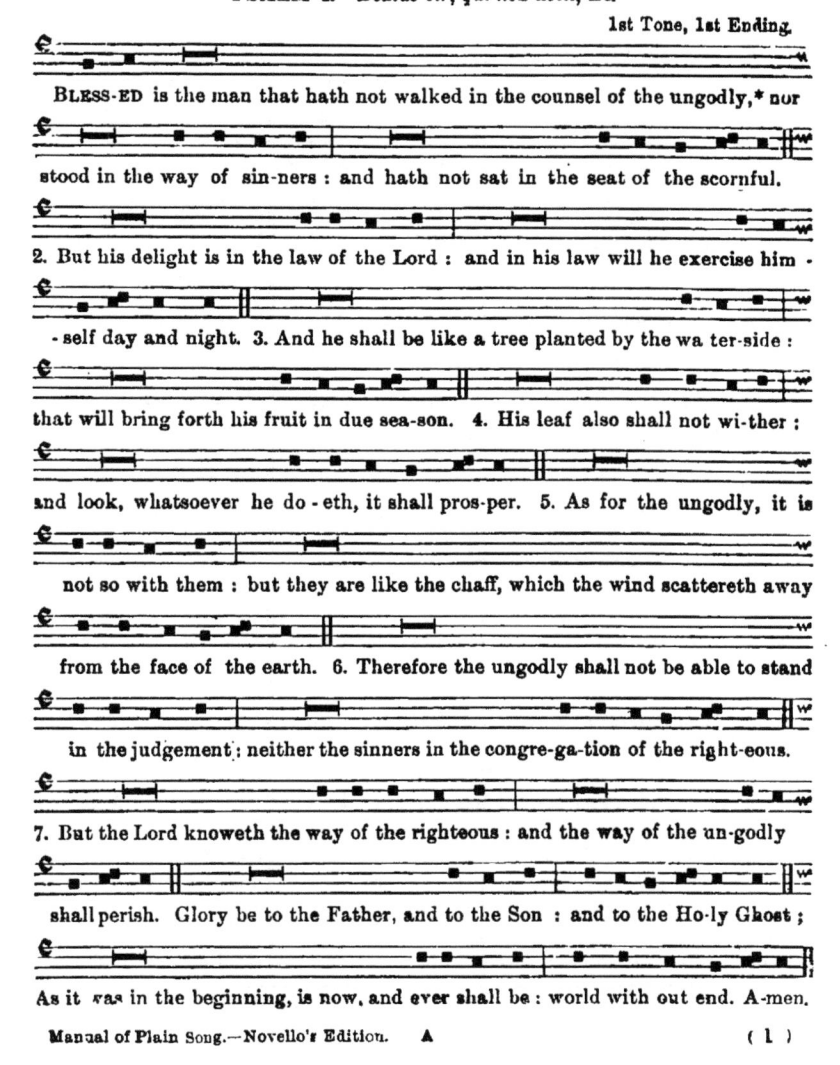

BLESS-ED is the man that hath not walked in the counsel of the ungodly,* nor stood in the way of sin-ners : and hath not sat in the seat of the scornful.

2. But his delight is in the law of the Lord : and in his law will he exercise him - self day and night. 3. And he shall be like a tree planted by the wa ter-side : that will bring forth his fruit in due sea-son. 4. His leaf also shall not wi-ther : and look, whatsoever he do - eth, it shall pros-per. 5. As for the ungodly, it is not so with them : but they are like the chaff, which the wind scattereth away from the face of the earth. 6. Therefore the ungodly shall not be able to stand in the judgement : neither the sinners in the congre-ga-tion of the right-eous.

7. But the Lord knoweth the way of the righteous : and the way of the un-godly shall perish. Glory be to the Father, and to the Son : and to the Ho-ly Ghost ; As it was in the beginning, is now, and ever shall be : world with out end. A-men.

Manual of Plain Song.—Novello's Edition.   A

Day 1.   MORNING PRAYER.

PSALM II.—*Quare fremuerunt gentes?*

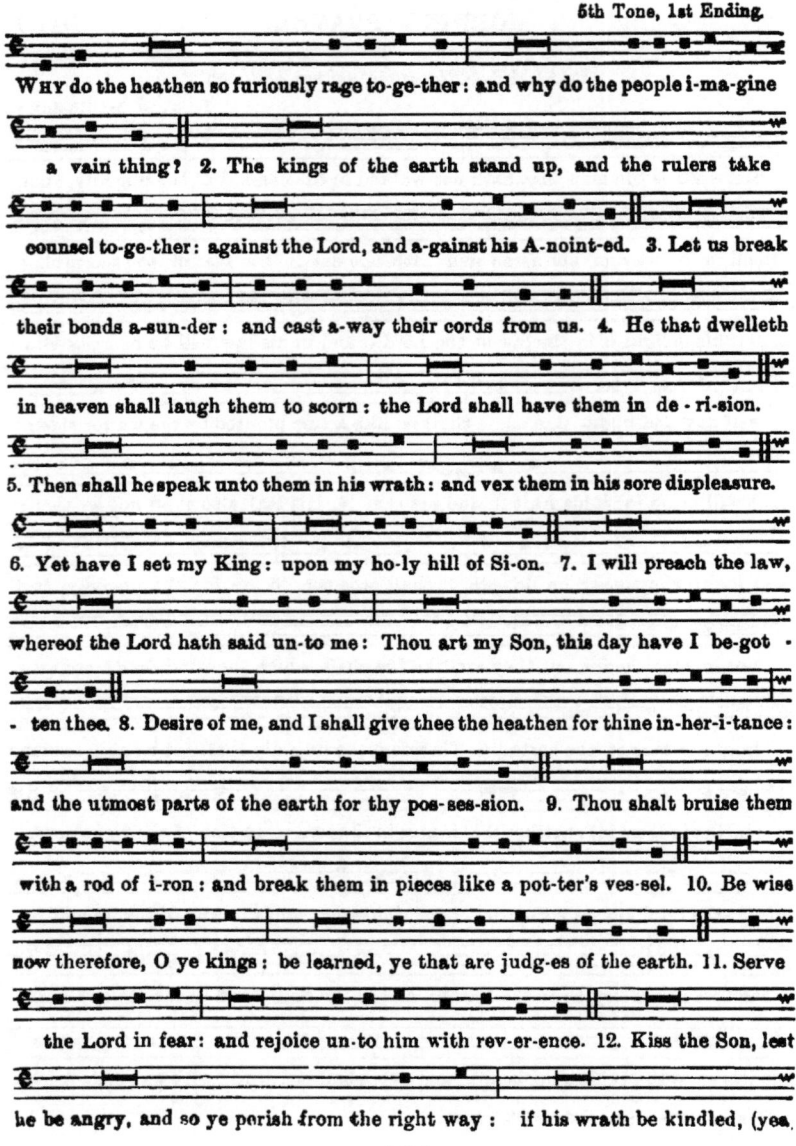

5th Tone, 1st Ending.

WHY do the heathen so furiously rage to-ge-ther : and why do the people i-ma-gine a vain thing? 2. The kings of the earth stand up, and the rulers take counsel to-ge-ther: against the Lord, and a-gainst his A-noint-ed. 3. Let us break their bonds a-sun-der : and cast a-way their cords from us. 4. He that dwelleth in heaven shall laugh them to scorn : the Lord shall have them in de-ri-sion. 5. Then shall he speak unto them in his wrath : and vex them in his sore displeasure. 6. Yet have I set my King : upon my ho-ly hill of Si-on. 7. I will preach the law, whereof the Lord hath said un-to me : Thou art my Son, this day have I be-got-ten thee. 8. Desire of me, and I shall give thee the heathen for thine in-her-i-tance : and the utmost parts of the earth for thy pos-ses-sion. 9. Thou shalt bruise them with a rod of i-ron : and break them in pieces like a pot-ter's ves-sel. 10. Be wise now therefore, O ye kings : be learned, ye that are judg-es of the earth. 11. Serve the Lord in fear : and rejoice un-to him with rev-er-ence. 12. Kiss the Son, lest he be angry, and so ye perish from the right way : if his wrath be kindled, (yea,

MORNING PRAYER. DAY 1.

but a little,) blessed are all they that put their trust in him. Glory be to the Father,

and to the Son : and to the Ho - ly Ghost ; As it was in the beginning, is now

and ever shall be : world with-out end. A-men.

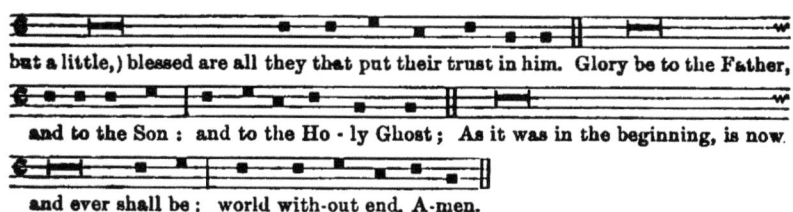

PSALM III.—*Domine, quid multiplicati?*

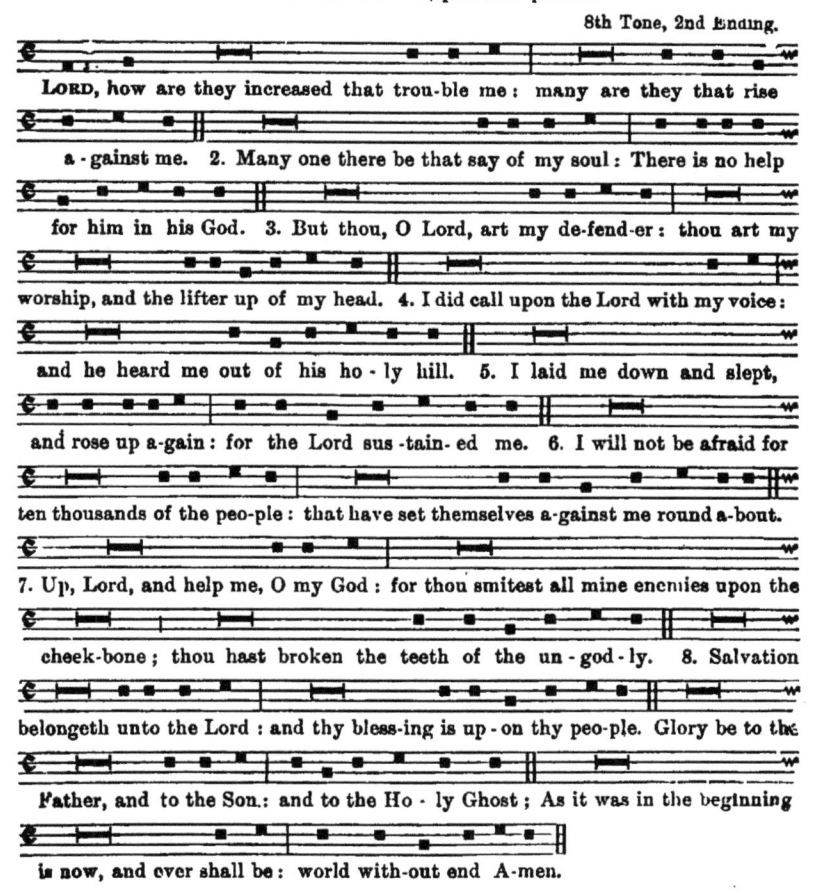

8th Tone, 2nd Ending.

LORD, how are they increased that trou-ble me : many are they that rise

a - gainst me. 2. Many one there be that say of my soul : There is no help

for him in his God. 3. But thou, O Lord, art my de-fend-er : thou art my

worship, and the lifter up of my head. 4. I did call upon the Lord with my voice :

and he heard me out of his ho - ly hill. 5. I laid me down and slept,

and rose up a-gain : for the Lord sus-tain-ed me. 6. I will not be afraid for

ten thousands of the peo-ple : that have set themselves a-gainst me round a-bout.

7. Up, Lord, and help me, O my God : for thou smitest all mine enemies upon the

cheek-bone ; thou hast broken the teeth of the un - god - ly. 8. Salvation

belongeth unto the Lord : and thy bless-ing is up - on thy peo-ple. Glory be to the

Father, and to the Son.: and to the Ho - ly Ghost ; As it was in the beginning

is now, and ever shall be : world with-out end A-men.

Day 1.   MORNING PRAYER.

PSALM IV.—*Cum invocarem.*

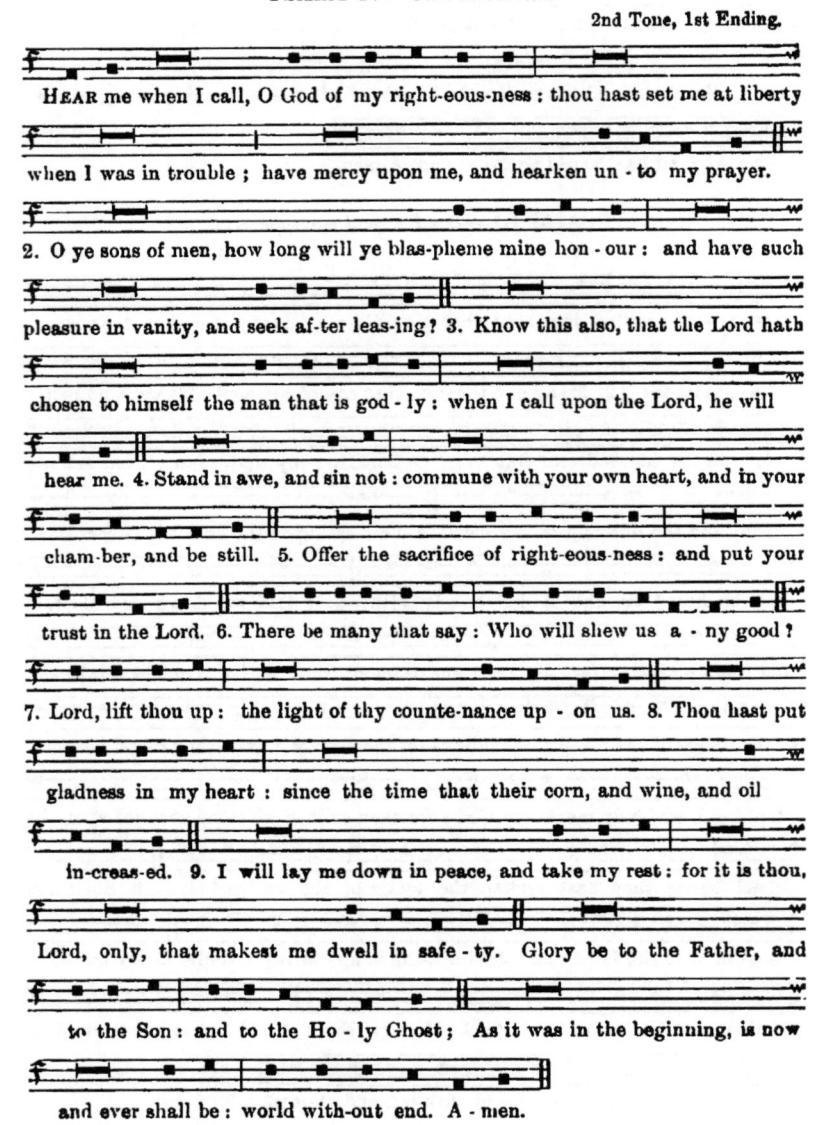

2nd Tone, 1st Ending.

Hear me when I call, O God of my right-eous-ness : thou hast set me at liberty when I was in trouble ; have mercy upon me, and hearken un - to my prayer.

2. O ye sons of men, how long will ye blas-pheme mine hon - our : and have such pleasure in vanity, and seek af-ter leas-ing ? 3. Know this also, that the Lord hath chosen to himself the man that is god - ly : when I call upon the Lord, he will hear me. 4. Stand in awe, and sin not : commune with your own heart, and in your cham-ber, and be still. 5. Offer the sacrifice of right-eous-ness : and put your trust in the Lord. 6. There be many that say : Who will shew us a - ny good ? 7. Lord, lift thou up : the light of thy counte-nance up - on us. 8. Thou hast put gladness in my heart : since the time that their corn, and wine, and oil in-creas-ed. 9. I will lay me down in peace, and take my rest : for it is thou, Lord, only, that makest me dwell in safe - ty. Glory be to the Father, and to the Son : and to the Ho - ly Ghost ; As it was in the beginning, is now and ever shall be : world with-out end. A - men.

MORNING PRAYER.

DAY 1.

PSALM V.—*Verba mea auribus.*

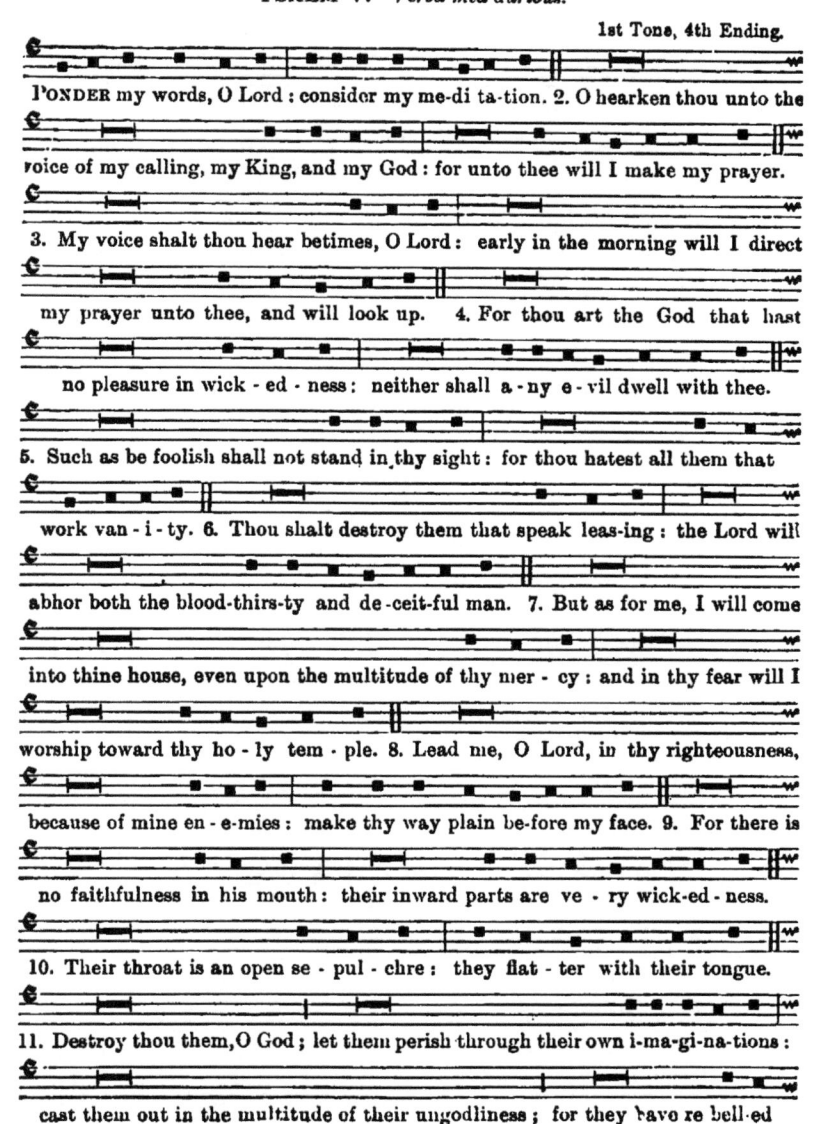

1st Tone, 4th Ending.

PONDER my words, O Lord : consider my me-di ta-tion. 2. O hearken thou unto the voice of my calling, my King, and my God : for unto thee will I make my prayer.

3. My voice shalt thou hear betimes, O Lord : early in the morning will I direct my prayer unto thee, and will look up. 4. For thou art the God that hast no pleasure in wick-ed-ness : neither shall a-ny e-vil dwell with thee.

5. Such as be foolish shall not stand in thy sight : for thou hatest all them that work van-i-ty. 6. Thou shalt destroy them that speak leas-ing : the Lord will abhor both the blood-thirs-ty and de-ceit-ful man. 7. But as for me, I will come into thine house, even upon the multitude of thy mer-cy : and in thy fear will I worship toward thy ho-ly tem-ple. 8. Lead me, O Lord, in thy righteousness, because of mine en-e-mies : make thy way plain be-fore my face. 9. For there is no faithfulness in his mouth : their inward parts are ve-ry wick-ed-ness.

10. Their throat is an open se-pul-chre : they flat-ter with their tongue.

11. Destroy thou them, O God ; let them perish through their own i-ma-gi-na-tions : cast them out in the multitude of their ungodliness ; for they have re-bell-ed

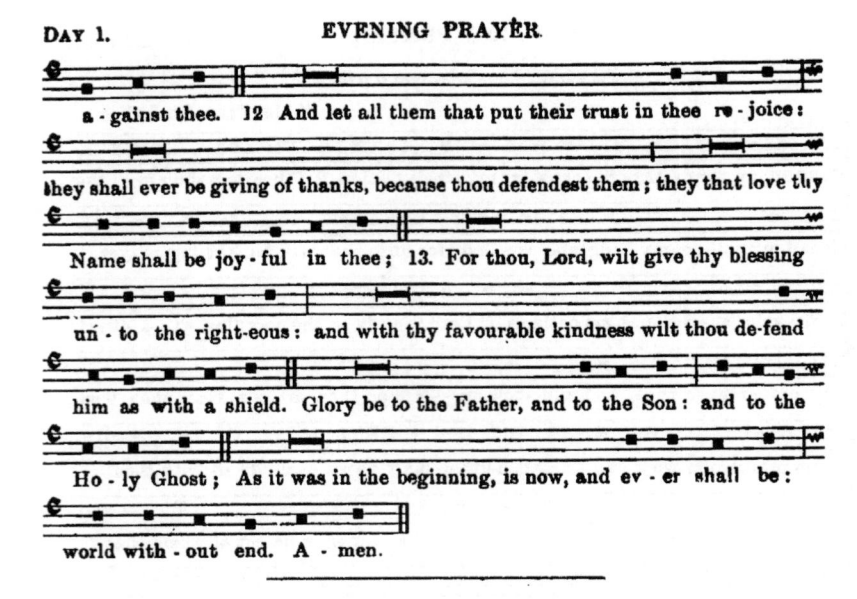

DAY 1.   EVENING PRAYER.

a - gainst thee. 12 And let all them that put their trust in thee re - joice:

they shall ever be giving of thanks, because thou defendest them; they that love thy

Name shall be joy - ful in thee; 13. For thou, Lord, wilt give thy blessing

un - to the right-eous: and with thy favourable kindness wilt thou de-fend

him as with a shield. Glory be to the Father, and to the Son: and to the

Ho - ly Ghost; As it was in the beginning, is now, and ev - er shall be:

world with - out end. A - men.

EVENING PRAYER.

PSALM VI.—*Domine, ne in furore.*

2nd Tone, 1st Ending.

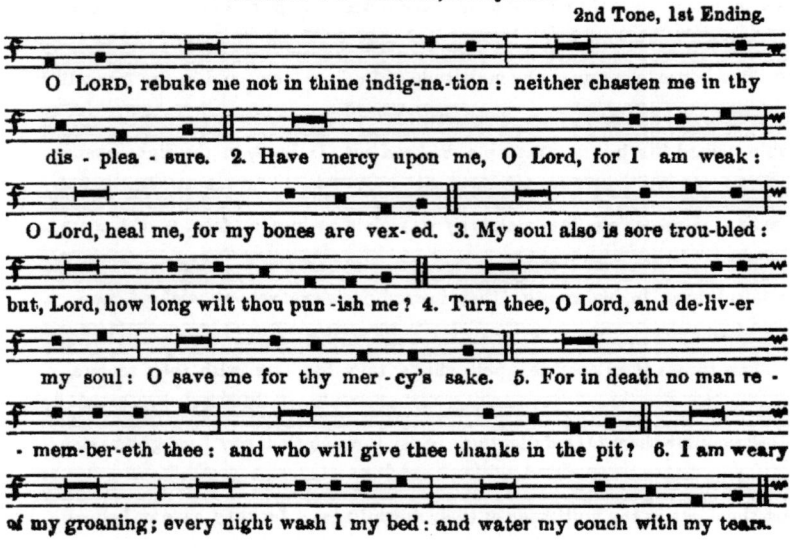

O LORD, rebuke me not in thine indig-na-tion: neither chasten me in thy

dis - plea - sure. 2. Have mercy upon me, O Lord, for I am weak:

O Lord, heal me, for my bones are vex- ed. 3. My soul also is sore trou-bled:

but, Lord, how long wilt thou pun -ish me? 4. Turn thee, O Lord, and de-liv-er

my soul: O save me for thy mer - cy's sake. 5. For in death no man re -

- mem-ber-eth thee: and who will give thee thanks in the pit? 6. I am weary

of my groaning; every night wash I my bed: and water my couch with my tears.

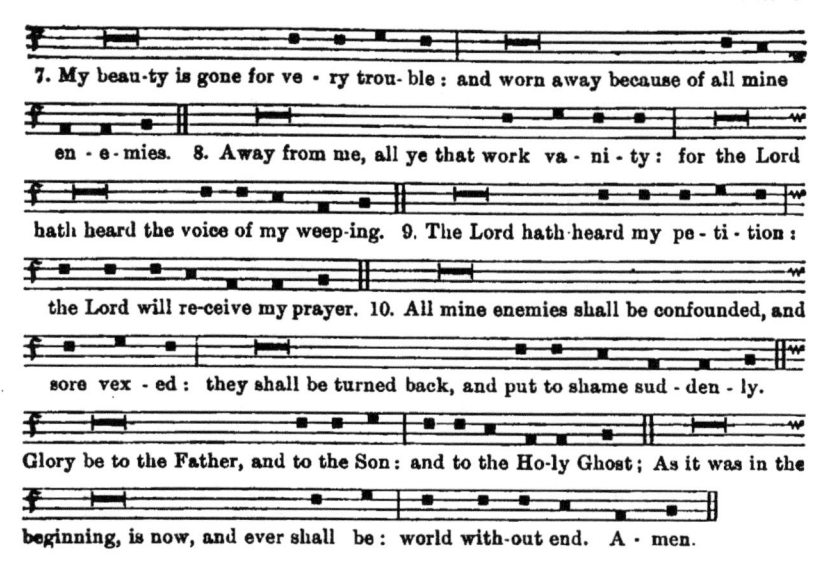

7. My beau-ty is gone for ve - ry trou- ble : and worn away because of all mine en - e - mies. 8. Away from me, all ye that work va - ni - ty : for the Lord hath heard the voice of my weep-ing. 9. The Lord hath heard my pe - ti - tion : the Lord will re-ceive my prayer. 10. All mine enemies shall be confounded, and sore vex - ed : they shall be turned back, and put to shame sud - den - ly.

Glory be to the Father, and to the Son : and to the Ho-ly Ghost; As it was in the beginning, is now, and ever shall be : world with-out end. A - men.

PSALM VII.—*Domine, Deus meus.*

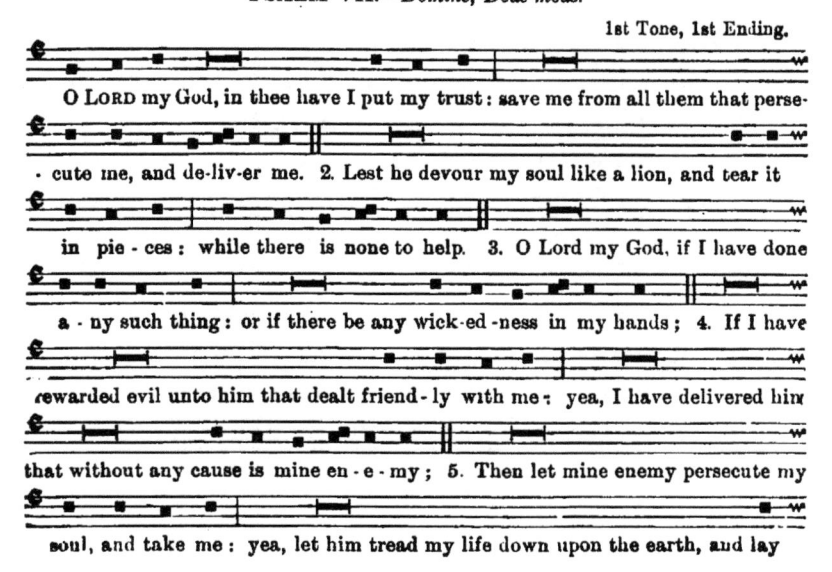

1st Tone, 1st Ending.

O LORD my God, in thee have I put my trust : save me from all them that perse- cute me, and de-liv-er me. 2. Lest he devour my soul like a lion, and tear it in pie - ces : while there is none to help. 3. O Lord my God, if I have done a - ny such thing : or if there be any wick-ed -ness in my hands ; 4. If I have rewarded evil unto him that dealt friend - ly with me : yea, I have delivered him that without any cause is mine en - e - my ; 5. Then let mine enemy persecute my soul, and take me : yea, let him tread my life down upon the earth, and lay

Day 1. EVENING PRAYER.

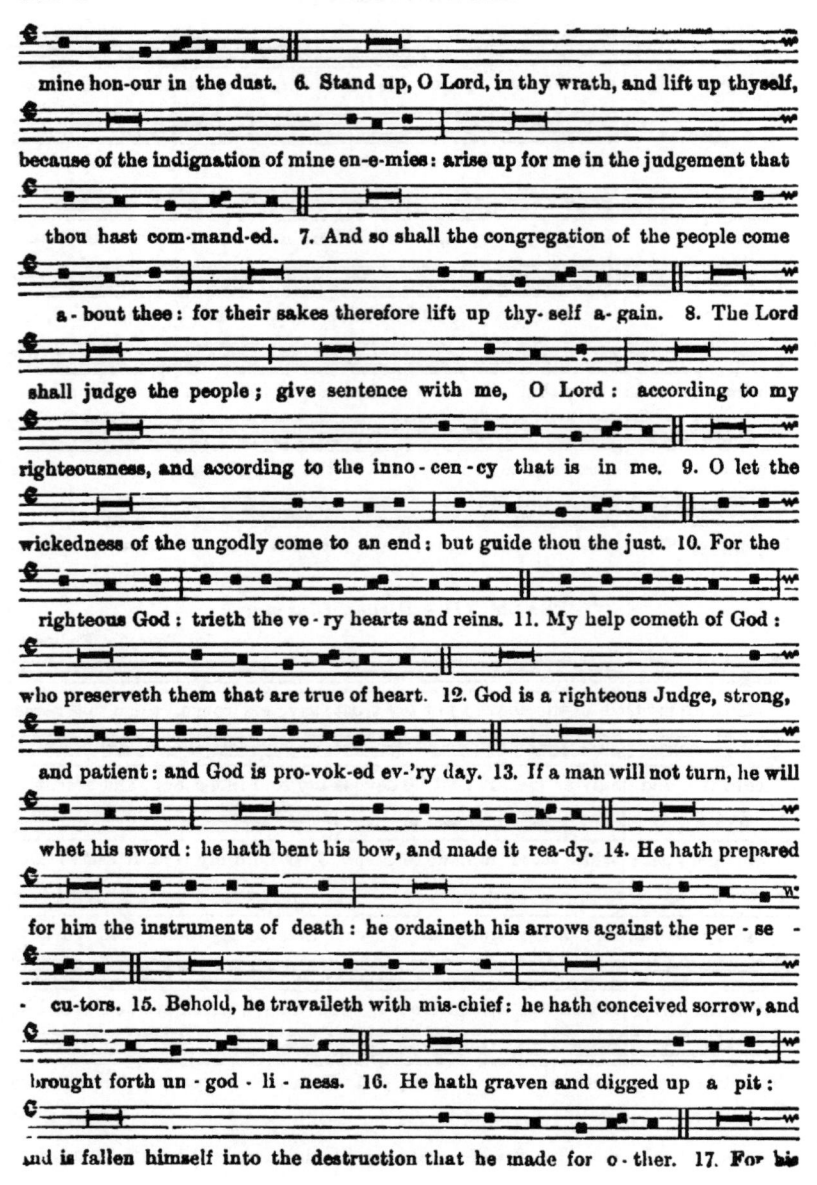

mine hon-our in the dust. 6. Stand up, O Lord, in thy wrath, and lift up thyself,

because of the indignation of mine en-e-mies: arise up for me in the judgement that

thou hast com-mand-ed. 7. And so shall the congregation of the people come

a-bout thee: for their sakes therefore lift up thy-self a-gain. 8. The Lord

shall judge the people; give sentence with me, O Lord: according to my

righteousness, and according to the inno-cen-cy that is in me. 9. O let the

wickedness of the ungodly come to an end: but guide thou the just. 10. For the

righteous God: trieth the ve-ry hearts and reins. 11. My help cometh of God:

who preserveth them that are true of heart. 12. God is a righteous Judge, strong,

and patient: and God is pro-vok-ed ev-'ry day. 13. If a man will not turn, he will

whet his sword: he hath bent his bow, and made it rea-dy. 14. He hath prepared

for him the instruments of death: he ordaineth his arrows against the per-se-

-cu-tors. 15. Behold, he travaileth with mis-chief: he hath conceived sorrow, and

brought forth un-god-li-ness. 16. He hath graven and digged up a pit:

and is fallen himself into the destruction that he made for o-ther. 17. For his

(8)

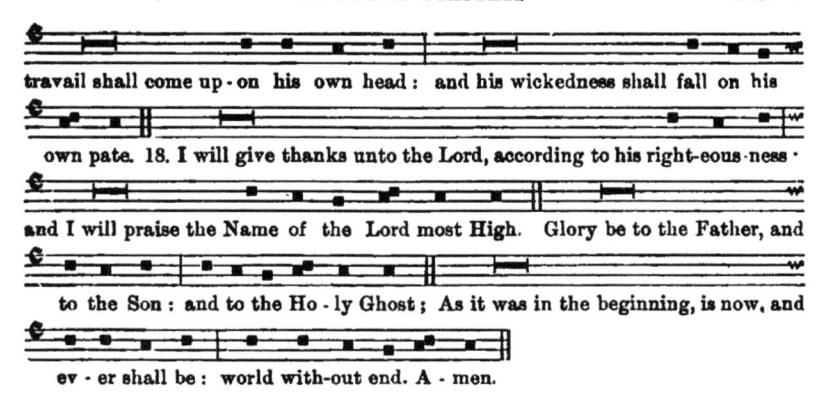

EVENING PRAYER. DAY 1

travail shall come up-on his own head: and his wickedness shall fall on his own pate. 18. I will give thanks unto the Lord, according to his right-eous-ness · and I will praise the Name of the Lord most High. Glory be to the Father, and to the Son: and to the Ho-ly Ghost; As it was in the beginning, is now, and ev-er shall be: world with-out end. A-men.

PSALM VIII.—*Domine, Dominus noster.*

8th Tone, 1st Ending.

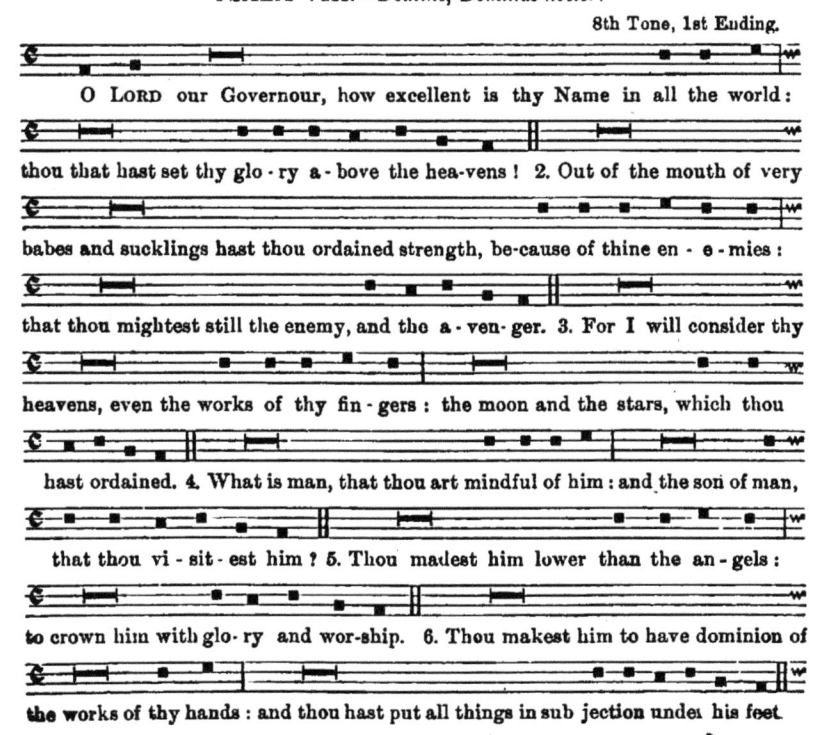

O LORD our Governour, how excellent is thy Name in all the world: thou that hast set thy glo-ry a-bove the hea-vens! 2. Out of the mouth of very babes and sucklings hast thou ordained strength, be-cause of thine en-e-mies: that thou mightest still the enemy, and the a-ven-ger. 3. For I will consider thy heavens, even the works of thy fin-gers: the moon and the stars, which thou hast ordained. 4. What is man, that thou art mindful of him: and the son of man, that thou vi-sit-est him? 5. Thou madest him lower than the an-gels: to crown him with glo-ry and wor-ship. 6. Thou makest him to have dominion of the works of thy hands: and thou hast put all things in sub jection under his feet.

(9)

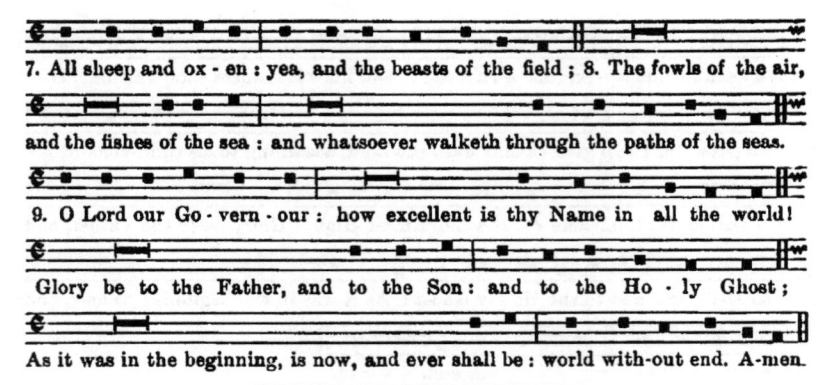

DAY 2.   MORNING PRAYER.

7. All sheep and ox-en : yea, and the beasts of the field ; 8. The fowls of the air,

and the fishes of the sea : and whatsoever walketh through the paths of the seas.

9. O Lord our Go-vern-our : how excellent is thy Name in all the world!

Glory be to the Father, and to the Son : and to the Ho-ly Ghost ;

As it was in the beginning, is now, and ever shall be : world with-out end. A-men.

DAY 2.   MORNING PRAYER.

PSALM IX.—*Confitebor tibi.*

6th Tone.

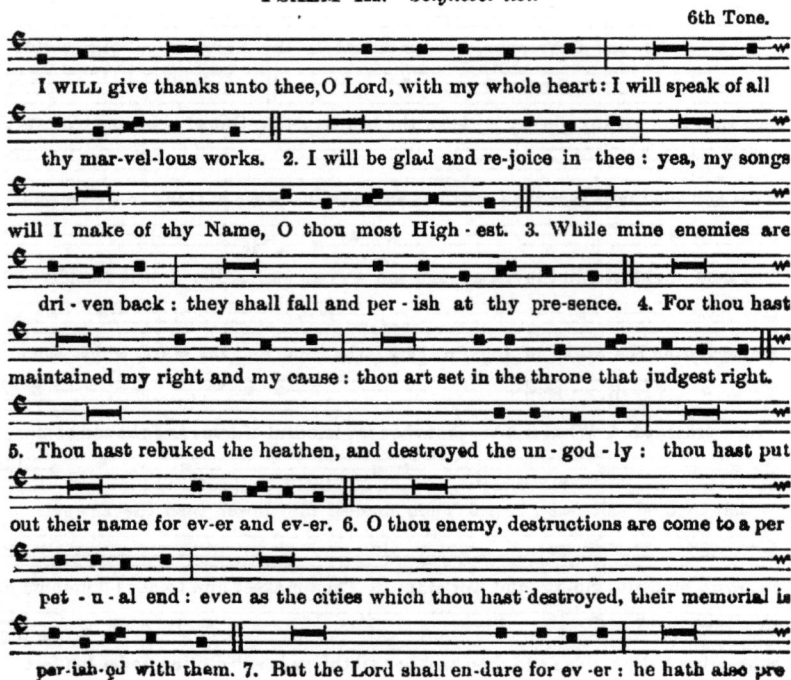

I WILL give thanks unto thee, O Lord, with my whole heart : I will speak of all

thy mar-vel-lous works. 2. I will be glad and re-joice in thee : yea, my songs

will I make of thy Name, O thou most High-est. 3. While mine enemies are

dri-ven back : they shall fall and per-ish at thy pre-sence. 4. For thou hast

maintained my right and my cause : thou art set in the throne that judgest right.

5. Thou hast rebuked the heathen, and destroyed the un-god-ly : thou hast put

out their name for ev-er and ev-er. 6. O thou enemy, destructions are come to a per

pet-u-al end : even as the cities which thou hast destroyed, their memorial is

per-ish-ed with them. 7. But the Lord shall en-dure for ev-er : he hath also pre

MORNING PRAYER. DAY 2.

- par - ed his seat for judge-ment. 8. For he shall judge the world in right -

- eous-ness : and minister true judgement un - to the peo - ple. 9. The Lord also

will be a defence for the op - press - ed : even a refuge in due time of trou - ble.

10. And they that know thy Name will put their trust in thee : for thou, Lord,

hast never fail - ed them that seek thee. 11. O praise the Lord which dwell-eth

in Si-on : shew the peo-ple of his do-ings. 12. For, when he maketh inquisition

for blood, he re-mem-ber-eth them : and forgetteth not the complaint of the poor.

13. Have mercy upon me, O Lord ; consider the trouble which I suffer of them

that hate me : thou that liftest me up from the gates of death. 14. That I may

shew all thy praises within the ports of the daugh-ter of Si - on : I will re-joice

in thy sal-va-tion. 15. The heathen are sunk down in the pit that they made :

in the same net, which they hid privily, is their foot tak-en. 16. The Lord is known to

ex - e - cute judge-ment : the ungodly is trapped in the work of his own hands.

17 The wicked shall be turned in-to hell : and all the peo-ple that for-get God.

18. For the poor shall not alway be for - got - ten : the patient abiding of the

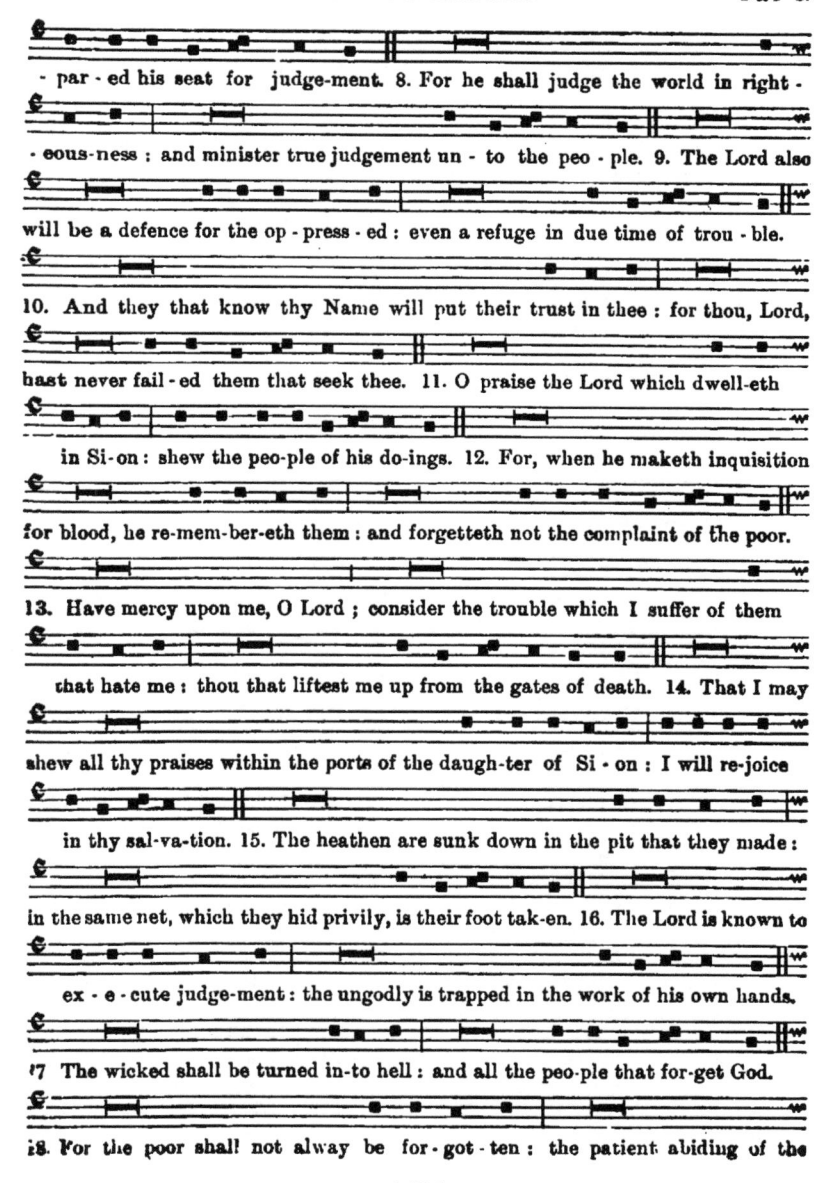

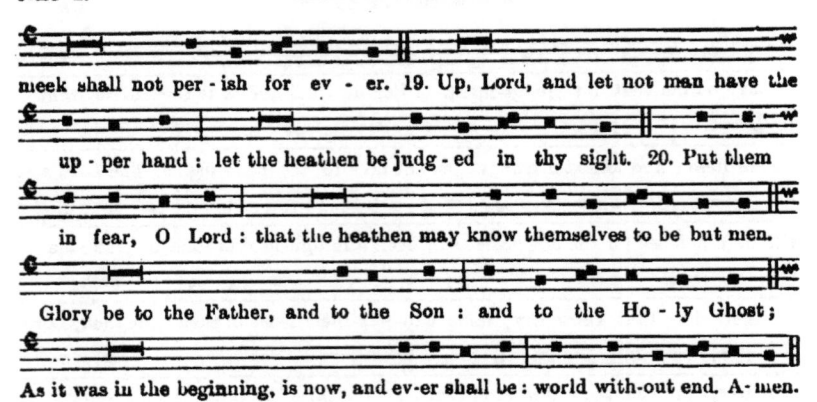

DAY 2.　　　　　MORNING PRAYER.

meek shall not per-ish for ev-er. 19. Up, Lord, and let not man have the

up-per hand : let the heathen be judg-ed in thy sight. 20. Put them

in fear, O Lord : that the heathen may know themselves to be but men.

Glory be to the Father, and to the Son : and to the Ho-ly Ghost;

As it was in the beginning, is now, and ev-er shall be : world with-out end. A-men.

PSALM X.—*Ut quid, Domine?*

4th Tone, 4th Ending.

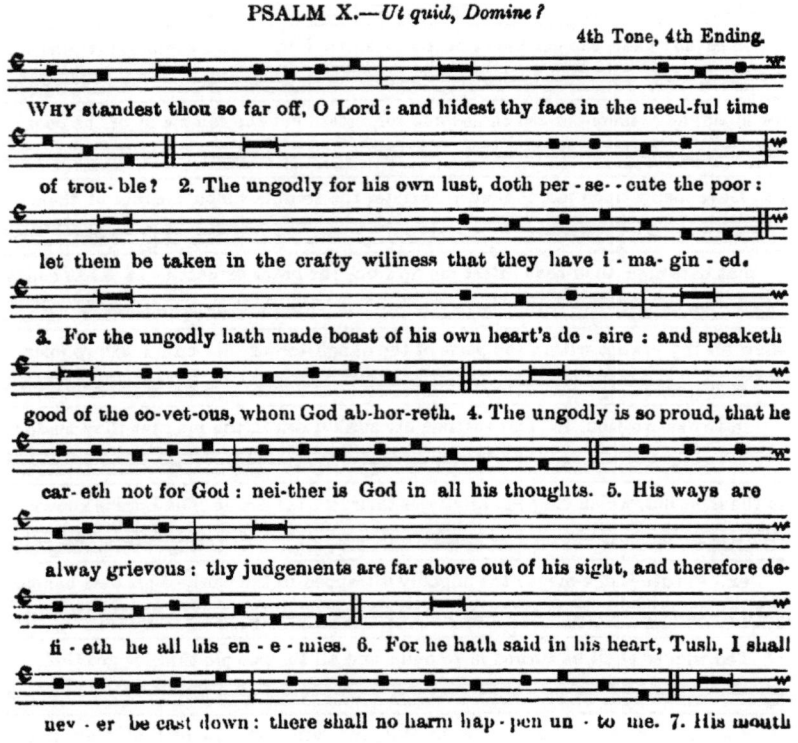

WHY standest thou so far off, O Lord : and hidest thy face in the need-ful time

of trou-ble? 2. The ungodly for his own lust, doth per-se--cute the poor :

let them be taken in the crafty wiliness that they have i-ma-gin-ed.

3. For the ungodly hath made boast of his own heart's de-sire : and speaketh

good of the co-vet-ous, whom God ab-hor-reth. 4. The ungodly is so proud, that he

car-eth not for God : nei-ther is God in all his thoughts. 5. His ways are

alway grievous : thy judgements are far above out of his sight, and therefore de-

fi-eth he all his en-e-mies. 6. For he hath said in his heart, Tush, I shall

nev-er be cast down : there shall no harm hap-pen un-to me. 7. His mouth

MORNING PRAYER.   DAY 2.

is full of curs-ing, de - ceit, and fraud : under his tongue is un-god-li-ness and van - i - ty. 8. He sitteth lurking in the thievish cor-ners of the streets : and privily in his lurking dens doth he murder the innocent ; his eyes are set a-gainst the poor. 9. For he lieth waiting secretly, even as a lion lurk-eth he in his den : that he may rav - ish the poor. 10. He doth rav- ish the poor : when he get- teth him in - to his net. 11. He falleth down, and hum-bleth himself : that the congregation of the poor may fall in - to the hands of his cap-tains. 12. He hath said in his heart, Tush, God hath for- got - ten : he hideth away his face, and he will nev- er see it. 13. Arise, O Lord God, and lift up thine hand : for - get not the poor. 14. Wherefore should the wick-ed blas-pheme God : while he doth say in his heart, Tush, thou God car - est not for it ? 15. Sure-ly thou hast seen it : for thou be-hold-est un-god - li - ness and wrong. 16. That thou mayest take the matter in - to thine hand : the poor committeth himself unto thee ; for thou art the help-er of the friend-less. 17. Break thou the power of the un-god- ly and ma - li- cious : take away his un - god-li-ness, and thou shalt find none. 18. The Lord is King for ev-er and ev -er :

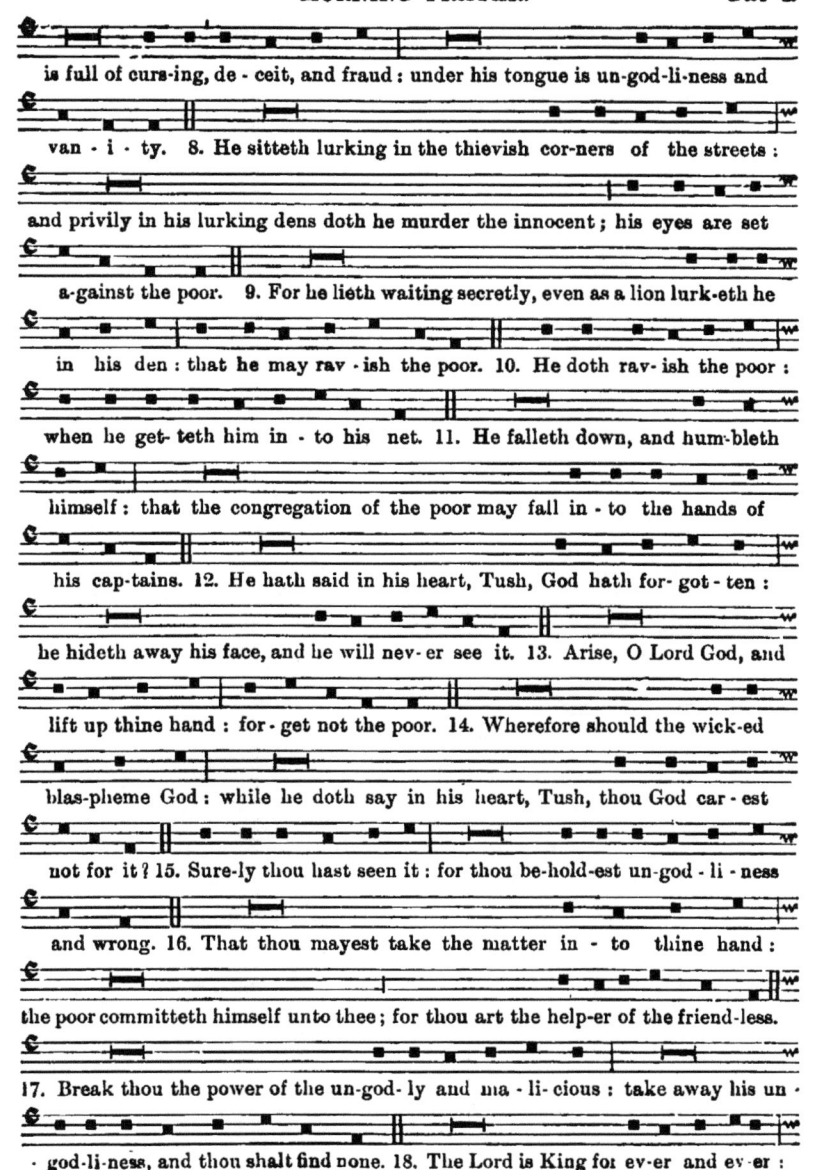

(13)

DAY 2. MORNING PRAYER.

and the heathen are per-ish-ed out of the land. 19. Lord, thou hast heard the de

- sire of the poor: thou preparest their heart, and thine ear heark - en - eth

there-to; 20. To help the fatherless and poor un-to their right: that the man of

the earth be no more ex - alt - ed a-gainst them. Glory be to the Father, and

to the Son: and to the Ho - ly Ghost; As it was in the beginning, is now, and

ev - er shall be: world with-out end. A - men.

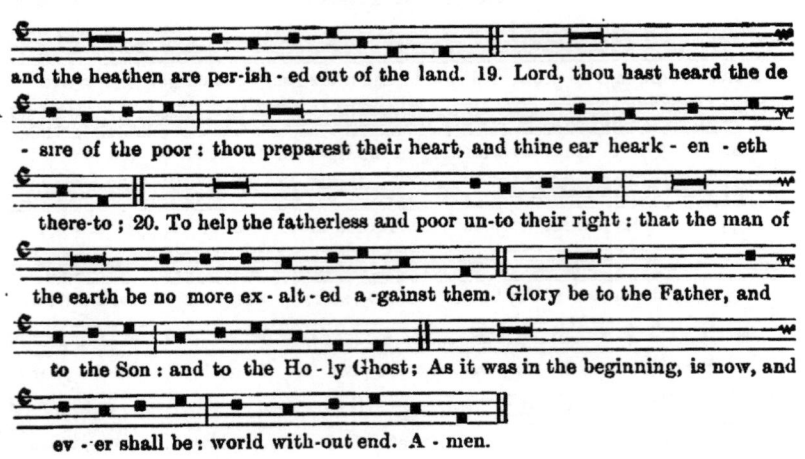

PSALM XI.—*In Domino confido.*

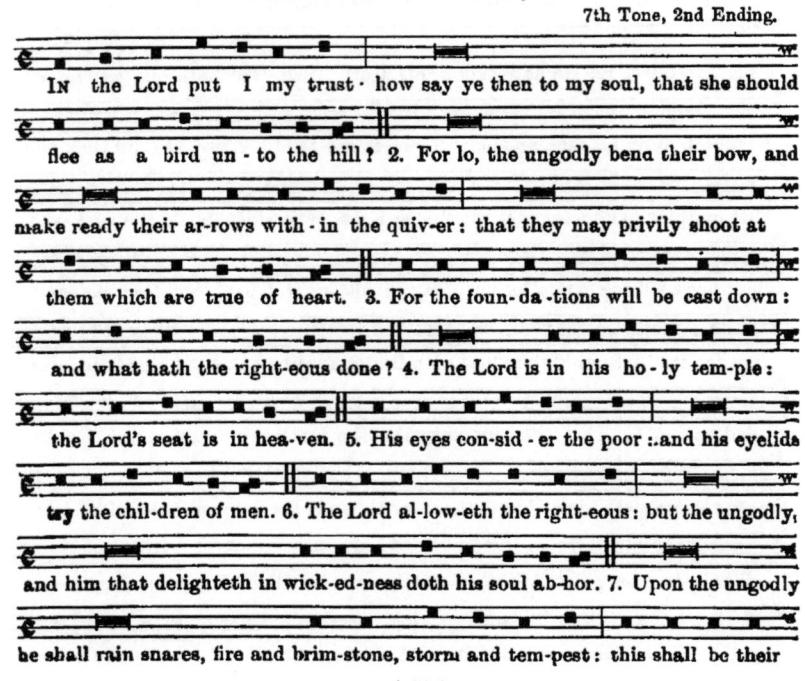

7th Tone, 2nd Ending.

IN the Lord put I my trust · how say ye then to my soul, that she should

flee as a bird un - to the hill? 2. For lo, the ungodly bend their bow, and

make ready their ar-rows with - in the quiv-er: that they may privily shoot at

them which are true of heart. 3. For the foun- da -tions will be cast down:

and what hath the right-eous done? 4. The Lord is in his ho - ly tem-ple:

the Lord's seat is in hea-ven. 5. His eyes con-sid - er the poor :.and his eyelids

try the chil-dren of men. 6. The Lord al-low-eth the right-eous: but the ungodly,

and him that delighteth in wick-ed-ness doth his soul ab-hor. 7. Upon the ungodly

he shall rain snares, fire and brim-stone, storm and tem-pest: this shall be their

(14)

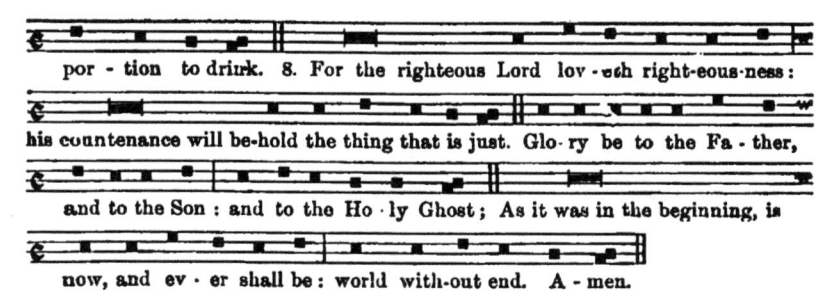

EVENING PRAYER. DAY 2

por - tion to drink. 8. For the righteous Lord lov - eth right-eous-ness: his countenance will be-hold the thing that is just. Glo - ry be to the Fa - ther, and to the Son : and to the Ho - ly Ghost ; As it was in the beginning, is now, and ev - er shall be : world with-out end. A - men.

EVENING PRAYER.

PSALM XII.—*Salvum me fac.*

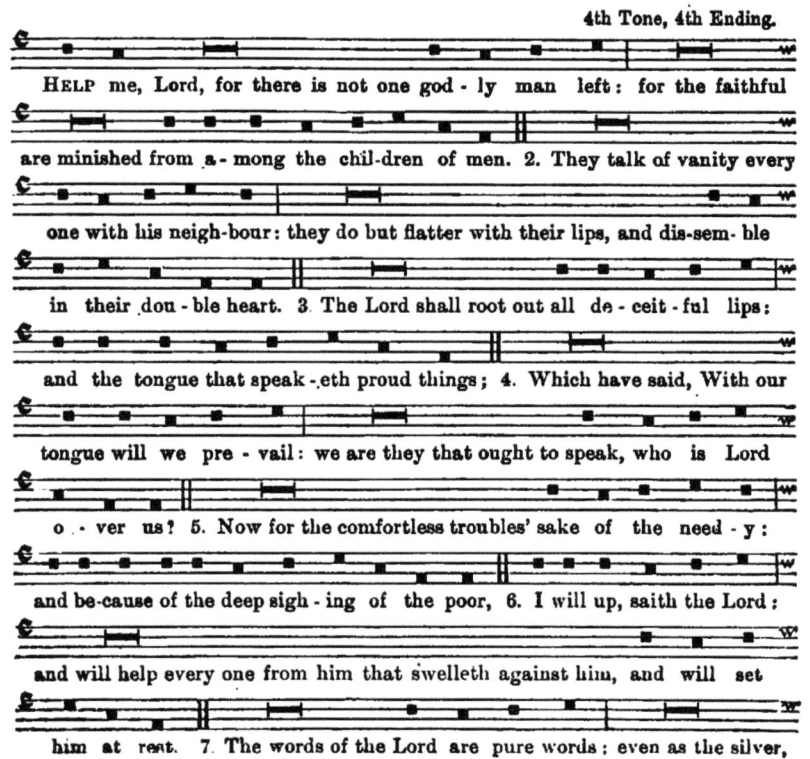

4th Tone, 4th Ending.

HELP me, Lord, for there is not one god - ly man left : for the faithful are minished from a - mong the chil-dren of men. 2. They talk of vanity every one with his neigh-bour: they do but flatter with their lips, and dis-sem- ble in their dou - ble heart. 3. The Lord shall root out all de - ceit - ful lips: and the tongue that speak - eth proud things; 4. Which have said, With our tongue will we pre - vail : we are they that ought to speak, who is Lord o - ver us? 5. Now for the comfortless troubles' sake of the need - y : and be-cause of the deep sigh - ing of the poor, 6. I will up, saith the Lord : and will help every one from him that swelleth against him, and will set him at rest. 7. The words of the Lord are pure words ; even as the silver,

{ 15 }

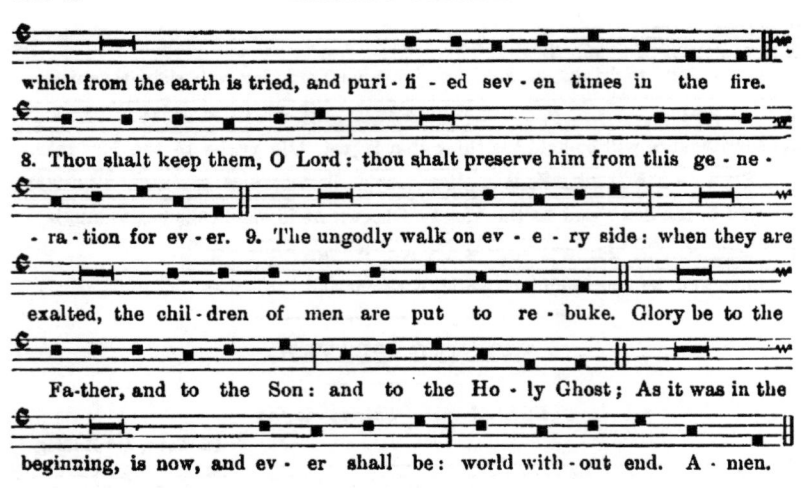

DAY 2. EVENING PRAYER.

which from the earth is tried, and puri-fi-ed sev-en times in the fire.

8. Thou shalt keep them, O Lord : thou shalt preserve him from this ge-ne-

-ra-tion for ev-er. 9. The ungodly walk on ev-e-ry side: when they are

exalted, the chil-dren of men are put to re-buke. Glory be to the

Fa-ther, and to the Son : and to the Ho-ly Ghost; As it was in the

beginning, is now, and ev-er shall be: world with-out end. A-men.

PSALM XIII.—*Usque quo, Domine?*

3rd Tone, 4th Ending.

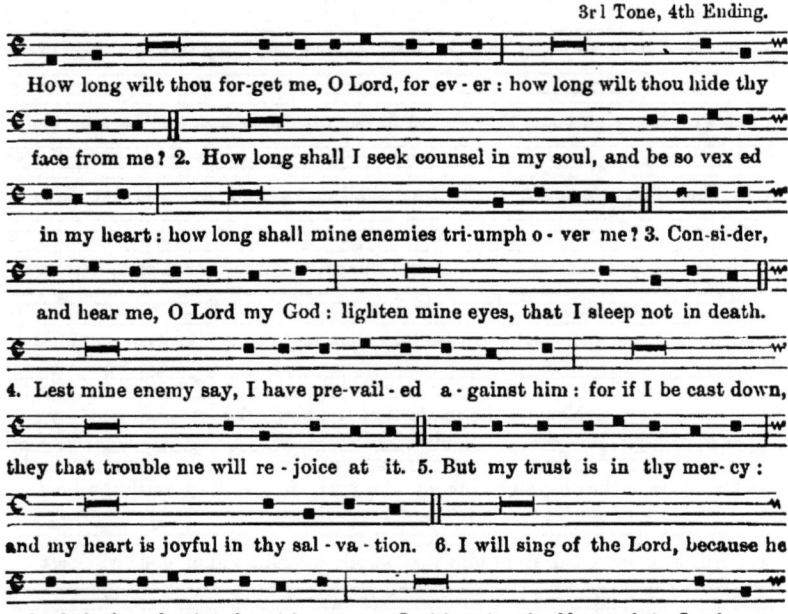

How long wilt thou for-get me, O Lord, for ev-er : how long wilt thou hide thy

face from me? 2. How long shall I seek counsel in my soul, and be so vexed

in my heart : how long shall mine enemies tri-umph o-ver me? 3. Con-si-der,

and hear me, O Lord my God : lighten mine eyes, that I sleep not in death.

4. Lest mine enemy say, I have pre-vail-ed a-gainst him : for if I be cast down,

they that trouble me will re-joice at it. 5. But my trust is in thy mer-cy :

and my heart is joyful in thy sal-va-tion. 6. I will sing of the Lord, because he

hath dealt so lov-ing-ly with me : yea, I will praise the Name of the Lord most

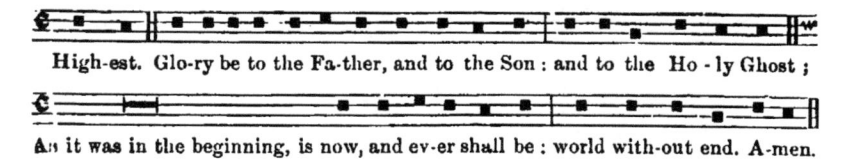

EVENING PRAYER. DAY 2.

High-est. Glo-ry be to the Fa-ther, and to the Son : and to the Ho - ly Ghost ;

As it was in the beginning, is now, and ev-er shall be : world with-out end. A-men.

PSALM XIV.—*Dixit insipiens.*

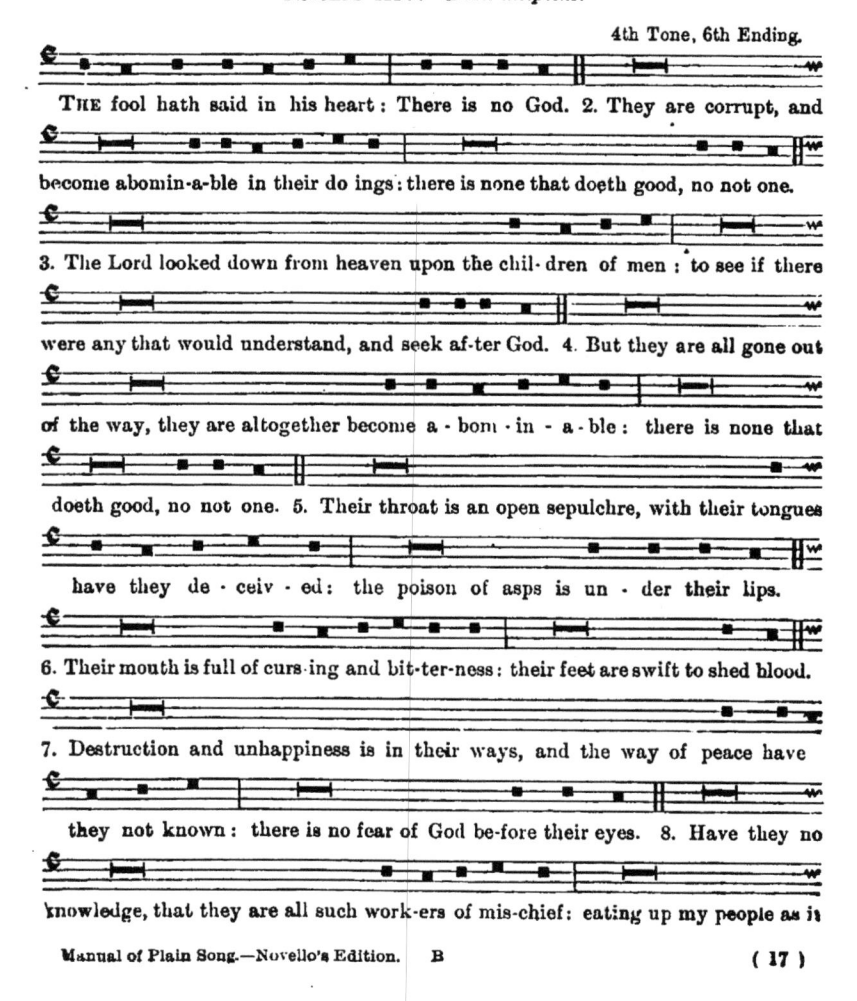

4th Tone, 6th Ending.

The fool hath said in his heart : There is no God. 2. They are corrupt, and

become abomin-a-ble in their do ings : there is none that doeth good, no not one.

3. The Lord looked down from heaven upon the chil-dren of men : to see if there

were any that would understand, and seek af-ter God. 4. But they are all gone out

of the way, they are altogether become a - bom - in - a - ble : there is none that

doeth good, no not one. 5. Their throat is an open sepulchre, with their tongues

have they de - ceiv - ed : the poison of asps is un - der their lips.

6. Their mouth is full of curs-ing and bit-ter-ness : their feet are swift to shed blood.

7. Destruction and unhappiness is in their ways, and the way of peace have

they not known : there is no fear of God be-fore their eyes. 8. Have they no

knowledge, that they are all such work-ers of mis-chief : eating up my people as it

Manual of Plain Song.—Novello's Edition. B (17)

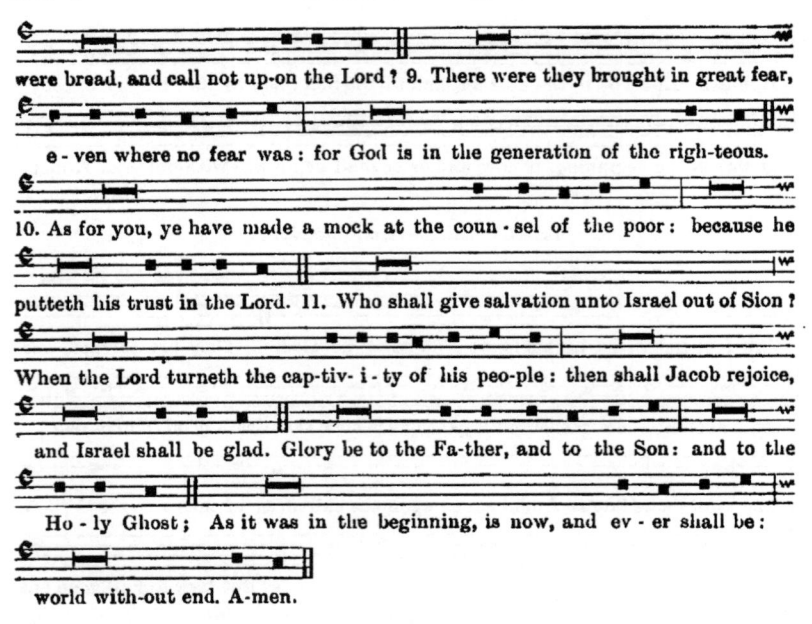

DAY 3.   MORNING PRAYER.

were bread, and call not up-on the Lord? 9. There were they brought in great fear,

e - ven where no fear was: for God is in the generation of the righ-teous.

10. As for you, ye have made a mock at the coun - sel of the poor: because he

putteth his trust in the Lord. 11. Who shall give salvation unto Israel out of Sion?

When the Lord turneth the cap-tiv- i - ty of his peo-ple: then shall Jacob rejoice,

and Israel shall be glad. Glory be to the Fa-ther, and to the Son: and to the

Ho - ly Ghost; As it was in the beginning, is now, and ev - er shall be:

world with-out end. A-men.

DAY 3.   MORNING PRAYER.

PSALM XV.—*Domine, quis habitabit?*

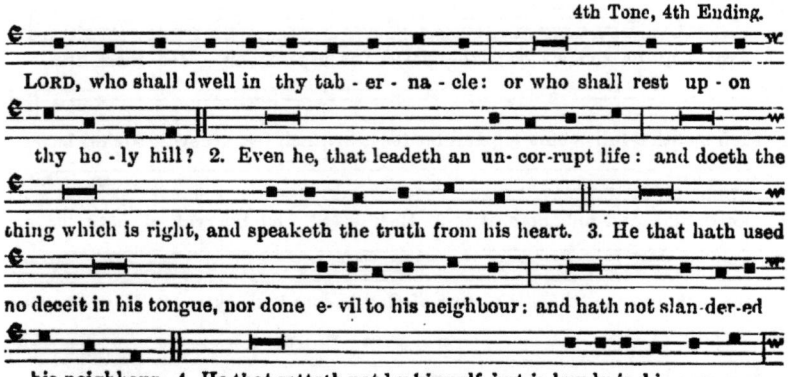

4th Tone, 4th Ending.

LORD, who shall dwell in thy tab - er - na - cle: or who shall rest up - on

thy ho - ly hill? 2. Even he, that leadeth an un- cor-rupt life: and doeth the

thing which is right, and speaketh the truth from his heart. 3. He that hath used

no deceit in his tongue, nor done e- vil to his neighbour: and hath not slan-der-ed

his neighbour. 4. He that setteth not by himself, but is low-ly in his own eyes:

(18)

MORNING PRAYER. DAY 3.

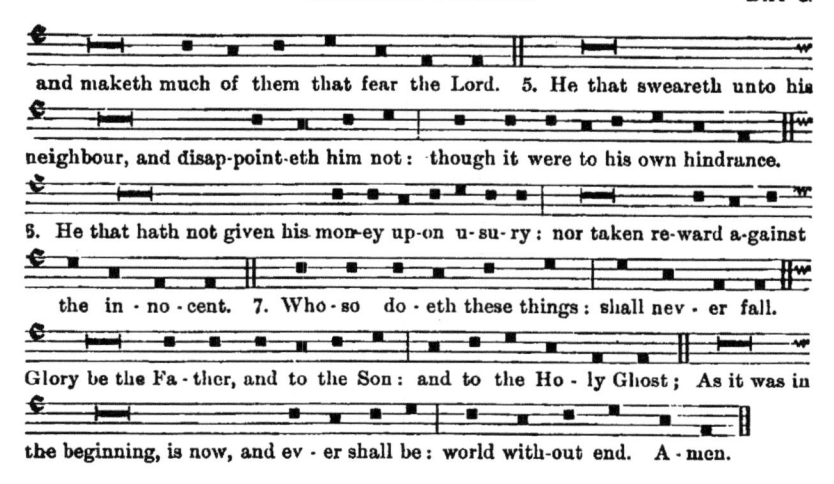

and maketh much of them that fear the Lord. 5. He that sweareth unto his neighbour, and disap-point-eth him not: though it were to his own hindrance.

6. He that hath not given his mon-ey up-on u-su-ry: nor taken re-ward a-gainst the in-no-cent. 7. Who-so do-eth these things: shall nev-er fall.

Glory be the Fa-ther, and to the Son: and to the Ho-ly Ghost; As it was in the beginning, is now, and ev-er shall be: world with-out end. A-men.

PSALM XVI.—*Conserva me, Domine.*

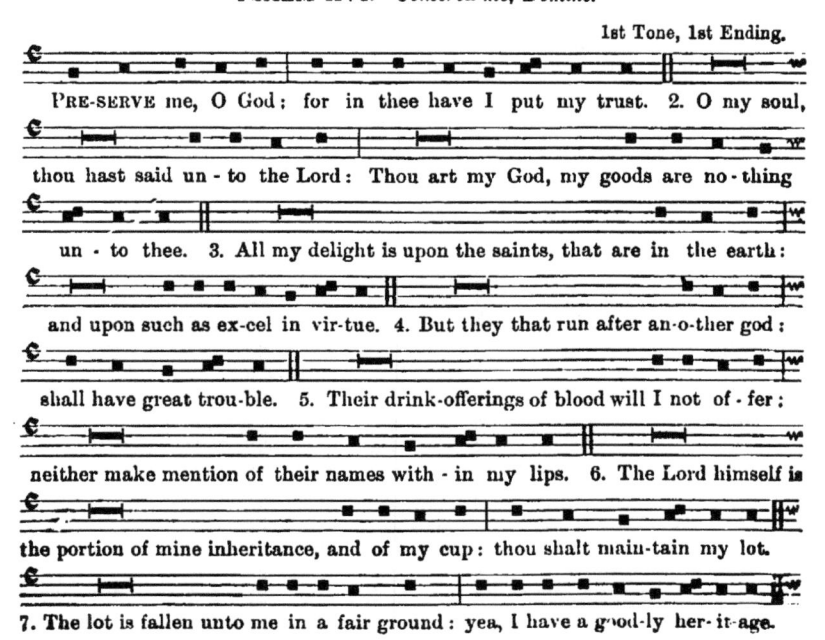

1st Tone, 1st Ending.

PRE-SERVE me, O God; for in thee have I put my trust. 2. O my soul, thou hast said un-to the Lord: Thou art my God, my goods are no-thing un-to thee. 3. All my delight is upon the saints, that are in the earth: and upon such as ex-cel in vir-tue. 4. But they that run after an-o-ther god: shall have great trou-ble. 5. Their drink-offerings of blood will I not of-fer; neither make mention of their names with-in my lips. 6. The Lord himself is the portion of mine inheritance, and of my cup: thou shalt main-tain my lot. 7. The lot is fallen unto me in a fair ground: yea, I have a good-ly her-it-age.

(19)

DAY 3. MORNING PRAYER.

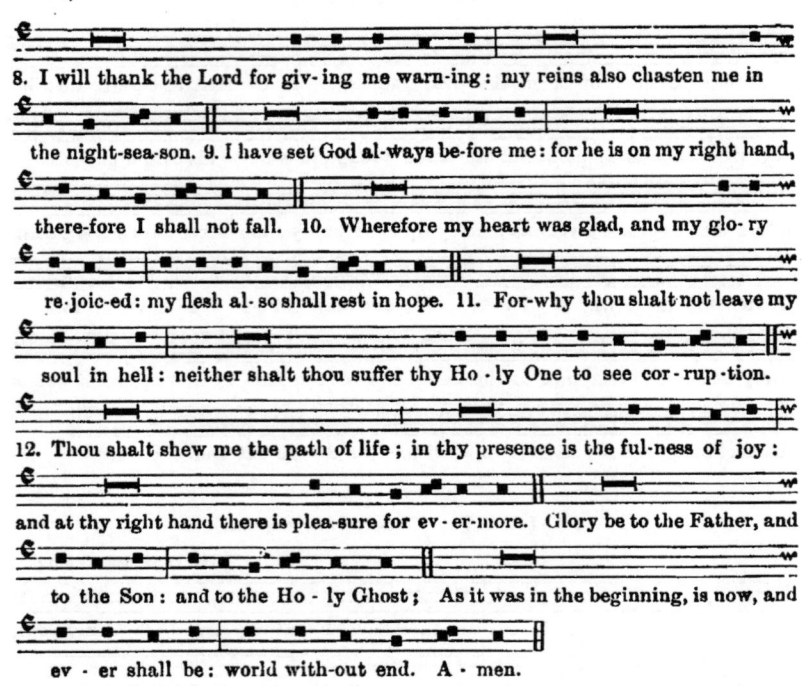

8. I will thank the Lord for giv-ing me warn-ing: my reins also chasten me in the night-sea-son. 9. I have set God al-ways be-fore me: for he is on my right hand, there-fore I shall not fall. 10. Wherefore my heart was glad, and my glo-ry re-joic-ed: my flesh al- so shall rest in hope. 11. For-why thou shalt not leave my soul in hell: neither shalt thou suffer thy Ho - ly One to see cor-rup-tion. 12. Thou shalt shew me the path of life; in thy presence is the ful-ness of joy: and at thy right hand there is plea-sure for ev - er-more. Glory be to the Father, and to the Son: and to the Ho - ly Ghost; As it was in the beginning, is now, and ev - er shall be: world with-out end. A - men.

PSALM XVII.—*Exaudi, Domine.*

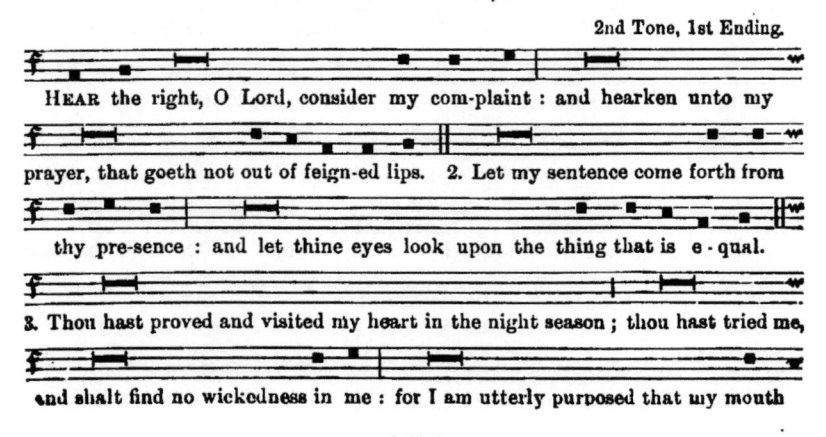

2nd Tone, 1st Ending.

HEAR the right, O Lord, consider my com-plaint: and hearken unto my prayer, that goeth not out of feign-ed lips. 2. Let my sentence come forth from thy pre-sence: and let thine eyes look upon the thing that is e - qual. 3. Thou hast proved and visited my heart in the night season; thou hast tried me, and shalt find no wickedness in me: for I am utterly purposed that my mouth

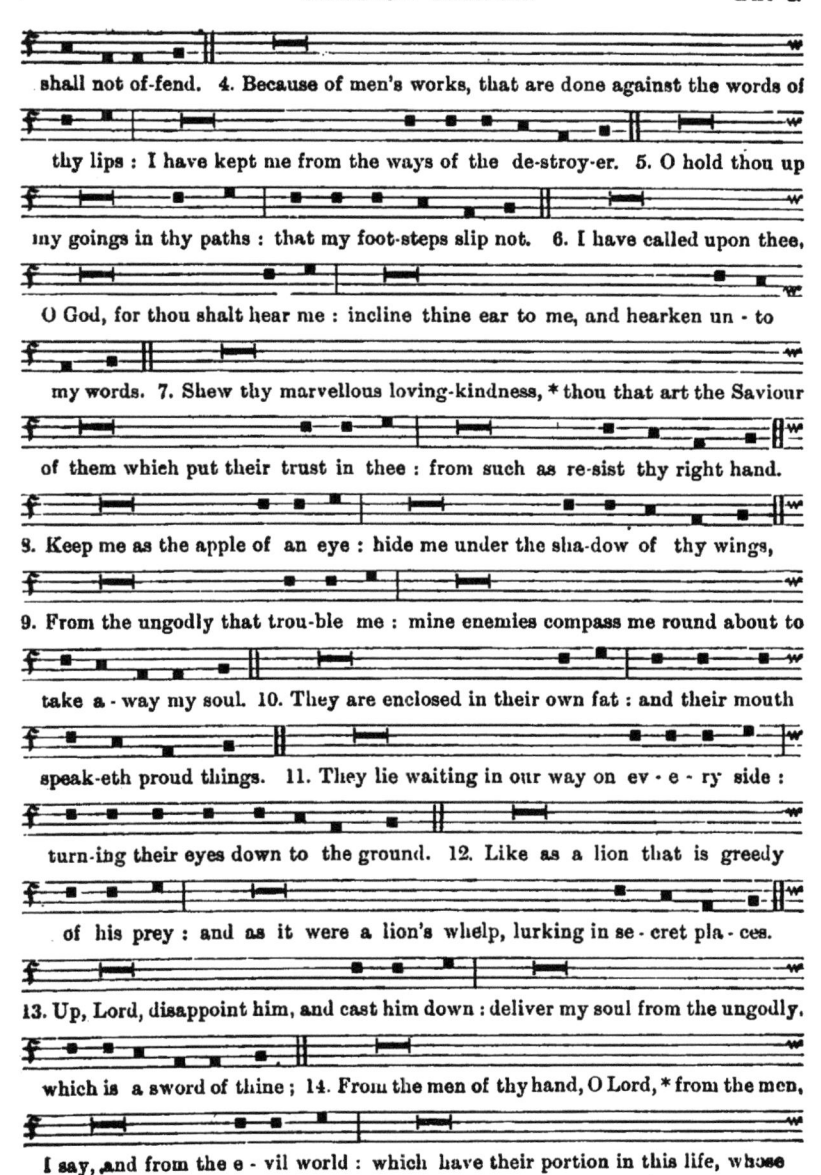

MORNING PRAYER. DAY 3.

shall not offend. 4. Because of men's works, that are done against the words of thy lips : I have kept me from the ways of the destroyer. 5. O hold thou up my goings in thy paths : that my foot-steps slip not. 6. I have called upon thee, O God, for thou shalt hear me : incline thine ear to me, and hearken un-to my words. 7. Shew thy marvellous loving-kindness, * thou that art the Saviour of them which put their trust in thee : from such as resist thy right hand.

8. Keep me as the apple of an eye : hide me under the shadow of thy wings,

9. From the ungodly that trouble me : mine enemies compass me round about to take away my soul. 10. They are enclosed in their own fat : and their mouth speaketh proud things. 11. They lie waiting in our way on every side : turning their eyes down to the ground. 12. Like as a lion that is greedy of his prey : and as it were a lion's whelp, lurking in secret places.

13. Up, Lord, disappoint him, and cast him down : deliver my soul from the ungodly, which is a sword of thine ; 14. From the men of thy hand, O Lord, * from the men, I say, and from the evil world : which have their portion in this life, whose

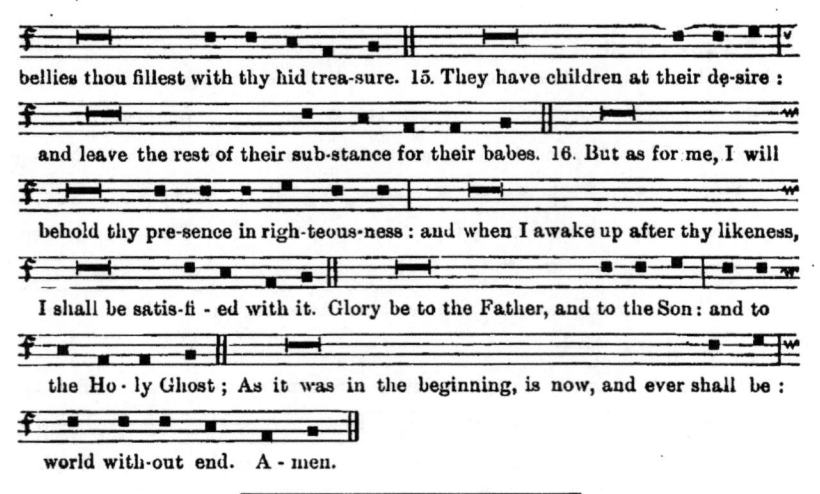

DAY 3   EVENING PRAYER.

bellies thou fillest with thy hid trea-sure. 15. They have children at their de-sire :

and leave the rest of their sub-stance for their babes. 16. But as for me, I will

behold thy pre-sence in righ-teous-ness : and when I awake up after thy likeness,

I shall be satis-fi - ed with it. Glory be to the Father, and to the Son : and to

the Ho - ly Ghost ; As it was in the beginning, is now, and ever shall be :

world with-out end. A - men.

EVENING PRAYER.

PSALM XVIII.—*Diligam te, Domine.*

1st Tone. 2nd Ending.

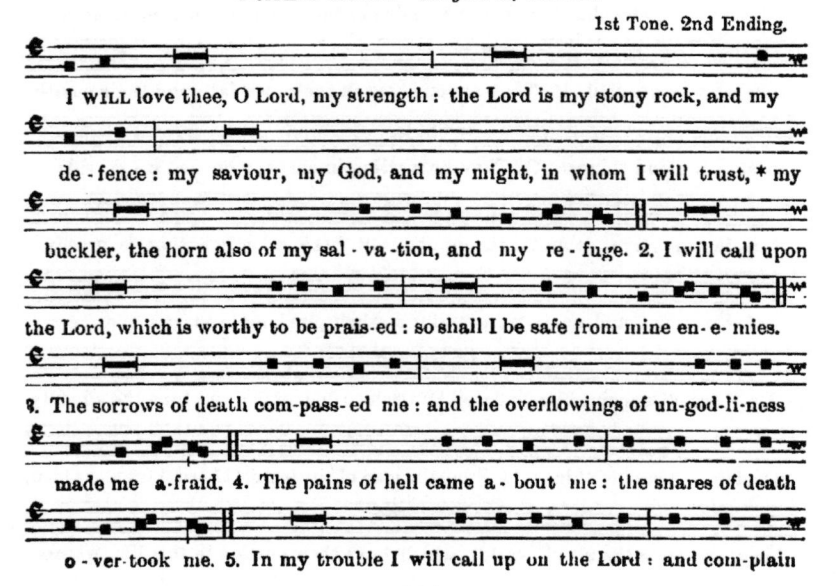

I WILL love thee, O Lord, my strength : the Lord is my stony rock, and my

de - fence : my saviour, my God, and my might, in whom I will trust, * my

buckler, the horn also of my sal - va-tion, and my re - fuge. 2. I will call upon

the Lord, which is worthy to be prais-ed : so shall I be safe from mine en- e- mies.

3. The sorrows of death com-pass- ed me : and the overflowings of un-god-li-ness

made me a-fraid. 4. The pains of hell came a - bout me : the snares of death

o - ver-took me. 5. In my trouble I will call up on the Lord : and com-plain

EVENING PRAYER. DAY 3.

un - to my God. 6. So shall he hear my voice out of his ho - ly tem - ple :

and my complaint shall come before him, it shall enter e - ven in - to his ears.

7. The earth trem-bled and quak- ed : the very foundations also of the hills shook,

and were re-mov - ed, be - cause he was wroth. 8. There went a smoke out in

his pre - sence ; and a consuming fire out of his mouth, so that coals were

kin-dled at it. 9. He bowed the heavens al - so, and came down : and it was

dark un - der his feet. 10. He rode upon the cherubims, and did fly :

he came flying up - on the wings of the wind. 11. He made darkness his

se-cret place : his pavilion round about him with dark water, and thick clouds

to cov- er him. 12. At the brightness of his presence his clouds re -mov- ed :

hail-stones, and coals of fire. 13. The Lord also thundered out of heaven,

and the Highest gave his thun-der : hail-stones, and coals of fire. 14. He sent out

his arrows, and scat-ter-ed them : he cast forth lightnings, and de-stroy-ed them.

15. The springs of waters were seen,* and the foundations of the round world were

discovered, at thy chid - ing, O Lord : at the blasting of the breath of thy

DAY 3.   EVENING PRAYER.

dis-plea-sure. 16. He shall send down from on high to fetch me:

and shall take me out of ma-ny wa-ters. 17. He shall deliver me from my

strongest enemy, and from them which hate me: for they are too mighty for me.

18. They prevented me in the day of my trou-ble: but the Lord was my

up-hold-er, 19. He brought me forth also into a place of lib-er-ty:

he brought me forth, even because he had a fa-vour un-to me. 20. The Lord shall

reward me after my right-eous deal-ing: according to the cleanness of my hands

shall he re-com-pense me. 21. Because I have kept the ways of the Lord :

and have not forsaken my God, as the wick-ed doth. 22. For I have an eye unto

all his laws: and will not cast out his com-mand-ments from me.

23. I was also uncor-rupt be-fore him: and es-chew-ed mine own wick-ed-ness.

24. Therefore shall the Lord reward me after my right-eous deal-ing : and according

unto the cleanness of my hands in his eye-sight. 25. With the holy thou shalt

be ho-ly: and with a perfect man thou shalt be per-fect. 26. With the clean

thou shalt be clean: and with the froward thou shalt learn fro-ward-ness.

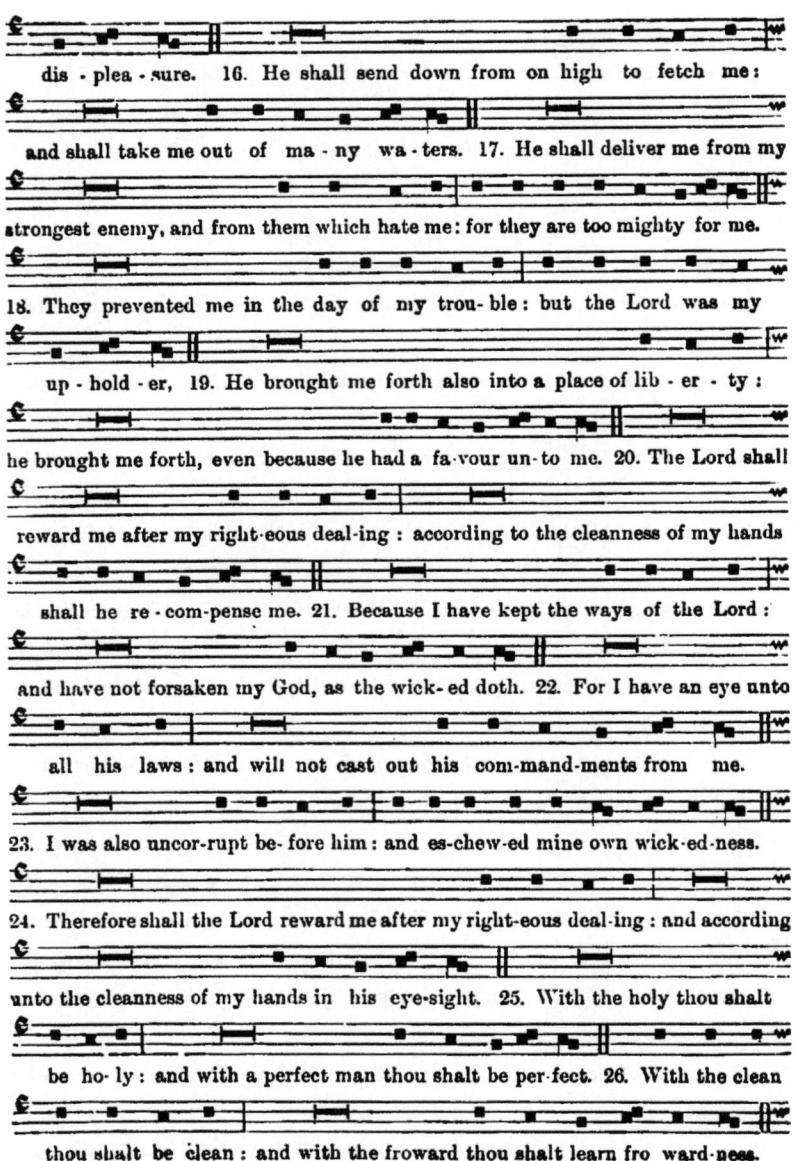

27. For thou shalt save the people that are in ad - ver - si - ty : and shalt bring down the high looks of the proud. 28. Thou also shalt light my can - dle : the Lord my God shall make my dark - ness to be light. 29. For in thee I shall discomfit an host of men : and with the help of my God I shall leap o - ver the wall. 30. The way of God is an unde - fil - ed way : the word of the Lord also is tried in the fire ; he is the defender of all them that put their trust in him. 31. For who is God, but the Lord : or who hath a ny strength, ex - cept our God ? 32. It is God, that girdeth me with strength of war : and mak - eth my way per - fect. 33. He maketh my feet like harts' feet : and set - teth me up on high. 34. He teach - eth mine hands to fight : and mine arms shall break e - ven a bow of steel. 35 Thou hast given me the defence of thy sal - va - tion : thy right hand also shall hold me up, and thy loving cor - rec - tion shall make me great. 36. Thou shalt make room enough under me for to go : that my foot-steps shall not slide. 37. I will follow upon mine enemies, and o - ver-take them : neither will I turn again till I have

(25)

DAY 8. EVENING PRAYER.

de-stroy-ed them. 38. I will smite them, that they shall not be a-ble to stand:

but fall un-der my feet. 39. Thou hast girded me with strength un-to

the bat-tle: thou shalt throw down mine en-e-mies un-der me.

40. Thou hast made mine enemies also to turn their backs up-on me:

and I shall de-stroy them that hate me. 41. They shall cry, but there shall be

none to help them: yea, even unto the Lord shall they cry, but he shall

not hear them. 42. I will beat them as small as the dust be-fore the wind;

I will cast them out as the clay in the streets. 43. Thou shalt deliver me from

the strivings of the peo-ple: and thou shalt make me the head of the heathen.

44. A people whom I have not known: shall serve me. 45. As soon as they

hear of me, they shall o-bey me: but the strange children shall dis-sem-ble

with me. 46. The strange children shall fail: and be afraid out of their pri-sons.

47. The Lord liveth, and blessed be my strong help-er: and praised be the

God of my sal-va-tion. 48. Even the God that seeth that I be a-veng-ed:

and sub-du-eth the peo-ple un-to me. 49. It is he that delivereth me from

my cruel enemies,* and setteth me up above mine ad-ver-sa-ries thou shalt rid me

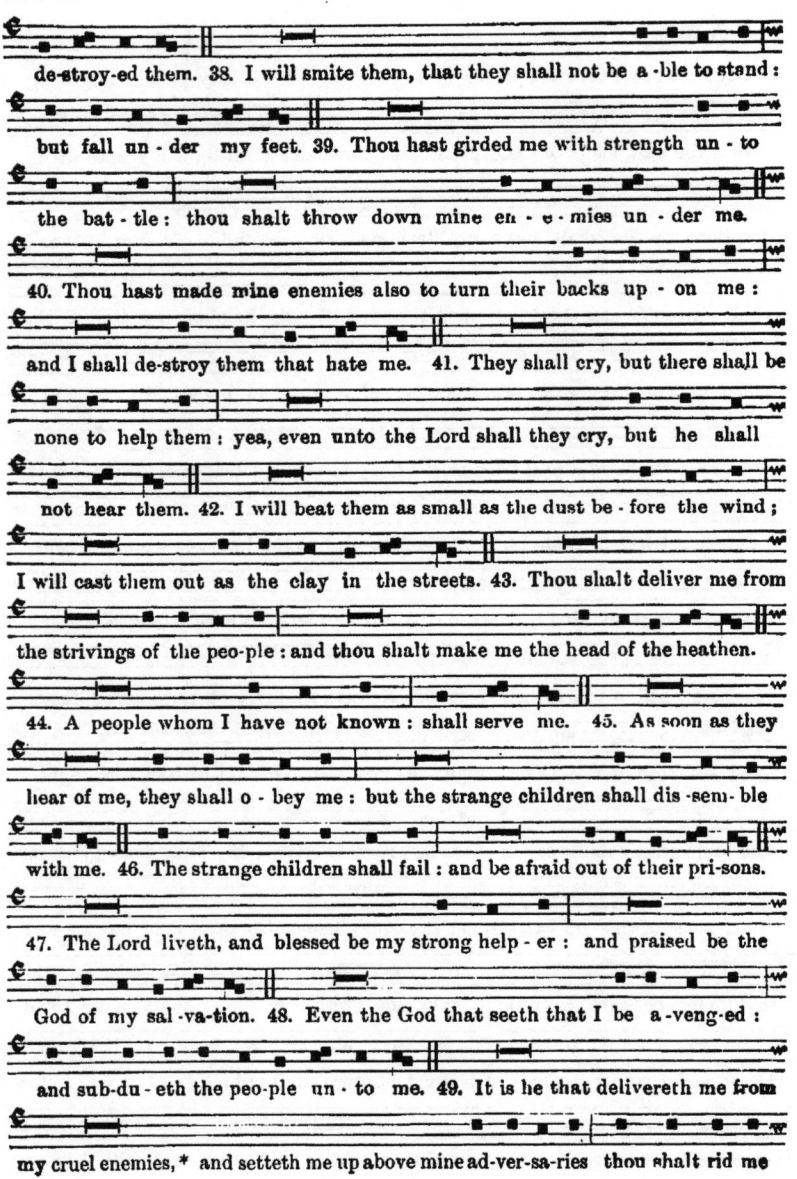

(26)

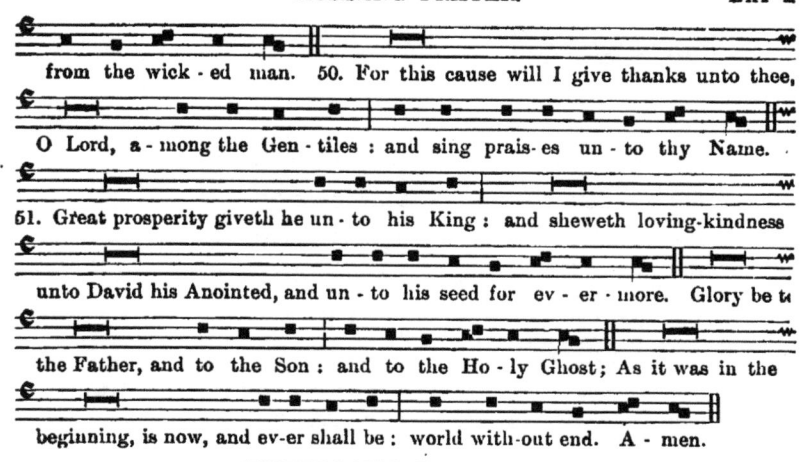

MORNING PRAYER. DAY 4.

from the wick-ed man. 50. For this cause will I give thanks unto thee,

O Lord, a-mong the Gen-tiles : and sing prais-es un-to thy Name.

51. Great prosperity giveth he un-to his King : and sheweth loving-kindness

unto David his Anointed, and un-to his seed for ev-er-more. Glory be to

the Father, and to the Son : and to the Ho-ly Ghost; As it was in the

beginning, is now, and ev-er shall be : world with-out end. A-men.

MORNING PRAYER. DAY 4.

PSALM XIX.—*Cæli enarrant.*

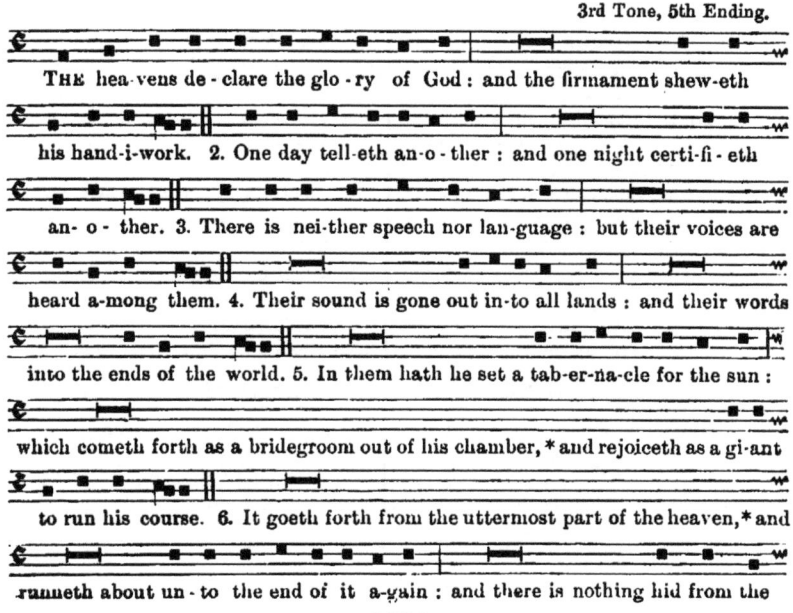

3rd Tone, 5th Ending.

THE hea-vens de-clare the glo-ry of God : and the firmament shew-eth

his hand-i-work. 2. One day tell-eth an-o-ther : and one night certi-fi-eth

an-o-ther. 3. There is nei-ther speech nor lan-guage : but their voices are

heard a-mong them. 4. Their sound is gone out in-to all lands : and their words

into the ends of the world. 5. In them hath he set a tab-er-na-cle for the sun :

which cometh forth as a bridegroom out of his chamber, * and rejoiceth as a gi-ant

to run his course. 6. It goeth forth from the uttermost part of the heaven, * and

runneth about un-to the end of it a-gain : and there is nothing hid from the

(27)

DAY 4. MORNING PRAYER.

heat there-of. 7. The law of the Lord is an undefiled law, con-vert-ing the soul: the testimony of the Lord is sure, and giveth wisdom un-to the sim-ple. 8. The statutes of the Lord are right, and re-joice the heart: the commandment of the Lord is pure, and giveth light un-to the eyes. 9. The fear of the Lord is clean, and en-dur-eth for ev-er: the judgements of the Lord are true, and righteous al-to-ge-ther. 10. More to be desired are they than gold, yea, than much fine gold: sweeter also than honey, and the hon-ey-comb. 11. Moreover, by them is thy ser-vant taught: and in keeping of them there is great re-ward. 12. Who can tell how oft he of-fend-eth: O cleanse thou me from my secret faults. 13. Keep thy servant also from presumptuous sins, lest they get the do-min-ion o-ver me: so shall I be undefiled, and innocent from the great of-fence. 14. Let the words of my mouth, and the me-di-ta-tion of my heart: be alway ac--cept-a-ble in thy sight. 15. O Lord: my strength, and my re-deem-er. Glo-ry be to the Fa-ther, and to the Son: and to the Ho-ly Ghost; As it was in the beginning, is now, and ever shall be: world without end. A-men.

(28)

MORNING PRAYER. DAY 4.

PSALM XX.—*Exaudiat te Dominus.*

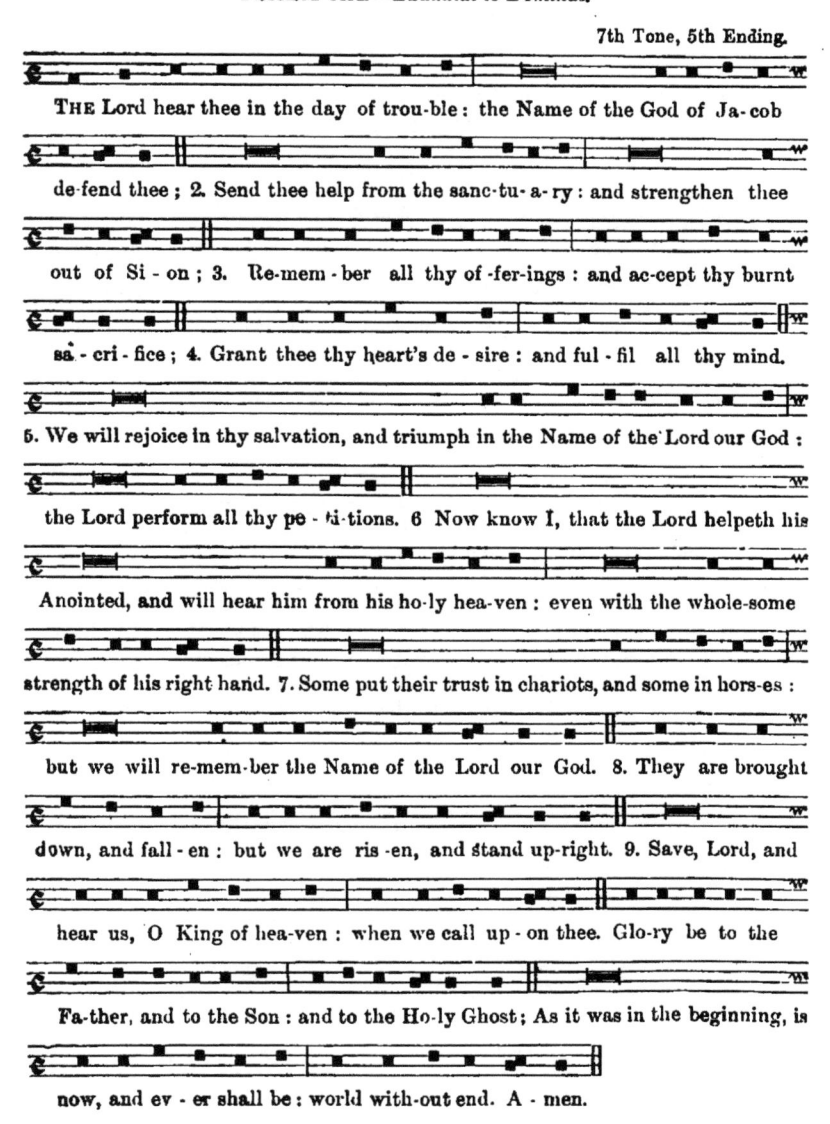

7th Tone, 5th Ending.

THE Lord hear thee in the day of trou-ble : the Name of the God of Ja-cob de-fend thee ; 2. Send thee help from the sanc-tu-a-ry : and strengthen thee out of Si-on ; 3. Re-mem-ber all thy of-fer-ings : and ac-cept thy burnt sa-cri-fice ; 4. Grant thee thy heart's de-sire : and ful-fil all thy mind. 5. We will rejoice in thy salvation, and triumph in the Name of the Lord our God : the Lord perform all thy pe-ti-tions. 6 Now know I, that the Lord helpeth his Anointed, and will hear him from his ho-ly hea-ven : even with the whole-some strength of his right hand. 7. Some put their trust in chariots, and some in hors-es : but we will re-mem-ber the Name of the Lord our God. 8. They are brought down, and fall-en : but we are ris-en, and stand up-right. 9. Save, Lord, and hear us, O King of hea-ven : when we call up-on thee. Glo-ry be to the Fa-ther, and to the Son : and to the Ho-ly Ghost ; As it was in the beginning, is now, and ev-er shall be : world with-out end. A-men.

(29)

Day 4.   MORNING PRAYER.

PSALM XXI.—*Domine, in virtute tua.*

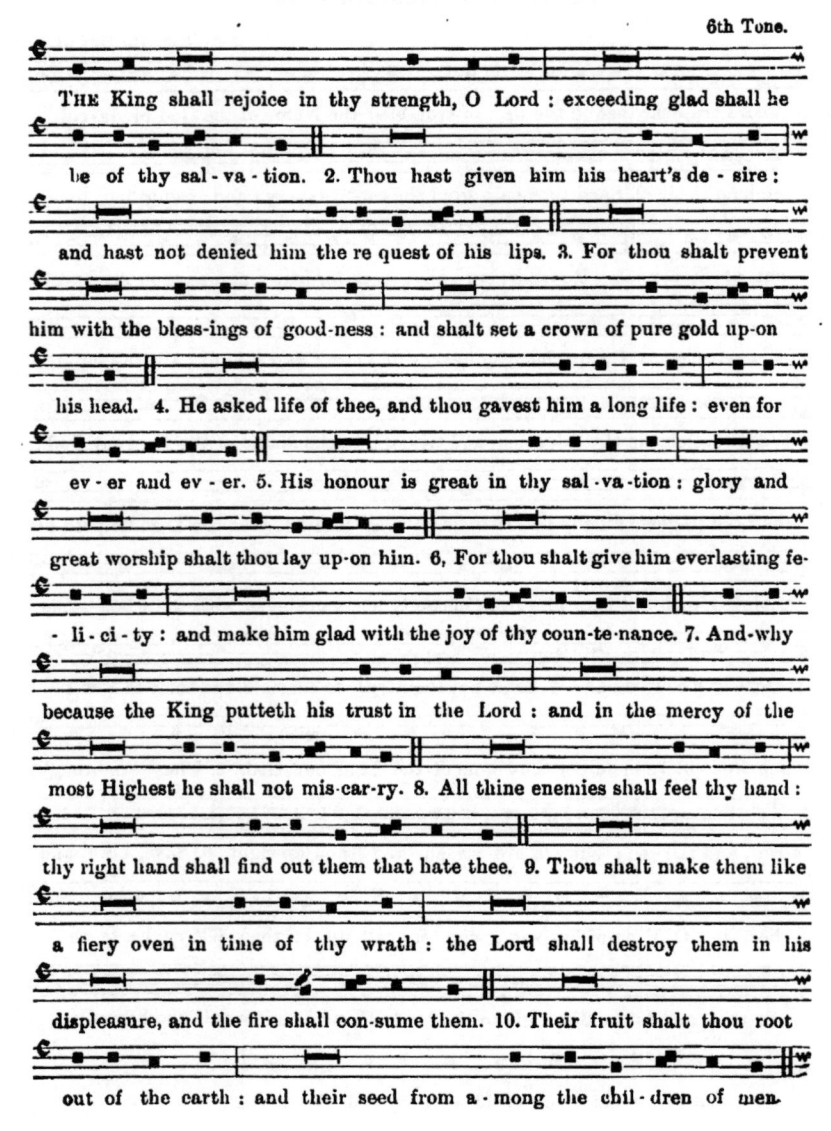

6th Tone.

The King shall rejoice in thy strength, O Lord : exceeding glad shall he be of thy sal-va-tion. 2. Thou hast given him his heart's de-sire : and hast not denied him the request of his lips. 3. For thou shalt prevent him with the bless-ings of good-ness : and shalt set a crown of pure gold up-on his head. 4. He asked life of thee, and thou gavest him a long life : even for ev-er and ev-er. 5. His honour is great in thy sal-va-tion : glory and great worship shalt thou lay up-on him. 6. For thou shalt give him everlasting fe- li-ci-ty : and make him glad with the joy of thy coun-te-nance. 7. And why because the King putteth his trust in the Lord : and in the mercy of the most Highest he shall not mis-car-ry. 8. All thine enemies shall feel thy hand : thy right hand shall find out them that hate thee. 9. Thou shalt make them like a fiery oven in time of thy wrath : the Lord shall destroy them in his displeasure, and the fire shall con-sume them. 10. Their fruit shalt thou root out of the earth : and their seed from a-mong the chil-dren of men.

(30)

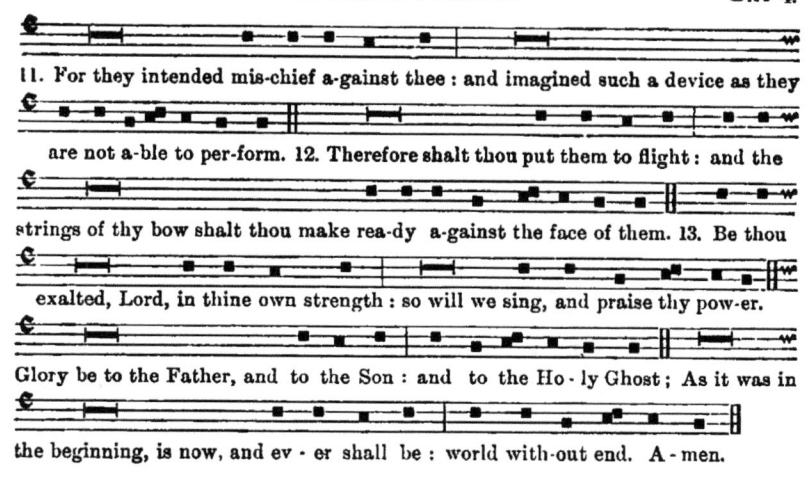

EVENING PRAYER. DAY 4.

11. For they intended mis-chief a-gainst thee : and imagined such a device as they are not a-ble to per-form. 12. Therefore shalt thou put them to flight : and the strings of thy bow shalt thou make rea-dy a-gainst the face of them. 13. Be thou exalted, Lord, in thine own strength : so will we sing, and praise thy pow-er.

Glory be to the Father, and to the Son : and to the Ho-ly Ghost; As it was in the beginning, is now, and ev-er shall be : world with-out end. A-men.

EVENING PRAYER.

PSALM XXII.—*Deus, Deus meus.*

2nd Tone, 1st Ending.

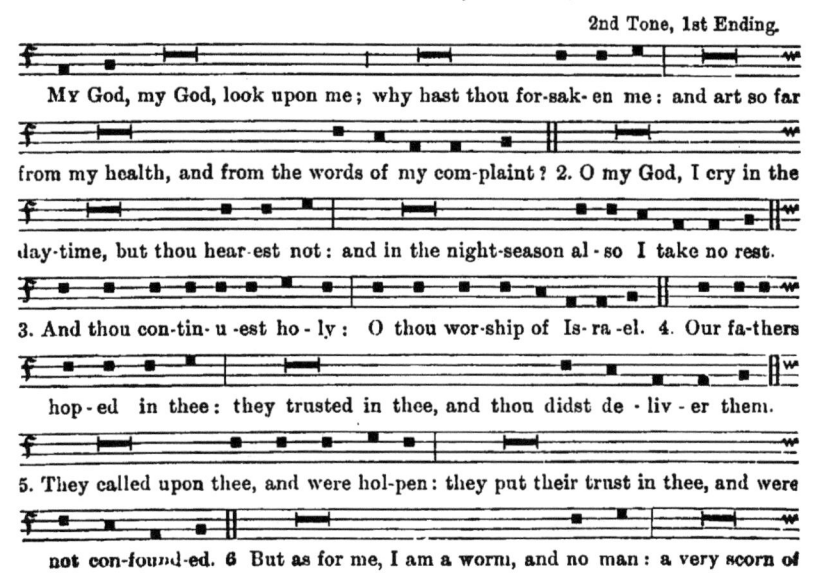

My God, my God, look upon me; why hast thou for-sak-en me : and art so far from my health, and from the words of my com-plaint? 2. O my God, I cry in the day-time, but thou hear-est not : and in the night-season al-so I take no rest. 3. And thou con-tin-u-est ho-ly : O thou wor-ship of Is-ra-el. 4. Our fa-thers hop-ed in thee : they trusted in thee, and thou didst de-liv-er them. 5. They called upon thee, and were hol-pen: they put their trust in thee, and were not con-found-ed. 6 But as for me, I am a worm, and no man : a very scorn of

(31)

DAY 4. EVENING PRAYER.

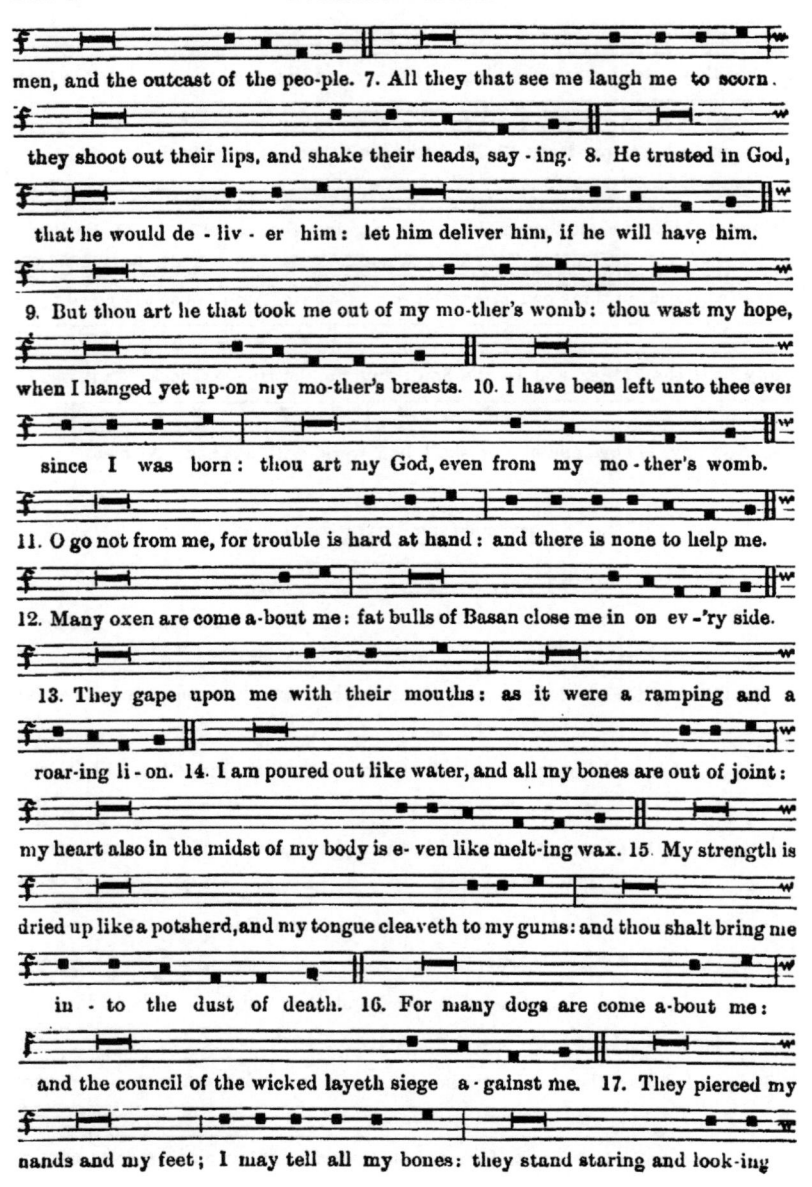

men, and the outcast of the peo-ple. 7. All they that see me laugh me to scorn.

they shoot out their lips, and shake their heads, say - ing. 8. He trusted in God,

that he would de - liv - er him: let him deliver him, if he will have him.

9. But thou art he that took me out of my mo-ther's womb: thou wast my hope,

when I hanged yet up-on my mo-ther's breasts. 10. I have been left unto thee ever

since I was born: thou art my God, even from my mo - ther's womb.

11. O go not from me, for trouble is hard at hand: and there is none to help me.

12. Many oxen are come a-bout me: fat bulls of Basan close me in on ev -'ry side.

13. They gape upon me with their mouths: as it were a ramping and a

roar-ing li - on. 14. I am poured out like water, and all my bones are out of joint:

my heart also in the midst of my body is e- ven like melt-ing wax. 15. My strength is

dried up like a potsherd, and my tongue cleaveth to my gums: and thou shalt bring me

in - to the dust of death. 16. For many dogs are come a-bout me:

and the council of the wicked layeth siege a - gainst me. 17. They pierced my

hands and my feet; I may tell all my bones: they stand staring and look-ing

(32)

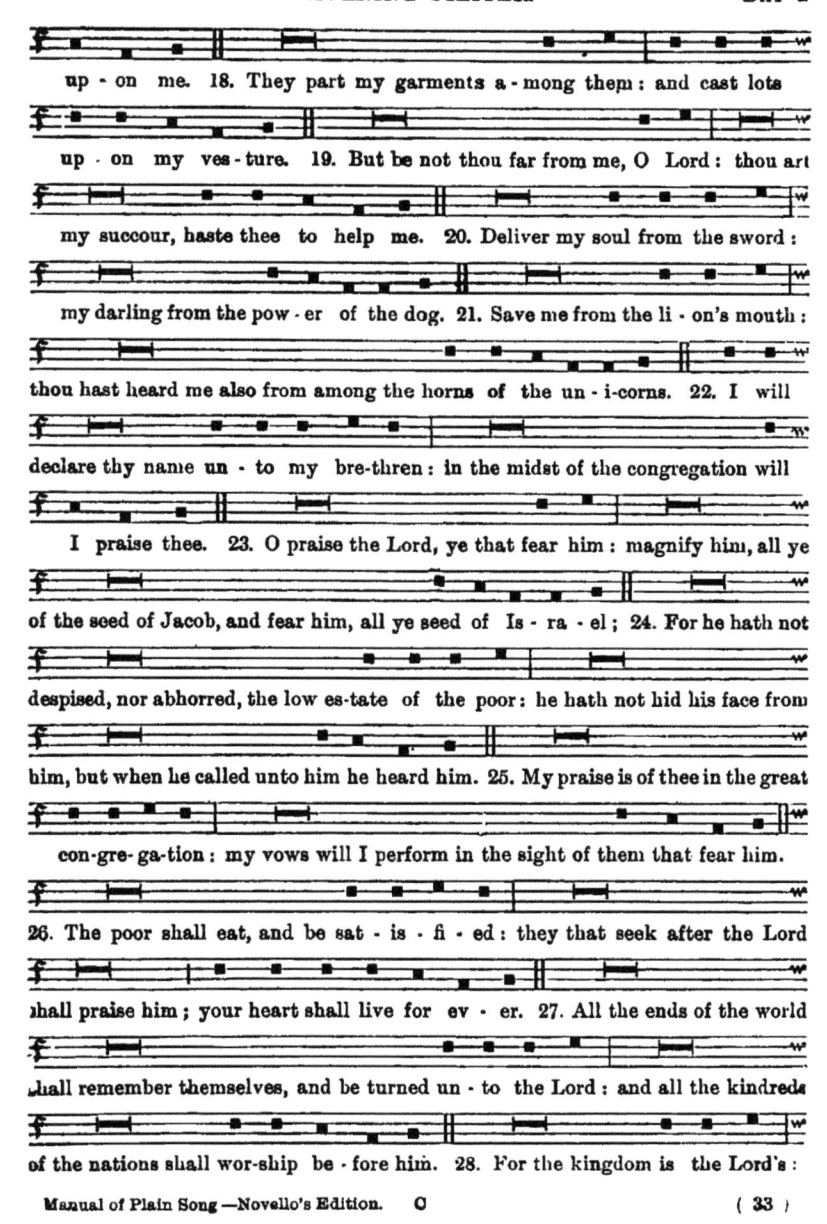

EVENING PRAYER.   DAY 4.

up - on me. 18. They part my garments a - mong them: and cast lots

up - on my ves - ture. 19. But be not thou far from me, O Lord: thou art

my succour, haste thee to help me. 20. Deliver my soul from the sword:

my darling from the pow - er of the dog. 21. Save me from the li - on's mouth:

thou hast heard me also from among the horns of the un - i-corns. 22. I will

declare thy name un - to my bre-thren: in the midst of the congregation will

I praise thee. 23. O praise the Lord, ye that fear him: magnify him, all ye

of the seed of Jacob, and fear him, all ye seed of Is - ra - el; 24. For he hath not

despised, nor abhorred, the low es-tate of the poor: he hath not hid his face from

him, but when he called unto him he heard him. 25. My praise is of thee in the great

con-gre-ga-tion: my vows will I perform in the sight of them that fear him.

26. The poor shall eat, and be sat - is - fi - ed: they that seek after the Lord

shall praise him; your heart shall live for ev - er. 27. All the ends of the world

shall remember themselves, and be turned un - to the Lord: and all the kindreds

of the nations shall wor-ship be - fore him. 28. For the kingdom is the Lord's:

Day 1.　　　　EVENING PRAYER.

and he is the Governour a-mong the peo-ple. 29. All such as be fat up - on earth.

have eat - en, and wor-ship-ped. 30. All they that go down into the dust shall

kneel be-fore him: and no man hath quick-en - ed his own soul. 31. My seed shall

serve him: they shall be counted unto the Lord for a ge - ne - ra tion.

32. They shall come, and the heavens shall de - clare his righ - teous -ness:

unto a people that shall be born, whom the Lord hath made. Glory be to the

Father, and to the Son: and to the Ho - ly Ghost; As it was in the beginning,

is now, and ever shall be: world with- out end. A - men.

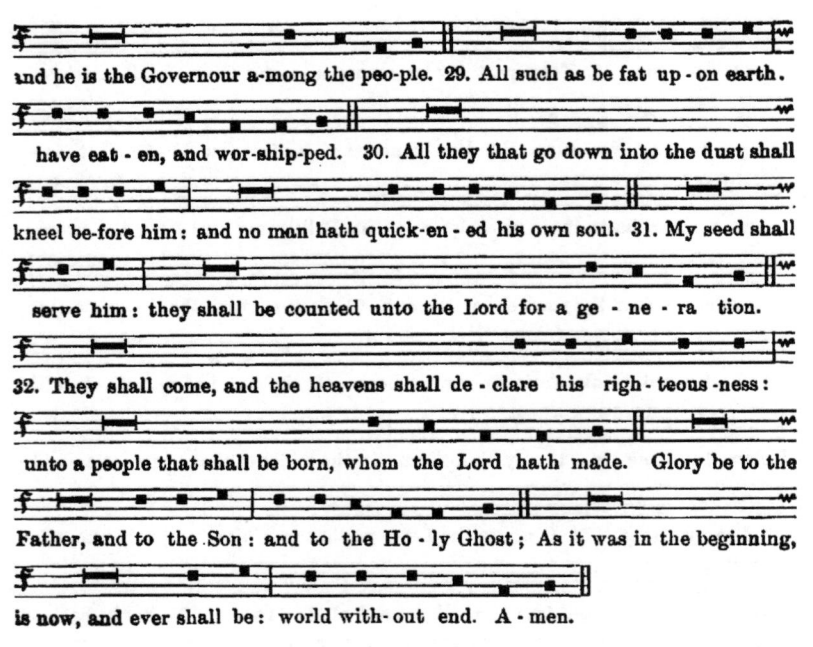

PSALM XXIII.—*Dominus regit me.*

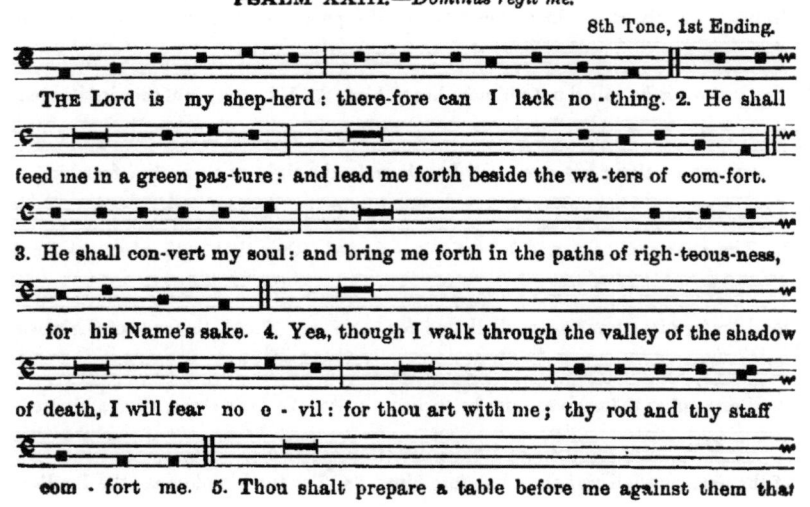

8th Tone, 1st Ending.

THE Lord is my shep-herd: there-fore can I lack no - thing. 2. He shall

feed me in a green pas-ture: and lead me forth beside the wa.-ters of com-fort.

3. He shall con-vert my soul: and bring me forth in the paths of righ-teous-ness,

for his Name's sake. 4. Yea, though I walk through the valley of the shadow

of death, I will fear no e - vil: for thou art with me; thy rod and thy staff

com - fort me. 5. Thou shalt prepare a table before me against them that

(34)

MORNING PRAYER. DAY 5

trou-ble me: thou hast anointed my head with oil, and my cup shall be full

5. But thy loving-kindness and mercy shall follow me all the days of my life:

and I will dwell in the house of the Lord for ev - er. Glory be to the

Father, and to the Son: and to the Ho - ly Ghost; As it was in the beginning,

is now, and ever shall be: world with-out end. A - men.

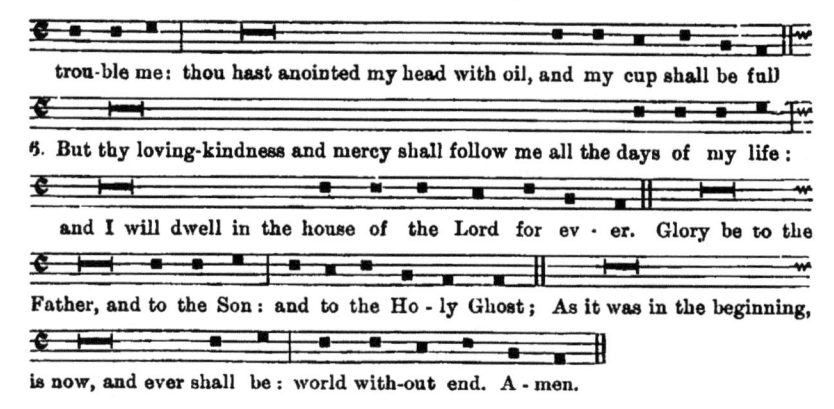

MORNING PRAYER. DAY 5.

PSALM XXIV.—*Domini est terra.*

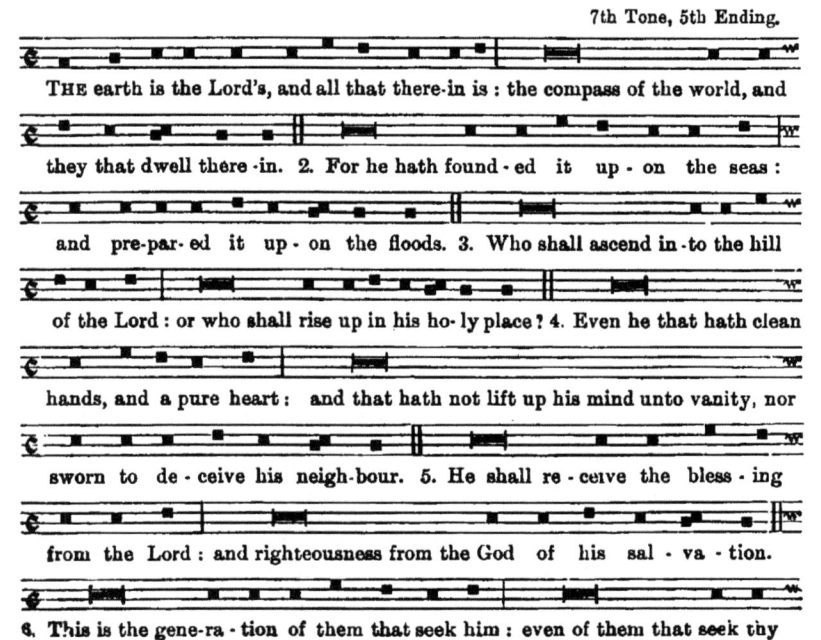

7th Tone, 5th Ending.

THE earth is the Lord's, and all that there-in is: the compass of the world, and

they that dwell there -in. 2. For he hath found - ed it up - on the seas:

and pre-par- ed it up - on the floods. 3. Who shall ascend in -to the hill

of the Lord: or who shall rise up in his ho- ly place? 4. Even he that hath clean

hands, and a pure heart: and that hath not lift up his mind unto vanity, nor

sworn to de - ceive his neigh-bour. 5. He shall re - ceive the bless - ing

from the Lord: and righteousness from the God of his sal - va - tion.

6. This is the gene-ra - tion of them that seek him: even of them that seek thy

(35)

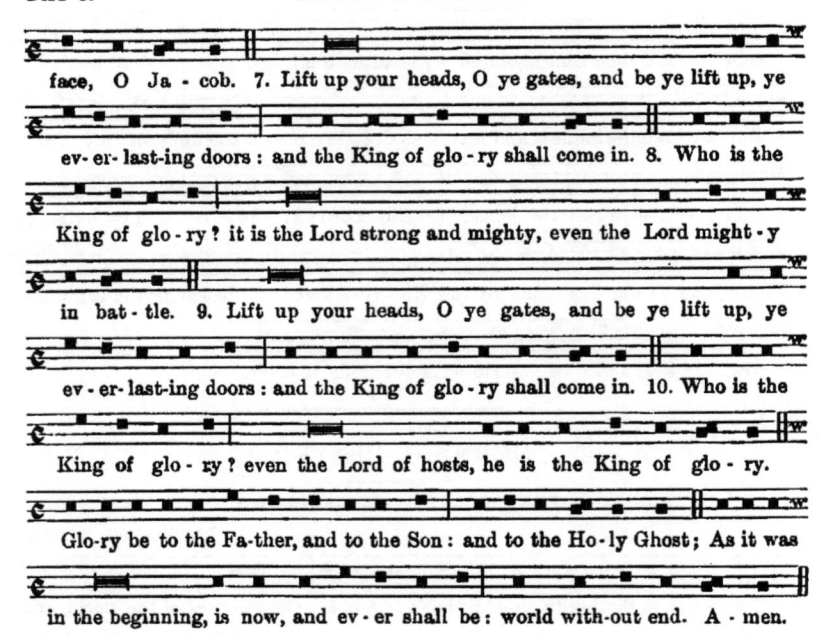

DAY 5. MORNING PRAYER.

face, O Ja - cob. 7. Lift up your heads, O ye gates, and be ye lift up, ye

ev- er- last-ing doors : and the King of glo - ry shall come in. 8. Who is the

King of glo - ry? it is the Lord strong and mighty, even the Lord might - y

in bat - tle. 9. Lift up your heads, O ye gates, and be ye lift up, ye

ev - er- last-ing doors : and the King of glo - ry shall come in. 10. Who is the

King of glo - ry? even the Lord of hosts, he is the King of glo - ry.

Glo-ry be to the Fa-ther, and to the Son : and to the Ho - ly Ghost; As it was

in the beginning, is now, and ev - er shall be : world with-out end. A - men.

PSALM XXV.—*Ad te, Domine, levavi.*

1st Tone, 1st Ending.

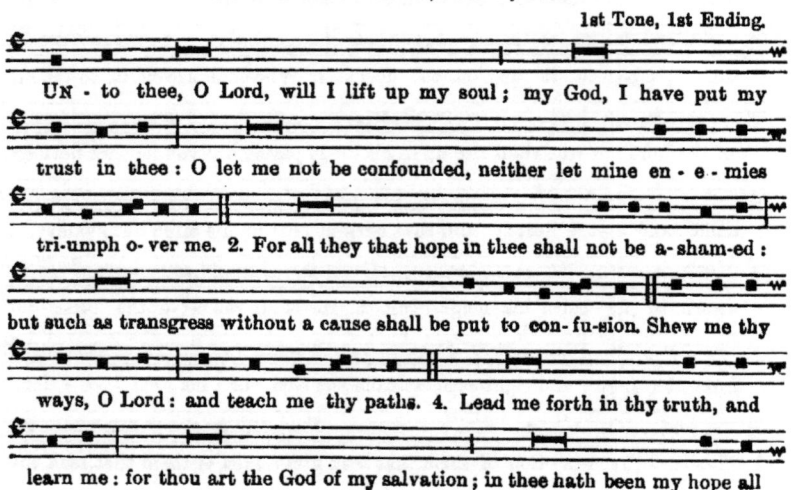

Un - to thee, O Lord, will I lift up my soul; my God, I have put my

trust in thee : O let me not be confounded, neither let mine en - e - mies

tri-umph o- ver me. 2. For all they that hope in thee shall not be a-sham-ed :

but such as transgress without a cause shall be put to con- fu-sion. Shew me thy

ways, O Lord : and teach me thy paths. 4. Lead me forth in thy truth, and

learn me : for thou art the God of my salvation ; in thee hath been my hope all

(36)

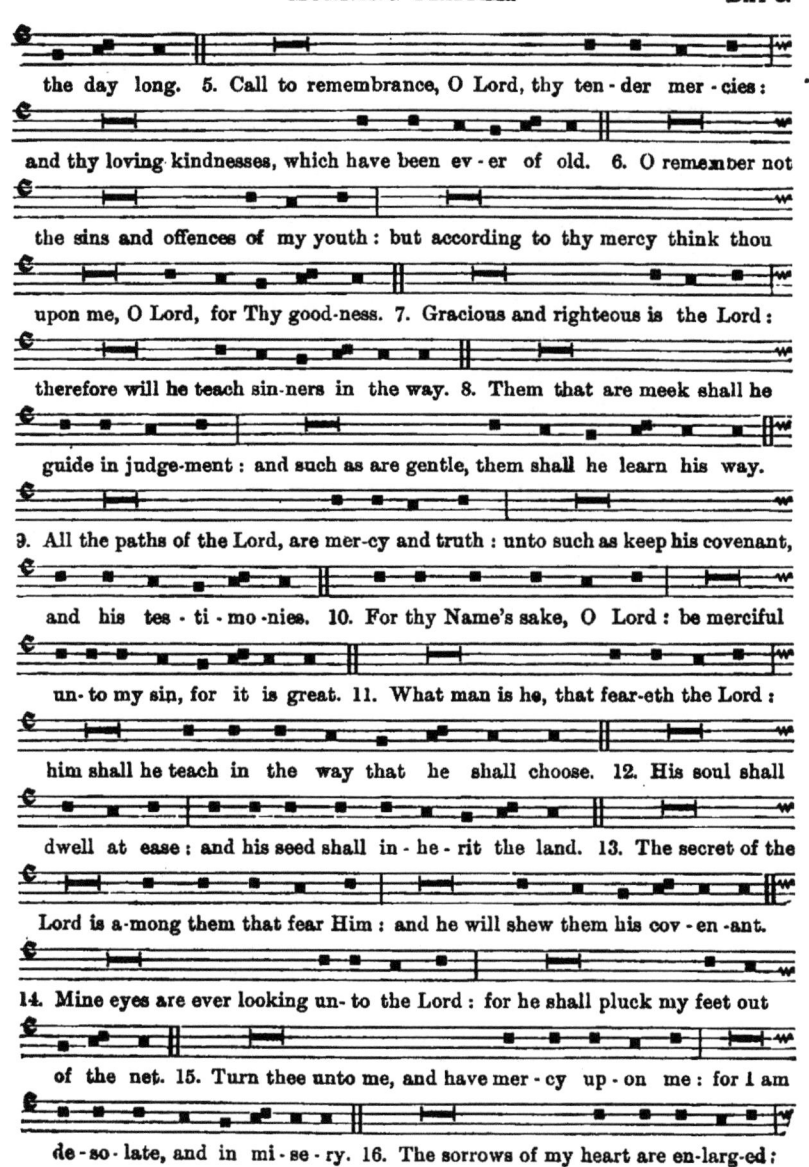

MORNING PRAYER.   Day 5.

the day long. 5. Call to remembrance, O Lord, thy ten-der mer-cies:

and thy loving kindnesses, which have been ev-er of old. 6. O remember not

the sins and offences of my youth: but according to thy mercy think thou

upon me, O Lord, for Thy good-ness. 7. Gracious and righteous is the Lord:

therefore will he teach sin-ners in the way. 8. Them that are meek shall he

guide in judge-ment: and such as are gentle, them shall he learn his way.

9. All the paths of the Lord, are mer-cy and truth : unto such as keep his covenant,

and his tes-ti-mo-nies. 10. For thy Name's sake, O Lord : be merciful

un-to my sin, for it is great. 11. What man is he, that fear-eth the Lord :

him shall he teach in the way that he shall choose. 12. His soul shall

dwell at ease : and his seed shall in-he-rit the land. 13. The secret of the

Lord is a-mong them that fear Him : and he will shew them his cov-en-ant.

14. Mine eyes are ever looking un-to the Lord : for he shall pluck my feet out

of the net. 15. Turn thee unto me, and have mer-cy up-on me : for I am

de-so-late, and in mi-se-ry. 16. The sorrows of my heart are en-larg-ed;

DAY 5. MORNING PRAYER.

O bring thou me out of my trou-bles. 17. Look upon my adversity and mi-se-ry:

and for-give me all my sin. 18. Consider mine enemies, how ma-ny they are:

and they bear a tyrannous hate a-gainst me. 19. O keep my soul, and de-liv-er me:

let me not be confounded, for I have put my trust in thee. 20. Let perfectness

and righteous dealing wait up-on me: for my hope hath been in thee.

21. Deliver Is-ra-el, O God: out of all his trou-bles. Glory be to the Father, and

to the Son: and to the Ho-ly Ghost; As it was in the beginning, is now, and

ev-er shall be: world with-out end. A-men.

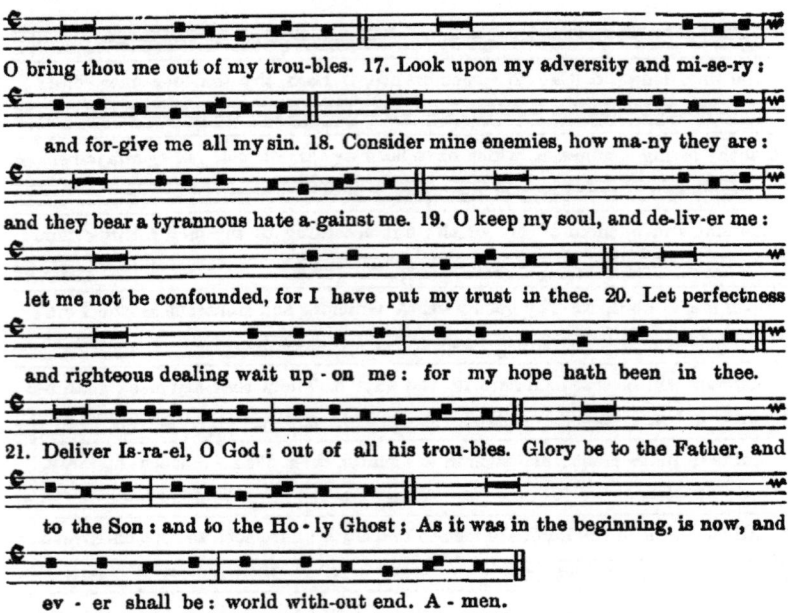

PSALM XXVI.—*Judica me, Domine.*

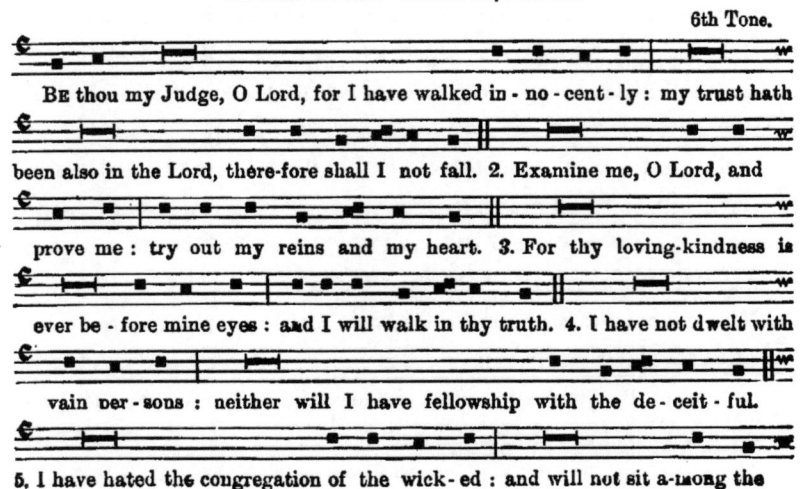

6th Tone.

Be thou my Judge, O Lord, for I have walked in-no-cent-ly: my trust hath

been also in the Lord, there-fore shall I not fall. 2. Examine me, O Lord, and

prove me: try out my reins and my heart. 3. For thy loving-kindness is

ever be-fore mine eyes: and I will walk in thy truth. 4. I have not dwelt with

vain per-sons: neither will I have fellowship with the de-ceit-ful.

5. I have hated the congregation of the wick-ed: and will not sit a-mong the

EVENING PRAYER. DAY 5.

un-god-ly. 6. I will wash my hands in inno-cen-cy, O Lord : and so will I go to thine al-tar. 7. That I may shew the voice of thanks-giv-ing : and tell of all thy won-drous works. 8. Lord, I have loved the habi-ta-tion of thy house : and the place where thine honour dwelleth. 9. O shut not up my soul with the sin-ners : nor my life with the blood thirs-ty; 10. In whose hands is wick-ed-ness : and their right hand is full of gifts. 11. But as for me, I will walk in-no-cent-ly : O deliver me, and be mer-ci-ful un-to me. 12. My foot stand-eth right : I will praise the Lord in the con-gre-ga-tions. Glory be to the Father, and to the Son : and to the Ho-ly Ghost ; As it was in the beginning, is now, and ev-er shall be : world with-out end. A-men.

EVENING PRAYER.

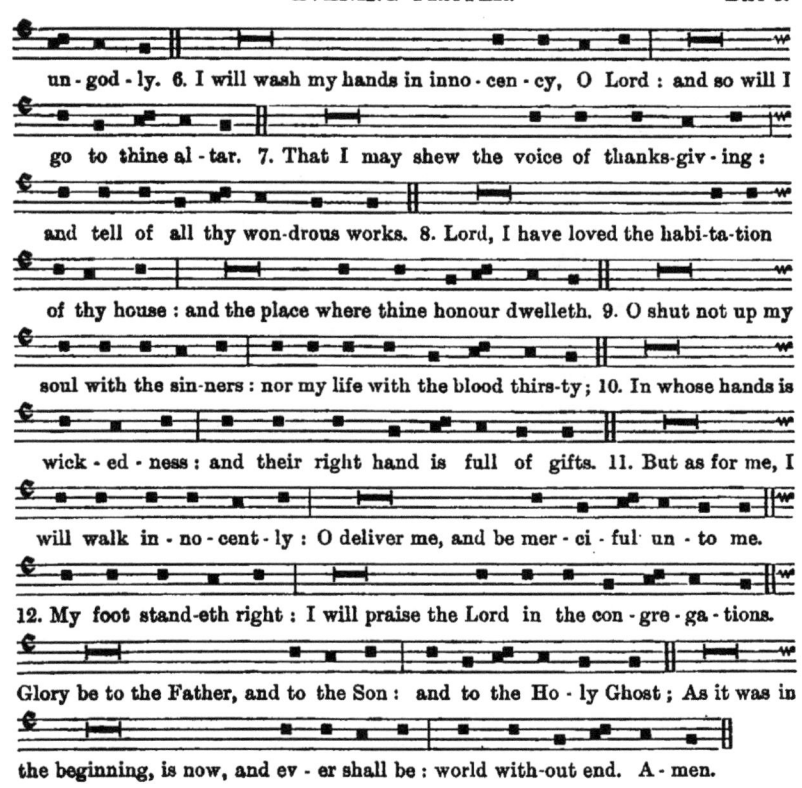

PSALM XXVII.—*Dominus illuminatio.*

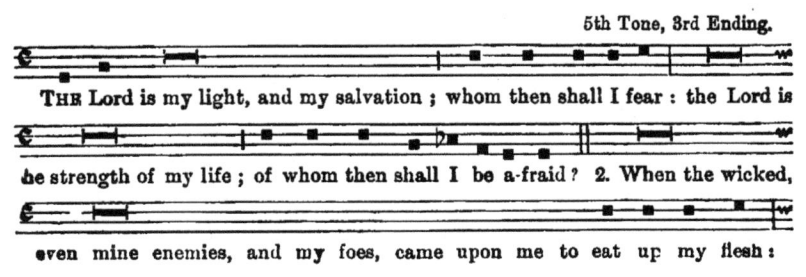

5th Tone, 3rd Ending.

The Lord is my light, and my salvation ; whom then shall I fear : the Lord is the strength of my life ; of whom then shall I be a-fraid ? 2. When the wicked, even mine enemies, and my foes, came upon me to eat up my flesh :

DAY 5.   EVENING PRAYER.

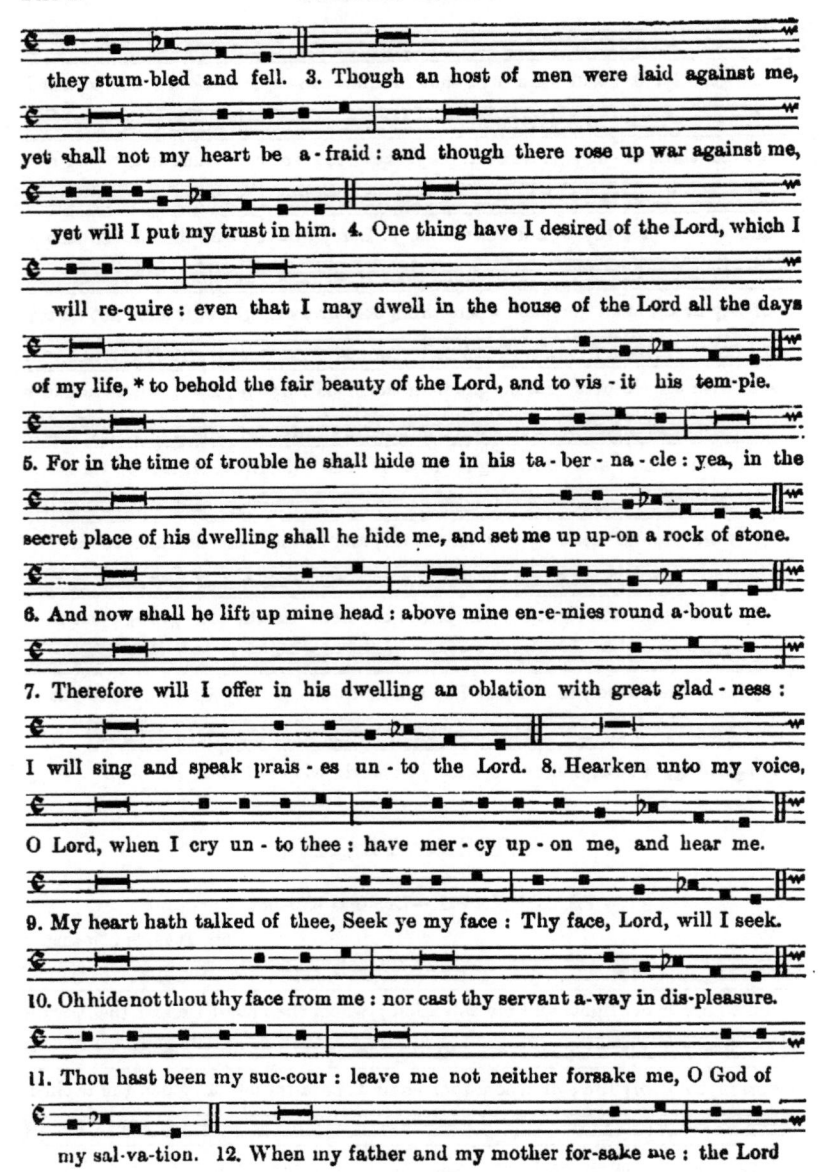

they stum-bled and fell. 3. Though an host of men were laid against me,

yet shall not my heart be a-fraid : and though there rose up war against me,

yet will I put my trust in him. 4. One thing have I desired of the Lord, which I

will re-quire : even that I may dwell in the house of the Lord all the days

of my life, * to behold the fair beauty of the Lord, and to vis-it his tem-ple.

5. For in the time of trouble he shall hide me in his ta-ber-na-cle : yea, in the

secret place of his dwelling shall he hide me, and set me up up-on a rock of stone.

6. And now shall he lift up mine head : above mine en-e-mies round a-bout me.

7. Therefore will I offer in his dwelling an oblation with great glad-ness :

I will sing and speak prais-es un-to the Lord. 8. Hearken unto my voice,

O Lord, when I cry un-to thee : have mer-cy up-on me, and hear me.

9. My heart hath talked of thee, Seek ye my face : Thy face, Lord, will I seek.

10. Oh hide not thou thy face from me : nor cast thy servant a-way in dis-pleasure.

11. Thou hast been my suc-cour : leave me not neither forsake me, O God of

my sal-va-tion. 12. When my father and my mother for-sake me : the Lord

(40)

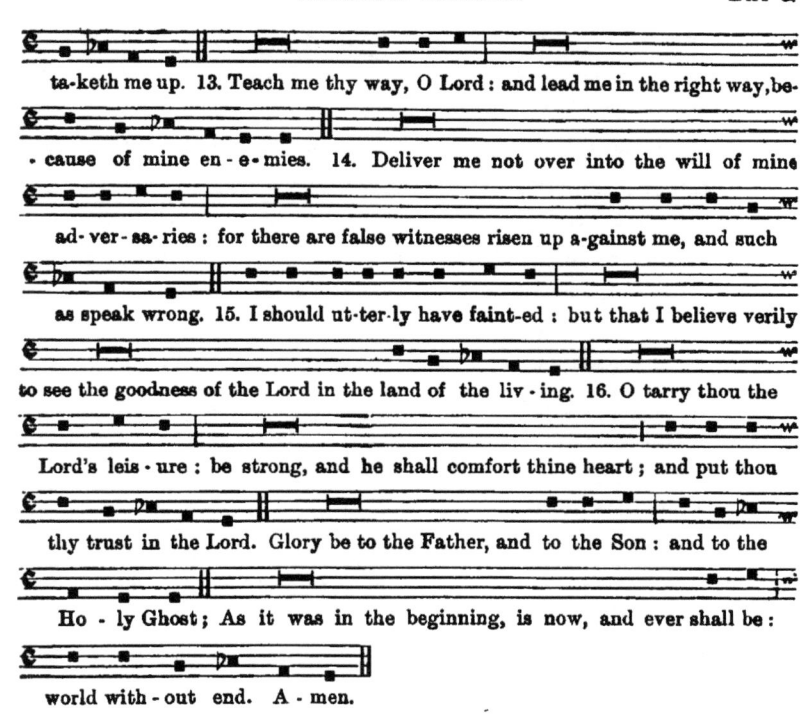

ta-keth me up. 13. Teach me thy way, O Lord : and lead me in the right way, be-
-cause of mine en-e-mies. 14. Deliver me not over into the will of mine
ad-ver-sa-ries : for there are false witnesses risen up a-gainst me, and such
as speak wrong. 15. I should ut-ter-ly have faint-ed : but that I believe verily
to see the goodness of the Lord in the land of the liv-ing. 16. O tarry thou the
Lord's leis-ure : be strong, and he shall comfort thine heart ; and put thou
thy trust in the Lord. Glory be to the Father, and to the Son : and to the
Ho-ly Ghost; As it was in the beginning, is now, and ever shall be :
world with-out end. A-men.

PSALM XXVIII.—*Ad te, Domine.*

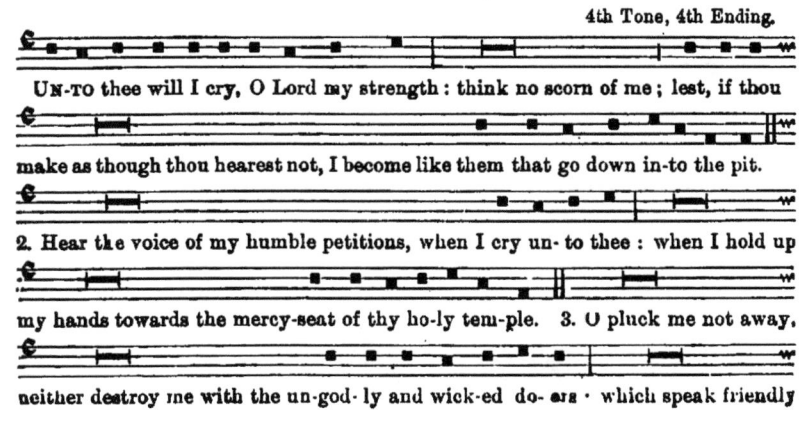

4th Tone, 4th Ending.

Un-to thee will I cry, O Lord my strength : think no scorn of me ; lest, if thou
make as though thou hearest not, I become like them that go down in-to the pit.
2. Hear the voice of my humble petitions, when I cry un-to thee : when I hold up
my hands towards the mercy-seat of thy ho-ly tem-ple. 3. O pluck me not away,
neither destroy me with the un-god-ly and wick-ed do-ers · which speak friendly

DAY 5.   EVENING PRAYER.

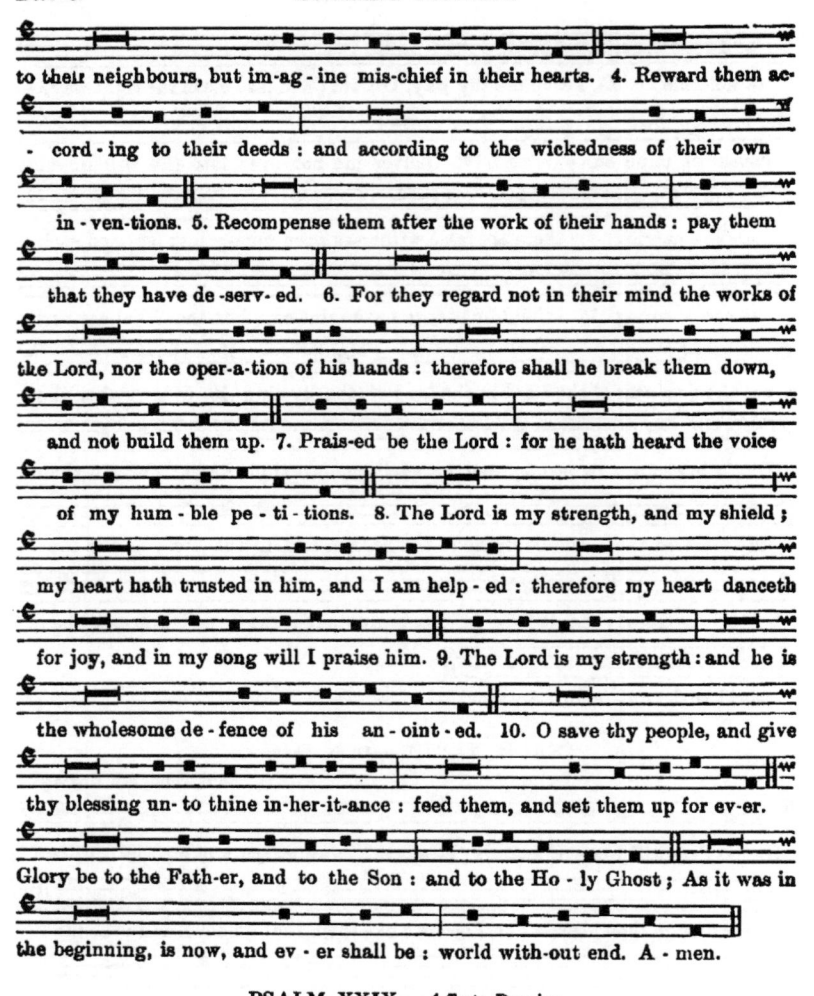

to their neighbours, but im-ag-ine mis-chief in their hearts. 4. Reward them ac-

- cord-ing to their deeds : and according to the wickedness of their own

in-ven-tions. 5. Recompense them after the work of their hands : pay them

that they have de-serv-ed. 6. For they regard not in their mind the works of

the Lord, nor the oper-a-tion of his hands : therefore shall he break them down,

and not build them up. 7. Prais-ed be the Lord : for he hath heard the voice

of my hum-ble pe-ti-tions. 8. The Lord is my strength, and my shield ;

my heart hath trusted in him, and I am help-ed : therefore my heart danceth

for joy, and in my song will I praise him. 9. The Lord is my strength : and he is

the wholesome de-fence of his an-oint-ed. 10. O save thy people, and give

thy blessing un-to thine in-her-it-ance : feed them, and set them up for ev-er.

Glory be to the Fath-er, and to the Son : and to the Ho-ly Ghost ; As it was in

the beginning, is now, and ev-er shall be : world with-out end. A-men.

            PSALM XXIX.—*Afferte Domino.*

                                             8th Tone, 1st Ending.

BRING un-to the Lord, O ye mighty, bring young rams un-to the Lord :

ascribe unto the Lord wor-ship and strength. 2. Give the Lord the honour due

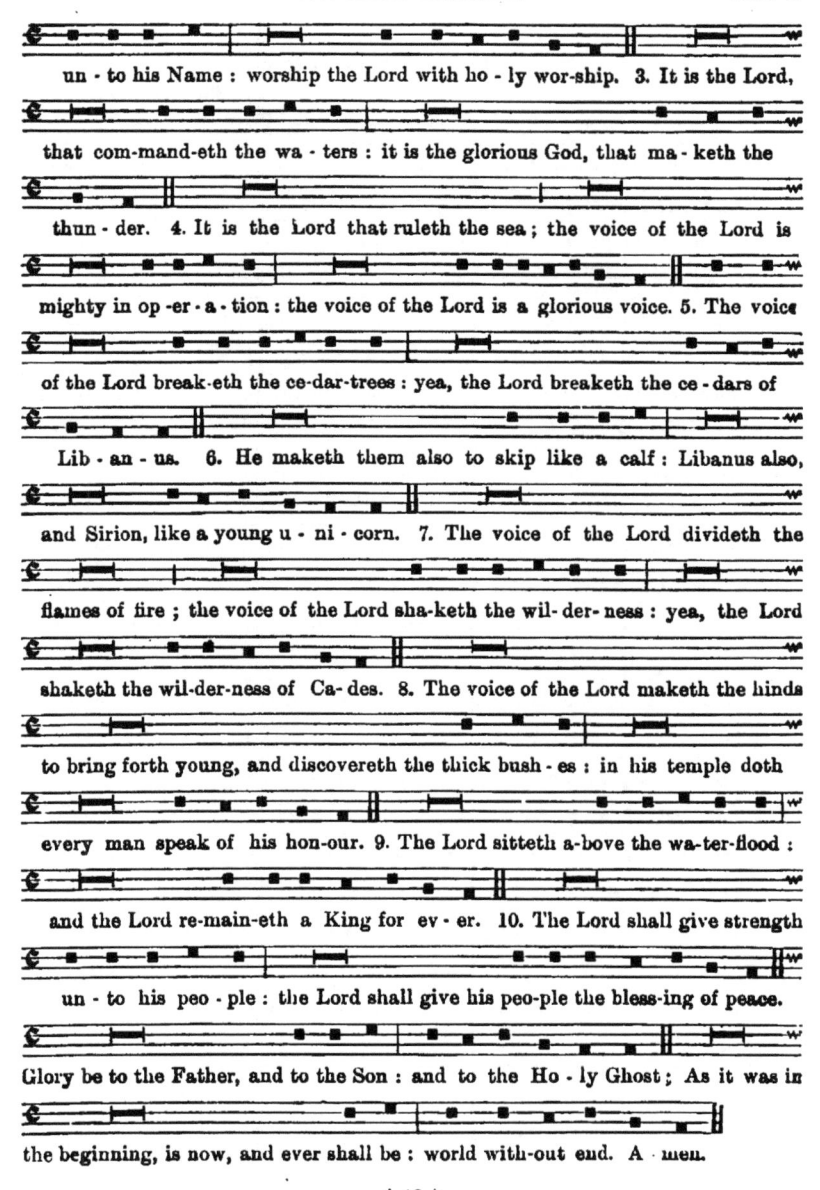

EVENING PRAYER. DAY 5.

un - to his Name : worship the Lord with ho - ly wor-ship. 3. It is the Lord, that com-mand-eth the wa - ters : it is the glorious God, that ma - keth the thun - der. 4. It is the Lord that ruleth the sea ; the voice of the Lord is mighty in op -er - a - tion : the voice of the Lord is a glorious voice. 5. The voice of the Lord break-eth the ce-dar-trees : yea, the Lord breaketh the ce - dars of Lib - an - us. 6. He maketh them also to skip like a calf : Libanus also, and Sirion, like a young u - ni - corn. 7. The voice of the Lord divideth the flames of fire ; the voice of the Lord sha-keth the wil- der- ness : yea, the Lord shaketh the wil-der-ness of Ca- des. 8. The voice of the Lord maketh the hinds to bring forth young, and discovereth the thick bush - es : in his temple doth every man speak of his hon-our. 9. The Lord sitteth a-bove the wa-ter-flood : and the Lord re-main-eth a King for ev - er. 10. The Lord shall give strength un - to his peo - ple : the Lord shall give his peo-ple the bless-ing of peace. Glory be to the Father, and to the Son : and to the Ho - ly Ghost ; As it was in the beginning, is now, and ever shall be : world with-out end. A - men.

Day 6. MORNING PRAYER.

PSALM XXX.—*Exaltabo te, Domine.*

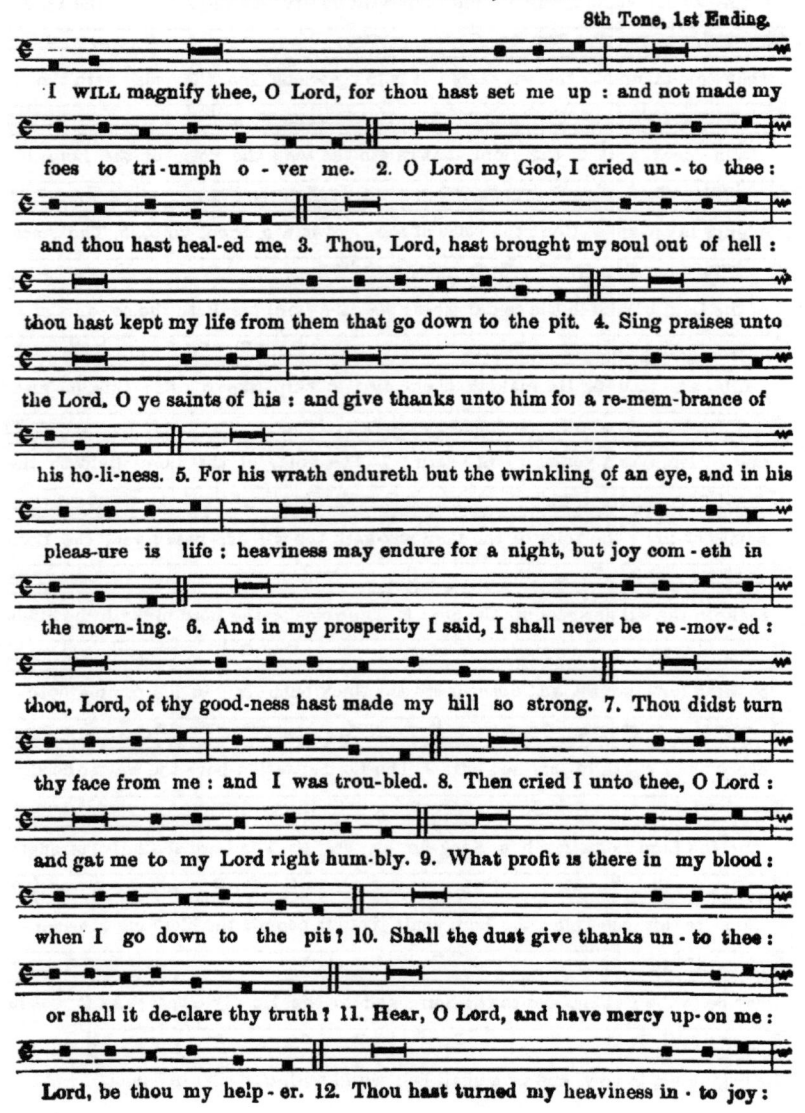

8th Tone, 1st Ending.

I will magnify thee, O Lord, for thou hast set me up : and not made my foes to tri-umph o-ver me. 2. O Lord my God, I cried un-to thee : and thou hast heal-ed me. 3. Thou, Lord, hast brought my soul out of hell : thou hast kept my life from them that go down to the pit. 4. Sing praises unto the Lord, O ye saints of his : and give thanks unto him for a re-mem-brance of his ho-li-ness. 5. For his wrath endureth but the twinkling of an eye, and in his pleas-ure is life : heaviness may endure for a night, but joy com-eth in the morn-ing. 6. And in my prosperity I said, I shall never be re-mov-ed : thou, Lord, of thy good-ness hast made my hill so strong. 7. Thou didst turn thy face from me : and I was trou-bled. 8. Then cried I unto thee, O Lord : and gat me to my Lord right hum-bly. 9. What profit is there in my blood : when I go down to the pit? 10. Shall the dust give thanks un-to thee : or shall it de-clare thy truth? 11. Hear, O Lord, and have mercy up-on me : Lord, be thou my help-er. 12. Thou hast turned my heaviness in-to joy :

MORNING PRAYER. DAY 6.

thou hast put off my sackcloth, and gird - ed me with glad - ness.

13. Therefore shall every good man sing of thy praise with - out ceas - ing:

O my God, I will give thanks un-to thee for ev - er. Glory be to the Father, and

to the Son: and to the Ho - ly Ghost; As it was in the beginning, is

now, and ever shall be : world with -out end. A - men.

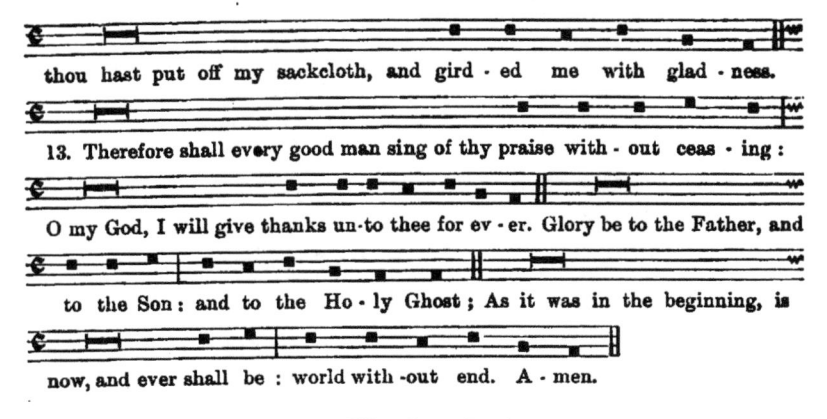

PSALM XXXI.—*In te, Domine, speravi.*

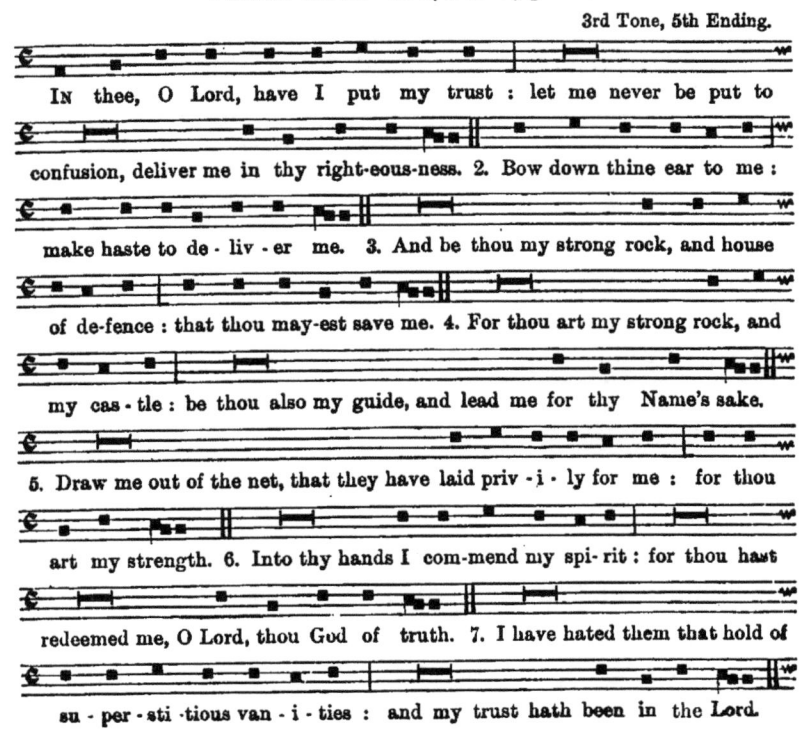

3rd Tone, 5th Ending.

In thee, O Lord, have I put my trust : let me never be put to

confusion, deliver me in thy right-eous-ness. 2. Bow down thine ear to me :

make haste to de - liv - er me. 3. And be thou my strong rock, and house

of de-fence : that thou may-est save me. 4. For thou art my strong rock, and

my cas - tle : be thou also my guide, and lead me for thy Name's sake.

5. Draw me out of the net, that they have laid priv - i - ly for me : for thou

art my strength. 6. Into thy hands I com-mend my spi - rit : for thou hast

redeemed me, O Lord, thou God of truth. 7. I have hated them that hold of

su - per - sti - tious van - i - ties : and my trust hath been in the Lord.

DAY 6. MORNING PRAYER.

8. I will be glad, and rejoice in thy mer - cy : for thou hast considered my trouble, and hast known my soul in ad - ver - si - ties. 9. Thou hast not shut me up in - to the hand of the en - e - my : but hast set my feet in a large room.

10. Have mercy upon me, O Lord, for I am in trou - ble : and mine eye is consumed for very heaviness ; yea, my soul and my bo - dy. 11. For my life is wax - en old with heav - i - ness : and my years with mourn - ing.

12. My strength faileth me, be-cause of mine in - i - qui - ty : and my bones are con - su - med. 13. I became a reproof among all mine enemies, but es - - pe - cial - ly a - mong my neigh-bours : and they of mine acquaintance were afraid of me ; and they that did see me without con-vey-ed them-selves from me.

14. I am clean forgotten, as a dead man out of mind : I am become like a bro-ken ves - sel. 15. For I have heard the blas-phe-my of the mul - ti-tude : and fear is on every side, while they conspire together against me, * and take their counsel to take a-way my life. 16. But my hope hath been in thee, O Lord : I have said, Thou art my God. 17. My time is in thy hand : deliver me

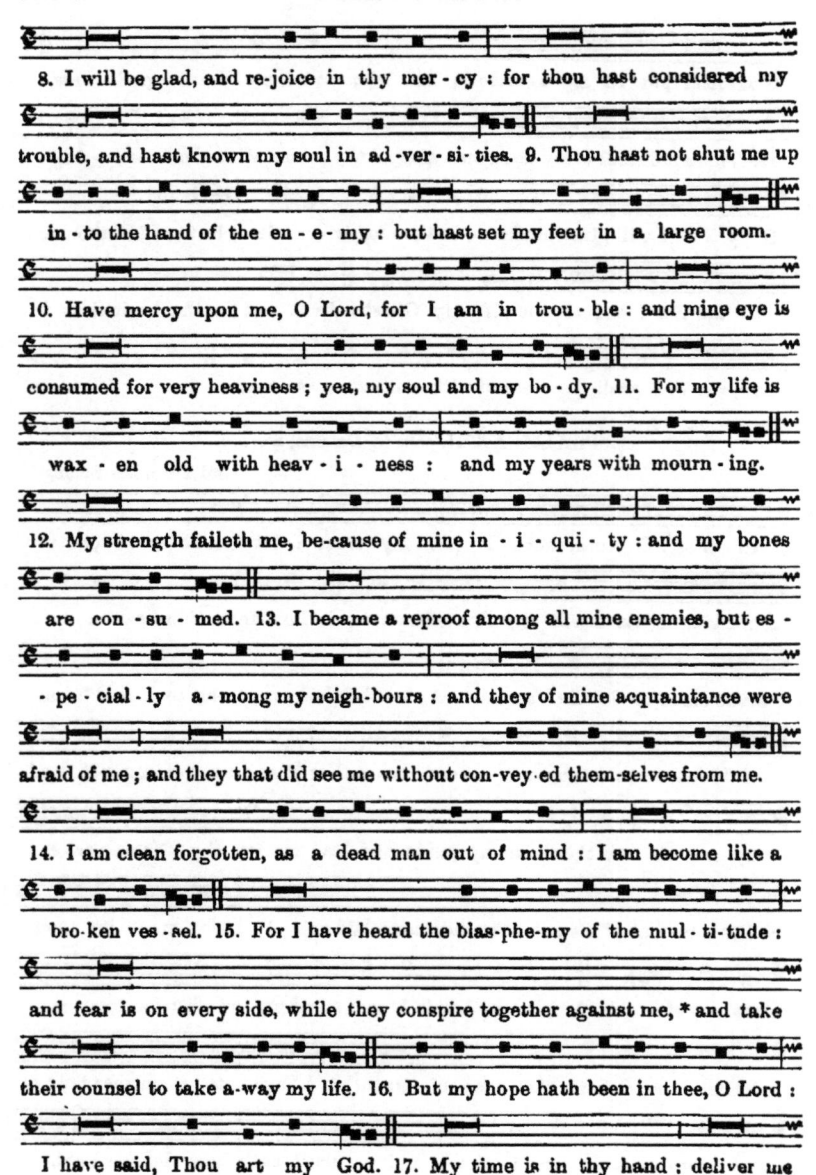

MORNING PRAYER. DAY 6

from the hand of mine en - e - mies : and from them that per-se-cute me. 18. Shew thy ser-vant the light of thy coun - ten - ance : and save me for thy mer - cy's sake. 19. Let me not be confounded, O Lord, for I have call - ed up - on thee : let the ungodly be put to confusion, and be put to si-lence in the grave. 20. Let the lying lips be put to si-lence : which cruelly, disdainfully, and despitefully, speak a - gainst the right-eous. 21. O how plentiful is thy goodness, which thou hast laid up for them that fear thee : and that thou hast prepared for them that put their trust in thee, even be-fore the sons of men! 22. Thou shalt hide them privily by thine own presence from the pro -vo - king of all men : thou shalt keep them secretly in thy tabernacle from the strife of tongues. 23. Thanks be to the Lord : for he hath shewed me marvellous great kindness in a strong ci - ty. 24. And when I made haste, I said : I am cast out of the sight of thine eyes. 25. Nevertheless, thou heard-est the voice of my pray- er : when I cri -ed un - to thee. 26. O love the Lord, all ye his saints : for the Lord preserveth them that are faithful,

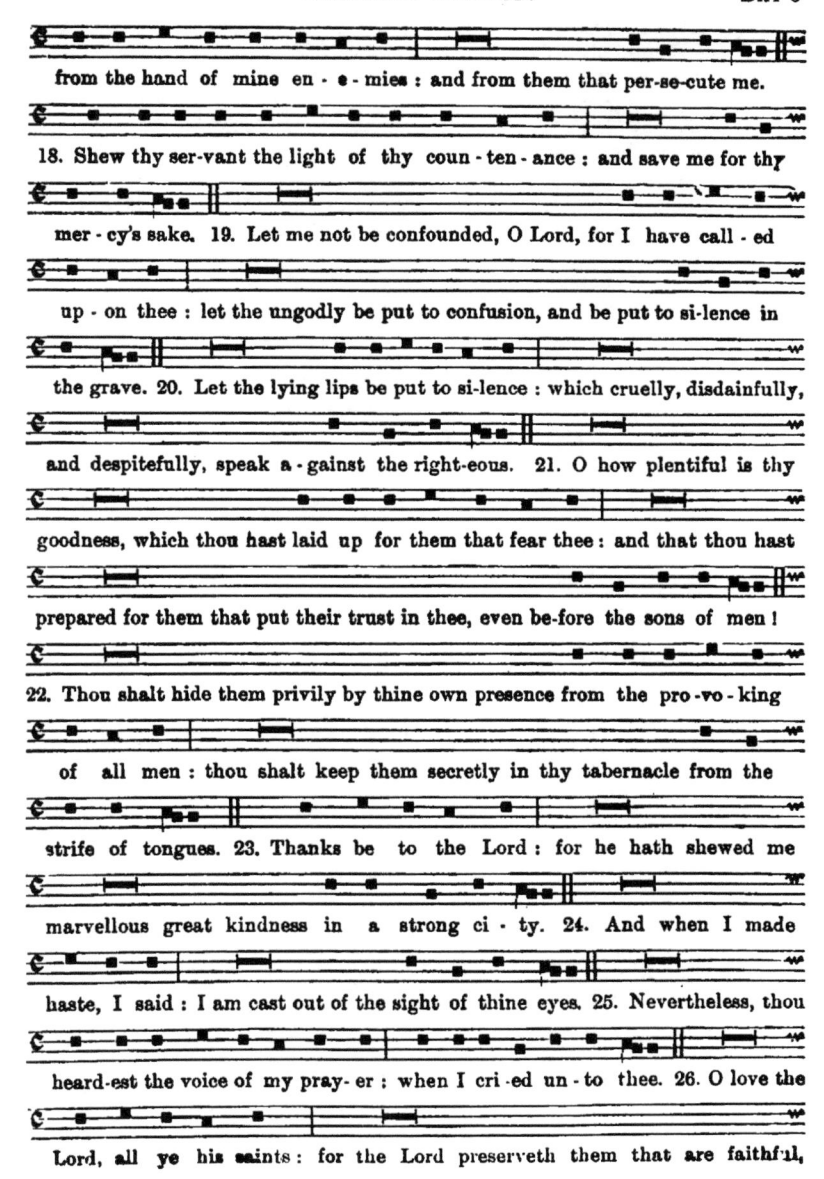

DAY 6. EVENING PRAYER.

and plenteously re-ward-eth the proud do-er. 27. Be strong, and he shall

es-tab-lish your heart : all ye that put your trust in the Lord. Glo-ry be to the

Fath-er, and to the Son : and to the Ho-ly Ghost; As it was in the beginning, is

now, and ev-er shall be : world with-out end. A-men.

EVENING PRAYER.

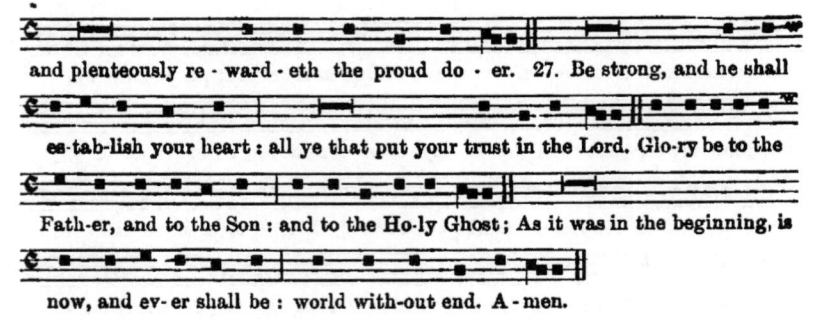

PSALM XXXII.—*Beati, quorum.*

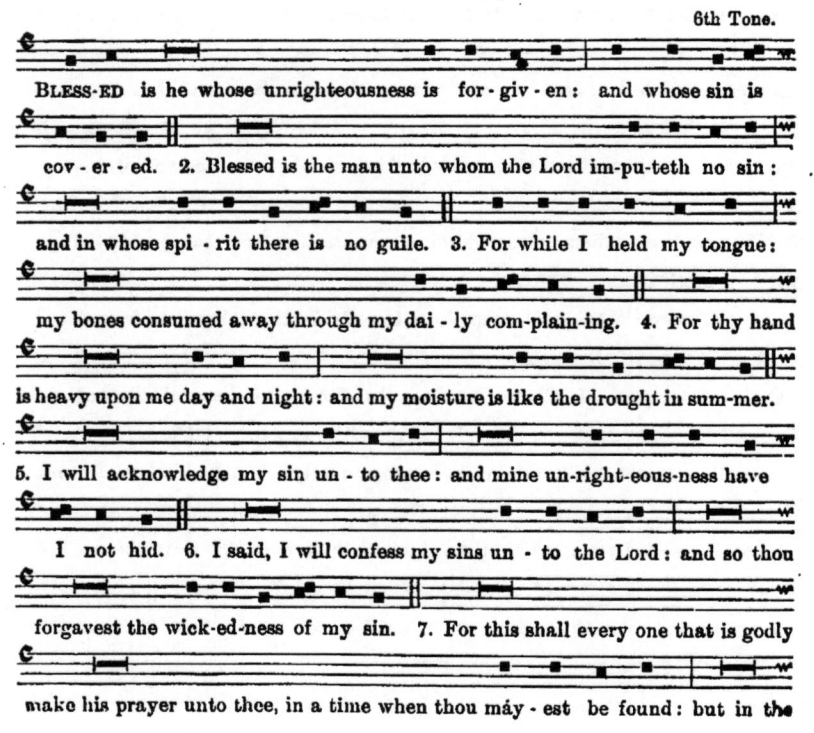

6th Tone.

BLESS-ED is he whose unrighteousness is for-giv-en : and whose sin is

cov-er-ed. 2. Blessed is the man unto whom the Lord im-pu-teth no sin :

and in whose spi-rit there is no guile. 3. For while I held my tongue:

my bones consumed away through my dai-ly com-plain-ing. 4. For thy hand

is heavy upon me day and night : and my moisture is like the drought in sum-mer.

5. I will acknowledge my sin un-to thee : and mine un-right-eous-ness have

I not hid. 6. I said, I will confess my sins un-to the Lord : and so thou

forgavest the wick-ed-ness of my sin. 7. For this shall every one that is godly

make his prayer unto thee, in a time when thou máy-est be found : but in the

(48)

EVENING PRAYER. DAY 6.

great water-floods they shall not come nigh him. 8. Thou art a place to hide

me in, thou shalt pre-serve me from trou-ble: thou shalt compass me about with

songs of de-liv-er-ance. 9. I will inform thee, and teach thee in the way where-

- in thou shalt go: and I will guide thee with mine eye. 10. Be ye not like to

horse and mule, which have no un-der-stand-ing: whose mouths must be held with

bit and bridle, lest they fall up-on thee. 11. Great plagues remain for the

un-god-ly: but whoso putteth his trust in the Lord, mercy em-bra-ceth him

on ev-'ry side. 12. Be glad, O ye righteous, and re-joice in the Lord:

and be joyful, all ye that are true of heart. Glory be to the Father, and

to the Son: and to the Ho-ly Ghost; As it was in the beginning, is now, and

ev-er shall be: world with-out end. A-men.

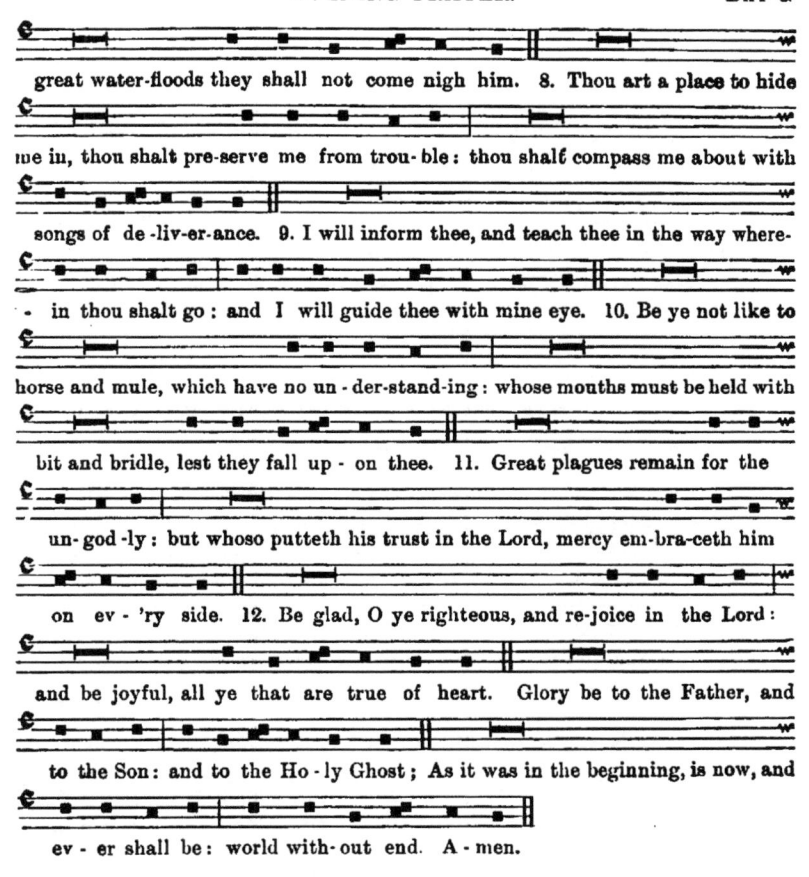

PSALM XXXIII.—*Exultate, justi.*

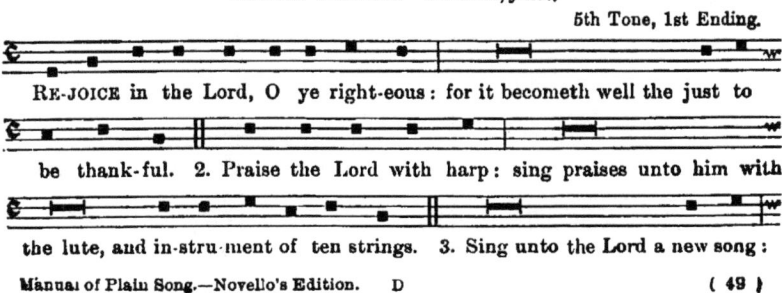

5th Tone, 1st Ending.

RE-JOICE in the Lord, O ye right-eous: for it becometh well the just to

be thank-ful. 2. Praise the Lord with harp: sing praises unto him with

the lute, and in-stru-ment of ten strings. 3. Sing unto the Lord a new song:

Manual of Plain Song.—Novello's Edition. D (49)

DAY 6.   EVENING PRAYER.

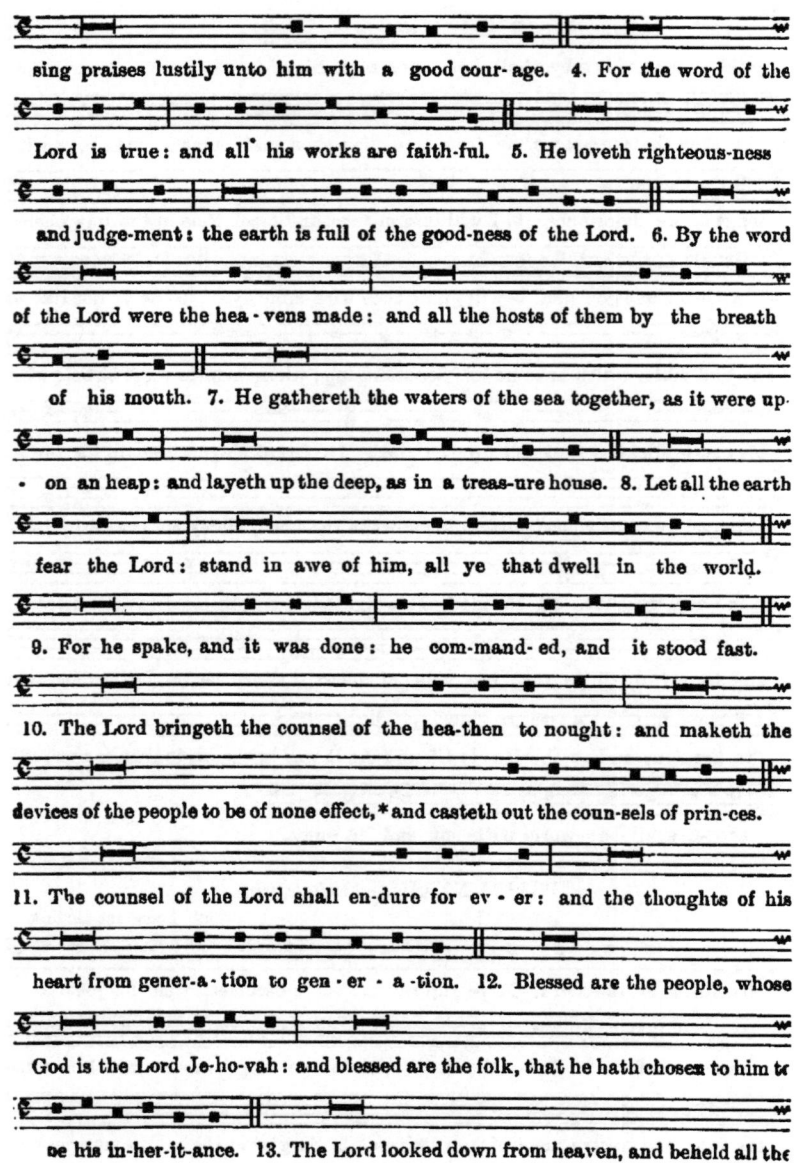

sing praises lustily unto him with a good cour-age. 4. For the word of the Lord is true: and all his works are faith-ful. 5. He loveth righteous-ness and judge-ment: the earth is full of the good-ness of the Lord. 6. By the word of the Lord were the hea-vens made: and all the hosts of them by the breath of his mouth. 7. He gathereth the waters of the sea together, as it were up- on an heap: and layeth up the deep, as in a treas-ure house. 8. Let all the earth fear the Lord: stand in awe of him, all ye that dwell in the world. 9. For he spake, and it was done: he com-mand-ed, and it stood fast. 10. The Lord bringeth the counsel of the hea-then to nought: and maketh the devices of the people to be of none effect,* and casteth out the coun-sels of prin-ces. 11. The counsel of the Lord shall en-dure for ev-er: and the thoughts of his heart from gener-a-tion to gen-er-a-tion. 12. Blessed are the people, whose God is the Lord Je-ho-vah: and blessed are the folk, that he hath chosen to him to be his in-her-it-ance. 13. The Lord looked down from heaven, and beheld all the chil-dren of men: from the habitation of his dwelling he considereth all them that dwell on the earth. 14. He fashioneth all the hearts of them: and un-der-stand-eth all their works. 15. There is no king that can be saved by the multitude of an host: neither is any mighty man de-liv-er-ed by much strength. 16. A horse is counted but a vain thing to save a man: neither shall he deliver any man by his great strength. 17. Behold, the eye of the Lord is upon them that fear him: and upon them that put their trust in his mer-cy; 18. To deliver their soul from death: and to feed them in the time of dearth. 19. Our soul hath patiently tarried for the Lord: for he is our help and our shield. 20. For our heart shall re-joice in him: because we have ho-ped in his ho-ly Name. 21. Let thy merciful kindness, O Lord, be up-on us: like as we do put our trust in thee. Glory be to the Father, and to the Son: and to the Ho-ly Ghost; As it was in the beginning, is now, and ever shall be: world with-out end. A-men.

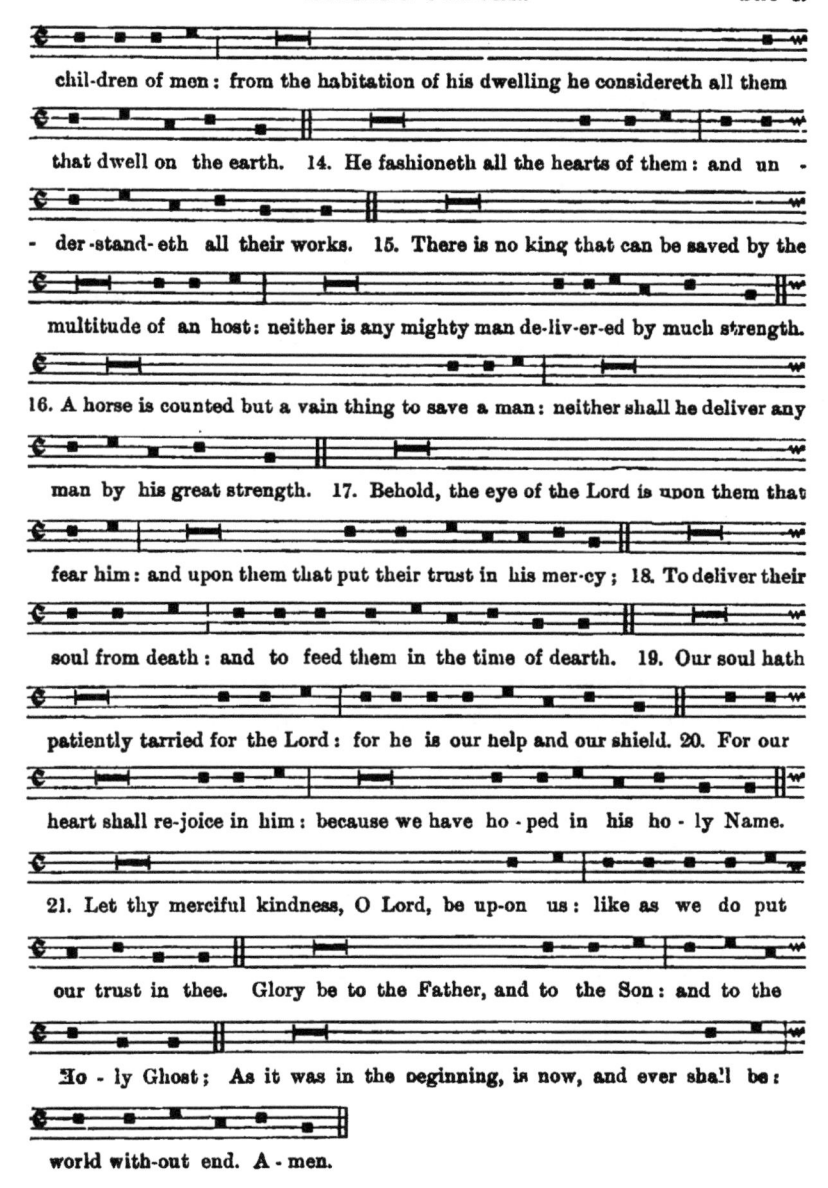

Day 6. EVENING PRAYER.

PSALM XXXIV.—*Benedicam Domino.*

7th Tone, 2nd Ending.

I WILL al-way give thanks un - to the Lord : his praise shall ev - er be in my mouth. 2. My soul shall make her boast in the Lord : the humble shall hear there-of and be glad. 3. O praise the Lord with me : and let us magni - fy his Name to - geth - er. 4. I sought the Lord, and he heard me : yea, he deliver-ed me out of all my fear. 5. They had an eye unto him, and were light - en - ed : and their fa-ces were not a - sha- med. 6. Lo, the poor crieth, and the Lord hear-eth him : yea, and saveth him out of all his trou-bles. 7. The angel of the Lord tarrieth round a-bout them that fear him : and de - liv - er - eth them. 8. O taste, and see, how gra-cious the Lord is : blessed is the man that trust-eth in him. 9. O fear the Lord, ye that are his saints : for they that fear him lack noth-ing. 10. The lions do lack, and suf-fer hun-ger : but they who seek the Lord shall want no man-ner of thing that is good. 11. Come, ye chil-dren, and heark- en un - to me : I will teach you the fear of the Lord. 12. What man is he that lust-eth to live : and would

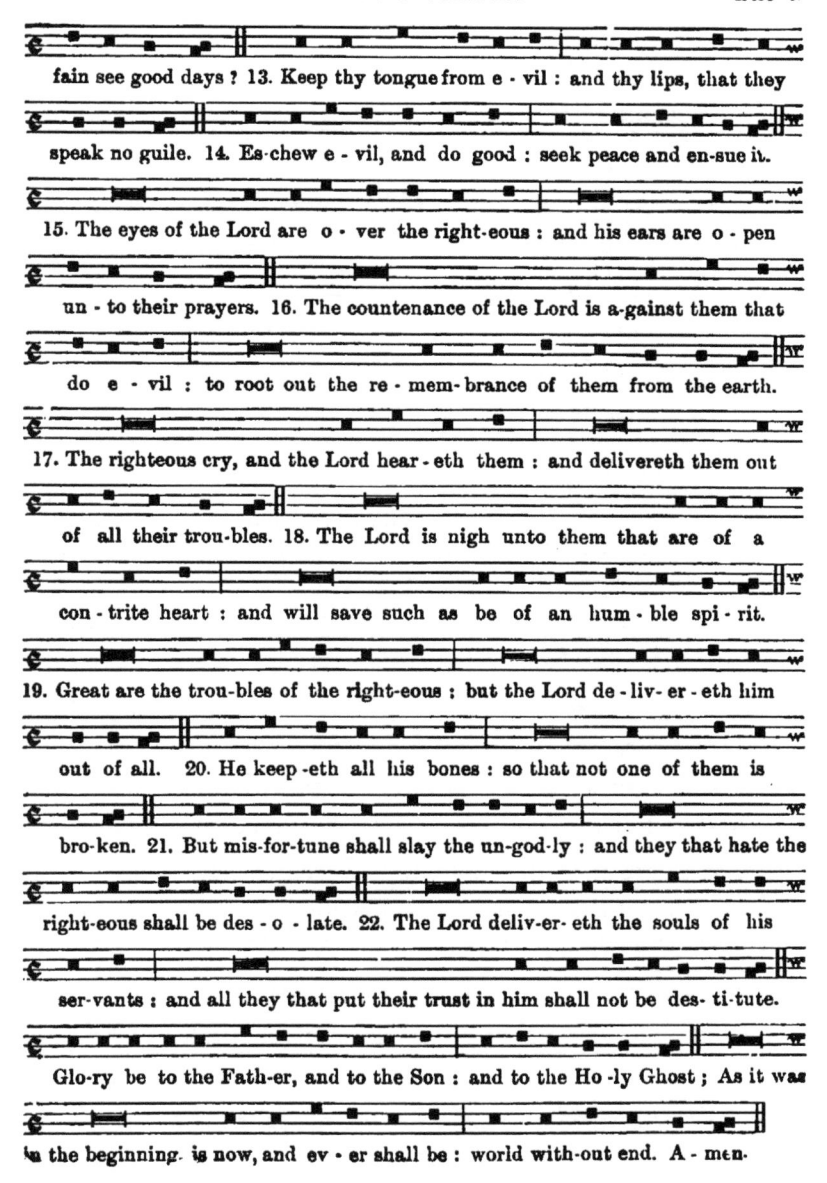

EVENING PRAYER. DAY 6

fain see good days? 13. Keep thy tongue from e-vil : and thy lips, that they speak no guile. 14. Es-chew e-vil, and do good : seek peace and en-sue it.

15. The eyes of the Lord are o-ver the right-eous : and his ears are o-pen un-to their prayers. 16. The countenance of the Lord is a-gainst them that do e-vil : to root out the re-mem-brance of them from the earth.

17. The righteous cry, and the Lord hear-eth them : and delivereth them out of all their trou-bles. 18. The Lord is nigh unto them that are of a con-trite heart : and will save such as be of an hum-ble spi-rit.

19. Great are the trou-bles of the right-eous : but the Lord de-liv-er-eth him out of all. 20. He keep-eth all his bones : so that not one of them is bro-ken. 21. But mis-for-tune shall slay the un-god-ly : and they that hate the right-eous shall be des-o-late. 22. The Lord deliv-er-eth the souls of his ser-vants : and all they that put their trust in him shall not be des-ti-tute.

Glo-ry be to the Fath-er, and to the Son : and to the Ho-ly Ghost ; As it was in the beginning, is now, and ev-er shall be : world with-out end. A-men.

(53)

DAY 7　　　　MORNING PRAYER

PSALM XXXV.—*Judica, Domine.*

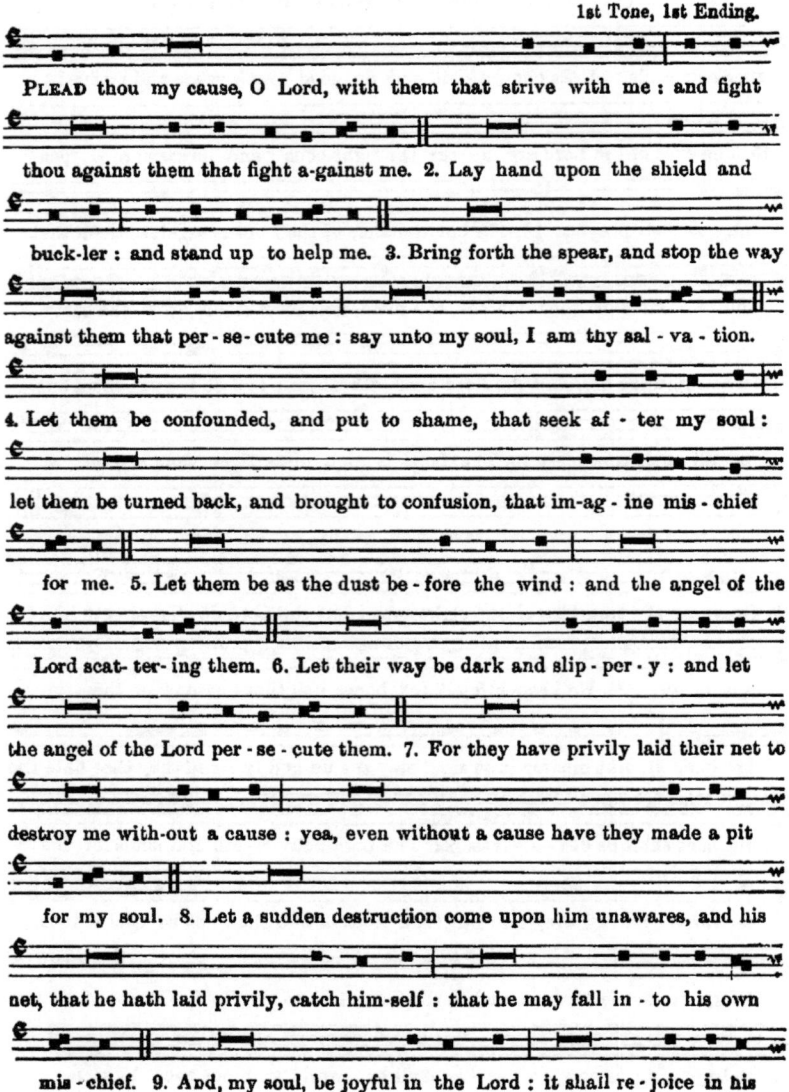

1st Tone, 1st Ending.

PLEAD thou my cause, O Lord, with them that strive with me : and fight thou against them that fight a-gainst me. 2. Lay hand upon the shield and buck-ler : and stand up to help me. 3. Bring forth the spear, and stop the way against them that per - se - cute me : say unto my soul, I am thy sal - va - tion. 4. Let them be confounded, and put to shame, that seek af - ter my soul : let them be turned back, and brought to confusion, that im-ag - ine mis - chief for me. 5. Let them be as the dust be - fore the wind : and the angel of the Lord scat- ter- ing them. 6. Let their way be dark and slip - per - y : and let the angel of the Lord per - se - cute them. 7. For they have privily laid their net to destroy me with-out a cause : yea, even without a cause have they made a pit for my soul. 8. Let a sudden destruction come upon him unawares, and his net, that he hath laid privily, catch him-self : that he may fall in - to his own mis -chief. 9. And, my soul, be joyful in the Lord : it shall re - joice in his

MORNING PRAYER. DAY 7.

sal - va - tion. 10. All my bones shall say, * Lord, who is like unto thee, who

deliverest the poor from him that is too strong for him : yea, the poor, and him

that is in mis - er - y, from him that spoil-eth him? 11. False witness-es did

rise up : they laid to my charge things that I knew not. 12. They rewarded me

e - vil for good : to the great dis-com-fort of my soul. 13. Nevertheless, when

they were sick, I put on sackcloth and humbled my soul with fast - ing :

and my prayer shall turn in - to mine own bo - som. 14. I behaved myself as

though it had been my friend, or my broth - er : I went heavily, as one that

mourn- eth for his moth - er. 15. But in mine adversity they rejoiced, and

gathered them-selves to - geth - er : yea, the very abjects came together against

me unawares, making mouths at me and ceas-ed not. 16. With the flatterers were

bu - sy mock-ers : who gnash-ed up - on me with their teeth. 17. Lord, how

long wilt thou look up - on this : O deliver my soul from the calamities which they

bring on me, and my dar- ling from the li - ons. 18. So will I give thee thanks

in the great con-gre-ga-tion : I will praise thee a-mong much peo ple. 19. O let not

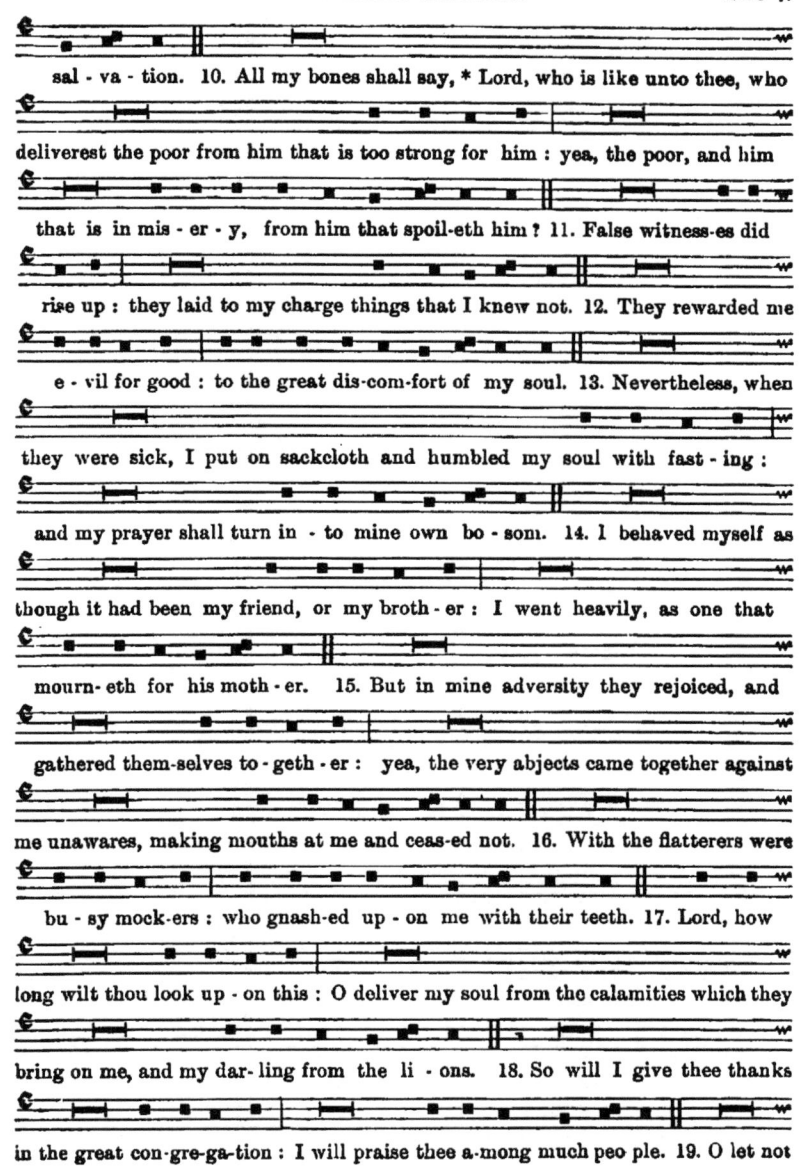

DAY 7. MORNING PRAYER.

them that are mine enemies triumph over me un-god-ly : neither let them wink

with their eyes that hate me with-out a cause. 20. And-why their communing is

not for peace : but they imagine deceitful words against them that are

qui-et in the land. 21. They gaped upon me with their mouths, and said,

Fie on thee, fie on thee, we saw it with our eyes. 22. This thou hast seen,

O Lord : hold not thy tongue then, go not far from me, O Lord. 23. Awake, and

stand up to judge my quar-rel : avenge thou my cause, my God and my Lord.

24. Judge me, O Lord my God, according to thy right-eous-ness : and let them

not tri-umph o-ver me. 25. Let them not say in their hearts, There, there,

so would we have it : neither let them say, We have de-vour-ed him.

26. Let them be put to confusion and shame together, that re-joice at my

trou-ble : let them be clothed with rebuke and dishonour, that boast them -

- selves a-gainst me. 27. Let them be glad and rejoice, that favour my

right-eous deal-ing : yea, let them say alway, Blessed be the Lord, who hath

pleasure in the pros-pe-ri-ty of his ser-vant. 28. And as for my tongue, it shall

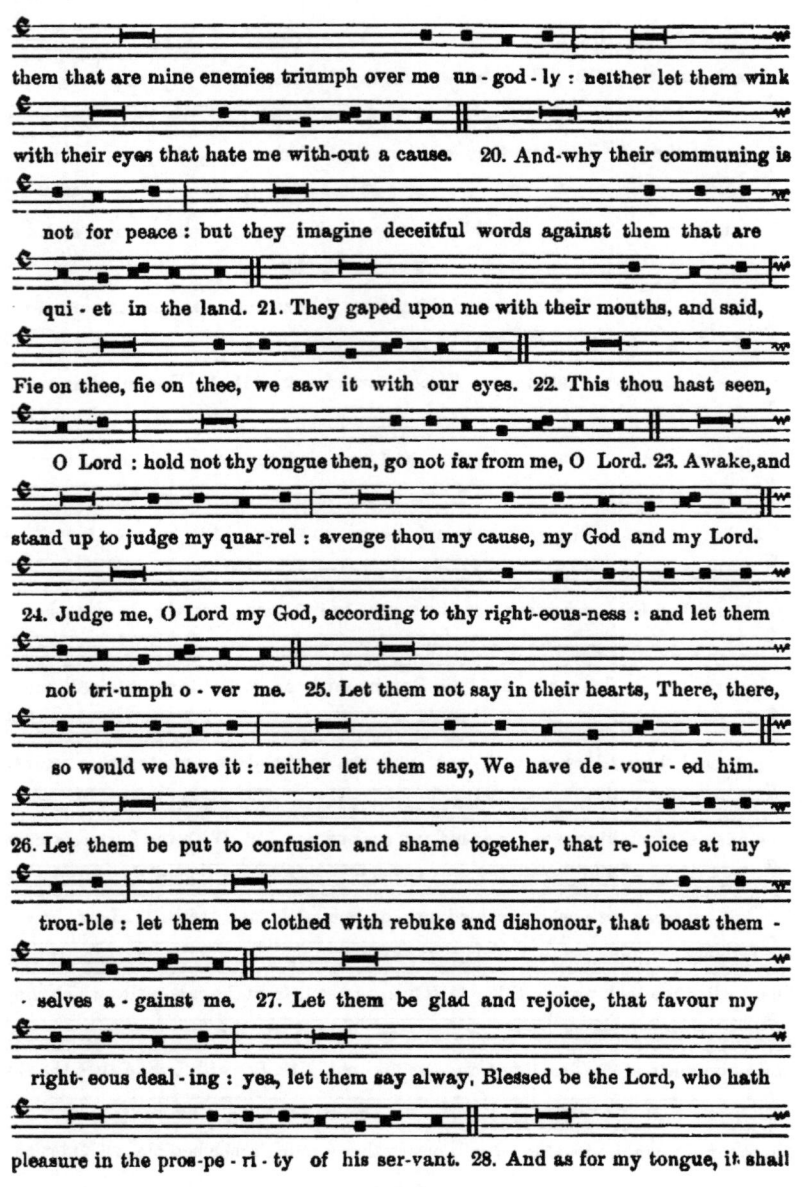

(56)

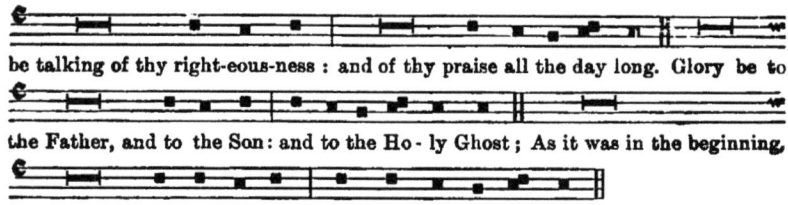

MORNING PRAYER. DAY 7.

be talking of thy right-eous-ness : and of thy praise all the day long. Glory be to the Father, and to the Son: and to the Ho - ly Ghost ; As it was in the beginning, is now, and ev - er shall be : world with-out end. A - men.

PSALM XXXVI.—*Dixit injustus.*

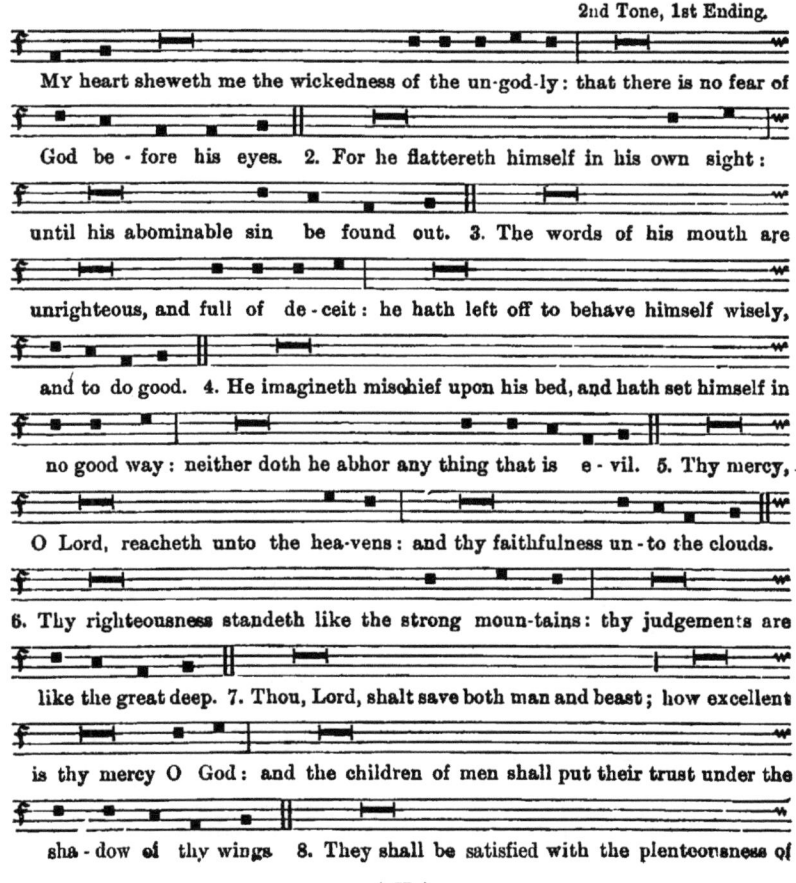

2nd Tone, 1st Ending.

MY heart sheweth me the wickedness of the un-god-ly : that there is no fear of God be - fore his eyes. 2. For he flattereth himself in his own sight: until his abominable sin be found out. 3. The words of his mouth are unrighteous, and full of de-ceit : he hath left off to behave himself wisely, and to do good. 4. He imagineth mischief upon his bed, and hath set himself in no good way : neither doth he abhor any thing that is e - vil. 5. Thy mercy, O Lord, reacheth unto the hea-vens : and thy faithfulness un - to the clouds. 6. Thy righteousness standeth like the strong moun-tains : thy judgements are like the great deep. 7. Thou, Lord, shalt save both man and beast ; how excellent is thy mercy O God : and the children of men shall put their trust under the sha - dow of thy wings. 8. They shall be satisfied with the plenteousness of

DAY 7. EVENING PRAYER.

thy house: and thou shalt give them drink of thy pleasures, as out of the riv-er.

9. For with thee is the well of life: and in thy light shall we see light.

10. O continue forth thy loving-kindness unto them that know thee:

and thy righteousness unto them that are true of heart. 11. O let not the foot

of pride come a-gainst me: and let not the hand of the un-god-ly cast me down.

12. There are they fallen, all that work wick - ed - ness: they are cast down,

and shall not be a - ble to stand. Glory be to the Father, and to the Son:

and to the Ho - ly Ghost ; As it was in the beginning, is now, and ever shall be:

world with-out end. A - men.

EVENING PRAYER.

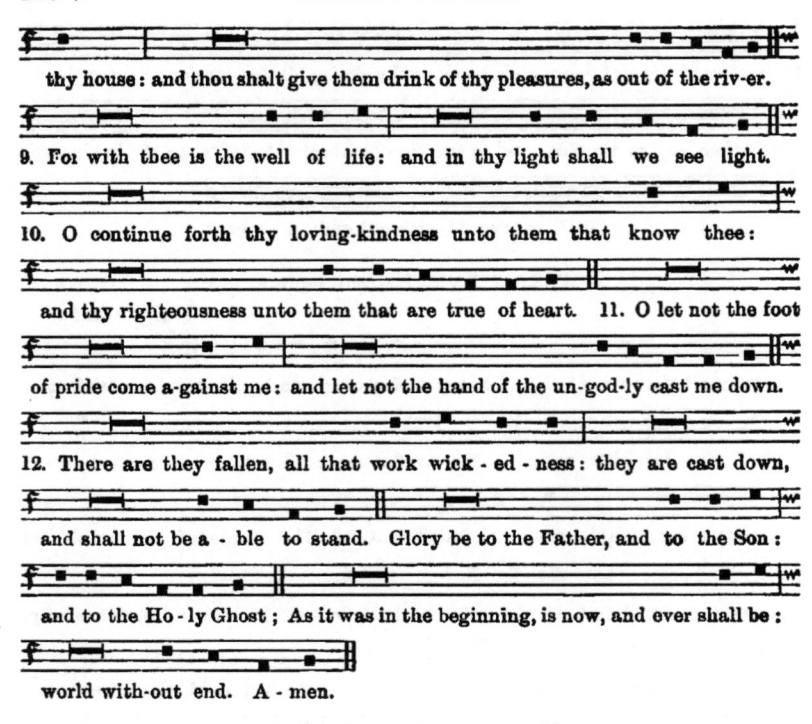

PSALM XXXVII.—*Noli æmulari.*

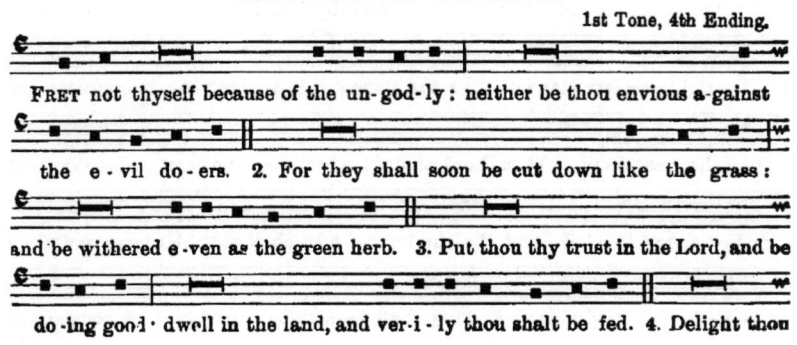

1st Tone, 4th Ending.

FRET not thyself because of the un-god-ly: neither be thou envious a-gainst

the e - vil do - ers. 2. For they shall soon be cut down like the grass:

and be withered e -ven as the green herb. 3. Put thou thy trust in the Lord, and be

do -ing good · dwell in the land, and ver-i - ly thou shalt be fed. 4. Delight thou

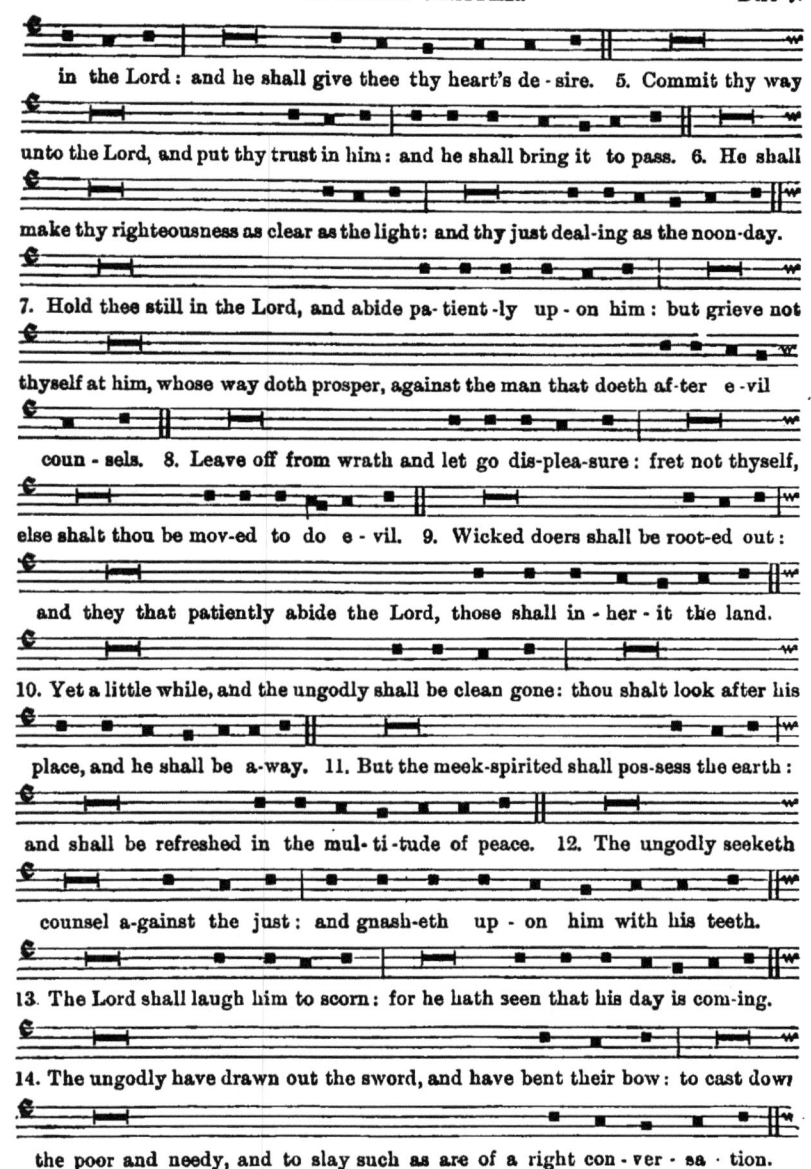

EVENING PRAYER. DAY 7.

in the Lord: and he shall give thee thy heart's de-sire. 5. Commit thy way

unto the Lord, and put thy trust in him: and he shall bring it to pass. 6. He shall

make thy righteousness as clear as the light: and thy just deal-ing as the noon-day.

7. Hold thee still in the Lord, and abide pa-tient-ly up-on him: but grieve not

thyself at him, whose way doth prosper, against the man that doeth af-ter e-vil

coun-sels. 8. Leave off from wrath and let go dis-plea-sure: fret not thyself,

else shalt thou be mov-ed to do e-vil. 9. Wicked doers shall be root-ed out:

and they that patiently abide the Lord, those shall in-her-it the land.

10. Yet a little while, and the ungodly shall be clean gone: thou shalt look after his

place, and he shall be a-way. 11. But the meek-spirited shall pos-sess the earth:

and shall be refreshed in the mul-ti-tude of peace. 12. The ungodly seeketh

counsel a-gainst the just: and gnash-eth up-on him with his teeth.

13. The Lord shall laugh him to scorn: for he hath seen that his day is com-ing.

14. The ungodly have drawn out the sword, and have bent their bow: to cast down

the poor and needy, and to slay such as are of a right con-ver-sa-tion.

DAY 7. EVENING PRAYER.

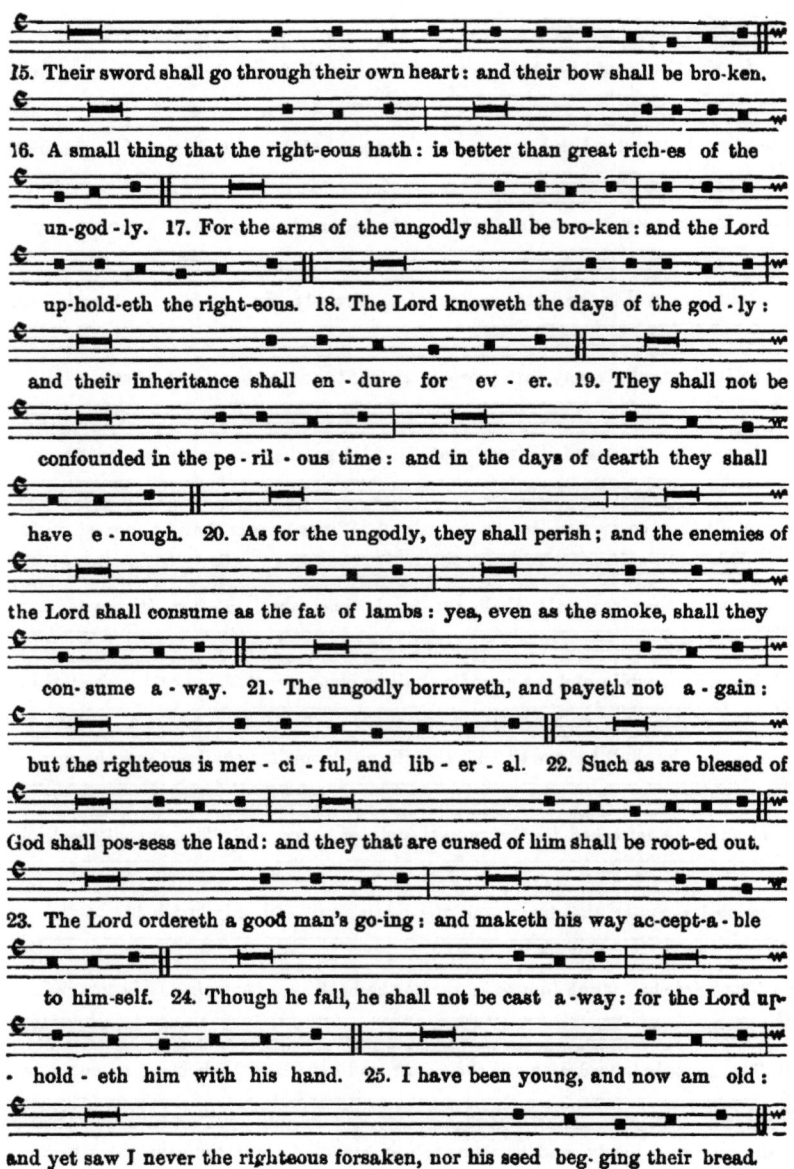

15. Their sword shall go through their own heart : and their bow shall be bro-ken.

16. A small thing that the right-eous hath : is better than great rich-es of the un-god-ly. 17. For the arms of the ungodly shall be bro-ken : and the Lord up-hold-eth the right-eous. 18. The Lord knoweth the days of the god-ly : and their inheritance shall en-dure for ev-er. 19. They shall not be confounded in the pe-ril-ous time : and in the days of dearth they shall have e-nough. 20. As for the ungodly, they shall perish ; and the enemies of the Lord shall consume as the fat of lambs : yea, even as the smoke, shall they con-sume a-way. 21. The ungodly borroweth, and payeth not a-gain : but the righteous is mer-ci-ful, and lib-er-al. 22. Such as are blessed of God shall pos-sess the land : and they that are cursed of him shall be root-ed out. 23. The Lord ordereth a good man's go-ing : and maketh his way ac-cept-a-ble to him-self. 24. Though he fall, he shall not be cast a-way : for the Lord up--hold-eth him with his hand. 25. I have been young, and now am old : and yet saw I never the righteous forsaken, nor his seed beg-ging their bread.

(60)

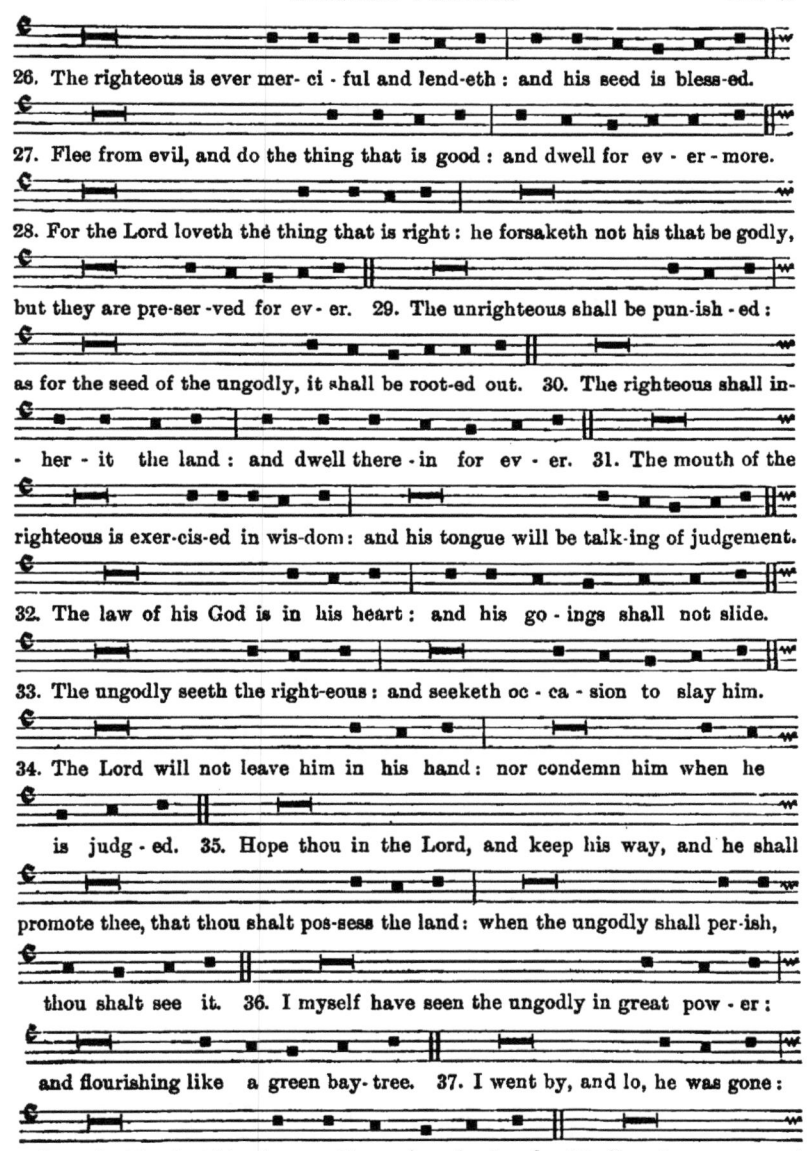

EVENING PRAYER. DAY 7.

26. The righteous is ever mer- ci - ful and lend-eth : and his seed is bless-ed.

27. Flee from evil, and do the thing that is good : and dwell for ev - er - more.

28. For the Lord loveth the thing that is right : he forsaketh not his that be godly, but they are pre-ser -ved for ev- er. 29. The unrighteous shall be pun-ish - ed : as for the seed of the ungodly, it shall be root-ed out. 30. The righteous shall in- - her - it the land : and dwell there - in for ev - er. 31. The mouth of the righteous is exer-cis-ed in wis-dom : and his tongue will be talk-ing of judgement.

32. The law of his God is in his heart : and his go - ings shall not slide.

33. The ungodly seeth the right-eous : and seeketh oc - ca - sion to slay him.

34. The Lord will not leave him in his hand : nor condemn him when he is judg - ed. 35. Hope thou in the Lord, and keep his way, and he shall promote thee, that thou shalt pos-sess the land : when the ungodly shall per-ish, thou shalt see it. 36. I myself have seen the ungodly in great pow - er : and flourishing like a green bay- tree. 37. I went by, and lo, he was gone : I sought him, but his place could no-where be found. 38. Keep innocency, and

DAY 8. MORNING PRAYER.

take heed unto the thing that is right: for that shall bring a man peace at the last.

39. As for the transgressors, they shall per - ish to-geth - er : and the end of the ungodly is, they shall be root - ed out at the last. 40. But the salvation of the righteous cometh of the Lord : who is also their strength in the time of trou-ble.

41. And the Lord shall stand by them, and save them : he shall deliver them from the ungodly, and shall save them, be - cause they put their trust in him.

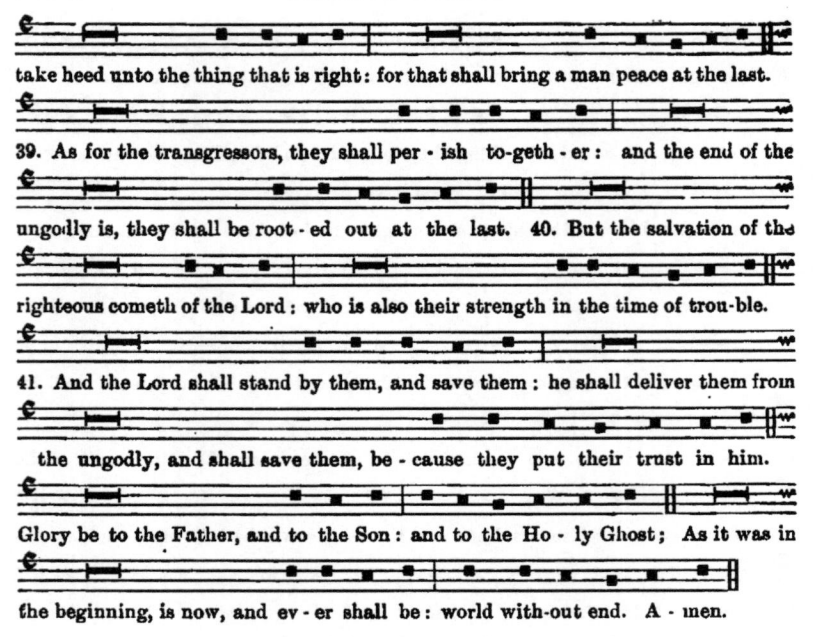

Glory be to the Father, and to the Son : and to the Ho - ly Ghost ; As it was in the beginning, is now, and ev - er shall be : world with-out end. A - men.

DAY 8.   MORNING PRAYER.

PSALM XXXVIII.—*Domine, ne in furore.*

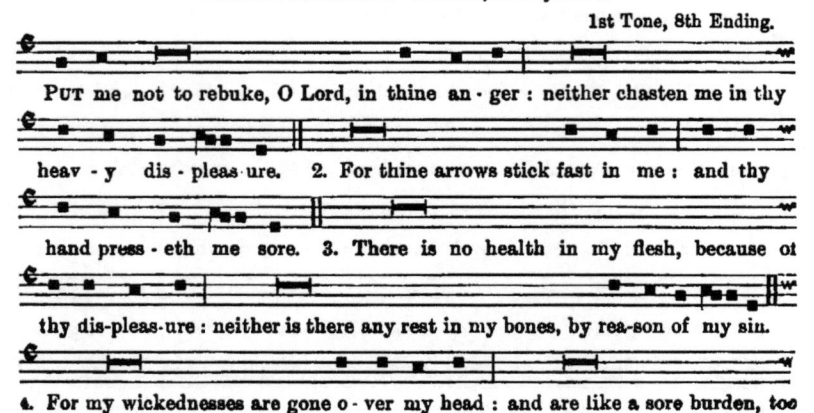

1st Tone, 8th Ending.

PUT me not to rebuke, O Lord, in thine an - ger : neither chasten me in thy heav - y dis - pleas-ure. 2. For thine arrows stick fast in me : and thy hand press - eth me sore. 3. There is no health in my flesh, because of thy dis-pleas-ure : neither is there any rest in my bones, by rea-son of my sin.

4. For my wickednesses are gone o - ver my head : and are like a sore burden, too

(62)

MORNING PRAYER. DAY 8.

heav y for me to bear. 5. My wounds stink, and are cor-rupt : through my fool-ish-ness. 6. I am brought into so great trouble and mis-er-y : that I go mourn-ing all the day long. 7. For my loins are filled with a sore dis-ease : and there is no whole part in my bo-dy. 8. I am feeble, and sore smit-ten : I have roared for the very dis-qui-et-ness of my heart. 9. Lord, thou knowest all my de-sire : and my groan-ing is not hid from thee. 10. My heart panteth, my strength hath fail-ed me : and the sight of mine eyes is gone from me.

11. My lovers and my neighbours did stand looking up-on my trou-ble : and my kins-men stood a-far off. 12. They also that sought after my life laid snares for me : and they that went about to do me evil talked of wickedness, and imagined de-ceit all the day long. 13. As for me, I was like a deaf man, and heard not : and as one that is dumb, who doth not o-pen his mouth. 14. I became even as a man that hear-eth not : and in whose mouth are no re-proofs. 15. For in thee, O Lord, have I put my trust : thou shalt an-swer for me, O Lord, my God. 16. I have required that they, even mine enemies,

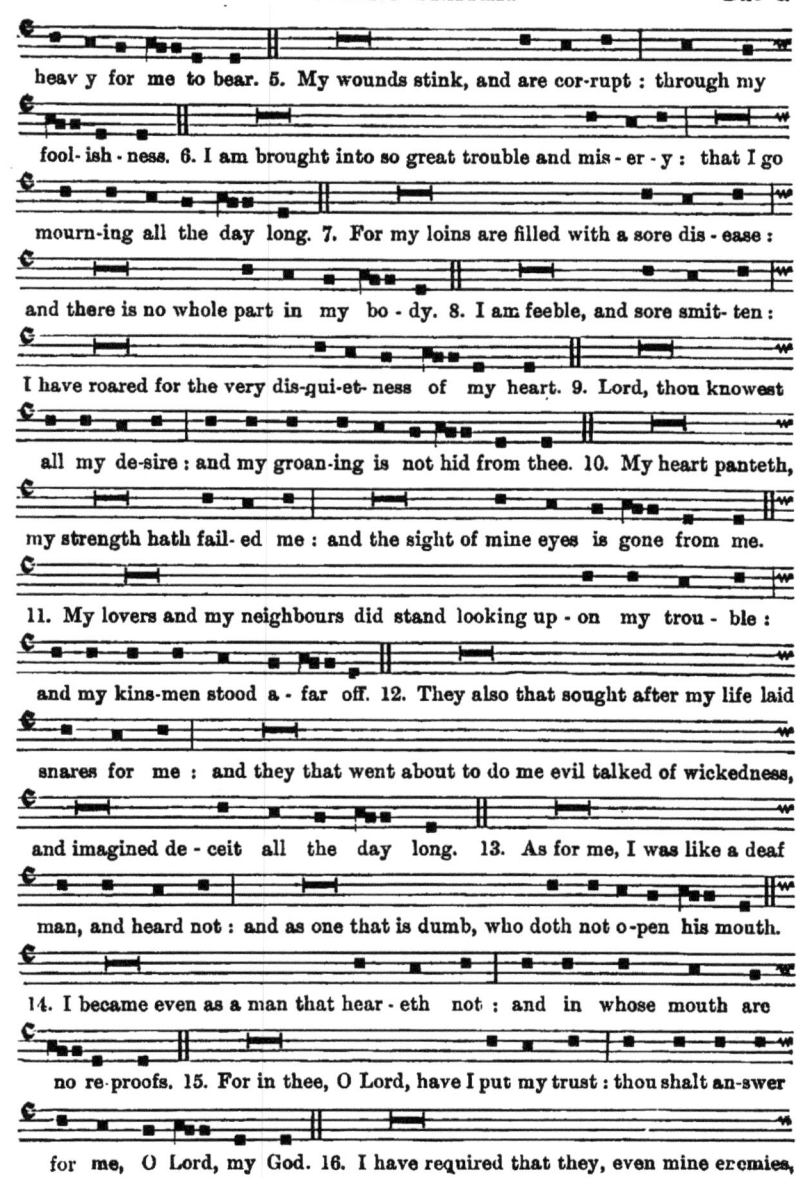

(63)

DAY 8. MORNING PRAYER.

should not triumph o- ver me : for when my foot slipped, they rejoiced great-ly

a- gainst me. 17. And I, truly, am set in the plague : and my heaviness is

ev - er in my sight. 18. For I will confess my wick-ed-ness : and be sor- ry

for my sin. 19. But mine enemies live, and are might- y : and they that hate

me wrongfully are ma - ny in num-ber. 20. They also that reward evil for good

are a-gainst me : be-cause I fol-low the thing that good is. 21. Forsake me not, O

Lord my God : be not thou far from me. 22. Haste thee to help me : O Lord

God of my sal-va - tion. Glory be to the Father, and to the Son : and to the

Ho - ly Ghost; As it was in the beginning, is now, and ev - er shall be :

world with-out end. A - men.

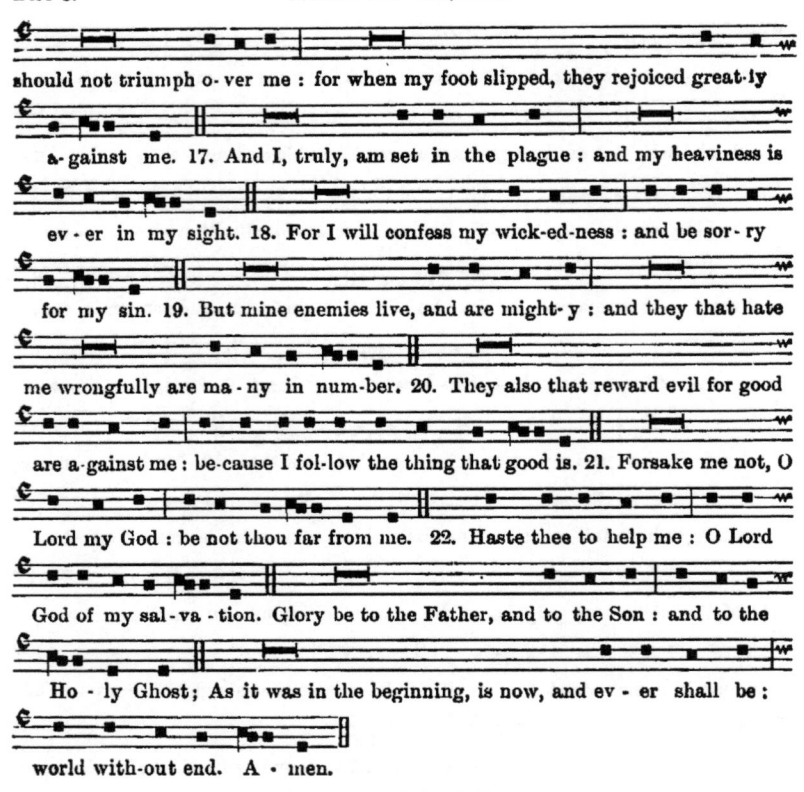

PSALM XXXIX.—*Dixi, custodiam.*

2nd Tone, 1st Ending.

I SAID, I will take heed to my ways : that I of-fend not in my tongue.

2. I will keep my mouth as it were with a bri-dle : while the un-god-ly is

in my sight. 3. I held my tongue, and spake noth-ing : I kept silence, yea,

even from good words; but it was pain and grief to me. 4. My heart was hot

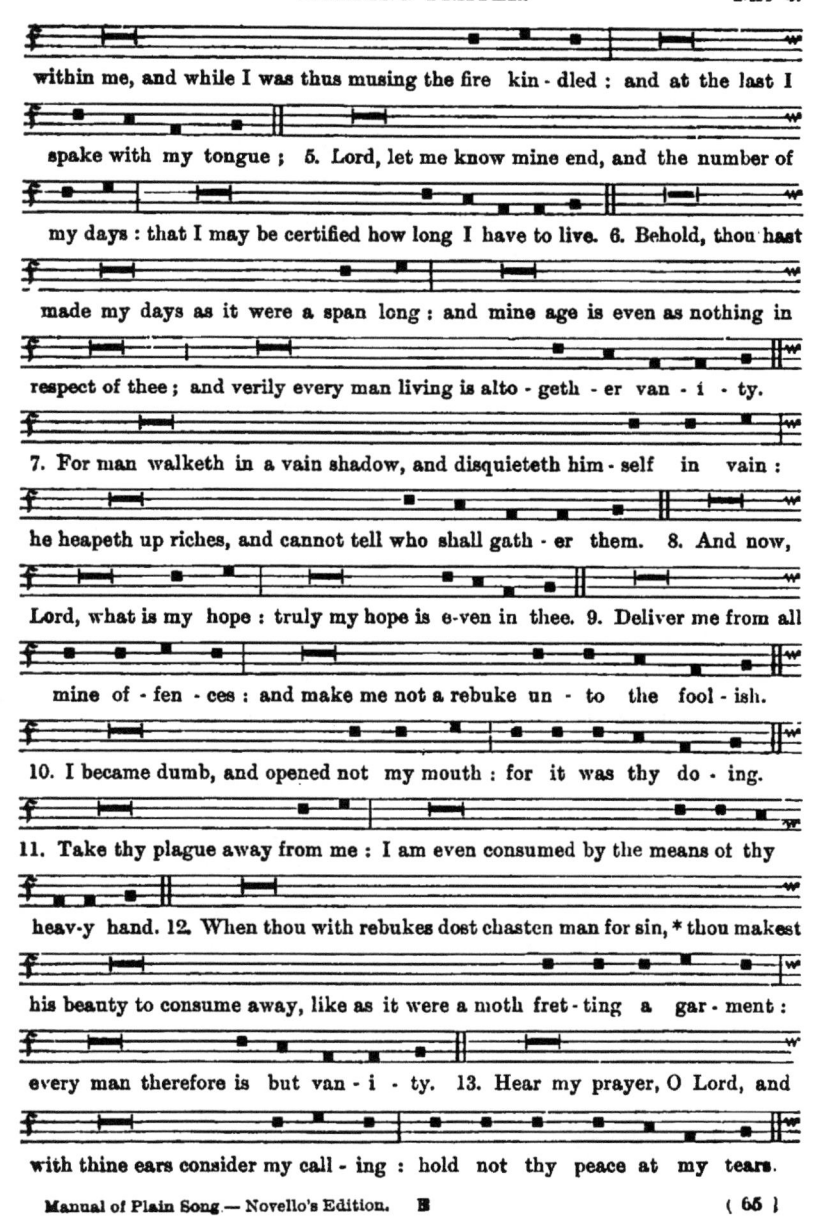

MORNING PRAYER. DAY 8.

within me, and while I was thus musing the fire kin-dled: and at the last I spake with my tongue; 5. Lord, let me know mine end, and the number of my days: that I may be certified how long I have to live. 6. Behold, thou hast made my days as it were a span long: and mine age is even as nothing in respect of thee; and verily every man living is alto-geth-er van-i-ty.

7. For man walketh in a vain shadow, and disquieteth him-self in vain: he heapeth up riches, and cannot tell who shall gath-er them. 8. And now, Lord, what is my hope: truly my hope is e-ven in thee. 9. Deliver me from all mine of-fen-ces: and make me not a rebuke un-to the fool-ish.

10. I became dumb, and opened not my mouth: for it was thy do-ing.

11. Take thy plague away from me: I am even consumed by the means of thy heav-y hand. 12. When thou with rebukes dost chasten man for sin, * thou makest his beauty to consume away, like as it were a moth fret-ting a gar-ment: every man therefore is but van-i-ty. 13. Hear my prayer, O Lord, and with thine ears consider my call-ing: hold not thy peace at my tears.

Manual of Plain Song.— Novello's Edition. B

DAY 8. MORNING PRAYER.

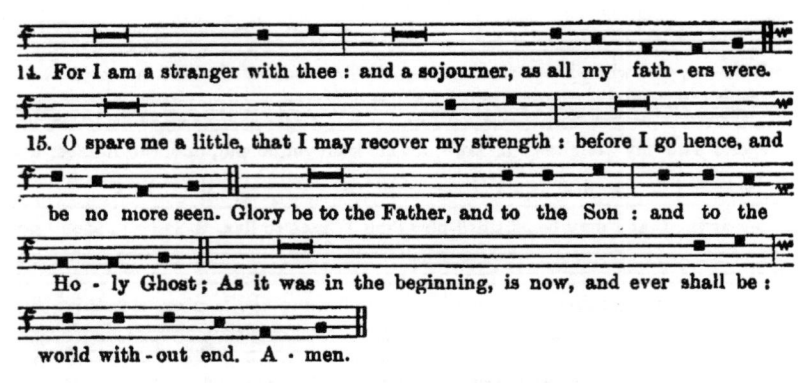

14. For I am a stranger with thee : and a sojourner, as all my fath-ers were.

15. O spare me a little, that I may recover my strength : before I go hence, and be no more seen. Glory be to the Father, and to the Son : and to the Ho-ly Ghost; As it was in the beginning, is now, and ever shall be : world with-out end. A·men.

PSALM XL.—*Expectans expectavi.*

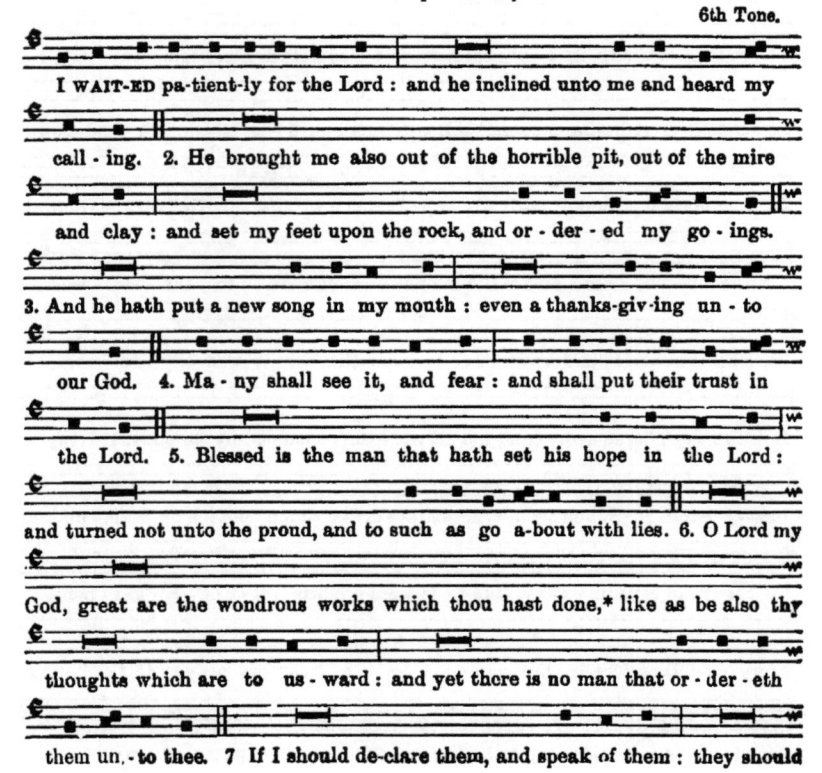

6th Tone.

I WAIT-ED pa-tient-ly for the Lord : and he inclined unto me and heard my call-ing. 2. He brought me also out of the horrible pit, out of the mire and clay : and set my feet upon the rock, and or-der-ed my go-ings. 3. And he hath put a new song in my mouth : even a thanks-giv-ing un-to our God. 4. Ma-ny shall see it, and fear : and shall put their trust in the Lord. 5. Blessed is the man that hath set his hope in the Lord : and turned not unto the proud, and to such as go a-bout with lies. 6. O Lord my God, great are the wondrous works which thou hast done,* like as be also thy thoughts which are to us-ward : and yet there is no man that or-der-eth them un.-to thee. 7 If I should de-clare them, and speak of them : they should

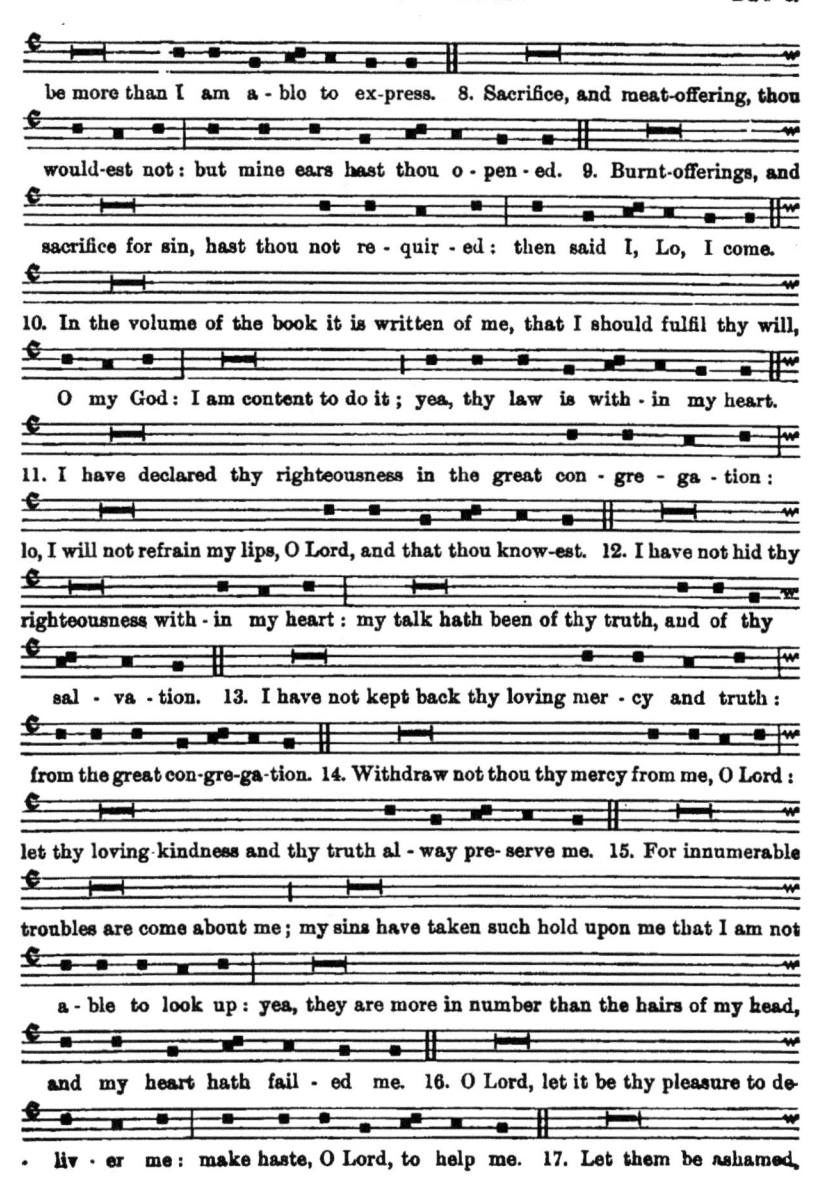

MORNING PRAYER. DAY 8.

be more than I am a-ble to ex-press. 8. Sacrifice, and meat-offering, thou would-est not: but mine ears hast thou o-pen-ed. 9. Burnt-offerings, and sacrifice for sin, hast thou not re-quir-ed: then said I, Lo, I come. 10. In the volume of the book it is written of me, that I should fulfil thy will, O my God: I am content to do it; yea, thy law is with-in my heart. 11. I have declared thy righteousness in the great con-gre-ga-tion: lo, I will not refrain my lips, O Lord, and that thou know-est. 12. I have not hid thy righteousness with-in my heart: my talk hath been of thy truth, and of thy sal-va-tion. 13. I have not kept back thy loving mer-cy and truth: from the great con-gre-ga-tion. 14. Withdraw not thou thy mercy from me, O Lord: let thy loving-kindness and thy truth al-way pre-serve me. 15. For innumerable troubles are come about me; my sins have taken such hold upon me that I am not a-ble to look up: yea, they are more in number than the hairs of my head, and my heart hath fail-ed me. 16. O Lord, let it be thy pleasure to de- liv-er me: make haste, O Lord, to help me. 17. Let them be ashamed,

(67)

DAY 8.   EVENING PRAYER.

and confounded together, that seek after my soul to des-troy it : let them be driven

backward, and put to re-buke, that wish me e-vil. 18. Let them be desolate, and re-

- ward - ed with shame : that say unto me, Fie up - on thee, fie up - on thee.

19. Let all those that seek thee be joyful and glad in thee : and let such as love

thy salvation say al - way, The Lord be prais - ed. 20. As for me, I am poor

and need - y : but the Lord ca - reth for me. 21. Thou art my helper and

re-deem-er : make no long tar- ry -ing, O my God. Glory be to the Father, and

to the Son : and to the Ho - ly Ghost ; As it was in the beginning, is now, and

ev - er shall be : world with - out end. A - men.

EVENING PRAYER.

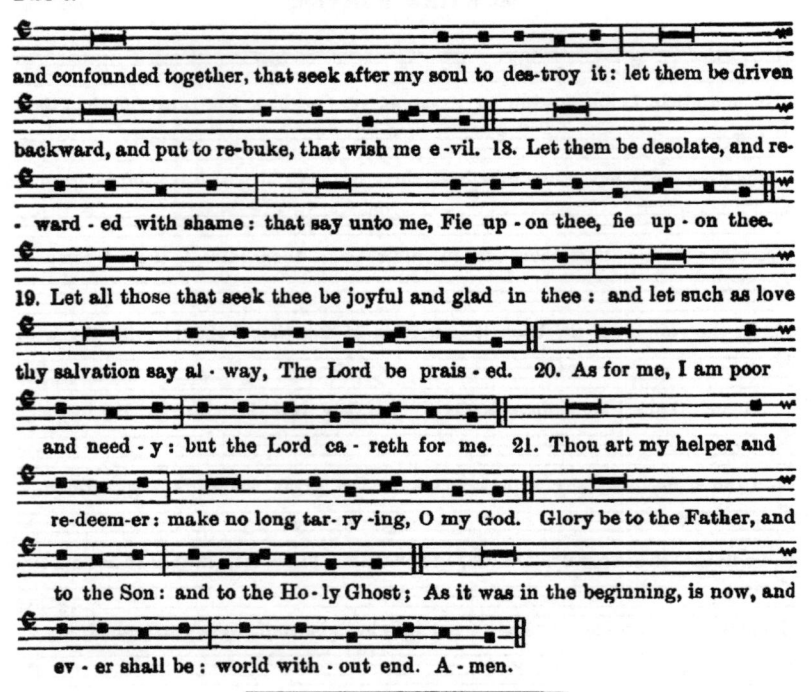

PSALM XLI.—*Beatus qui intelligit.*

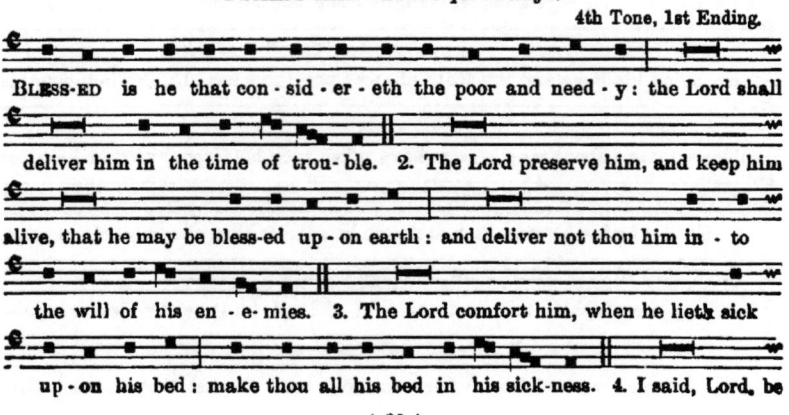

4th Tone, 1st Ending.

BLESS-ED is he that con - sid - er - eth the poor and need - y : the Lord shall

deliver him in the time of trou- ble. 2. The Lord preserve him, and keep him

alive, that he may be bless-ed up - on earth : and deliver not thou him in - to

the will of his en - e- mies. 3. The Lord comfort him, when he lieth sick

up - on his bed : make thou all his bed in his sick-ness. 4. I said, Lord, be mer - ci - ful un - to me : heal my soul, for I have sin - ned a - gainst thee.

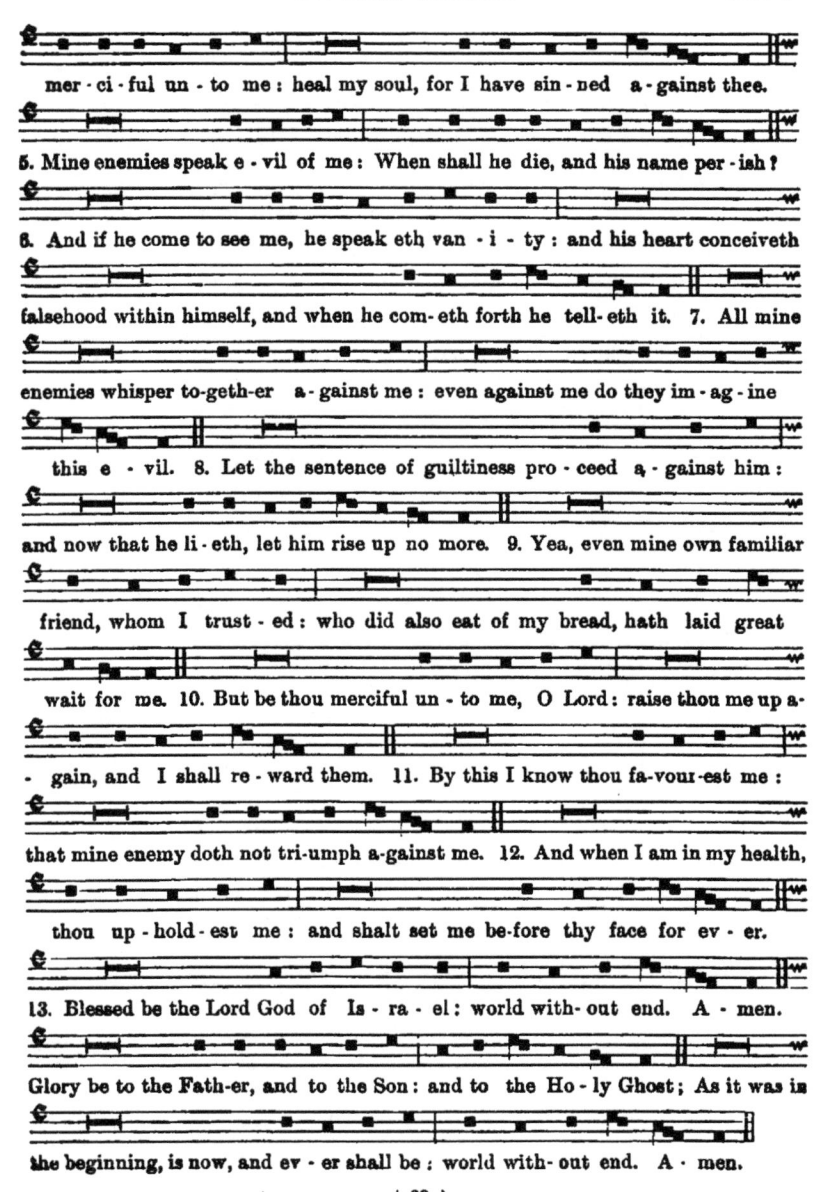

5. Mine enemies speak e - vil of me : When shall he die, and his name per - ish ?

6. And if he come to see me, he speak eth van - i - ty : and his heart conceiveth falsehood within himself, and when he com - eth forth he tell - eth it. 7. All mine enemies whisper to-geth-er a - gainst me : even against me do they im - ag - ine this e - vil. 8. Let the sentence of guiltiness pro - ceed a - gainst him : and now that he li - eth, let him rise up no more. 9. Yea, even mine own familiar friend, whom I trust - ed : who did also eat of my bread, hath laid great wait for me. 10. But be thou merciful un - to me, O Lord : raise thou me up a - gain, and I shall re - ward them. 11. By this I know thou fa-vour-est me : that mine enemy doth not tri-umph a-gainst me. 12. And when I am in my health, thou up - hold - est me : and shalt set me be-fore thy face for ev - er.

13. Blessed be the Lord God of Is - ra - el : world with- out end. A - men.

Glory be to the Fath-er, and to the Son : and to the Ho - ly Ghost ; As it was in the beginning, is now, and ev - er shall be : world with- out end. A - men.

Day 8. EVENING PRAYER.

PSALM XLII.—*Quemadmodum.*

3rd Tone, 4th Ending.

Like as the hart de-sir-eth the wa-ter-brooks : so longeth my soul af-ter thee, O God. 2. My soul is athirst for God, yea, e-ven for the liv-ing God : when shall I come to appear before the pres-ence of God. 3. My tears have been my meat day and night : while they daily say unto me, Where is now thy God? 4. Now when I think thereupon, I pour out my heart by my-self : for I went with the multitude, and brought them forth in-to the house of God ; 5. In the voice of praise and thanks-giv-ing : a-mong such as keep ho-ly day. 6. Why art thou so full of heav-i-ness, O my soul : and why art thou so dis qui-et-ed with-in me? 7. Put thy trust in God : for I will yet give him thanks for the help of his coun-ten-ance. 8. My God, my soul is vex-ed with-in me : therefore will I remember thee concerning the land of Jordan, and the little hill of Her-mon. 9. One deep calleth another, because of the noise of the wa-ter-pipes : all thy waves and storms are gone o-ver me. 10. The Lord hath granted his loving-kind-ness in the day-time : and in the night-season did I sing of him, and made my prayer unto the God of my life. 11. I will say unto the God of my strength, Why hast thou for-got-ten me : why go I thus heavily, while the en-e-my op-press-eth me? 12. My bones are smit-ten a-sun-der as with a sword : while mine enemies that trouble me cast me in the teeth; 13. Namely, while they say dai-ly un-to me : Where is now thy God? 14. Why art thou so vex-ed, O my soul : and why art thou so dis-qui-et-ed with-in me? 15. O put thy trust in God : for I will yet thank him, which is the help of my coun-ten-ance, and my God. Glo-ry be to the Fath-er, and to the Son : and to the Ho-ly Ghost; As it was in the beginning, is now and ev-er shall be : world with-out end. A-men.

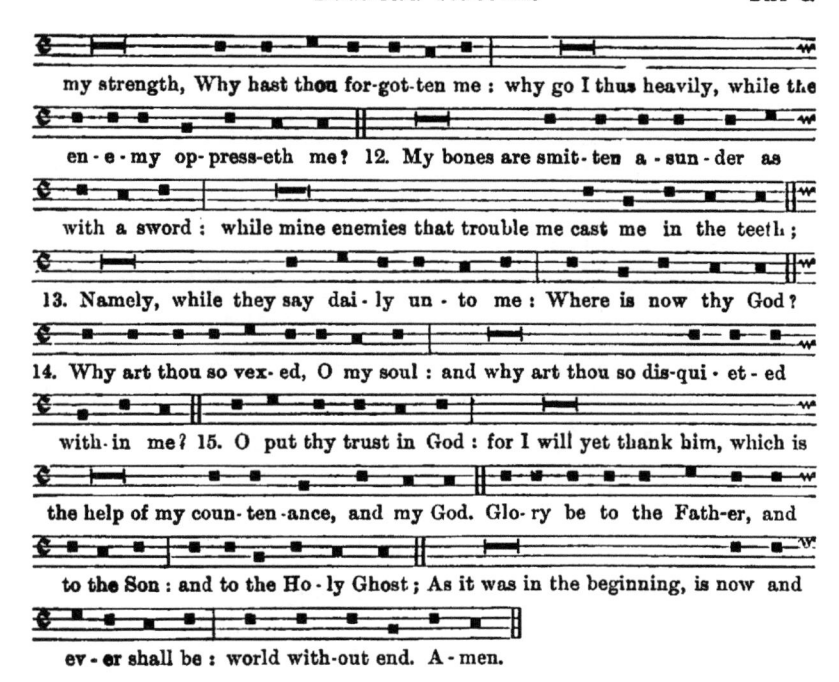

PSALM XLIII.—*Judica me, Deus.*

3rd Tone, 4th Ending.

GIVE sentence with me, O God, and defend my cause a-gainst the un-god-ly peo-ple : O deliver me from the de-ceit-ful and wick-ed man. 2. For thou art the God of my strength, why hast thou put me from thee : and why go I so heavily, while the en-e-my op-press-eth me ? 3. O send out thy light and thy truth, that they may lead me : and bring me unto thy holy hill, and to thy dwell-ing. 4. And that I may go unto the altar of God even unto the God

DAY 9. MORNING PRAYER.

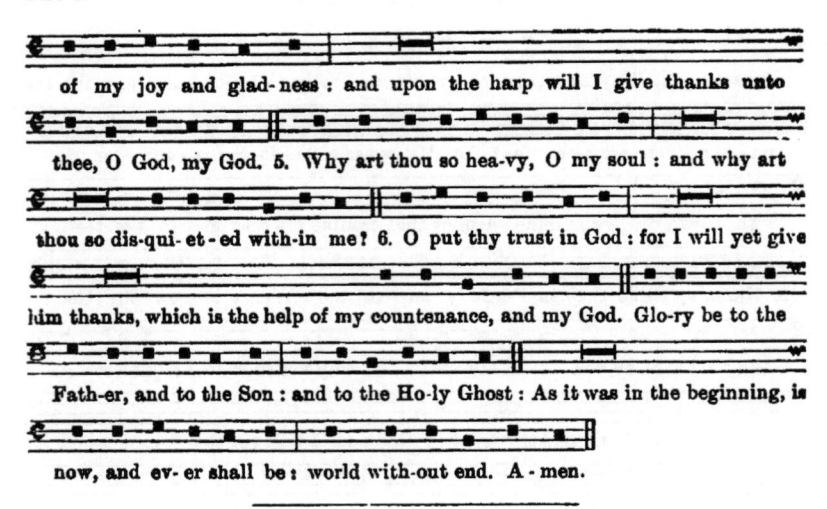

of my joy and glad-ness : and upon the harp will I give thanks unto thee, O God, my God. 5. Why art thou so hea-vy, O my soul : and why art thou so dis-qui-et-ed with-in me? 6. O put thy trust in God : for I will yet give him thanks, which is the help of my countenance, and my God. Glo-ry be to the Fath-er, and to the Son : and to the Ho-ly Ghost : As it was in the beginning, is now, and ev-er shall be: world with-out end. A-men.

DAY 9. MORNING PRAYER.

PSALM XLIV.—*Deus, auribus.*

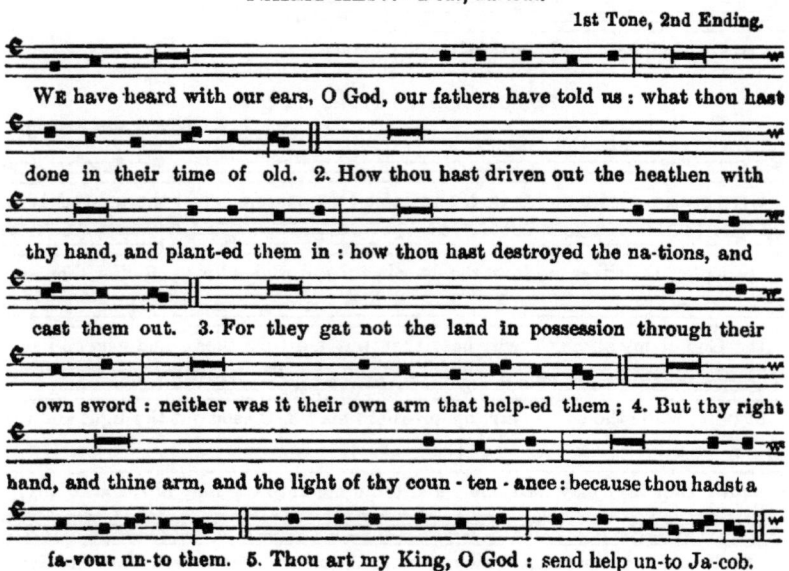

1st Tone, 2nd Ending.

WE have heard with our ears, O God, our fathers have told us : what thou hast done in their time of old. 2. How thou hast driven out the heathen with thy hand, and plant-ed them in : how thou hast destroyed the na-tions, and cast them out. 3. For they gat not the land in possession through their own sword : neither was it their own arm that help-ed them ; 4. But thy right hand, and thine arm, and the light of thy coun-ten-ance: because thou hadst a fa-vour un-to them. 5. Thou art my King, O God : send help un-to Ja-cob.

MORNING PRAYER.   DAY 9.

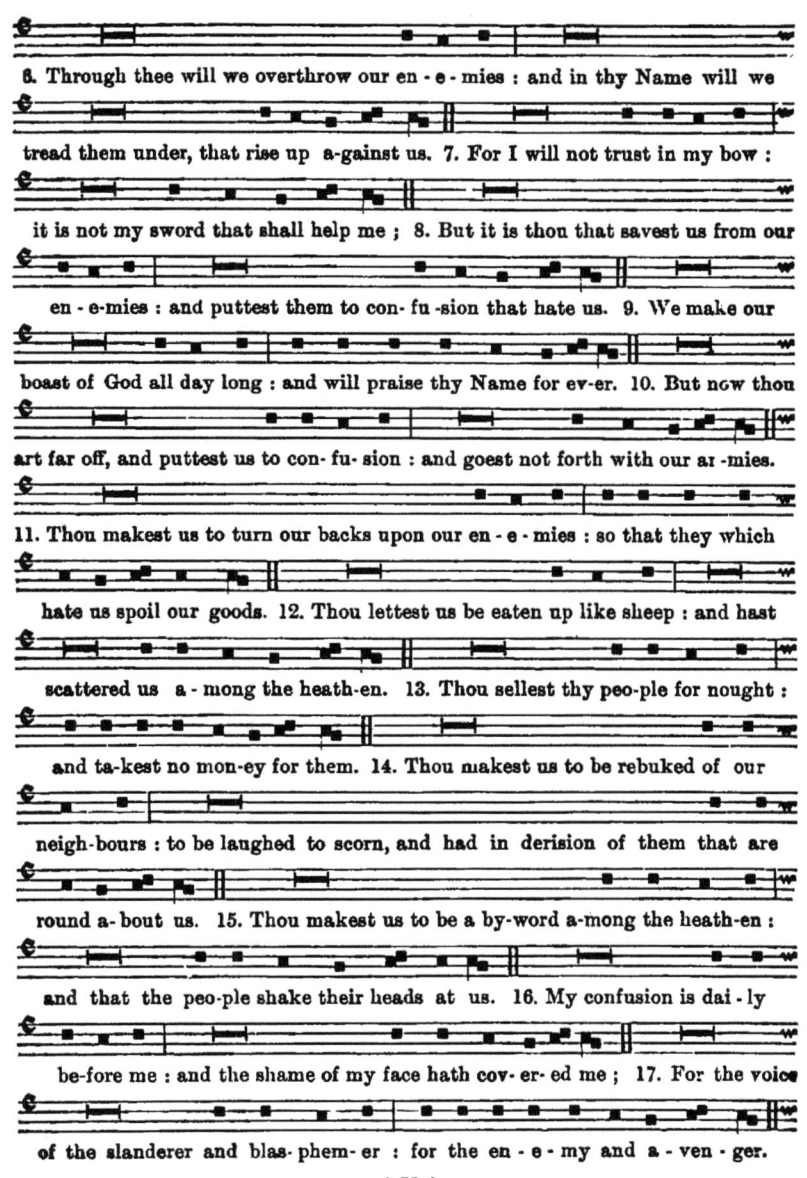

6. Through thee will we overthrow our en - e - mies : and in thy Name will we tread them under, that rise up a-gainst us. 7. For I will not trust in my bow : it is not my sword that shall help me ; 8. But it is thou that savest us from our en - e-mies : and puttest them to con- fu -sion that hate us. 9. We make our boast of God all day long : and will praise thy Name for ev-er. 10. But now thou art far off, and puttest us to con- fu- sion : and goest not forth with our ar -mies. 11. Thou makest us to turn our backs upon our en - e - mies : so that they which hate us spoil our goods. 12. Thou lettest us be eaten up like sheep : and hast scattered us a - mong the heath-en. 13. Thou sellest thy peo-ple for nought : and ta-kest no mon-ey for them. 14. Thou makest us to be rebuked of our neigh-bours : to be laughed to scorn, and had in derision of them that are round a- bout us. 15. Thou makest us to be a by-word a-mong the heath-en : and that the peo-ple shake their heads at us. 16. My confusion is dai - ly be-fore me : and the shame of my face hath cov- er- ed me ; 17. For the voice of the slanderer and blas- phem- er : for the en - e - my and a - ven - ger.

DAY 9. MORNING PRAYER.

18. And though all this be come up-on us, yet do we not for-get thee: nor behave ourselves fro-ward-ly in thy co-ve-nant. 19. Our heart is not turn-ed back: neither our steps gone out of thy way; 20. No, not when thou hast smitten us into the place of drag-ons: and covered us with the shad-ow of death. 21. If we have forgotten the Name of our God, and holden up our hands to a-ny strange god: shall not God search it out? for he knoweth the ve-ry se-crets of the heart. 22. For thy sake also are we killed all the day long: and are counted as sheep ap-point-ed to be slain. 23. Up, Lord, why sleep-est thou: awake, and be not ab-sent from us for ev-er. 24. Wherefore hidest thou thy face: and forgettest our mis-e-ry and trou-ble? 25. For our soul is brought low, even un-to the dust: our bel-ly cleav-eth un-to the ground. 26. A-rise and help us: and de-liv-er us for thy mer-cy's sake. Glory be to the Father, and to the Son: and to the Ho-ly Ghost; As it was in the beginning, is now, and ev-er shall be: world with-out end. A-men.

(74)

MORNING PRAYER.

PSALM XLV.—*Eructavit cor meum.*

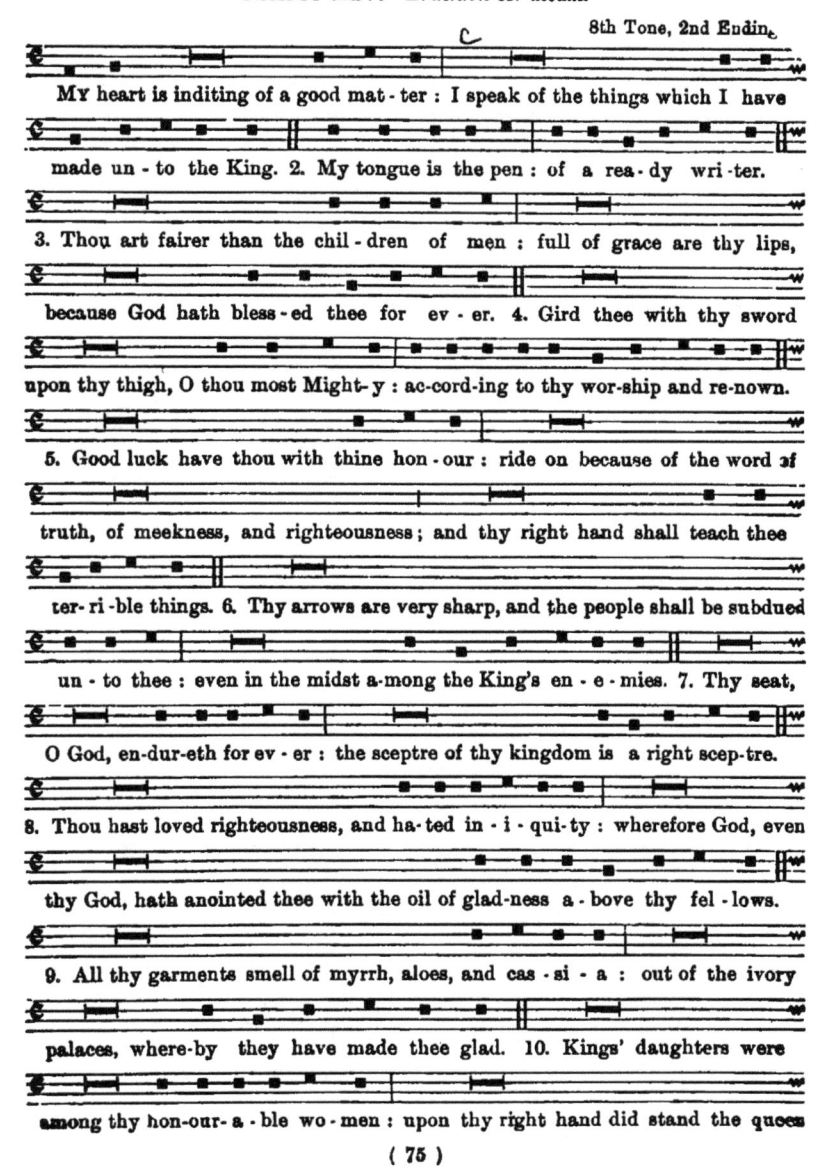

8th Tone, 2nd Ending.

MY heart is inditing of a good mat-ter : I speak of the things which I have made un-to the King. 2. My tongue is the pen : of a rea-dy wri-ter.

3. Thou art fairer than the chil-dren of men : full of grace are thy lips, because God hath bless-ed thee for ev-er. 4. Gird thee with thy sword upon thy thigh, O thou most Might-y : ac-cord-ing to thy wor-ship and re-nown.

5. Good luck have thou with thine hon-our : ride on because of the word of truth, of meekness, and righteousness; and thy right hand shall teach thee ter-ri-ble things. 6. Thy arrows are very sharp, and the people shall be subdued un-to thee : even in the midst a-mong the King's en-e-mies. 7. Thy seat, O God, en-dur-eth for ev-er : the sceptre of thy kingdom is a right scep-tre.

8. Thou hast loved righteousness, and ha-ted in-i-qui-ty : wherefore God, even thy God, hath anointed thee with the oil of glad-ness a-bove thy fel-lows.

9. All thy garments smell of myrrh, aloes, and cas-si-a : out of the ivory palaces, where-by they have made thee glad. 10. Kings' daughters were among thy hon-our-a-ble wo-men : upon thy right hand did stand the queen

DAY 9   MORNING PRAYER.

in a vesture of gold, wrought about with divers colours. 11. Hearken, O daughter, and consider, incline thine ear : forget also thine own people and thy father's house. 12. So shall the King have pleasure in thy beauty : for he is thy Lord God, and worship thou him. 13. And the daughter of Tyre shall be there with a gift : like as the rich also among the people shall make their supplication before thee. 14. The King's daughter is all glorious within : her clothing is of wrought gold. 15. She shall be brought unto the King in raiment of needlework : the virgins that be her fellows shall bear her company, and shall be brought unto thee. 16. With joy and gladness shall they be brought : and shall enter into the King's palace. 17. Instead of thy fathers thou shalt have children : whom thou mayest make princes in all lands. 18. I will remember thy Name from one generation to another : therefore shall the people give thanks unto thee, world without end. Glory be to the Father, and to the Son : and to the Holy Ghost; As it was in the beginning, is now, and ever shall be : world without end. Amen.

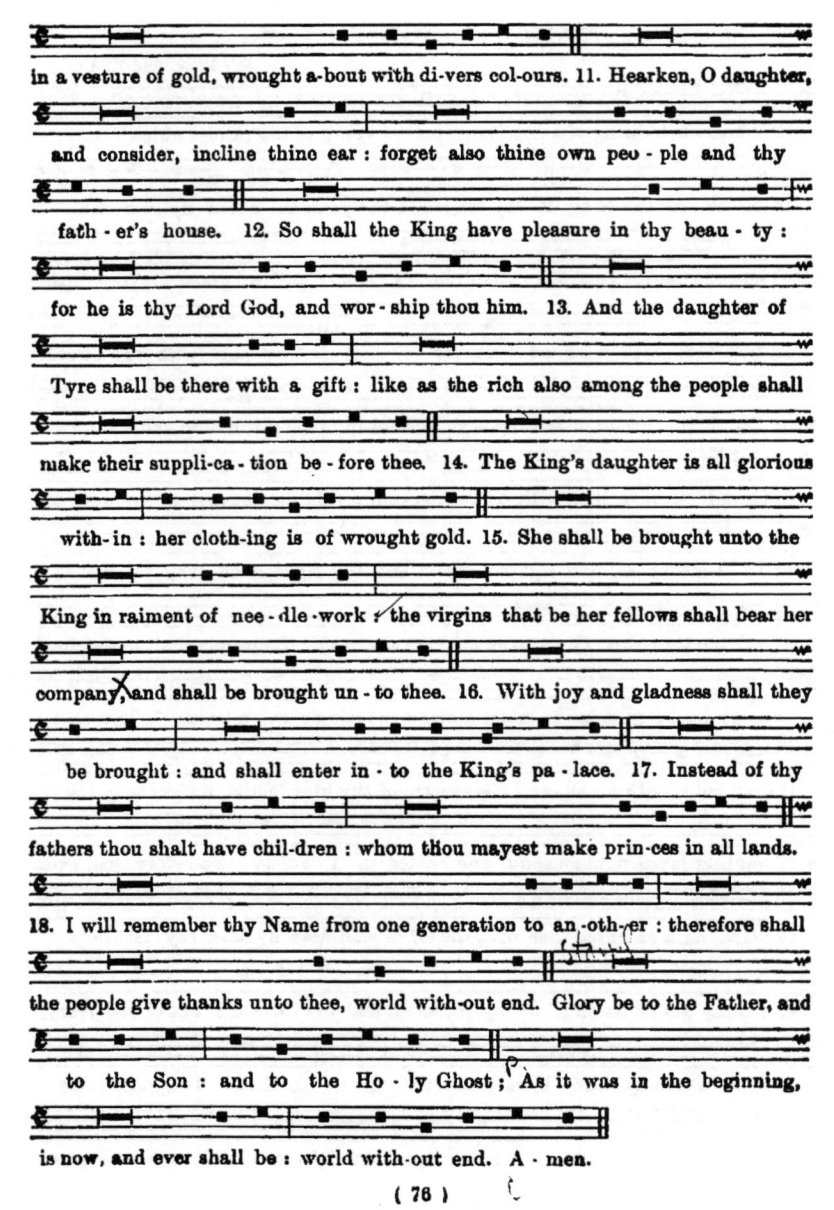

(76)

MORNING PRAYER. DAY 9.

PSALM XLVI.—*Deus noster refugium.*

5th Tone, 1st Ending.

GOD is our hope and strength : a ve - ry pres- ent help in trou - ble.

2. Therefore will we not fear, though the earth be mov - ed : and though the hills be carried in - to the midst of the sea. 3. Though the waters thereof rage and swell : and though the mountains shake at the tem-pest of the same.

4. The rivers of the flood thereof shall make glad the city of God : the holy place of the taber-na-cle of the most High- est. 5. God is in the midst of her, therefore shall she not be re-mov-ed : God shall help her, and that right ear - ly.

6. The heathen make much ado, and the kingdoms are mov - ed : but God hath shewed his voice, and the earth shall melt a - way. 7. The Lord of hosts is with us : the God of Ja - cob is our ref - uge. 8. O come hither, and behold the works of the Lord : what destruction he hath brought up- on the earth.

9. He maketh wars to cease in all the world : he breaketh the bow, and knappeth the spear in sunder, and burn- eth the cha- ri - ots in the fire. 10. Be still then, and know that I am God : I will be exalted among the heathen, and I will

(77)

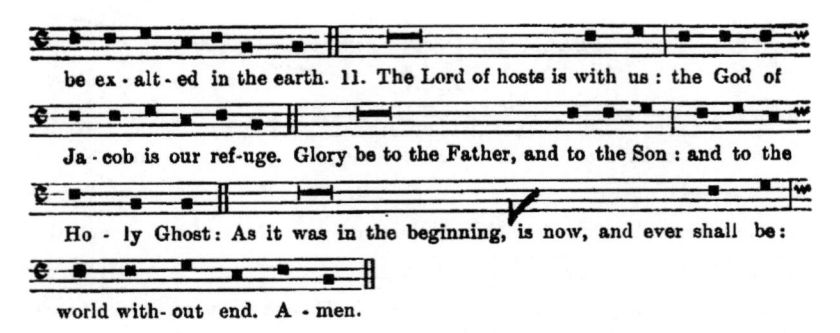

DAY 9. EVENING PRAYER.

be ex-alt-ed in the earth. 11. The Lord of hosts is with us : the God of Ja-cob is our ref-uge. Glory be to the Father, and to the Son : and to the Ho-ly Ghost: As it was in the beginning, is now, and ever shall be: world with-out end. A-men.

EVENING PRAYER.

PSALM XLVII.—*Omnes gentes, plaudite.*

7th Tone, 4th Ending.

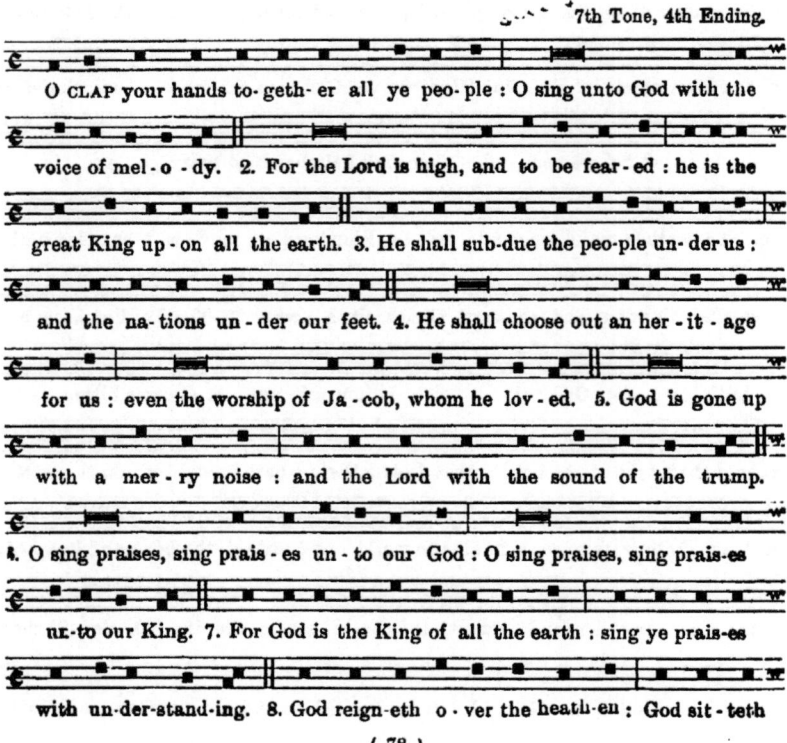

O CLAP your hands to-geth-er all ye peo-ple : O sing unto God with the voice of mel-o-dy. 2. For the Lord is high, and to be fear-ed : he is the great King up-on all the earth. 3. He shall sub-due the peo-ple un-der us : and the na-tions un-der our feet. 4. He shall choose out an her-it-age for us : even the worship of Ja-cob, whom he lov-ed. 5. God is gone up with a mer-ry noise : and the Lord with the sound of the trump. 6. O sing praises, sing prais-es un-to our God : O sing praises, sing prais-es un-to our King. 7. For God is the King of all the earth : sing ye prais-es with un-der-stand-ing. 8. God reign-eth o-ver the heath-en : God sit-teth

EVENING PRAYER. DAY 9.

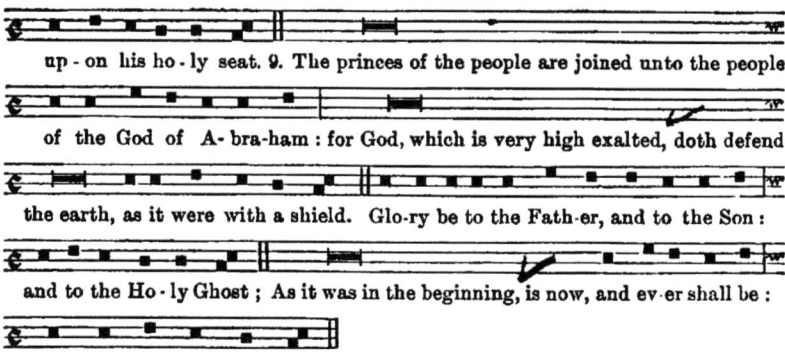

up - on his ho - ly seat. 9. The princes of the people are joined unto the people of the God of A- bra-ham : for God, which is very high exalted, doth defend the earth, as it were with a shield. Glo-ry be to the Fath-er, and to the Son : and to the Ho - ly Ghost ; As it was in the beginning, is now, and ev-er shall be : world with-out end. A - men.

PSALM XLVIII.—*Magnus Dominus.*

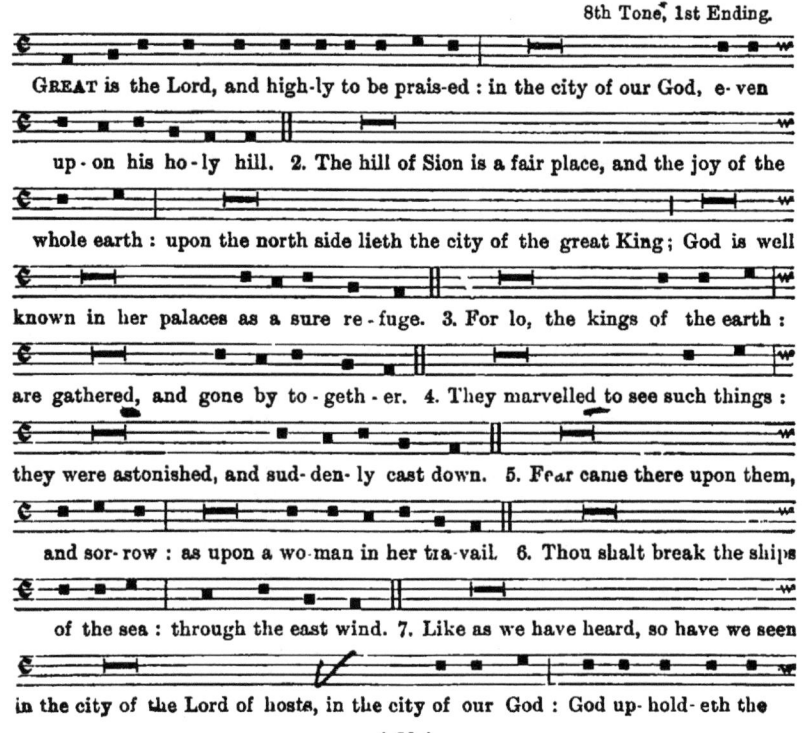

8th Tone, 1st Ending.

GREAT is the Lord, and high-ly to be prais-ed : in the city of our God, e- ven up - on his ho - ly hill. 2. The hill of Sion is a fair place, and the joy of the whole earth : upon the north side lieth the city of the great King ; God is well known in her palaces as a sure re - fuge. 3. For lo, the kings of the earth : are gathered, and gone by to - geth - er. 4. They marvelled to see such things : they were astonished, and sud- den- ly cast down. 5. Fear came there upon them, and sor- row : as upon a wo-man in her tra-vail. 6. Thou shalt break the ships of the sea : through the east wind. 7. Like as we have heard, so have we seen in the city of the Lord of hosts, in the city of our God : God up- hold- eth the

DAY 9.   EVENING PRAYER.

same for ev - er. 8. We wait for thy loving-kindness, O God : in the midst

of thy tem - ple. 9. O God, according to thy Name, so is thy praise unto the

world's end : thy right hand is full of right-eous-ness. 10. Let the mount Sion

rejoice, and the daughter of Judah be glad : be-cause of thy judge-ments.

11. Walk about Sion, and go round a-bout her : and tell the tow-ers there-of.

12. Mark well her bulwarks, set up her hous-es : that ye may tell them that

come af - ter. 13. For this God is our God for ev -er and ev - er : he shall be

our guide un-to death.   Glory be to the Father, and to the Son : and to the

Ho - ly Ghost; As it was in the beginning, is now, and ever shall be :

world with - out end. A - men.

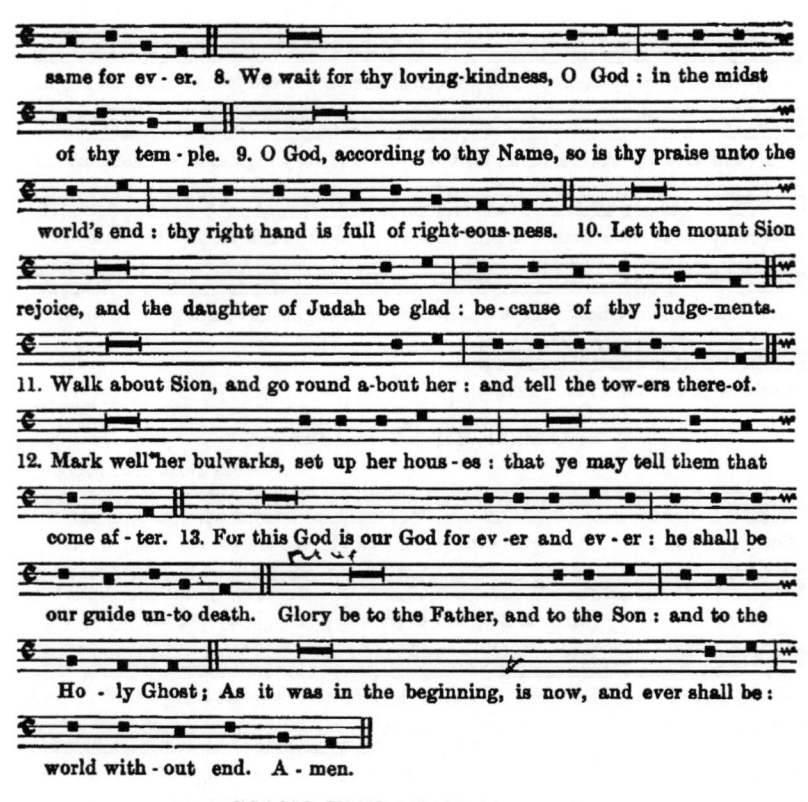

PSALM XLIX.—*Audite hoc, omnes.*

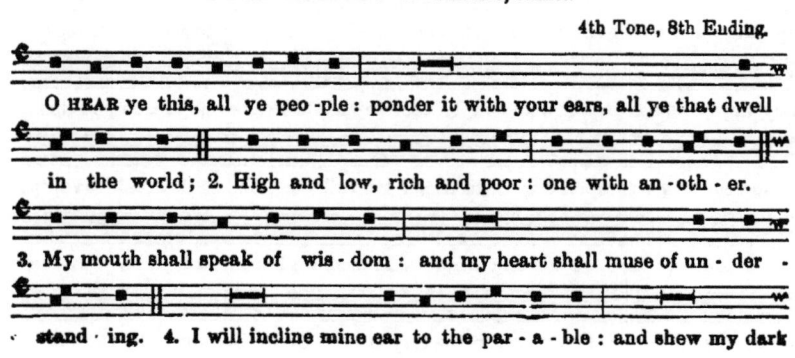

4th Tone, 8th Ending.

O HEAR ye this, all ye peo -ple : ponder it with your ears, all ye that dwell

in the world; 2. High and low, rich and poor : one with an -oth - er.

3. My mouth shall speak of wis - dom : and my heart shall muse of un - der -

- stand - ing. 4. I will incline mine ear to the par - a - ble : and shew my dark speech up-on the harp. 5. Wherefore should I fear in the days of wick-ed-ness : and when the wickedness of my heels compasseth me round a-bout? 6. There be some that put their trust in their goods : and boast themselves in the multitude of their rich-es. 7. But no man may de-liv-er his broth-er : nor make agreement un-to God for him ; 8. For it cost more to re-deem their souls : so that he must let that a-lone for ev-er ; 9. Yea, though he live long : and see not the grave. 10. For he seeth that wise men also die, and per-ish to-geth-er : as well as the ignorant and foolish, and leave their riches for oth-er. 11. And yet they think that their houses shall con-tin-ue for ev-er : and that their dwelling-places shall endure from one generation to another ; and call the lands after their own names. 12. Nevertheless, man will not a-bide in hon-our : seeing he may be compared unto the beasts that perish ; this is the way of them. 13. This is their fool-ish-ness : and their posterity praise their say-ing. 14. They lie in the hell like sheep,* death gnaweth upon them, and the righteous shall have domination over them in the morn-ing : their beauty shall consume in the sepulchre out of

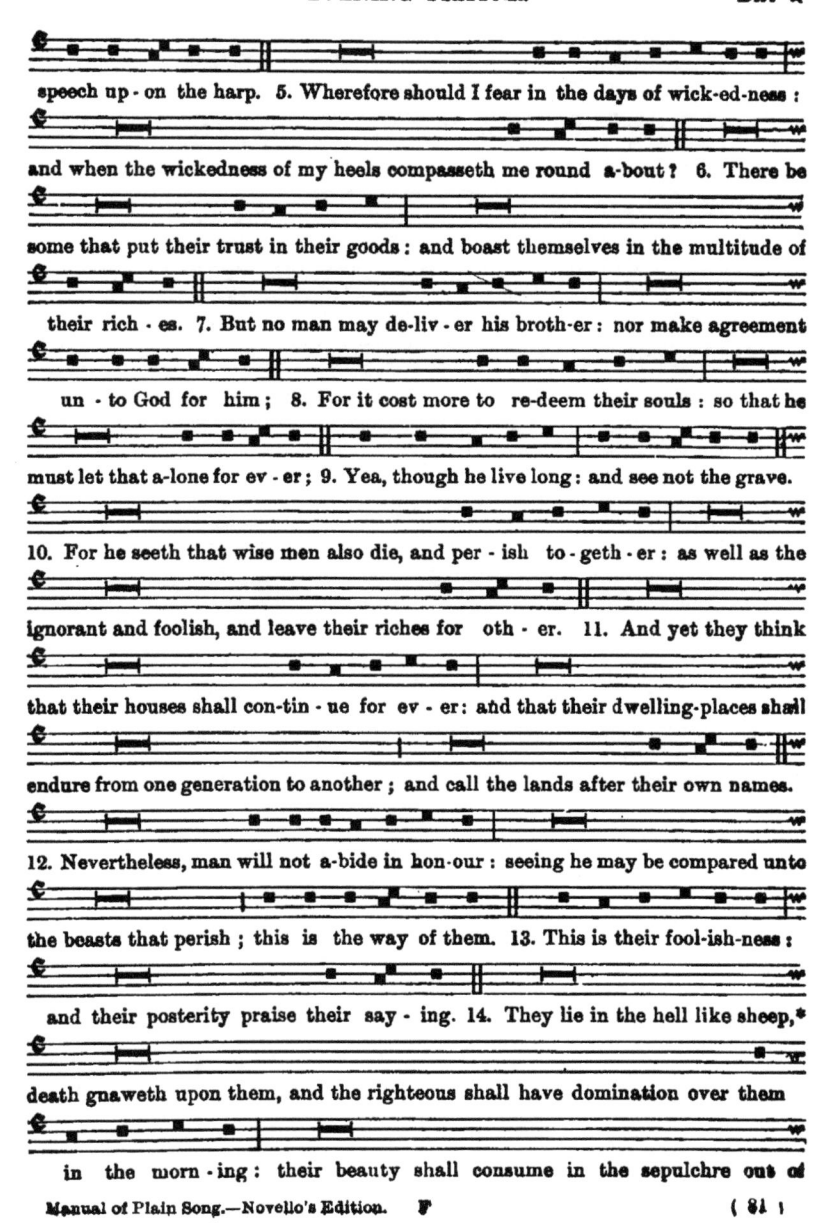

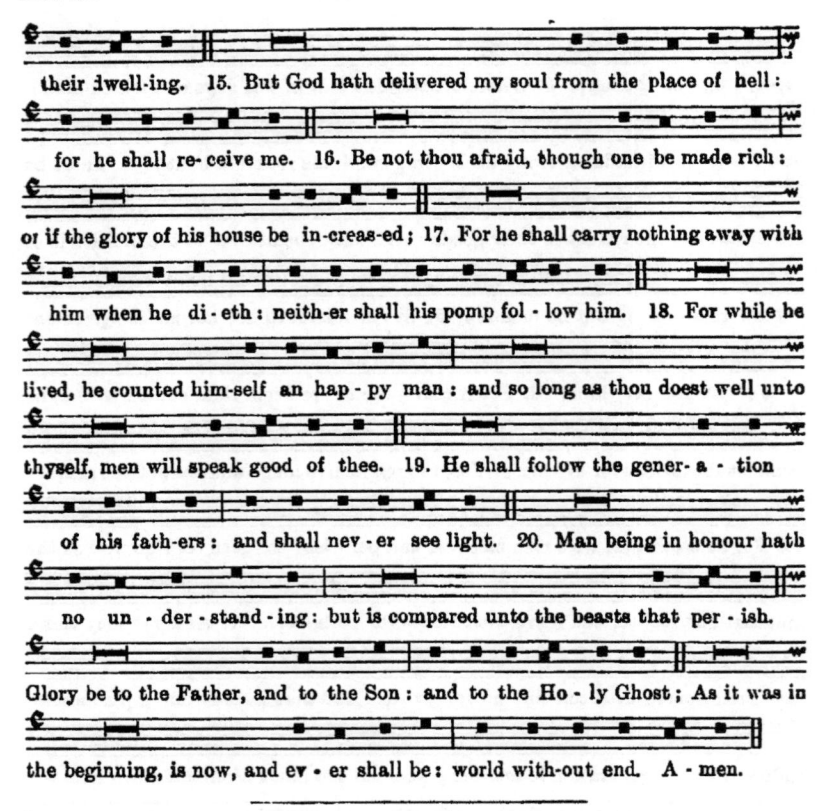

Day 10.   MORNING PRAYER.

their dwell-ing. 15. But God hath delivered my soul from the place of hell: for he shall re-ceive me. 16. Be not thou afraid, though one be made rich: or if the glory of his house be in-creas-ed; 17. For he shall carry nothing away with him when he di-eth: neith-er shall his pomp fol-low him. 18. For while he lived, he counted him-self an hap-py man: and so long as thou doest well unto thyself, men will speak good of thee. 19. He shall follow the gener-a-tion of his fath-ers: and shall nev-er see light. 20. Man being in honour hath no un-der-stand-ing: but is compared unto the beasts that per-ish.

Glory be to the Father, and to the Son: and to the Ho-ly Ghost; As it was in the beginning, is now, and ev-er shall be: world with-out end. A-men.

Day 10.   MORNING PRAYER.

PSALM L.—*Deus deorum.*

3rd Tone, 2nd Ending.

The Lord, e-ven the most might-y God, hath spo-ken: and called the world, from the rising up of the sun, un-to the go-ing down there-of. 2. Out of Sion hath God ap-pear-ed: in per-fect beau-ty. 3. Our God shall come, and shall

MORNING PRAYER. DAY 10.

not keep si-lence : there shall go before him a consuming fire, and a mighty tempest shall be stir-red up round a-bout him. 4. He shall call the heav-en from a-bove : and the earth, that he may judge his peo-ple. 5. Gather my saints to-geth-er un-to me : those that have made a covenant with me with sac-ri-fice. 6. And the heavens shall de-clare his right-eous-ness : for God is Judge him-self. 7. Hear, O my peo-ple, and I will speak : I myself will testify against thee, O Israel ; for I am God, e-ven thy God. 8. I will not reprove thee because of thy sacrifices, or for thy burnt of-fer-ings : because they were not al-way be-fore me. 9. I will take no bul-lock out of thine house : nor he-goat out of thy folds. 10. For all the beasts of the for-est are mine : and so are the cat-tle up-on a thou-sand hills. 11. I know all the fowls up-on the moun-tains : and the wild beasts of the field are in my sight. 12. If I be hungry, I will not tell thee : for the whole world is mine, and all that is there-in. 13. Think-est thou that I will eat bulls' flesh : and drink the blood of goats ? 14. Of-fer un-to God thanks-

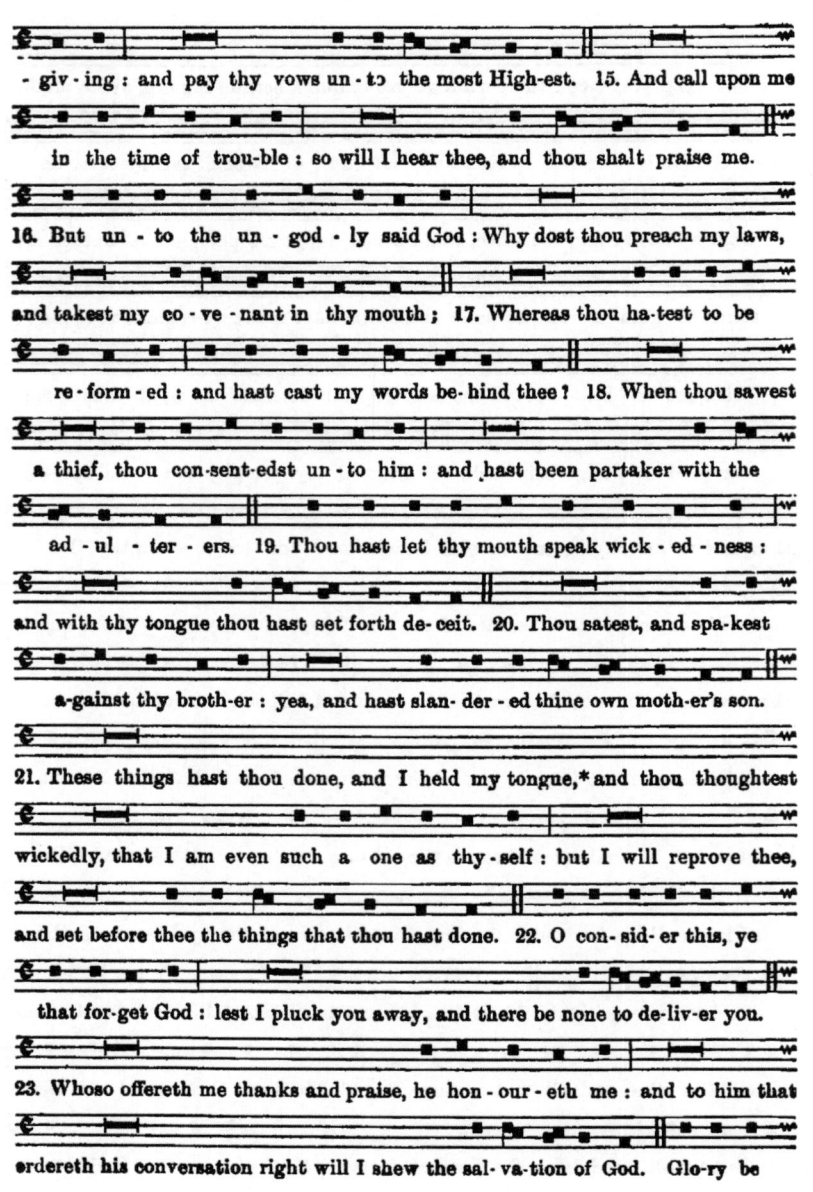

DAY 10. MORNING PRAYER.

- giv - ing : and pay thy vows un - to the most High-est. 15. And call upon me

in the time of trou-ble : so will I hear thee, and thou shalt praise me.

16. But un - to the un - god - ly said God : Why dost thou preach my laws,

and takest my co - ve - nant in thy mouth ; 17. Whereas thou ha-test to be

re - form - ed : and hast cast my words be- hind thee? 18. When thou sawest

a thief, thou con-sent-edst un - to him : and hast been partaker with the

ad - ul - ter - ers. 19. Thou hast let thy mouth speak wick - ed - ness :

and with thy tongue thou hast set forth de-ceit. 20. Thou satest, and spa-kest

a-gainst thy broth-er : yea, and hast slan- der - ed thine own moth-er's son.

21. These things hast thou done, and I held my tongue,* and thou thoughtest

wickedly, that I am even such a one as thy-self : but I will reprove thee,

and set before thee the things that thou hast done. 22. O con- sid- er this, ye

that for-get God : lest I pluck you away, and there be none to de-liv-er you.

23. Whoso offereth me thanks and praise, he hon - our - eth me : and to him that

ordereth his conversation right will I shew the sal- va-tion of God. Glo-ry be

(84)

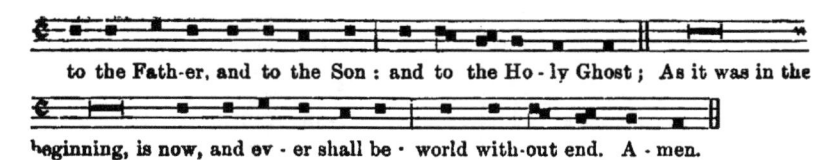

MORNING PRAYER　　　　　　DAY 10.

to the Fath-er, and to the Son : and to the Ho - ly Ghost ; As it was in the beginning, is now, and ev - er shall be · world with-out end. A - men.

PSALM LI.—*Miserere mei, Deus.*

4th Tone, 4th Ending.

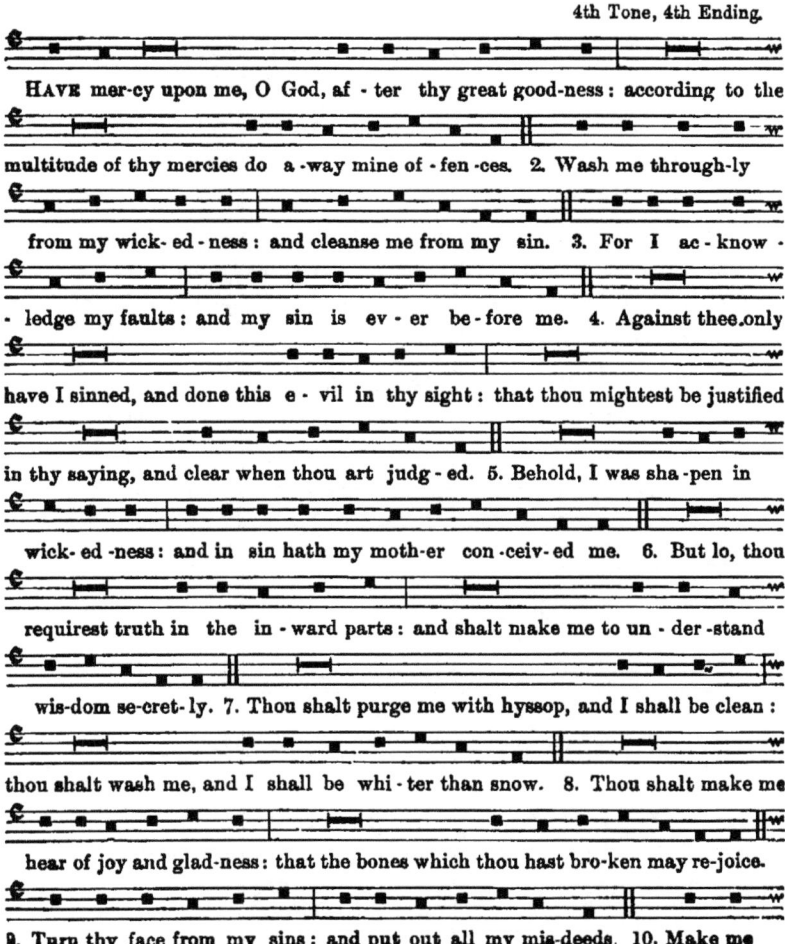

HAVE mer-cy upon me, O God, af - ter thy great good-ness : according to the multitude of thy mercies do a -way mine of - fen -ces. 2. Wash me through-ly from my wick- ed - ness : and cleanse me from my sin. 3. For I ac - know - ledge my faults : and my sin is ev - er be - fore me. 4. Against thee, only have I sinned, and done this e - vil in thy sight : that thou mightest be justified in thy saying, and clear when thou art judg - ed. 5. Behold, I was sha -pen in wick- ed -ness : and in sin hath my moth-er con -ceiv- ed me. 6. But lo, thou requirest truth in the in - ward parts : and shalt make me to un - der -stand wis-dom se-cret- ly. 7. Thou shalt purge me with hyssop, and I shall be clean : thou shalt wash me, and I shall be whi - ter than snow. 8. Thou shalt make me hear of joy and glad-ness : that the bones which thou hast bro-ken may re-joice. 9. Turn thy face from my sins : and put out all my mis-deeds. 10. Make me

(95)

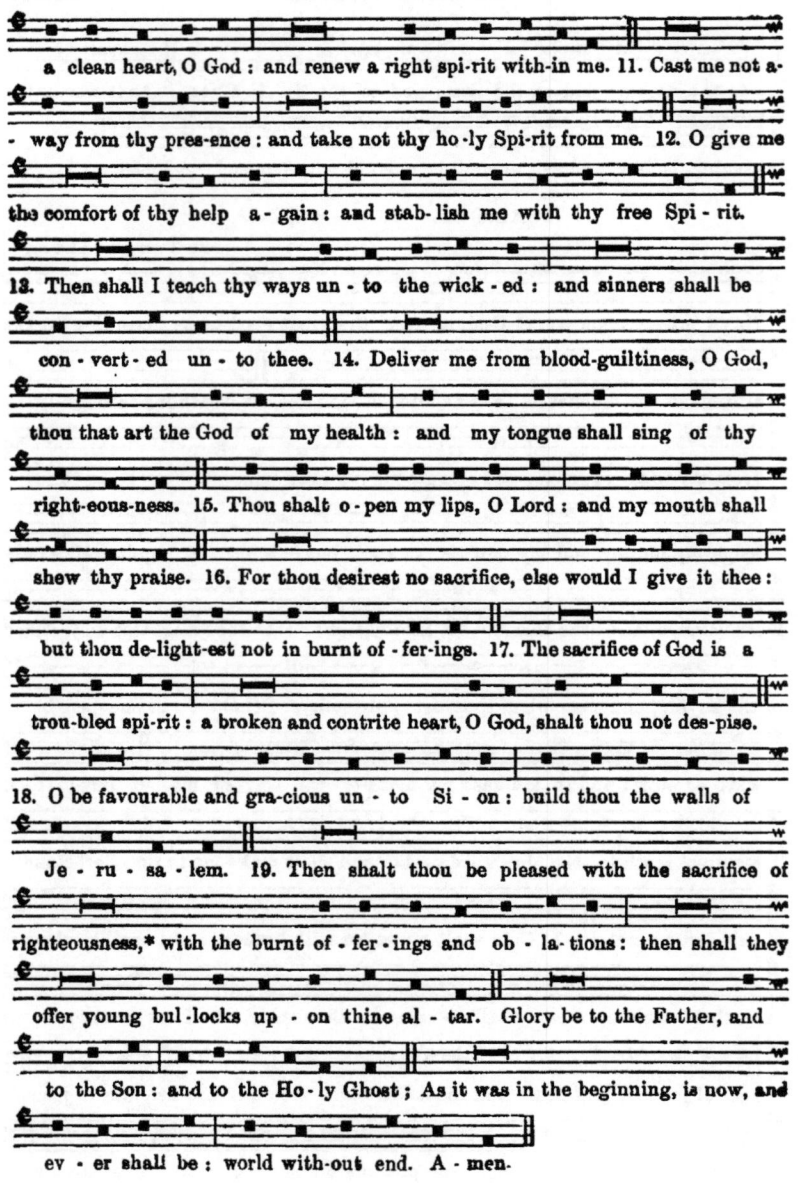

DAY 10. MORNING PRAYER.

a clean heart, O God : and renew a right spi-rit with-in me. 11. Cast me not a- way from thy pres-ence: and take not thy ho-ly Spi-rit from me. 12. O give me the comfort of thy help a-gain: and stab-lish me with thy free Spi-rit. 13. Then shall I teach thy ways un-to the wick-ed: and sinners shall be con-vert-ed un-to thee. 14. Deliver me from blood-guiltiness, O God, thou that art the God of my health: and my tongue shall sing of thy right-eous-ness. 15. Thou shalt o-pen my lips, O Lord: and my mouth shall shew thy praise. 16. For thou desirest no sacrifice, else would I give it thee: but thou de-light-est not in burnt of-fer-ings. 17. The sacrifice of God is a trou-bled spi-rit: a broken and contrite heart, O God, shalt thou not des-pise. 18. O be favourable and gra-cious un-to Si-on: build thou the walls of Je-ru-sa-lem. 19. Then shalt thou be pleased with the sacrifice of righteousness,* with the burnt of-fer-ings and ob-la-tions: then shall they offer young bul-locks up-on thine al-tar. Glory be to the Father, and to the Son: and to the Ho-ly Ghost; As it was in the beginning, is now, and ev-er shall be: world with-out end. A-men.

MORNING PRAYER. DAY 10.

PSALM LII.—*Quid gloriaris?*

7th Tone, 7th Ending.

WHY boast-est thou thy-self, thou ty-rant: that thou canst do mis-chief;

2. Where-as the good-ness of God: en-dur-eth yet dai-ly? 3. Thy tongue

im-ag-in-eth wick-ed-ness: and with lies thou cuttest like a sharp ra-zor.

4. Thou hast loved un-right-eous-ness more than good-ness: and to talk of lies

more than right-eous-ness. 5. Thou hast loved to speak all words that

may do hurt: O thou false tongue. 6. There-fore shall God de-stroy

thee for ev-er: he shall take thee, and pluck thee out of thy dwelling,

and root thee out of the land of the liv-ing. 7. The righteous also shall

see this, and fear: and shall laugh him to scorn. 8. Lo, this is the man that

took not God for his strength: but trusted unto the multitude of his riches,

and strengthened him-self in his wick-ed-ness. 9. As for me, I am like a

green olive-tree in the house of God: my trust is in the tender mercy of God

for ev-er and ev-er. 10. I will always give thanks unto thee for that

thou hast done: and I will hope in thy Name, for thy saints like it well.

Glo-ry be to the Fath-er, and to the Son: and to the Ho-ly Ghost; As it was

in the beginning, is now, and ev-er shall be: world with-out end. A men.

Day 10.   EVENING PRAYER.

PSALM LIII.—*Dixit insipiens.*

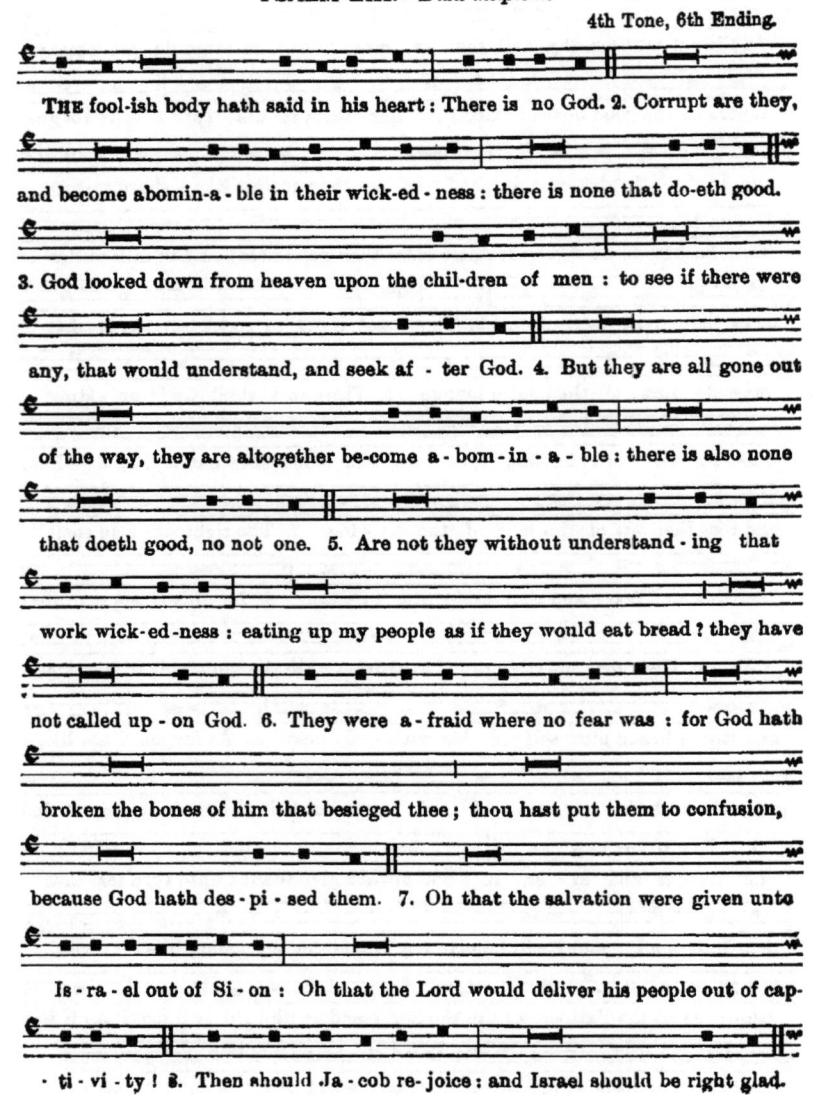

4th Tone, 6th Ending.

THE fool-ish body hath said in his heart : There is no God. 2. Corrupt are they, and become abomin-a-ble in their wick-ed-ness : there is none that do-eth good.

3. God looked down from heaven upon the chil-dren of men : to see if there were any, that would understand, and seek af-ter God. 4. But they are all gone out of the way, they are altogether be-come a-bom-in-a-ble : there is also none that doeth good, no not one. 5. Are not they without understand-ing that work wick-ed-ness : eating up my people as if they would eat bread ? they have not called up-on God. 6. They were a-fraid where no fear was : for God hath broken the bones of him that besieged thee ; thou hast put them to confusion, because God hath des-pi-sed them. 7. Oh that the salvation were given unto Is-ra-el out of Si-on : Oh that the Lord would deliver his people out of cap--ti-vi-ty ! 8. Then should Ja-cob re-joice : and Israel should be right glad.

(85)

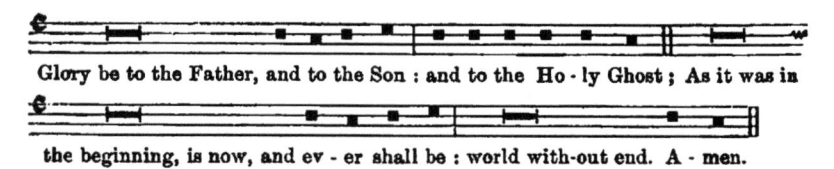

EVENING PRAYER. DAY 10.

Glory be to the Father, and to the Son : and to the Ho - ly Ghost ; As it was in the beginning, is now, and ev - er shall be : world with-out end. A - men.

PSALM LIV.—*Deus, in nomine.*

6th Tone.

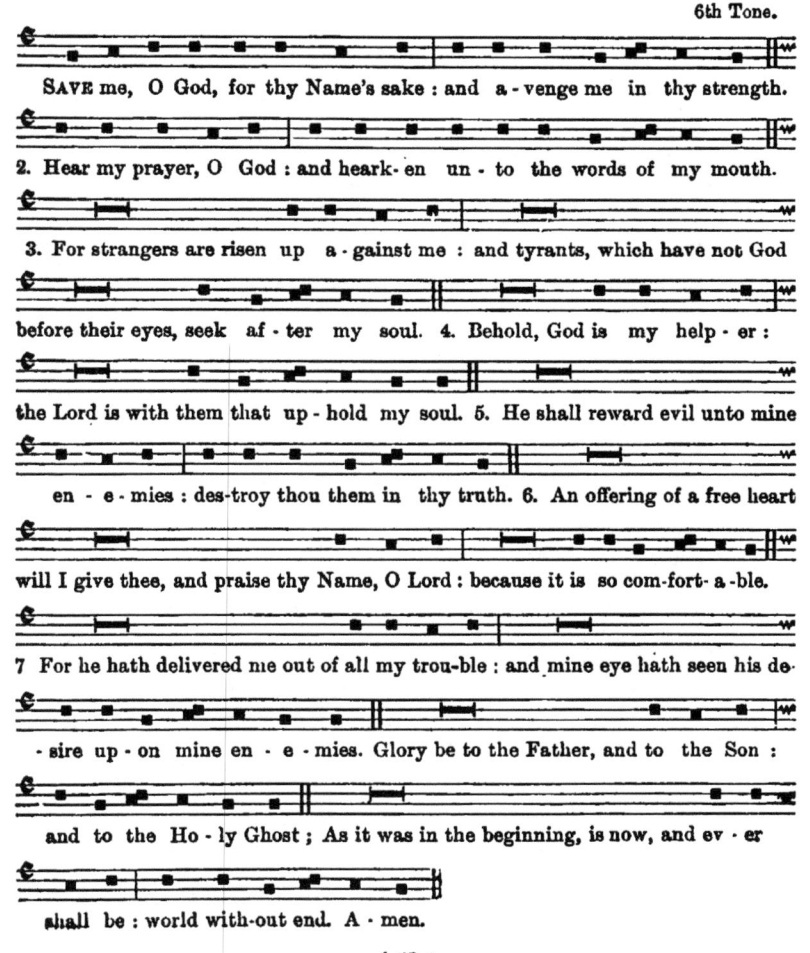

SAVE me, O God, for thy Name's sake : and a - venge me in thy strength.

2. Hear my prayer, O God : and heark- en un - to the words of my mouth.

3. For strangers are risen up a - gainst me : and tyrants, which have not God before their eyes, seek af - ter my soul. 4. Behold, God is my help - er : the Lord is with them that up - hold my soul. 5. He shall reward evil unto mine en - e - mies : des-troy thou them in thy truth. 6. An offering of a free heart will I give thee, and praise thy Name, O Lord : because it is so com-fort- a -ble.

7 For he hath delivered me out of all my trou-ble : and mine eye hath seen his de- - sire up - on mine en - e - mies. Glory be to the Father, and to the Son : and to the Ho - ly Ghost ; As it was in the beginning, is now, and ev - er shall be : world with-out end. A - men.

DAY 10.　　　　　EVENING PRAYER.

PSALM LV.—*Exaudi, Deus.*

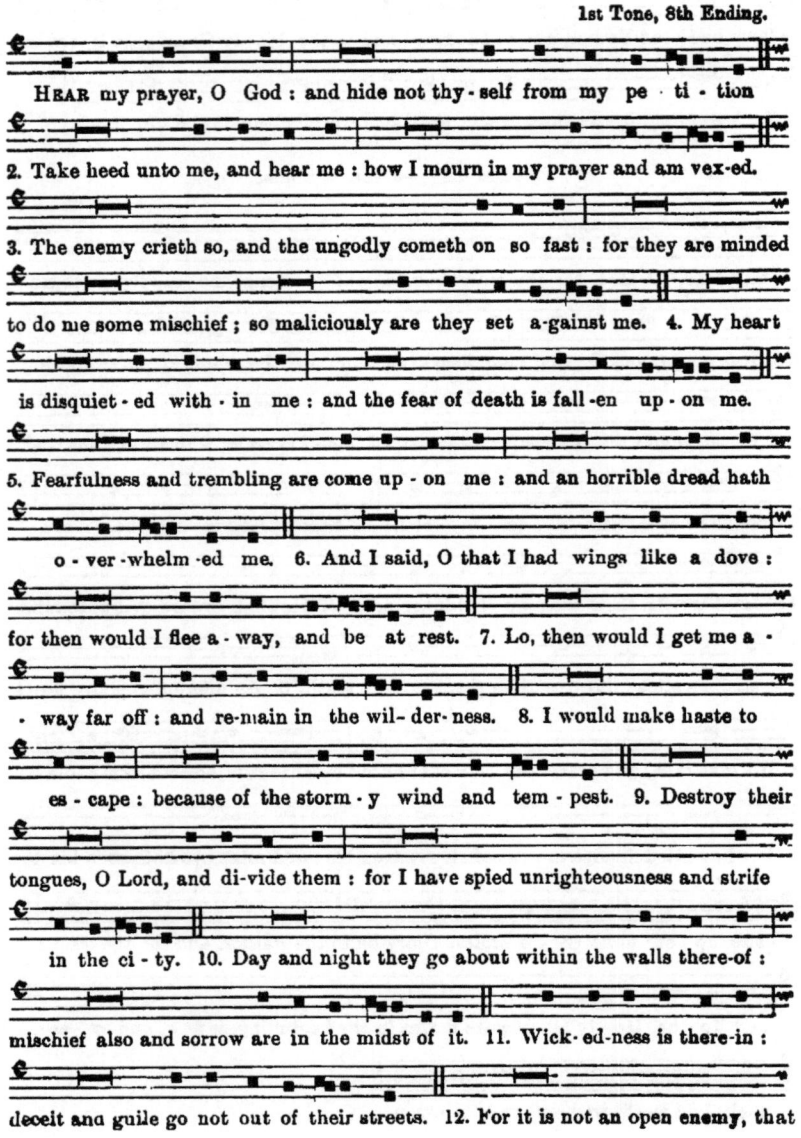

1st Tone, 8th Ending.

HEAR my prayer, O God : and hide not thy-self from my pe - ti - tion

2. Take heed unto me, and hear me : how I mourn in my prayer and am vex-ed.

3. The enemy crieth so, and the ungodly cometh on so fast : for they are minded to do me some mischief ; so maliciously are they set a-gainst me. 4. My heart is disquiet - ed with - in me : and the fear of death is fall -en up - on me.

5. Fearfulness and trembling are come up - on me : and an horrible dread hath o - ver -whelm -ed me. 6. And I said, O that I had wings like a dove : for then would I flee a - way, and be at rest. 7. Lo, then would I get me a - - way far off : and re-main in the wil - der- ness. 8. I would make haste to es - cape : because of the storm - y wind and tem - pest. 9. Destroy their tongues, O Lord, and di-vide them : for I have spied unrighteousness and strife in the ci - ty. 10. Day and night they go about within the walls there-of : mischief also and sorrow are in the midst of it. 11. Wick- ed-ness is there-in : deceit and guile go not out of their streets. 12. For it is not an open enemy, that

EVENING PRAYER. DAY 10.

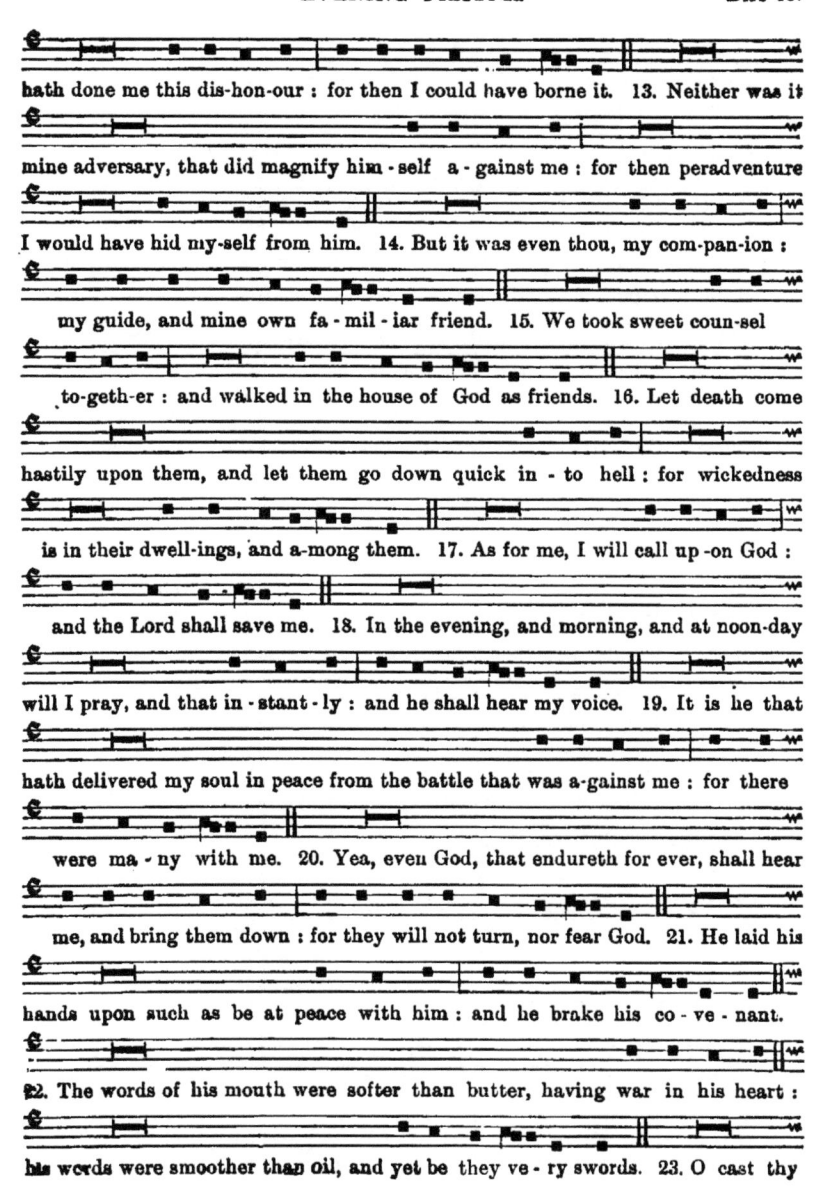

hath done me this dis-hon-our : for then I could have borne it. 13. Neither was it mine adversary, that did magnify him-self a-gainst me : for then peradventure I would have hid my-self from him. 14. But it was even thou, my com-pan-ion : my guide, and mine own fa-mil-iar friend. 15. We took sweet coun-sel to-geth-er : and walked in the house of God as friends. 16. Let death come hastily upon them, and let them go down quick in-to hell : for wickedness is in their dwell-ings, and a-mong them. 17. As for me, I will call up-on God : and the Lord shall save me. 18. In the evening, and morning, and at noon-day will I pray, and that in-stant-ly : and he shall hear my voice. 19. It is he that hath delivered my soul in peace from the battle that was a-gainst me : for there were ma-ny with me. 20. Yea, even God, that endureth for ever, shall hear me, and bring them down : for they will not turn, nor fear God. 21. He laid his hands upon such as be at peace with him : and he brake his co-ve-nant. 22. The words of his mouth were softer than butter, having war in his heart : his words were smoother than oil, and yet be they ve-ry swords. 23. O cast thy

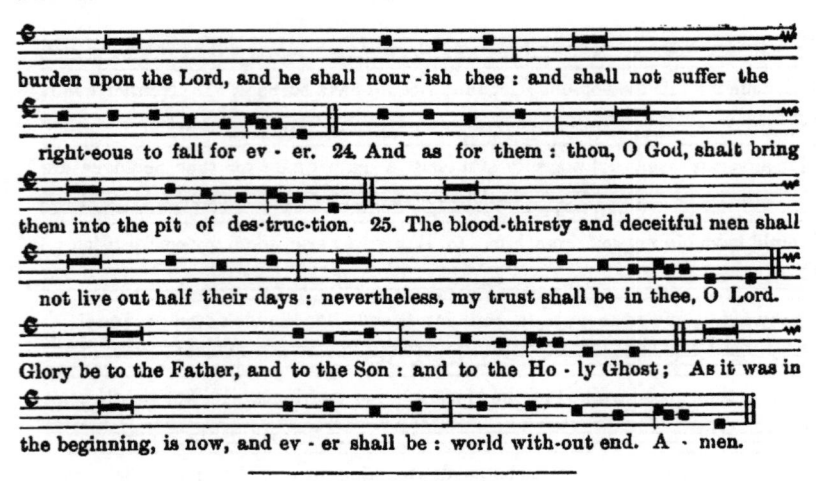

DAY 11. MORNING PRAYER.

burden upon the Lord, and he shall nour-ish thee : and shall not suffer the right-eous to fall for ev - er. 24. And as for them : thou, O God, shalt bring them into the pit of des-truc-tion. 25. The blood-thirsty and deceitful men shall not live out half their days : nevertheless, my trust shall be in thee, O Lord. Glory be to the Father, and to the Son : and to the Ho - ly Ghost ; As it was in the beginning, is now, and ev - er shall be : world with-out end. A - men.

DAY 11. MORNING PRAYER.

PSALM LVI.—*Miserere mei, Deus.*

1st Tone, 2nd Ending.

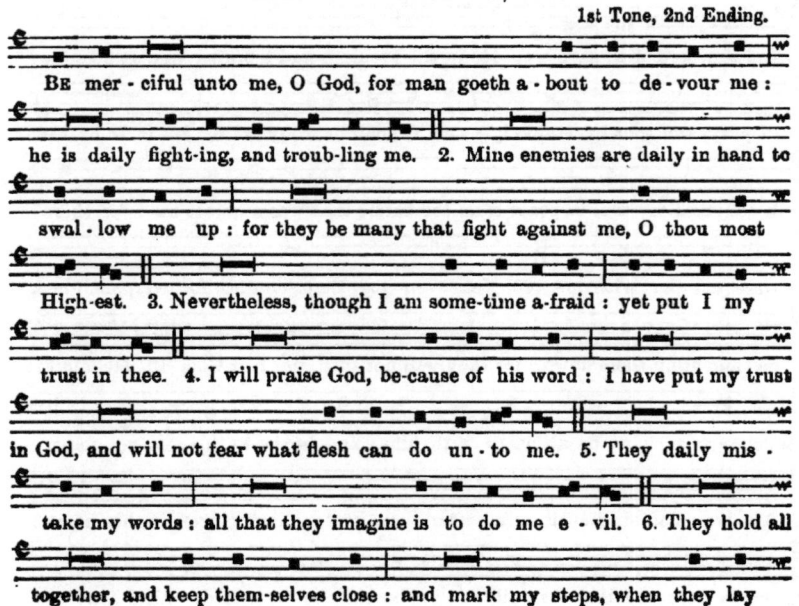

BE mer - ciful unto me, O God, for man goeth a - bout to de - vour me : he is daily fight-ing, and troub-ling me. 2. Mine enemies are daily in hand to swal - low me up : for they be many that fight against me, O thou most High-est. 3. Nevertheless, though I am some-time a-fraid : yet put I my trust in thee. 4. I will praise God, be-cause of his word : I have put my trust in God, and will not fear what flesh can do un - to me. 5. They daily mis - take my words : all that they imagine is to do me e - vil. 6. They hold all together, and keep them-selves close : and mark my steps, when they lay

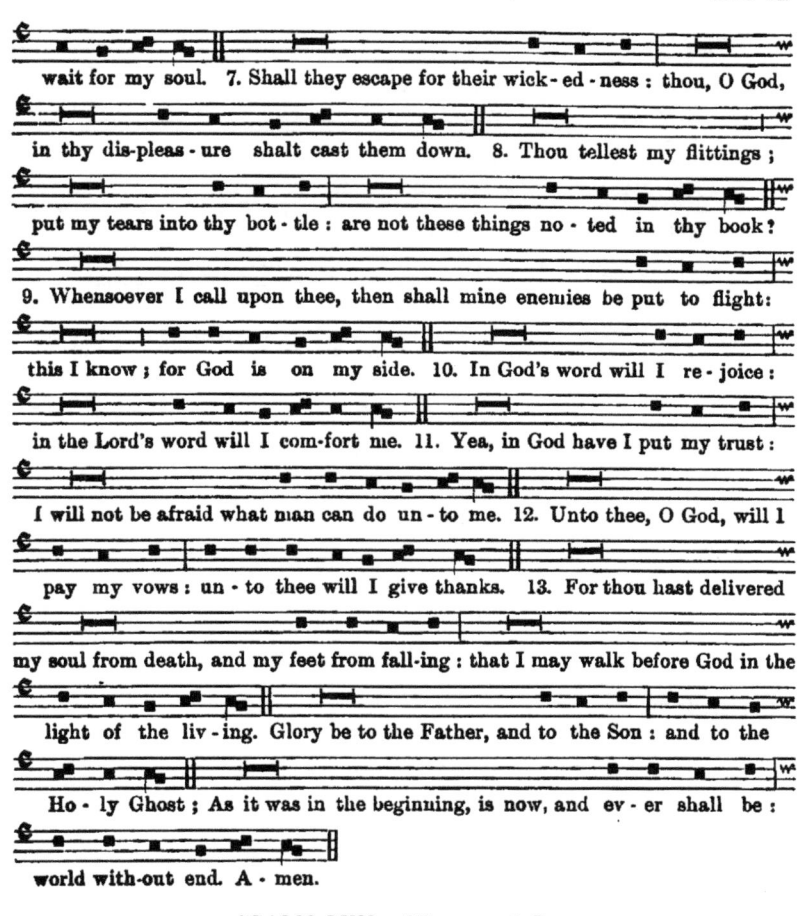

MORNING PRAYER. DAY 11.

wait for my soul. 7. Shall they escape for their wick-ed-ness: thou, O God, in thy dis-pleas-ure shalt cast them down. 8. Thou tellest my flittings; put my tears into thy bot-tle: are not these things no-ted in thy book? 9. Whensoever I call upon thee, then shall mine enemies be put to flight: this I know; for God is on my side. 10. In God's word will I re-joice: in the Lord's word will I com-fort me. 11. Yea, in God have I put my trust: I will not be afraid what man can do un-to me. 12. Unto thee, O God, will I pay my vows: un-to thee will I give thanks. 13. For thou hast delivered my soul from death, and my feet from fall-ing: that I may walk before God in the light of the liv-ing. Glory be to the Father, and to the Son: and to the Ho-ly Ghost; As it was in the beginning, is now, and ev-er shall be: world with-out end. A-men.

PSALM LVII.—*Miserere mei, Deus.*

8th Tone, 1st Ending.

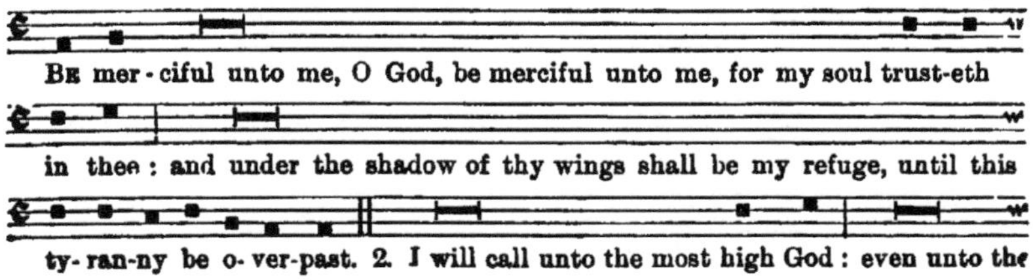

BE mer-ciful unto me, O God, be merciful unto me, for my soul trust-eth in thee: and under the shadow of thy wings shall be my refuge, until this ty-ran-ny be o-ver-past. 2. I will call unto the most high God: even unto the

(93)

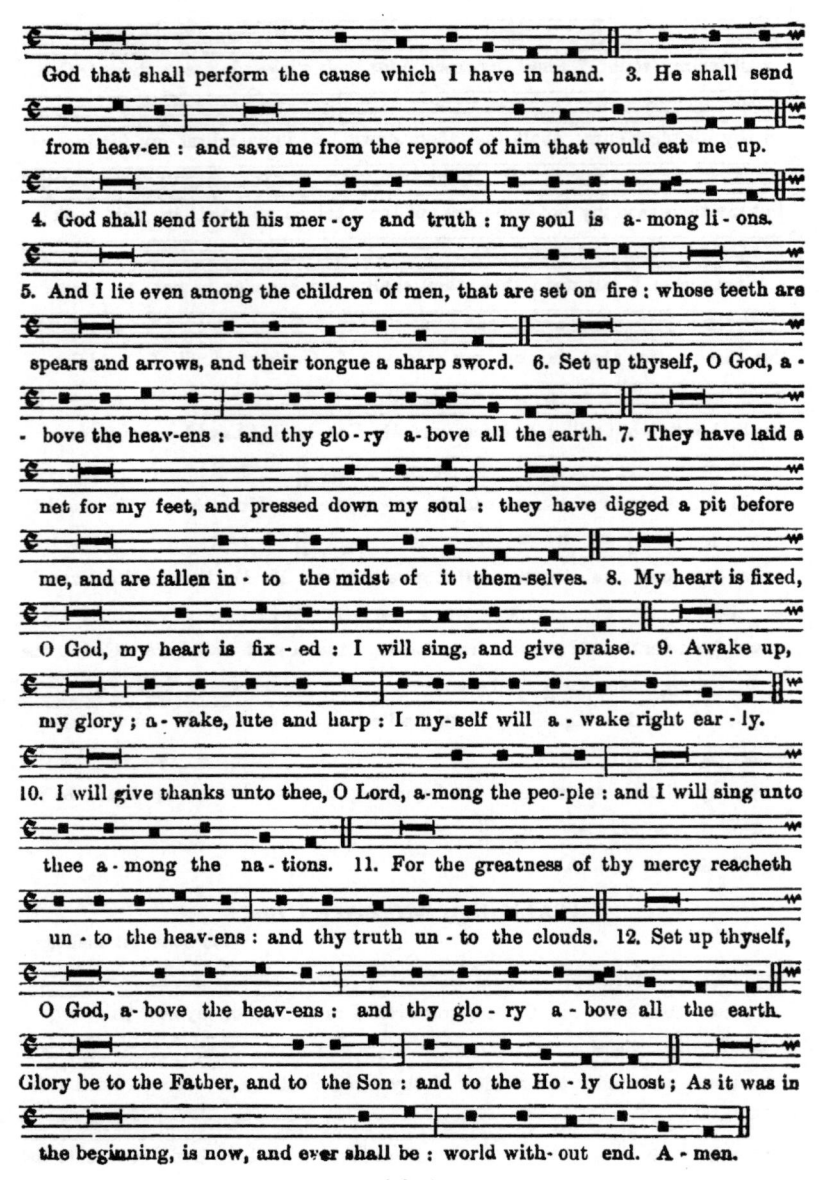

Day 11.   MORNING PRAYER.

God that shall perform the cause which I have in hand. 3. He shall send from heav-en : and save me from the reproof of him that would eat me up.

4. God shall send forth his mer-cy and truth : my soul is a-mong li-ons.

5. And I lie even among the children of men, that are set on fire : whose teeth are spears and arrows, and their tongue a sharp sword. 6. Set up thyself, O God, a-bove the heav-ens : and thy glo-ry a-bove all the earth. 7. They have laid a net for my feet, and pressed down my soul : they have digged a pit before me, and are fallen in-to the midst of it them-selves. 8. My heart is fixed, O God, my heart is fix-ed : I will sing, and give praise. 9. Awake up, my glory ; a-wake, lute and harp : I my-self will a-wake right ear-ly.

10. I will give thanks unto thee, O Lord, a-mong the peo-ple : and I will sing unto thee a-mong the na-tions. 11. For the greatness of thy mercy reacheth un-to the heav-ens : and thy truth un-to the clouds. 12. Set up thyself, O God, a-bove the heav-ens : and thy glo-ry a-bove all the earth.

Glory be to the Father, and to the Son : and to the Ho-ly Ghost ; As it was in the beginning, is now, and ever shall be : world with-out end. A-men.

MORNING PRAYER. DAY 11.

PSALM LVIII.—*Si vere, utique.*

2nd Tone, 1st Ending.

ARE your minds set upon righteousness, O ye con-gre-ga-tion : and do ye judge the thing that is right, O ye sons of men? 2. Yea, ye imagine mischief in your heart up-on the earth : and your hands deal with wick-ed-ness.

3. The ungodly are froward, even from their moth-er's womb : as soon as they are born, they go a-stray, and speak lies. 4. They are as venomous as the poison of a ser-pent : even like the deaf adder that stop-peth her ears; 5. Which re-fuseth to hear the voice of the charm-er : charm he nev-er so wise-ly.

6. Break their teeth, O God, in their mouths ; smite the jaw-bones of the lions, O Lord : let them fall away like water that runneth apace ; and, when they shoot their arrows, let them be root-ed out. 7. Let them consume away like a snail, and be like the untimely fruit of a wo-man : and let them not see the sun.

8. Or ever your pots be made hot with thorns : so let indignation vex him, even as a thing that is raw. 9. The righteous shall rejoice when he se-eth the ven-geance : he shall wash his footsteps in the blood of the un-god-ly. 10. So that a man shall say, Verily there is a reward for the right-eous : doubtless there is a God that

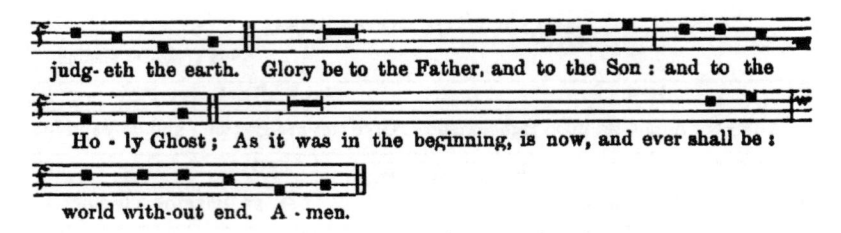

DAY 11. EVENING PRAYER.

judg-eth the earth. Glory be to the Father, and to the Son : and to the Ho-ly Ghost ; As it was in the beginning, is now, and ever shall be : world with-out end. A-men.

EVENING PRAYER.

PSALM LIX.—*Eripe me de inimicis.*

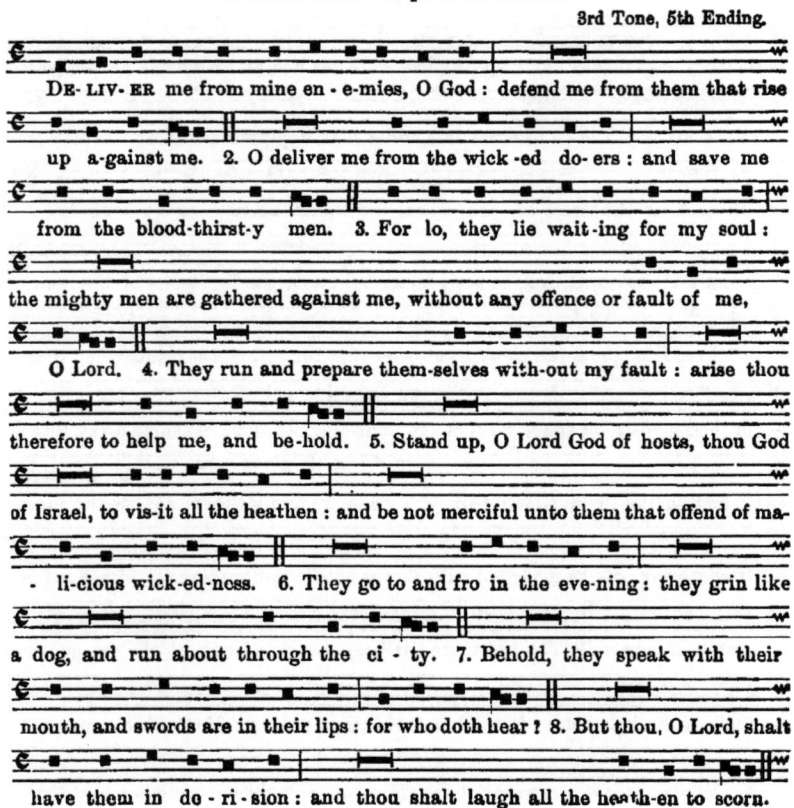

3rd Tone, 5th Ending.

DE-LIV-ER me from mine en-e-mies, O God : defend me from them that rise up a-gainst me. 2. O deliver me from the wick-ed do-ers : and save me from the blood-thirst-y men. 3. For lo, they lie wait-ing for my soul : the mighty men are gathered against me, without any offence or fault of me, O Lord. 4. They run and prepare them-selves with-out my fault : arise thou therefore to help me, and be-hold. 5. Stand up, O Lord God of hosts, thou God of Israel, to vis-it all the heathen : and be not merciful unto them that offend of ma- -li-cious wick-ed-ness. 6. They go to and fro in the eve-ning : they grin like a dog, and run about through the ci-ty. 7. Behold, they speak with their mouth, and swords are in their lips : for who doth hear ? 8. But thou, O Lord, shalt have them in de-ri-sion : and thou shalt laugh all the heath-en to scorn.

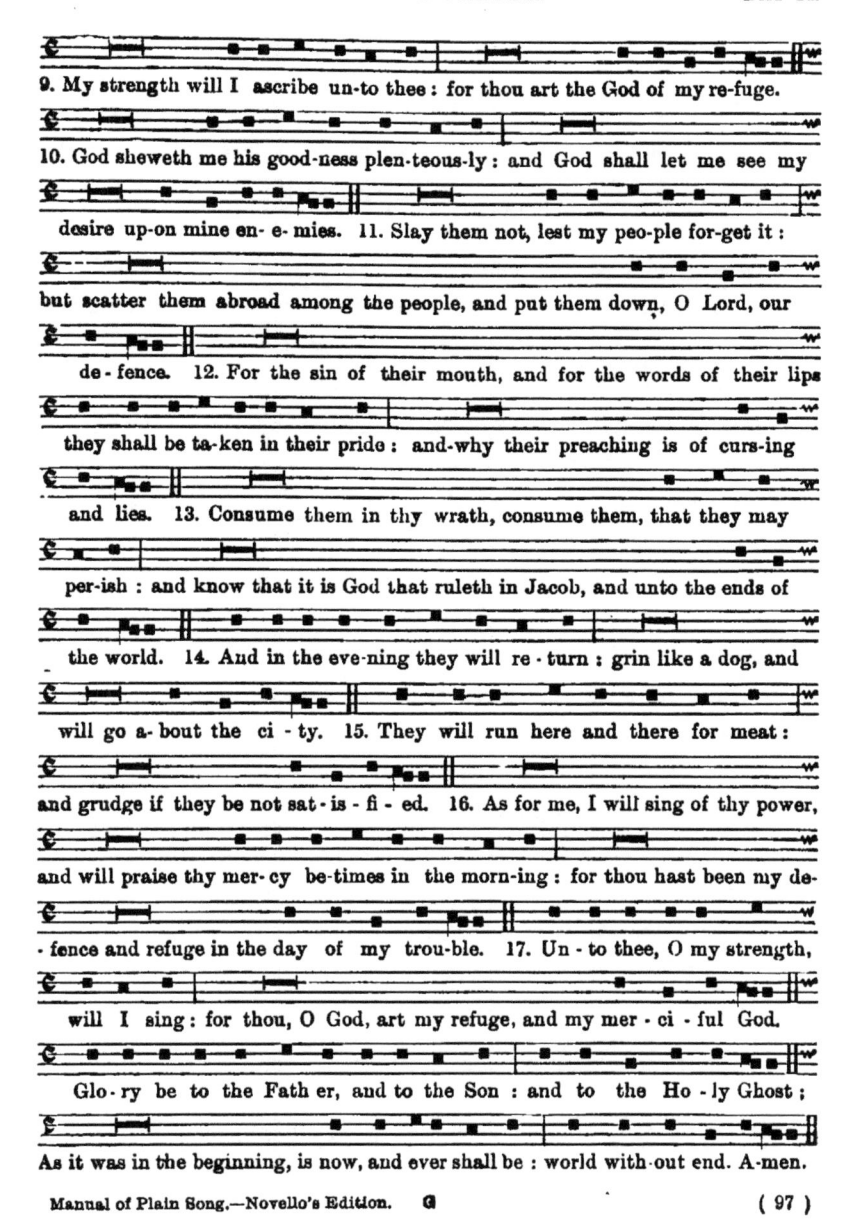

9. My strength will I ascribe un-to thee : for thou art the God of my re-fuge.

10. God sheweth me his good-ness plen-teous-ly : and God shall let me see my desire up-on mine en- e- mies. 11. Slay them not, lest my peo-ple for-get it : but scatter them abroad among the people, and put them down, O Lord, our de - fence. 12. For the sin of their mouth, and for the words of their lips they shall be ta-ken in their pride : and-why their preaching is of curs-ing and lies. 13. Consume them in thy wrath, consume them, that they may per-ish : and know that it is God that ruleth in Jacob, and unto the ends of the world. 14. And in the eve-ning they will re - turn : grin like a dog, and will go a- bout the ci - ty. 15. They will run here and there for meat : and grudge if they be not sat - is - fi - ed. 16. As for me, I will sing of thy power, and will praise thy mer- cy be-times in the morn-ing : for thou hast been my de- - fence and refuge in the day of my trou-ble. 17. Un - to thee, O my strength, will I sing : for thou, O God, art my refuge, and my mer - ci - ful God.

Glo - ry be to the Fath er, and to the Son : and to the Ho - ly Ghost ; As it was in the beginning, is now, and ever shall be : world with-out end. A-men.

DAY 11.   EVENING PRAYER.

PSALM LX.—*Deus, repulisti nos.*

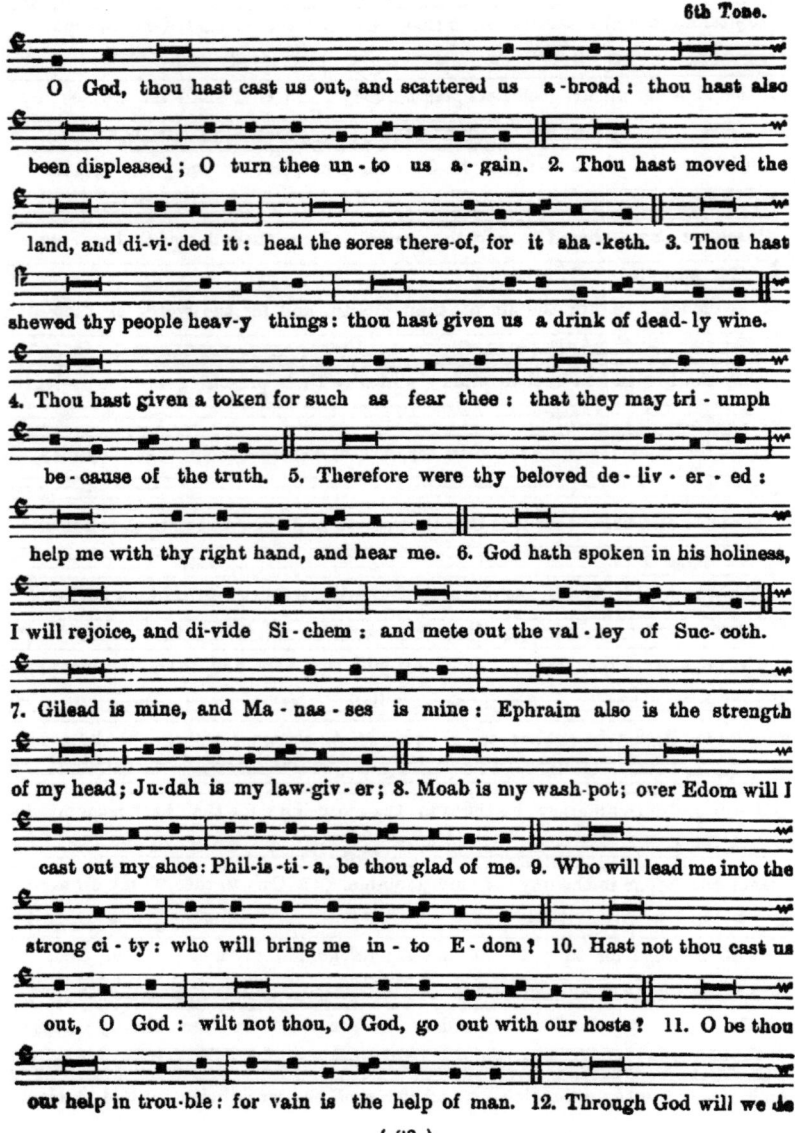

6th Tone.

O God, thou hast cast us out, and scattered us a-broad: thou hast also been displeased; O turn thee un-to us a-gain. 2. Thou hast moved the land, and di-vi-ded it: heal the sores there-of, for it sha-keth. 3. Thou hast shewed thy people heav-y things: thou hast given us a drink of dead-ly wine. 4. Thou hast given a token for such as fear thee: that they may tri-umph be-cause of the truth. 5. Therefore were thy beloved de-liv-er-ed: help me with thy right hand, and hear me. 6. God hath spoken in his holiness, I will rejoice, and di-vide Si-chem: and mete out the val-ley of Suc-coth. 7. Gilead is mine, and Ma-nas-ses is mine: Ephraim also is the strength of my head; Ju-dah is my law-giv-er; 8. Moab is my wash-pot; over Edom will I cast out my shoe: Phil-is-ti-a, be thou glad of me. 9. Who will lead me into the strong ci-ty: who will bring me in-to E-dom? 10. Hast not thou cast us out, O God: wilt not thou, O God, go out with our hosts? 11. O be thou our help in trou-ble: for vain is the help of man. 12. Through God will we do

(98)

EVENING PRAYER. DAY 11.

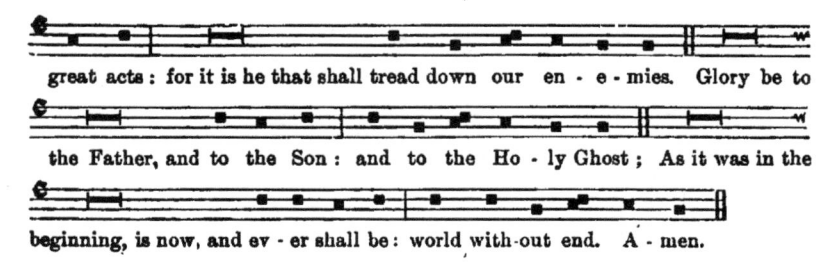

great acts: for it is he that shall tread down our en - e - mies. Glory be to the Father, and to the Son: and to the Ho - ly Ghost; As it was in the beginning, is now, and ev - er shall be: world with-out end. A - men.

PSALM LXI.—*Exaudi Deus.*

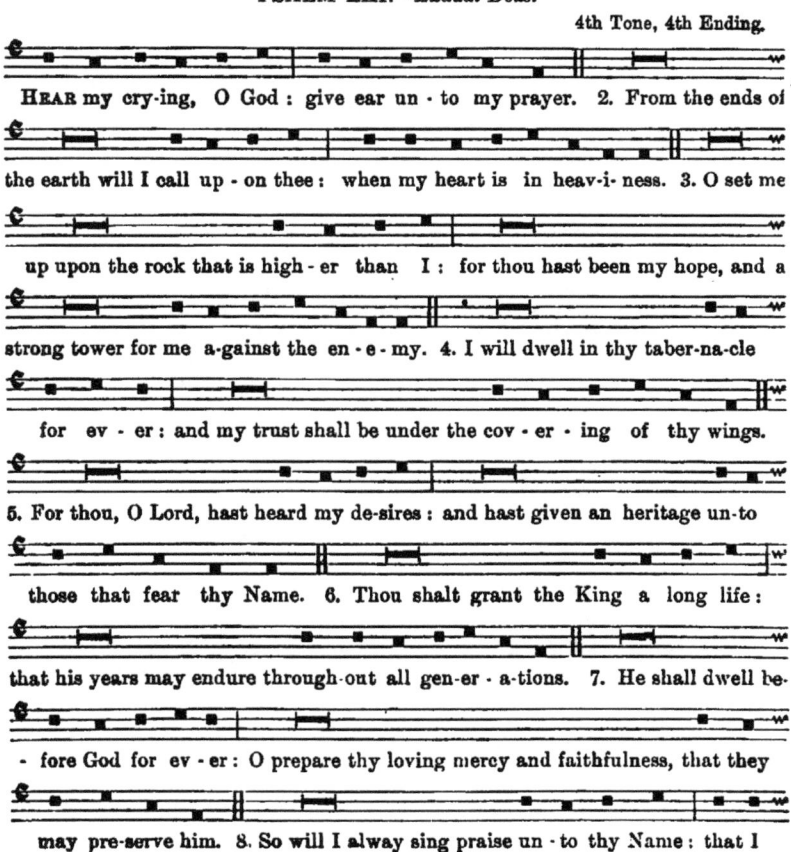

4th Tone, 4th Ending.

HEAR my cry-ing, O God: give ear un - to my prayer. 2. From the ends of the earth will I call up - on thee: when my heart is in heav-i- ness. 3. O set me up upon the rock that is high - er than I: for thou hast been my hope, and a strong tower for me a-gainst the en - e - my. 4. I will dwell in thy taber-na-cle for ev - er: and my trust shall be under the cov - er - ing of thy wings. 5. For thou, O Lord, hast heard my de-sires: and hast given an heritage un-to those that fear thy Name. 6. Thou shalt grant the King a long life: that his years may endure through-out all gen-er - a-tions. 7. He shall dwell be- - fore God for ev - er: O prepare thy loving mercy and faithfulness, that they may pre-serve him. 8. So will I alway sing praise un - to thy Name: that I

(99)

DAY 12. MORNING PRAYER.

may dai-ly per-form my vows. Glory be to the Father, and to the Son: and to the Ho-ly Ghost; As it was in the beginning, is now, and ev-er shall be: world with-out end. A-men.

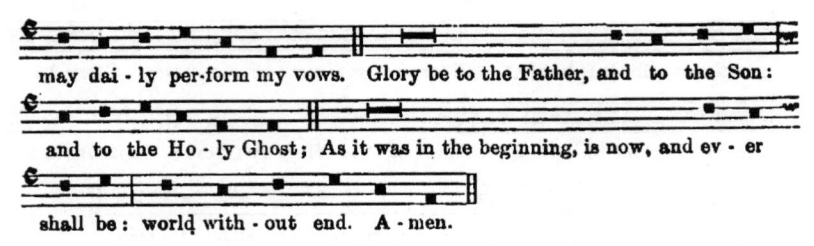

MORNING PRAYER.

PSALM LXII.—*Nonne Deo?*

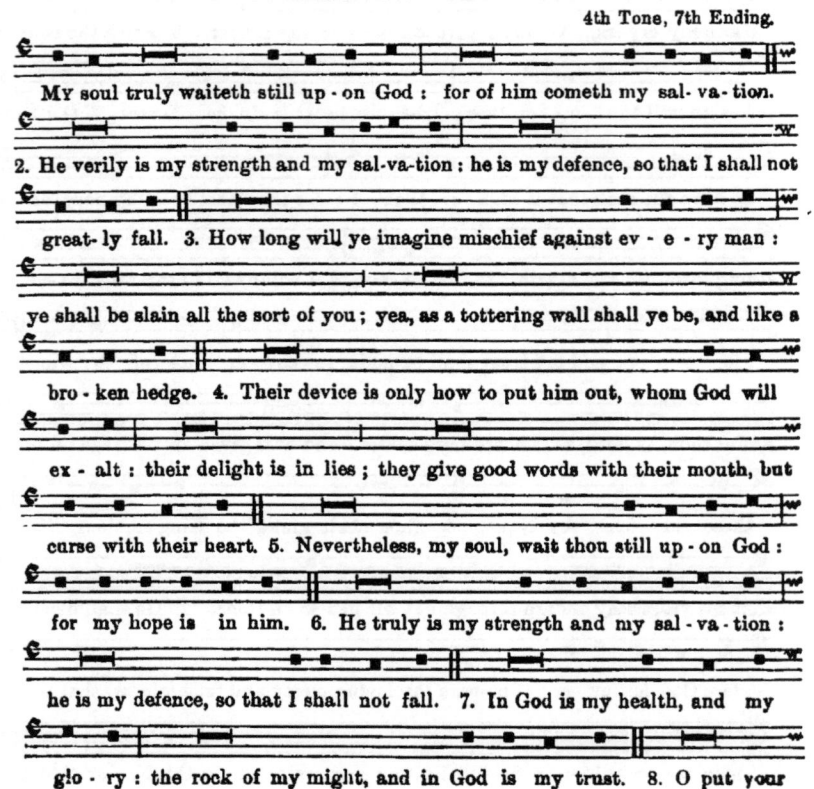

4th Tone, 7th Ending.

My soul truly waiteth still up-on God : for of him cometh my sal-va-tion. 2. He verily is my strength and my sal-va-tion : he is my defence, so that I shall not great-ly fall. 3. How long will ye imagine mischief against ev-e-ry man : ye shall be slain all the sort of you; yea, as a tottering wall shall ye be, and like a bro-ken hedge. 4. Their device is only how to put him out, whom God will ex-alt : their delight is in lies; they give good words with their mouth, but curse with their heart. 5. Nevertheless, my soul, wait thou still up-on God : for my hope is in him. 6. He truly is my strength and my sal-va-tion : he is my defence, so that I shall not fall. 7. In God is my health, and my glo-ry : the rock of my might, and in God is my trust. 8. O put your

MORNING PRAYER. DAY 12

trust in him al-way, ye peo-ple : pour out your hearts before him, for God is our hope. 9. As for the children of men, they are but van-i-ty: the children of men are deceitful upon the weights,* they are altogether lighter than van-i-ty it-self. 10. O trust not in wrong and robbery, give not your-selves un-to van-i-ty: if riches increase, set not your heart up-on them. 11. God spake once, and twice I have al-so heard the same : that power belongeth un-to God. 12. And that thou, Lord, art mer-ci-ful : for thou rewardest every man ac-cord-ing to his work. Glory be to the Father, and to the Son : and to the Ho-ly Ghost ; As it was in the beginning, is now, and ev-er shall be : world with-out end. A-men.

PSALM LXIII.—*Deus, Deus meus.*

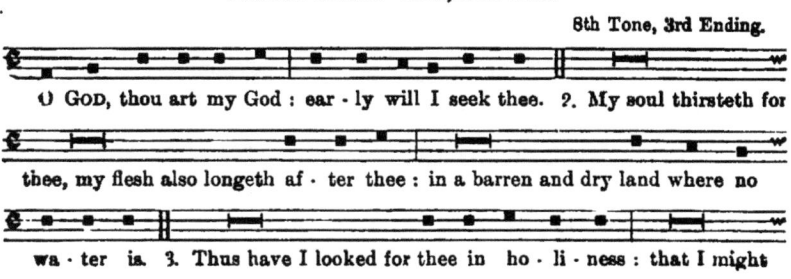

8th Tone, 3rd Ending.

O GOD, thou art my God : ear-ly will I seek thee. 2. My soul thirsteth for thee, my flesh also longeth af-ter thee : in a barren and dry land where no wa-ter is. 3. Thus have I looked for thee in ho-li-ness : that I might

(101)

DAY 12. MORNING PRAYER.

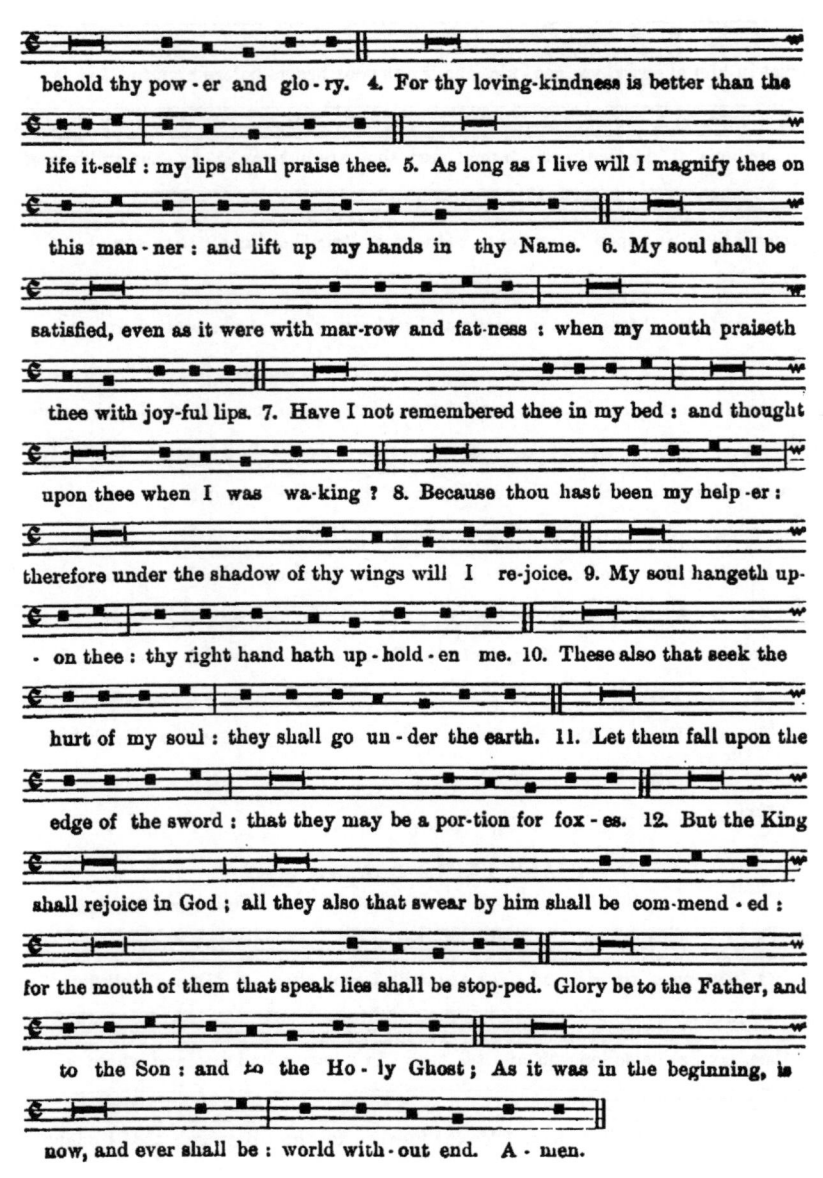

behold thy pow-er and glo-ry. 4. For thy loving-kindness is better than the life it-self : my lips shall praise thee. 5. As long as I live will I magnify thee on this man-ner : and lift up my hands in thy Name. 6. My soul shall be satisfied, even as it were with mar-row and fat-ness : when my mouth praiseth thee with joy-ful lips. 7. Have I not remembered thee in my bed : and thought upon thee when I was wa-king ? 8. Because thou hast been my help-er : therefore under the shadow of thy wings will I re-joice. 9. My soul hangeth up- -on thee : thy right hand hath up-hold-en me. 10. These also that seek the hurt of my soul : they shall go un-der the earth. 11. Let them fall upon the edge of the sword : that they may be a por-tion for fox-es. 12. But the King shall rejoice in God ; all they also that swear by him shall be com-mend-ed : for the mouth of them that speak lies shall be stop-ped. Glory be to the Father, and to the Son : and to the Ho-ly Ghost ; As it was in the beginning, is now, and ever shall be : world with-out end. A-men.

(102)

MORNING PRAYER.

PSALM LXIV.—*Exaudi, Deus.*

2nd Tone, 1st Ending.

HEAR my voice, O God, in my prayer : preserve my life from fear of the en - e - my. 2. Hide me from the gathering together of the fro-ward : and from the insurrection of wick -ed do - ers ; 3. Who have whet their tongue like a sword : and shoot out their arrows, e - ven bit- ter words ; 4. That they may privily shoot at him that is per - fect : suddenly do they hit him, and fear not. 5. They encourage them-selves in mis-chief : and commune among themselves how they may lay snares, and say, that no man shall see them. 6. They imagine wickedness, and prac-tise it : that they keep secret among them-selves, every man in the deep of his heart. 7. But God shall suddenly shoot at them with a swift ar - row : that they shall be wound-ed. 8. Yea, their own tongues shall make them fall : insomuch that whoso seeth them shall laugh them to scorn. 9. And all men that see it shall say, This hath God done : for they shall perceive that it is his work. 10. The righteous shall rejoice in the

DAY 12.   EVENING PRAYER.

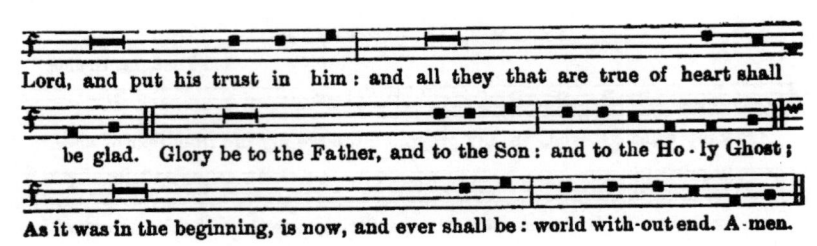

Lord, and put his trust in him : and all they that are true of heart shall be glad. Glory be to the Father, and to the Son : and to the Ho-ly Ghost; As it was in the beginning, is now, and ever shall be : world with-out end. A-men.

EVENING PRAYER.

PSALM LXV.—*Te decet hymnus.*

8th Tone, 1st Ending.

THOU, O God, art prais-ed in Si-on : and unto thee shall the vow be per-form-ed in Je-ru-sa-lem. 2. Thou that hear-est the prayer : un-to thee shall all flesh come. 3. My misdeeds prevail a-gainst me : O be thou mer-ci-ful un-to our sins. 4. Blessed is the man, whom thou choosest, and receivest un-to thee : he shall dwell in thy court, and shall be satisfied with the pleasures of thy house,* even of thy ho-ly tem-ple. 5. Thou shalt shew us wonderful things in thy righteousness, O God of our sal-va-tion : thou that art the hope of all the ends of the earth, and of them that re-main in the broad sea. 6 Who in his strength settest fast the moun-tains : and is gird-ed a-bout with pow-er. 7. Who stilleth the raging of the sea : and the noise of his waves,

(104)

EVENING PRAYER. DAY 12.

and the mad-ness of the peo-ple. 8. They also that dwell in the uttermost parts of the earth shall be afraid at thy to-kens: thou that makest the outgoings of the morning and eve-ning to praise thee. 9. Thou visitest the earth, and bless-est it: thou ma-kest it ve-ry plen-teous. 10. The river of God is full of wa-ter: thou preparest their corn, for so thou pro-vi-dest for the earth. 11. Thou waterest her furrows, thou sendest rain into the little valleys there-of: thou makest it soft with the drops of rain, and bless-est the in--crease of it. 12. Thou crownest the year with thy good-ness: and thy clouds drop fat-ness. 13. They shall drop upon the dwellings of the wil-der-ness: and the little hills shall re-joice on ev-'ry side. 14. The folds shall be full of sheep: the valleys also shall stand so thick with corn, that they shall laugh and sing. Glory be to the Father, and to the Son: and to the Ho-ly Ghost; As it was in the beginning, is now, and ever shall be : world with-out end. A-men.

DAY 12.   EVENING PRAYER.

PSALM LXVI.—*Jubilate Deo.*

1st Tone, 3rd Ending.

O be joy-ful in God, all ye lands : sing praises unto the honour of his Name, make his praise to be glo-ri-ous. 2. Say unto God, O how wonderful art thou in thy works : through the greatness of thy power shall thine enemies be found li-ars un-to thee. 3. For all the world shall wor-ship thee : sing of thee, and praise thy Name. 4. O come hither, and behold the works of God : how wonderful he is in his doing to-ward the chil-dren of men. 5. He turned the sea in-to dry land : so that they went through the water on foot; there did we re-joice there-of. 6. He ruleth with his power for ever; his eyes be-hold the peo-ple : and such as will not believe, shall not be a-ble to ex-alt them-selves. 7. O praise our God, ye peo-ple : and make the voice of his praise to be heard. 8. Who holdeth our soul in life : and suf-fer-eth not our feet to slip. 9. For thou, O God, hast prov-ed us : thou also hast tried us, like as sil-ver is tri-ed. 10. Thou broughtest us in to the snare :

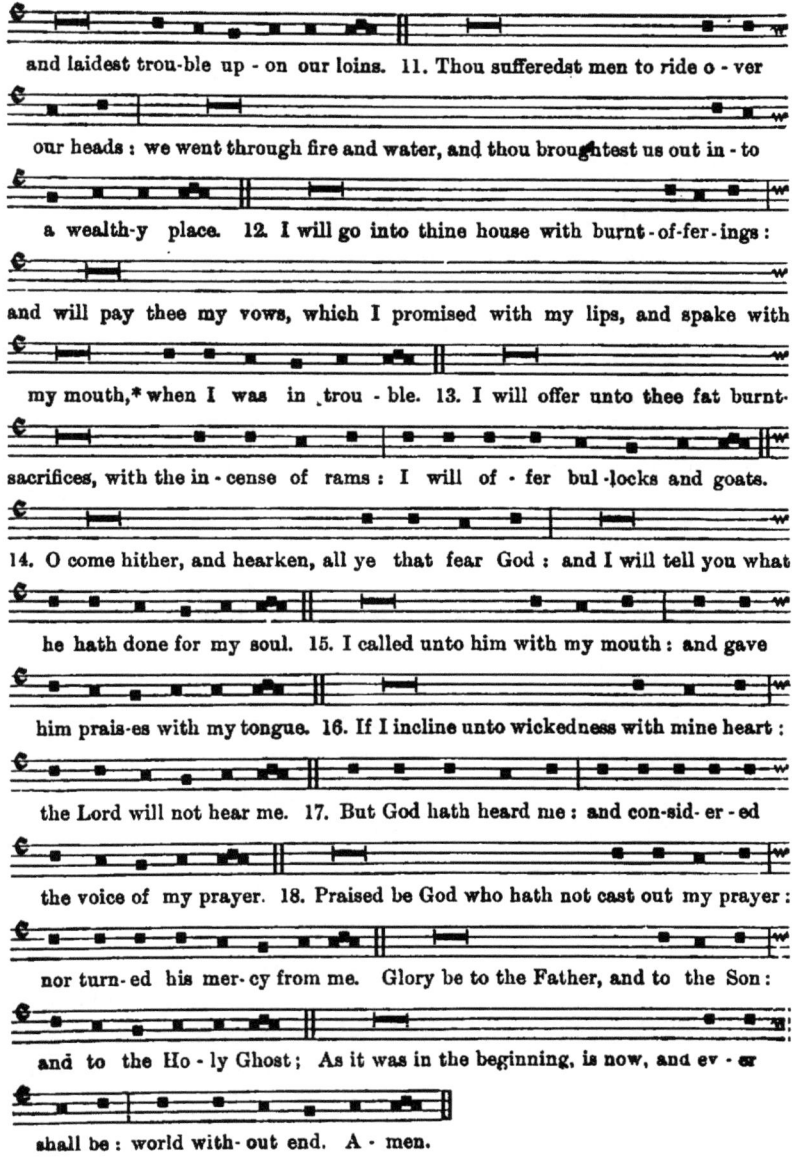

EVENING PRAYER. DAY 12.

and laidest trou-ble up - on our loins. 11. Thou sufferedst men to ride o - ver our heads : we went through fire and water, and thou broughtest us out in - to a wealth-y place. 12. I will go into thine house with burnt-of-fer-ings : and will pay thee my vows, which I promised with my lips, and spake with my mouth,* when I was in trou - ble. 13. I will offer unto thee fat burnt-sacrifices, with the in - cense of rams : I will of - fer bul-locks and goats. 14. O come hither, and hearken, all ye that fear God : and I will tell you what he hath done for my soul. 15. I called unto him with my mouth : and gave him prais-es with my tongue. 16. If I incline unto wickedness with mine heart : the Lord will not hear me. 17. But God hath heard me : and con-sid-er-ed the voice of my prayer. 18. Praised be God who hath not cast out my prayer : nor turn-ed his mer-cy from me. Glory be to the Father, and to the Son : and to the Ho - ly Ghost; As it was in the beginning, is now, and ev - er shall be : world with-out end. A - men.

Day 12.　　　　　EVENING PRAYER.

PSALM LXVII.—*Deus misereatur.*

7th Tone, 2nd Ending.

God be mer-ci-ful un-to us, and bless us : and shew us the light of his countenance, and be mer-ci-ful un-to us ; 2. That thy way may be known up-on earth : thy saving health a-mong all na-tions. 3. Let the peo-ple praise thee, O God : yea, let all the peo-ple praise thee. 4. O let the na-tions re-joice and be glad : for thou shalt judge the folk righteously, and gov-ern the na-tions up-on earth. 5. Let the peo-ple praise thee, O God : let all the peo-ple praise thee. 6. Then shall the earth bring forth her in-crease : and God, even our own God, shall give us his bless-ing. 7. God shall bless us : and all the ends of the world shall fear him. Glo-ry be to the Fath-er, and to the Son : and to the Ho-ly Ghost ; As it was in beginning, is now, and ev-er shall be : world with-out end. A-men.

Day 13.　　　　　MORNING PRAYER.

PSALM LXVIII.—*Exurgat Deus.*

5th Tone, 1st Ending.

Let God arise, and let his enemies be scat-ter-ed : let them also that hate him flee be-fore him　2. Like as the smoke vanisheth, so shalt thou drive them

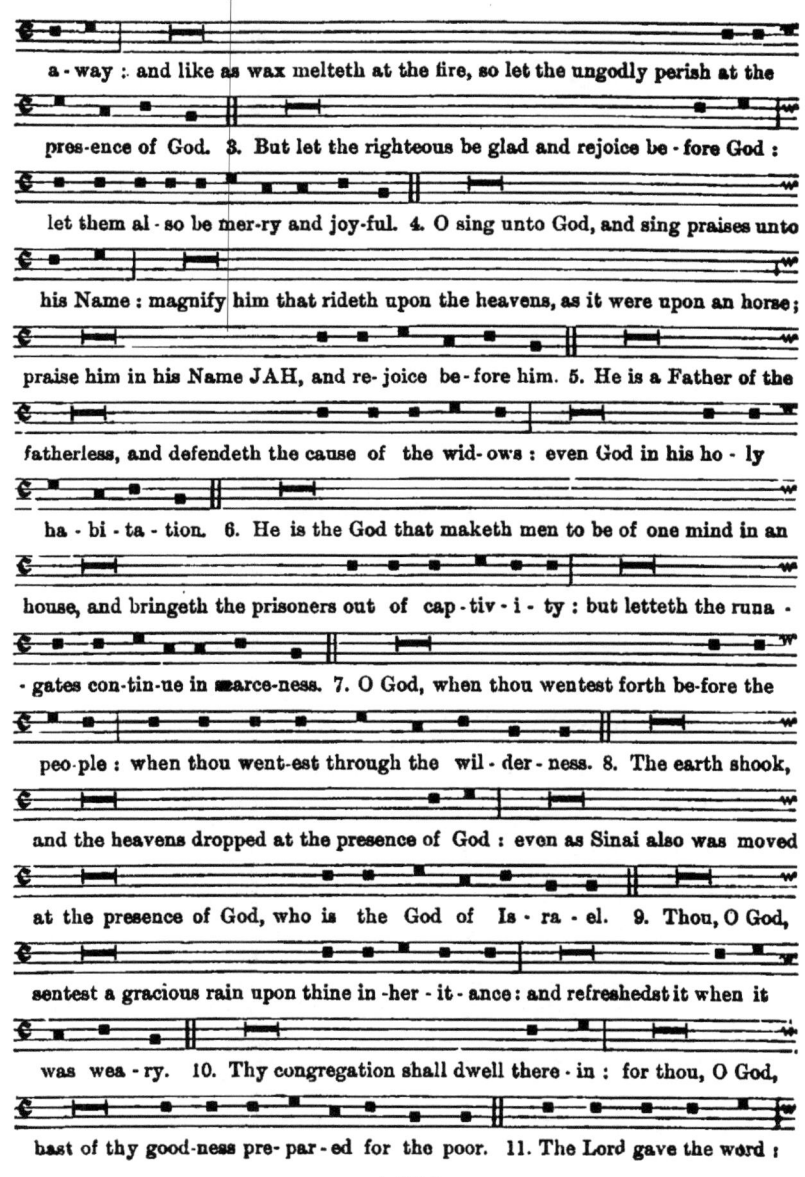

MORNING PRAYER. Day 13.

a-way : and like as wax melteth at the fire, so let the ungodly perish at the pres-ence of God. 3. But let the righteous be glad and rejoice be-fore God : let them al-so be mer-ry and joy-ful. 4. O sing unto God, and sing praises unto his Name : magnify him that rideth upon the heavens, as it were upon an horse; praise him in his Name JAH, and re-joice be-fore him. 5. He is a Father of the fatherless, and defendeth the cause of the wid-ows : even God in his ho-ly ha-bi-ta-tion. 6. He is the God that maketh men to be of one mind in an house, and bringeth the prisoners out of cap-tiv-i-ty : but letteth the runa-gates con-tin-ue in scarce-ness. 7. O God, when thou wentest forth be-fore the peo-ple : when thou went-est through the wil-der-ness. 8. The earth shook, and the heavens dropped at the presence of God : even as Sinai also was moved at the presence of God, who is the God of Is-ra-el. 9. Thou, O God, sentest a gracious rain upon thine in-her-it-ance : and refreshedst it when it was wea-ry. 10. Thy congregation shall dwell there-in : for thou, O God, hast of thy good-ness pre-par-ed for the poor. 11. The Lord gave the word :

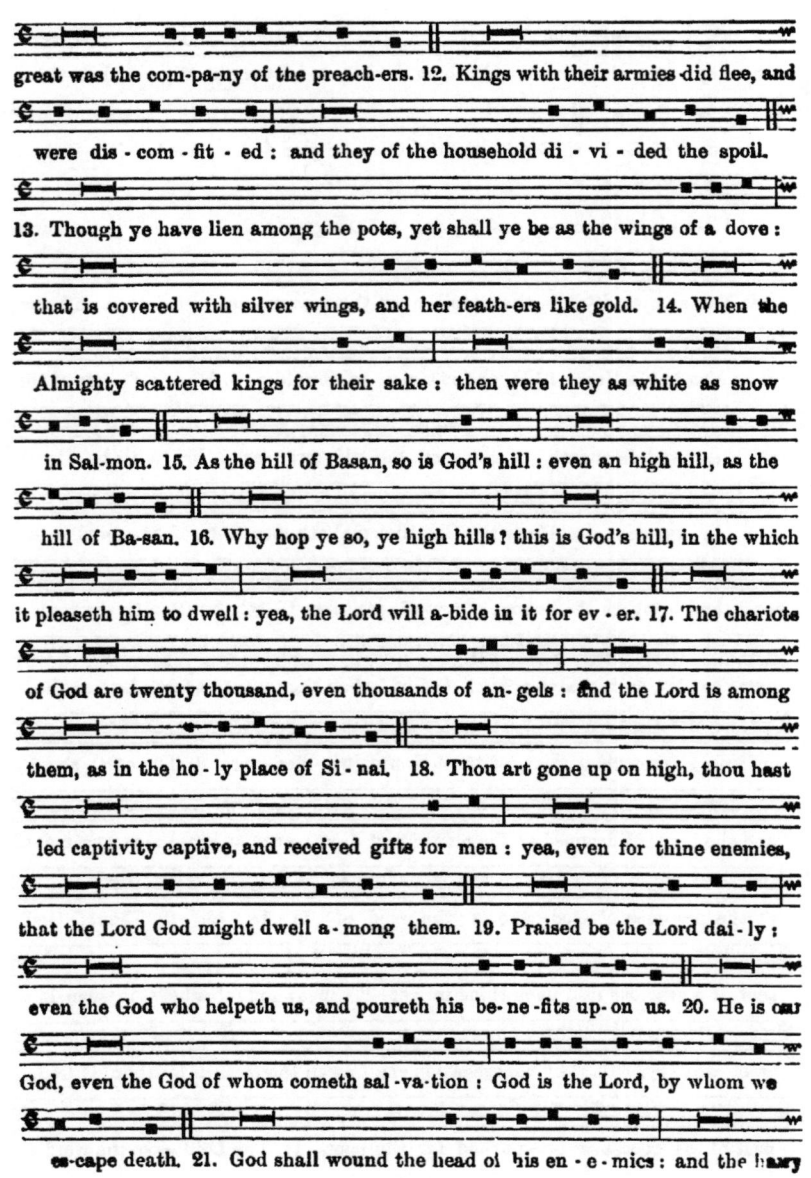

DAY 13. MORNING PRAYER.

great was the com-pa-ny of the preach-ers. 12. Kings with their armies did flee, and were dis-com-fit-ed: and they of the household di-vi-ded the spoil. 13. Though ye have lien among the pots, yet shall ye be as the wings of a dove: that is covered with silver wings, and her feath-ers like gold. 14. When the Almighty scattered kings for their sake: then were they as white as snow in Sal-mon. 15. As the hill of Basan, so is God's hill: even an high hill, as the hill of Ba-san. 16. Why hop ye so, ye high hills? this is God's hill, in the which it pleaseth him to dwell: yea, the Lord will a-bide in it for ev-er. 17. The chariots of God are twenty thousand, even thousands of an-gels: and the Lord is among them, as in the ho-ly place of Si-nai. 18. Thou art gone up on high, thou hast led captivity captive, and received gifts for men: yea, even for thine enemies, that the Lord God might dwell a-mong them. 19. Praised be the Lord dai-ly: even the God who helpeth us, and poureth his be-ne-fits up-on us. 20. He is our God, even the God of whom cometh sal-va-tion: God is the Lord, by whom we es-cape death. 21. God shall wound the head of his en-e-mics: and the hairy

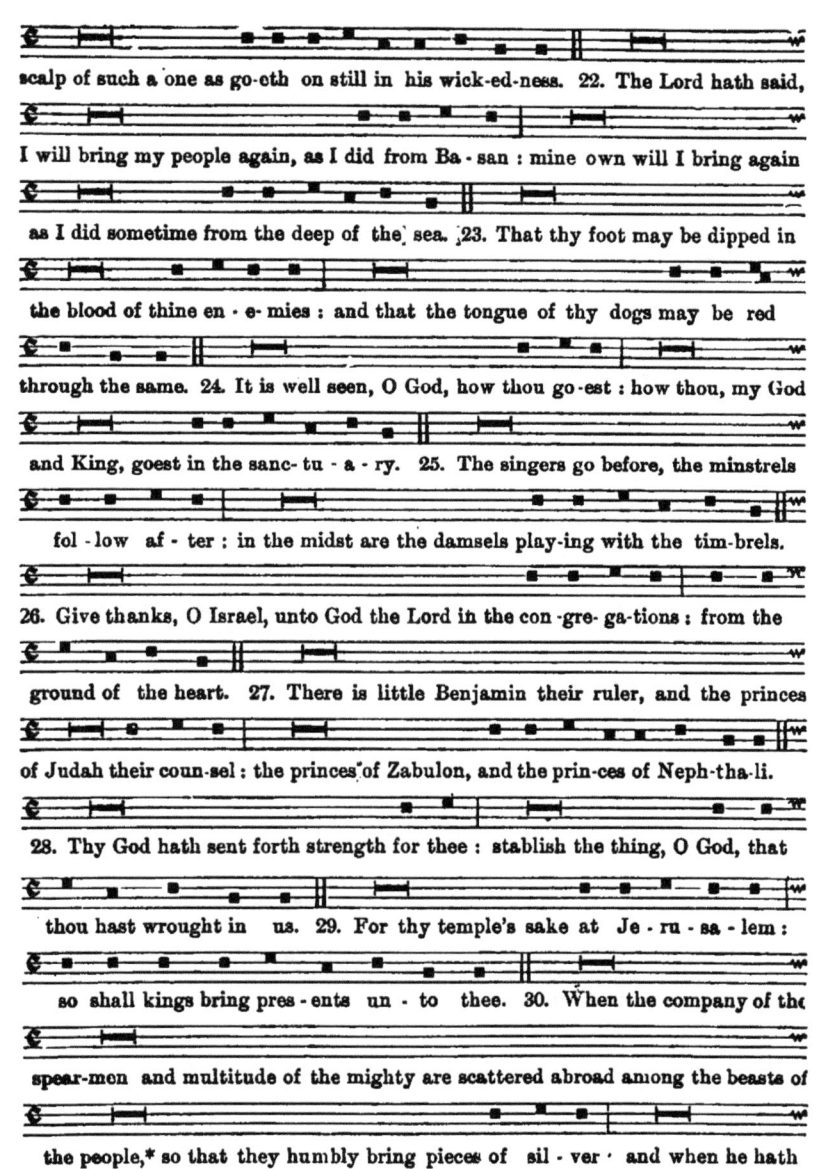

MORNING PRAYER.

scalp of such a one as goeth on still in his wickedness. 22. The Lord hath said, I will bring my people again, as I did from Ba-san : mine own will I bring again as I did sometime from the deep of the sea. 23. That thy foot may be dipped in the blood of thine en-e-mies : and that the tongue of thy dogs may be red through the same. 24. It is well seen, O God, how thou goest : how thou, my God and King, goest in the sanc-tu-a-ry. 25. The singers go before, the minstrels fol-low af-ter : in the midst are the damsels play-ing with the tim-brels. 26. Give thanks, O Israel, unto God the Lord in the con-gre-ga-tions : from the ground of the heart. 27. There is little Benjamin their ruler, and the princes of Judah their coun-sel : the princes of Zabulon, and the prin-ces of Neph-tha-li. 28. Thy God hath sent forth strength for thee : stablish the thing, O God, that thou hast wrought in us. 29. For thy temple's sake at Je-ru-sa-lem : so shall kings bring pres-ents un-to thee. 30. When the company of the spear-men and multitude of the mighty are scattered abroad among the beasts of the people,* so that they humbly bring pieces of sil-ver · and when he hath

(111)

DAY 13. EVENING PRAYER.

scattered the peo-ple that de-light in war ; 31. Then shall the princes come out of E-gypt : the Morians' land shall soon stretch out her hands un - to God.

32. Sing unto God, O ye kingdoms of the earth : O sing prais-es un-to the Lord ;

33. Who sitteth in the heavens over all from the be-gin-ning : lo, he doth send out his voice, yea, and that a might-y voice. 34. Ascribe ye the power to God o - ver Is - ra - el : his wor-ship and strength is in the clouds. 35. O God, wonderful art thou in thy ho - ly pla-ces : even the God of Israel ; he will give strength and power unto his people ; bless-ed be God. Glory be to the Father, and to the Son : and to the Ho - ly Ghost ; As it was in the beginning, is now and ever shall be : world with-out end. A - men.

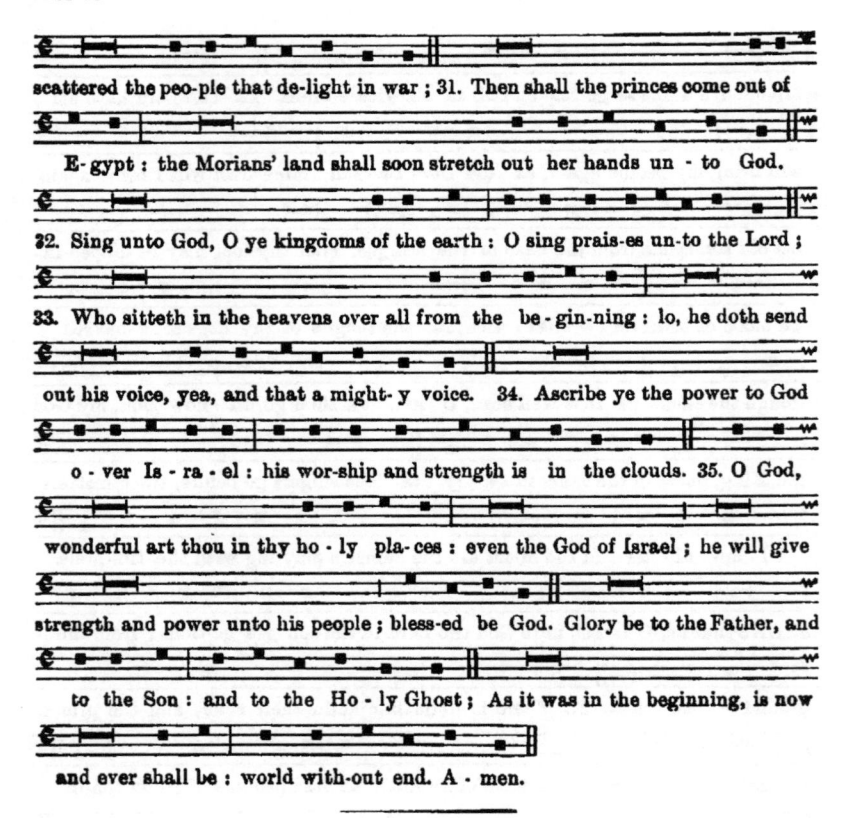

EVENING PRAYER.

PSALM LXIX.—*Salvum me fac.*

4th Tone, 4th Ending.

SAVE me, O God : for the waters are come in, e - ven un - to my soul.

2. I stick fast in the deep mire, where no ground is : I am come into deep waters, so that the floods run o-ver me. 3. I am weary of crying, my throat is dry :

(112)

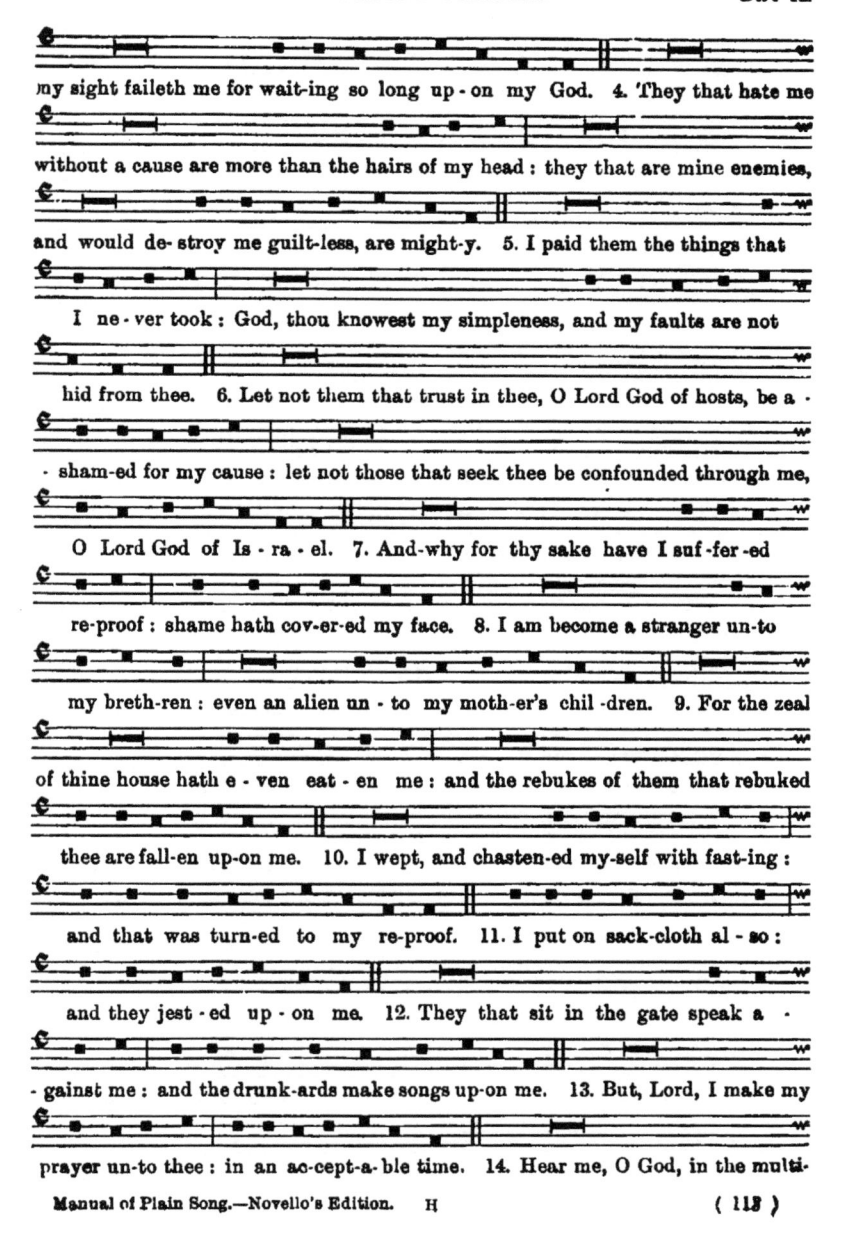

EVENING PRAYER.

my sight faileth me for wait-ing so long up-on my God. 4. They that hate me without a cause are more than the hairs of my head: they that are mine enemies, and would de-stroy me guilt-less, are might-y. 5. I paid them the things that I ne-ver took: God, thou knowest my simpleness, and my faults are not hid from thee. 6. Let not them that trust in thee, O Lord God of hosts, be a-sham-ed for my cause: let not those that seek thee be confounded through me, O Lord God of Is-ra-el. 7. And why for thy sake have I suf-fer-ed re-proof: shame hath cov-er-ed my face. 8. I am become a stranger un-to my breth-ren: even an alien un-to my moth-er's chil-dren. 9. For the zeal of thine house hath e-ven eat-en me: and the rebukes of them that rebuked thee are fall-en up-on me. 10. I wept, and chasten-ed my-self with fast-ing: and that was turn-ed to my re-proof. 11. I put on sack-cloth al-so: and they jest-ed up-on me. 12. They that sit in the gate speak a-gainst me: and the drunk-ards make songs up-on me. 13. But, Lord, I make my prayer un-to thee: in an ac-cept-a-ble time. 14. Hear me, O God, in the multi-

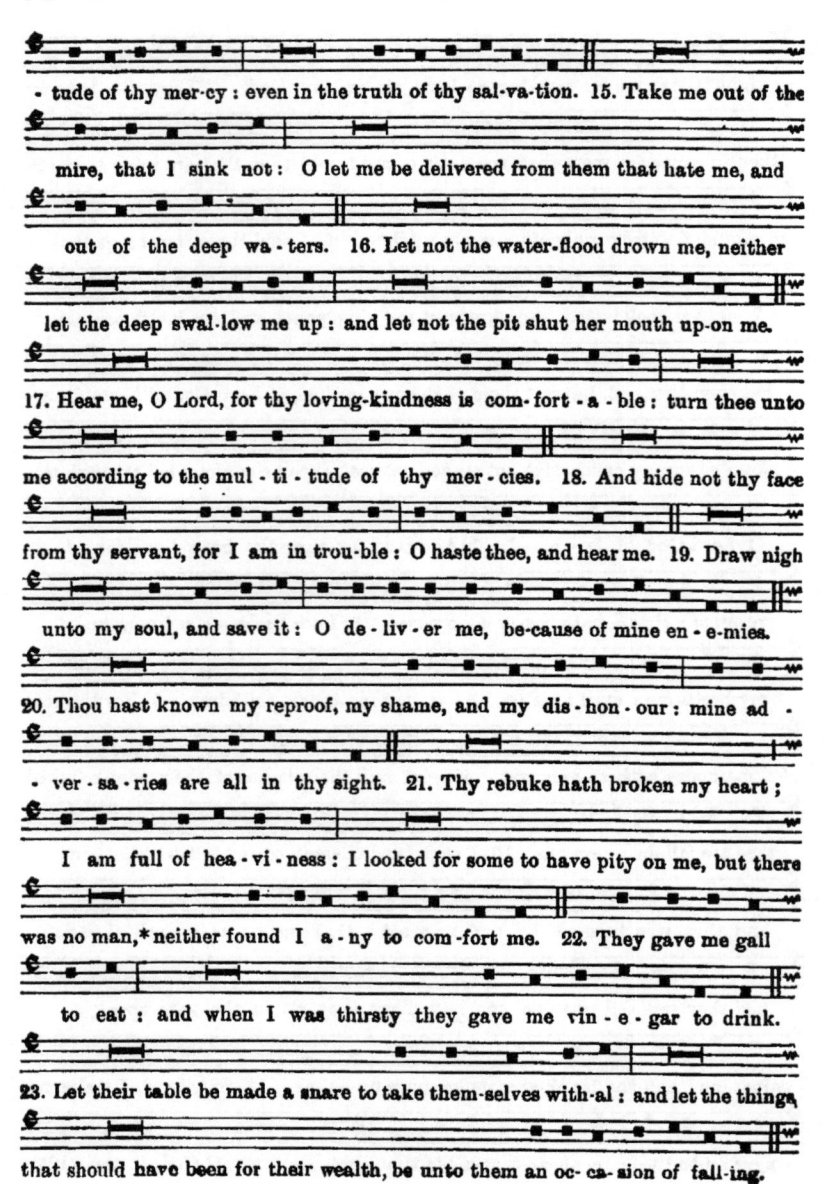

DAY 13. EVENING PRAYER.

- tude of thy mer-cy : even in the truth of thy sal-va-tion. 15. Take me out of the mire, that I sink not : O let me be delivered from them that hate me, and out of the deep wa-ters. 16. Let not the water-flood drown me, neither let the deep swal-low me up : and let not the pit shut her mouth up-on me. 17. Hear me, O Lord, for thy loving-kindness is com-fort-a-ble : turn thee unto me according to the mul-ti-tude of thy mer-cies. 18. And hide not thy face from thy servant, for I am in trou-ble : O haste thee, and hear me. 19. Draw nigh unto my soul, and save it : O de-liv-er me, be-cause of mine en-e-mies. 20. Thou hast known my reproof, my shame, and my dis-hon-our : mine ad-ver-sa-ries are all in thy sight. 21. Thy rebuke hath broken my heart ; I am full of hea-vi-ness : I looked for some to have pity on me, but there was no man,* neither found I a-ny to com-fort me. 22. They gave me gall to eat : and when I was thirsty they gave me vin-e-gar to drink. 23. Let their table be made a snare to take them-selves with-al : and let the things that should have been for their wealth, be unto them an oc-ca-sion of fall-ing.

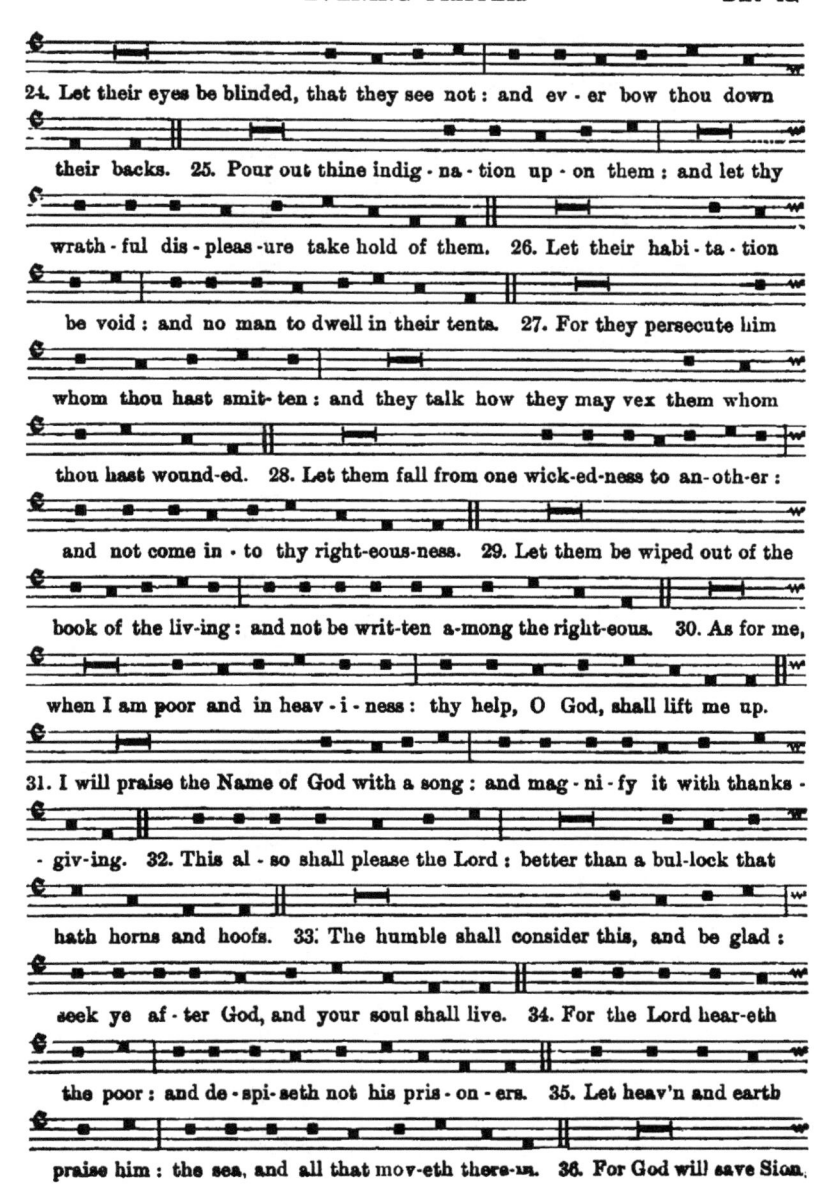

EVENING PRAYER. DAY 12.

24. Let their eyes be blinded, that they see not : and ev-er bow thou down their backs. 25. Pour out thine indig-na-tion up-on them : and let thy wrath-ful dis-pleas-ure take hold of them. 26. Let their habi-ta-tion be void : and no man to dwell in their tents. 27. For they persecute him whom thou hast smit-ten : and they talk how they may vex them whom thou hast wound-ed. 28. Let them fall from one wick-ed-ness to an-oth-er : and not come in-to thy right-eous-ness. 29. Let them be wiped out of the book of the liv-ing : and not be writ-ten a-mong the right-eous. 30. As for me, when I am poor and in heav-i-ness : thy help, O God, shall lift me up. 31. I will praise the Name of God with a song : and mag-ni-fy it with thanks--giv-ing. 32. This al-so shall please the Lord : better than a bul-lock that hath horns and hoofs. 33. The humble shall consider this, and be glad : seek ye af-ter God, and your soul shall live. 34. For the Lord hear-eth the poor : and de-spi-seth not his pris-on-ers. 35. Let heav'n and earth praise him : the sea, and all that mov-eth there-in. 36. For God will save Sion,

(115)

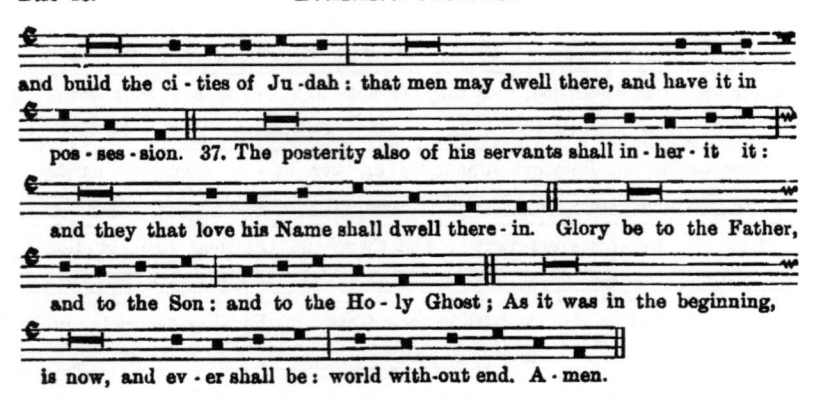

DAY 13. EVENING PRAYER.

and build the ci - ties of Ju -dah : that men may dwell there, and have it in pos - ses - sion. 37. The posterity also of his servants shall in - her - it it : and they that love his Name shall dwell there - in. Glory be to the Father, and to the Son : and to the Ho - ly Ghost ; As it was in the beginning, is now, and ev - er shall be : world with-out end. A - men.

PSALM LXX.—*Deus in adjutorium.*

2nd Tone, 1st Ending.

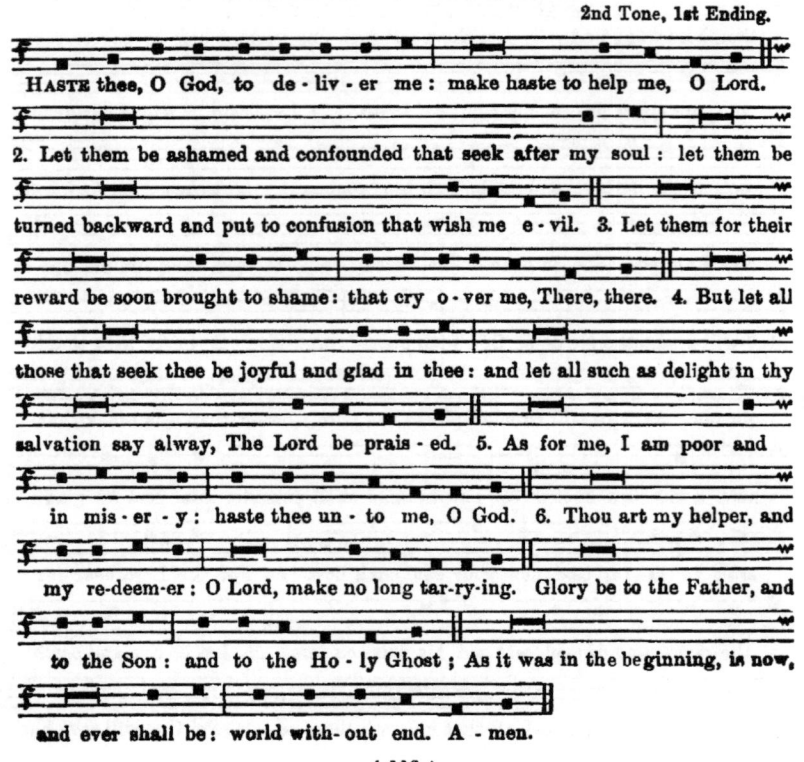

HASTE thee, O God, to de - liv - er me : make haste to help me, O Lord. 2. Let them be ashamed and confounded that seek after my soul : let them be turned backward and put to confusion that wish me e - vil. 3. Let them for their reward be soon brought to shame : that cry o - ver me, There, there. 4. But let all those that seek thee be joyful and glad in thee : and let all such as delight in thy salvation say alway, The Lord be prais - ed. 5. As for me, I am poor and in mis - er - y : haste thee un - to me, O God. 6. Thou art my helper, and my re-deem-er : O Lord, make no long tar-ry-ing. Glory be to the Father, and to the Son : and to the Ho - ly Ghost ; As it was in the beginning, is now, and ever shall be : world with- out end. A - men.

MORNING PRAYER.   Day 14.

PSALM LXXI.—*In te, Domine, speravi.*

3rd Tone, 2nd Ending.

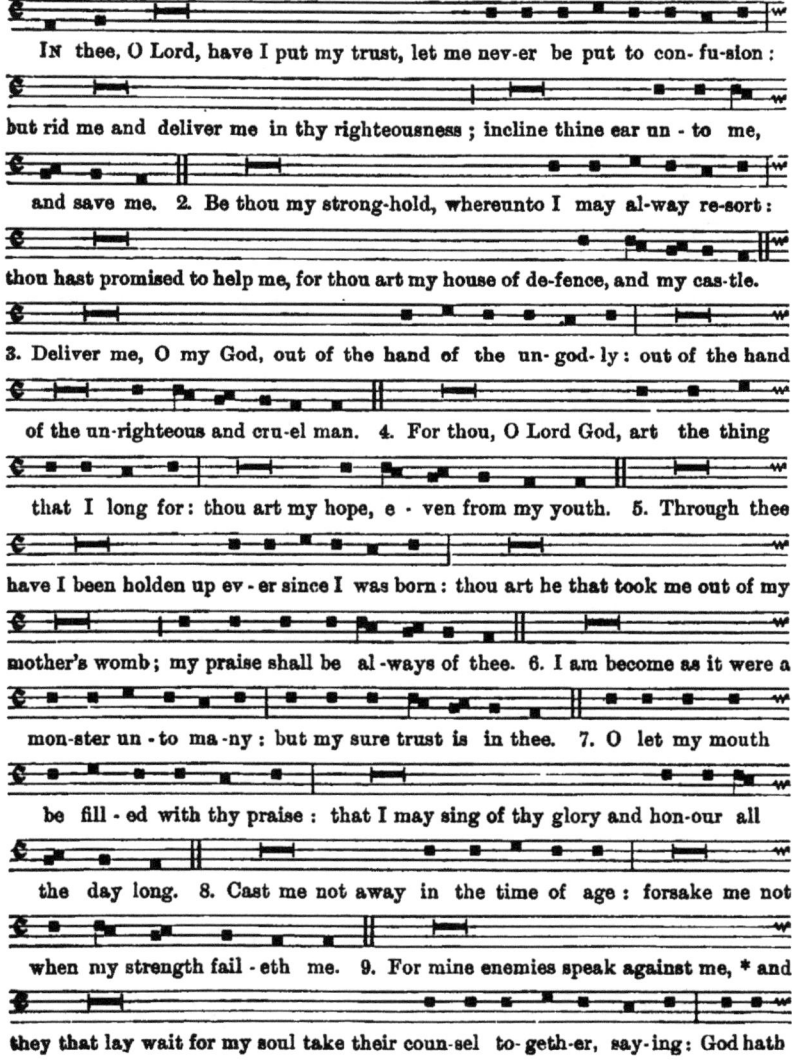

In thee, O Lord, have I put my trust, let me nev-er be put to con-fu-sion:

but rid me and deliver me in thy righteousness; incline thine ear un - to me,

and save me. 2. Be thou my strong-hold, whereunto I may al-way re-sort:

thou hast promised to help me, for thou art my house of de-fence, and my cas-tle.

3. Deliver me, O my God, out of the hand of the un-god-ly: out of the hand

of the un-righteous and cru-el man. 4. For thou, O Lord God, art the thing

that I long for: thou art my hope, e - ven from my youth. 5. Through thee

have I been holden up ev - er since I was born: thou art he that took me out of my

mother's womb; my praise shall be al-ways of thee. 6. I am become as it were a

mon-ster un - to ma-ny: but my sure trust is in thee. 7. O let my mouth

be fill - ed with thy praise: that I may sing of thy glory and hon-our all

the day long. 8. Cast me not away in the time of age: forsake me not

when my strength fail - eth me. 9. For mine enemies speak against me, * and

they that lay wait for my soul take their coun-sel to-geth-er, say-ing: God hath

DAY 14. MORNING PRAYER.

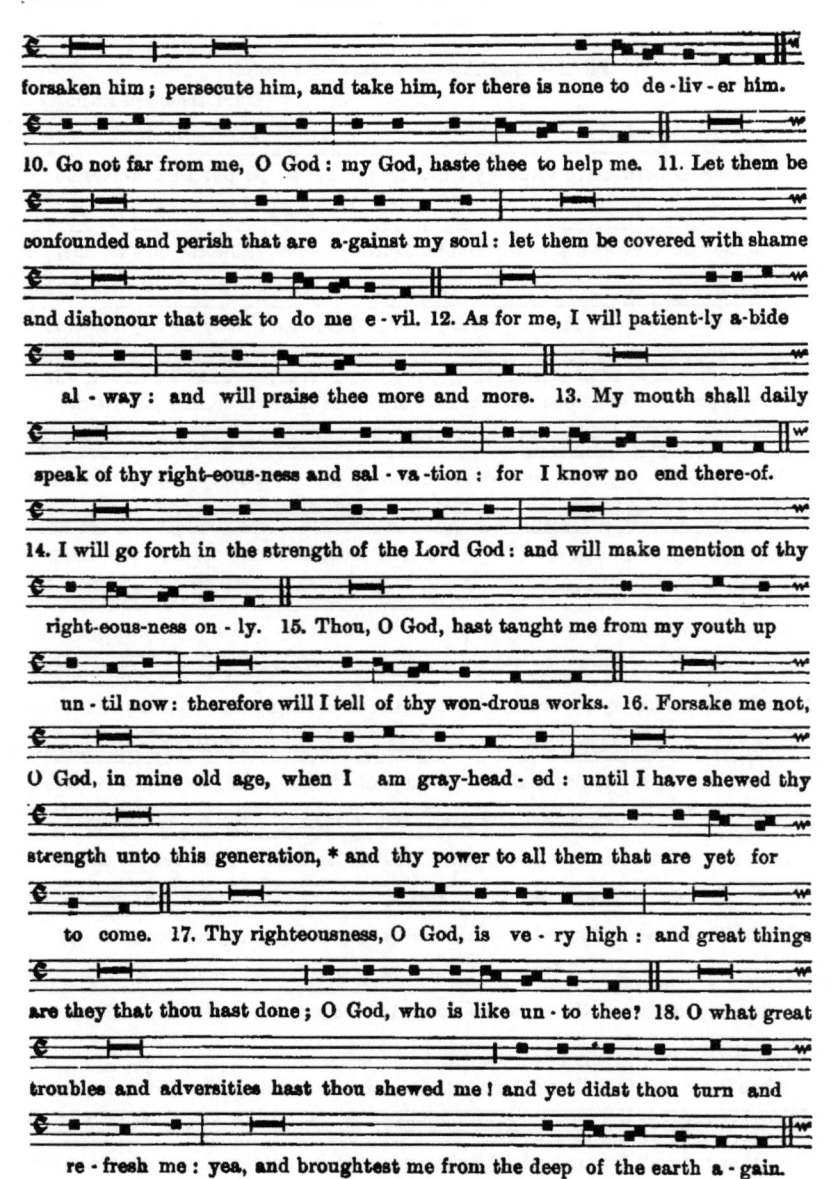

forsaken him; persecute him, and take him, for there is none to de-liv-er him. 10. Go not far from me, O God: my God, haste thee to help me. 11. Let them be confounded and perish that are a-gainst my soul: let them be covered with shame and dishonour that seek to do me e-vil. 12. As for me, I will patient-ly a-bide al-way: and will praise thee more and more. 13. My mouth shall daily speak of thy right-eous-ness and sal-va-tion: for I know no end there-of. 14. I will go forth in the strength of the Lord God: and will make mention of thy right-eous-ness on-ly. 15. Thou, O God, hast taught me from my youth up un-til now: therefore will I tell of thy won-drous works. 16. Forsake me not, O God, in mine old age, when I am gray-head-ed: until I have shewed thy strength unto this generation, * and thy power to all them that are yet for to come. 17. Thy righteousness, O God, is ve-ry high: and great things are they that thou hast done; O God, who is like un-to thee? 18. O what great troubles and adversities hast thou shewed me! and yet didst thou turn and re-fresh me: yea, and broughtest me from the deep of the earth a-gain.

(118)

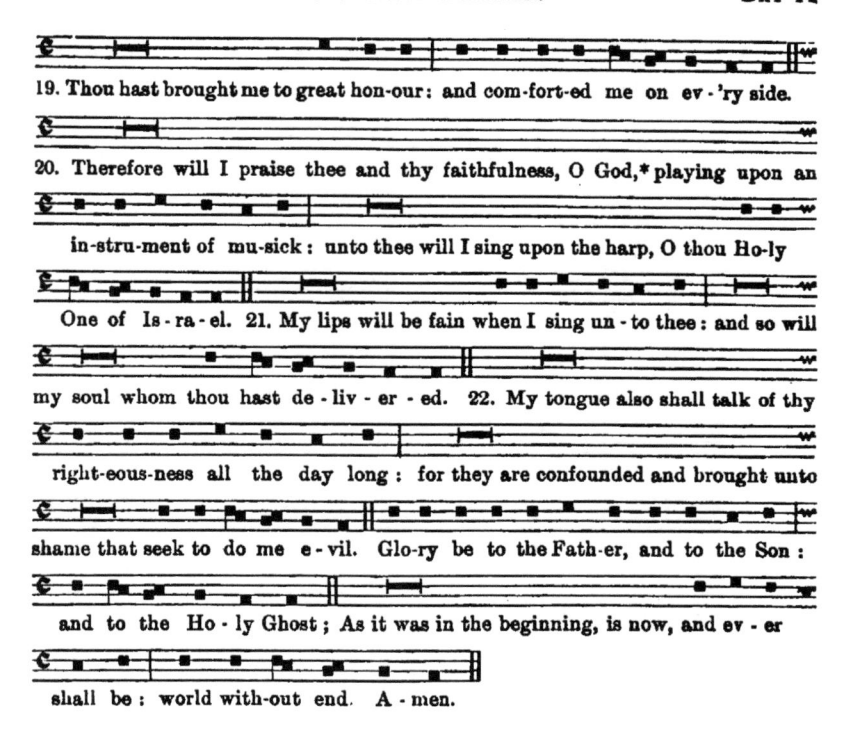

19. Thou hast brought me to great hon-our: and com-fort-ed me on ev-'ry side.

20. Therefore will I praise thee and thy faithfulness, O God,* playing upon an in-stru-ment of mu-sick: unto thee will I sing upon the harp, O thou Ho-ly One of Is-ra-el. 21. My lips will be fain when I sing un-to thee: and so will my soul whom thou hast de-liv-er-ed. 22. My tongue also shall talk of thy right-eous-ness all the day long: for they are confounded and brought unto shame that seek to do me e-vil. Glo-ry be to the Fath-er, and to the Son: and to the Ho-ly Ghost; As it was in the beginning, is now, and ev-er shall be: world with-out end. A-men.

PSALM LXXII.—*Deus, judicium.*

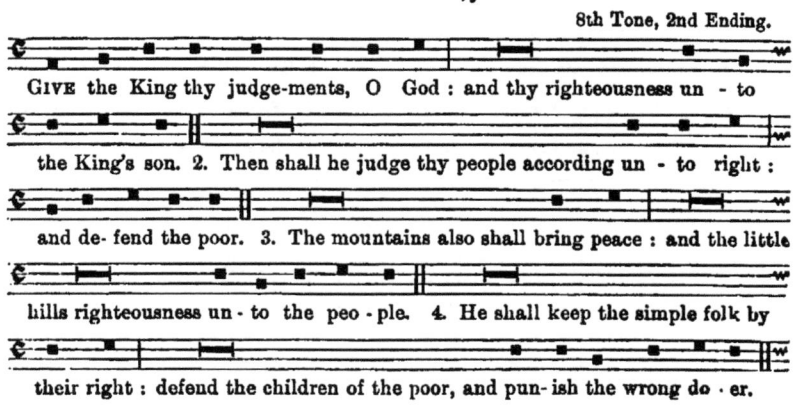

8th Tone, 2nd Ending.

GIVE the King thy judge-ments, O God: and thy righteousness un-to the King's son. 2. Then shall he judge thy people according un-to right: and de-fend the poor. 3. The mountains also shall bring peace: and the little hills righteousness un-to the peo-ple. 4. He shall keep the simple folk by their right: defend the children of the poor, and pun-ish the wrong do-er.

(119)

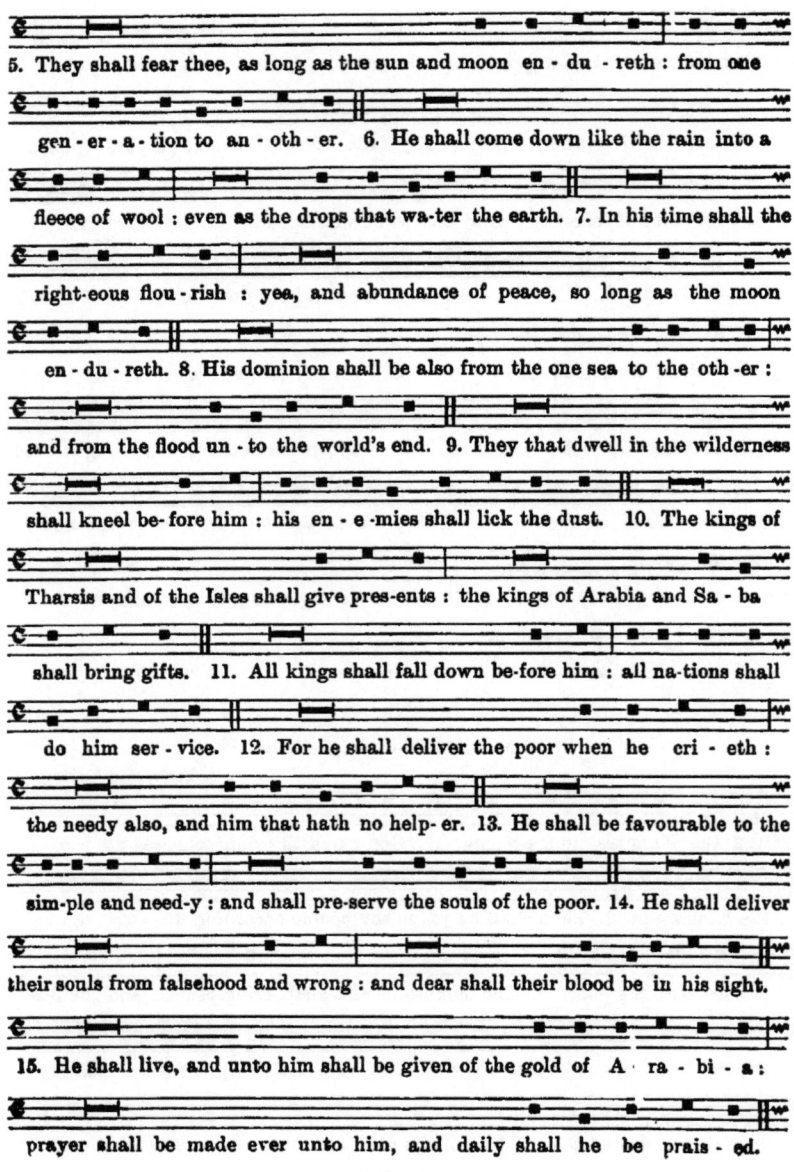

Day 14.   MORNING PRAYER.

5. They shall fear thee, as long as the sun and moon en-du-reth : from one gen-er-a-tion to an-oth-er. 6. He shall come down like the rain into a fleece of wool : even as the drops that wa-ter the earth. 7. In his time shall the right-eous flou-rish : yea, and abundance of peace, so long as the moon en-du-reth. 8. His dominion shall be also from the one sea to the oth-er : and from the flood un-to the world's end. 9. They that dwell in the wilderness shall kneel be-fore him : his en-e-mies shall lick the dust. 10. The kings of Tharsis and of the Isles shall give pres-ents : the kings of Arabia and Sa-ba shall bring gifts. 11. All kings shall fall down be-fore him : all na-tions shall do him ser-vice. 12. For he shall deliver the poor when he cri-eth : the needy also, and him that hath no help-er. 13. He shall be favourable to the sim-ple and need-y : and shall pre-serve the souls of the poor. 14. He shall deliver their souls from falsehood and wrong : and dear shall their blood be in his sight.

15. He shall live, and unto him shall be given of the gold of A-ra-bi-a : prayer shall be made ever unto him, and daily shall he be prais-ed.

EVENING PRAYER. DAY 14.

16. There shall be an heap of corn in the earth, high up-on the hills: his fruit shall shake like Libanus, and shall be green in the city like grass up-on the earth. 17. His Name shall endure for ever; his Name shall remain under the sun among the pos-ter-i-ties: which shall be blessed through him; and all the heath-en shall praise him. 18. Blessed be the Lord God, even the God of Is-ra-el: which on-ly do-eth won-drous things. 19. And blessed be the name of his majesty for ev-er: and all the earth shall be filled with his ma-jes-ty. A-men, A-men. Glory be to the Father, and to the Son: and to the Ho-ly Ghost; As it was in the beginning, is now, and ever shall be: world with-out end. A-men.

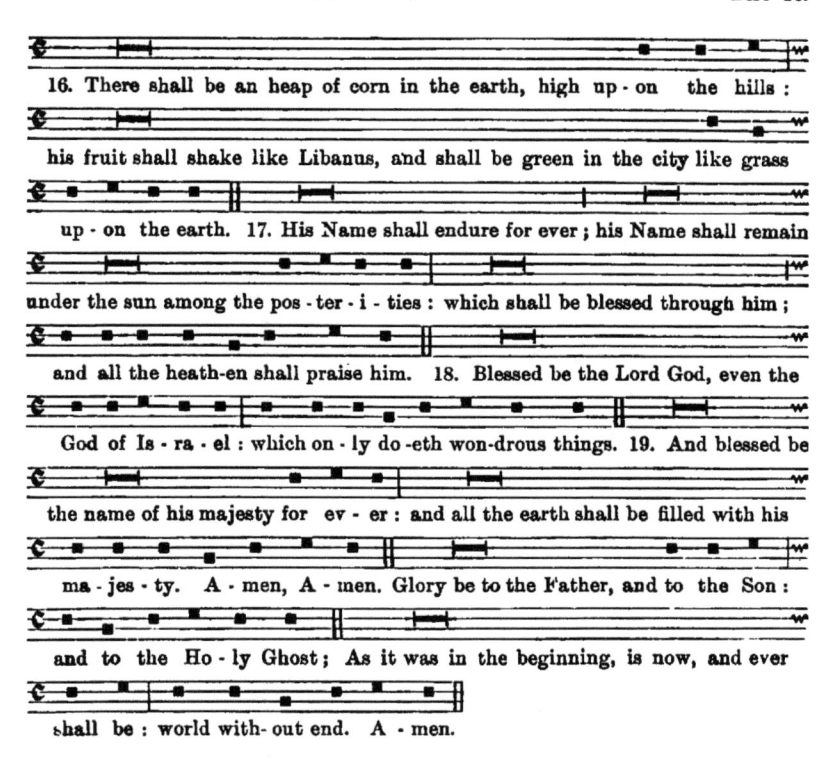

EVENING PRAYER.

PSALM LXXIII.—*Quam bonus Israel.*

1st Tone, 4th Ending.

TRU-LY God is loving unto Is-ra-el: even unto such as are of a clean heart.

2. Nevertheless, my feet were al-most gone: my tread-ings had well-nigh slipt.

3. And-why I was grieved at the wick-ed: I do also see the un-god-ly in such

(121)

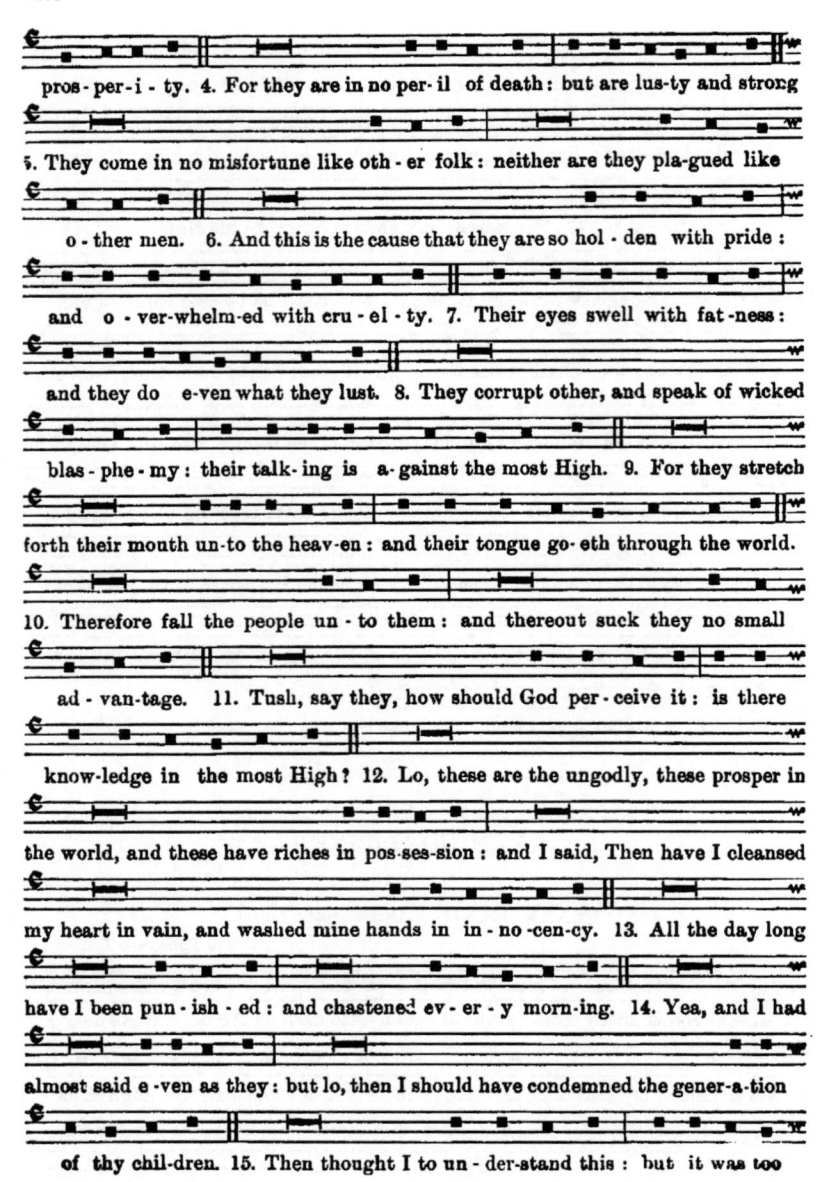

pros-per-i-ty. 4. For they are in no per-il of death: but are lus-ty and strong 5. They come in no misfortune like oth-er folk: neither are they pla-gued like o-ther men. 6. And this is the cause that they are so hol-den with pride: and o-ver-whelm-ed with cru-el-ty. 7. Their eyes swell with fat-ness: and they do e-ven what they lust. 8. They corrupt other, and speak of wicked blas-phe-my: their talk-ing is a-gainst the most High. 9. For they stretch forth their mouth un-to the heav-en: and their tongue go-eth through the world. 10. Therefore fall the people un-to them: and thereout suck they no small ad-van-tage. 11. Tush, say they, how should God per-ceive it: is there know-ledge in the most High? 12. Lo, these are the ungodly, these prosper in the world, and these have riches in pos-ses-sion: and I said, Then have I cleansed my heart in vain, and washed mine hands in in-no-cen-cy. 13. All the day long have I been pun-ish-ed: and chastened ev-er-y morn-ing. 14. Yea, and I had almost said e-ven as they: but lo, then I should have condemned the gener-a-tion of thy chil-dren. 15. Then thought I to un-der-stand this: but it was too

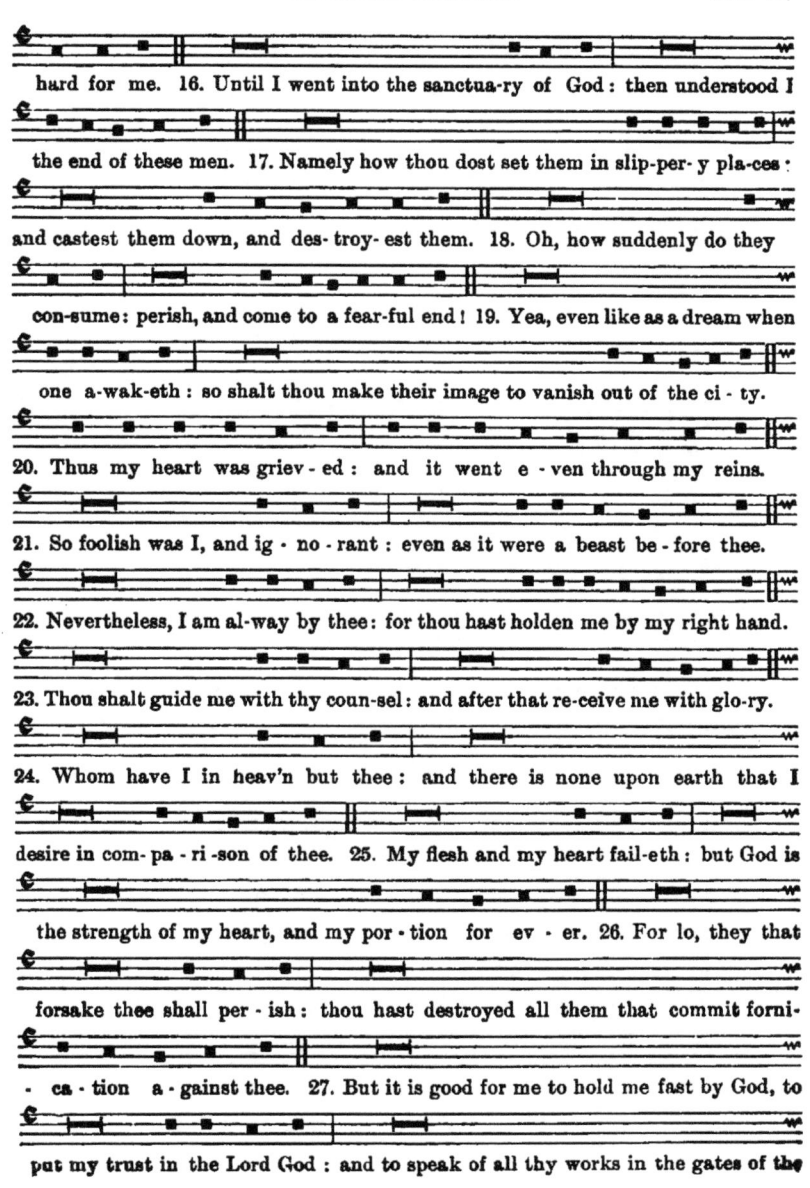

EVENING PRAYER. DAY 14.

hard for me. 16. Until I went into the sanctua-ry of God: then understood I the end of these men. 17. Namely how thou dost set them in slip-per-y pla-ces: and castest them down, and des-troy-est them. 18. Oh, how suddenly do they con-sume: perish, and come to a fear-ful end! 19. Yea, even like as a dream when one a-wak-eth: so shalt thou make their image to vanish out of the ci-ty. 20. Thus my heart was griev-ed: and it went e-ven through my reins. 21. So foolish was I, and ig-no-rant: even as it were a beast be-fore thee. 22. Nevertheless, I am al-way by thee: for thou hast holden me by my right hand. 23. Thou shalt guide me with thy coun-sel: and after that re-ceive me with glo-ry. 24. Whom have I in heav'n but thee: and there is none upon earth that I desire in com-pa-ri-son of thee. 25. My flesh and my heart fail-eth: but God is the strength of my heart, and my por-tion for ev-er. 26. For lo, they that forsake thee shall per-ish: thou hast destroyed all them that commit forni- -ca-tion a-gainst thee. 27. But it is good for me to hold me fast by God, to put my trust in the Lord God: and to speak of all thy works in the gates of the

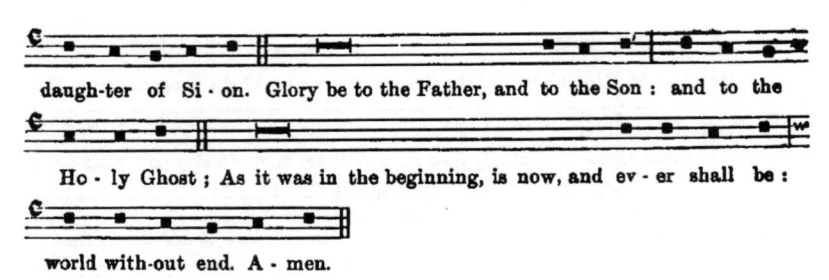

DAY 14. EVENING PRAYER.

daugh-ter of Si-on. Glory be to the Father, and to the Son : and to the

Ho-ly Ghost ; As it was in the beginning, is now, and ev-er shall be :

world with-out end. A-men.

PSALM LXXIV.—*Ut quid, Deus?*

7th Tone, 7th Ending.

O GOD, where-fore art thou ab-sent from us so long : why is thy wrath so hot a-gainst the sheep of thy pas-ture ? 2. O think up-on thy con-gre-ga-tion : whom thou hast purchased, and re-deem-ed of old. 3. Think upon the tribe of thine in-her-it-ance : and mount Sion, where-in thou hast dwelt. 4. Lift up thy feet, that thou mayest utterly de-stroy ev-er-y en-e-my : which hath done evil in thy sanc-tu-a-ry. 5. Thine adversaries roar in the midst of thy con-gre-ga-tions : and set up their ban-ners for to-kens. 6. He that hewed timber a-fore out of the thick trees : was known to bring it to an ex-cel-lent work. 7. But now they break down all the car-ved work there-of : with ax-es and ham-mers.

(124)

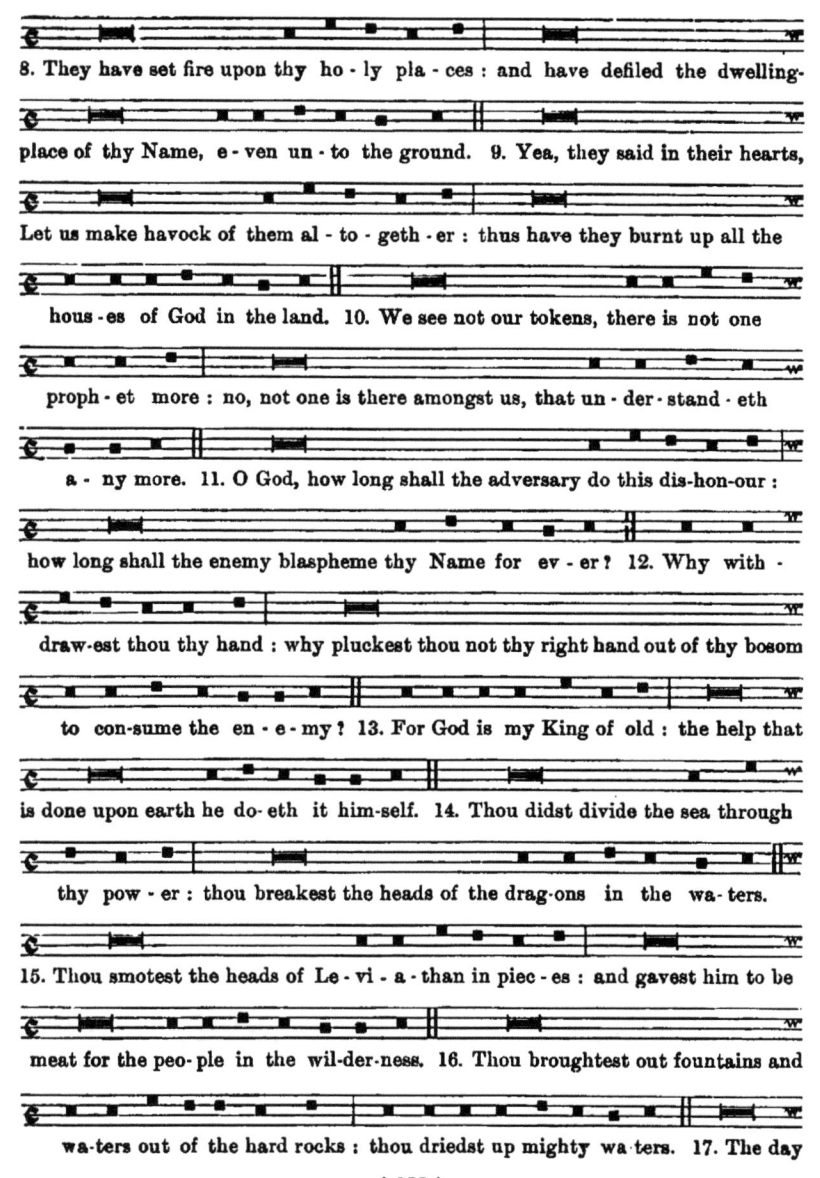

EVENING PRAYER. DAY 14.

8. They have set fire upon thy ho - ly pla - ces : and have defiled the dwelling-place of thy Name, e - ven un - to the ground. 9. Yea, they said in their hearts, Let us make havock of them al - to - geth - er : thus have they burnt up all the hous - es of God in the land. 10. We see not our tokens, there is not one proph - et more : no, not one is there amongst us, that un - der - stand - eth a - ny more. 11. O God, how long shall the adversary do this dis-hon-our : how long shall the enemy blaspheme thy Name for ev - er? 12. Why with - draw-est thou thy hand : why pluckest thou not thy right hand out of thy bosom to con-sume the en - e - my? 13. For God is my King of old : the help that is done upon earth he do-eth it him-self. 14. Thou didst divide the sea through thy pow - er : thou breakest the heads of the drag-ons in the wa- ters. 15. Thou smotest the heads of Le - vi - a - than in piec - es : and gavest him to be meat for the peo- ple in the wil-der-ness. 16. Thou broughtest out fountains and wa-ters out of the hard rocks : thou driedst up mighty wa-ters. 17. The day

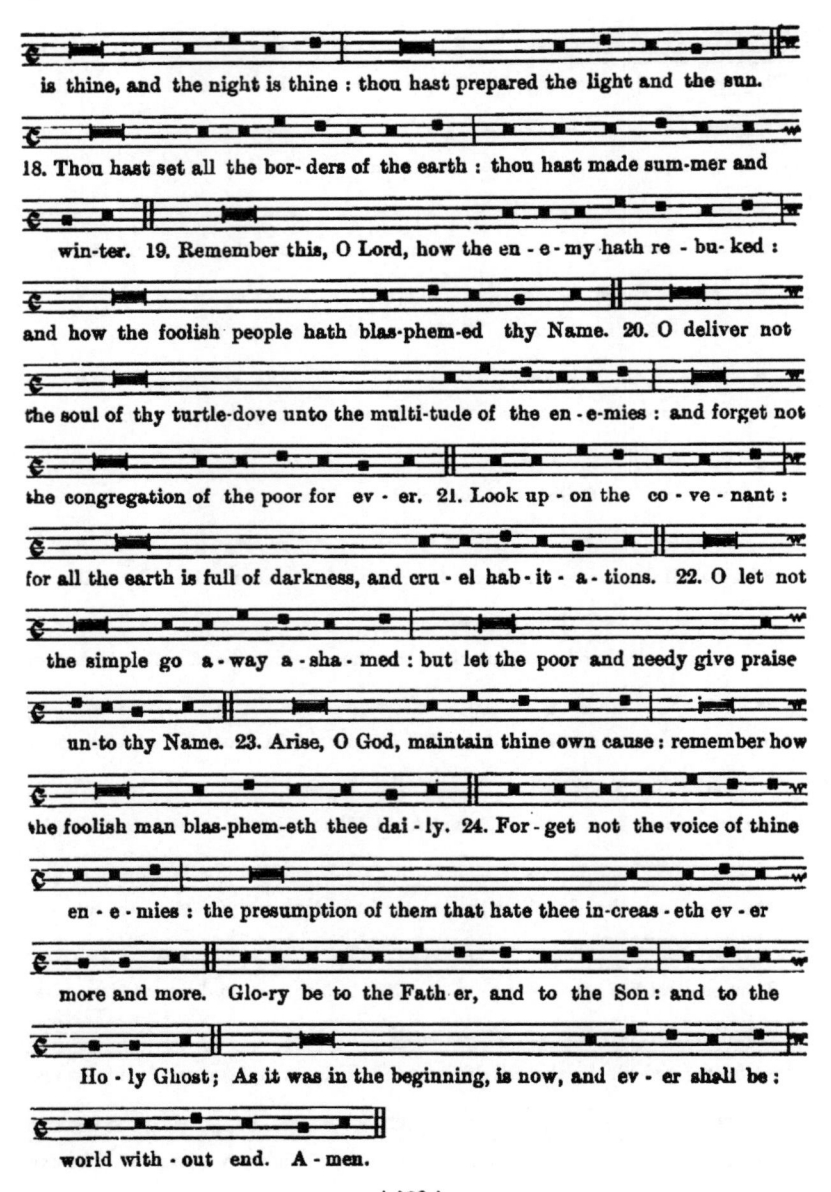

DAY 14. EVENING PRAYER.

is thine, and the night is thine : thou hast prepared the light and the sun.

18. Thou hast set all the bor- ders of the earth : thou hast made sum-mer and

win-ter. 19. Remember this, O Lord, how the en - e - my hath re - bu- ked :

and how the foolish people hath blas-phem-ed thy Name. 20. O deliver not

the soul of thy turtle-dove unto the multi-tude of the en - e-mies : and forget not

the congregation of the poor for ev - er. 21. Look up - on the co - ve - nant :

for all the earth is full of darkness, and cru - el hab - it - a - tions. 22. O let not

the simple go a - way a - sha - med : but let the poor and needy give praise

un-to thy Name. 23. Arise, O God, maintain thine own cause : remember how

the foolish man blas-phem-eth thee dai - ly. 24. For - get not the voice of thine

en - e - mies : the presumption of them that hate thee in-creas - eth ev - er

more and more. Glo-ry be to the Fath er, and to the Son : and to the

Ho - ly Ghost; As it was in the beginning, is now, and ev - er shall be :

world with - out end. A - men.

MORNING PRAYER. DAY 15.

PSALM LXXV.—*Confitebimur tibi.*

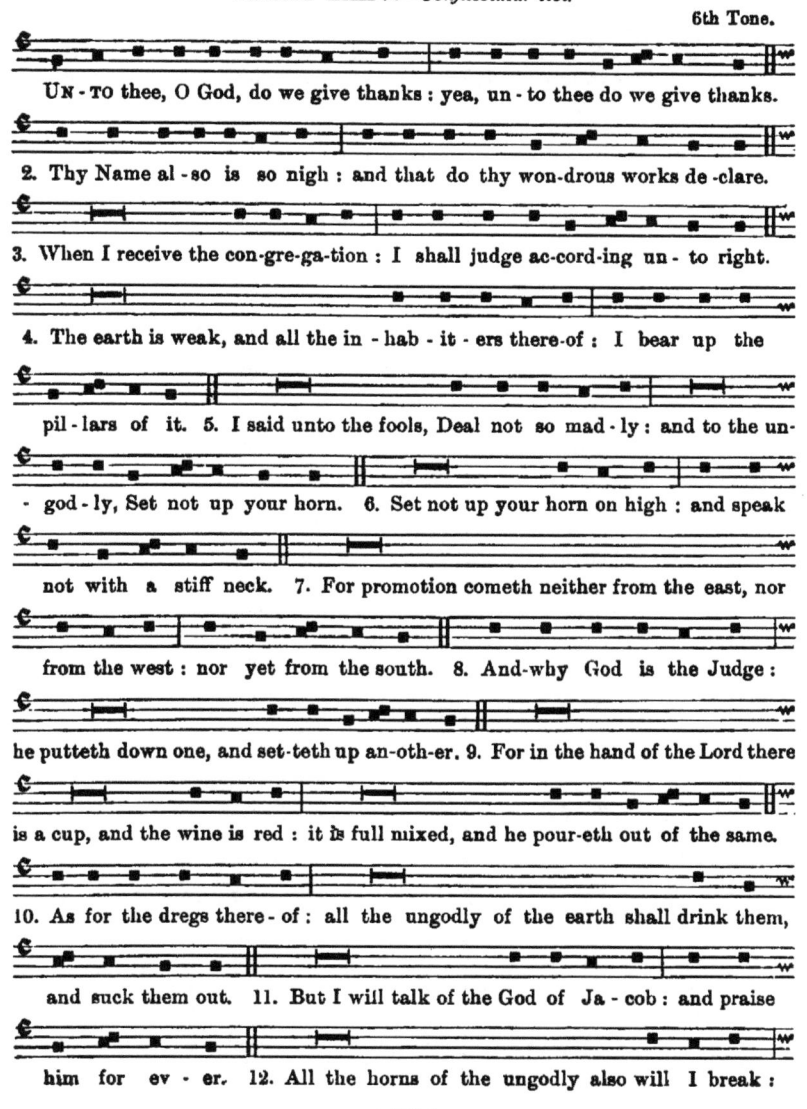

6th Tone.

UN - TO thee, O God, do we give thanks : yea, un - to thee do we give thanks.

2. Thy Name al - so is so nigh : and that do thy won-drous works de -clare.

3. When I receive the con-gre-ga-tion : I shall judge ac-cord-ing un - to right.

4. The earth is weak, and all the in - hab - it - ers there-of : I bear up the

pil - lars of it. 5. I said unto the fools, Deal not so mad - ly : and to the un-

- god - ly, Set not up your horn. 6. Set not up your horn on high : and speak

not with a stiff neck. 7. For promotion cometh neither from the east, nor

from the west : nor yet from the south. 8. And-why God is the Judge :

he putteth down one, and set-teth up an-oth-er. 9. For in the hand of the Lord there

is a cup, and the wine is red : it is full mixed, and he pour-eth out of the same.

10. As for the dregs there - of : all the ungodly of the earth shall drink them,

and suck them out. 11. But I will talk of the God of Ja - cob : and praise

him for ev - er. 12. All the horns of the ungodly also will I break :

DAY 15. MORNING PRAYER.

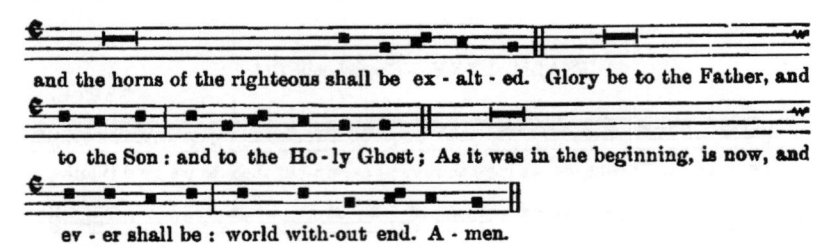

and the horns of the righteous shall be ex - alt - ed. Glory be to the Father, and to the Son : and to the Ho - ly Ghost; As it was in the beginning, is now, and ev - er shall be : world with-out end. A - men.

PSALM LXXVI.—*Notus in Judæa.*

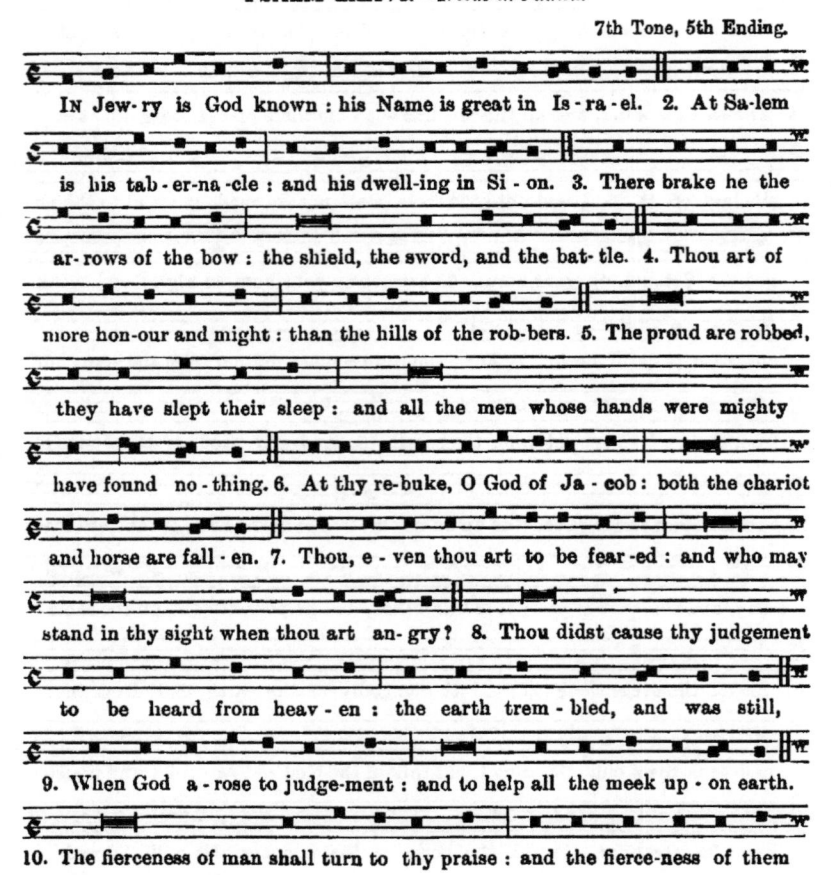

7th Tone, 5th Ending.

IN Jew-ry is God known : his Name is great in Is - ra - el. 2. At Sa-lem is his tab - er-na -cle : and his dwell-ing in Si - on. 3. There brake he the ar- rows of the bow : the shield, the sword, and the bat- tle. 4. Thou art of more hon-our and might : than the hills of the rob-bers. 5. The proud are robbed, they have slept their sleep : and all the men whose hands were mighty have found no - thing. 6. At thy re-buke, O God of Ja - cob: both the chariot and horse are fall - en. 7. Thou, e - ven thou art to be fear -ed : and who may stand in thy sight when thou art an - gry? 8. Thou didst cause thy judgement to be heard from heav - en : the earth trem - bled, and was still, 9. When God a - rose to judge-ment : and to help all the meek up - on earth. 10. The fierceness of man shall turn to thy praise : and the fierce-ness of them

(128)

MORNING PRAYER.

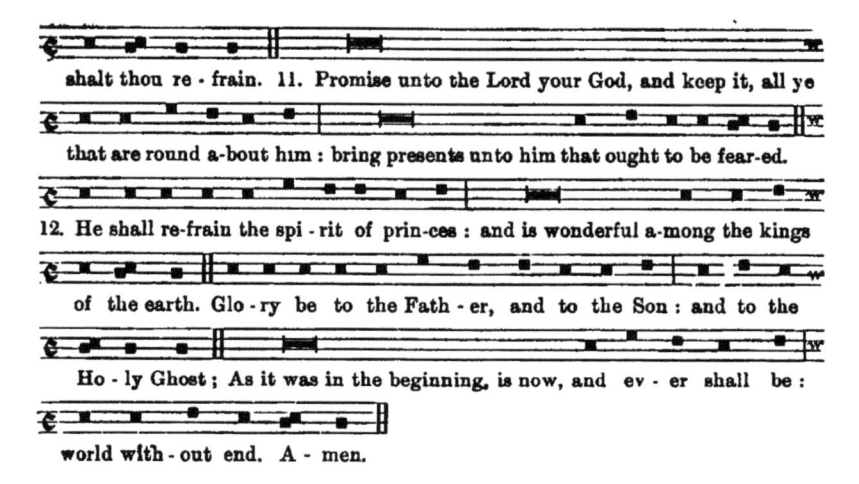

shalt thou re - frain. 11. Promise unto the Lord your God, and keep it, all ye that are round a-bout him : bring presents unto him that ought to be fear-ed. 12. He shall re-frain the spi - rit of prin-ces : and is wonderful a-mong the kings of the earth. Glo - ry be to the Fath - er, and to the Son : and to the Ho - ly Ghost ; As it was in the beginning, is now, and ev - er shall be : world with - out end. A - men.

PSALM LXXVII. - *Voce mea ad Dominum.*

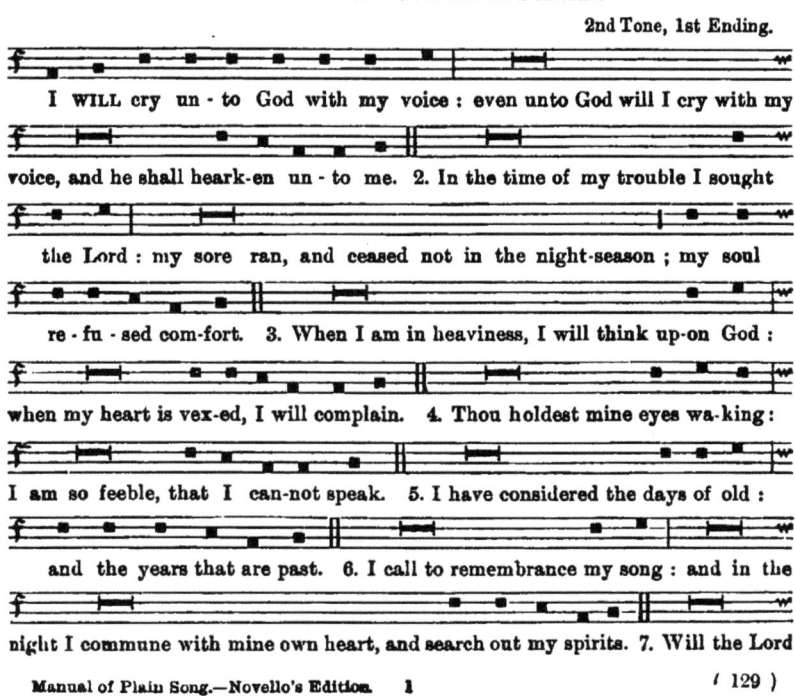

2nd Tone, 1st Ending.

I WILL cry un - to God with my voice : even unto God will I cry with my voice, and he shall heark-en un - to me. 2. In the time of my trouble I sought the Lord : my sore ran, and ceased not in the night-season ; my soul re - fu - sed com-fort. 3. When I am in heaviness, I will think up-on God : when my heart is vex-ed, I will complain. 4. Thou holdest mine eyes wa-king : I am so feeble, that I can-not speak. 5. I have considered the days of old : and the years that are past. 6. I call to remembrance my song : and in the night I commune with mine own heart, and search out my spirits. 7. Will the Lord

Manual of Plain Song.—Novello's Edition. 1

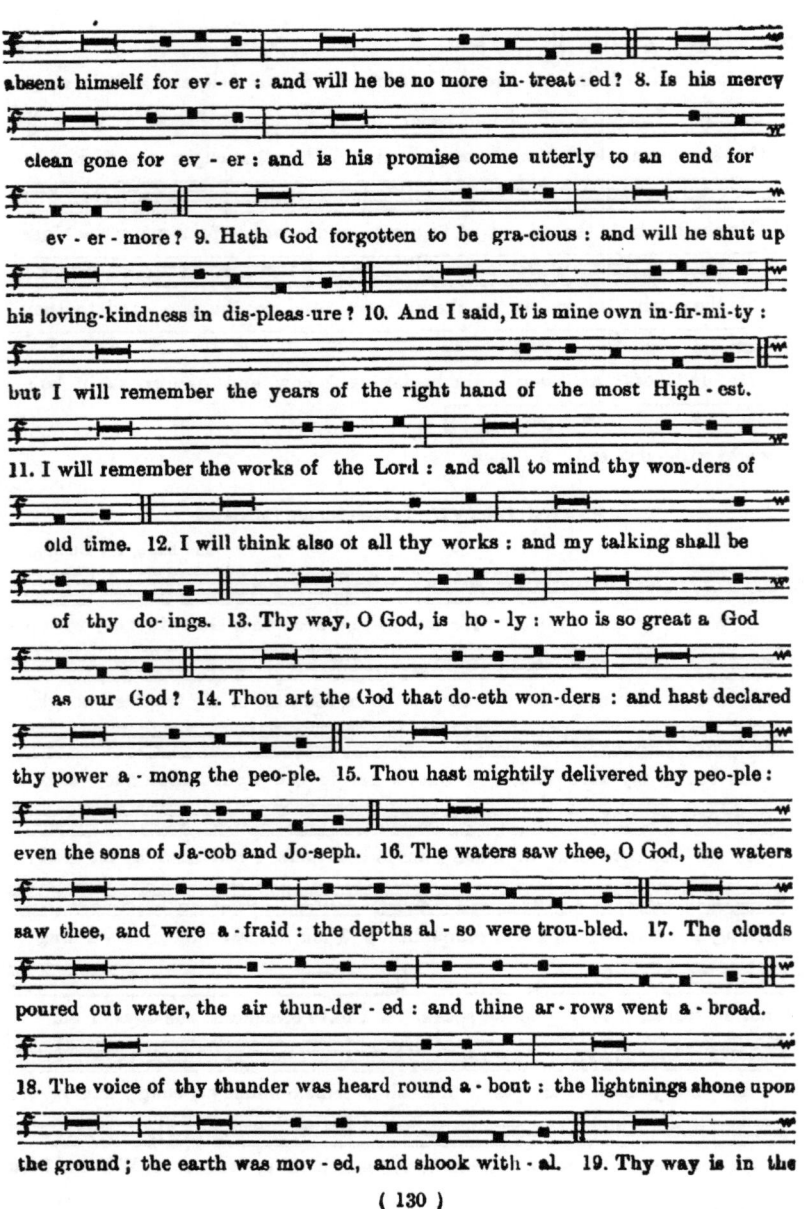

Day 15.   MORNING PRAYER.

absent himself for ev - er : and will he be no more in-treat-ed? 8. Is his mercy clean gone for ev - er : and is his promise come utterly to an end for ev - er - more? 9. Hath God forgotten to be gra-cious : and will he shut up his loving-kindness in dis-pleas-ure? 10. And I said, It is mine own in-fir-mi-ty : but I will remember the years of the right hand of the most High - est. 11. I will remember the works of the Lord : and call to mind thy won-ders of old time. 12. I will think also of all thy works : and my talking shall be of thy do-ings. 13. Thy way, O God, is ho - ly : who is so great a God as our God? 14. Thou art the God that do-eth won-ders : and hast declared thy power a - mong the peo-ple. 15. Thou hast mightily delivered thy peo-ple : even the sons of Ja-cob and Jo-seph. 16. The waters saw thee, O God, the waters saw thee, and were a - fraid : the depths al - so were trou-bled. 17. The clouds poured out water, the air thun-der - ed : and thine ar - rows went a - broad. 18. The voice of thy thunder was heard round a - bout : the lightnings shone upon the ground; the earth was mov - ed, and shook with - al. 19. Thy way is in the

EVENING PRAYER. DAY 15.

sea, and thy paths in the great wa-ters : and thy foot-steps are not known.

20. Thou leddest thy people like sheep : by the hand of Mo-ses and Aa-ron.

Glory be to the Father, and to the Son : and to the Ho-ly Ghost ; As it was in

the beginning, is now, and ever shall be : world with-out end. A-men.

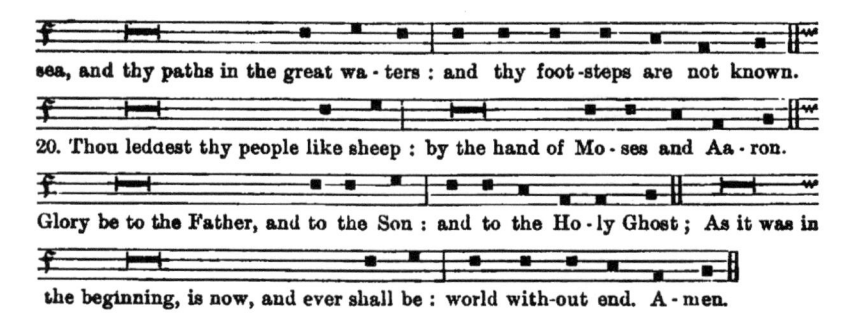

EVENING PRAYER.

PSALM LXXVIII.—*Attendite, popule.*

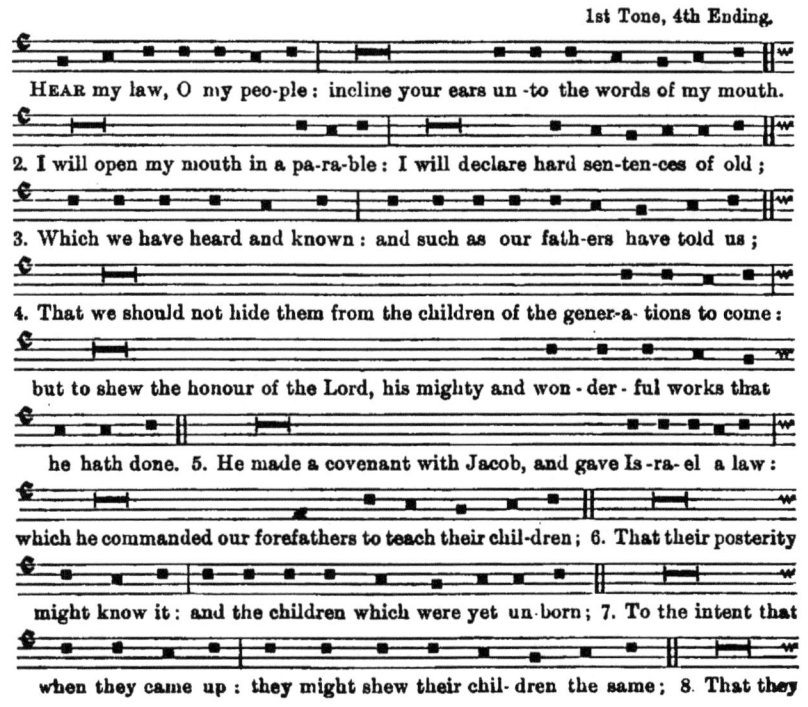

1st Tone, 4th Ending.

HEAR my law, O my peo-ple : incline your ears un-to the words of my mouth.

2. I will open my mouth in a pa-ra-ble : I will declare hard sen-ten-ces of old ;

3. Which we have heard and known : and such as our fath-ers have told us ;

4. That we should not hide them from the children of the gener-a-tions to come :

but to shew the honour of the Lord, his mighty and won-der-ful works that

he hath done. 5. He made a covenant with Jacob, and gave Is-ra-el a law :

which he commanded our forefathers to teach their chil-dren; 6. That their posterity

might know it : and the children which were yet un-born; 7. To the intent that

when they came up : they might shew their chil-dren the same ; 8. That they

DAY 15. EVENING PRAYER

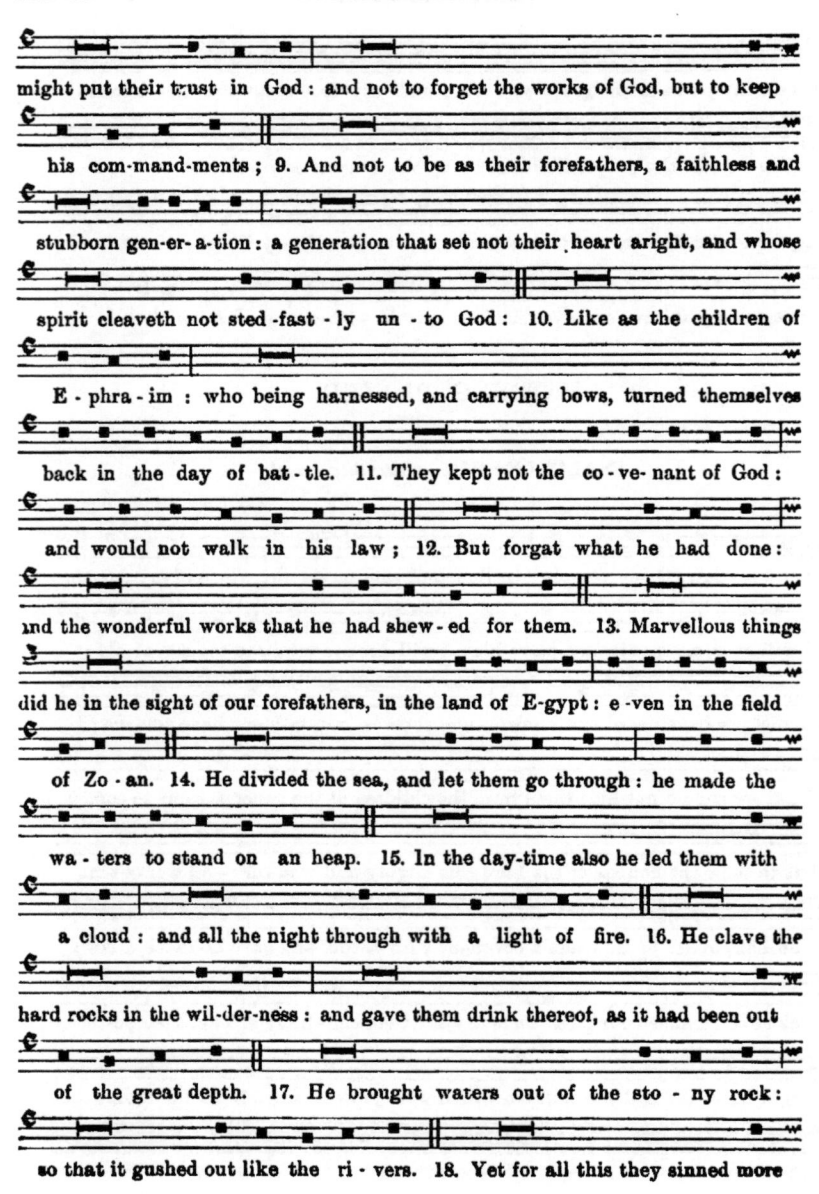

might put their trust in God : and not to forget the works of God, but to keep his com-mand-ments ; 9. And not to be as their forefathers, a faithless and stubborn gen-er-a-tion : a generation that set not their heart aright, and whose spirit cleaveth not sted-fast-ly un-to God : 10. Like as the children of E-phra-im : who being harnessed, and carrying bows, turned themselves back in the day of bat-tle. 11. They kept not the co-ve-nant of God : and would not walk in his law ; 12. But forgat what he had done : and the wonderful works that he had shew-ed for them. 13. Marvellous things did he in the sight of our forefathers, in the land of E-gypt : e-ven in the field of Zo-an. 14. He divided the sea, and let them go through : he made the wa-ters to stand on an heap. 15. In the day-time also he led them with a cloud : and all the night through with a light of fire. 16. He clave the hard rocks in the wil-der-ness : and gave them drink thereof, as it had been out of the great depth. 17. He brought waters out of the sto-ny rock : so that it gushed out like the ri-vers. 18. Yet for all this they sinned more a - gainst him : and provoked the Most High - est in the wil - der -ness.

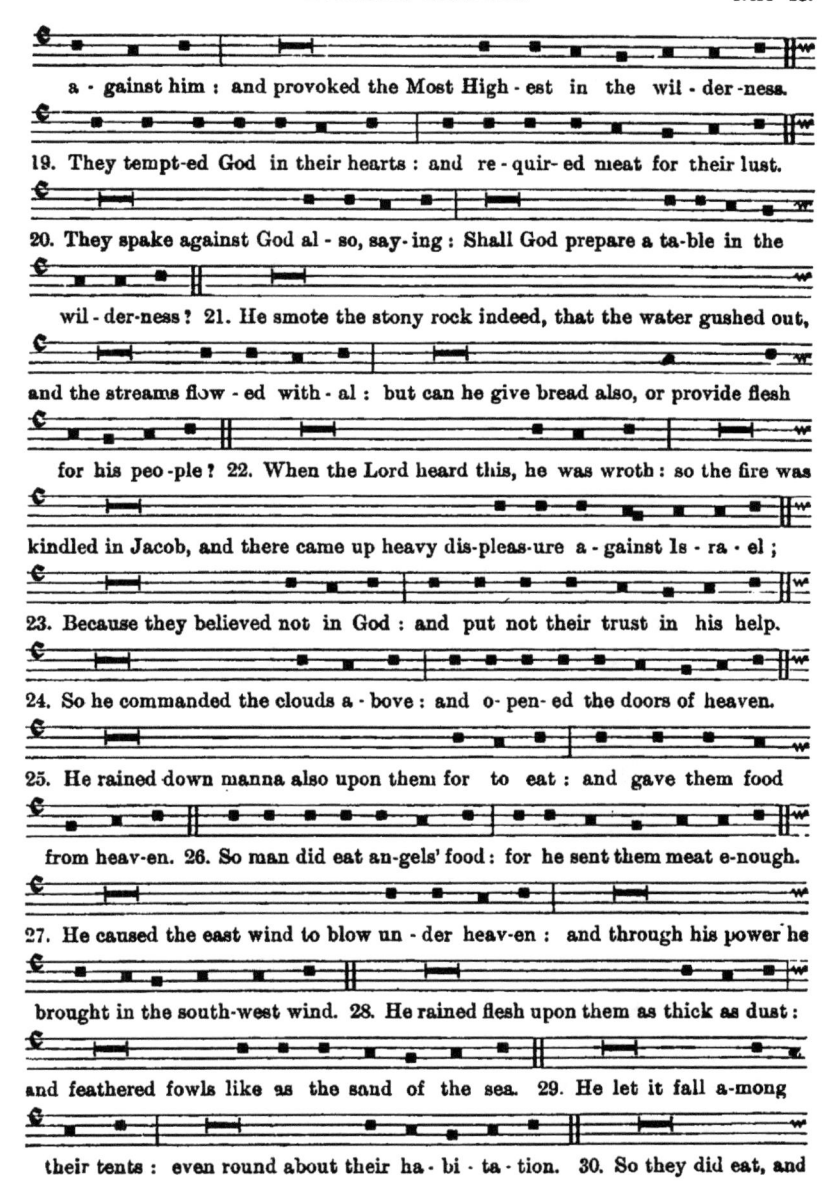

19. They tempt-ed God in their hearts : and re - quir- ed meat for their lust.

20. They spake against God al - so, say-ing : Shall God prepare a ta-ble in the

wil - der-ness ? 21. He smote the stony rock indeed, that the water gushed out,

and the streams flow - ed with - al : but can he give bread also, or provide flesh

for his peo -ple ? 22. When the Lord heard this, he was wroth : so the fire was

kindled in Jacob, and there came up heavy dis-pleas-ure a - gainst Is - ra - el ;

23. Because they believed not in God : and put not their trust in his help.

24. So he commanded the clouds a - bove : and o- pen- ed the doors of heaven.

25. He rained down manna also upon them for to eat : and gave them food

from heav-en. 26. So man did eat an-gels' food : for he sent them meat e-nough.

27. He caused the east wind to blow un - der heav-en : and through his power he

brought in the south-west wind. 28. He rained flesh upon them as thick as dust :

and feathered fowls like as the sand of the sea. 29. He let it fall a-mong

their tents : even round about their ha - bi - ta - tion. 30. So they did eat, and

DAY 15   EVENING PRAYER.

were well filled; for he gave them their own de-sire: they were not disappoint-ed of their lust. 31. But while the meat was yet in their mouths, the heavy wrath of God came upon them, and slew the wealth-i-est of them: yea, and smote down the chosen men that were in Is-ra-el. 32. But for all this they sin-ned yet more: and be-liev-ed not his won-drous works. 33. Therefore their days did he consume in van-i-ty: and their years in trou-ble. 34. When he slew them, they sought him: and turned them early, and en-quir-ed af-ter God. 35. And they remembered that God was their strength: and that the high God was their re-deem-er. 36. Nevertheless, they did but flatter him with their mouth: and dis-sem-bled with him in their tongue. 37. For their heart was not whole with him: neither continued they sted-fast in his co-ve-nant 38. But he was so merciful, that he for-gave their mis-deeds: and des-troy-ed them not. 39. Yea, many a time turned he his wrath a-way: and would not suffer his whole dis-pleas-ure to a-rise. 40. For he considered that they were but flesh: and that they were even a wind that passeth away, and

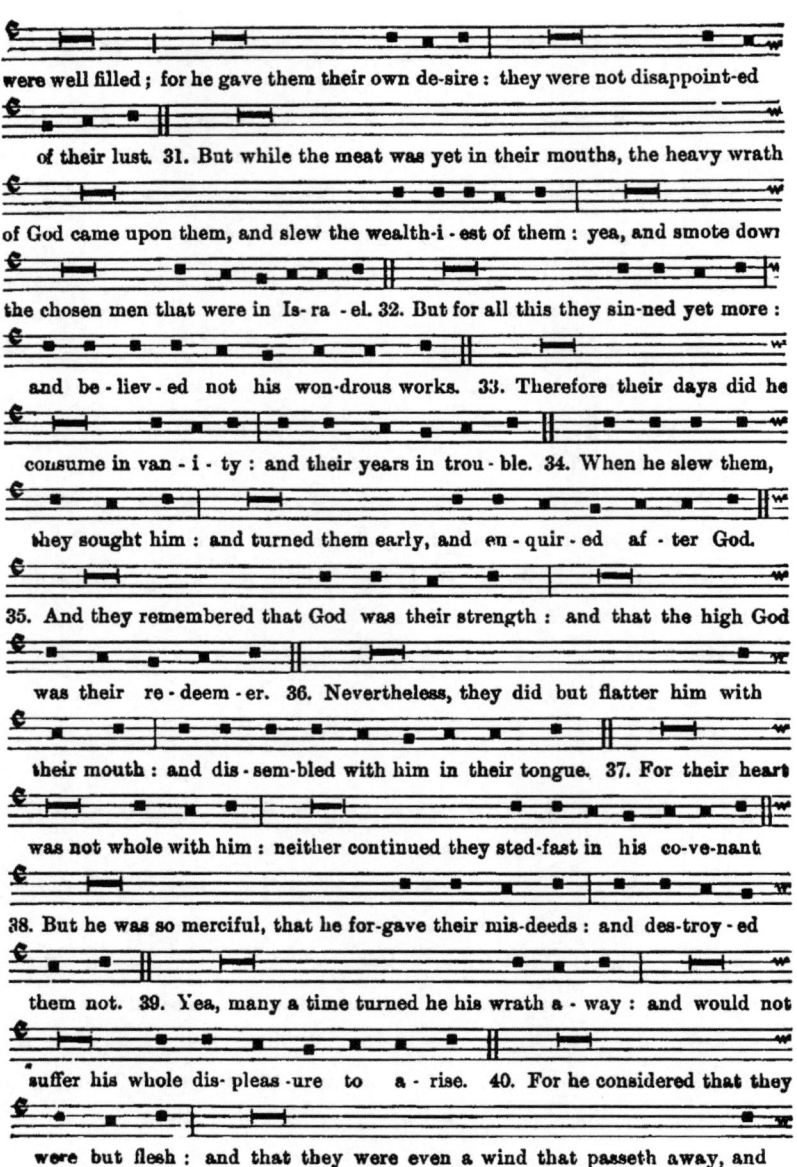

EVENING PRAYER. DAY 15.

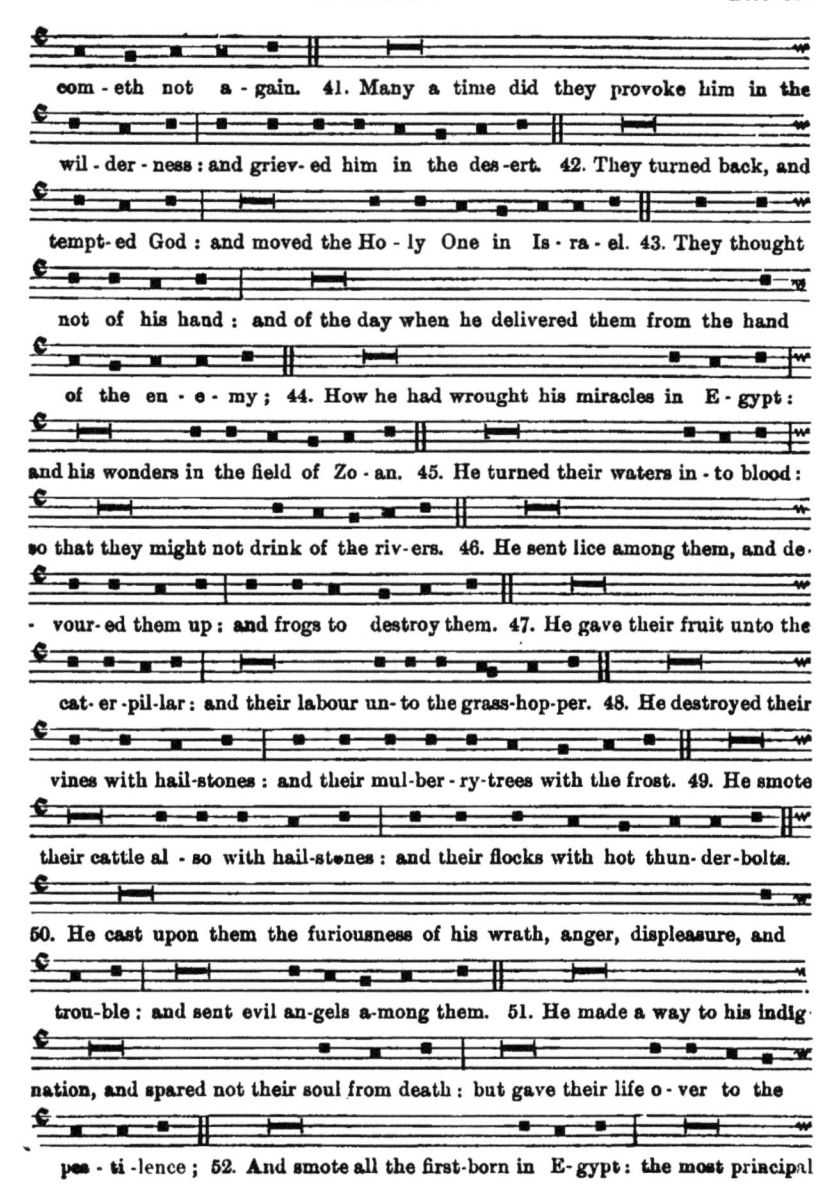

com-eth not a-gain. 41. Many a time did they provoke him in the wil-der-ness: and griev-ed him in the des-ert. 42. They turned back, and tempt-ed God: and moved the Ho-ly One in Is-ra-el. 43. They thought not of his hand: and of the day when he delivered them from the hand of the en-e-my; 44. How he had wrought his miracles in E-gypt: and his wonders in the field of Zo-an. 45. He turned their waters in-to blood: so that they might not drink of the riv-ers. 46. He sent lice among them, and de- vour-ed them up: and frogs to destroy them. 47. He gave their fruit unto the cat-er-pil-lar: and their labour un-to the grass-hop-per. 48. He destroyed their vines with hail-stones: and their mul-ber-ry-trees with the frost. 49. He smote their cattle al-so with hail-stones: and their flocks with hot thun-der-bolts. 50. He cast upon them the furiousness of his wrath, anger, displeasure, and trou-ble: and sent evil an-gels a-mong them. 51. He made a way to his indig- nation, and spared not their soul from death: but gave their life o-ver to the pes-ti-lence; 52. And smote all the first-born in E-gypt: the most principal and mightiest in the dwell-ings of Ham. 53. But as for his own people, he led them forth like sheep: and carried them in the wil-der-ness like a flock. 54. He brought them out safely, that they should not fear: and overwhelmed their en-e-mies with the sea. 55. And brought them within the borders of his sanc-tu-a-ry: even to his mountain which he pur-chas-ed with his right hand. 56. He cast out the heathen al-so be-fore them: caused their land to be divided among them for an heritage, and made the tribes of Israel to dwell in their tents. 57. So they tempted, and displeased the most high God: and kept not his tes-ti-mon-ies; 58. But turned their backs, and fell away like their fore-fath-ers: start-ing a-side like a bro-ken bow. 59. For they grieved him with their hill-al-tars: and provoked him to dis-pleas-ure with their im-a-ges. 60. When God heard this, he was wroth: and took sore dis-pleas-ure at Is-ra-el. 61. So that he forsook the tabernacle in Si-lo: even the tent that he had pitch-ed a-mong men. 62. He delivered their power into cap-ti-vi-ty: and their beauty in-to the en-e-my's hand. 63. He gave his people over also un-to the sword:

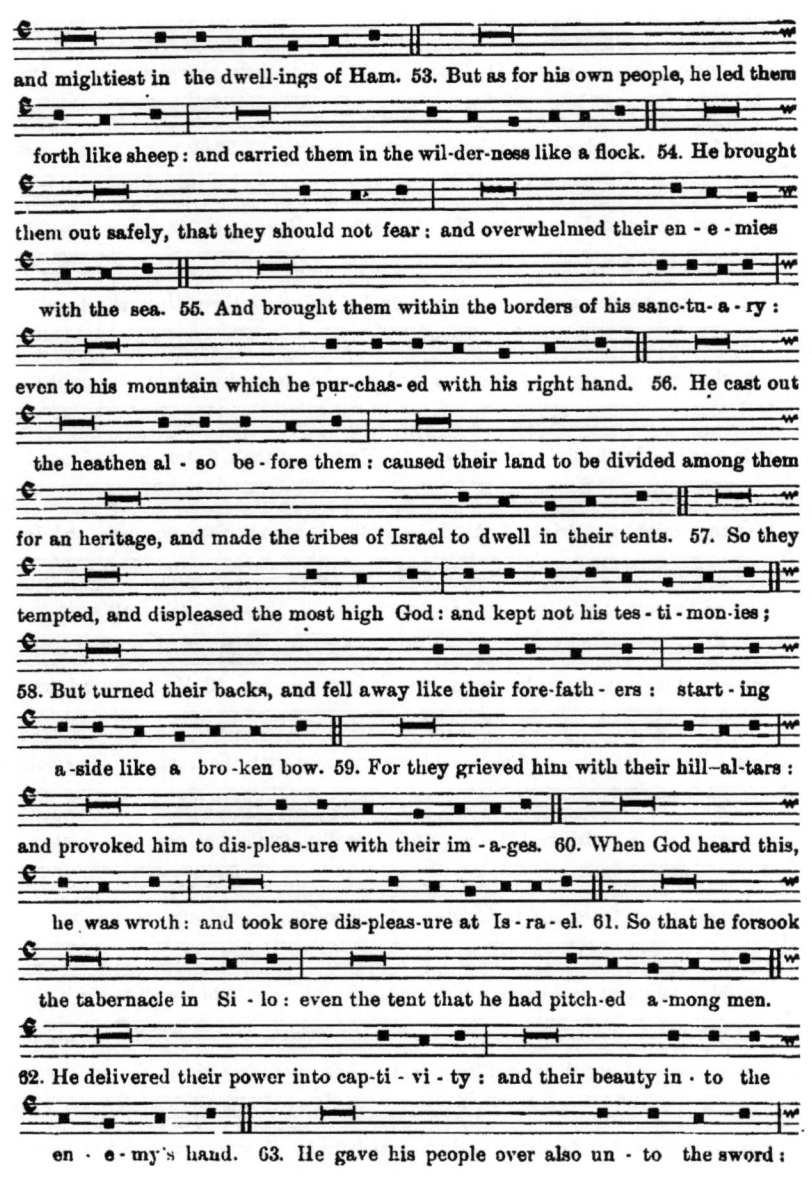

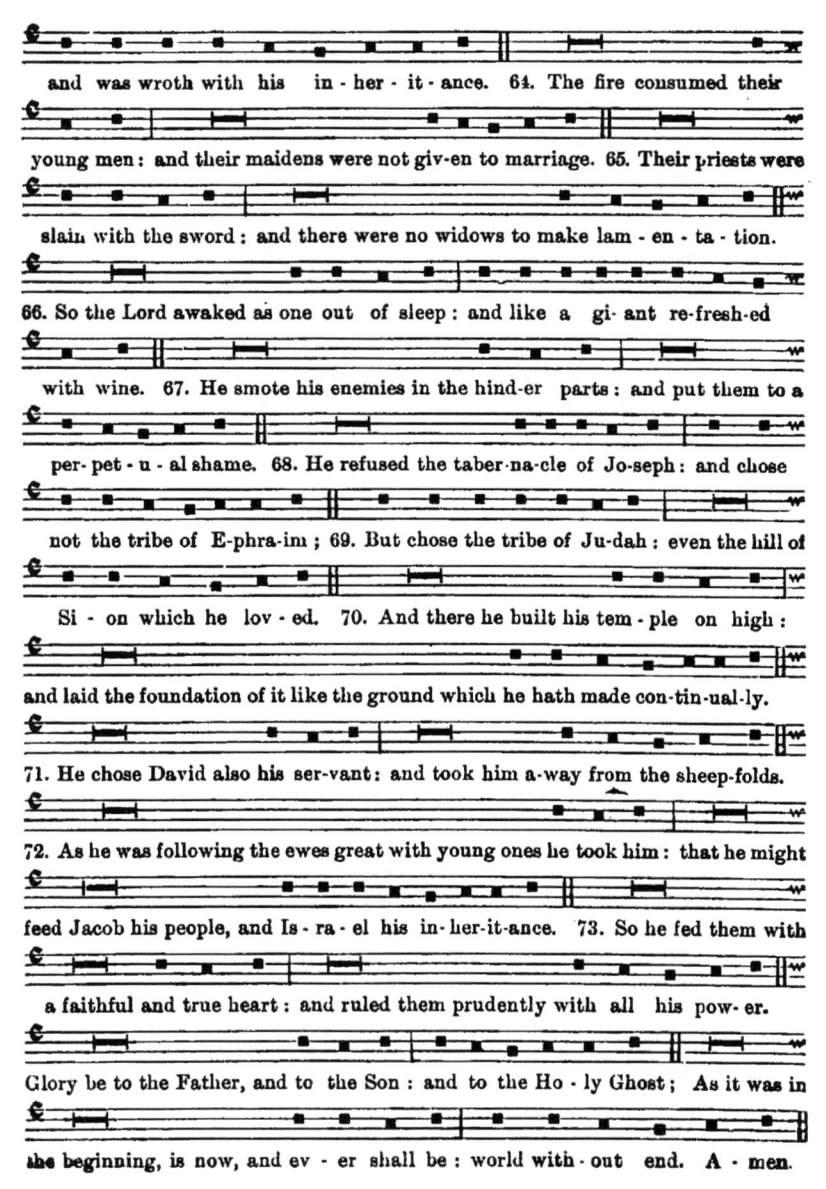

and was wroth with his in-her-it-ance. 64. The fire consumed their young men: and their maidens were not giv-en to marriage. 65. Their priests were slain with the sword: and there were no widows to make lam-en-ta-tion. 66. So the Lord awaked as one out of sleep: and like a gi-ant re-fresh-ed with wine. 67. He smote his enemies in the hind-er parts: and put them to a per-pet-u-al shame. 68. He refused the taber-na-cle of Jo-seph: and chose not the tribe of E-phra-im; 69. But chose the tribe of Ju-dah: even the hill of Si-on which he lov-ed. 70. And there he built his tem-ple on high: and laid the foundation of it like the ground which he hath made con-tin-ual-ly. 71. He chose David also his ser-vant: and took him a-way from the sheep-folds. 72. As he was following the ewes great with young ones he took him: that he might feed Jacob his people, and Is-ra-el his in-her-it-ance. 73. So he fed them with a faithful and true heart: and ruled them prudently with all his pow-er. Glory be to the Father, and to the Son: and to the Ho-ly Ghost; As it was in the beginning, is now, and ev-er shall be: world with-out end. A-men.

Day 16. MORNING PRAYER.

PSALM LXXIX.—*Deus, venerunt.*

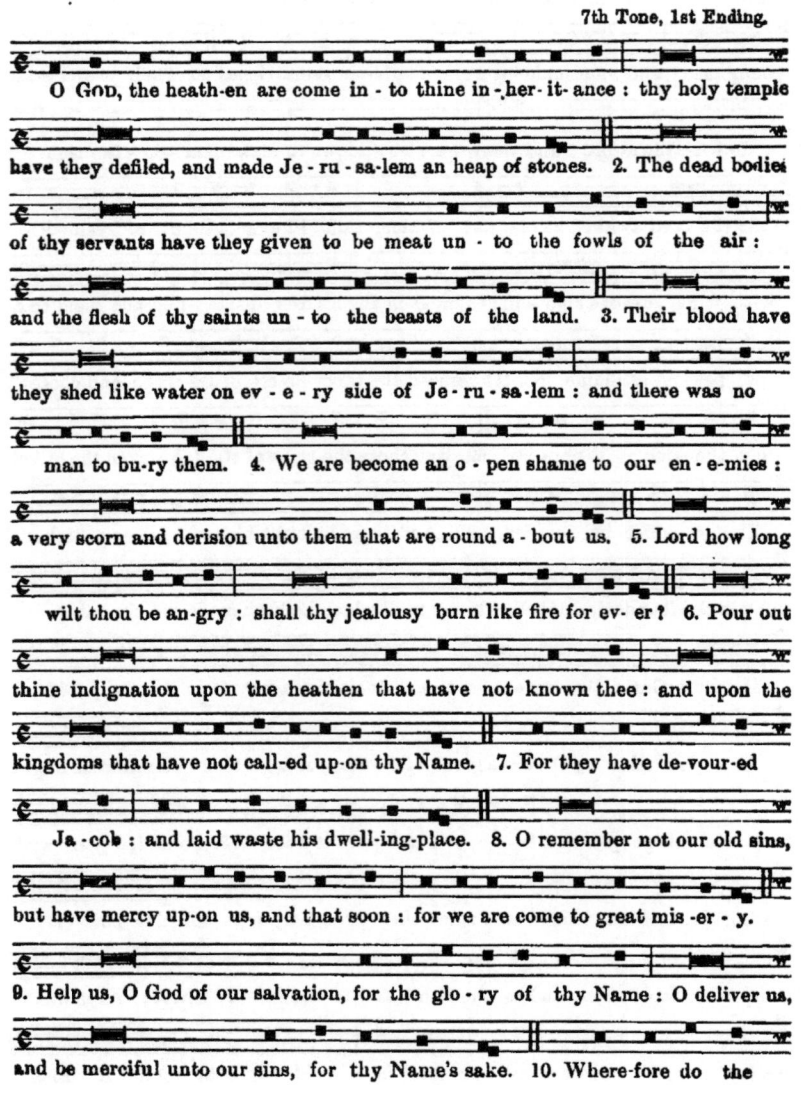

7th Tone, 1st Ending.

O God, the heath-en are come in - to thine in - her- it- ance : thy holy temple have they defiled, and made Je - ru - sa-lem an heap of stones. 2. The dead bodies of thy servants have they given to be meat un - to the fowls of the air : and the flesh of thy saints un - to the beasts of the land. 3. Their blood have they shed like water on ev - e - ry side of Je - ru - sa-lem : and there was no man to bu-ry them. 4. We are become an o - pen shame to our en - e-mies : a very scorn and derision unto them that are round a - bout us. 5. Lord how long wilt thou be an-gry : shall thy jealousy burn like fire for ev- er ? 6. Pour out thine indignation upon the heathen that have not known thee : and upon the kingdoms that have not call-ed up-on thy Name. 7. For they have de-vour-ed Ja -cob : and laid waste his dwell-ing-place. 8. O remember not our old sins, but have mercy up-on us, and that soon : for we are come to great mis -er - y. 9. Help us, O God of our salvation, for the glo - ry of thy Name : O deliver us, and be merciful unto our sins, for thy Name's sake. 10. Where-fore do the

(138)

MORNING PRAYER. DAY 16

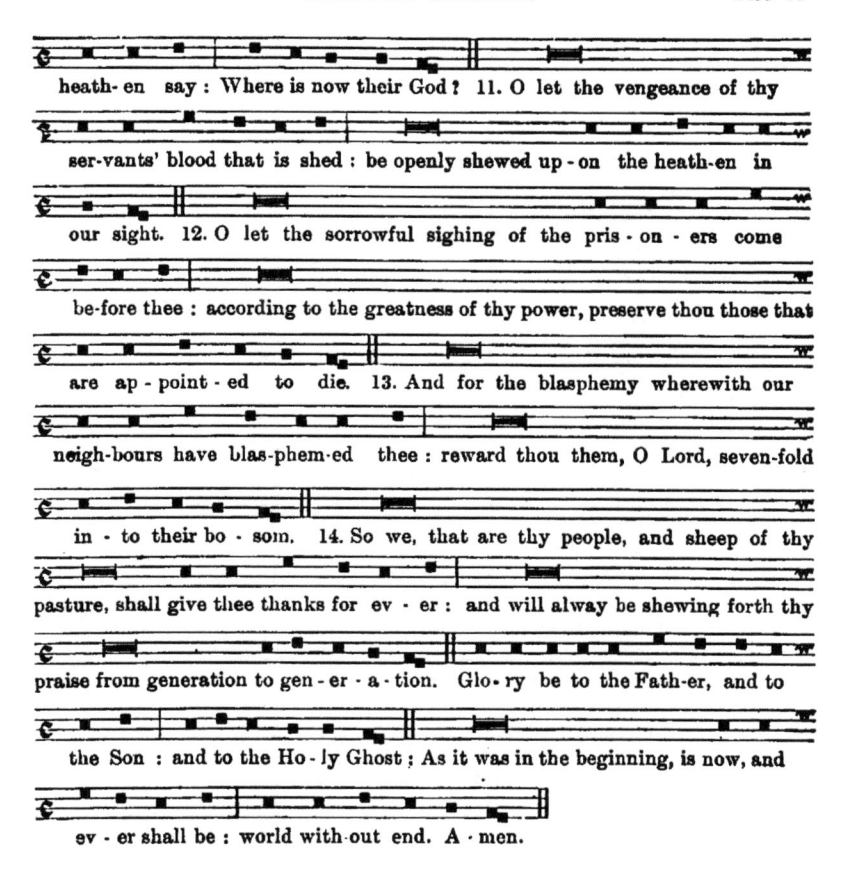

heath-en say : Where is now their God ? 11. O let the vengeance of thy ser-vants' blood that is shed : be openly shewed up-on the heath-en in our sight. 12. O let the sorrowful sighing of the pris-on-ers come be-fore thee : according to the greatness of thy power, preserve thou those that are ap-point-ed to die. 13. And for the blasphemy wherewith our neigh-bours have blas-phem-ed thee : reward thou them, O Lord, seven-fold in-to their bo-som. 14. So we, that are thy people, and sheep of thy pasture, shall give thee thanks for ev-er : and will alway be shewing forth thy praise from generation to gen-er-a-tion. Glo-ry be to the Fath-er, and to the Son : and to the Ho-ly Ghost ; As it was in the beginning, is now, and ev-er shall be : world with-out end. A-men.

PSALM LXXX.—*Qui regis Israel.*

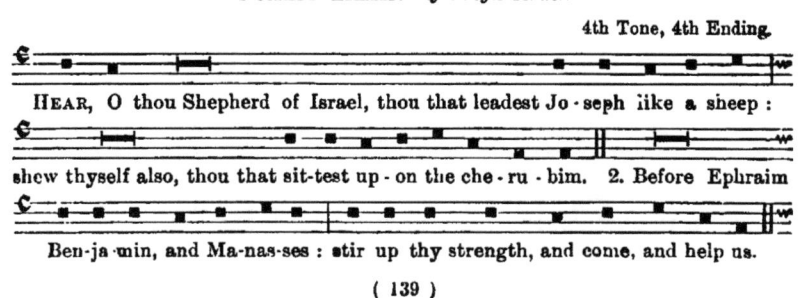

4th Tone, 4th Ending.

HEAR, O thou Shepherd of Israel, thou that leadest Jo-seph like a sheep : shew thyself also, thou that sit-test up-on the che-ru-bim. 2. Before Ephraim Ben-ja-min, and Ma-nas-ses : stir up thy strength, and come, and help us.

(139)

DAY 16. MORNING PRAYER.

3. Turn us a-gain, O God : shew the light of thy coun-ten-ance, and we shall be whole. 4. O Lord God of hosts : how long wilt thou be angry with thy peo-ple that pray-eth? 5. Thou feedest them with the bread of tears : and givest them plen-teous-ness of tears to drink. 6. Thou hast made us a very strife un-to our neigh-bours : and our en-e-mies laugh us to scorn. 7. Turn us again, thou God of hosts : shew the light of thy coun-te-nance, and we shall be whole. 8. Thou hast brought a vine out of E-gypt : thou hast cast out the heath-en, and plant-ed it. 9. Thou ma-dest room for it : and when it had taken root it fill-ed the land. 10. The hills were covered with the sha-dow of it : and the boughs thereof were like the good-ly ce-dar-trees. 11. She stretched out her branches un-to the sea : and her boughs un-to the riv-er. 12. Why hast thou then bro-ken down her hedge : that all they that go by pluck off her grapes? 13. The wild boar out of the wood doth root it up : and the wild beasts of the field de-vour it. 14. Turn thee again, thou God of hosts, look down from heav-en : be-hold, and vis-it this vine;

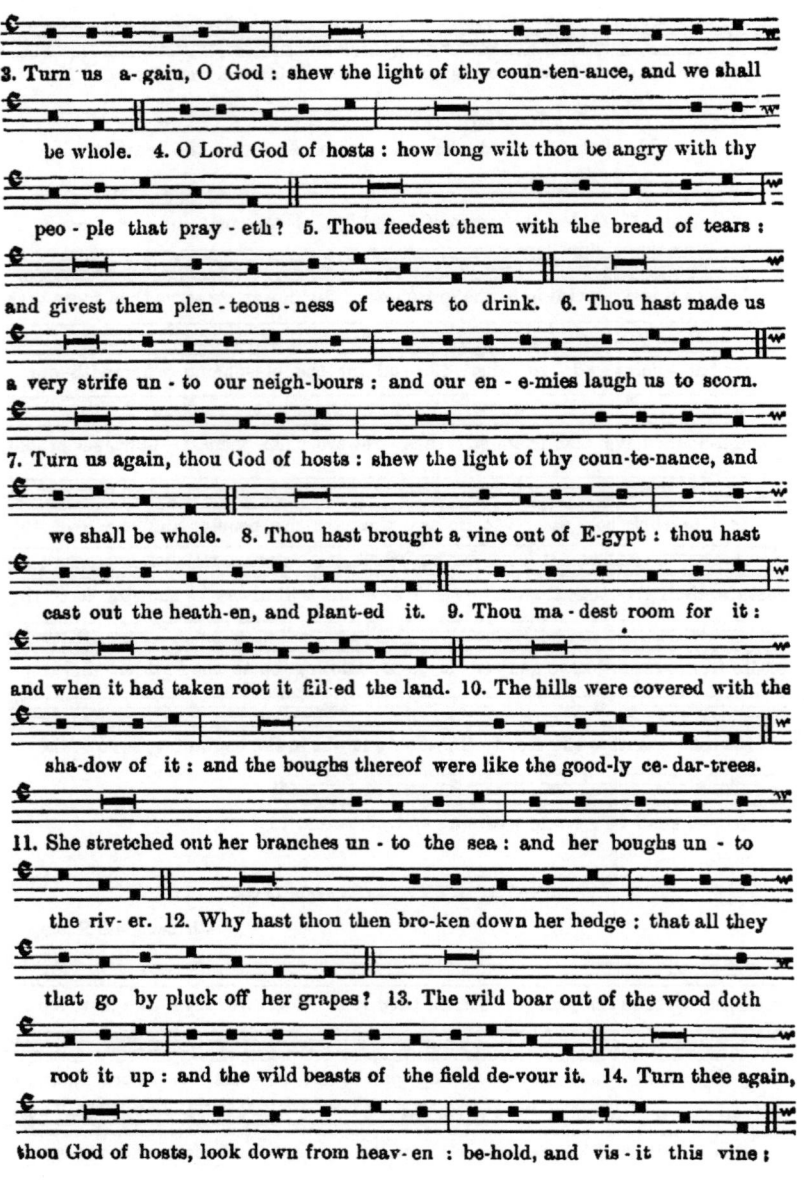

MORNING PRAYER. DAY 16.

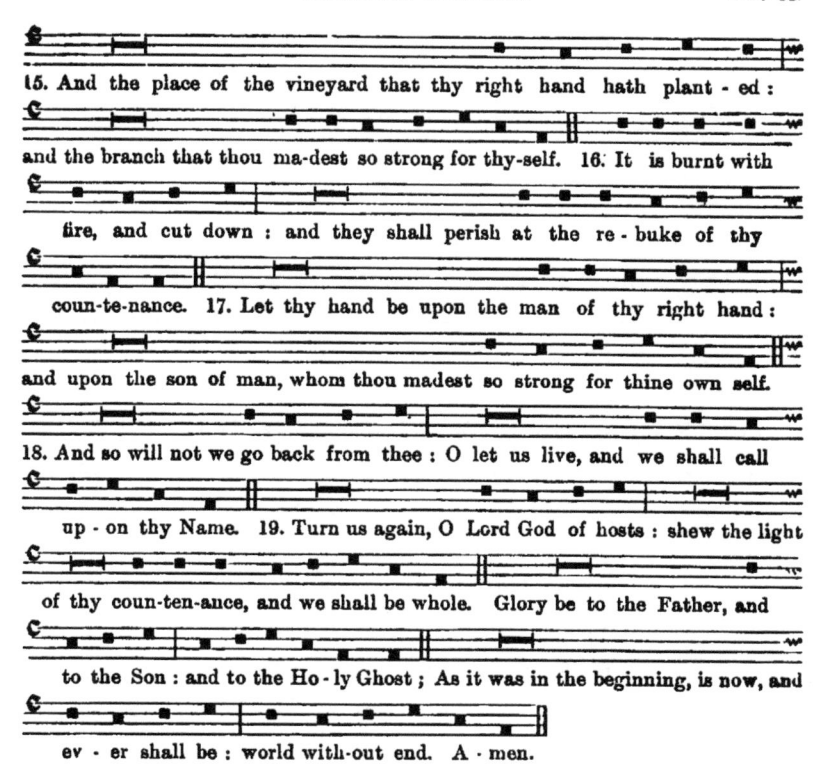

15. And the place of the vineyard that thy right hand hath plant - ed : and the branch that thou ma-dest so strong for thy-self. 16. It is burnt with fire, and cut down : and they shall perish at the re - buke of thy coun-te-nance. 17. Let thy hand be upon the man of thy right hand : and upon the son of man, whom thou madest so strong for thine own self. 18. And so will not we go back from thee : O let us live, and we shall call up - on thy Name. 19. Turn us again, O Lord God of hosts : shew the light of thy coun-ten-ance, and we shall be whole. Glory be to the Father, and to the Son : and to the Ho - ly Ghost ; As it was in the beginning, is now, and ev - er shall be : world with-out end. A - men.

PSALM LXXXI.—*Exultate Deo.*

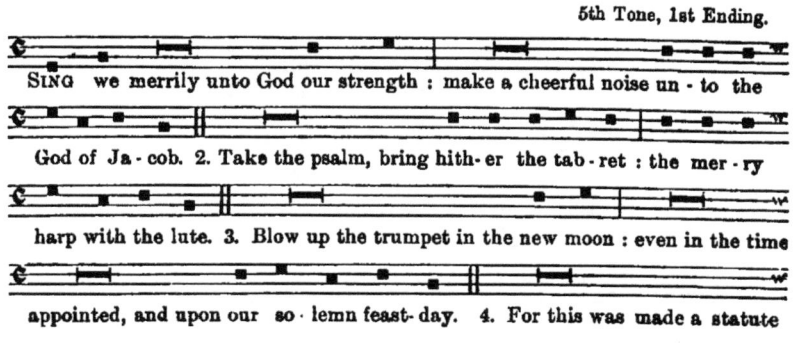

5th Tone, 1st Ending.

Sing we merrily unto God our strength : make a cheerful noise un - to the God of Ja - cob. 2. Take the psalm, bring hith- er the tab- ret : the mer - ry harp with the lute. 3. Blow up the trumpet in the new moon : even in the time appointed, and upon our so - lemn feast- day. 4. For this was made a statute

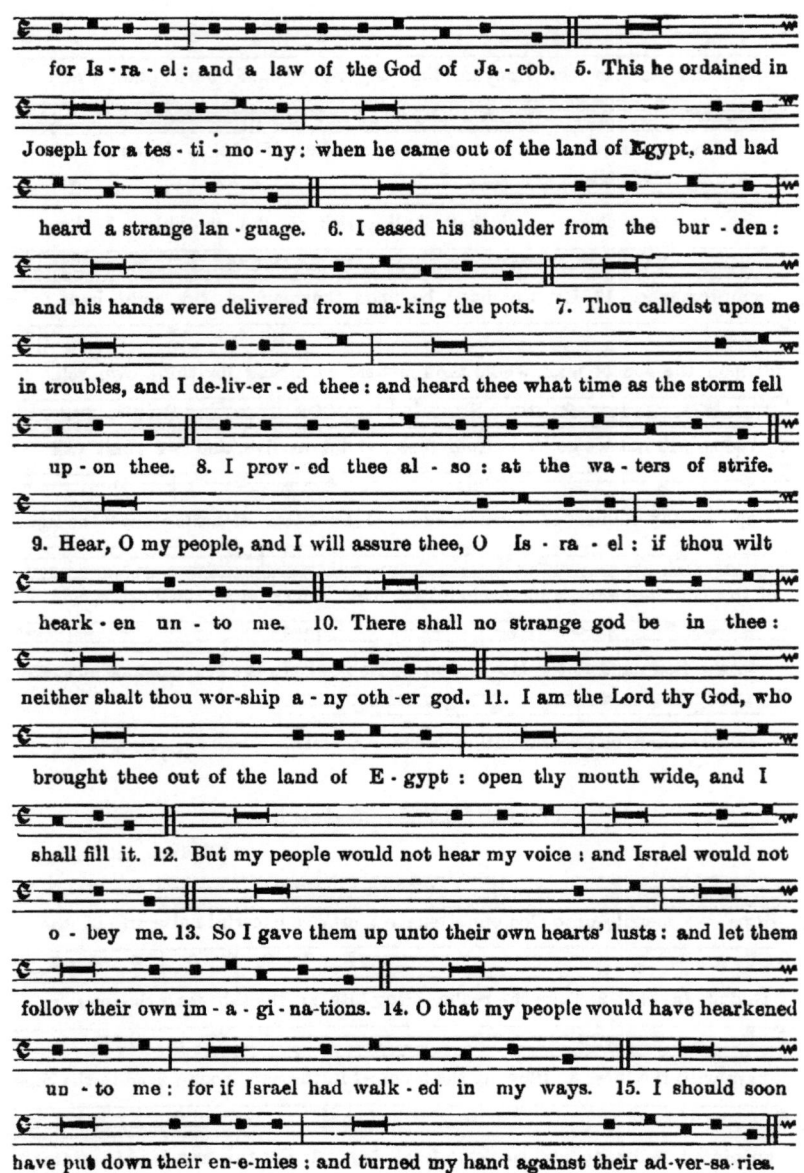

DAY 16. MORNING PRAYER.

for Is-ra-el: and a law of the God of Ja-cob. 5. This he ordained in Joseph for a tes-ti-mo-ny: when he came out of the land of Egypt, and had heard a strange lan-guage. 6. I eased his shoulder from the bur-den: and his hands were delivered from ma-king the pots. 7. Thou calledst upon me in troubles, and I de-liv-er-ed thee: and heard thee what time as the storm fell up-on thee. 8. I prov-ed thee al-so: at the wa-ters of strife. 9. Hear, O my people, and I will assure thee, O Is-ra-el: if thou wilt heark-en un-to me. 10. There shall no strange god be in thee: neither shalt thou wor-ship a-ny oth-er god. 11. I am the Lord thy God, who brought thee out of the land of E-gypt: open thy mouth wide, and I shall fill it. 12. But my people would not hear my voice: and Israel would not o-bey me. 13. So I gave them up unto their own hearts' lusts: and let them follow their own im-a-gi-na-tions. 14. O that my people would have hearkened un-to me: for if Israel had walk-ed in my ways. 15. I should soon have put down their en-e-mies: and turned my hand against their ad-ver-sa-ries.

(142)

EVENING PRAYER. DAY 16

16. The haters of the Lord should have been found li - ars : but their time should have en -dur - ed for ev - er. 17. He should have fed them also with the finest wheat flour : and with honey out of the stony rock should I have sat-is-fi-ed thee.

Glory be to the Father, and to the Son : and to the Ho -ly Ghost ; As it was in the beginning, is now, and ever shall be : world with - out end. A - men.

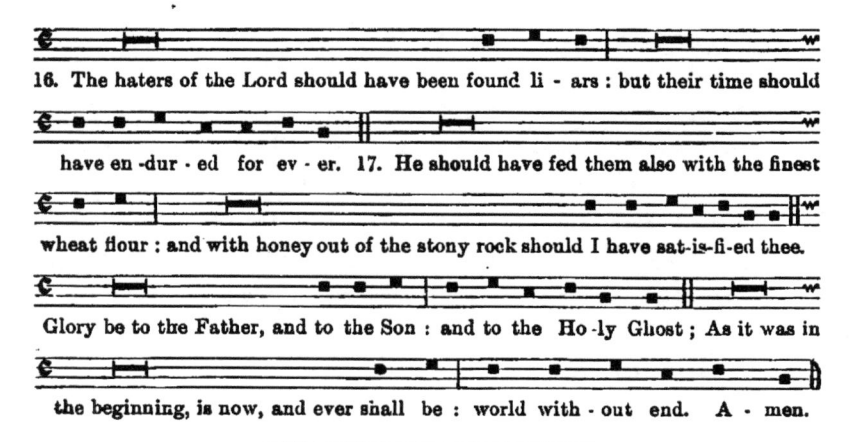

EVENING PRAYER.

PSALM LXXXII.—*Deus stetit.*

8th Tone, 2nd Ending.

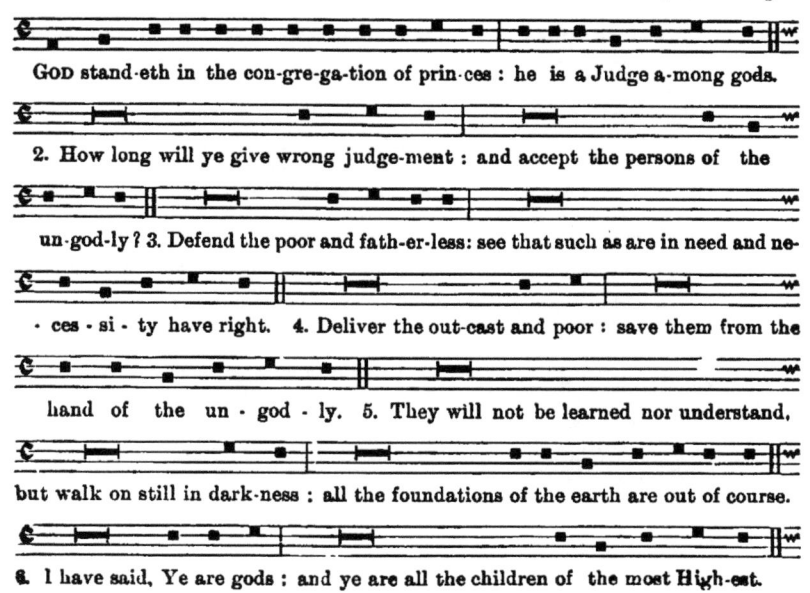

God stand-eth in the con-gre-ga-tion of prin-ces : he is a Judge a-mong gods.

2. How long will ye give wrong judge-ment : and accept the persons of the un-god-ly? 3. Defend the poor and fath-er-less: see that such as are in need and ne- - ces - si - ty have right. 4. Deliver the out-cast and poor : save them from the hand of the un - god - ly. 5. They will not be learned nor understand, but walk on still in dark-ness : all the foundations of the earth are out of course.

6. I have said, Ye are gods : and ye are all the children of the most High-est.

(143)

Day 16. EVENING PRAYER.

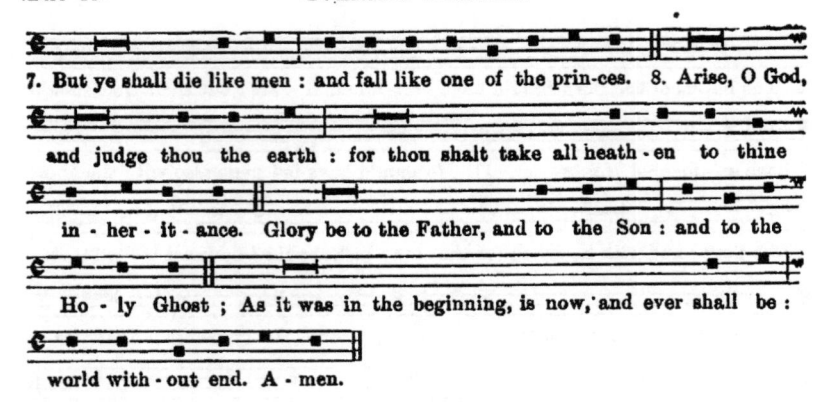

7. But ye shall die like men : and fall like one of the prin-ces. 8. Arise, O God, and judge thou the earth : for thou shalt take all heath-en to thine in-her-it-ance. Glory be to the Father, and to the Son : and to the Ho-ly Ghost ; As it was in the beginning, is now, and ever shall be : world with-out end. A-men.

PSALM LXXXIII.—*Deus, quis similis?*

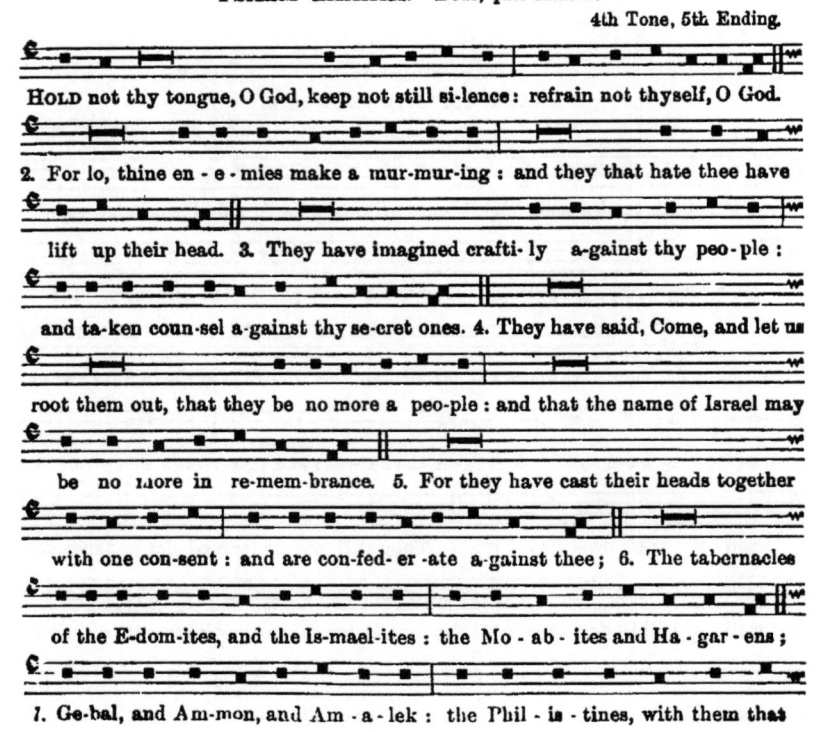

4th Tone, 5th Ending.

HOLD not thy tongue, O God, keep not still si-lence: refrain not thyself, O God. 2. For lo, thine en-e-mies make a mur-mur-ing : and they that hate thee have lift up their head. 3. They have imagined crafti-ly a-gainst thy peo-ple : and ta-ken coun-sel a-gainst thy se-cret ones. 4. They have said, Come, and let us root them out, that they be no more a peo-ple : and that the name of Israel may be no more in re-mem-brance. 5. For they have cast their heads together with one con-sent : and are con-fed-er-ate a-gainst thee ; 6. The tabernacles of the E-dom-ites, and the Is-mael-ites : the Mo-ab-ites and Ha-gar-ens ; 7. Ge-bal, and Am-mon, and Am-a-lek : the Phil-is-tines, with them that

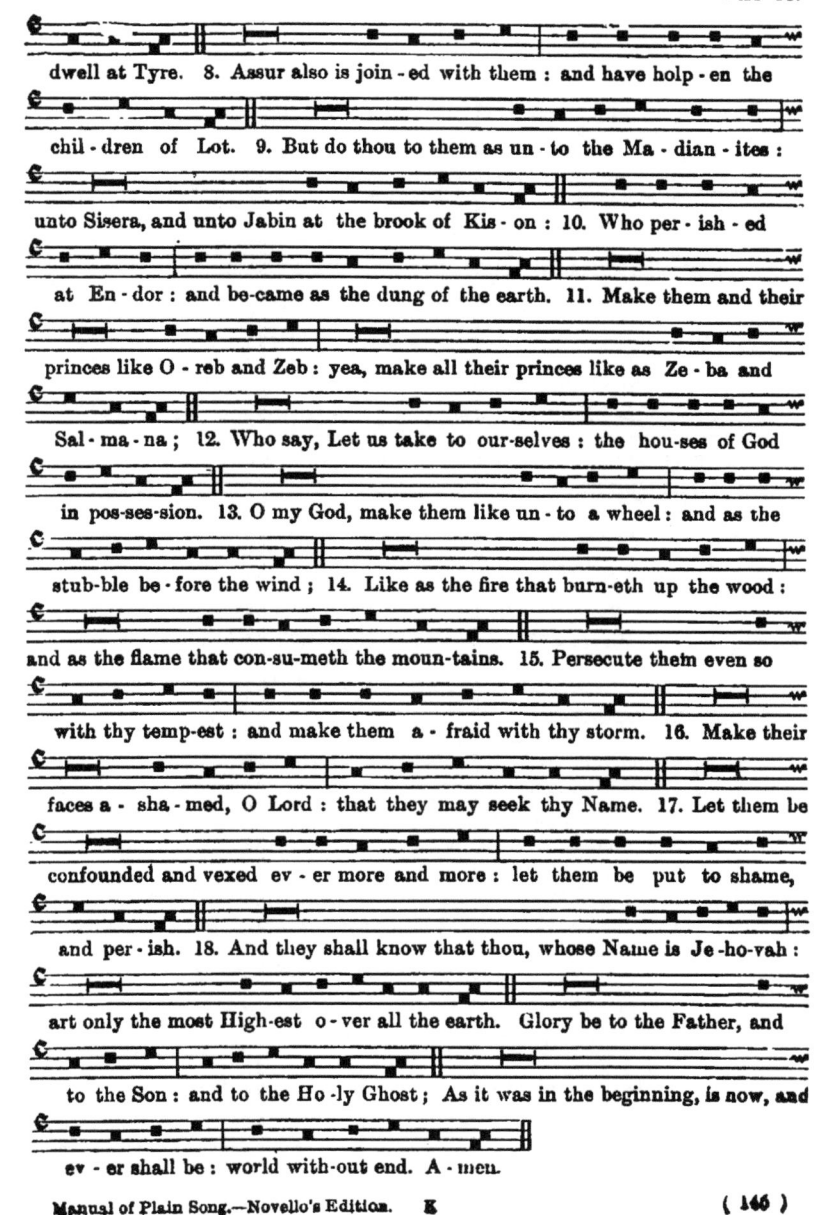

EVENING PRAYER. DAY 16.

dwell at Tyre. 8. Assur also is join - ed with them : and have holp - en the chil - dren of Lot. 9. But do thou to them as un - to the Ma - dian - ites : unto Sisera, and unto Jabin at the brook of Kis - on : 10. Who per - ish - ed at En - dor : and be-came as the dung of the earth. 11. Make them and their princes like O - reb and Zeb : yea, make all their princes like as Ze - ba and Sal - ma - na ; 12. Who say, Let us take to our-selves : the hou-ses of God in pos-ses-sion. 13. O my God, make them like un - to a wheel : and as the stub-ble be - fore the wind ; 14. Like as the fire that burn-eth up the wood : and as the flame that con-su-meth the moun-tains. 15. Persecute them even so with thy temp-est : and make them a - fraid with thy storm. 16. Make their faces a - sha - med, O Lord : that they may seek thy Name. 17. Let them be confounded and vexed ev - er more and more : let them be put to shame, and per - ish. 18. And they shall know that thou, whose Name is Je -ho-vah : art only the most High-est o - ver all the earth. Glory be to the Father, and to the Son : and to the Ho -ly Ghost ; As it was in the beginning, is now, and ev - er shall be : world with-out end. A - men.

Manual of Plain Song.—Novello's Edition. K (146)

DAY 16. **EVENING PRAYER.**

PSALM LXXXIV.—*Quam dilecta.*

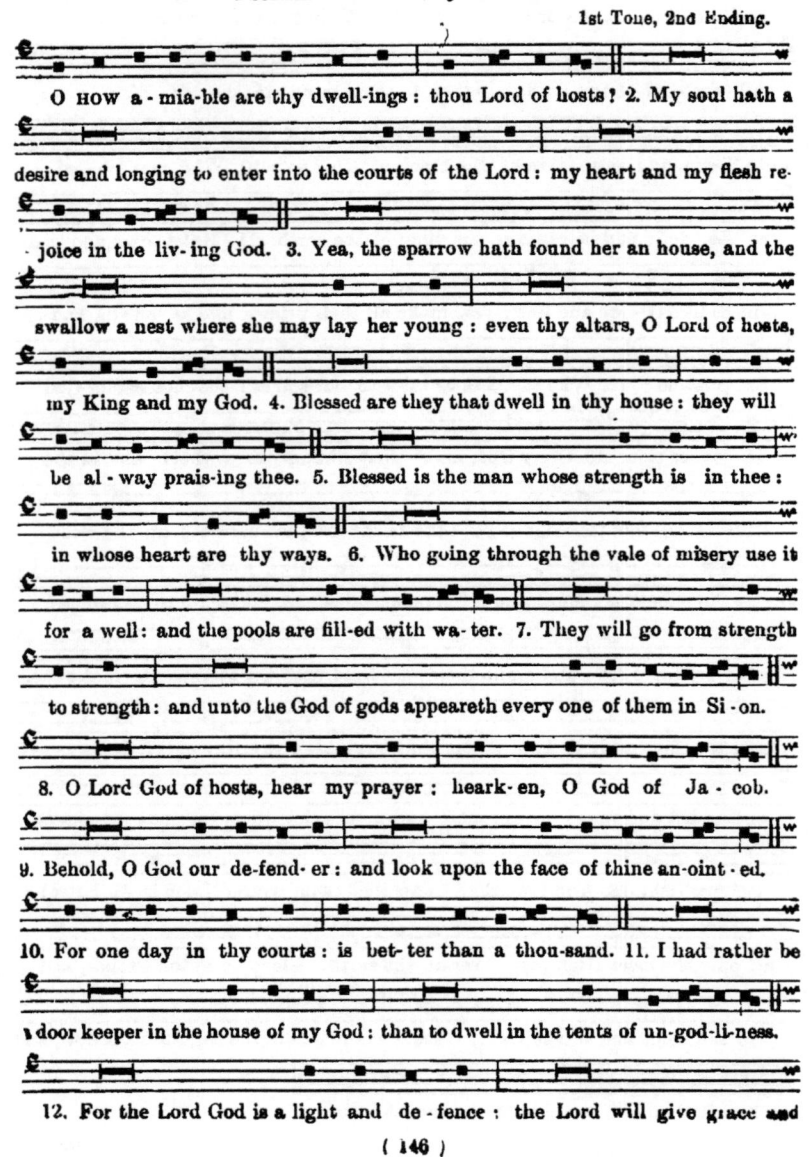

1st Tone, 2nd Ending.

O HOW a-mia-ble are thy dwell-ings : thou Lord of hosts? 2. My soul hath a

desire and longing to enter into the courts of the Lord : my heart and my flesh re-

joice in the liv-ing God. 3. Yea, the sparrow hath found her an house, and the

swallow a nest where she may lay her young : even thy altars, O Lord of hosts,

my King and my God. 4. Blessed are they that dwell in thy house : they will

be al-way prais-ing thee. 5. Blessed is the man whose strength is in thee :

in whose heart are thy ways. 6. Who going through the vale of misery use it

for a well : and the pools are fill-ed with wa-ter. 7. They will go from strength

to strength : and unto the God of gods appeareth every one of them in Si-on.

8. O Lord God of hosts, hear my prayer : heark-en, O God of Ja-cob.

9. Behold, O God our de-fend-er : and look upon the face of thine an-oint-ed.

10. For one day in thy courts : is bet-ter than a thou-sand. 11. I had rather be

a door keeper in the house of my God : than to dwell in the tents of un-god-li-ness.

12. For the Lord God is a light and de-fence : the Lord will give grace and

EVENING PRAYER. DAY 16.

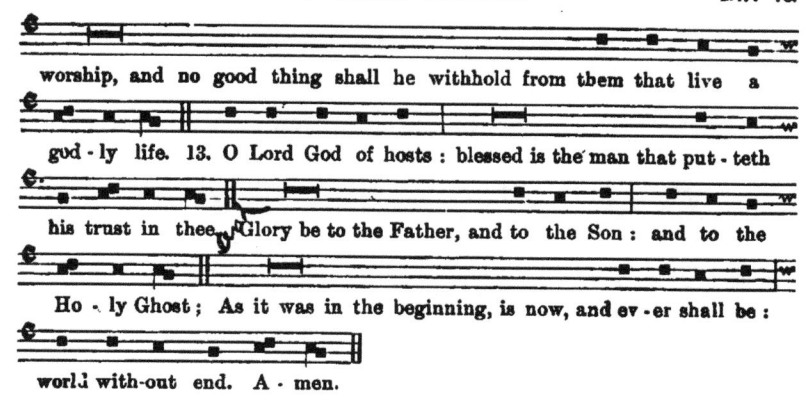

worship, and no good thing shall he withhold from them that live a godly life. 13. O Lord God of hosts : blessed is the man that putteth his trust in thee. Glory be to the Father, and to the Son : and to the Holy Ghost ; As it was in the beginning, is now, and ever shall be : world without end. A men.

PSALM LXXXV.—*Benedixisti, Domine.*

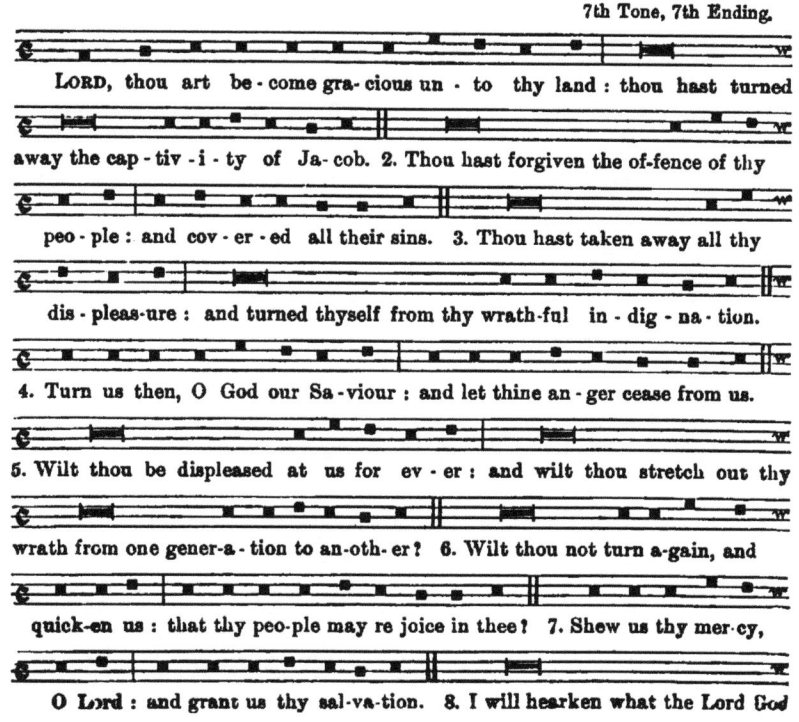

7th Tone, 7th Ending.

LORD, thou art become gracious unto thy land : thou hast turned away the captivity of Jacob. 2. Thou hast forgiven the offence of thy people : and covered all their sins. 3. Thou hast taken away all thy displeasure : and turned thyself from thy wrathful indignation. 4. Turn us then, O God our Saviour : and let thine anger cease from us. 5. Wilt thou be displeased at us for ever : and wilt thou stretch out thy wrath from one generation to another? 6. Wilt thou not turn again, and quicken us : that thy people may rejoice in thee? 7. Shew us thy mercy, O Lord : and grant us thy salvation. 8. I will hearken what the Lord God

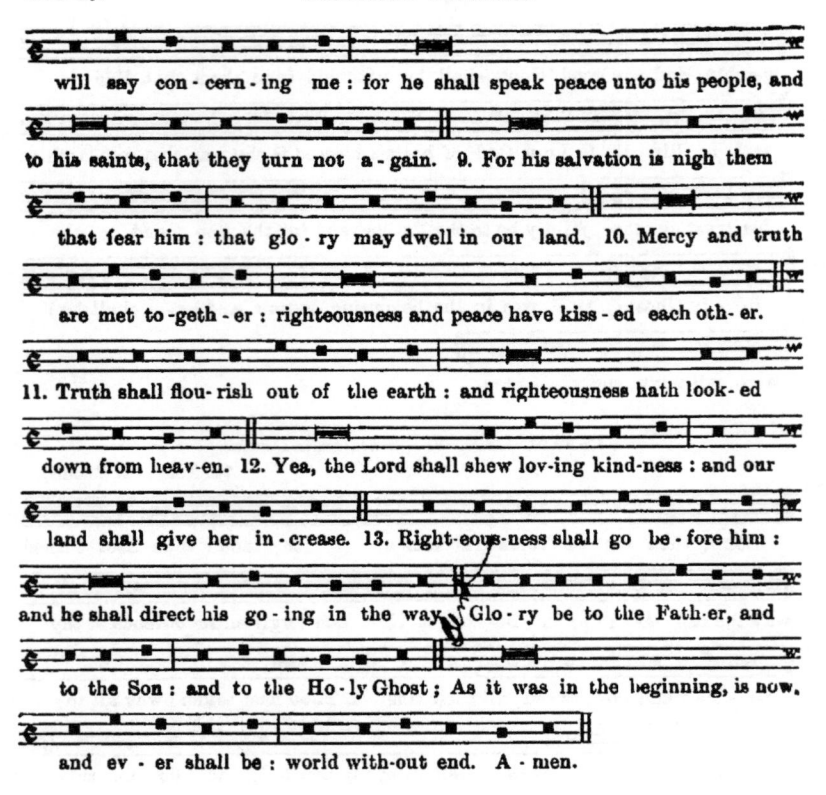

DAY 17. MORNING PRAYER.

will say con-cern-ing me: for he shall speak peace unto his people, and to his saints, that they turn not a-gain. 9. For his salvation is nigh them that fear him: that glo-ry may dwell in our land. 10. Mercy and truth are met to-geth-er: righteousness and peace have kiss-ed each oth-er. 11. Truth shall flou-rish out of the earth: and righteousness hath look-ed down from heav-en. 12. Yea, the Lord shall shew lov-ing kind-ness: and our land shall give her in-crease. 13. Right-eous-ness shall go be-fore him: and he shall direct his go-ing in the way. Glo-ry be to the Fath-er, and to the Son: and to the Ho-ly Ghost; As it was in the beginning, is now, and ev-er shall be: world with-out end. A-men.

DAY 17. MORNING PRAYER.

PSALM LXXXVI.—*Inclina, Domine.*

4th Tone, 8th Ending.

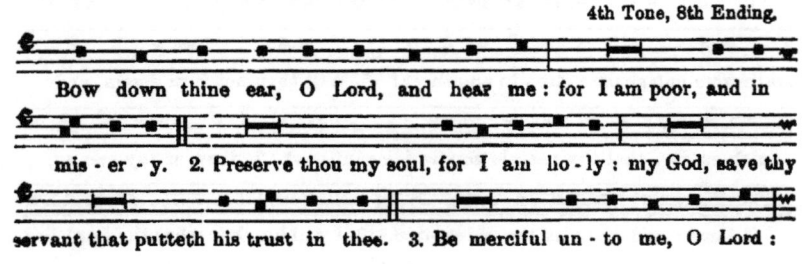

Bow down thine ear, O Lord, and hear me: for I am poor, and in mis-er-y. 2. Preserve thou my soul, for I am ho-ly: my God, save thy servant that putteth his trust in thee. 3. Be merciful un-to me, O Lord:

(148)

MORNING PRAYER. DAY 17.

for I will call daily up - on thee. 4. Com - fort the soul of thy ser - vant :
for unto thee, O Lord, do I lift up my soul. 5. For thou, Lord, art good and
gra - cious : and of great mercy unto all them that call up - on thee.
6. Give ear, Lord, un - to my prayer : and ponder the voice of my hum - ble
de- sires. 7. In the time of my trouble I will call up - on thee : for thou
hear- est me. 8. Among the gods there is none like un - to thee, O Lord :
there is not one that can do as thou do- est. 9. All nations whom thou hast made
shall come and wor - ship thee, O Lord : and shall glo - ri - fy thy Name.
10. For thou art great, and do - est won- drous things : thou art God a - lone.
11. Teach me thy way, O Lord, and I will walk in thy truth : O knit my heart
unto thee, that I may fear thy Name. 12. I will thank thee, O Lord my God,
with all my heart : and will praise thy Name for ev · er - more.
13. For great is thy mer-cy to-ward me : and thou hast delivered my soul from the
neth-er-most hell. 14. O God, the proud are ris - en a-gainst me : and the congregations of naughty men. have sought after my soul,* and have not set thee be ·

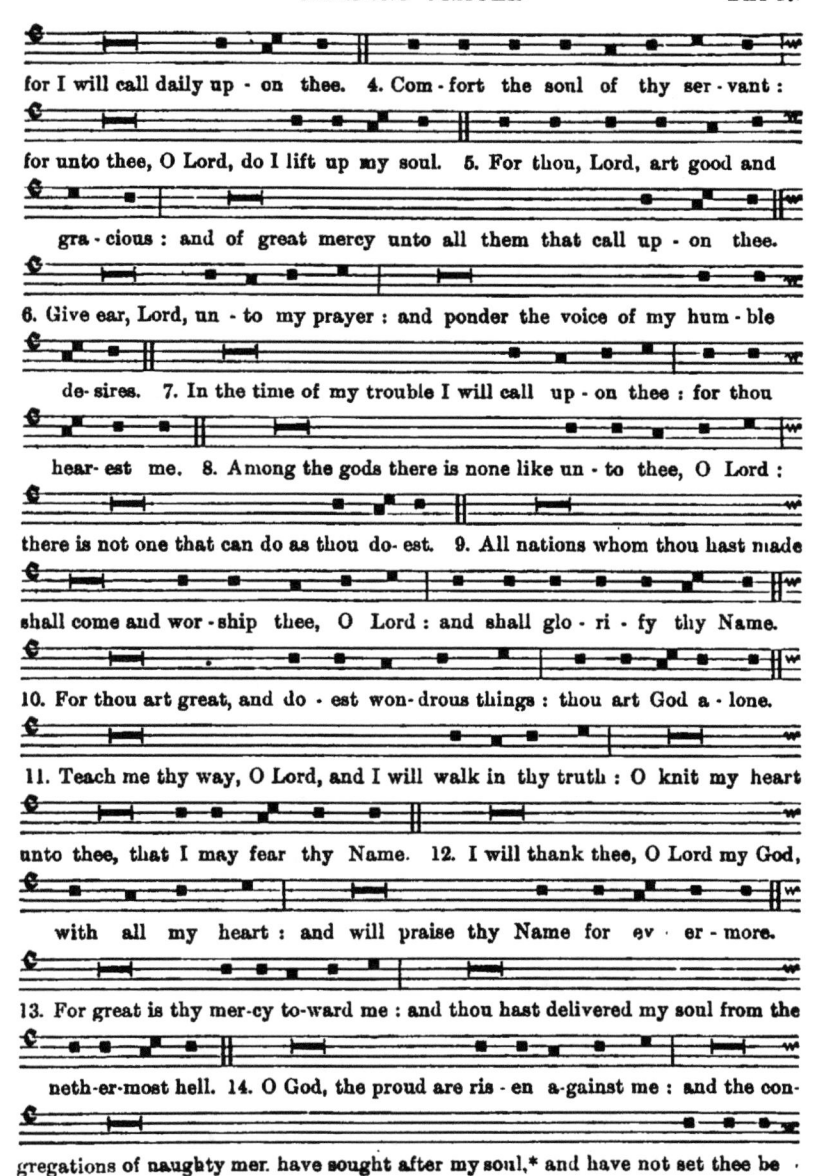

DAY 17. MORNING PRAYER.

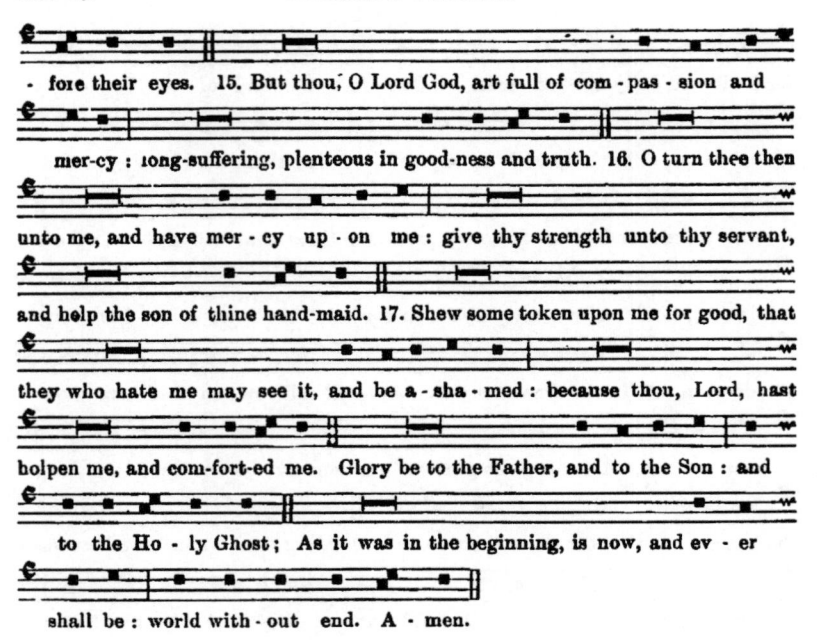

- fore their eyes. 15. But thou, O Lord God, art full of com - pas - sion and mer-cy : long-suffering, plenteous in good-ness and truth. 16. O turn thee then unto me, and have mer - cy up - on me : give thy strength unto thy servant, and help the son of thine hand-maid. 17. Shew some token upon me for good, that they who hate me may see it, and be a - sha - med : because thou, Lord, hast holpen me, and com-fort-ed me. Glory be to the Father, and to the Son : and to the Ho - ly Ghost ; As it was in the beginning, is now, and ev - er shall be : world with - out end. A - men.

PSALM LXXXVII.—*Fundamenta ejus.*

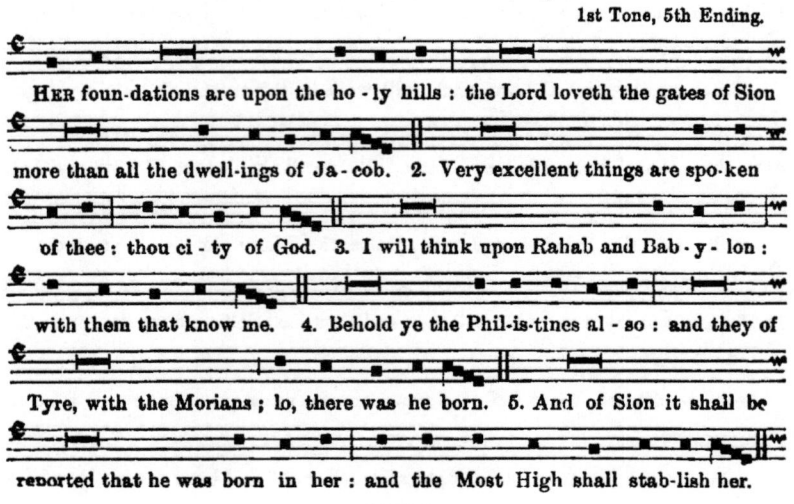

1st Tone, 5th Ending.

HER foun-dations are upon the ho - ly hills : the Lord loveth the gates of Sion more than all the dwell-ings of Ja - cob. 2. Very excellent things are spo-ken of thee : thou ci - ty of God. 3. I will think upon Rahab and Bab - y - lon : with them that know me. 4. Behold ye the Phil-is-tines al - so : and they of Tyre, with the Morians ; lo, there was he born. 5. And of Sion it shall be reported that he was born in her : and the Most High shall stab-lish her.

(150)

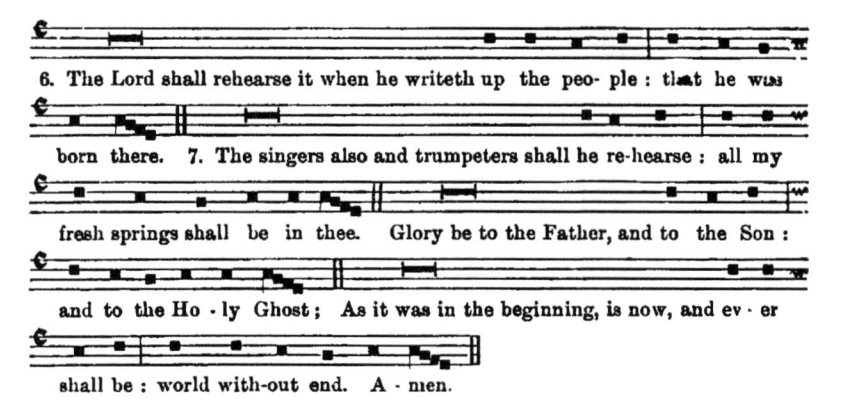

MORNING PRAYER. DAY 17.

6. The Lord shall rehearse it when he writeth up the peo- ple : that he was born there. 7. The singers also and trumpeters shall he re-hearse : all my fresh springs shall be in thee. Glory be to the Father, and to the Son : and to the Ho - ly Ghost ; As it was in the beginning, is now, and ev - er shall be : world with-out end. A - men.

PSALM LXXXVIII.—*Domine Deus.*

2nd Tone, 1st Ending.

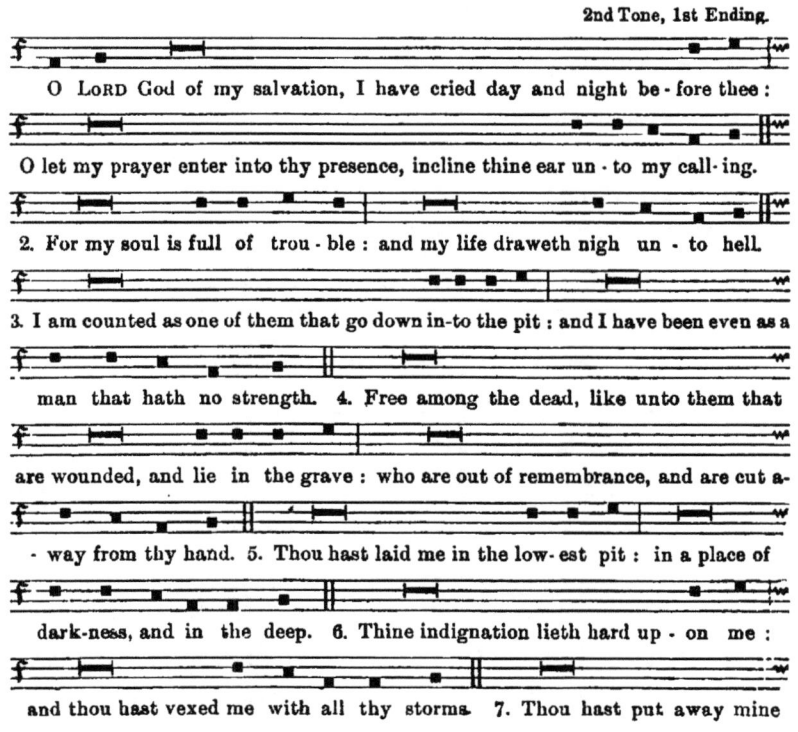

O LORD God of my salvation, I have cried day and night be - fore thee : O let my prayer enter into thy presence, incline thine ear un - to my call- ing. 2. For my soul is full of trou - ble : and my life draweth nigh un - to hell. 3. I am counted as one of them that go down in-to the pit : and I have been even as a man that hath no strength. 4. Free among the dead, like unto them that are wounded, and lie in the grave : who are out of remembrance, and are cut a- - way from thy hand. 5. Thou hast laid me in the low- est pit : in a place of dark-ness, and in the deep. 6. Thine indignation lieth hard up - on me : and thou hast vexed me with all thy storms. 7. Thou hast put away mine

(151)

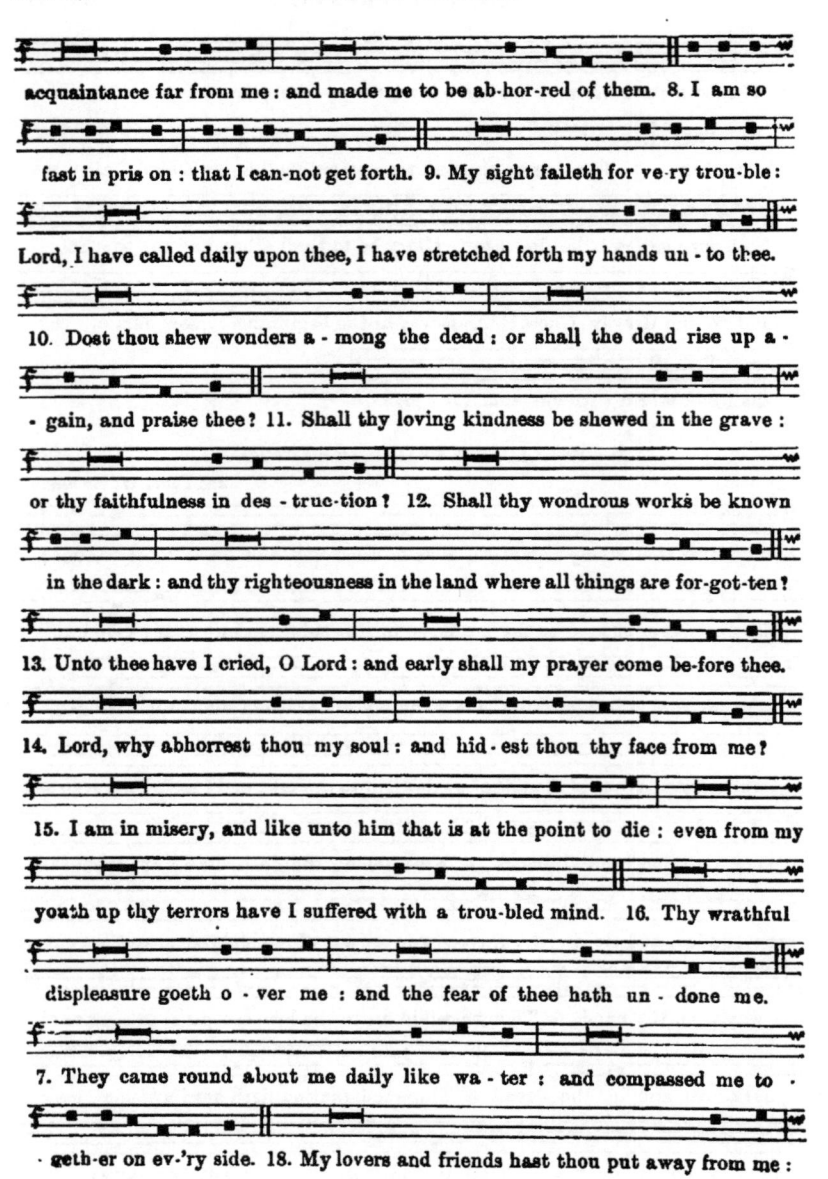

Day 17. MORNING PRAYER.

acquaintance far from me : and made me to be ab-hor-red of them. 8. I am so fast in pris on : that I can-not get forth. 9. My sight faileth for ve-ry trou-ble : Lord, I have called daily upon thee, I have stretched forth my hands un - to thee. 10. Dost thou shew wonders a - mong the dead : or shall the dead rise up a - gain, and praise thee? 11. Shall thy loving kindness be shewed in the grave : or thy faithfulness in des - truc-tion? 12. Shall thy wondrous works be known in the dark : and thy righteousness in the land where all things are for-got-ten? 13. Unto thee have I cried, O Lord : and early shall my prayer come be-fore thee. 14. Lord, why abhorrest thou my soul : and hid-est thou thy face from me? 15. I am in misery, and like unto him that is at the point to die : even from my youth up thy terrors have I suffered with a trou-bled mind. 16. Thy wrathful displeasure goeth o - ver me : and the fear of thee hath un - done me. 7. They came round about me daily like wa - ter : and compassed me to - geth-er on ev-'ry side. 18. My lovers and friends hast thou put away from me :

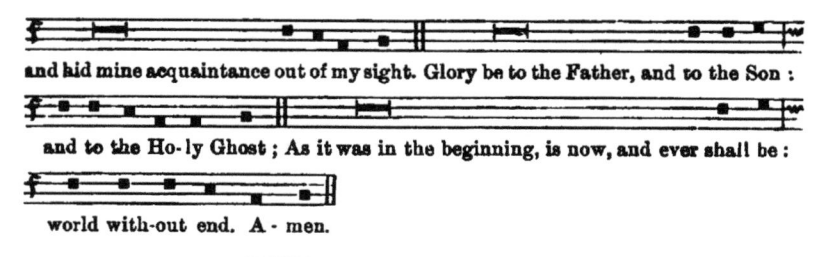

EVENING PRAYER. DAY 17.

and hid mine acquaintance out of my sight. Glory be to the Father, and to the Son :

and to the Ho-ly Ghost ; As it was in the beginning, is now, and ever shall be :

world with-out end. A - men.

EVENING PRAYER.

PSALM LXXXIX.—*Misericordias Domini.*

1st Tone, 1st Ending.

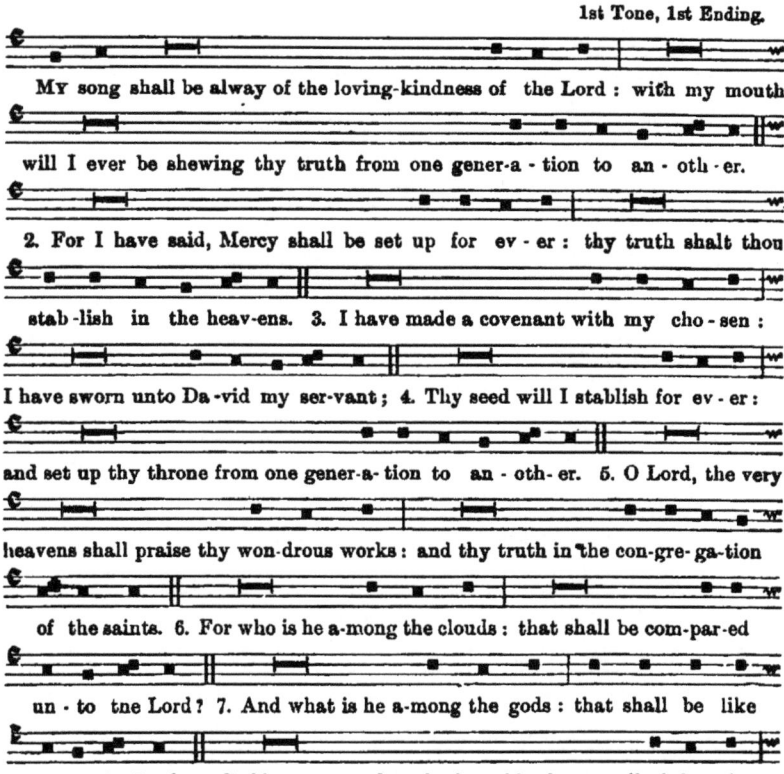

My song shall be alway of the loving-kindness of the Lord : with my mouth

will I ever be shewing thy truth from one gener-a - tion to an - oth - er.

2. For I have said, Mercy shall be set up for ev - er : thy truth shalt thou

stab -lish in the heav-ens. 3. I have made a covenant with my cho - sen :

I have sworn unto Da -vid my ser-vant ; 4. Thy seed will I stablish for ev - er :

and set up thy throne from one gener-a- tion to an - oth- er. 5. O Lord, the very

heavens shall praise thy won-drous works : and thy truth in the con-gre- ga-tion

of the saints. 6. For who is he a-mong the clouds : that shall be com-par-ed

un - to the Lord ? 7. And what is he a-mong the gods : that shall be like

un -to the Lord ? 8. God is very greatly to be feared in the council of the saints :

DAY 17. EVENING PRAYER.

and to be had in reverence of all them that are round a-bout him. 9. O Lord God of hosts, who is like un-to thee? thy truth, most mighty Lord, is on ev-'ry side. 10. Thou rulest the raging of the sea : thou stillest the waves there-of when they a-rise. 11. Thou hast subdued Egypt, and des-troy-ed it : thou hast scattered thine enemies a-broad with thy might-y arm. 12. The heavens are thine, the earth al-so is thine : thou hast laid the foundation of the round world, and all that there-in is. 13. Thou hast made the north and the south : Tabor and Hermon shall re-joice in thy Name. 14. Thou hast a might-y arm : strong is thy hand, and high is thy right hand. 15. Righteousness and equity are the habitation of thy seat : mer-cy and truth shall go be-fore thy face. 16. Blessed is the people, O Lord, that can re-joice in thee : they shall walk in the light of thy coun-te-nance. 17. Their delight shall be dai-ly in thy Name : and in thy right-eous-ness shall they make their boast. 18. For thou art the glo-ry of their strength : and in thy loving kindness thou shalt lift up our horns. 19. For the Lord is our de-fence : the Holy One of Is-ra-el is our King.

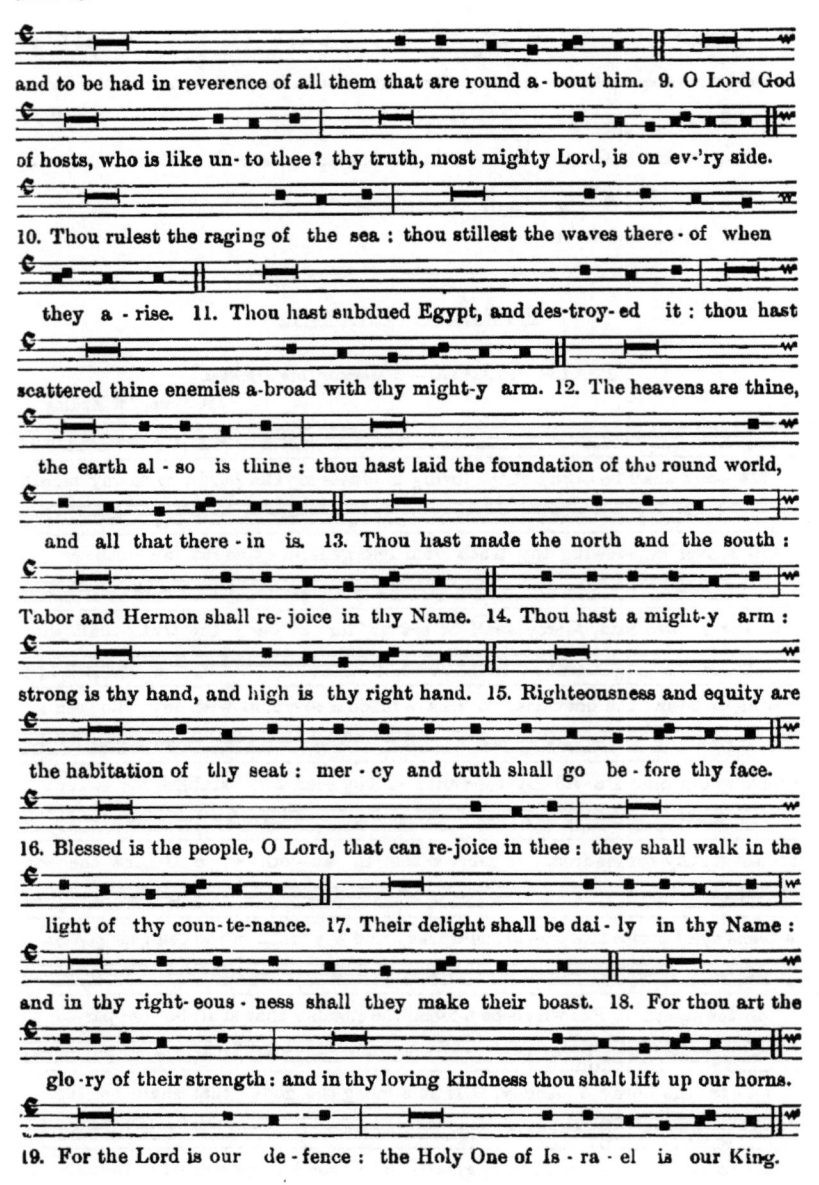

EVENING PRAYER. DAY 17.

20. Thou spakest sometime in visions unto thy saints, and saidst: I have laid help upon one that is mighty ; I have exalted one chosen out of the peo - ple.

21. I have found David my ser-vant : with my holy oil have I an-oint-ed him.

22. My hand shall hold him fast : and my arm shall strength - en him.

23. The enemy shall not be able to do him vi - o -lence : the son of wick-ed ness shall not hurt him. 24. I will smite down his foes be-fore his face : and plague them that hate him. 25. My truth also and my mercy shall be with him : and in my Name shall his horn be ex - alt - ed. 26. I will set his dominion also in the sea : and his right hand in the floods. 27. He shall call me, Thou art my Fath - er : my God, and my strong sal - va-tion. 28. And I will make him my first-born : high- er than the kings of the earth. 29. My mercy will I keep for him for ev - er - more : and my covenant shall stand fast with him.

30. His seed also will I make to en-dure for ev - er : and his throne as the days of heav - en. 31. But if his children for-sake my law : and walk not in my judge-ments ; 32. If they break my statutes, and keep not my commandments :

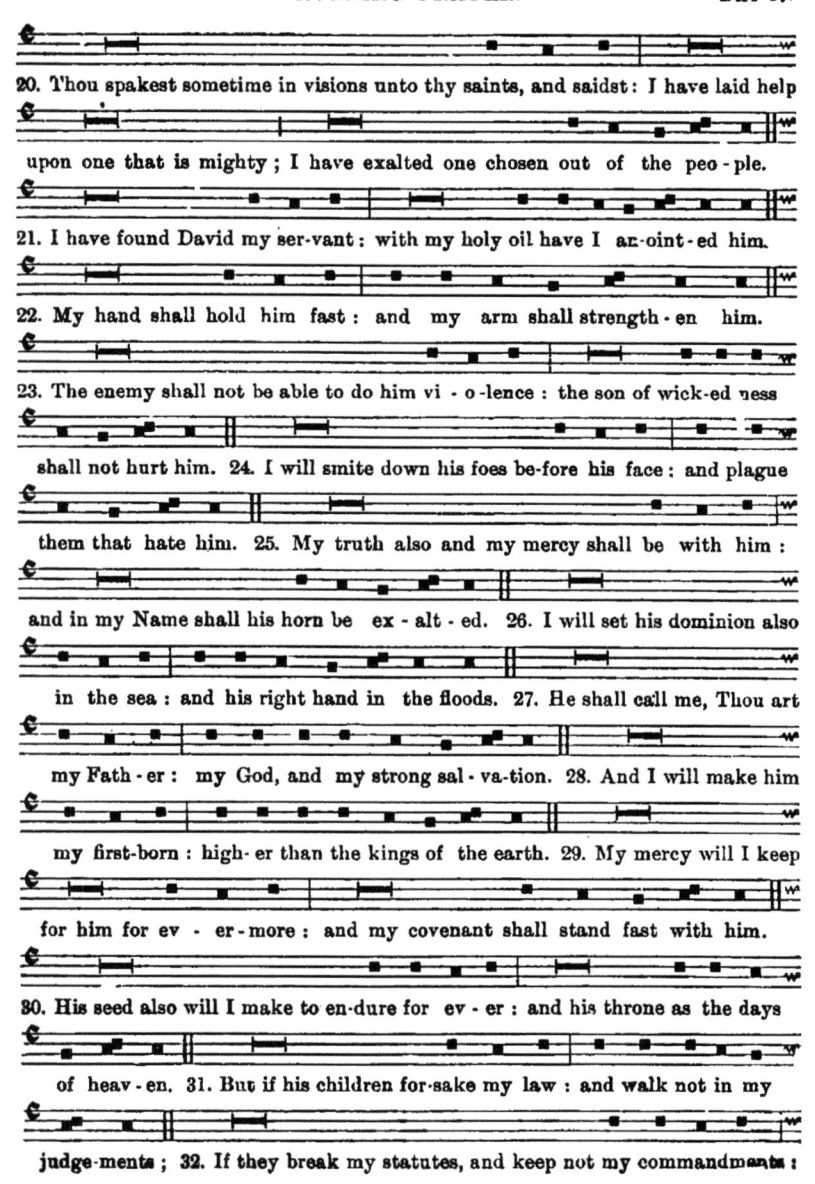

DAY 17　　　　　EVENING PRAYER.

I will visit their offences with the rod, and their sin with scour-ges.

33. Nevertheless, my loving-kindness will I not utterly take from him:

nor suf-fer my truth to fail. 34. My covenant will I not break, nor alter the

thing that is gone out of my lips : I have sworn once by my holiness, that I will

not fail Da-vid. 35. His seed shall en-dure for ev-er : and his seat is like as

the sun be-fore me. 36. He shall stand fast for evermore as the moon :

and as the faithful wit-ness in heav-en. 37. But thou hast abhorred and forsaken

thine an-oint-ed : and art dis-pleas-ed at him. 38. Thou hast broken the

covenant of thy ser-vant : and cast his crown to the ground. 39. Thou hast

overthrown all his hed-ges : and bro-ken down his strong holds. 40. All they that

go by spoil him : and he is become a re-proach to his neigh-bours.

41. Thou hast set up the right hand of his en-e-mies : and made all his

ad-ver-sar-ies to re-joice. 42. Thou hast taken away the edge of his sword :

and givest him not vic-to-ry in the bat-tle. 43. Thou hast put out his glo-ry :

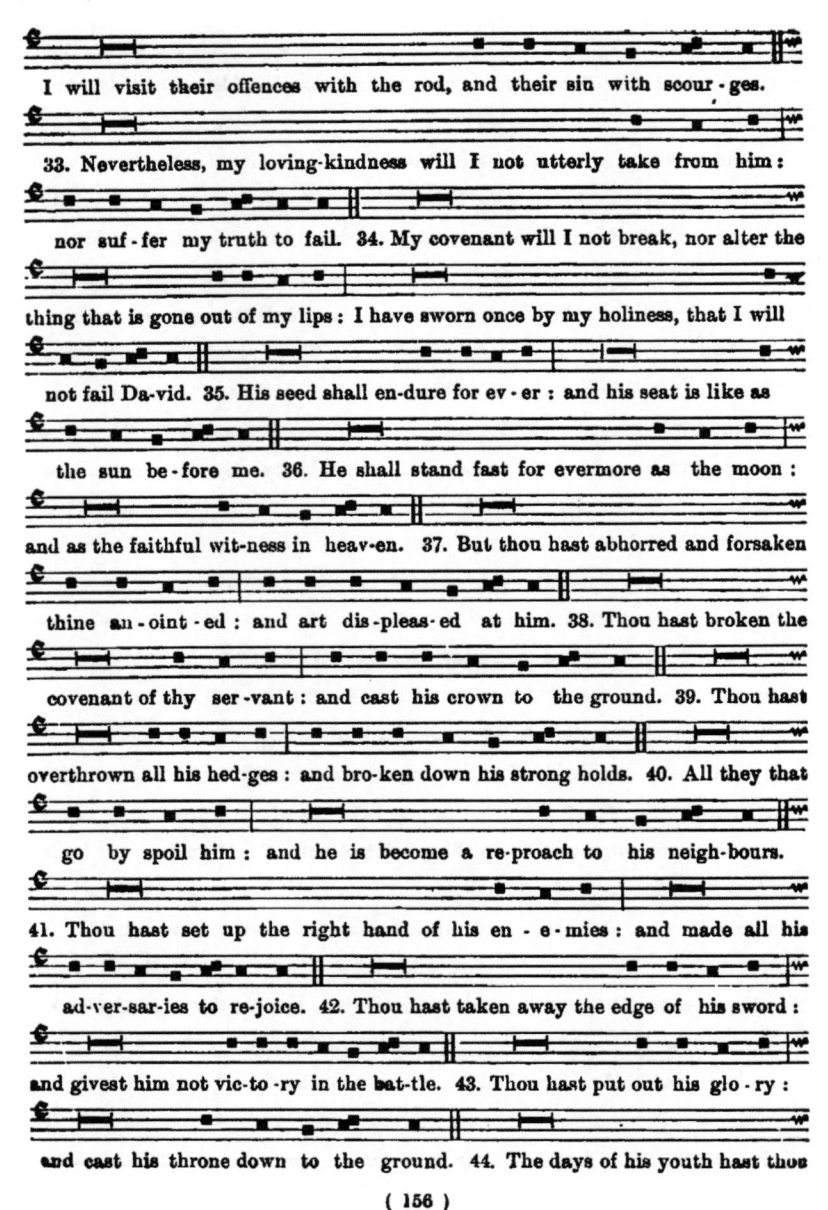

and cast his throne down to the ground. 44. The days of his youth hast thou short-en-ed : and covered him with dis-hon-our. 45. Lord, how long wilt thou hide thyself, for ev-er : and shall thy wrath burn like fire? 46. O remember how short my time is : where-fore hast thou made all men for nought? 47. What man is he that liveth, and shall not see death : and shall he deliver his soul from the hand of hell? 48. Lord, where are thy old loving-kind-ness-es : which thou swarest unto Da-vid in thy truth? 49. Remember, Lord, the rebuke that thy ser-vants have: and how I do bear in my bosom the re-bukes of ma,ny peo-ple ; 50. Where-with thine enemies have blasphemed thee. and slandered the footsteps of thine an-oint-ed : Praised be the Lord for evermore. A-men, and A-men.

Glory be to the Father, and to the Son : and to the Ho-ly Ghost; As it was in the beginning, is now, and ev-er shall be : world with-out end. A-men.

MORNING PRAYER. DAY 18.

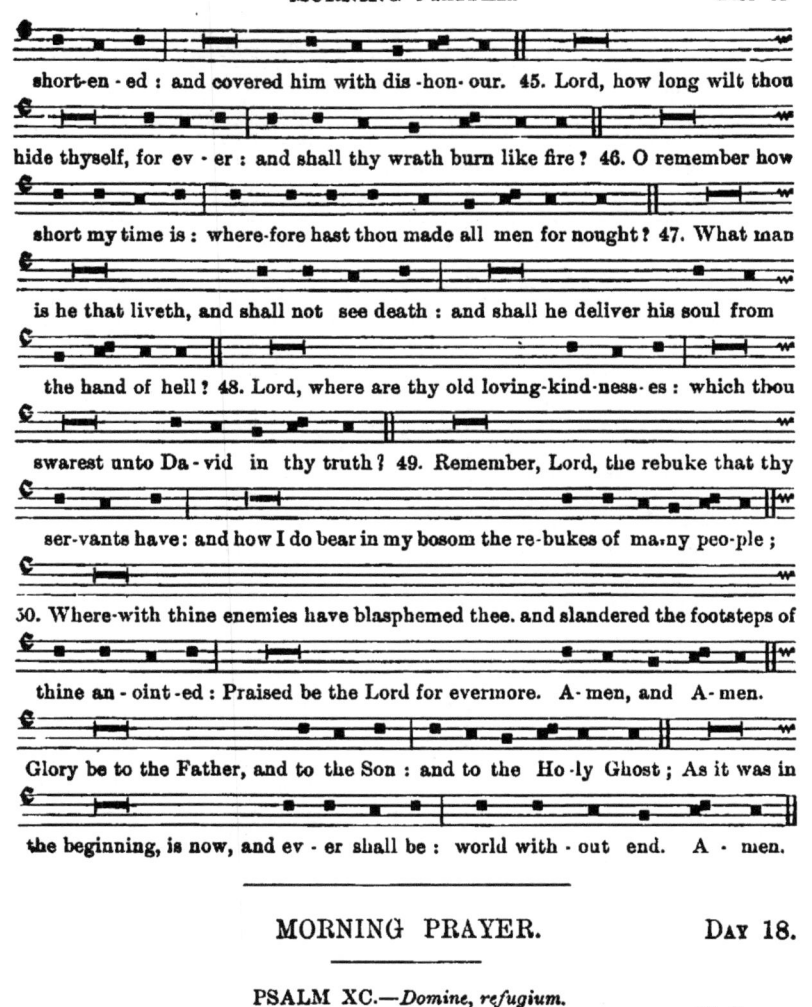

PSALM XC.—*Domine, refugium.*

6th Tone.

LORD, thou hast been our re-fuge : from one gener-a-tion to an-oth-er.

2. Before the mountains were brought forth, or ever the earth and the world

(157)

DAY 18.   MORNING PRAYER.

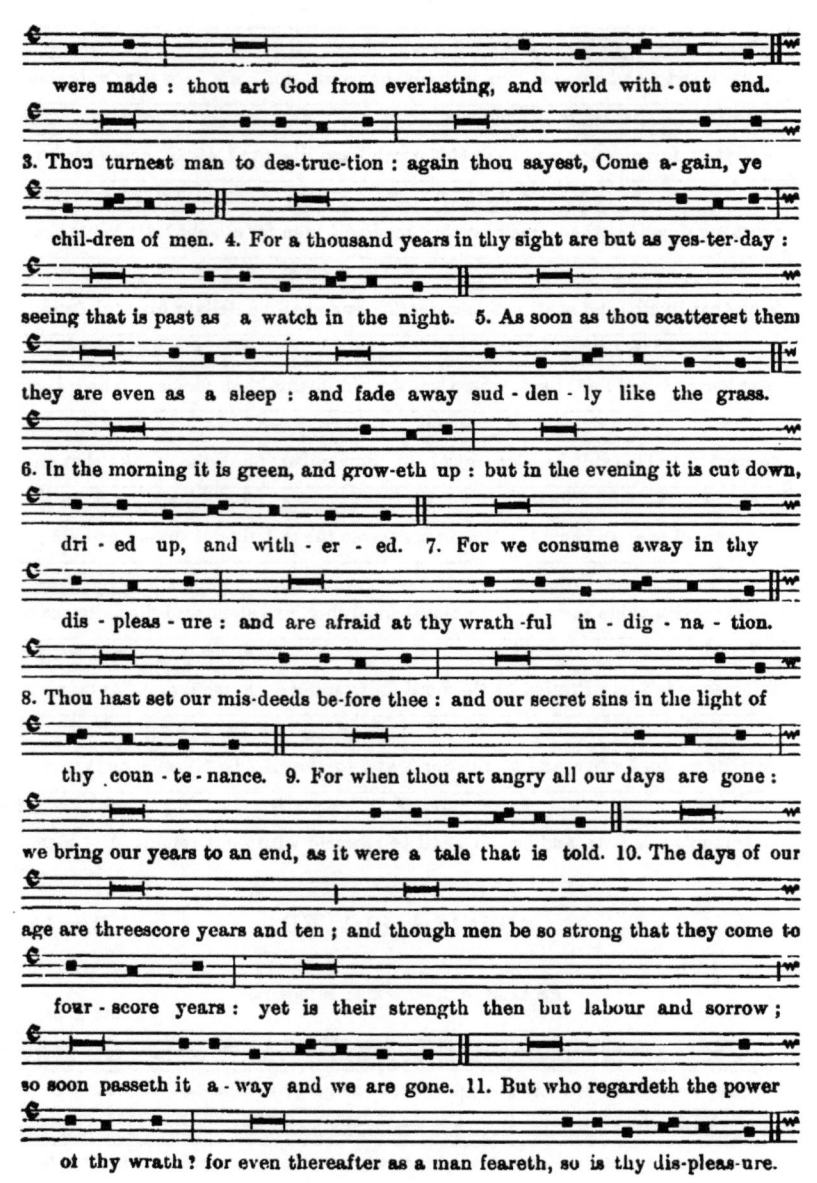

were made : thou art God from everlasting, and world with-out end.

3. Thou turnest man to des-truc-tion : again thou sayest, Come a-gain, ye chil-dren of men. 4. For a thousand years in thy sight are but as yes-ter-day : seeing that is past as a watch in the night. 5. As soon as thou scatterest them they are even as a sleep : and fade away sud-den-ly like the grass.

6. In the morning it is green, and grow-eth up : but in the evening it is cut down, dri-ed up, and with-er-ed. 7. For we consume away in thy dis-pleas-ure : and are afraid at thy wrath-ful in-dig-na-tion.

8. Thou hast set our mis-deeds be-fore thee : and our secret sins in the light of thy coun-te-nance. 9. For when thou art angry all our days are gone : we bring our years to an end, as it were a tale that is told. 10. The days of our age are threescore years and ten ; and though men be so strong that they come to four-score years : yet is their strength then but labour and sorrow ; so soon passeth it a-way and we are gone. 11. But who regardeth the power of thy wrath ? for even thereafter as a man feareth, so is thy dis-pleas-ure.

MORNING PRAYER. DAY 18.

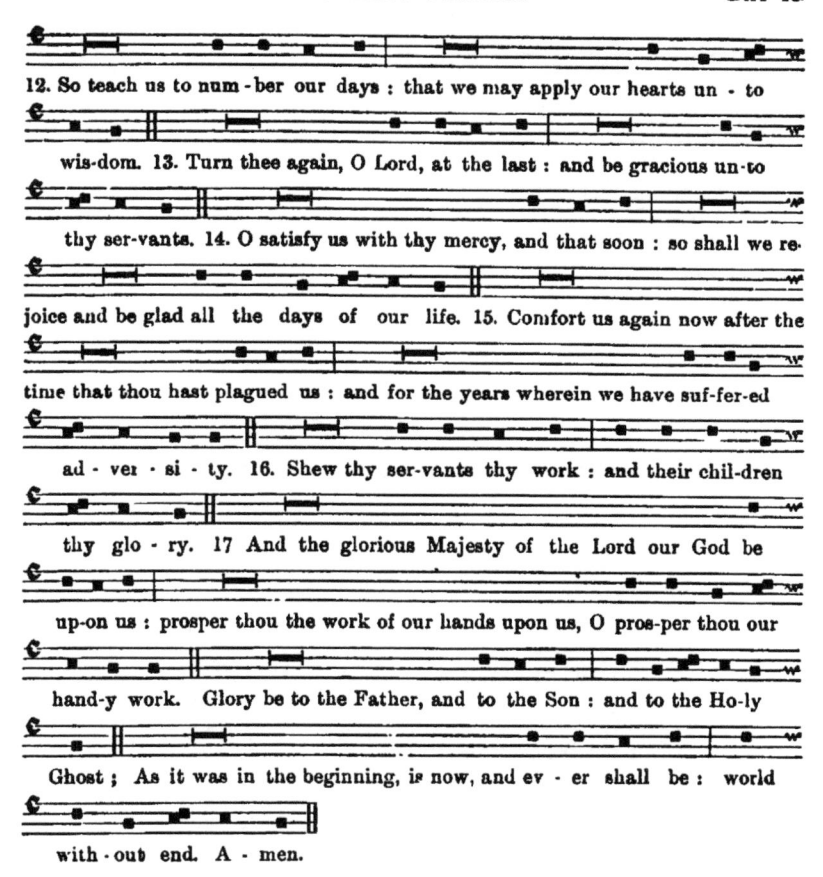

12. So teach us to num-ber our days : that we may apply our hearts un - to wis-dom. 13. Turn thee again, O Lord, at the last : and be gracious un-to thy ser-vants. 14. O satisfy us with thy mercy, and that soon : so shall we rejoice and be glad all the days of our life. 15. Comfort us again now after the time that thou hast plagued us : and for the years wherein we have suf-fer-ed ad - ver - si - ty. 16. Shew thy ser-vants thy work : and their chil-dren thy glo - ry. 17 And the glorious Majesty of the Lord our God be up-on us : prosper thou the work of our hands upon us, O pros-per thou our hand-y work. Glory be to the Father, and to the Son : and to the Ho-ly Ghost ; As it was in the beginning, is now, and ev - er shall be : world with - out end. A - men.

PSALM XCI.—*Qui habitat.*

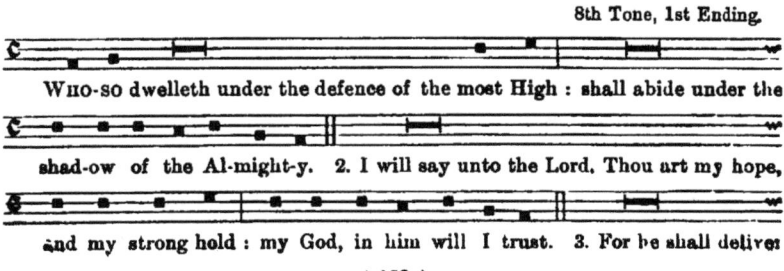

8th Tone, 1st Ending.

Who-so dwelleth under the defence of the most High : shall abide under the shad-ow of the Al-might-y. 2. I will say unto the Lord, Thou art my hope, and my strong hold : my God, in him will I trust. 3. For he shall deliver

(159)

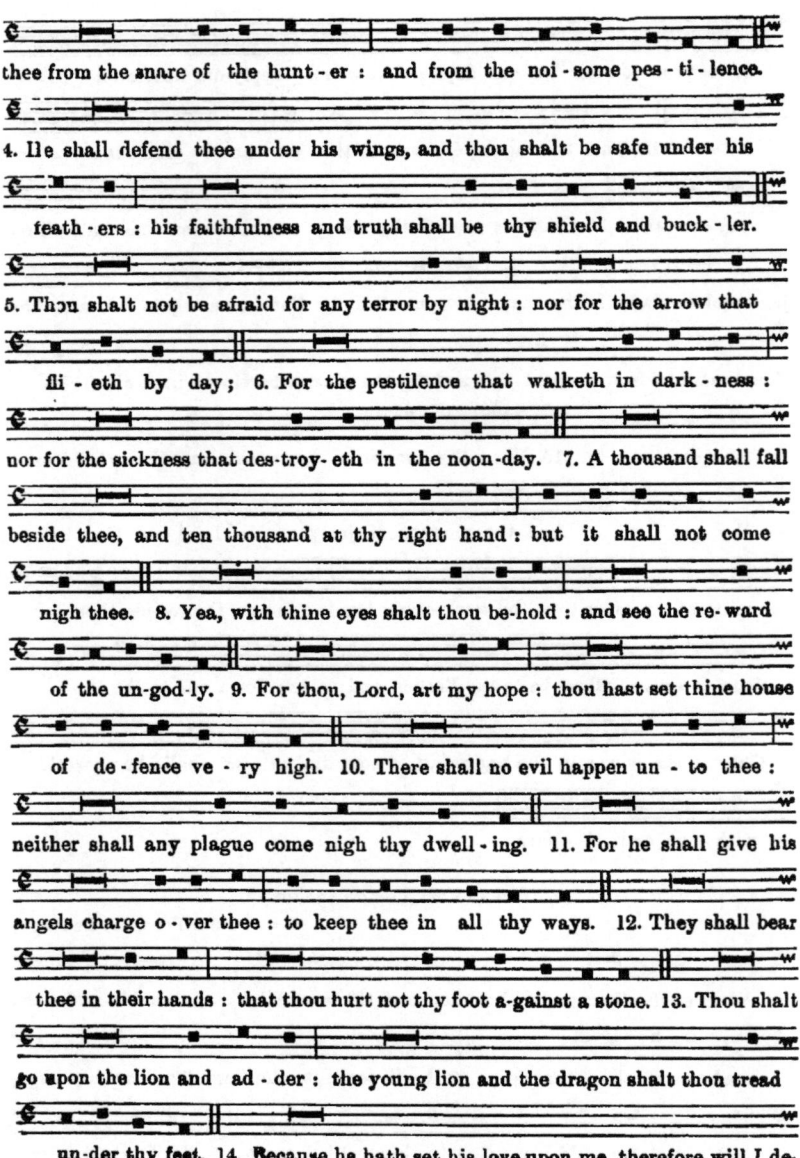

thee from the snare of the hunt-er : and from the noi-some pes-ti-lence.

4. He shall defend thee under his wings, and thou shalt be safe under his feath-ers : his faithfulness and truth shall be thy shield and buck-ler.

5. Thou shalt not be afraid for any terror by night : nor for the arrow that fli-eth by day; 6. For the pestilence that walketh in dark-ness : nor for the sickness that des-troy-eth in the noon-day. 7. A thousand shall fall beside thee, and ten thousand at thy right hand : but it shall not come nigh thee. 8. Yea, with thine eyes shalt thou be-hold : and see the re-ward of the un-god-ly. 9. For thou, Lord, art my hope : thou hast set thine house of de-fence ve-ry high. 10. There shall no evil happen un-to thee : neither shall any plague come nigh thy dwell-ing. 11. For he shall give his angels charge o-ver thee : to keep thee in all thy ways. 12. They shall bear thee in their hands : that thou hurt not thy foot a-gainst a stone. 13. Thou shalt go upon the lion and ad-der : the young lion and the dragon shalt thou tread un-der thy feet. 14. Because he hath set his love upon me, therefore will I de-

MORNING PRAYER. DAY 18.

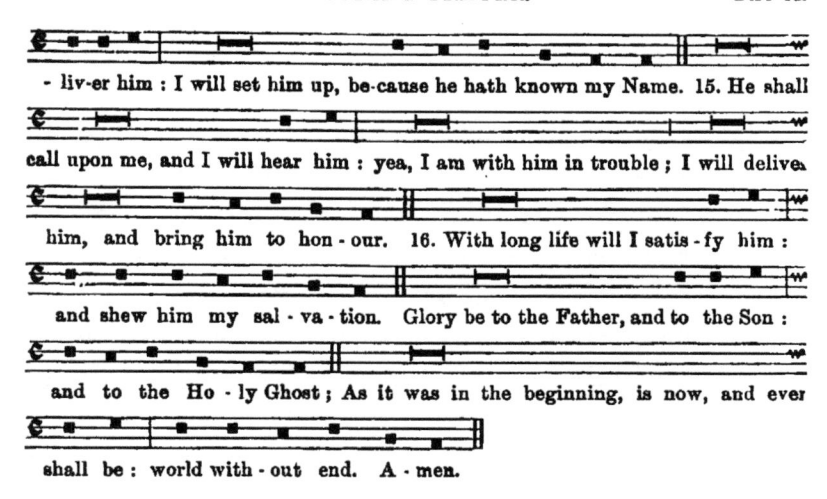

-liv-er him : I will set him up, be-cause he hath known my Name. 15. He shall call upon me, and I will hear him : yea, I am with him in trouble ; I will deliver him, and bring him to hon-our. 16. With long life will I satis-fy him : and shew him my sal-va-tion. Glory be to the Father, and to the Son : and to the Ho-ly Ghost ; As it was in the beginning, is now, and ever shall be : world with-out end. A-men.

PSALM XCII.—*Bonum est confiteri.*

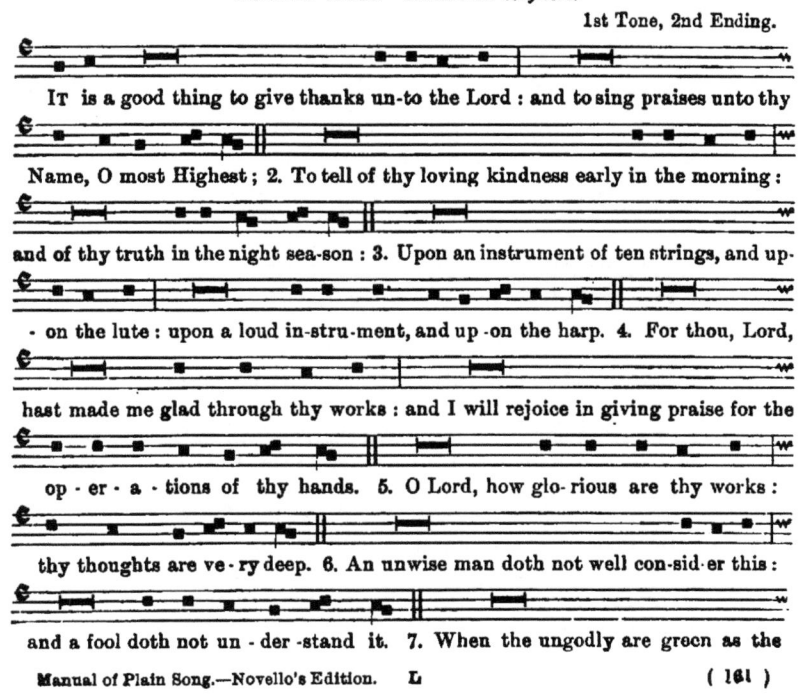

1st Tone, 2nd Ending.

IT is a good thing to give thanks un-to the Lord : and to sing praises unto thy Name, O most Highest ; 2. To tell of thy loving kindness early in the morning : and of thy truth in the night sea-son : 3. Upon an instrument of ten strings, and up- -on the lute : upon a loud in-stru-ment, and up-on the harp. 4. For thou, Lord, hast made me glad through thy works : and I will rejoice in giving praise for the op-er-a-tions of thy hands. 5. O Lord, how glo-rious are thy works : thy thoughts are ve-ry deep. 6. An unwise man doth not well con-sid-er this : and a fool doth not un-der-stand it. 7. When the ungodly are green as the

Manual of Plain Song.—Novello's Edition.   L

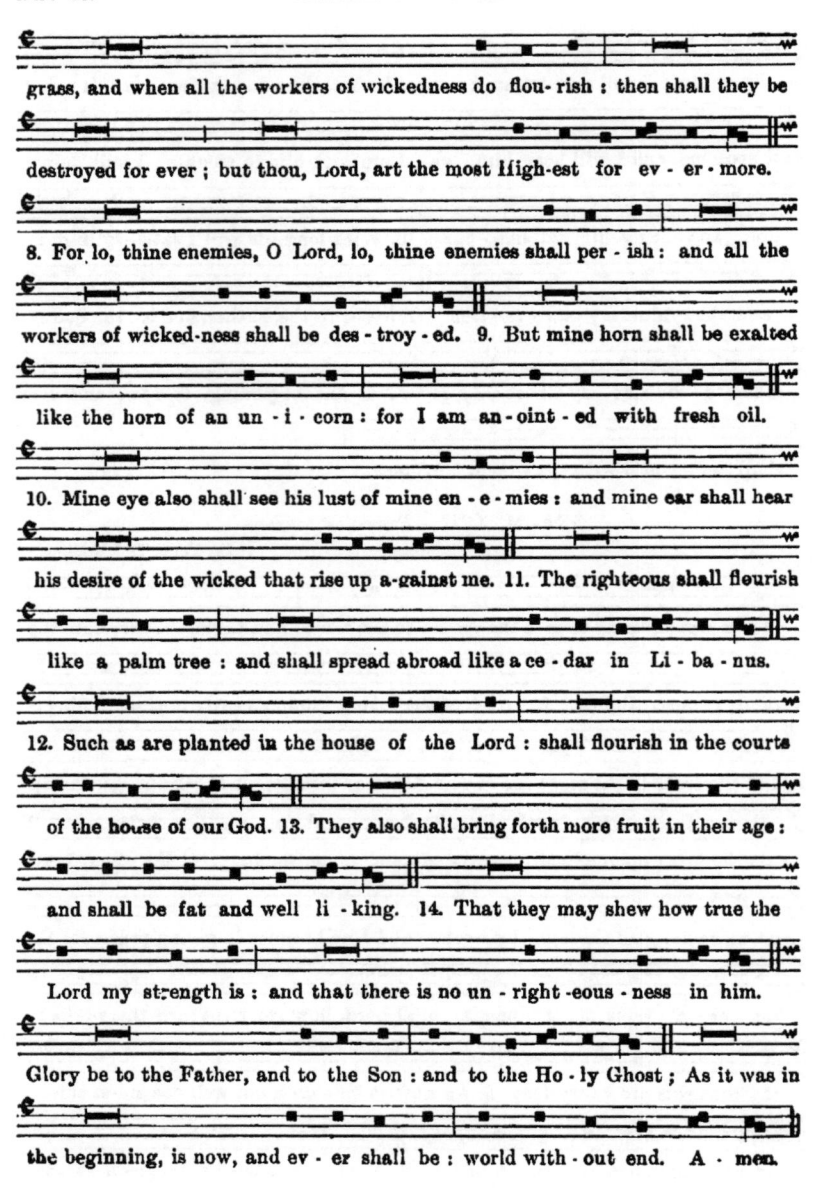

grass, and when all the workers of wickedness do flou-rish : then shall they be destroyed for ever ; but thou, Lord, art the most High-est for ev-er-more.

8. For lo, thine enemies, O Lord, lo, thine enemies shall per-ish : and all the workers of wicked-ness shall be des-troy-ed. 9. But mine horn shall be exalted like the horn of an un-i-corn : for I am an-oint-ed with fresh oil.

10. Mine eye also shall see his lust of mine en-e-mies : and mine ear shall hear his desire of the wicked that rise up a-gainst me. 11. The righteous shall flourish like a palm tree : and shall spread abroad like a ce-dar in Li-ba-nus.

12. Such as are planted in the house of the Lord : shall flourish in the courts of the house of our God. 13. They also shall bring forth more fruit in their age : and shall be fat and well li-king. 14. That they may shew how true the Lord my strength is : and that there is no un-right-eous-ness in him.

Glory be to the Father, and to the Son : and to the Ho-ly Ghost ; As it was in the beginning, is now, and ev-er shall be : world with-out end. A-men.

EVENING PRAYER.

DAY 18.

PSALM XCIII.—*Dominus regnavit.*

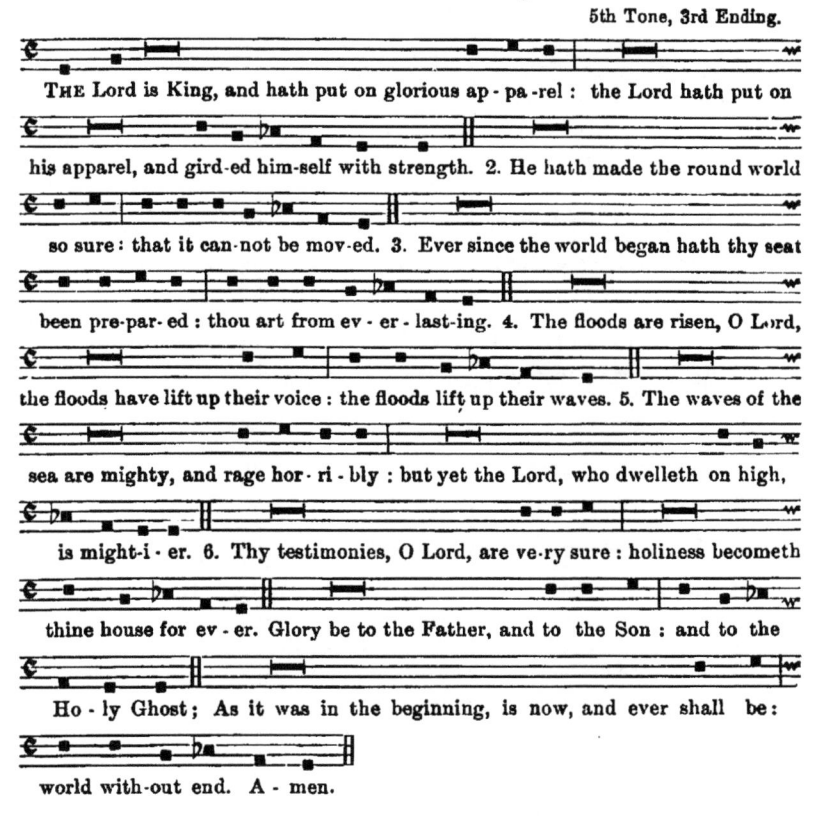

5th Tone, 3rd Ending.

The Lord is King, and hath put on glorious ap - pa -rel : the Lord hath put on his apparel, and gird-ed him-self with strength. 2. He hath made the round world so sure: that it can-not be mov-ed. 3. Ever since the world began hath thy seat been pre-par-ed : thou art from ev - er - last-ing. 4. The floods are risen, O Lord, the floods have lift up their voice : the floods lift up their waves. 5. The waves of the sea are mighty, and rage hor - ri - bly : but yet the Lord, who dwelleth on high, is might-i - er. 6. Thy testimonies, O Lord, are ve-ry sure : holiness becometh thine house for ev - er. Glory be to the Father, and to the Son : and to the Ho - ly Ghost ; As it was in the beginning, is now, and ever shall be : world with-out end. A - men.

PSALM XCIV.—*Deus ultionum.*

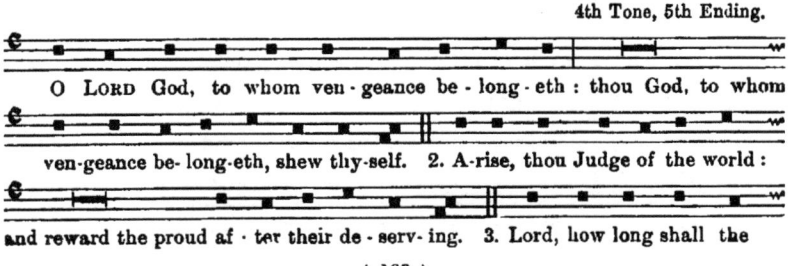

4th Tone, 5th Ending.

O Lord God, to whom ven - geance be - long - eth : thou God, to whom ven-geance be- long-eth, shew thy-self. 2. A-rise, thou Judge of the world : and reward the proud af - ter their de - serv- ing. 3. Lord, how long shall the

(163)

DAY 18. EVENING PRAYER.

un-god-ly : how long shall the un-god-ly tri-umph? 4. How long shall

all wicked doers speak so dis-dain-ful-ly : and make such proud boast-ing?

5. They smite down thy peo-ple, O Lord : and trou-ble thine her-it-age.

6. They murder the wid-ow, and the stran-ger : and put the fath-er-less to death.

7. And yet they say, Tush, the Lord shall not see : neither shall the God of

Ja-cob re-gard it. 8. Take heed, ye un-wise a-mong the peo-ple : O ye

fools, when will ye un-der-stand? 9. He that planted the ear, shall he

not hear : or he that made the eye, shall he not see? 10. Or he that

nur-tur-eth the heath-en : it is he that teacheth man know-ledge, shall not

he pun-ish? 11. The Lord know-eth the thoughts of man · that they are

but vain. 12. Blessed is the man whom thou chas-ten-est, O Lord : and

teach-est him in thy law; 13. That thou mayest give him patience in time

of ad-ver-si-ty : until the pit be digged up for the un-god-ly. 14. For the Lord

will not fail his peo-ple : nei-ther will he for-sake his in-her-it-ance;

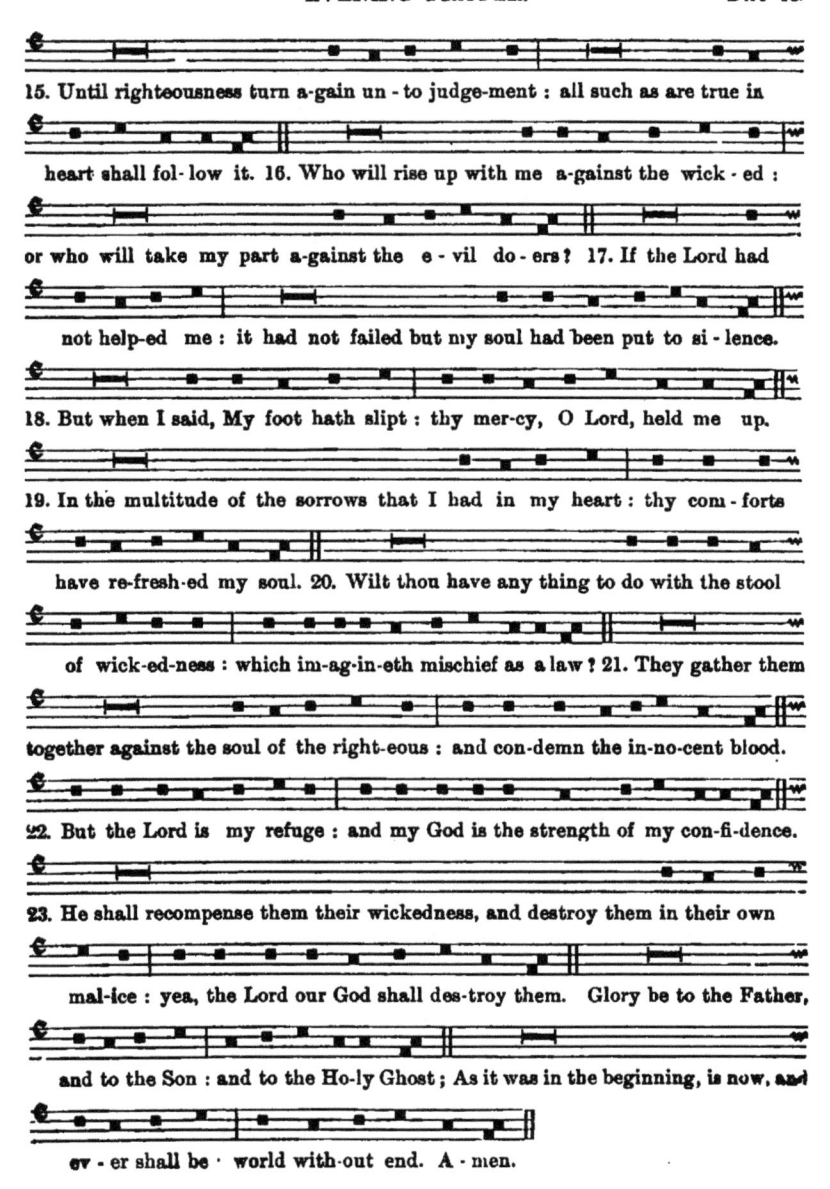

EVENING PRAYER. DAY 18.

15. Until righteousness turn a-gain un - to judge-ment : all such as are true in heart shall fol-low it. 16. Who will rise up with me a-gainst the wick - ed : or who will take my part a-gainst the e - vil do - ers? 17. If the Lord had not help-ed me : it had not failed but my soul had been put to si - lence. 18. But when I said, My foot hath slipt : thy mer-cy, O Lord, held me up. 19. In the multitude of the sorrows that I had in my heart : thy com - forts have re-fresh-ed my soul. 20. Wilt thou have any thing to do with the stool of wick-ed-ness : which im-ag-in-eth mischief as a law? 21. They gather them together against the soul of the right-eous : and con-demn the in-no-cent blood. 22. But the Lord is my refuge : and my God is the strength of my con-fi-dence. 23. He shall recompense them their wickedness, and destroy them in their own mal-ice : yea, the Lord our God shall des-troy them. Glory be to the Father, and to the Son : and to the Ho-ly Ghost ; As it was in the beginning, is now, and ev - er shall be · world with-out end. A - men.

DAY 19.   MORNING PRAYER.

PSALM XCV.—*Venite, exultemus Domino.*

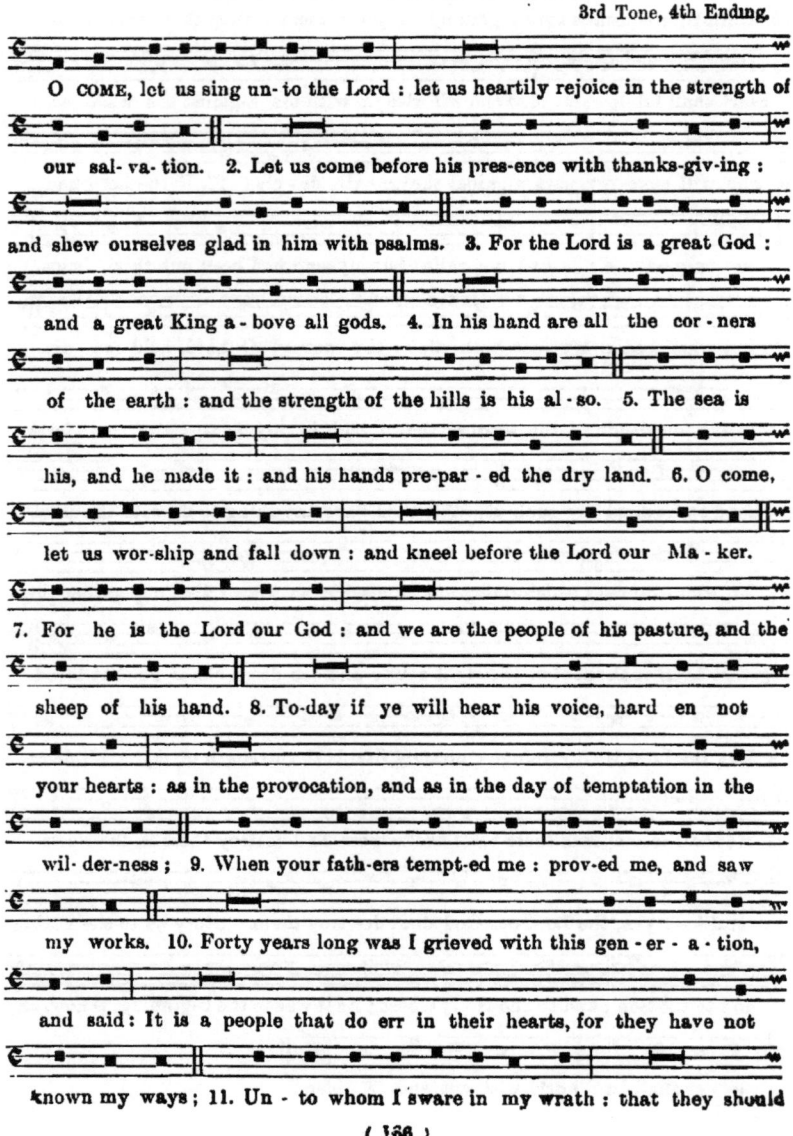

3rd Tone, 4th Ending.

O COME, let us sing un- to the Lord : let us heartily rejoice in the strength of

our sal- va- tion. 2. Let us come before his pres-ence with thanks-giv-ing :

and shew ourselves glad in him with psalms. 3. For the Lord is a great God :

and a great King a- bove all gods. 4. In his hand are all the cor- ners

of the earth : and the strength of the hills is his al- so. 5. The sea is

his, and he made it : and his hands pre-par- ed the dry land. 6. O come,

let us wor-ship and fall down : and kneel before the Lord our Ma- ker.

7. For he is the Lord our God : and we are the people of his pasture, and the

sheep of his hand. 8. To-day if ye will hear his voice, hard en not

your hearts : as in the provocation, and as in the day of temptation in the

wil- der-ness ; 9. When your fath-ers tempt-ed me : prov-ed me, and saw

my works. 10. Forty years long was I grieved with this gen- er- a- tion,

and said : It is a people that do err in their hearts, for they have not

known my ways ; 11. Un - to whom I sware in my wrath : that they should

(166)

MORNING PRAYER. DAY 19.

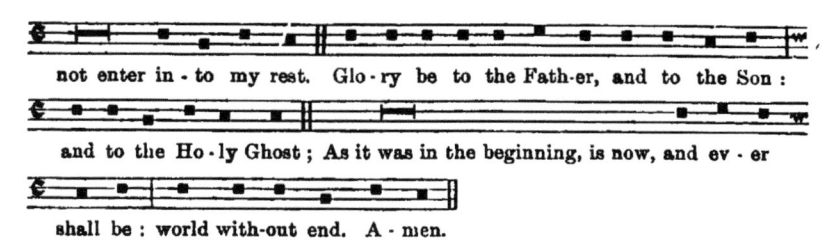

not enter in-to my rest. Glo-ry be to the Fath-er, and to the Son:

and to the Ho-ly Ghost; As it was in the beginning, is now, and ev-er

shall be: world with-out end. A-men.

PSALM XCVI.—*Cantate Domino.*

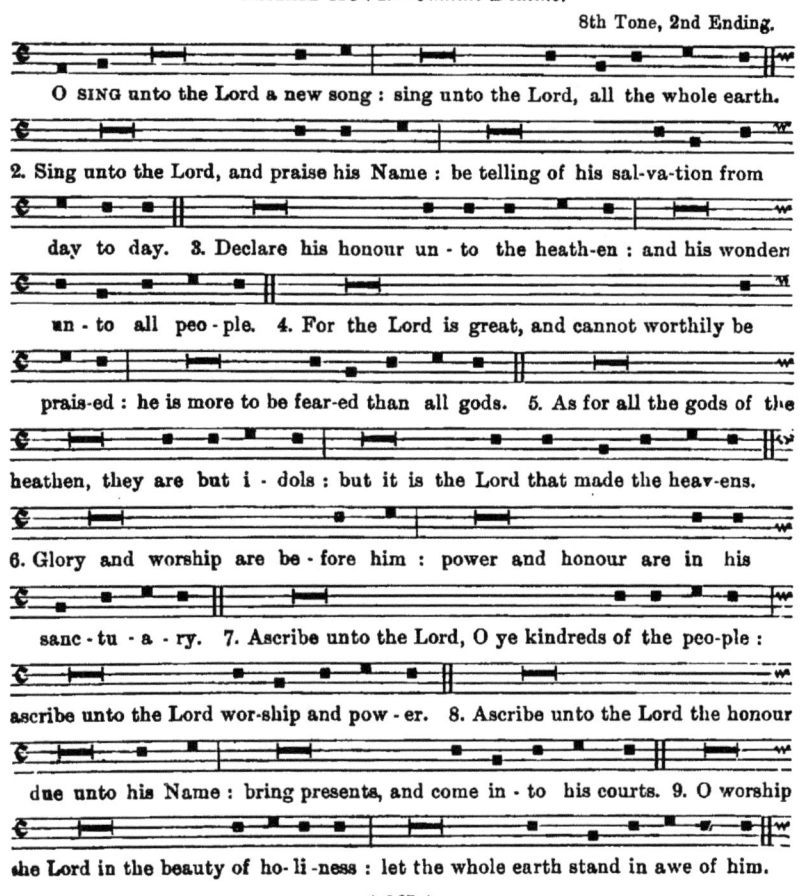

8th Tone, 2nd Ending.

O SING unto the Lord a new song: sing unto the Lord, all the whole earth.

2. Sing unto the Lord, and praise his Name: be telling of his sal-va-tion from

day to day. 3. Declare his honour un-to the heath-en: and his wonders

un-to all peo-ple. 4. For the Lord is great, and cannot worthily be

prais-ed: he is more to be fear-ed than all gods. 5. As for all the gods of the

heathen, they are but i-dols: but it is the Lord that made the heav-ens.

6. Glory and worship are be-fore him: power and honour are in his

sanc-tu-a-ry. 7. Ascribe unto the Lord, O ye kindreds of the peo-ple:

ascribe unto the Lord wor-ship and pow-er. 8. Ascribe unto the Lord the honour

due unto his Name: bring presents, and come in-to his courts. 9. O worship

the Lord in the beauty of ho-li-ness: let the whole earth stand in awe of him.

(167)

DAY 19   MORNING PRAYER.

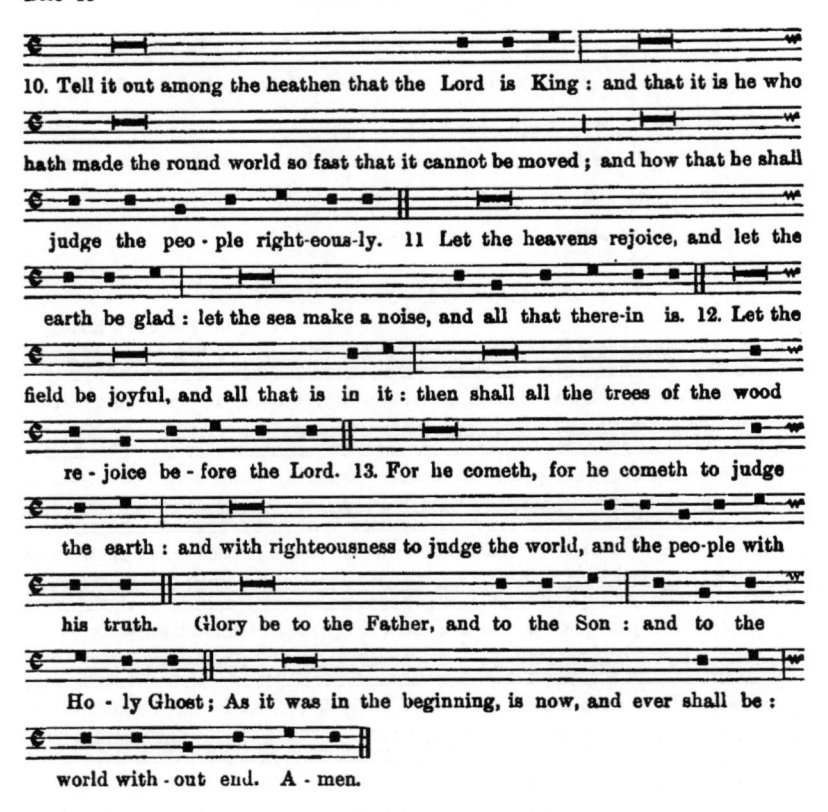

10. Tell it out among the heathen that the Lord is King : and that it is he who hath made the round world so fast that it cannot be moved ; and how that he shall judge the peo - ple right-eous-ly. 11 Let the heavens rejoice, and let the earth be glad : let the sea make a noise, and all that there-in is. 12. Let the field be joyful, and all that is in it : then shall all the trees of the wood re - joice be - fore the Lord. 13. For he cometh, for he cometh to judge the earth : and with righteousness to judge the world, and the peo-ple with his truth. Glory be to the Father, and to the Son : and to the Ho - ly Ghost ; As it was in the beginning, is now, and ever shall be : world with - out end. A - men.

PSALM XCVII.—*Dominus regnavit.*

5th Tone, 1st Ending.

The Lord is King, the earth may be glad there-of : yea, the multitude of the isles may be glad there - of. 2. Clouds and darkness are round a - bout him : righteousness and judgement are the hab-it - a - tion of his seat. 3. There shall go a fire be-fore him : and burn up his en - e-mies on ev-'ry side. 4. His lightnings

(168)

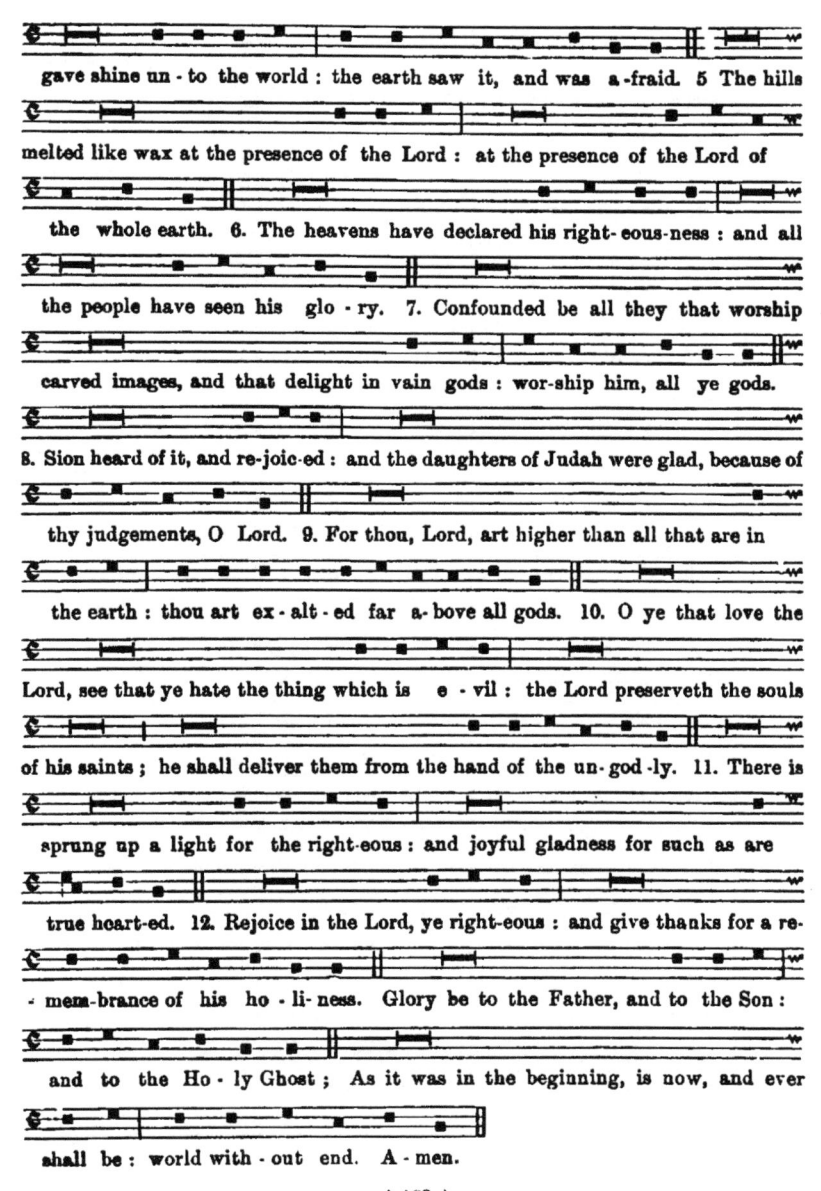

MORNING PRAYER. DAY 19.

gave shine un-to the world : the earth saw it, and was a-fraid. 5 The hills melted like wax at the presence of the Lord : at the presence of the Lord of the whole earth. 6. The heavens have declared his right-eous-ness : and all the people have seen his glo-ry. 7. Confounded be all they that worship carved images, and that delight in vain gods : wor-ship him, all ye gods.

8. Sion heard of it, and re-joic-ed : and the daughters of Judah were glad, because of thy judgements, O Lord. 9. For thou, Lord, art higher than all that are in the earth : thou art ex-alt-ed far a-bove all gods. 10. O ye that love the Lord, see that ye hate the thing which is e-vil : the Lord preserveth the souls of his saints; he shall deliver them from the hand of the un-god-ly. 11. There is sprung up a light for the right-eous : and joyful gladness for such as are true heart-ed. 12. Rejoice in the Lord, ye right-eous : and give thanks for a re-mem-brance of his ho-li-ness. Glory be to the Father, and to the Son : and to the Ho-ly Ghost ; As it was in the beginning, is now, and ever shall be : world with-out end. A-men.

DAY 19.   EVENING PRAYER.

PSALM XCVIII.—*Cantate Domino.*

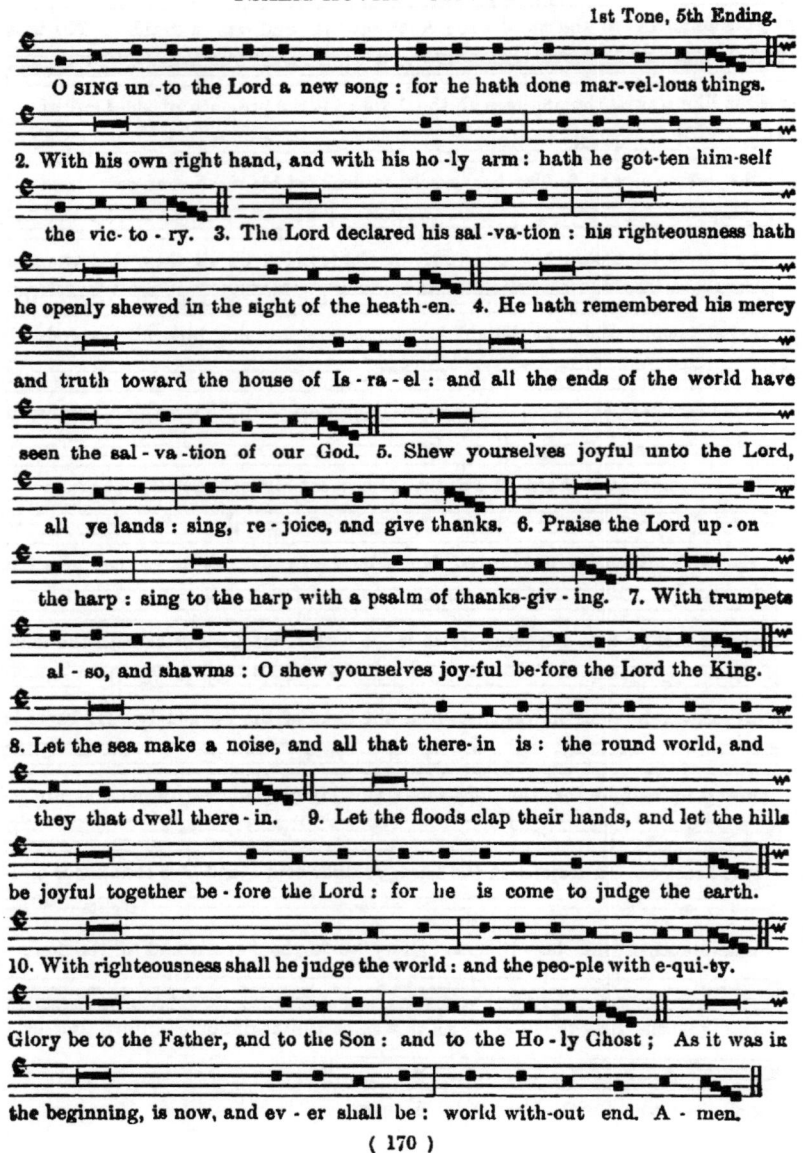

1st Tone, 5th Ending.

O SING un-to the Lord a new song : for he hath done mar-vel-lous things.

2. With his own right hand, and with his ho-ly arm : hath he got-ten him-self the vic-to-ry. 3. The Lord declared his sal-va-tion : his righteousness hath he openly shewed in the sight of the heath-en. 4. He hath remembered his mercy and truth toward the house of Is-ra-el : and all the ends of the world have seen the sal-va-tion of our God. 5. Shew yourselves joyful unto the Lord, all ye lands : sing, re-joice, and give thanks. 6. Praise the Lord up-on the harp : sing to the harp with a psalm of thanks-giv-ing. 7. With trumpets al-so, and shawms : O shew yourselves joy-ful be-fore the Lord the King. 8. Let the sea make a noise, and all that there-in is : the round world, and they that dwell there-in. 9. Let the floods clap their hands, and let the hills be joyful together be-fore the Lord : for he is come to judge the earth. 10. With righteousness shall he judge the world : and the peo-ple with e-qui-ty.

Glory be to the Father, and to the Son : and to the Ho-ly Ghost ; As it was in the beginning, is now, and ev-er shall be : world with-out end. A-men.

EVENING PRAYER. DAY 19.

PSALM XCIX.—*Dominus regnavit.*

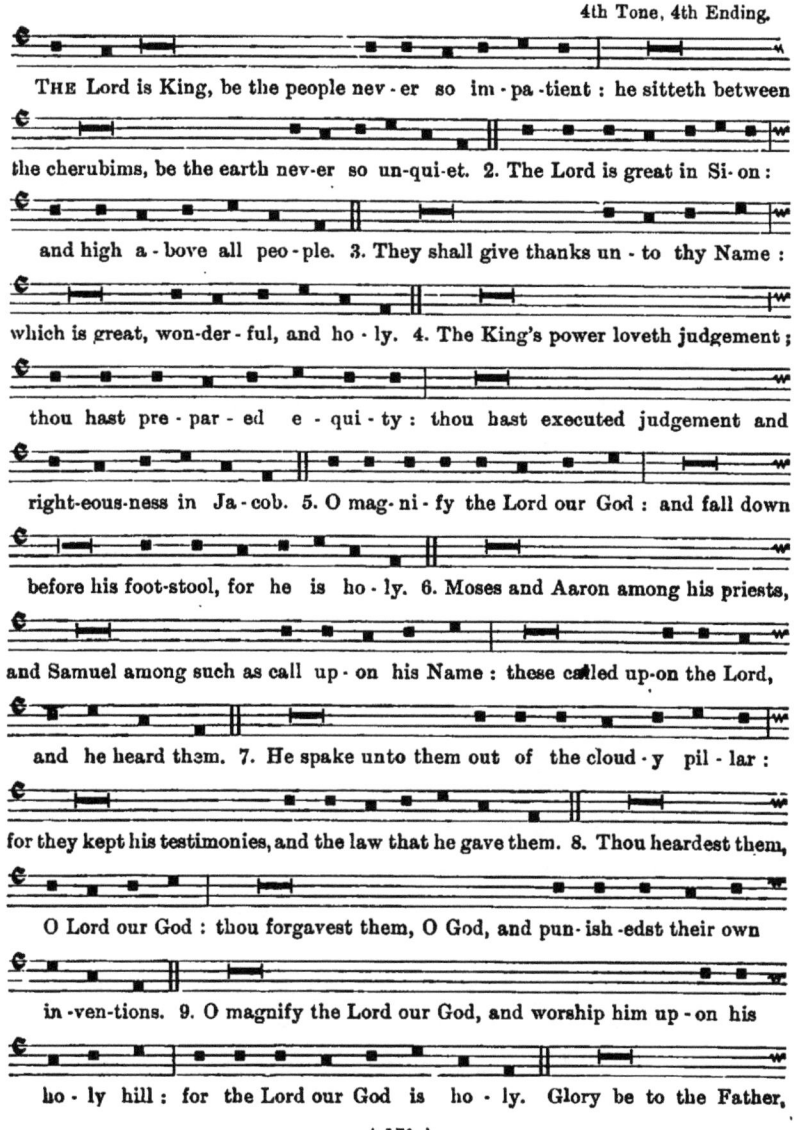

4th Tone, 4th Ending.

THE Lord is King, be the people nev-er so im-pa-tient: he sitteth between the cherubims, be the earth nev-er so un-qui-et. 2. The Lord is great in Si-on: and high a-bove all peo-ple. 3. They shall give thanks un-to thy Name: which is great, won-der-ful, and ho-ly. 4. The King's power loveth judgement; thou hast pre-par-ed e-qui-ty: thou hast executed judgement and right-eous-ness in Ja-cob. 5. O mag-ni-fy the Lord our God: and fall down before his foot-stool, for he is ho-ly. 6. Moses and Aaron among his priests, and Samuel among such as call up-on his Name: these called up-on the Lord, and he heard them. 7. He spake unto them out of the cloud-y pil-lar: for they kept his testimonies, and the law that he gave them. 8. Thou heardest them, O Lord our God: thou forgavest them, O God, and pun-ish-edst their own in-ven-tions. 9. O magnify the Lord our God, and worship him up-on his ho-ly hill: for the Lord our God is ho-ly. Glory be to the Father,

(171)

DAY 19.   EVENING PRAYER.

and to the Son : and to the Ho-ly Ghost ; As it was in the beginning, is now, and ev-er shall be : world with-out end. A-men.

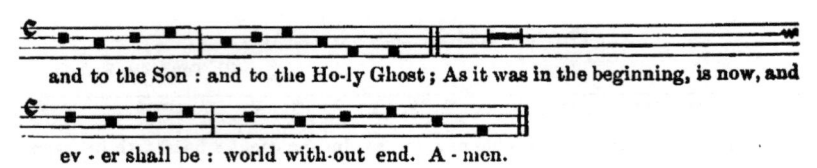

PSALM C.—*Jubilate Deo.*

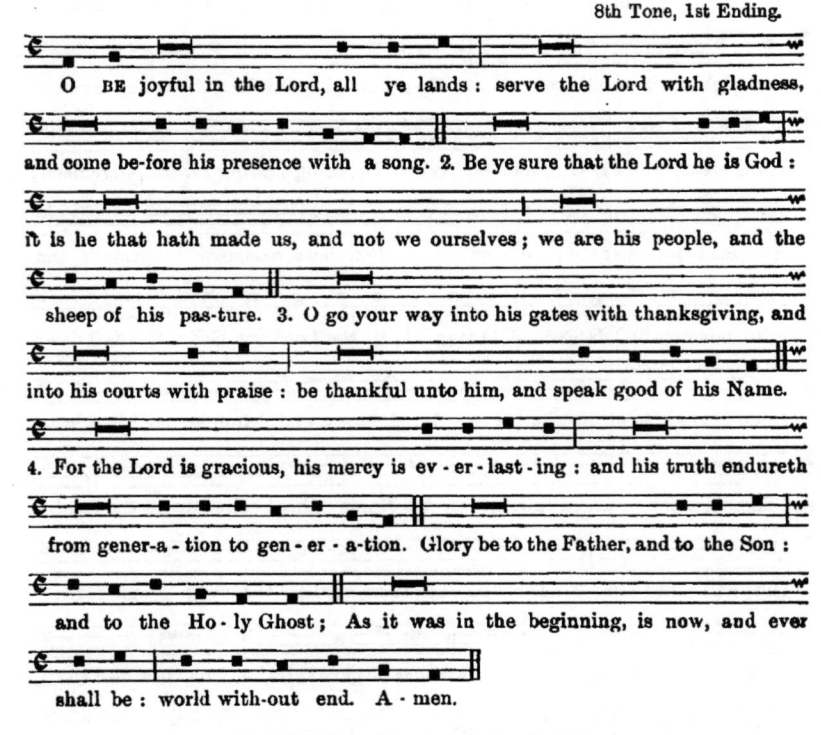

8th Tone, 1st Ending.

O BE joyful in the Lord, all ye lands : serve the Lord with gladness, and come be-fore his presence with a song. 2. Be ye sure that the Lord he is God : it is he that hath made us, and not we ourselves ; we are his people, and the sheep of his pas-ture. 3. O go your way into his gates with thanksgiving, and into his courts with praise : be thankful unto him, and speak good of his Name. 4. For the Lord is gracious, his mercy is ev-er-last-ing : and his truth endureth from gener-a-tion to gen-er-a-tion. Glory be to the Father, and to the Son : and to the Ho-ly Ghost ; As it was in the beginning, is now, and ever shall be : world with-out end. A-men.

PSALM CI.—*Misericordiam et judicium.*

1st Tone, 2nd Ending.

MY song shall be of mer-cy and judgement : un-to thee, O Lord, will I sing. 2. O let me have un-der-stand-ing : in the way of god-li-ness. 3. When wilt

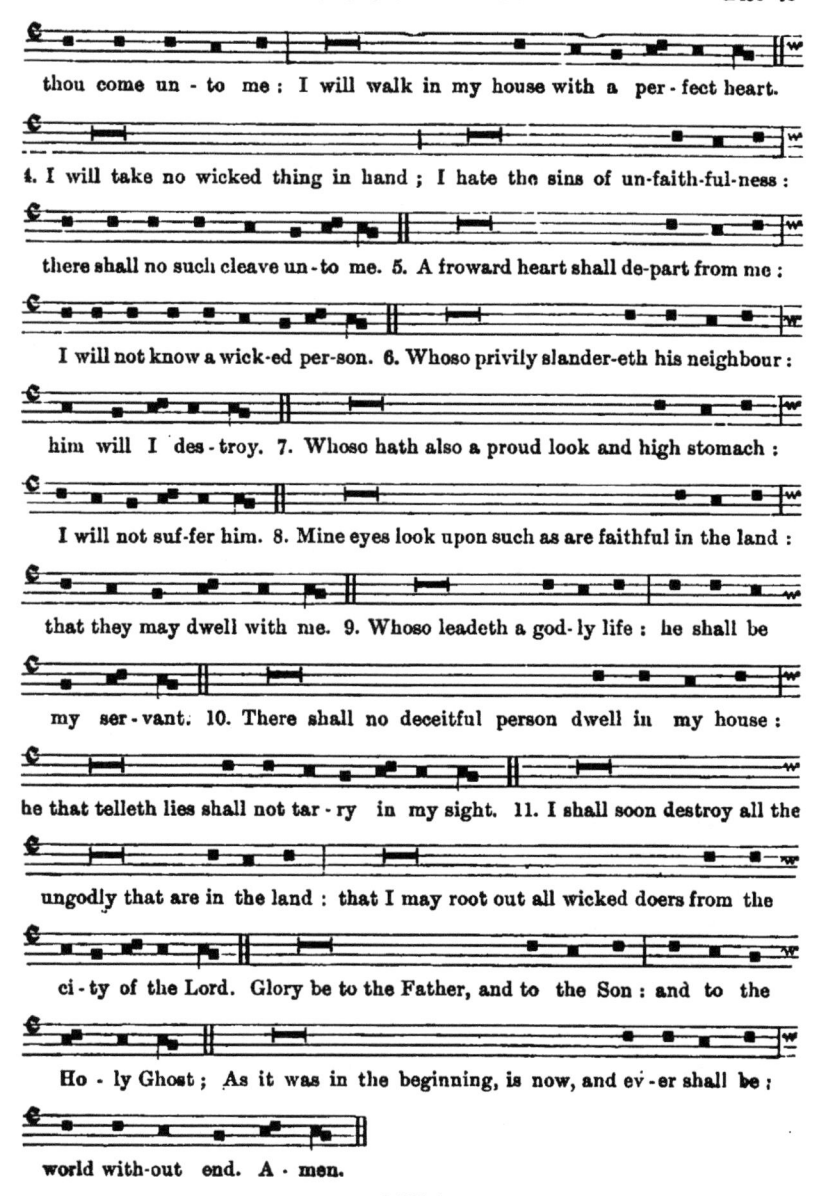

EVENING PRAYER. DAY 19

thou come un-to me : I will walk in my house with a per-fect heart.

4. I will take no wicked thing in hand ; I hate the sins of un-faith-ful-ness :

there shall no such cleave un-to me. 5. A froward heart shall de-part from me :

I will not know a wick-ed per-son. 6. Whoso privily slander-eth his neighbour :

him will I des-troy. 7. Whoso hath also a proud look and high stomach :

I will not suf-fer him. 8. Mine eyes look upon such as are faithful in the land :

that they may dwell with me. 9. Whoso leadeth a god-ly life : he shall be

my ser-vant. 10. There shall no deceitful person dwell in my house :

he that telleth lies shall not tar-ry in my sight. 11. I shall soon destroy all the

ungodly that are in the land : that I may root out all wicked doers from the

ci-ty of the Lord. Glory be to the Father, and to the Son : and to the

Ho-ly Ghost ; As it was in the beginning, is now, and ev-er shall be ;

world with-out end. A-men.

DAY 20.   MORNING PRAYER.

PSALM CII.—*Domine, exaudi.*

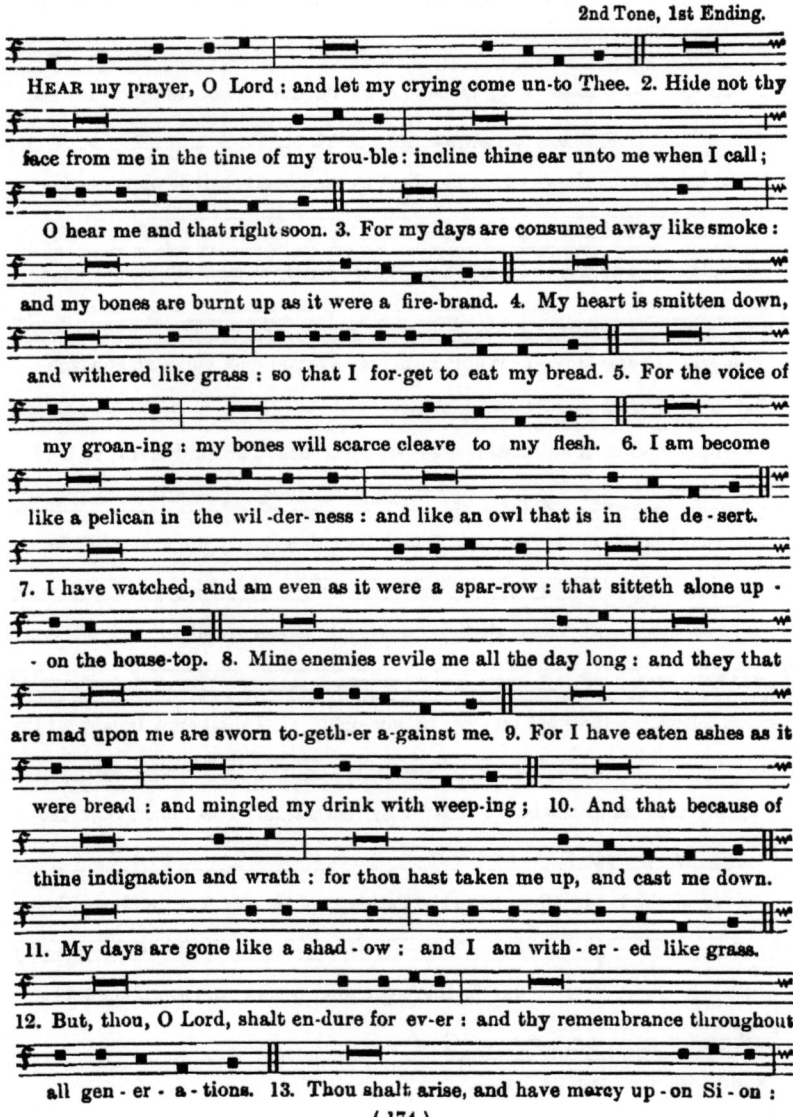

2nd Tone, 1st Ending.

HEAR my prayer, O Lord : and let my crying come un-to Thee. 2. Hide not thy face from me in the time of my trou-ble : incline thine ear unto me when I call ; O hear me and that right soon. 3. For my days are consumed away like smoke : and my bones are burnt up as it were a fire-brand. 4. My heart is smitten down, and withered like grass : so that I for-get to eat my bread. 5. For the voice of my groan-ing : my bones will scarce cleave to my flesh. 6. I am become like a pelican in the wil-der-ness : and like an owl that is in the de-sert. 7. I have watched, and am even as it were a spar-row : that sitteth alone up- -on the house-top. 8. Mine enemies revile me all the day long : and they that are mad upon me are sworn to-geth-er a-gainst me. 9. For I have eaten ashes as it were bread : and mingled my drink with weep-ing ; 10. And that because of thine indignation and wrath : for thou hast taken me up, and cast me down. 11. My days are gone like a shad-ow : and I am with-er-ed like grass. 12. But, thou, O Lord, shalt en-dure for ev-er : and thy remembrance throughout all gen-er-a-tions. 13. Thou shalt arise, and have mercy up-on Si-on :

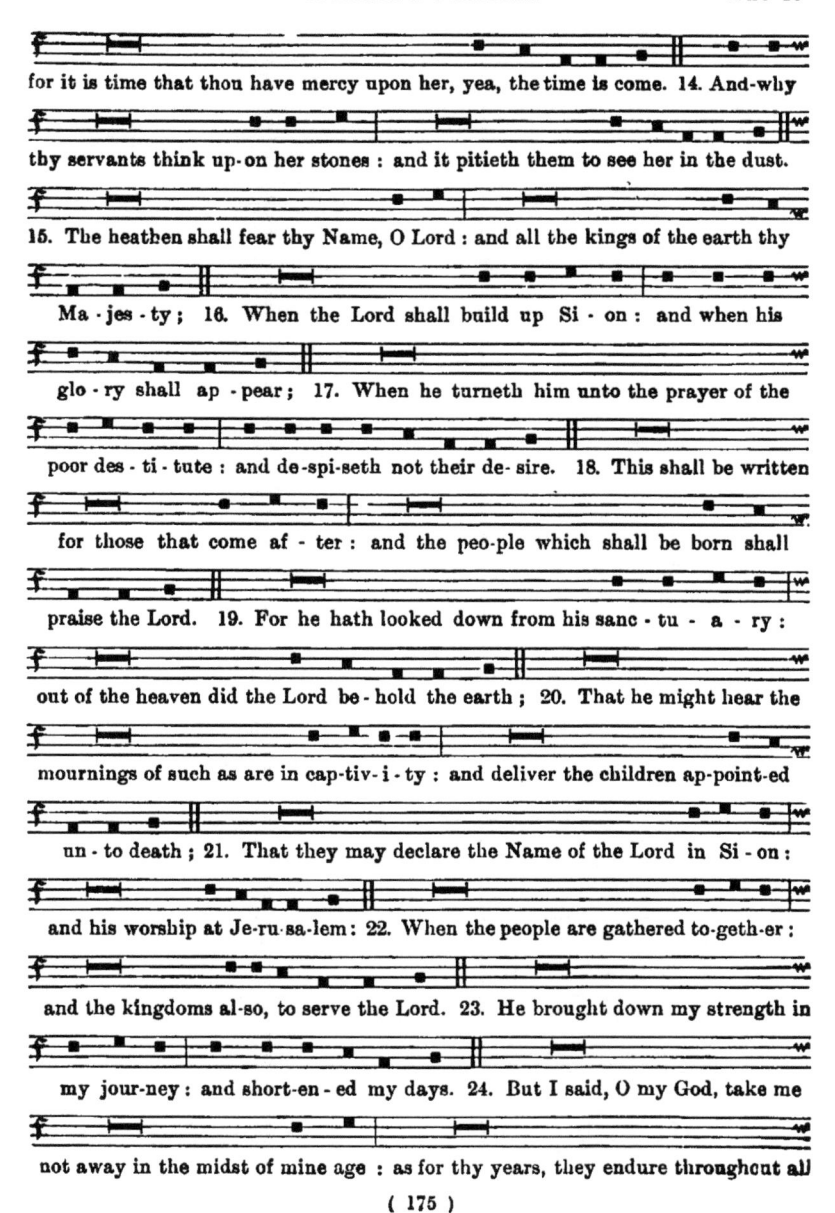

MORNING PRAYER. DAY 20.

for it is time that thou have mercy upon her, yea, the time is come. 14. And why thy servants think up-on her stones : and it pitieth them to see her in the dust.

15. The heathen shall fear thy Name, O Lord : and all the kings of the earth thy Ma-jes-ty; 16. When the Lord shall build up Si-on : and when his glo-ry shall ap-pear; 17. When he turneth him unto the prayer of the poor des-ti-tute : and de-spi-seth not their de-sire. 18. This shall be written for those that come af-ter : and the peo-ple which shall be born shall praise the Lord. 19. For he hath looked down from his sanc-tu-a-ry : out of the heaven did the Lord be-hold the earth ; 20. That he might hear the mournings of such as are in cap-tiv-i-ty : and deliver the children ap-point-ed un-to death ; 21. That they may declare the Name of the Lord in Si-on : and his worship at Je-ru-sa-lem: 22. When the people are gathered to-geth-er : and the kingdoms al-so, to serve the Lord. 23. He brought down my strength in my jour-ney : and short-en-ed my days. 24. But I said, O my God, take me not away in the midst of mine age : as for thy years, they endure throughout all

DAY 20. MORNING PRAYER.

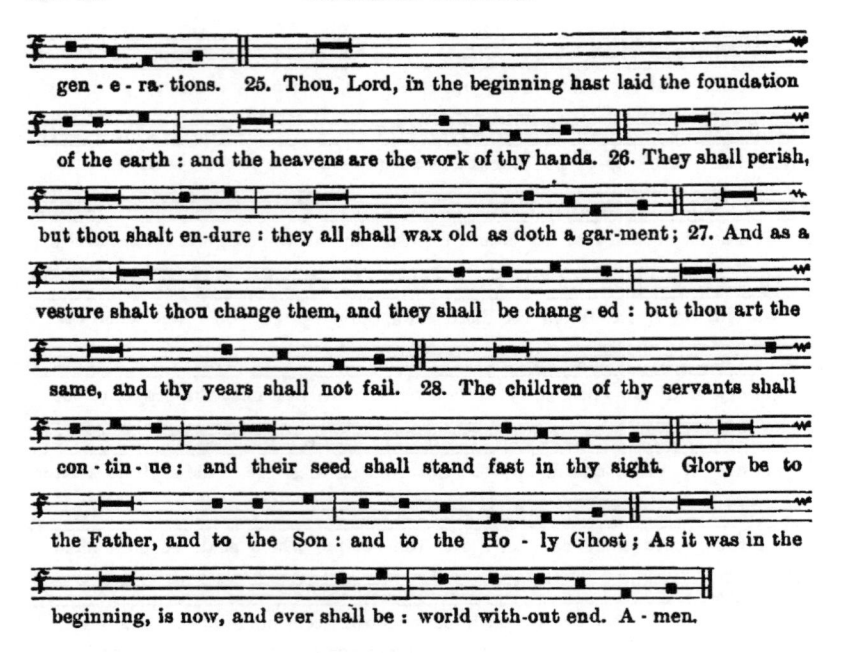

gen - e - ra - tions. 25. Thou, Lord, in the beginning hast laid the foundation of the earth : and the heavens are the work of thy hands. 26. They shall perish, but thou shalt en-dure : they all shall wax old as doth a gar-ment ; 27. And as a vesture shalt thou change them, and they shall be chang - ed : but thou art the same, and thy years shall not fail. 28. The children of thy servants shall con - tin - ue : and their seed shall stand fast in thy sight. Glory be to the Father, and to the Son : and to the Ho - ly Ghost ; As it was in the beginning, is now, and ever shall be : world with-out end. A - men.

PSALM CIII.—*Benedic, anima mea.*

8th Tone, 2nd Ending.

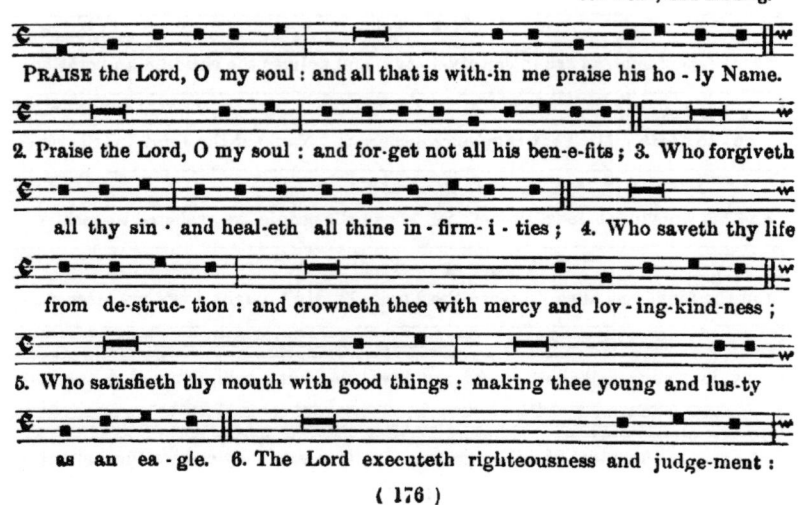

PRAISE the Lord, O my soul : and all that is with-in me praise his ho - ly Name. 2. Praise the Lord, O my soul : and for-get not all his ben-e-fits ; 3. Who forgiveth all thy sin · and heal-eth all thine in - firm- i - ties ; 4. Who saveth thy life from de-struc- tion : and crowneth thee with mercy and lov - ing-kind-ness ; 5. Who satisfieth thy mouth with good things : making thee young and lus-ty as an ea - gle. 6. The Lord executeth righteousness and judge-ment :

(176)

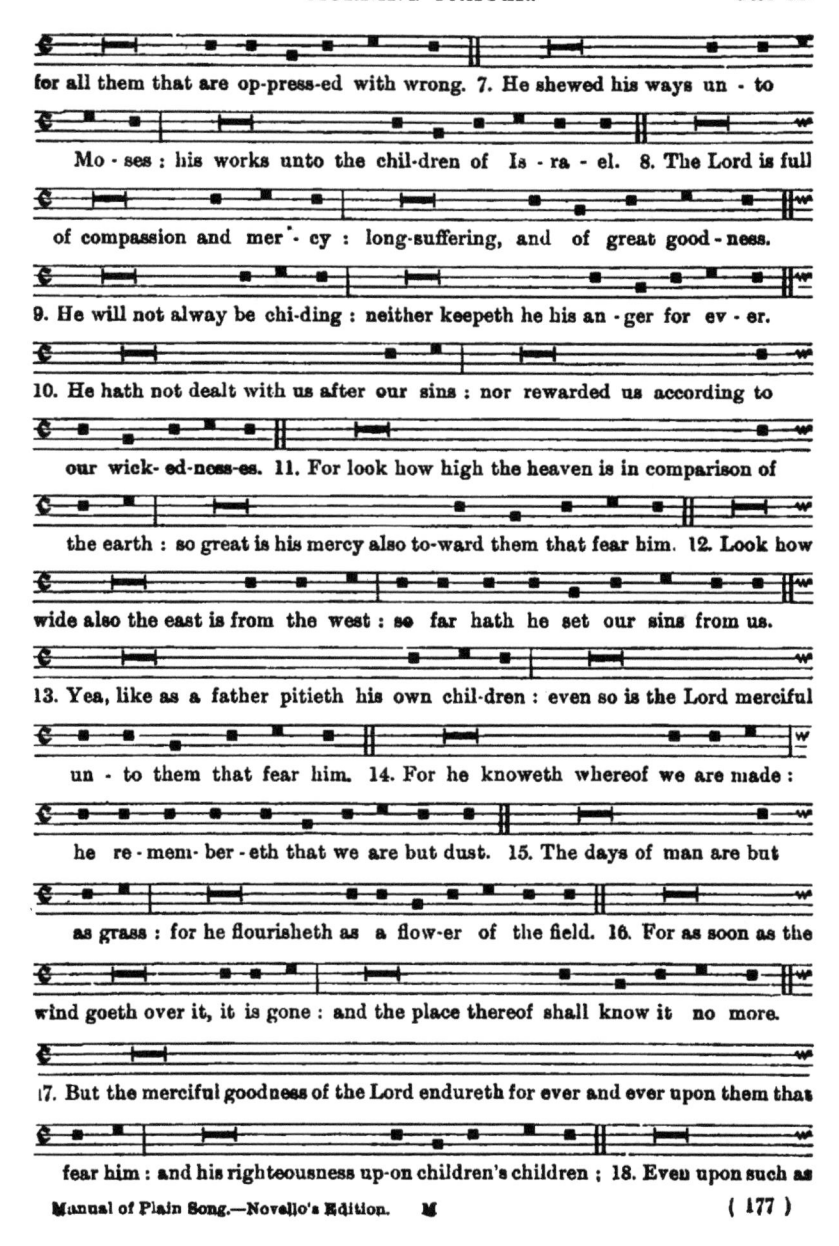

MORNING PRAYER. DAY 20.

for all them that are op-press-ed with wrong. 7. He shewed his ways un - to Mo - ses : his works unto the chil-dren of Is - ra - el. 8. The Lord is full of compassion and mer - cy : long-suffering, and of great good - ness. 9. He will not alway be chi-ding : neither keepeth he his an - ger for ev - er. 10. He hath not dealt with us after our sins : nor rewarded us according to our wick- ed-ness-es. 11. For look how high the heaven is in comparison of the earth : so great is his mercy also to-ward them that fear him. 12. Look how wide also the east is from the west : so far hath he set our sins from us. 13. Yea, like as a father pitieth his own chil-dren : even so is the Lord merciful un - to them that fear him. 14. For he knoweth whereof we are made : he re - mem- ber - eth that we are but dust. 15. The days of man are but as grass : for he flourisheth as a flow-er of the field. 16. For as soon as the wind goeth over it, it is gone : and the place thereof shall know it no more. 17. But the merciful goodness of the Lord endureth for ever and ever upon them that fear him : and his righteousness up-on children's children ; 18. Even upon such as

Manual of Plain Song.—Novello's Edition. M (177)

DAY 20.   EVENING PRAYER.

keep his co-ve-nant : and think upon his com-mand-ments to do them.

19. The Lord hath prepared his seat in heav-en : and his king-dom ru-leth

o-ver all. 20. O praise the Lord, ye angels of his, ye that excel in strength :

ye that fulfil his commandment, and hearken un-to the voice of his words.

21. O praise the Lord, all ye his hosts : ye servants of his that do his plea-sure.

22. O speak good of the Lord, all ye works of his, in all places of his do-min-ion :

praise thou the Lord, O my soul. Glory be to the Father, and to the Son :

and to the Ho-ly Ghost ; As it was in the beginning, is now, and ever

shall be : world with-out end. A-men.

EVENING PRAYER.

PSALM CIV.—*Benedic, anima mea.*

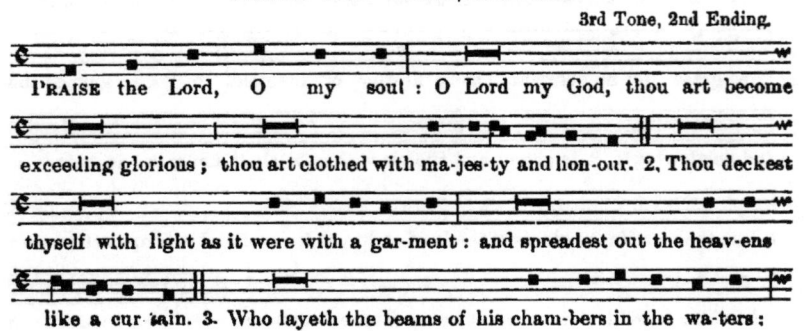

3rd Tone, 2nd Ending.

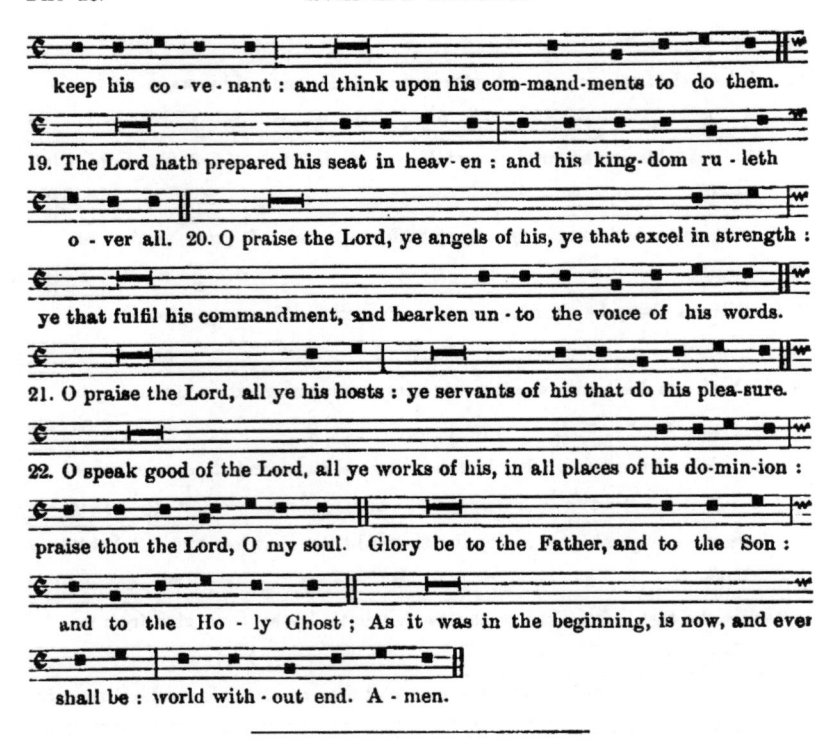

PRAISE the Lord, O my soul : O Lord my God, thou art become

exceeding glorious ; thou art clothed with ma-jes-ty and hon-our. 2. Thou deckest

thyself with light as it were with a gar-ment : and spreadest out the heav-ens

like a cur-tain. 3. Who layeth the beams of his cham-bers in the wa-ters :

EVENING PRAYER. DAY 20.

and maketh the clouds his chariot, and walketh up-on the wings of the wind.

4. He ma-keth his an - gels spir - its : and his min - is - ters a flam-ing fire.

5. He laid the foun-da-tions of the earth : that it nev - er should move at a - ny time. 6. Thou coveredst it with the deep like as with a gar-ment : the wa-ters stand in the hills. 7. At thy re-buke they flee : at the voice of thy thun-der they are a-fraid. 8. They go up as high as the hills, and down to the val-leys be-neath : even unto the place which thou hast ap-point-ed for them. 9. Thou hast set them their bounds which they shall not pass : neither turn a-gain to cov-er the earth. 10. He sendeth the springs in - to the ri - vers : which run a-mong the hills. 11. All beasts of the field drink there-of : and the wild ass - es quench their thirst. 12. Beside them shall the fowls of the air have their hab - it - a - tion : and sing a-mong the branch-es.

13. He wa-ter-eth the hills from a - bove : the earth is filled with the fruit of thy works. 14. He bringeth forth grass for the cat-tle : and green herb for the ser-vice of men. 15. That he may bring food out of the earth, and wine that

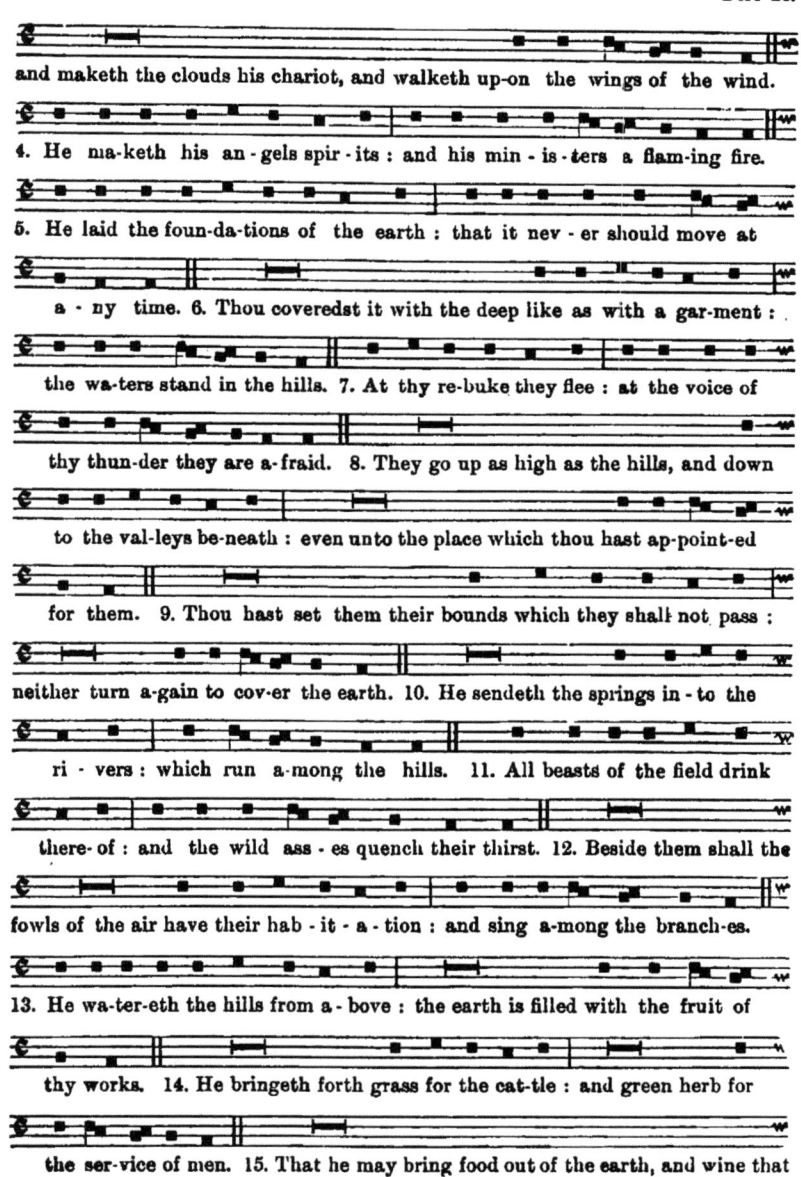

DAY 20. EVENING PRAYER.

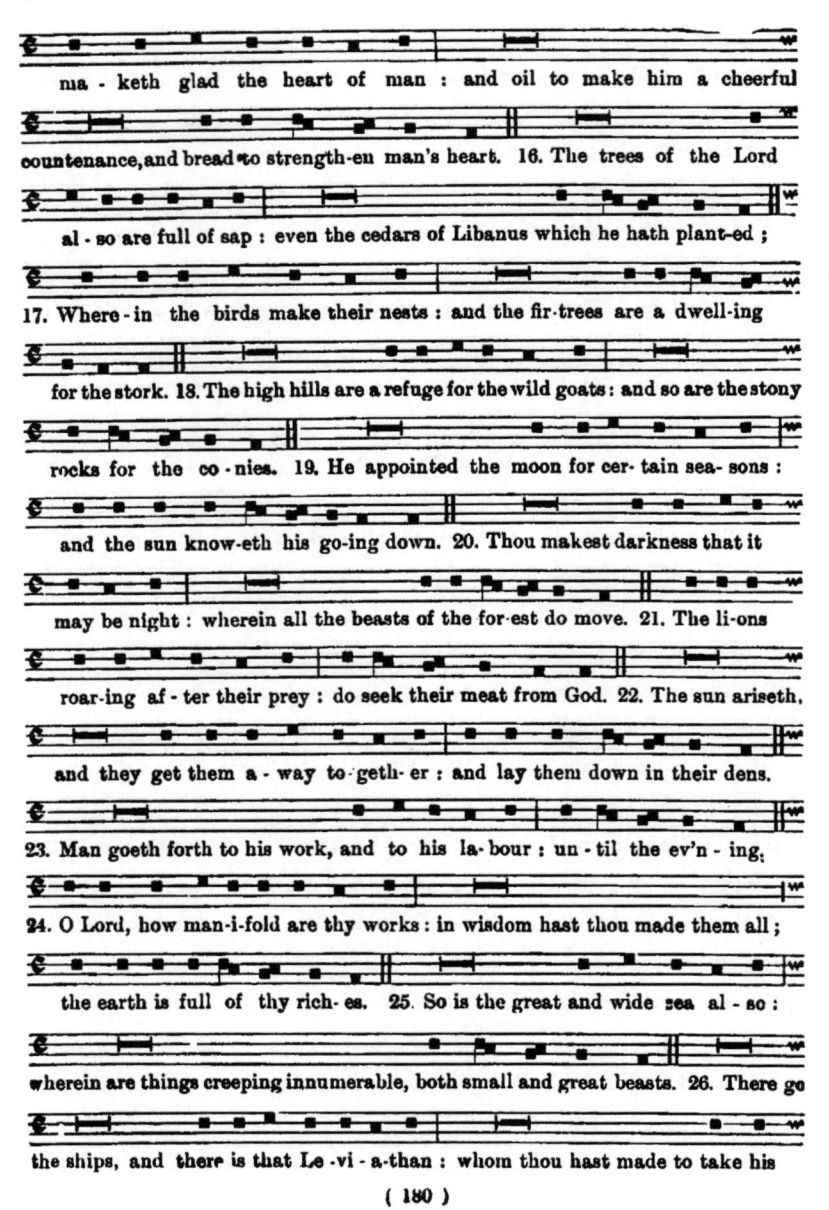

ma - keth glad the heart of man : and oil to make him a cheerful countenance, and bread to strength-en man's heart. 16. The trees of the Lord al - so are full of sap : even the cedars of Libanus which he hath plant-ed ; 17. Where - in the birds make their nests : and the fir-trees are a dwell-ing for the stork. 18. The high hills are a refuge for the wild goats : and so are the stony rocks for the co - nies. 19. He appointed the moon for cer- tain sea- sons : and the sun know-eth his go-ing down. 20. Thou makest darkness that it may be night : wherein all the beasts of the for-est do move. 21. The li-ons roar-ing af - ter their prey : do seek their meat from God. 22. The sun ariseth, and they get them a - way to-geth- er : and lay them down in their dens. 23. Man goeth forth to his work, and to his la- bour : un - til the ev'n - ing. 24. O Lord, how man-i-fold are thy works : in wisdom hast thou made them all ; the earth is full of thy rich- es. 25. So is the great and wide sea al - so : wherein are things creeping innumerable, both small and great beasts. 26. There go the ships, and there is that Le -vi - a-than : whom thou hast made to take his pas-time there-in. 27. These wait all up-on thee : that thou mayest give them meat in due sea-son. 28. When thou giv-est it them they gath-er it : and when thou openest thy hand they are fill-ed with good. 29. When thou hidest thy face they are trou-bled : when thou takest away their breath they die, and are turn-ed a-gain to their dust. 30. When thou lettest thy breath go forth they shall be made : and thou shalt re-new the face of the earth. 31. The glorious Majesty of the Lord shall en-dure for ev-er : the Lord shall re-joice in his works. 32. The earth shall trem-ble at the look of him : if he do but touch the hills, they shall smoke. 33. I will sing unto the Lord as long as I live : I will praise my God while I have my be-ing. 34. And so shall my words please him : my joy shall be in the Lord. 35. As for sinners they shall be consumed out of the earth, and the ungodly shall come to an end : praise thou the Lord, O my soul, praise the Lord. Glo-ry be to the Fath-er, and to the Son : and to the Ho-ly Ghost ; As it was in the beginning, is now, and ev-er shall be : world with-out end. A-men.

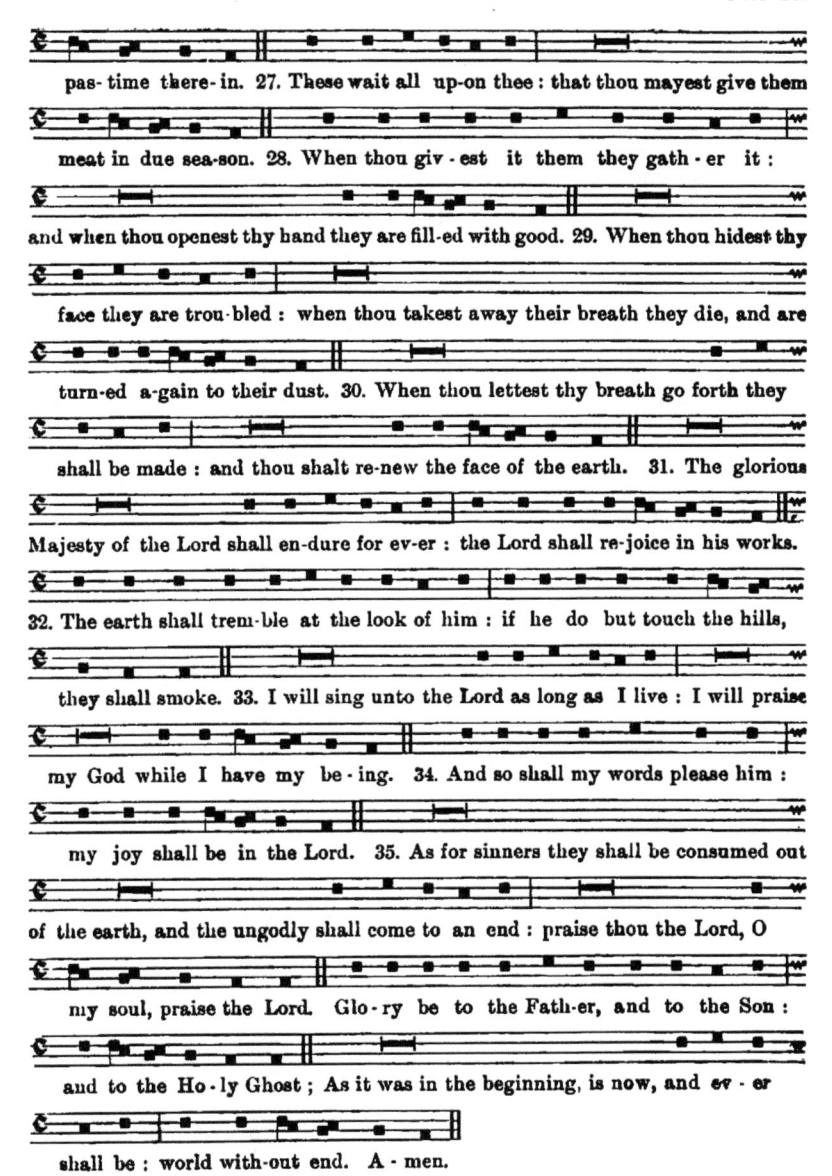

Day 21.   MORNING PRAYER.

PSALM CV.—*Confitemini Domino.*

7th Tone, 6th Ending.

O GIVE thanks un-to the Lord, and call up-on his Name : tell the peo-ple what things he hath done. 2. O let your songs be of him, and praise him : and let your talking be of all his won-drous works. 3. Re-joice in his ho-ly Name : let the heart of them re-joice that seek the Lord. 4. Seek the Lord and his strength : seek his face ev-er-more. 5. Remember the mar-vel-lous works that he hath done : his won-ders, and the judge-ments of his mouth. 6. O ye seed of A-bra-ham his ser-vant : ye chil-dren of Ja-cob his cho-sen. 7. He is the Lord our God : his judge-ments are in all the world. 8. He hath been alway mindful of his co-ve-nant and prom-ise : that he made to a thou-sand gen-e-ra-tions; 9. Even the covenant that he made with A-bra-ham : and the oath that he sware un-to I-saac; 10. And appointed the same un-to Ja-cob for a law : and to Israel for an ev-er-last-ing tes-ta-ment; 11. Saying, Unto thee will I give the land of Ca-na-an : the lot of your in-her-it-ance; 12. When there were yet but a few of them : and they

MORNING PRAYER. DAY 21.

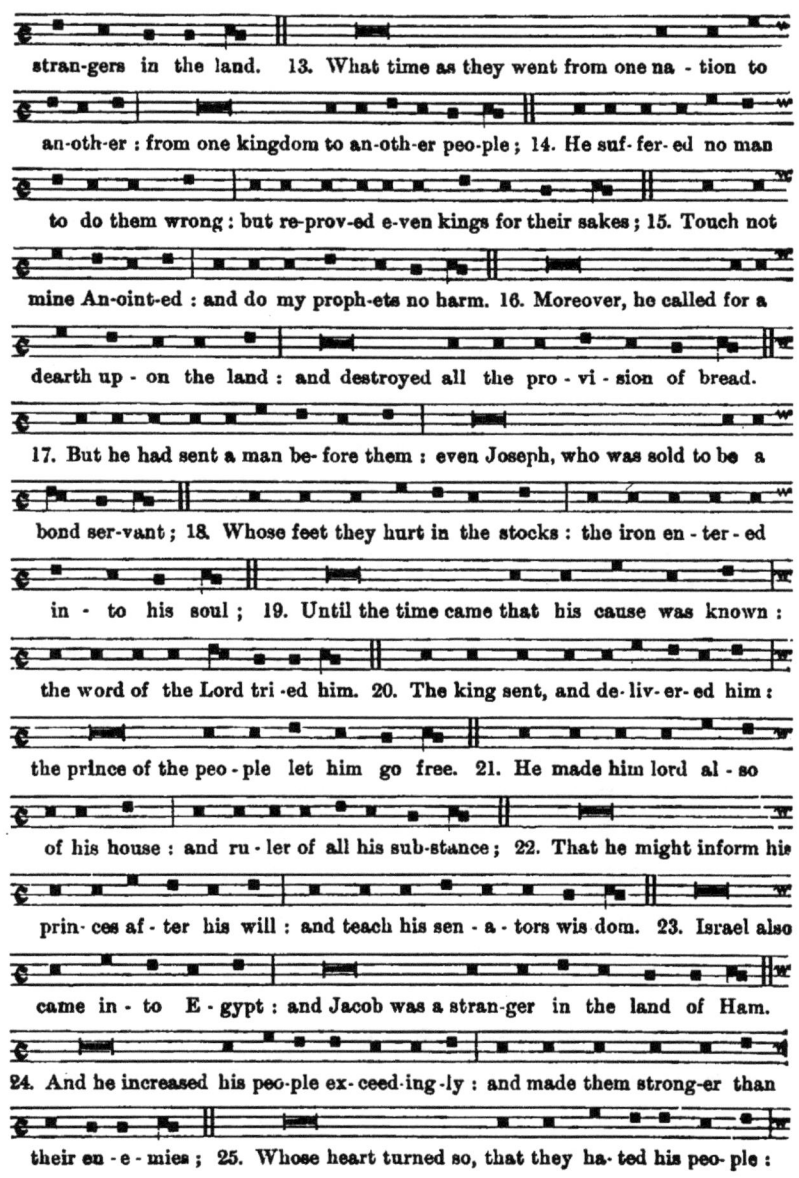

stran-gers in the land. 13. What time as they went from one na - tion to an-oth-er : from one kingdom to an-oth-er peo-ple ; 14. He suf-fer-ed no man to do them wrong : but re-prov-ed e-ven kings for their sakes ; 15. Touch not mine An-oint-ed : and do my proph-ets no harm. 16. Moreover, he called for a dearth up - on the land : and destroyed all the pro - vi - sion of bread. 17. But he had sent a man be- fore them : even Joseph, who was sold to be a bond ser-vant ; 18. Whose feet they hurt in the stocks : the iron en - ter - ed in - to his soul ; 19. Until the time came that his cause was known : the word of the Lord tri -ed him. 20. The king sent, and de- liv- er- ed him : the prince of the peo - ple let him go free. 21. He made him lord al - so of his house : and ru - ler of all his sub-stance ; 22. That he might inform his prin- ces af - ter his will : and teach his sen - a - tors wis dom. 23. Israel also came in - to E - gypt : and Jacob was a stran-ger in the land of Ham. 24. And he increased his peo-ple ex- ceed-ing -ly : and made them strong-er than their en - e - mies ; 25. Whose heart turned so, that they ha- ted his peo- ple :

(183)

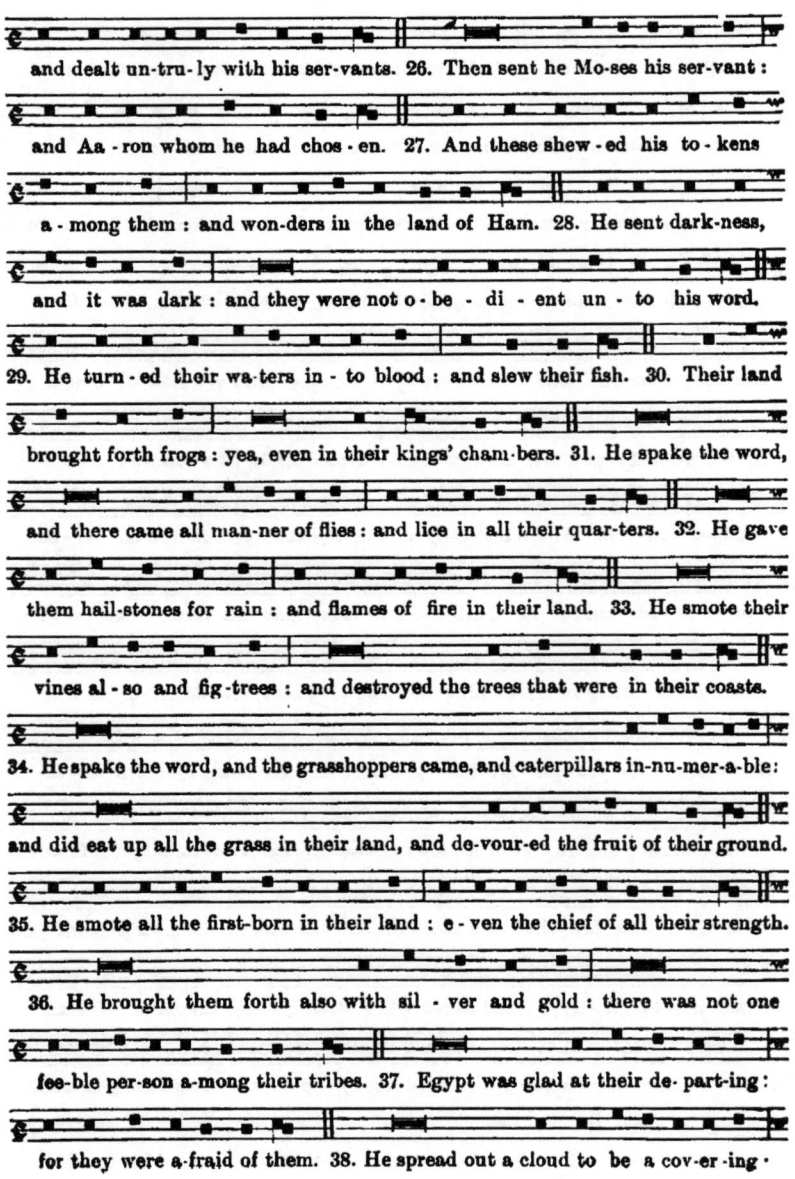

DAY 21   MORNING PRAYER.

and dealt un-tru-ly with his ser-vants. 26. Then sent he Mo-ses his ser-vant:

and Aa-ron whom he had chos-en. 27. And these shew-ed his to-kens

a-mong them : and won-ders in the land of Ham. 28. He sent dark-ness,

and it was dark : and they were not o-be-di-ent un-to his word.

29. He turn-ed their wa-ters in-to blood : and slew their fish. 30. Their land

brought forth frogs : yea, even in their kings' cham-bers. 31. He spake the word,

and there came all man-ner of flies : and lice in all their quar-ters. 32. He gave

them hail-stones for rain : and flames of fire in their land. 33. He smote their

vines al-so and fig-trees : and destroyed the trees that were in their coasts.

34. He spake the word, and the grasshoppers came, and caterpillars in-nu-mer-a-ble :

and did eat up all the grass in their land, and de-vour-ed the fruit of their ground.

35. He smote all the first-born in their land : e-ven the chief of all their strength.

36. He brought them forth also with sil-ver and gold : there was not one

fee-ble per-son a-mong their tribes. 37. Egypt was glad at their de-part-ing :

for they were a-fraid of them. 38. He spread out a cloud to be a cov-er-ing·

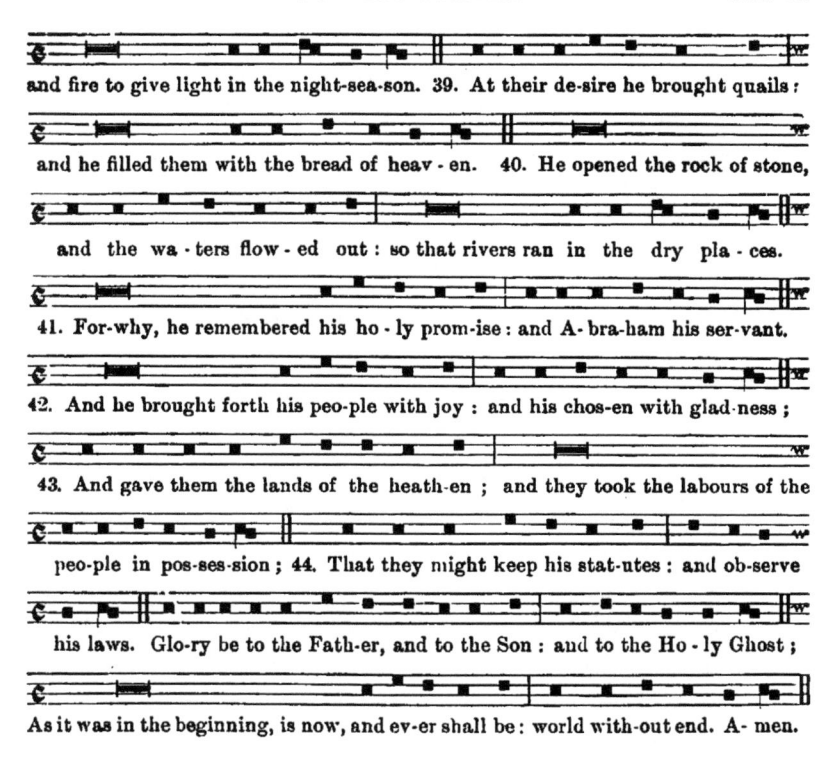

EVENING PRAYER. DAY 21.

and fire to give light in the night-sea-son. 39. At their de-sire he brought quails:

and he filled them with the bread of heav - en. 40. He opened the rock of stone,

and the wa - ters flow - ed out: so that rivers ran in the dry pla - ces.

41. For-why, he remembered his ho - ly prom-ise: and A- bra-ham his ser-vant.

42. And he brought forth his peo-ple with joy : and his chos-en with glad-ness ;

43. And gave them the lands of the heath-en ; and they took the labours of the

peo-ple in pos-ses-sion ; 44. That they might keep his stat-utes : and ob-serve

his laws. Glo-ry be to the Fath-er, and to the Son : and to the Ho - ly Ghost;

As it was in the beginning, is now, and ev-er shall be: world with-out end. A- men.

EVENING PRAYER.

PSALM CVI.—*Confitemini Domino.*

6th Tone.

O GIVE thanks unto the Lord, for he is gra-cious: and his mercy en-dur-eth

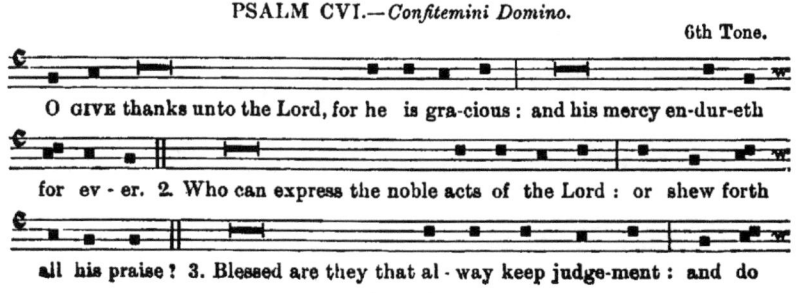

for ev - er. 2. Who can express the noble acts of the Lord : or shew forth

all his praise? 3. Blessed are they that al - way keep judge-ment : and do

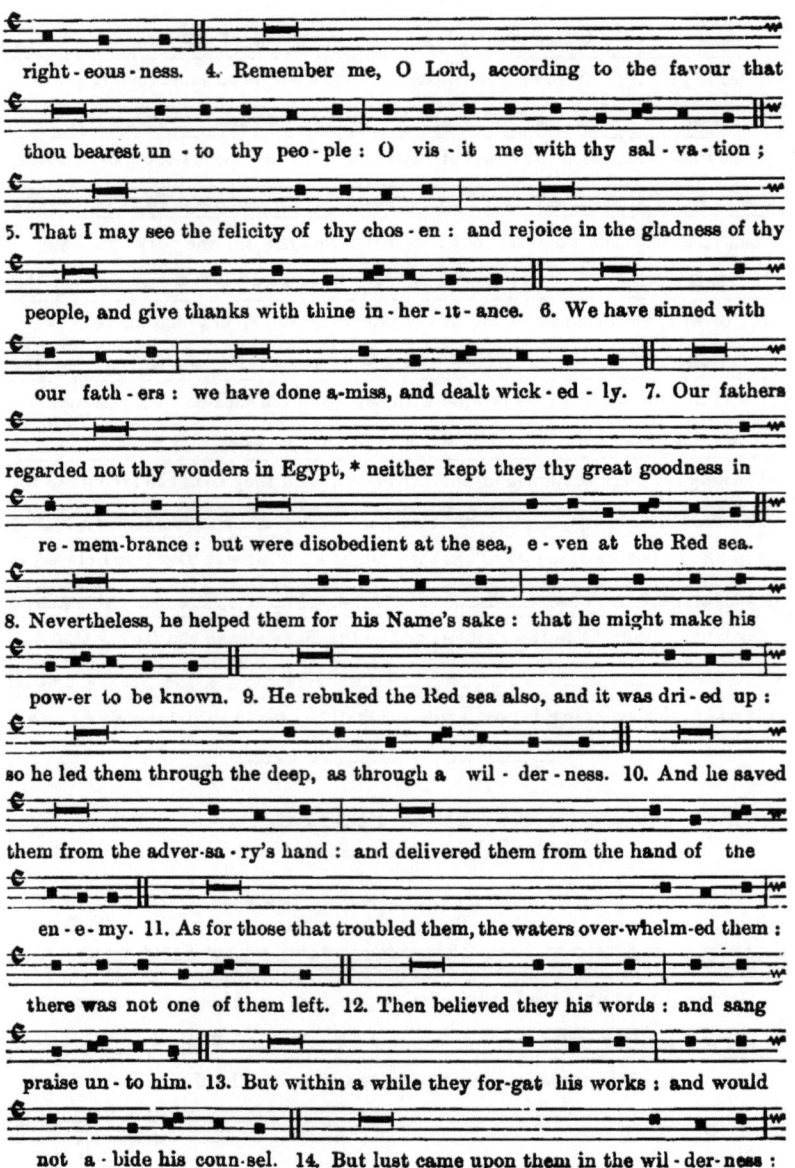

DAY 21   EVENING PRAYER.

right - eous - ness. 4. Remember me, O Lord, according to the favour that thou bearest un - to thy peo - ple : O vis - it me with thy sal - va - tion ;

5. That I may see the felicity of thy chos - en : and rejoice in the gladness of thy people, and give thanks with thine in - her - it - ance. 6. We have sinned with our fath - ers : we have done a-miss, and dealt wick - ed - ly. 7. Our fathers regarded not thy wonders in Egypt, * neither kept they thy great goodness in re - mem -brance : but were disobedient at the sea, e - ven at the Red sea.

8. Nevertheless, he helped them for his Name's sake : that he might make his pow-er to be known. 9. He rebuked the Red sea also, and it was dri - ed up : so he led them through the deep, as through a wil - der - ness. 10. And he saved them from the adver-sa - ry's hand : and delivered them from the hand of the en - e - my. 11. As for those that troubled them, the waters over-whelm-ed them : there was not one of them left. 12. Then believed they his words : and sang praise un - to him. 13. But within a while they for-gat his works : and would not a - bide his coun-sel. 14. But lust came upon them in the wil - der - ness :

EVENING PRAYER. DAY 21.

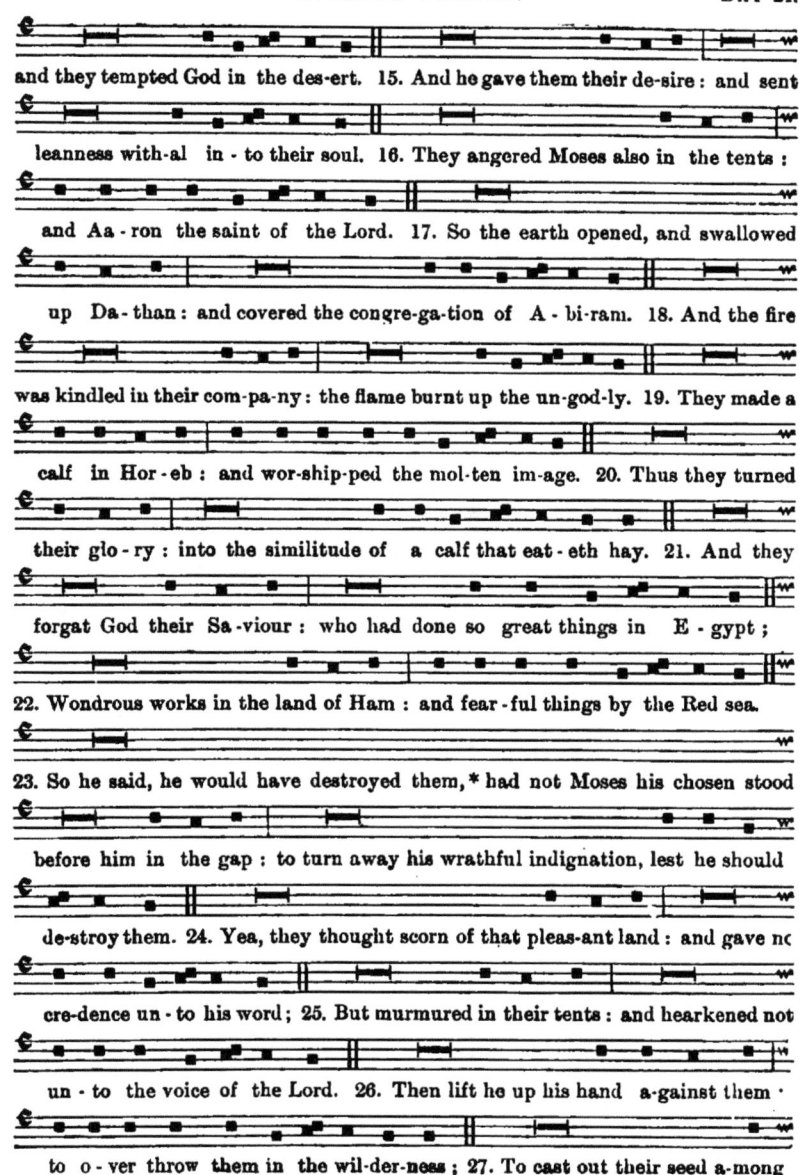

and they tempted God in the des-ert. 15. And he gave them their de-sire : and sent leanness with-al in - to their soul. 16. They angered Moses also in the tents : and Aa - ron the saint of the Lord. 17. So the earth opened, and swallowed up Da - than : and covered the congre-ga-tion of A - bi-ram. 18. And the fire was kindled in their com-pa-ny : the flame burnt up the un-god-ly. 19. They made a calf in Hor - eb : and wor-ship-ped the mol-ten im-age. 20. Thus they turned their glo - ry : into the similitude of a calf that eat - eth hay. 21. And they forgat God their Sa-viour : who had done so great things in E - gypt ; 22. Wondrous works in the land of Ham : and fear - ful things by the Red sea.

23. So he said, he would have destroyed them,* had not Moses his chosen stood before him in the gap : to turn away his wrathful indignation, lest he should de-stroy them. 24. Yea, they thought scorn of that pleas-ant land : and gave no cre-dence un - to his word ; 25. But murmured in their tents : and hearkened not un - to the voice of the Lord. 26. Then lift he up his hand a-gainst them · to o - ver throw them in the wil-der-ness ; 27. To cast out their seed a-mong

(187)

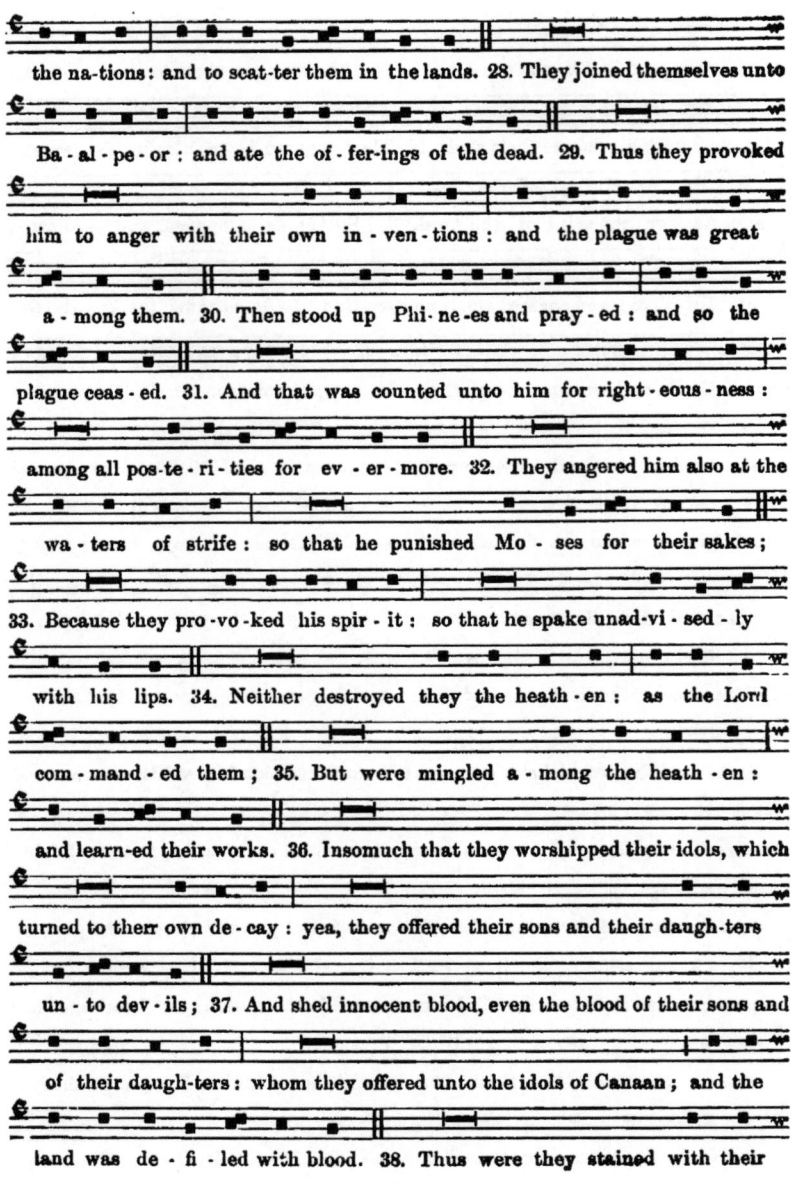

Day 21. EVENING PRAYER.

the na-tions: and to scat-ter them in the lands. 28. They joined themselves unto Ba - al - pe - or : and ate the of - fer-ings of the dead. 29. Thus they provoked him to anger with their own in - ven - tions : and the plague was great a - mong them. 30. Then stood up Phi - ne-es and pray - ed : and so the plague ceas - ed. 31. And that was counted unto him for right - eous - ness : among all pos-te - ri - ties for ev - er - more. 32. They angered him also at the wa - ters of strife : so that he punished Mo - ses for their sakes; 33. Because they pro -vo -ked his spir - it : so that he spake unad-vi - sed - ly with his lips. 34. Neither destroyed they the heath - en : as the Lord com - mand - ed them ; 35. But were mingled a - mong the heath - en : and learn-ed their works. 36. Insomuch that they worshipped their idols, which turned to their own de - cay : yea, they offered their sons and their daugh-ters un - to dev - ils ; 37. And shed innocent blood, even the blood of their sons and of their daugh-ters : whom they offered unto the idols of Canaan ; and the land was de - fi - led with blood. 38. Thus were they stained with their

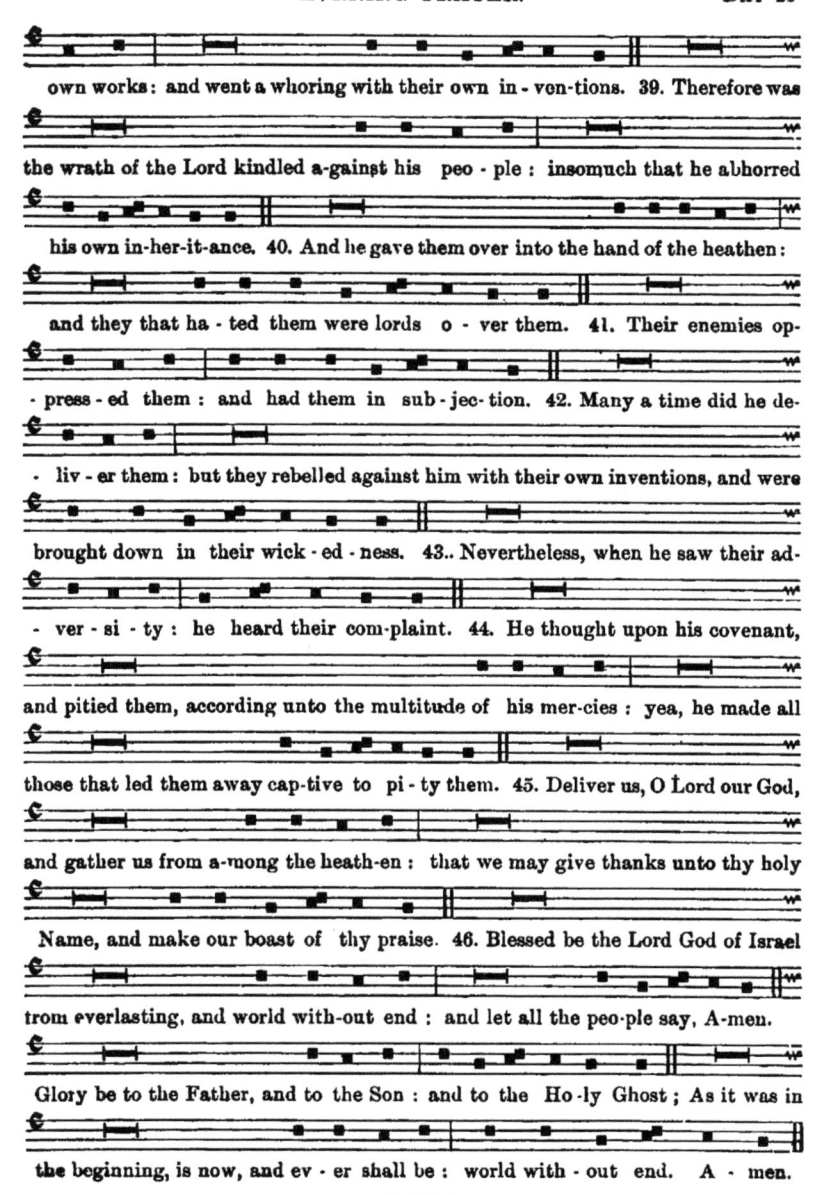

EVENING PRAYER. DAY 21

own works: and went a whoring with their own in-ven-tions. 39. Therefore was the wrath of the Lord kindled a-gainst his peo-ple: insomuch that he abhorred his own in-her-it-ance. 40. And he gave them over into the hand of the heathen: and they that ha-ted them were lords o-ver them. 41. Their enemies op--press-ed them: and had them in sub-jec-tion. 42. Many a time did he de--liv-er them: but they rebelled against him with their own inventions, and were brought down in their wick-ed-ness. 43. Nevertheless, when he saw their ad--ver-si-ty: he heard their com-plaint. 44. He thought upon his covenant, and pitied them, according unto the multitude of his mer-cies: yea, he made all those that led them away cap-tive to pi-ty them. 45. Deliver us, O Lord our God, and gather us from a-mong the heath-en: that we may give thanks unto thy holy Name, and make our boast of thy praise. 46. Blessed be the Lord God of Israel from everlasting, and world with-out end: and let all the peo-ple say, A-men.

Glory be to the Father, and to the Son: and to the Ho-ly Ghost; As it was in the beginning, is now, and ev-er shall be: world with-out end. A-men.

DAY 22. MORNING PRAYER.

PSALM CVII.—*Confitemini Domino.*

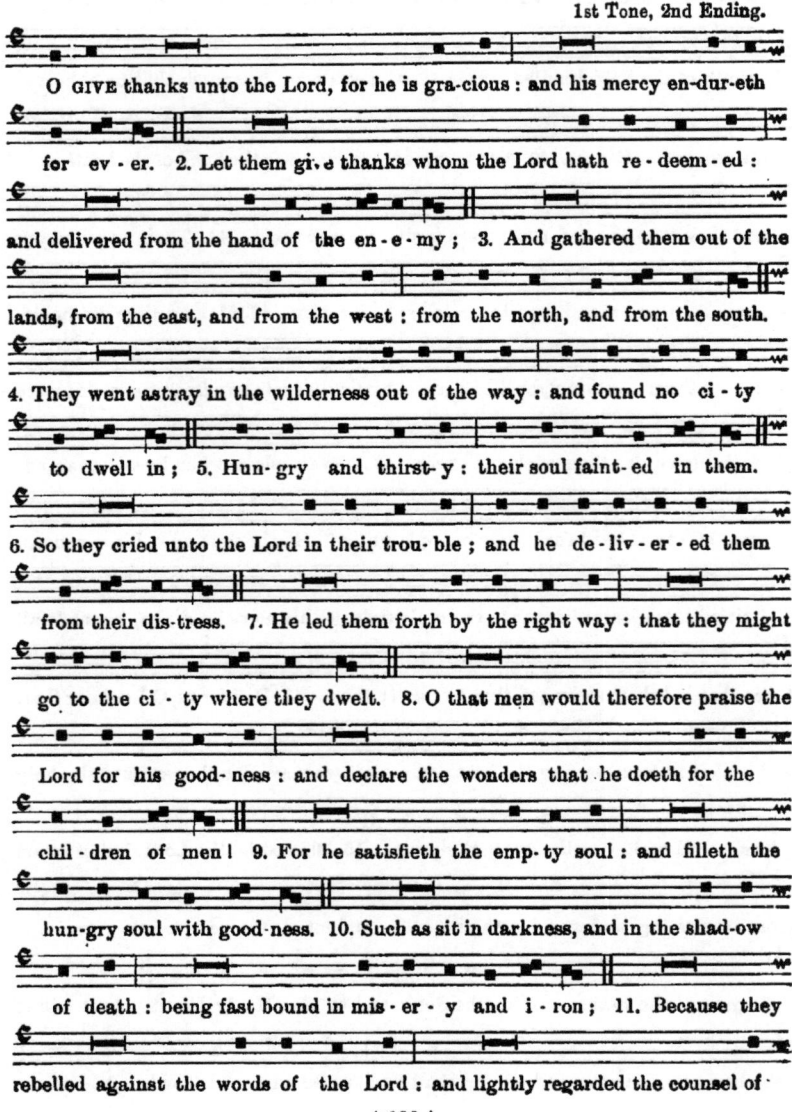

1st Tone, 2nd Ending.

O GIVE thanks unto the Lord, for he is gra-cious : and his mercy en-dur-eth for ev - er. 2. Let them give thanks whom the Lord hath re - deem - ed : and delivered from the hand of the en - e - my ; 3. And gathered them out of the lands, from the east, and from the west : from the north, and from the south. 4. They went astray in the wilderness out of the way : and found no ci - ty to dwell in ; 5. Hun- gry and thirst- y : their soul faint- ed in them. 6. So they cried unto the Lord in their trou- ble ; and he de - liv - er - ed them from their dis-tress. 7. He led them forth by the right way : that they might go to the ci - ty where they dwelt. 8. O that men would therefore praise the Lord for his good- ness : and declare the wonders that he doeth for the chil - dren of men ! 9. For he satisfieth the emp- ty soul : and filleth the hun-gry soul with good-ness. 10. Such as sit in darkness, and in the shad-ow of death : being fast bound in mis - er - y and i - ron ; 11. Because they rebelled against the words of the Lord : and lightly regarded the counsel of

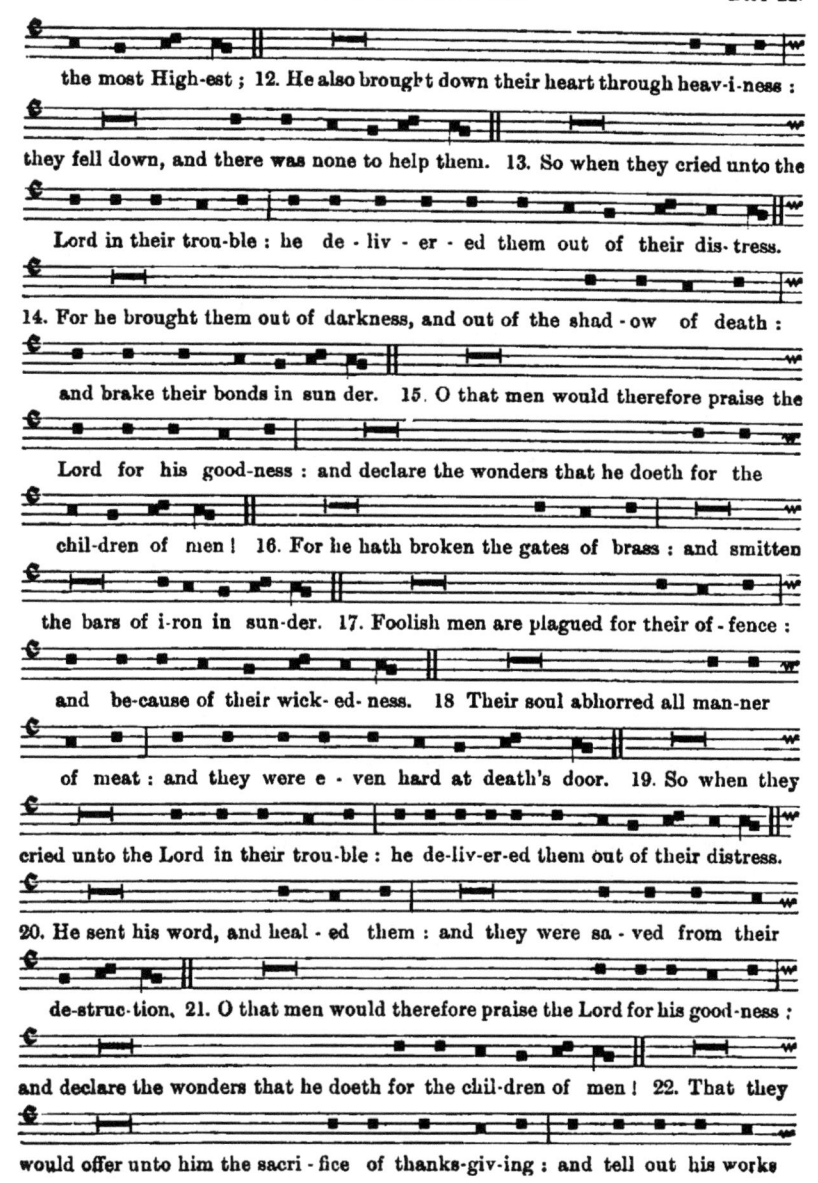

the most High-est ; 12. He also brought down their heart through heav-i-ness :
they fell down, and there was none to help them. 13. So when they cried unto the
Lord in their trou-ble : he de - liv - er - ed them out of their dis- tress.
14. For he brought them out of darkness, and out of the shad - ow of death :
and brake their bonds in sun der. 15. O that men would therefore praise the
Lord for his good-ness : and declare the wonders that he doeth for the
chil-dren of men! 16. For he hath broken the gates of brass : and smitten
the bars of i-ron in sun-der. 17. Foolish men are plagued for their of - fence :
and be-cause of their wick- ed- ness. 18 Their soul abhorred all man-ner
of meat : and they were e - ven hard at death's door. 19. So when they
cried unto the Lord in their trou-ble : he de-liv-er-ed them out of their distress.
20. He sent his word, and heal - ed them : and they were sa - ved from their
de-struc-tion, 21. O that men would therefore praise the Lord for his good-ness :
and declare the wonders that he doeth for the chil-dren of men! 22. That they
would offer unto him the sacri - fice of thanks-giv-ing : and tell out his works

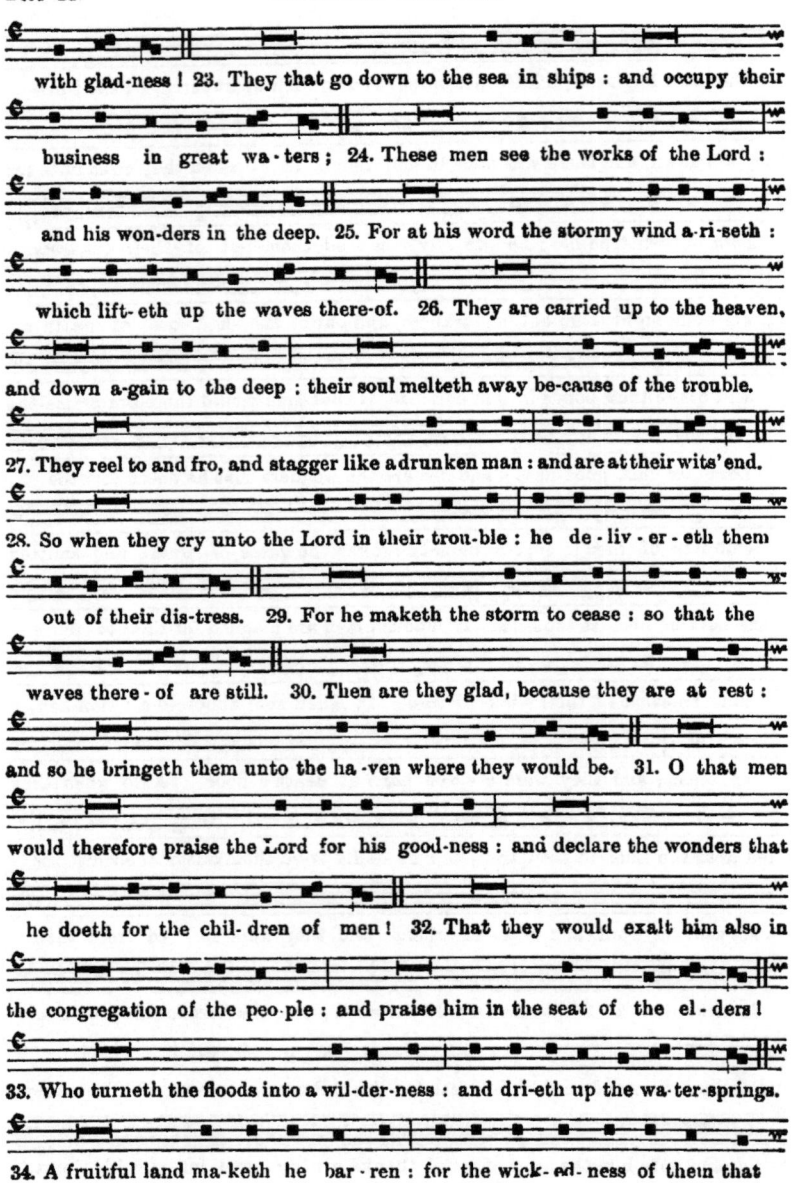

Day 22. MORNING PRAYER.

with glad-ness! 23. They that go down to the sea in ships : and occupy their

business in great wa-ters; 24. These men see the works of the Lord :

and his won-ders in the deep. 25. For at his word the stormy wind a-ri-seth :

which lift-eth up the waves there-of. 26. They are carried up to the heaven,

and down a-gain to the deep : their soul melteth away be-cause of the trouble.

27. They reel to and fro, and stagger like a drunken man : and are at their wits' end.

28. So when they cry unto the Lord in their trou-ble : he de-liv-er-eth them

out of their dis-tress. 29. For he maketh the storm to cease : so that the

waves there-of are still. 30. Then are they glad, because they are at rest :

and so he bringeth them unto the ha-ven where they would be. 31. O that men

would therefore praise the Lord for his good-ness : and declare the wonders that

he doeth for the chil-dren of men! 32. That they would exalt him also in

the congregation of the peo-ple : and praise him in the seat of the el-ders!

33. Who turneth the floods into a wil-der-ness : and dri-eth up the wa-ter-springs.

34. A fruitful land ma-keth he bar-ren : for the wick-ed-ness of them that

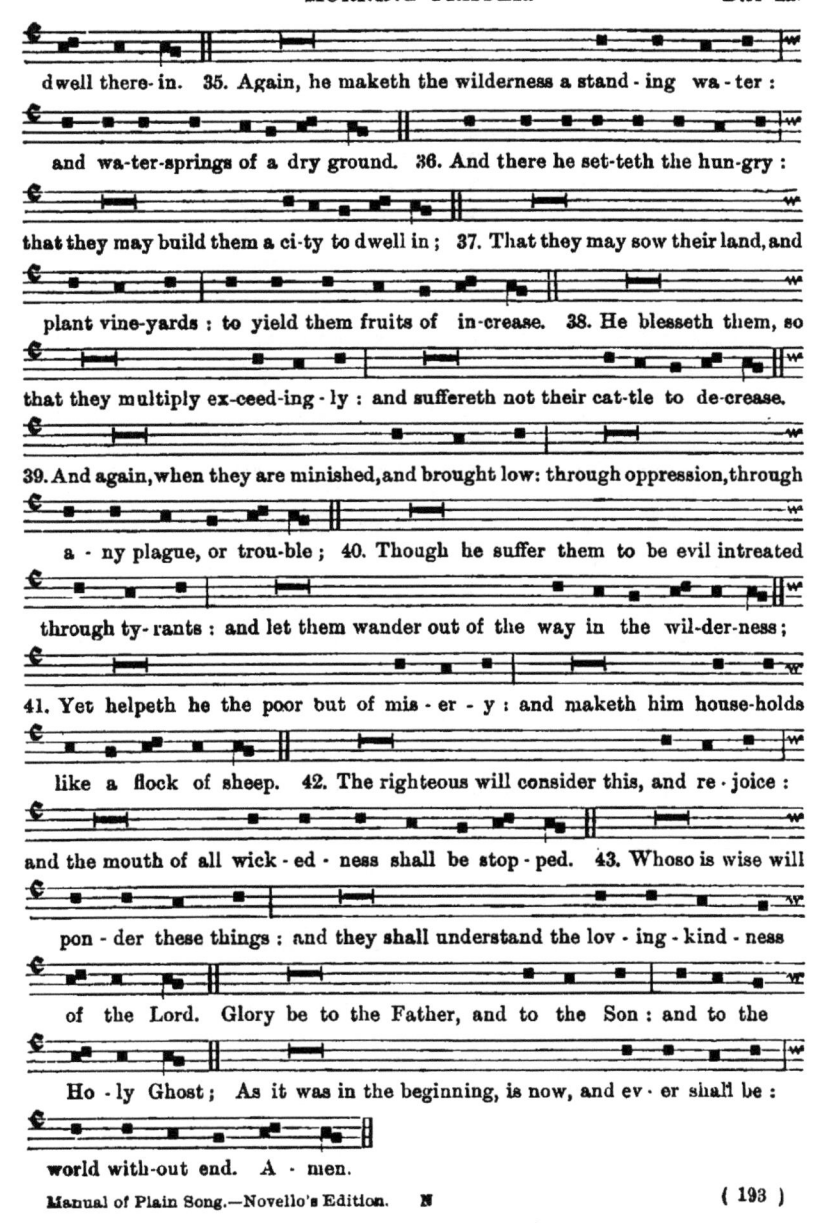

dwell there-in. 35. Again, he maketh the wilderness a stand-ing wa-ter:
and wa-ter-springs of a dry ground. 36. And there he set-teth the hun-gry:
that they may build them a ci-ty to dwell in; 37. That they may sow their land, and
plant vine-yards : to yield them fruits of in-crease. 38. He blesseth them, so
that they multiply ex-ceed-ing-ly : and suffereth not their cat-tle to de-crease.
39. And again, when they are minished, and brought low: through oppression, through
a-ny plague, or trou-ble; 40. Though he suffer them to be evil intreated
through ty-rants : and let them wander out of the way in the wil-der-ness;
41. Yet helpeth he the poor but of mis-er-y : and maketh him house-holds
like a flock of sheep. 42. The righteous will consider this, and re-joice :
and the mouth of all wick-ed-ness shall be stop-ped. 43. Whoso is wise will
pon-der these things : and they shall understand the lov-ing-kind-ness
of the Lord. Glory be to the Father, and to the Son: and to the
Ho-ly Ghost; As it was in the beginning, is now, and ev-er shall be :
world with-out end. A-men.

DAY 22.   EVENING PRAYER.

PSALM CVIII.—*Paratum cor meum.*

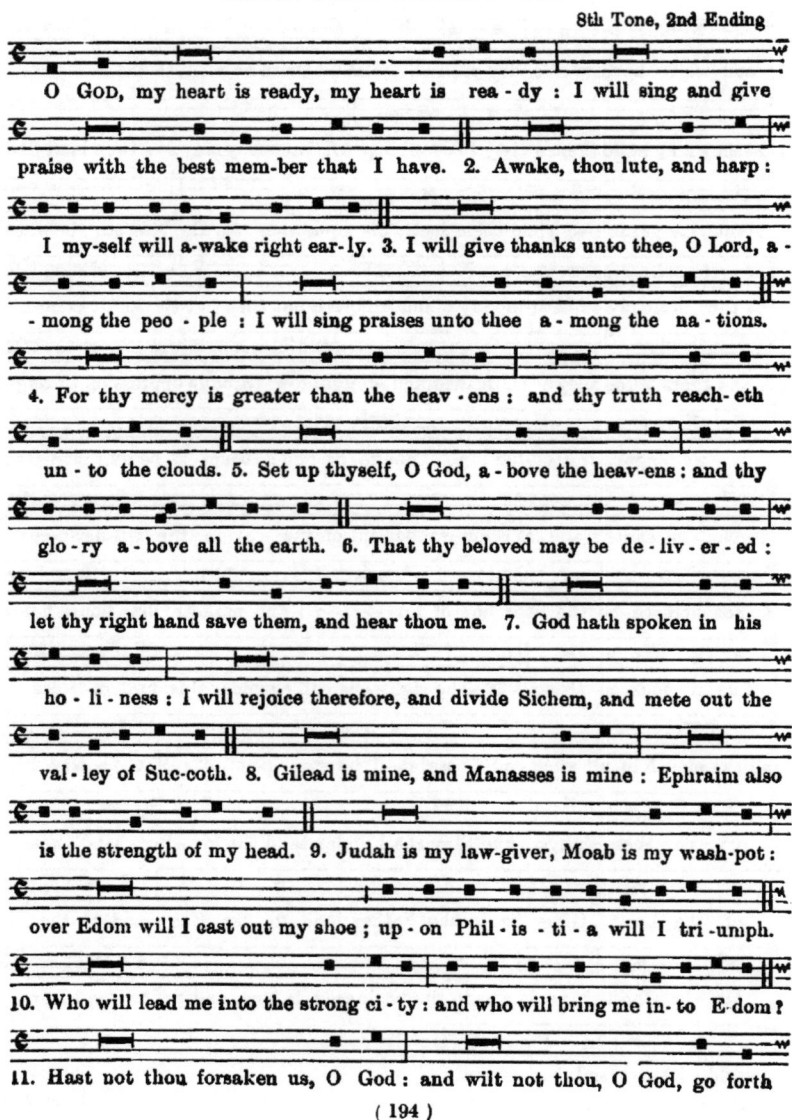

8th Tone, 2nd Ending

O GOD, my heart is ready, my heart is rea-dy : I will sing and give praise with the best mem-ber that I have. 2. Awake, thou lute, and harp : I my-self will a-wake right ear-ly. 3. I will give thanks unto thee, O Lord, a-mong the peo-ple : I will sing praises unto thee a-mong the na-tions. 4. For thy mercy is greater than the heav-ens : and thy truth reach-eth un-to the clouds. 5. Set up thyself, O God, a-bove the heav-ens : and thy glo-ry a-bove all the earth. 6. That thy beloved may be de-liv-er-ed : let thy right hand save them, and hear thou me. 7. God hath spoken in his ho-li-ness : I will rejoice therefore, and divide Sichem, and mete out the val-ley of Suc-coth. 8. Gilead is mine, and Manasses is mine : Ephraim also is the strength of my head. 9. Judah is my law-giver, Moab is my wash-pot : over Edom will I cast out my shoe ; up-on Phil-is-ti-a will I tri-umph. 10. Who will lead me into the strong ci-ty : and who will bring me in-to E-dom ? 11. Hast not thou forsaken us, O God : and wilt not thou, O God, go forth

EVENING PRAYER. DAY 22.

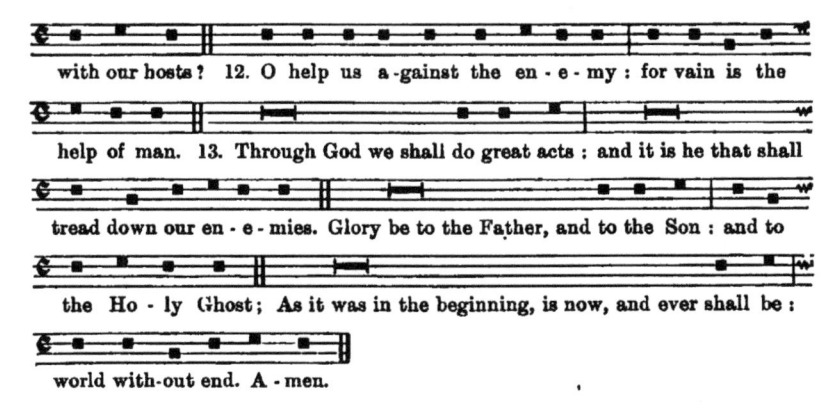

with our hosts? 12. O help us a-gainst the en-e-my: for vain is the help of man. 13. Through God we shall do great acts: and it is he that shall tread down our en-e-mies. Glory be to the Father, and to the Son: and to the Ho-ly Ghost; As it was in the beginning, is now, and ever shall be: world with-out end. A-men.

PSALM CIX.—*Deus laudum.*

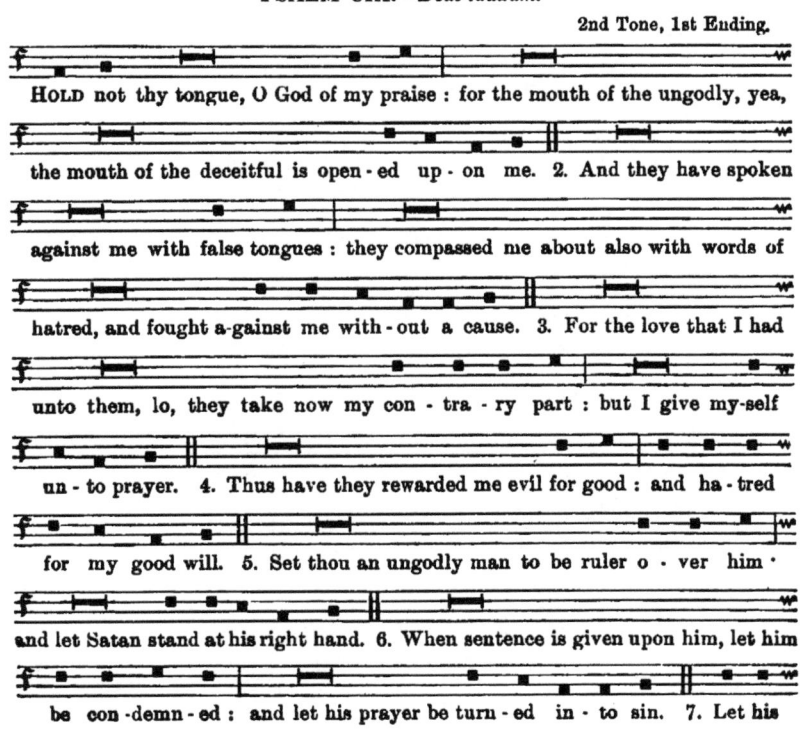

2nd Tone, 1st Ending.

HOLD not thy tongue, O God of my praise: for the mouth of the ungodly, yea, the mouth of the deceitful is open-ed up-on me. 2. And they have spoken against me with false tongues: they compassed me about also with words of hatred, and fought a-gainst me with-out a cause. 3. For the love that I had unto them, lo, they take now my con-tra-ry part: but I give my-self un-to prayer. 4. Thus have they rewarded me evil for good: and ha-tred for my good will. 5. Set thou an ungodly man to be ruler o-ver him· and let Satan stand at his right hand. 6. When sentence is given upon him, let him be con-demn-ed: and let his prayer be turn-ed in-to sin. 7. Let his

(195)

DAY 22.   EVENING PRAYER.

days be few : and let another take his ot - fice. 8. Let his children be fath - er - less : and his wife a wid -ow. 9. Let his children be vagabonds, and beg their bread : let them seek it also out of des - o - late pla - ces. 10. Let the extortioner consume all that he hath : and let the stranger spoil his la- bour. 11. Let there be no man to pi - ty him : nor to have compassion upon his fath - er - less chil-dren. 12. Let his posterity be des-troy - ed : and in the next generation let his name be clean put out. 13. Let the wickedness of his fathers be had in remembrance in the sight of the Lord : and let not the sin of his moth-er be done a - way. 14. Let them alway be be - fore the Lord : that he may root out the memorial of them from off the earth ; 15. And that, because his mind was not to do good : but persecuted the poor helpless man, that he might slay him that was vex - ed at the heart. 16. His delight was in cursing, and it shall happen un - to him : he loved not blessing, therefore shall it be far from him. 17. He clothed himself with cursing, like as with a rai-ment : and it shall come into his bowels like water, and like oil in - to his bones.

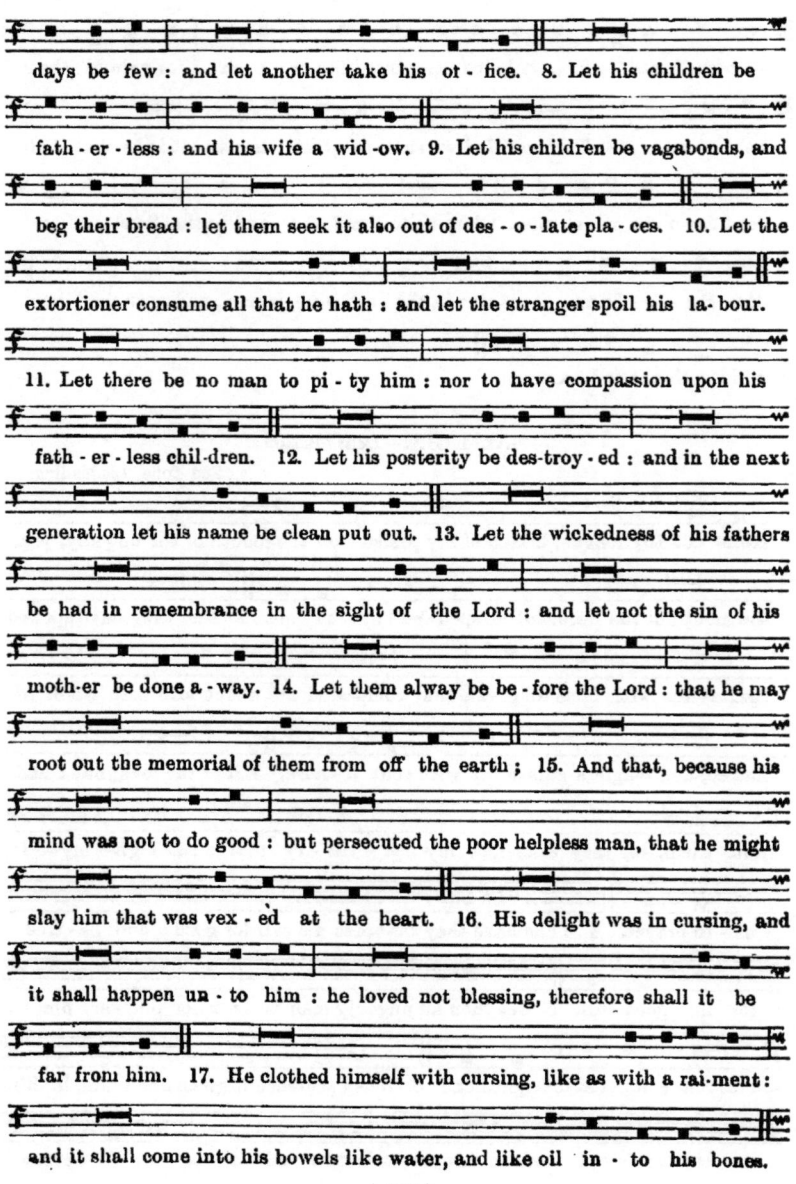

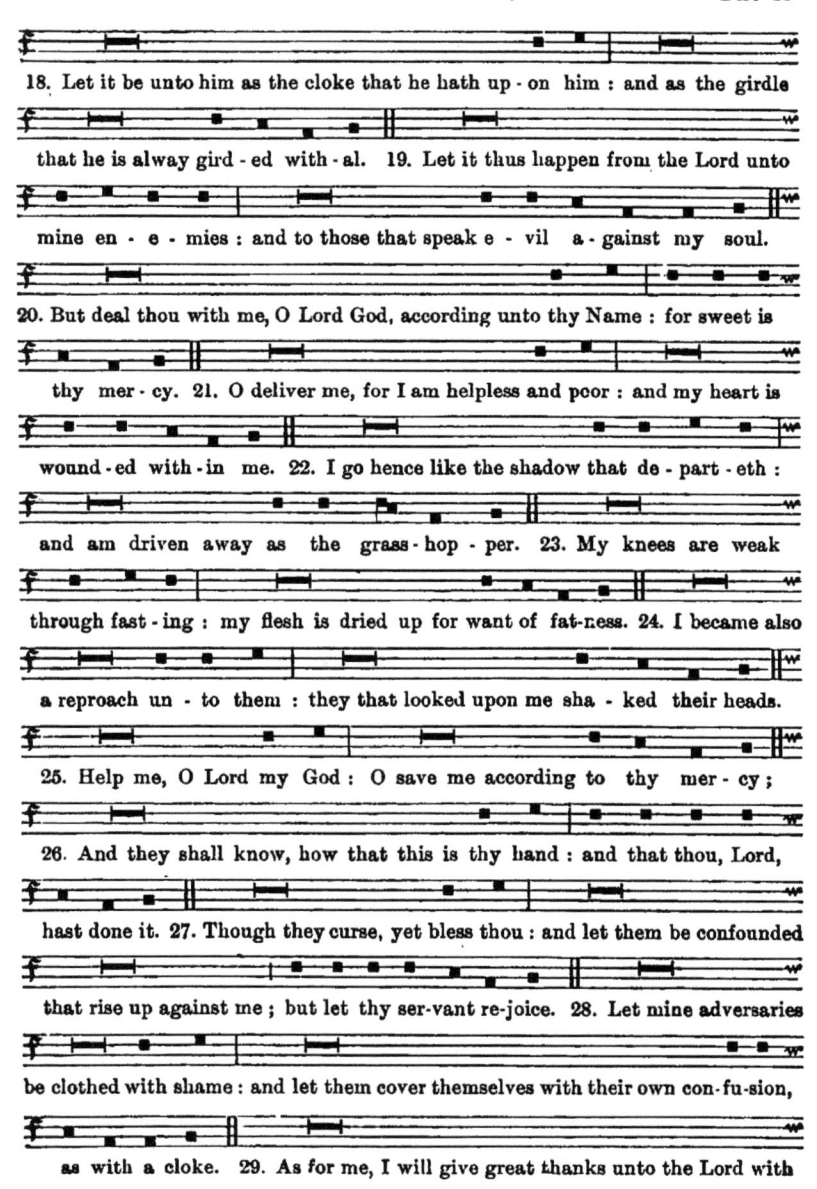

18. Let it be unto him as the cloke that he hath up - on him : and as the girdle that he is alway gird - ed with - al. 19. Let it thus happen from the Lord unto mine en - e - mies : and to those that speak e - vil a - gainst my soul.

20. But deal thou with me, O Lord God, according unto thy Name : for sweet is thy mer - cy. 21. O deliver me, for I am helpless and poor : and my heart is wound - ed with - in me. 22. I go hence like the shadow that de - part - eth : and am driven away as the grass - hop - per. 23. My knees are weak through fast - ing : my flesh is dried up for want of fat-ness. 24. I became also a reproach un - to them : they that looked upon me sha - ked their heads.

25. Help me, O Lord my God : O save me according to thy mer - cy ; 26. And they shall know, how that this is thy hand : and that thou, Lord, hast done it. 27. Though they curse, yet bless thou : and let them be confounded that rise up against me ; but let thy ser-vant re-joice. 28. Let mine adversaries be clothed with shame : and let them cover themselves with their own con-fu-sion, as with a cloke. 29. As for me, I will give great thanks unto the Lord with

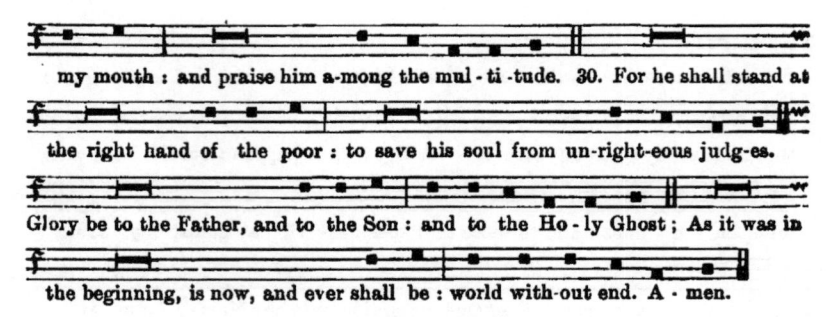

DAY 23.   MORNING PRAYER.

my mouth : and praise him a-mong the mul-ti-tude. 30. For he shall stand at

the right hand of the poor : to save his soul from un-right-eous judg-es.

Glory be to the Father, and to the Son : and to the Ho-ly Ghost ; As it was in

the beginning, is now, and ever shall be : world with-out end. A-men.

DAY 23.   MORNING PRAYER.

PSALM CX.—*Dixit Dominus.*

3rd Tone, 2nd Ending.

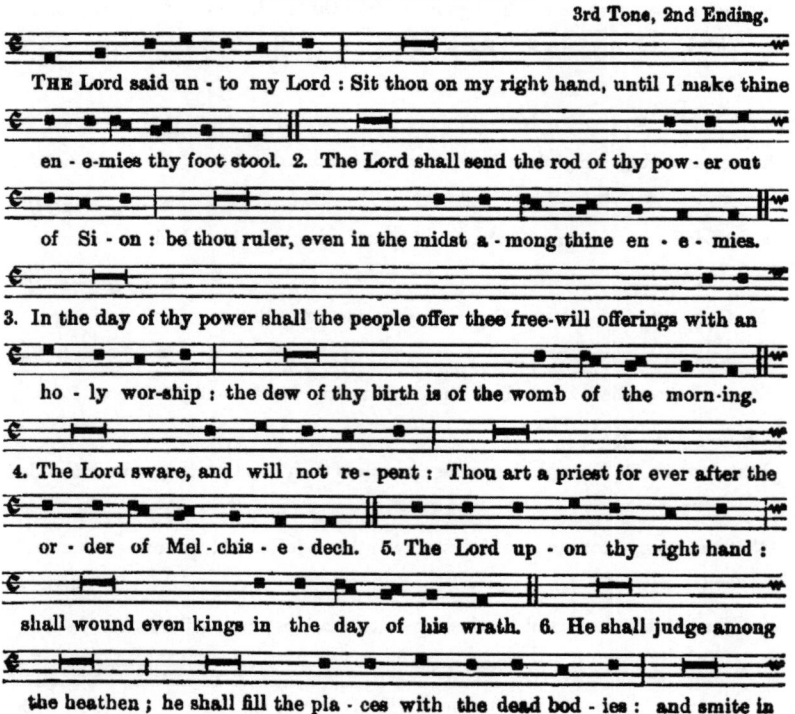

THE Lord said un-to my Lord : Sit thou on my right hand, until I make thine

en-e-mies thy foot-stool. 2. The Lord shall send the rod of thy pow-er out

of Si-on : be thou ruler, even in the midst a-mong thine en-e-mies.

3. In the day of thy power shall the people offer thee free-will offerings with an

ho-ly wor-ship : the dew of thy birth is of the womb of the morn-ing.

4. The Lord sware, and will not re-pent : Thou art a priest for ever after the

or-der of Mel-chis-e-dech. 5. The Lord up-on thy right hand :

shall wound even kings in the day of his wrath. 6. He shall judge among

the heathen ; he shall fill the pla-ces with the dead bod-ies : and smite in

MORNING PRAYER. DAY 23.

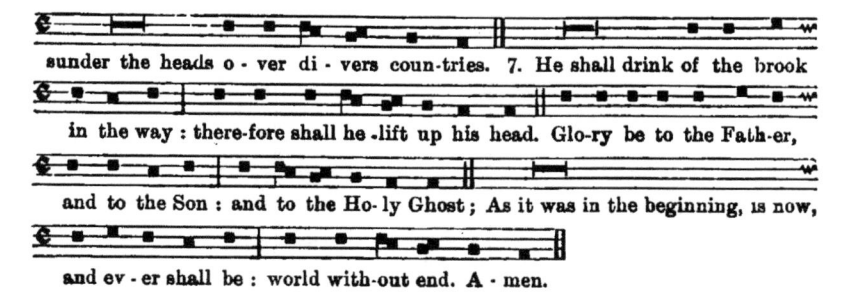

sunder the heads o-ver di-vers coun-tries. 7. He shall drink of the brook in the way : there-fore shall he lift up his head. Glo-ry be to the Fath-er, and to the Son : and to the Ho-ly Ghost ; As it was in the beginning, is now, and ev-er shall be : world with-out end. A-men.

PSALM CXI.—*Confitebor tibi.*

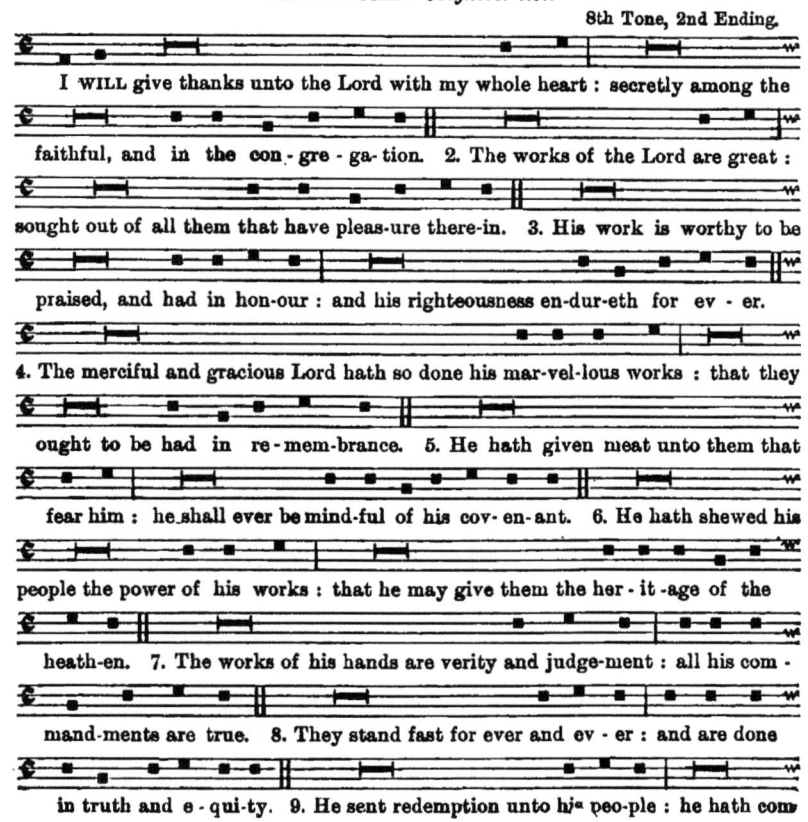

8th Tone, 2nd Ending.

I WILL give thanks unto the Lord with my whole heart : secretly among the faithful, and in the con-gre-ga-tion. 2. The works of the Lord are great : sought out of all them that have pleas-ure there-in. 3. His work is worthy to be praised, and had in hon-our : and his righteousness en-dur-eth for ev-er. 4. The merciful and gracious Lord hath so done his mar-vel-lous works : that they ought to be had in re-mem-brance. 5. He hath given meat unto them that fear him : he shall ever be mind-ful of his cov-en-ant. 6. He hath shewed his people the power of his works : that he may give them the her-it-age of the heath-en. 7. The works of his hands are verity and judge-ment : all his com-mand-ments are true. 8. They stand fast for ever and ev-er : and are done in truth and e-qui-ty. 9. He sent redemption unto his peo-ple : he hath com-

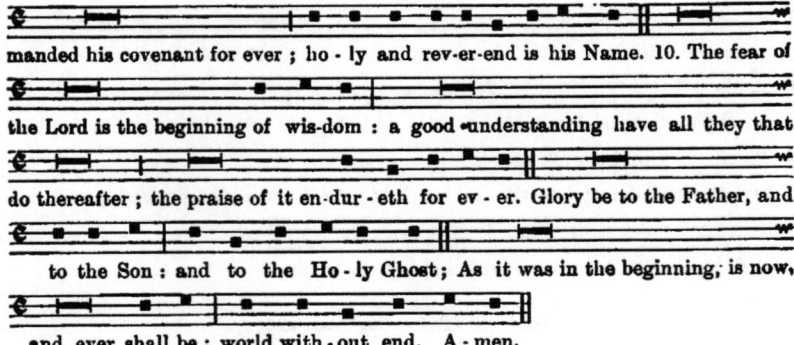

DAY 23. MORNING PRAYER

manded his covenant for ever ; ho - ly and rev-er-end is his Name. 10. The fear of the Lord is the beginning of wis-dom : a good understanding have all they that do thereafter ; the praise of it en-dur-eth for ev - er. Glory be to the Father, and to the Son : and to the Ho - ly Ghost ; As it was in the beginning, is now, and ever shall be : world with-out end. A-men.

PSALM CXII.—*Beatus vir.*

7th Tone, 5th Ending.

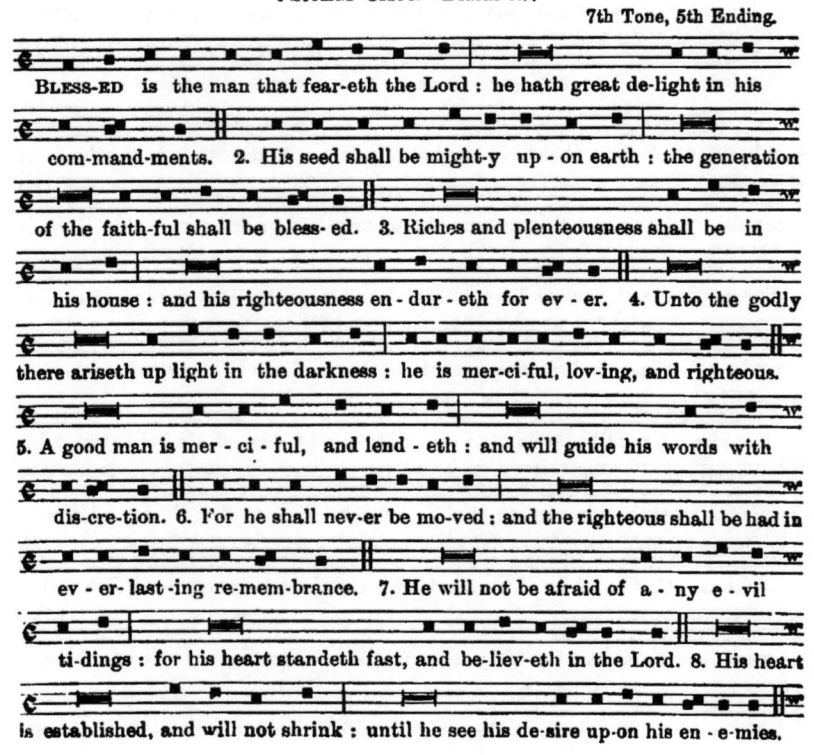

BLESS-ED is the man that fear-eth the Lord : he hath great de-light in his com-mand-ments. 2. His seed shall be might-y up - on earth : the generation of the faith-ful shall be bless-ed. 3. Riches and plenteousness shall be in his house : and his righteousness en - dur - eth for ev - er. 4. Unto the godly there ariseth up light in the darkness : he is mer-ci-ful, lov-ing, and righteous. 5. A good man is mer - ci - ful, and lend - eth : and will guide his words with dis-cre-tion. 6. For he shall nev-er be mo-ved : and the righteous shall be had in ev-er-last-ing re-mem-brance. 7. He will not be afraid of a - ny e - vil ti-dings : for his heart standeth fast, and be-liev-eth in the Lord. 8. His heart is established, and will not shrink : until he see his de-sire up-on his en - e-mies.

9. He hath dispersed abroad, and giv-en to the poor : and his righteousness remaineth for ever ; his horn shall be ex-alt-ed with hon-our. 10. The ungodly shall see it, and it shall grieve him : he shall gnash with his teeth, and consume away ; the desire of the un - god - ly shall per-ish. Glo-ry be to the Fath-er, and to the Son : and to the Ho- ly Ghost ; As it was in the beginning, is now, and ev - er shall be: world with-out end. A - men.

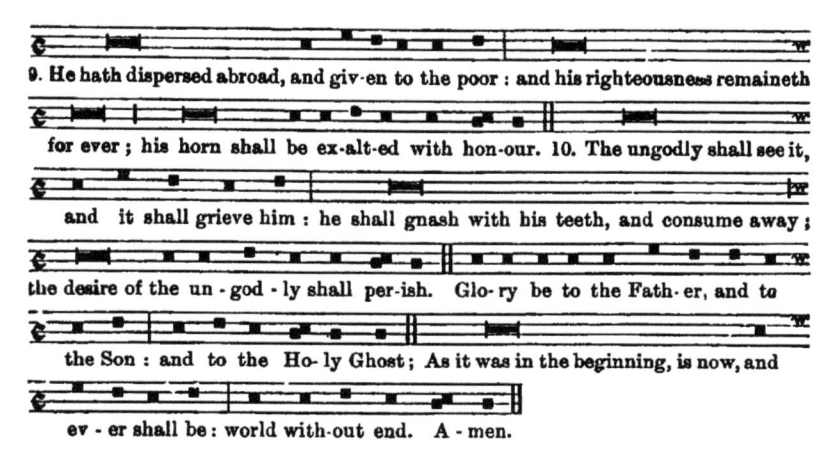

PSALM CXIII.—*Laudate pueri.*

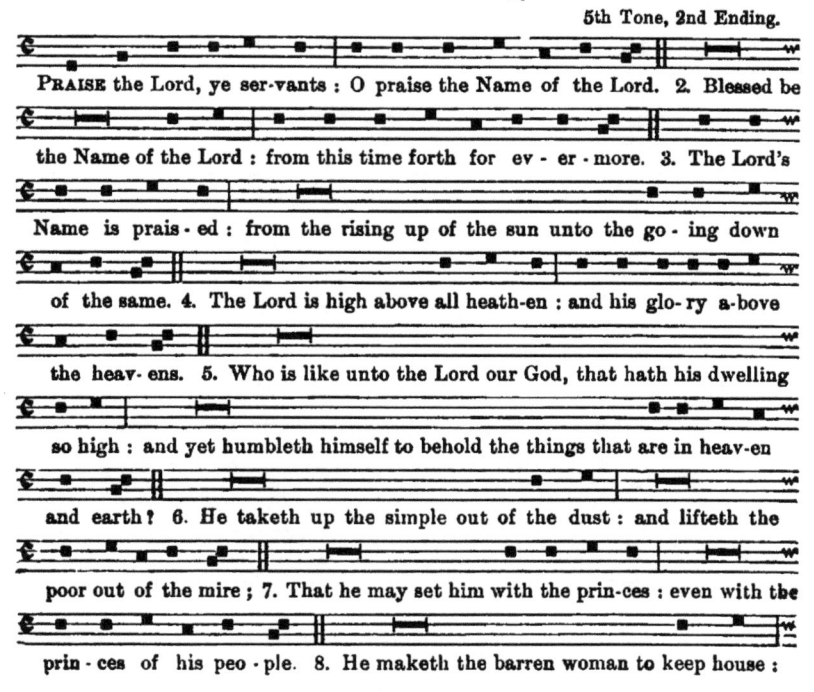

5th Tone, 2nd Ending.

PRAISE the Lord, ye ser-vants : O praise the Name of the Lord. 2. Blessed be the Name of the Lord : from this time forth for ev - er - more. 3. The Lord's Name is prais - ed : from the rising up of the sun unto the go - ing down of the same. 4. The Lord is high above all heath-en : and his glo-ry a-bove the heav-ens. 5. Who is like unto the Lord our God, that hath his dwelling so high : and yet humbleth himself to behold the things that are in heav-en and earth? 6. He taketh up the simple out of the dust : and lifteth the poor out of the mire ; 7. That he may set him with the prin-ces : even with the prin - ces of his peo - ple. 8. He maketh the barren woman to keep house :

DAY 23.   EVENING PRAYER.

and to be a joy-ful moth-er of chil-dren. Glory be to the Father, and to the Son :

and to the Ho-ly Ghost ; As it was in the beginning, is now, and ever shall be :

world with-out end. A - men.

EVENING PRAYER.

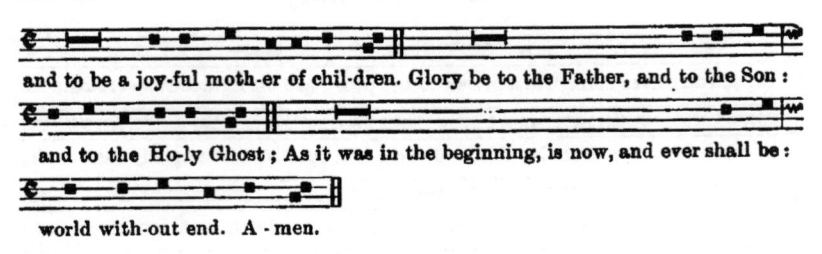

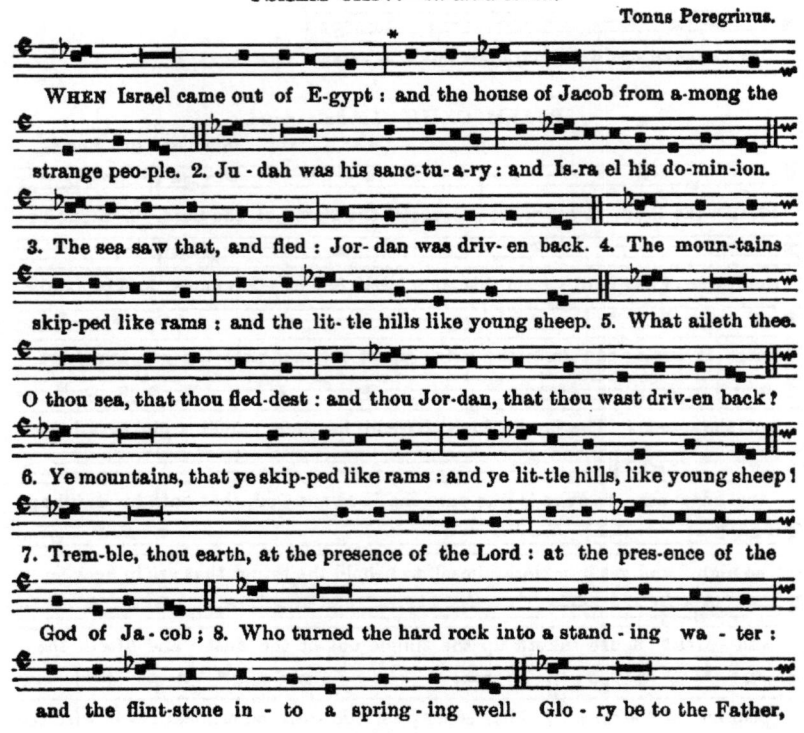

PSALM CXIV.—*In exitu Israel.*

Tonus Peregrinus.

WHEN Israel came out of E-gypt : and the house of Jacob from a-mong the

strange peo-ple. 2. Ju - dah was his sanc-tu- a-ry : and Is-ra el his do-min-ion.

3. The sea saw that, and fled : Jor- dan was driv- en back. 4. The moun-tains

skip-ped like rams : and the lit- tle hills like young sheep. 5. What aileth thee.

O thou sea, that thou fled-dest : and thou Jor-dan, that thou wast driv-en back ?

6. Ye mountains, that ye skip-ped like rams : and ye lit-tle hills, like young sheep ?

7. Trem-ble, thou earth, at the presence of the Lord : at the pres-ence of the

God of Ja - cob ; 8. Who turned the hard rock into a stand - ing wa - ter :

and the flint-stone in - to a spring - ing well. Glo - ry be to the Father,

* The notes of the intonation may be omitted in the second half of each verse, and the recitation begin at once on the G.

EVENING PRAYER. DAY 23.

and to the Son : and to the Ho-ly Ghost ; As it was in the beginning, is now, and ev - er shall be : world with-out end. A - men.

PSALM CXV.—*Non nobis, Domine.*

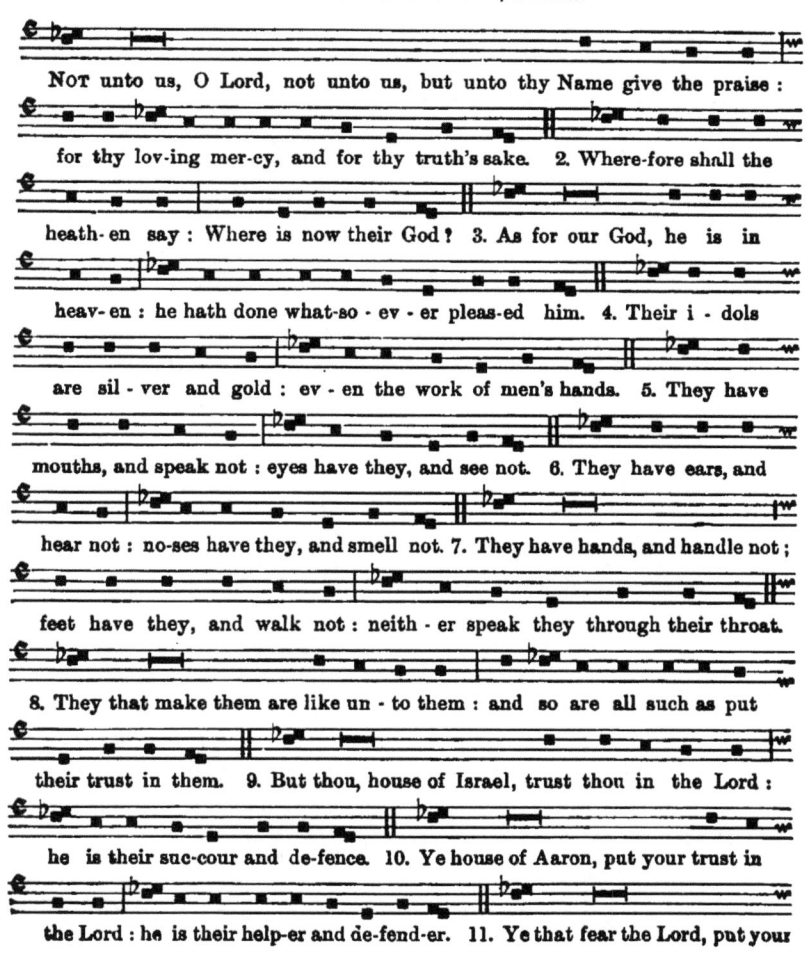

Not unto us, O Lord, not unto us, but unto thy Name give the praise : for thy lov-ing mer-cy, and for thy truth's sake. 2. Where-fore shall the heath-en say : Where is now their God? 3. As for our God, he is in heav- en : he hath done what-so - ev - er pleas-ed him. 4. Their i - dols are sil - ver and gold : ev - en the work of men's hands. 5. They have mouths, and speak not : eyes have they, and see not. 6. They have ears, and hear not : no-ses have they, and smell not. 7. They have hands, and handle not ; feet have they, and walk not : neith - er speak they through their throat. 8. They that make them are like un - to them : and so are all such as put their trust in them. 9. But thou, house of Israel, trust thou in the Lord : he is their suc-cour and de-fence. 10. Ye house of Aaron, put your trust in the Lord : he is their help-er and de-fend-er. 11. Ye that fear the Lord, put your

(203)

Day 24. MORNING PRAYER.

trust in the Lord : he is their help - er and de- fend-er. 12. The Lord hath been mindful of us, and he shall bless us : e-ven he shall bless the house of Israel, he shall bless the house of Aa - ron. 13. He shall bless them that fear the Lord : both small and great. 14. The Lord shall in - crease you more and more : you and your chil-dren. 15. Ye are the bless-ed of the Lord : who made heav - en and earth. 16. All the whole heav-ens are the Lord's : the earth hath he given to the chil-dren of men. 17. The dead praise not thee, O Lord : nei-ther all they that go down in-to si-lence. 18. But we will praise the Lord : from this time forth for ev-er-more. Praise the Lord. Glo-ry be to the Fath-er, and to the Son : and to the Ho - ly Ghost ; As it was in the beginning, is now, and ev - er shall be : world with-out end. A - men.

Day 24. MORNING PRAYER.

PSALM CXVI.—*Dilexi, quoniam.*

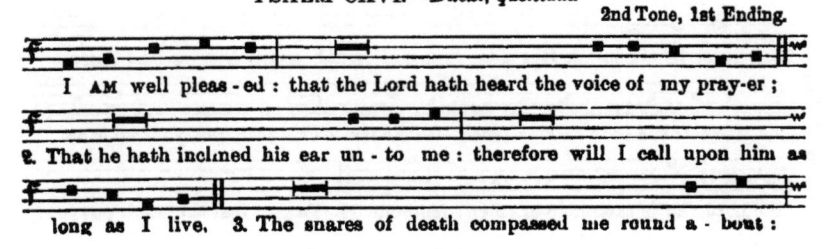

2nd Tone, 1st Ending.

I AM well pleas - ed : that the Lord hath heard the voice of my pray-er ; 2. That he hath inclined his ear un - to me : therefore will I call upon him as long as I live. 3. The snares of death compassed me round a - bout :

(204)

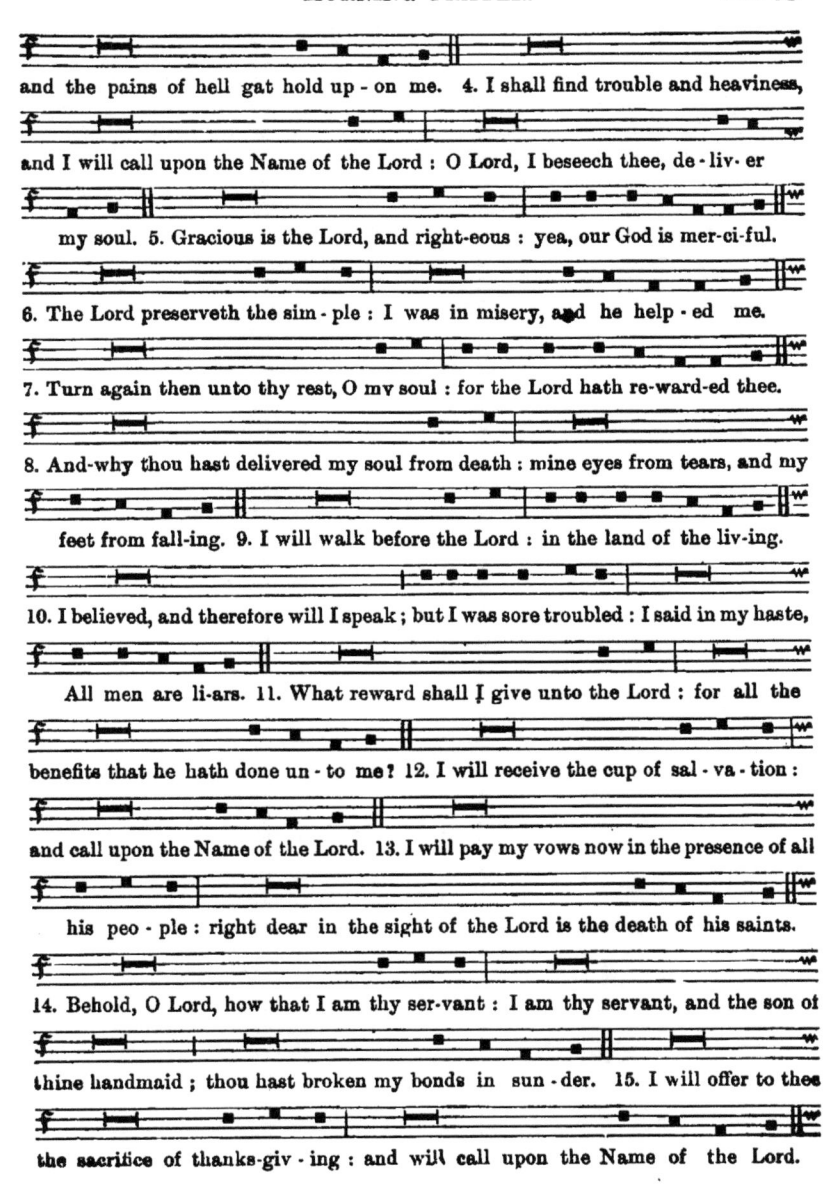

and the pains of hell gat hold up-on me. 4. I shall find trouble and heaviness,

and I will call upon the Name of the Lord : O Lord, I beseech thee, de-liv-er

my soul. 5. Gracious is the Lord, and right-eous : yea, our God is mer-ci-ful.

6. The Lord preserveth the sim-ple : I was in misery, and he help-ed me.

7. Turn again then unto thy rest, O my soul : for the Lord hath re-ward-ed thee.

8. And why thou hast delivered my soul from death : mine eyes from tears, and my

feet from fall-ing. 9. I will walk before the Lord : in the land of the liv-ing.

10. I believed, and therefore will I speak ; but I was sore troubled : I said in my haste,

All men are li-ars. 11. What reward shall I give unto the Lord : for all the

benefits that he hath done un-to me? 12. I will receive the cup of sal-va-tion :

and call upon the Name of the Lord. 13. I will pay my vows now in the presence of all

his peo-ple : right dear in the sight of the Lord is the death of his saints.

14. Behold, O Lord, how that I am thy ser-vant : I am thy servant, and the son of

thine handmaid ; thou hast broken my bonds in sun-der. 15. I will offer to thee

the sacrifice of thanks-giv-ing : and will call upon the Name of the Lord.

Day 24.   MORNING PRAYER.

16. I will pay my vows unto the Lord, in the sight of all his people: in the courts of the Lord's house, even in the midst of thee, O Je-ru-sa-lem. Praise the Lord.

Glory be to the Father, and to the Son: and to the Ho-ly Ghost; As it was in the beginning, is now, and ever shall be: world with-out end. A men.

PSALM CXVII.—*Laudate Dominum.*

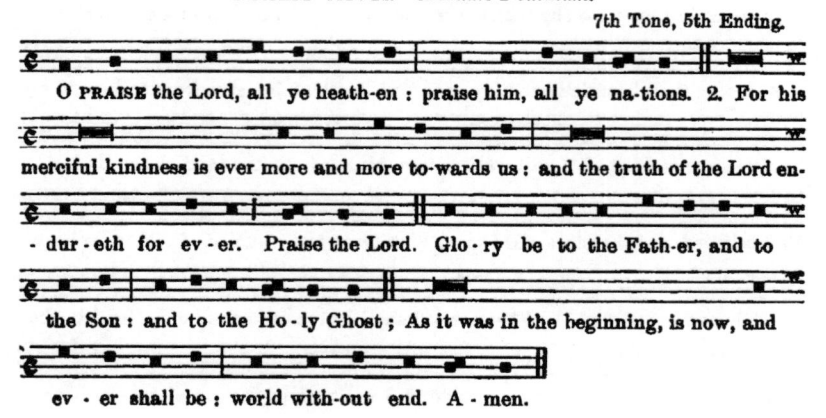

7th Tone, 5th Ending.

O PRAISE the Lord, all ye heath-en: praise him, all ye na-tions. 2. For his merciful kindness is ever more and more to-wards us: and the truth of the Lord en- -dur-eth for ev-er. Praise the Lord. Glo-ry be to the Fath-er, and to the Son: and to the Ho-ly Ghost; As it was in the beginning, is now, and ev-er shall be: world with-out end. A-men.

PSALM CXVIII.—*Confitemini Domino.*

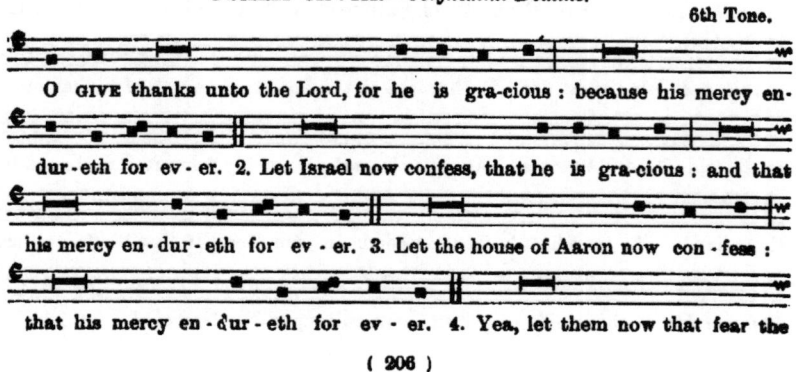

6th Tone.

O GIVE thanks unto the Lord, for he is gra-cious: because his mercy en- dur-eth for ev-er. 2. Let Israel now confess, that he is gra-cious: and that his mercy en-dur-eth for ev-er. 3. Let the house of Aaron now con-fess: that his mercy en-dur-eth for ev-er. 4. Yea, let them now that fear the

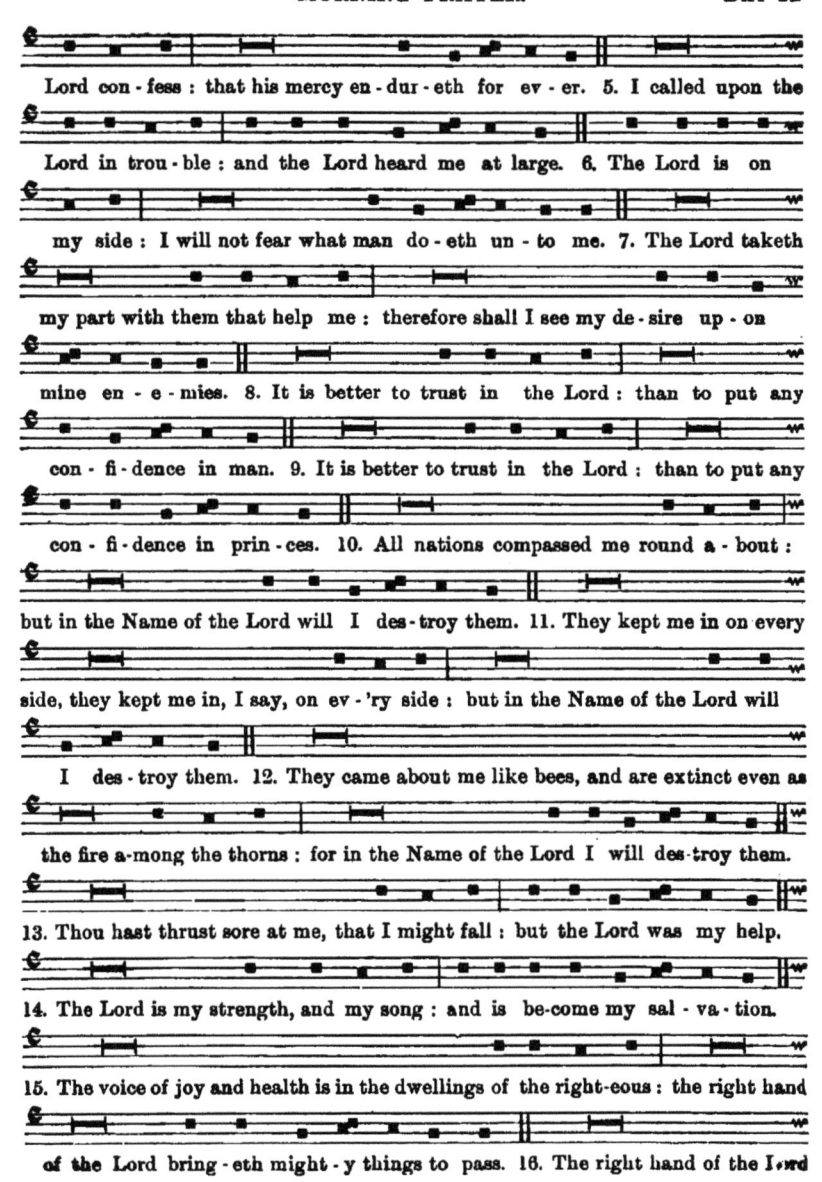

MORNING PRAYER. DAY 24.

Lord con-fess : that his mercy en-dur-eth for ev-er. 5. I called upon the Lord in trou-ble : and the Lord heard me at large. 6. The Lord is on my side : I will not fear what man do-eth un-to me. 7. The Lord taketh my part with them that help me : therefore shall I see my de-sire up-on mine en-e-mies. 8. It is better to trust in the Lord : than to put any con-fi-dence in man. 9. It is better to trust in the Lord : than to put any con-fi-dence in prin-ces. 10. All nations compassed me round a-bout : but in the Name of the Lord will I des-troy them. 11. They kept me in on every side, they kept me in, I say, on ev-'ry side : but in the Name of the Lord will I des-troy them. 12. They came about me like bees, and are extinct even as the fire a-mong the thorns : for in the Name of the Lord I will des-troy them. 13. Thou hast thrust sore at me, that I might fall : but the Lord was my help. 14. The Lord is my strength, and my song : and is be-come my sal-va-tion. 15. The voice of joy and health is in the dwellings of the right-eous : the right hand of the Lord bring-eth might-y things to pass. 16. The right hand of the Lord

(207)

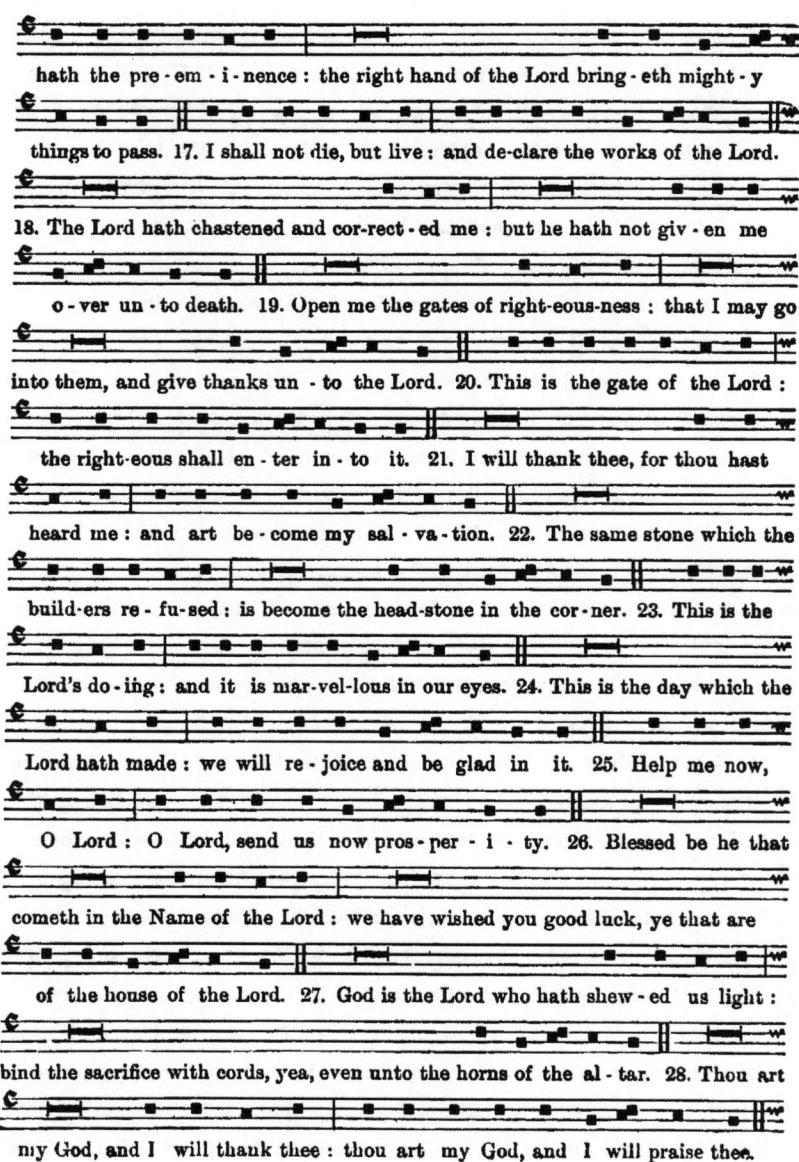

DAY 24. MORNING PRAYER.

hath the pre-em-i-nence : the right hand of the Lord bring-eth might-y things to pass. 17. I shall not die, but live : and de-clare the works of the Lord. 18. The Lord hath chastened and cor-rect-ed me : but he hath not giv-en me o-ver un-to death. 19. Open me the gates of right-eous-ness : that I may go into them, and give thanks un-to the Lord. 20. This is the gate of the Lord : the right-eous shall en-ter in-to it. 21. I will thank thee, for thou hast heard me : and art be-come my sal-va-tion. 22. The same stone which the build-ers re-fu-sed : is become the head-stone in the cor-ner. 23. This is the Lord's do-ing : and it is mar-vel-lous in our eyes. 24. This is the day which the Lord hath made : we will re-joice and be glad in it. 25. Help me now, O Lord : O Lord, send us now pros-per-i-ty. 26. Blessed be he that cometh in the Name of the Lord : we have wished you good luck, ye that are of the house of the Lord. 27. God is the Lord who hath shew-ed us light : bind the sacrifice with cords, yea, even unto the horns of the al-tar. 28. Thou art my God, and I will thank thee : thou art my God, and I will praise thee.

EVENING PRAYER.　　　　　　　　　DAY 24.

29. O give thanks unto the Lord, for he is gra-cious : and his mercy en-dur-eth for ev - er. Glory be to the Father, and to the Son : and to the Ho-ly Ghost ; As it was in the beginning, is now, and ev - er shall be : world with-out end. A - men.

EVENING PRAYER.

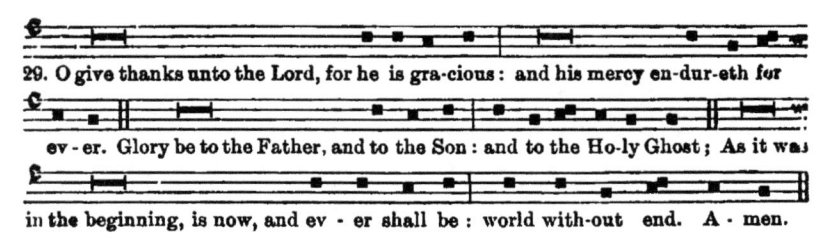

PSALM CXIX.—*Beati immaculati.*

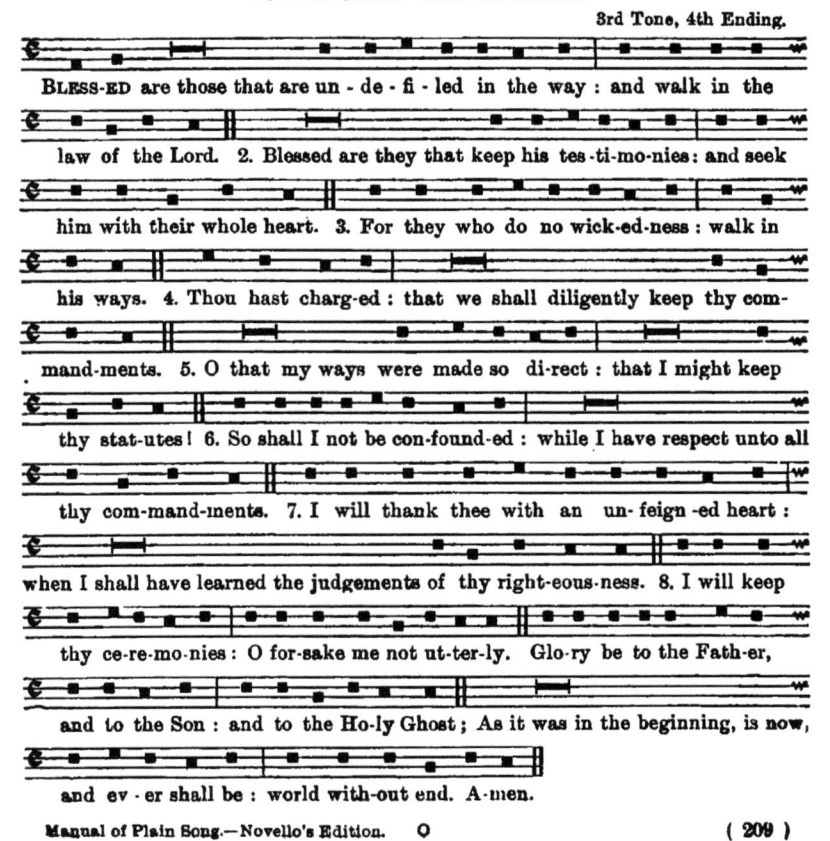

3rd Tone, 4th Ending.

BLESS-ED are those that are un - de - fi - led in the way : and walk in the law of the Lord. 2. Blessed are they that keep his tes-ti-mo-nies : and seek him with their whole heart. 3. For they who do no wick-ed-ness : walk in his ways. 4. Thou hast charg-ed : that we shall diligently keep thy com-mand-ments. 5. O that my ways were made so di-rect : that I might keep thy stat-utes! 6. So shall I not be con-found-ed : while I have respect unto all thy com-mand-ments. 7. I will thank thee with an un-feign-ed heart : when I shall have learned the judgements of thy right-eous-ness. 8. I will keep thy ce-re-mo-nies : O for-sake me not ut-ter-ly. Glo-ry be to the Fath-er, and to the Son : and to the Ho-ly Ghost ; As it was in the beginning, is now, and ev - er shall be : world with-out end. A-men.

Manual of Plain Song.—Novello's Edition.　　O

DAY 24. EVENING PRAYER.

In quo corriget?
3rd Tone, 4th Ending.

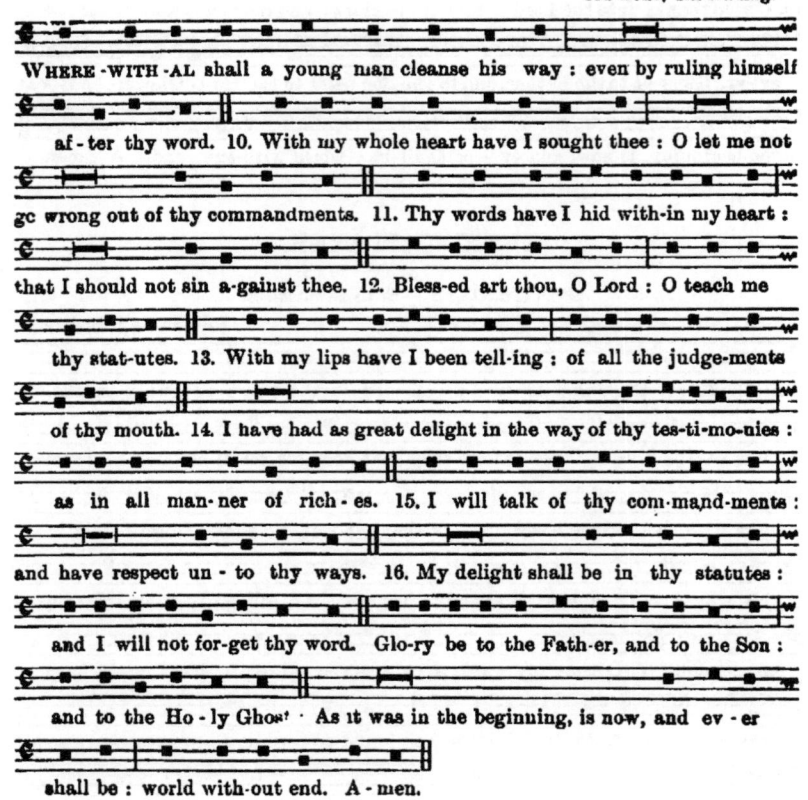

WHERE-WITH-AL shall a young man cleanse his way : even by ruling himself af-ter thy word. 10. With my whole heart have I sought thee : O let me not go wrong out of thy commandments. 11. Thy words have I hid with-in my heart : that I should not sin a-gainst thee. 12. Bless-ed art thou, O Lord : O teach me thy stat-utes. 13. With my lips have I been tell-ing : of all the judge-ments of thy mouth. 14. I have had as great delight in the way of thy tes-ti-mo-nies : as in all man-ner of rich-es. 15. I will talk of thy com-mand-ments : and have respect un-to thy ways. 16. My delight shall be in thy statutes : and I will not for-get thy word. Glo-ry be to the Fath-er, and to the Son : and to the Ho-ly Ghost. As it was in the beginning, is now, and ev-er shall be : world with-out end. A-men.

Retribue servo tuo.
6th Tone.

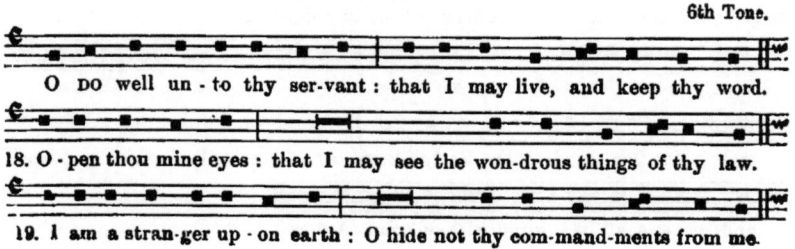

O DO well un-to thy ser-vant : that I may live, and keep thy word. 18. O-pen thou mine eyes : that I may see the won-drous things of thy law. 19. I am a stran-ger up-on earth : O hide not thy com-mand-ments from me.

(210)

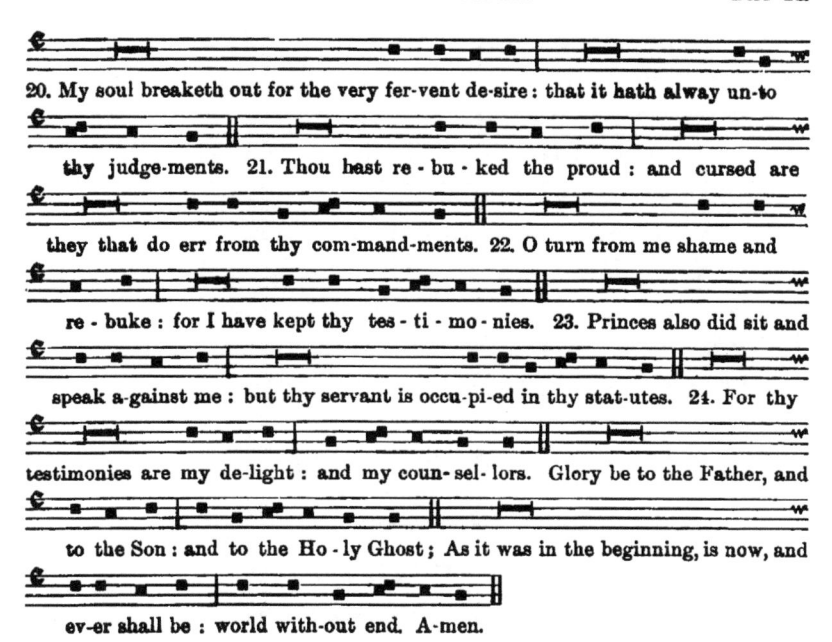

EVENING PRAYER. DAY 24.

20. My soul breaketh out for the very fer-vent de-sire : that it hath alway un-to thy judge-ments. 21. Thou hast re - bu - ked the proud : and cursed are they that do err from thy com-mand-ments. 22. O turn from me shame and re - buke : for I have kept thy tes - ti - mo - nies. 23. Princes also did sit and speak a-gainst me : but thy servant is occu-pi-ed in thy stat-utes. 24. For thy testimonies are my de-light : and my coun- sel- lors. Glory be to the Father, and to the Son : and to the Ho - ly Ghost ; As it was in the beginning, is now, and ev-er shall be : world with-out end. A-men.

Adhæsit pavimento.

6th Tone.

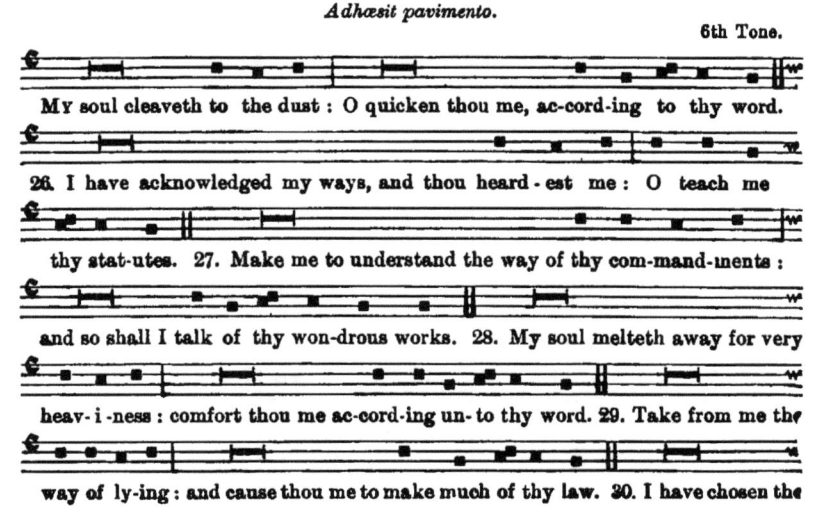

My soul cleaveth to the dust : O quicken thou me, ac-cord-ing to thy word. 26. I have acknowledged my ways, and thou heard - est me : O teach me thy stat-utes. 27. Make me to understand the way of thy com-mand-ments : and so shall I talk of thy won-drous works. 28. My soul melteth away for very heav- i -ness : comfort thou me ac-cord-ing un- to thy word. 29. Take from me the way of ly-ing : and cause thou me to make much of thy law. 30. I have chosen the

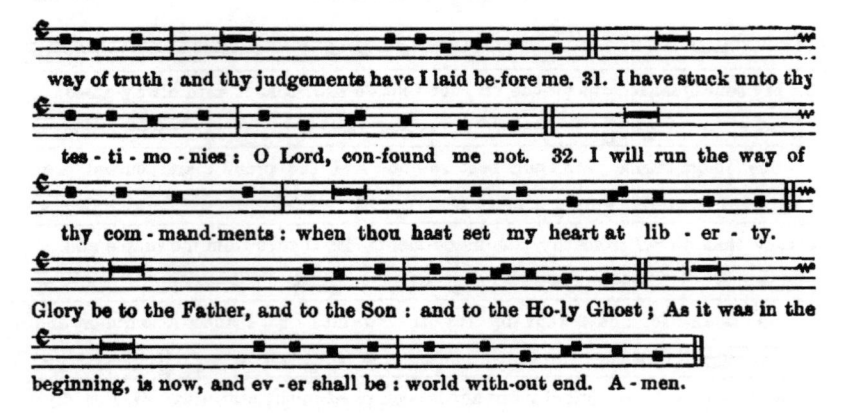

DAY 25. MORNING PRAYER.

way of truth: and thy judgements have I laid be-fore me. 31. I have stuck unto thy tes - ti - mo - nies: O Lord, con-found me not. 32. I will run the way of thy com - mand-ments: when thou hast set my heart at lib - er - ty. Glory be to the Father, and to the Son: and to the Ho-ly Ghost; As it was in the beginning, is now, and ev - er shall be: world with-out end. A - men.

DAY 25. MORNING PRAYER.

Legem pone.

8th Tone, 1st Ending.

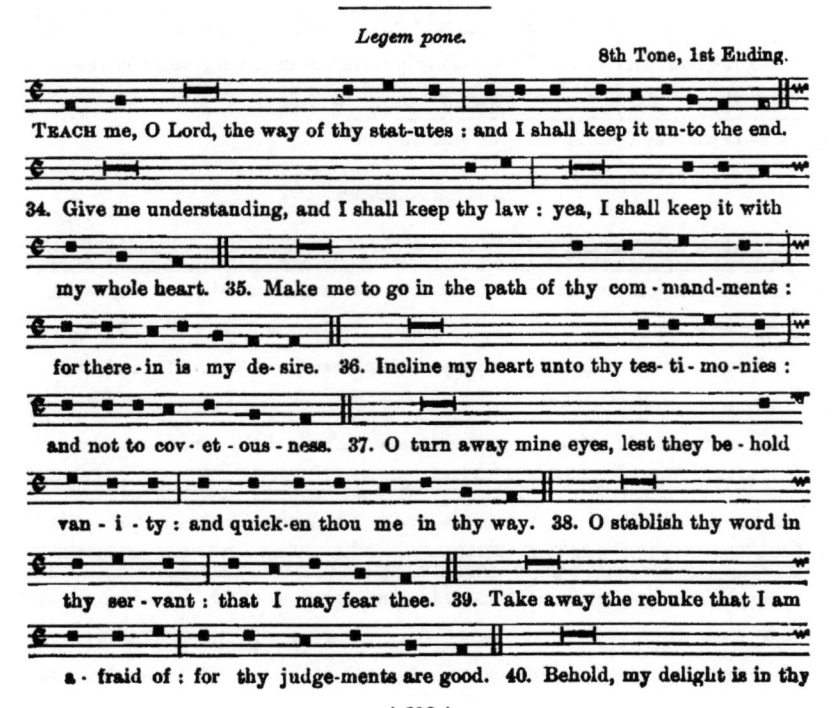

TEACH me, O Lord, the way of thy stat-utes: and I shall keep it un-to the end. 34. Give me understanding, and I shall keep thy law: yea, I shall keep it with my whole heart. 35. Make me to go in the path of thy com - mand-ments: for there-in is my de-sire. 36. Incline my heart unto thy tes- ti - mo -nies: and not to cov- et - ous - ness. 37. O turn away mine eyes, lest they be - hold van - i - ty: and quick-en thou me in thy way. 38. O stablish thy word in thy ser - vant: that I may fear thee. 39. Take away the rebuke that I am a - fraid of: for thy judge-ments are good. 40. Behold, my delight is in thy

(212)

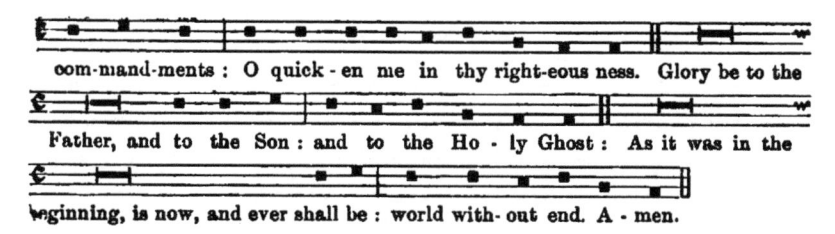

com-mand-ments : O quick-en me in thy right-eous ness. Glory be to the Father, and to the Son : and to the Ho-ly Ghost : As it was in the beginning, is now, and ever shall be : world with-out end. A-men.

Et veniat super me.

8th Tone, 1st Ending.

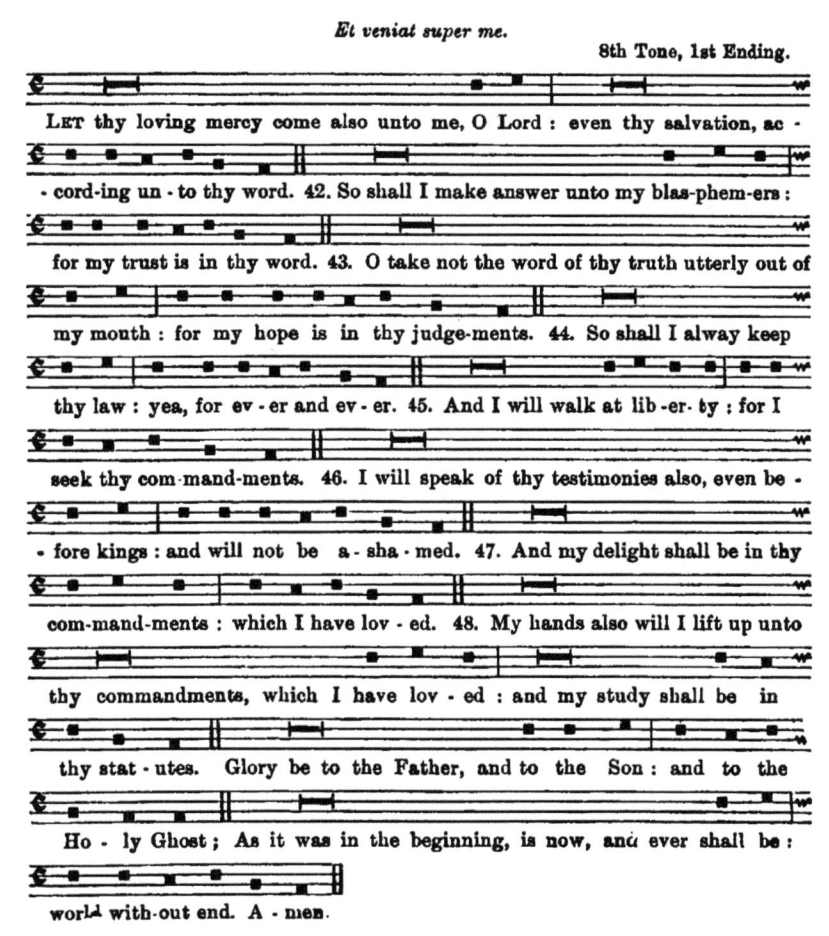

LET thy loving mercy come also unto me, O Lord : even thy salvation, ac- -cord-ing un-to thy word. 42. So shall I make answer unto my blas-phem-ers : for my trust is in thy word. 43. O take not the word of thy truth utterly out of my mouth : for my hope is in thy judge-ments. 44. So shall I alway keep thy law : yea, for ev-er and ev-er. 45. And I will walk at lib-er-ty : for I seek thy com-mand-ments. 46. I will speak of thy testimonies also, even be- -fore kings : and will not be a-sha-med. 47. And my delight shall be in thy com-mand-ments : which I have lov-ed. 48. My hands also will I lift up unto thy commandments, which I have lov-ed : and my study shall be in thy stat-utes. Glory be to the Father, and to the Son : and to the Ho-ly Ghost ; As it was in the beginning, is now, and ever shall be : world with-out end. A-men.

DAY 25.　　　　　MORNING PRAYER.

Memor esto servi tui.　　　　1st Tone, 3rd Ending.

O THINK upon thy servant, as con-cern-ing thy word : wherein thou hast caus-ed me to put my trust. 50. The same is my comfort in my trou-ble : for thy word hath quick-en-ed me. 51. The proud have had me exceedingly in de-ri-sion : yet have I not shrink-ed from thy law. 52. For I remembered thine everlasting judge-ments, O Lord : and re-ceiv-ed com-fort. 53. I am hor-ri-bly a-fraid : for the un-god-ly that for-sake thy law. 54. Thy statutes have been my songs : in the house of my pil-grim-age. 55. I have thought upon thy Name, O Lord, in the night-sea-son : and have kept thy law. 56. This I had : be-cause I kept thy commandments. Glory be to the Father, and to the Son : and to the Ho-ly Ghost; As it was in the beginning, is now, and ev-er shall be : world with-out end. A-men.

Portio mea, Domine.　　　　1st Tone, 3rd Ending.

THOU art my por-tion, O Lord : I have prom-is-ed to keep thy law. 58. I made my humble petition in thy presence with my whole heart : O be merciful unto me, ac-cord-ing to thy word. 59. I called mine own ways to re-mem-brance

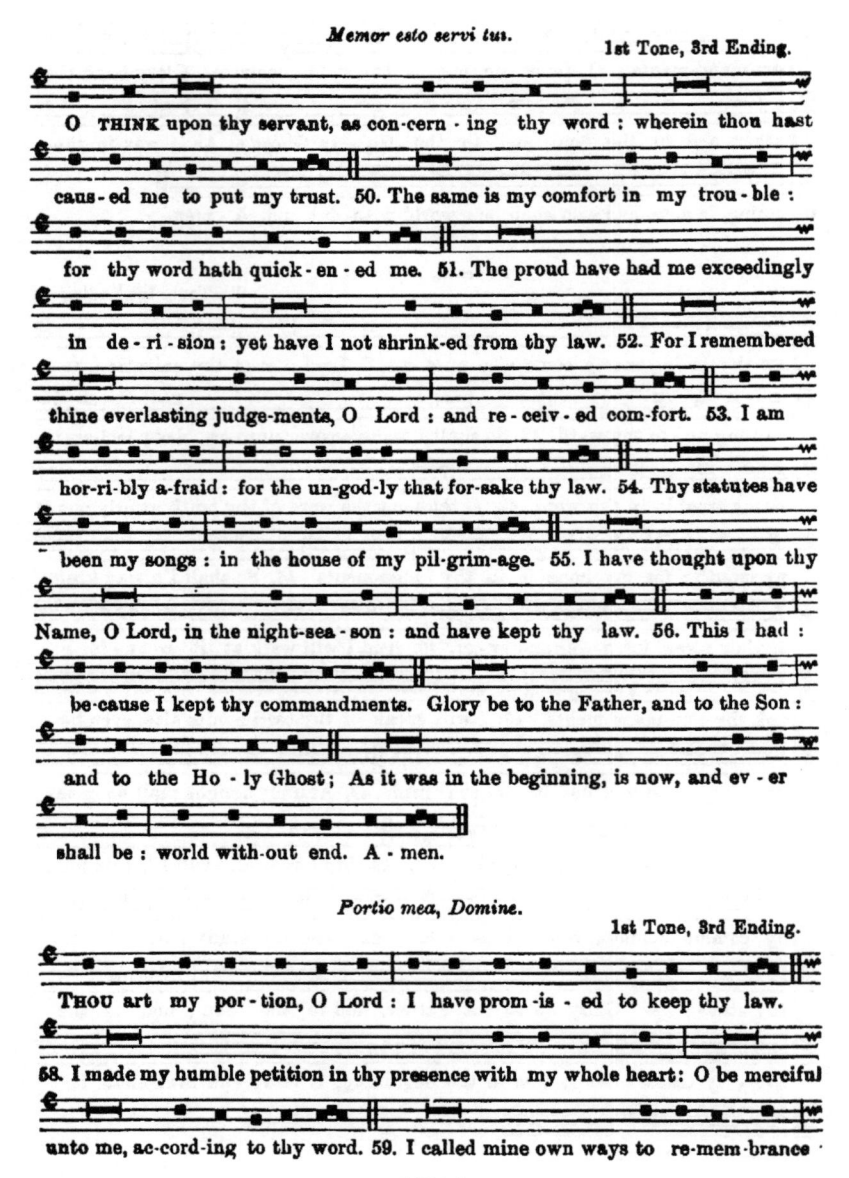

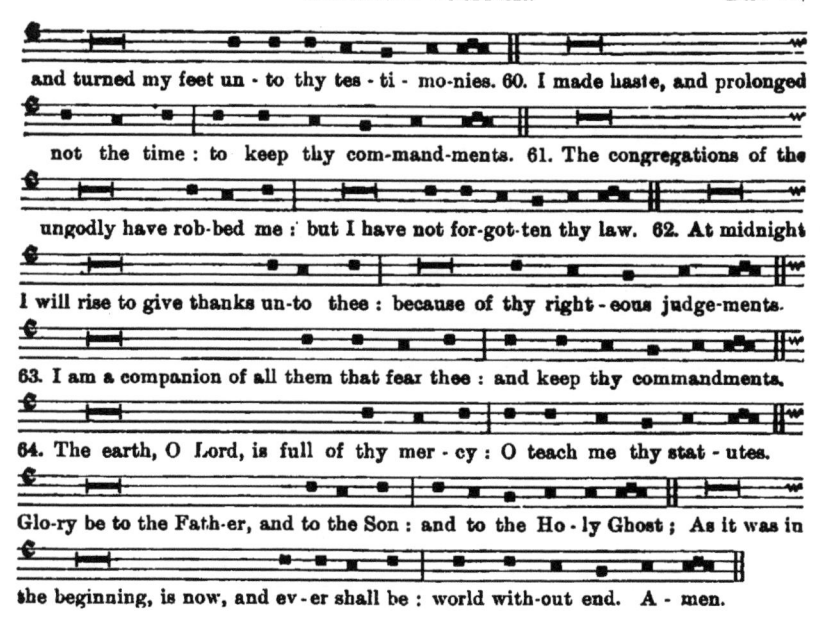

MORNING PRAYER. DAY 25.

and turned my feet un - to thy tes - ti - mo-nies. 60. I made haste, and prolonged not the time : to keep thy com-mand-ments. 61. The congregations of the ungodly have rob-bed me : but I have not for-got-ten thy law. 62. At midnight I will rise to give thanks un-to thee : because of thy right - eous judge-ments. 63. I am a companion of all them that fear thee : and keep thy commandments. 64. The earth, O Lord, is full of thy mer - cy : O teach me thy stat - utes. Glo-ry be to the Fath-er, and to the Son : and to the Ho - ly Ghost ; As it was in the beginning, is now, and ev-er shall be : world with-out end. A - men.

Bonitatem fecisti.

2nd Tone, 1st Endmg.

O LORD, thou hast dealt graciously with thy ser-vant : ac-cord-ing un - to thy word. 66. O learn me true understanding and know-ledge : for I have believed thy com-mand-ments. 67. Before I was troubled, I went wrong : but now have I kept thy word. 68. Thou art good and gra-cious : O teach me thy stat-utes. 69. The proud have imagined a lie a-gainst me : but I will keep thy commandments with my whole heart. 70. Their heart is as fat as brawn : but my delight hath

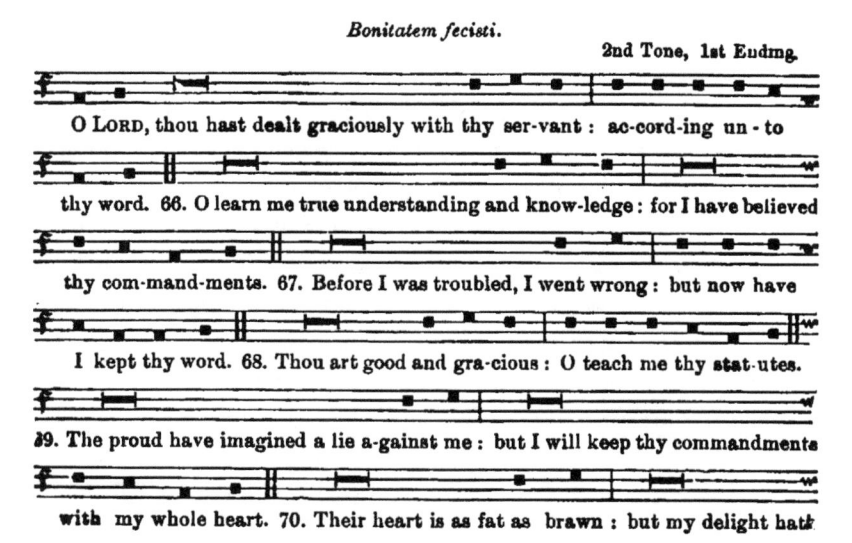

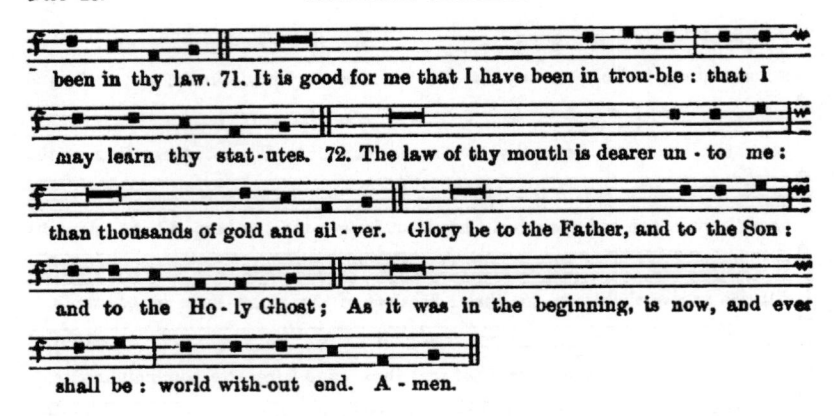

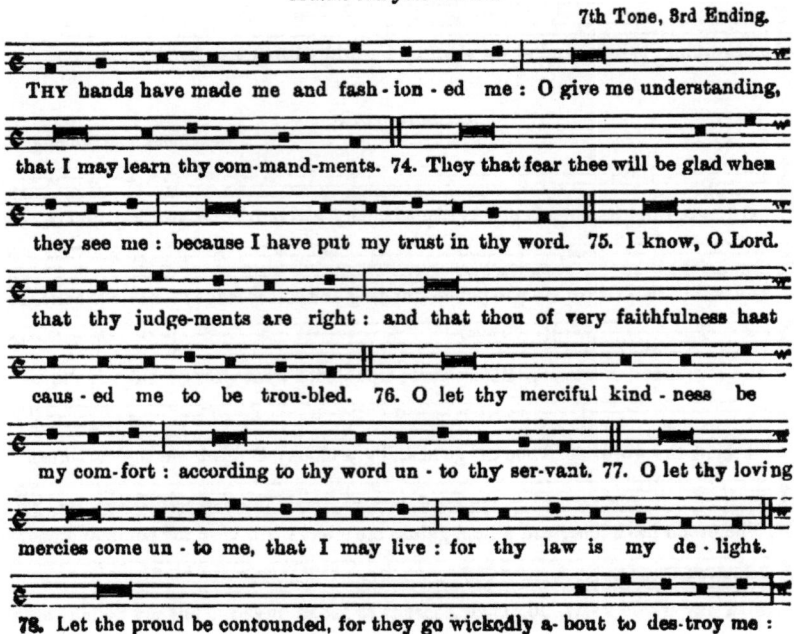

DAY 25. EVENING PRAYER.

been in thy law. 71. It is good for me that I have been in trou-ble : that I may learn thy stat-utes. 72. The law of thy mouth is dearer un - to me: than thousands of gold and sil - ver. Glory be to the Father, and to the Son : and to the Ho - ly Ghost; As it was in the beginning, is now, and ever shall be : world with-out end. A - men.

EVENING PRAYER.

Manus tuæ fecerunt me.

7th Tone, 3rd Ending.

THY hands have made me and fash-ion-ed me : O give me understanding, that I may learn thy com-mand-ments. 74. They that fear thee will be glad when they see me : because I have put my trust in thy word. 75. I know, O Lord, that thy judge-ments are right : and that thou of very faithfulness hast caus-ed me to be trou-bled. 76. O let thy merciful kind - ness be my com-fort : according to thy word un - to thy ser-vant. 77. O let thy loving mercies come un - to me, that I may live : for thy law is my de - light. 78. Let the proud be confounded, for they go wickedly a- bout to des-troy me :

EVENING PRAYER. DAY 25.

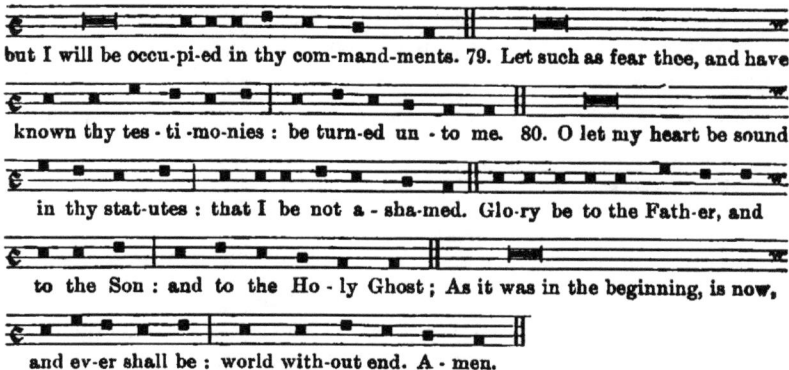

but I will be occu-pi-ed in thy com-mand-ments. 79. Let such as fear thee, and have known thy tes-ti-mo-nies : be turn-ed un-to me. 80. O let my heart be sound in thy stat-utes : that I be not a-sha-med. Glo-ry be to the Fath-er, and to the Son : and to the Ho-ly Ghost ; As it was in the beginning, is now, and ev-er shall be : world with-out end. A-men.

Defecit anima mea.

7th Tone, 3rd Ending.

My soul hath longed for thy sal-va-tion : and I have a good hope be-cause of thy word. 82. Mine eyes long sore for thy word : say-ing, O when wilt thou com-fort me ! 83. For I am become like a bot-tle in the smoke : yet do I not for-get thy stat-utes. 84. How many are the days of thy ser-vant : when wilt thou be avenged of them that per-se-cute me ? 85. The proud have dig-ged pits for me : which are not aft-er thy law. 86. All thy com-mand-ments are true : they persecute me falsely ; O be thou my help. 87. They had almost made an end of me up-on earth : but I forsook not thy com-mand-ments. 88. O quicken me after thy lov-ing-kind-ness : and so shall I keep the tes-ti-

Day 25.   EVENING PRAYER.

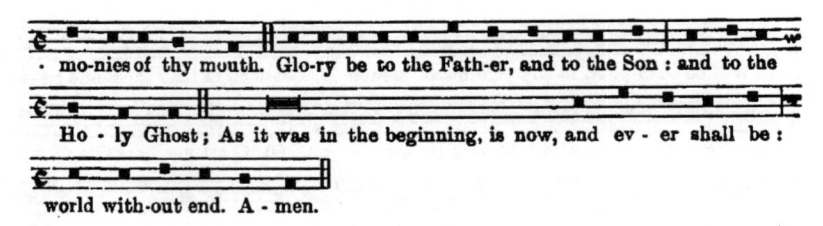

- mo-nies of thy mouth. Glo-ry be to the Fath-er, and to the Son : and to the Ho - ly Ghost; As it was in the beginning, is now, and ev - er shall be : world with-out end. A - men.

In æternum, Domine.

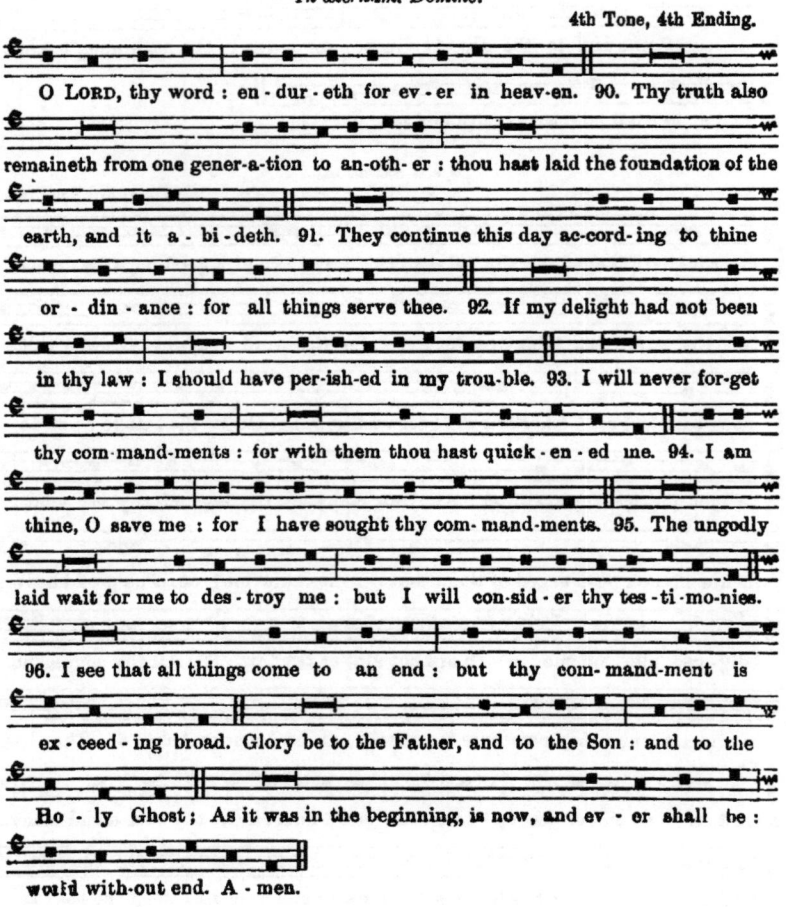

4th Tone, 4th Ending.

O LORD, thy word : en - dur - eth for ev - er in heav-en. 90. Thy truth also remaineth from one gener-a-tion to an-oth-er : thou hast laid the foundation of the earth, and it a - bi - deth. 91. They continue this day ac-cord-ing to thine or - din - ance : for all things serve thee. 92. If my delight had not been in thy law : I should have per-ish-ed in my trou-ble. 93. I will never for-get thy com-mand-ments : for with them thou hast quick - en - ed me. 94. I am thine, O save me : for I have sought thy com- mand-ments. 95. The ungodly laid wait for me to des - troy me : but I will con-sid - er thy tes -ti-mo-nies. 96. I see that all things come to an end : but thy com- mand-ment is ex - ceed - ing broad. Glory be to the Father, and to the Son : and to the Ho - ly Ghost; As it was in the beginning, is now, and ev - er shall be : world with-out end. A - men.

EVENING PRAYER. DAY 25.
Quomodo dilexi.

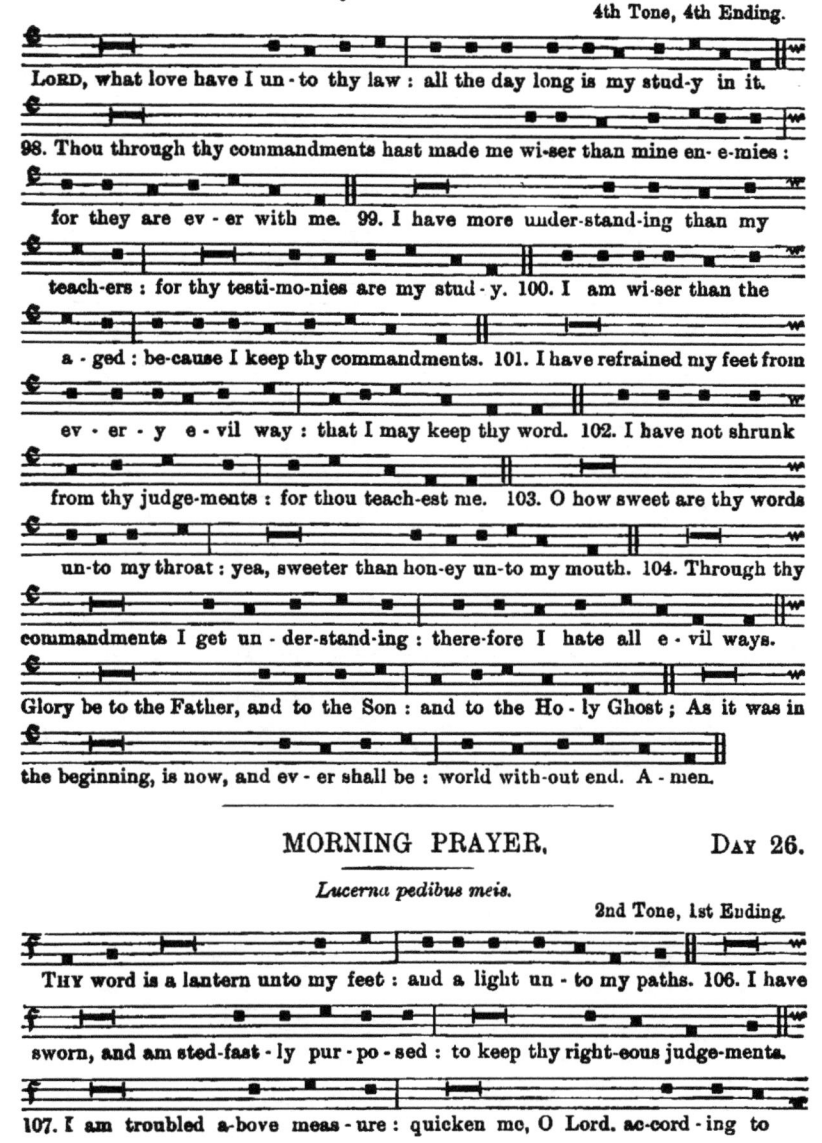

4th Tone, 4th Ending.

LORD, what love have I un-to thy law : all the day long is my stud-y in it.

98. Thou through thy commandments hast made me wi-ser than mine en- e-mies :

for they are ev - er with me. 99. I have more under-stand-ing than my

teach-ers : for thy testi-mo-nies are my stud - y. 100. I am wi-ser than the

a - ged : be-cause I keep thy commandments. 101. I have refrained my feet from

ev - er - y e - vil way : that I may keep thy word. 102. I have not shrunk

from thy judge-ments : for thou teach-est me. 103. O how sweet are thy words

un-to my throat : yea, sweeter than hon-ey un-to my mouth. 104. Through thy

commandments I get un - der-stand-ing : there-fore I hate all e - vil ways.

Glory be to the Father, and to the Son : and to the Ho - ly Ghost ; As it was in

the beginning, is now, and ev - er shall be : world with-out end. A - men.

MORNING PRAYER. DAY 26.
Lucerna pedibus meis.

2nd Tone, 1st Ending.

THY word is a lantern unto my feet : and a light un - to my paths. 106. I have

sworn, and am sted-fast - ly pur - po - sed : to keep thy right-eous judge-ments.

107. I am troubled a-bove meas - ure : quicken me, O Lord. ac-cord - ing to

(219)

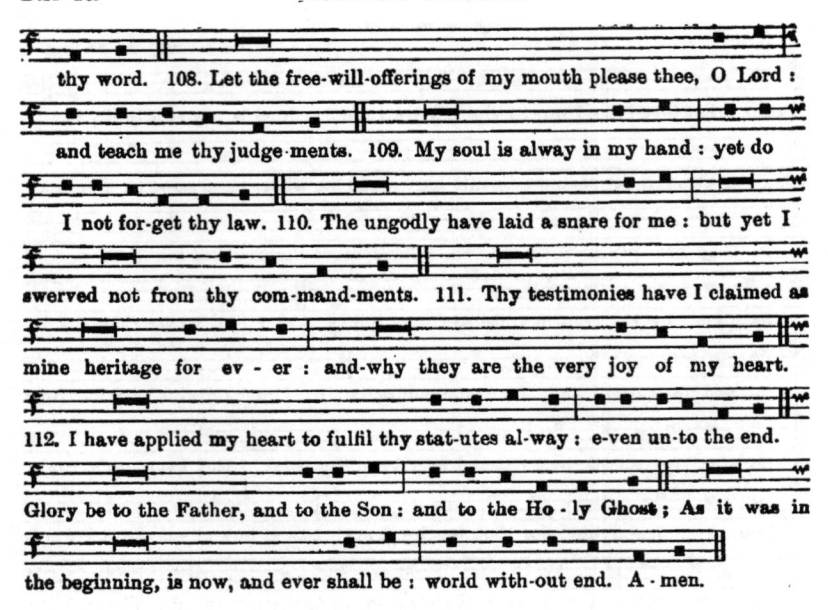

DAY 26.   MORNING PRAYER.

thy word. 108. Let the free-will-offerings of my mouth please thee, O Lord :

and teach me thy judge-ments. 109. My soul is alway in my hand : yet do

I not for-get thy law. 110. The ungodly have laid a snare for me : but yet I

swerved not from thy com-mand-ments. 111. Thy testimonies have I claimed as

mine heritage for ev - er : and-why they are the very joy of my heart.

112. I have applied my heart to fulfil thy stat-utes al-way : e-ven un-to the end.

Glory be to the Father, and to the Son : and to the Ho - ly Ghost ; As it was in

the beginning, is now, and ever shall be : world with-out end. A - men.

Iniquos odio habui.

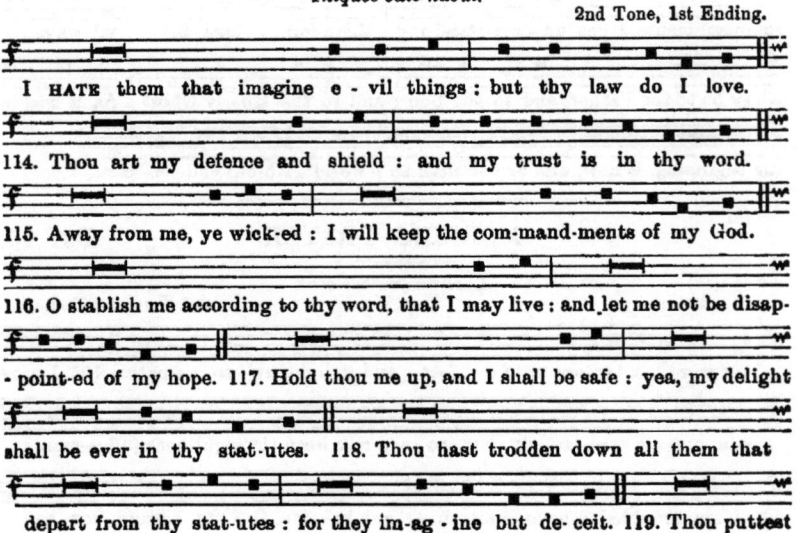

2nd Tone, 1st Ending.

I HATE them that imagine e - vil things : but thy law do I love.

114. Thou art my defence and shield : and my trust is in thy word.

115. Away from me, ye wick-ed : I will keep the com-mand-ments of my God.

116. O stablish me according to thy word, that I may live : and let me not be disap-

- point-ed of my hope. 117. Hold thou me up, and I shall be safe : yea, my delight

shall be ever in thy stat-utes. 118. Thou hast trodden down all them that

depart from thy stat-utes : for they im-ag - ine but de-ceit. 119. Thou puttest

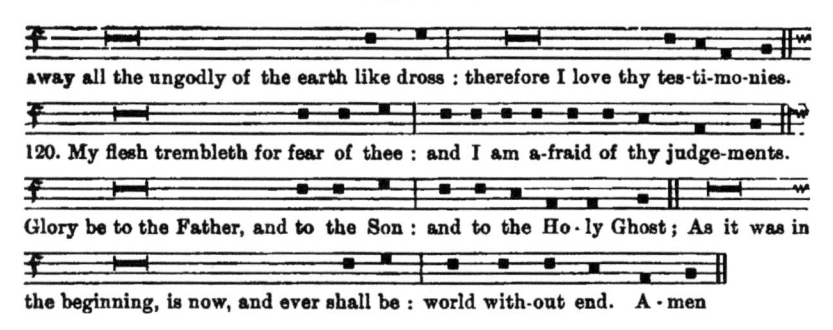

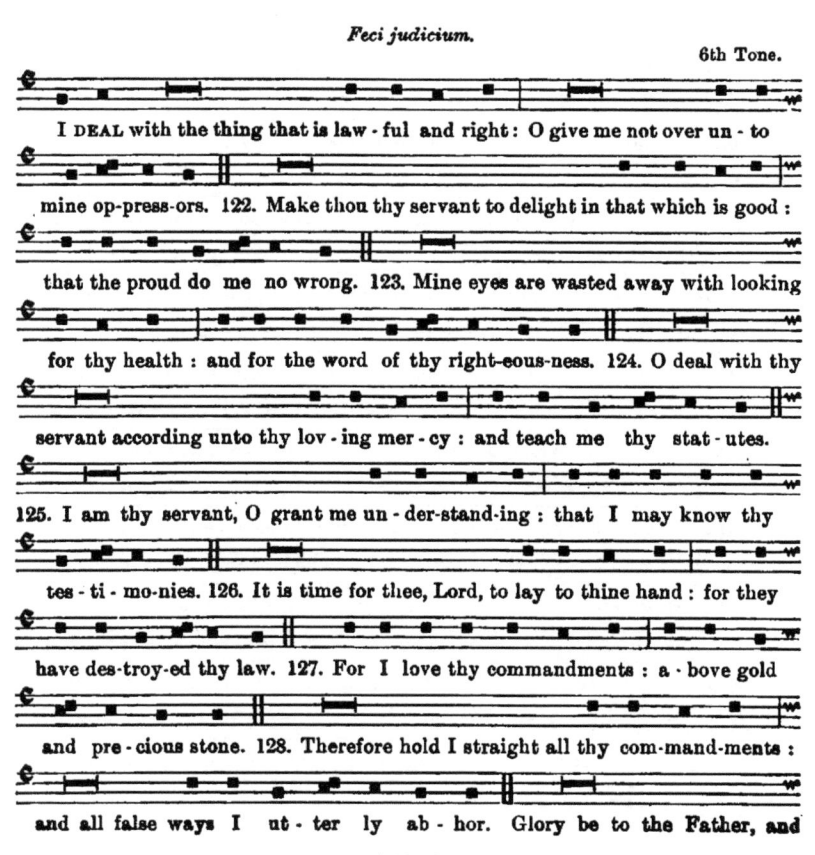

MORNING PRAYER. DAY 26.

away all the ungodly of the earth like dross : therefore I love thy tes-ti-mo-nies.

120. My flesh trembleth for fear of thee : and I am a-fraid of thy judge-ments.

Glory be to the Father, and to the Son : and to the Ho-ly Ghost ; As it was in the beginning, is now, and ever shall be : world with-out end. A - men

Feci judicium.

6th Tone.

I DEAL with the thing that is law - ful and right : O give me not over un - to mine op-press-ors. 122. Make thou thy servant to delight in that which is good : that the proud do me no wrong. 123. Mine eyes are wasted away with looking for thy health : and for the word of thy right-eous-ness. 124. O deal with thy servant according unto thy lov - ing mer - cy : and teach me thy stat - utes. 125. I am thy servant, O grant me un - der-stand-ing : that I may know thy tes - ti - mo-nies. 126. It is time for thee, Lord, to lay to thine hand : for they have des-troy-ed thy law. 127. For I love thy commandments : a - bove gold and pre - cious stone. 128. Therefore hold I straight all thy com-mand-ments : and all false ways I ut - ter - ly ab - hor. Glory be to the Father, and

DAY 26. MORNING PRAYER.

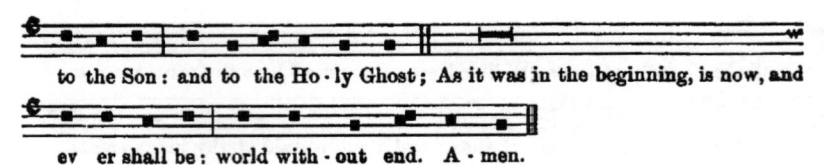

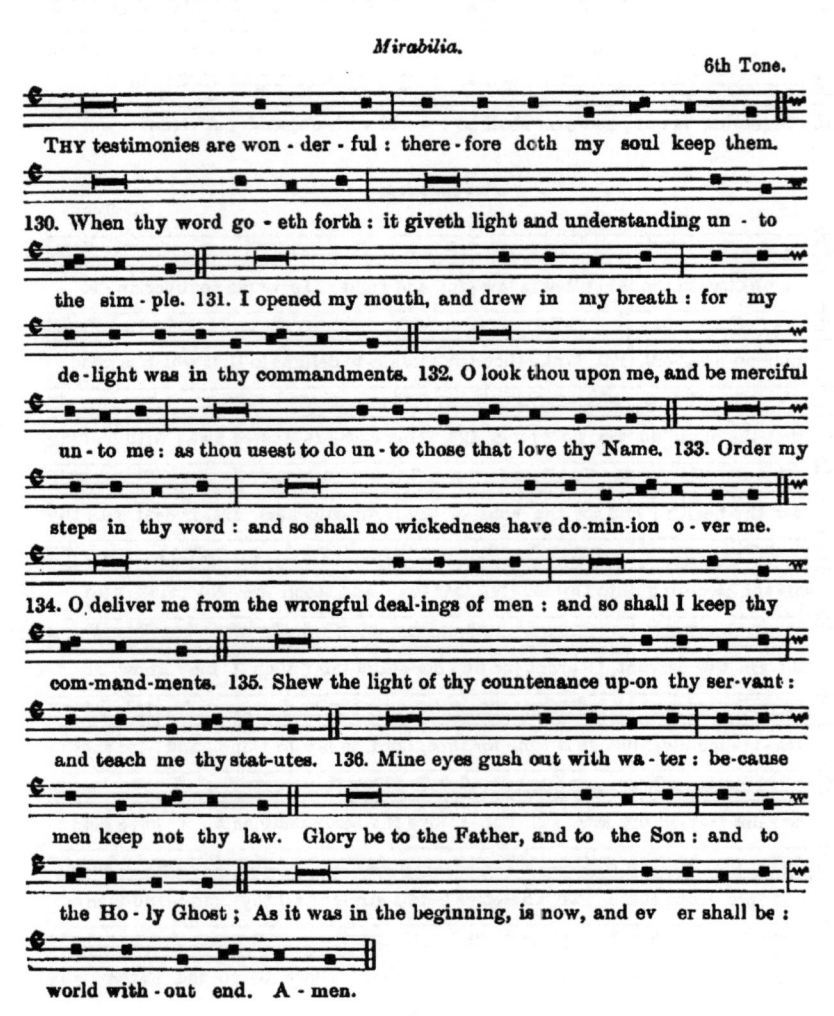

to the Son: and to the Ho-ly Ghost; As it was in the beginning, is now, and ev er shall be: world with-out end. A-men.

Mirabilia.

6th Tone.

THY testimonies are won-der-ful: there-fore doth my soul keep them. 130. When thy word go-eth forth: it giveth light and understanding un-to the sim-ple. 131. I opened my mouth, and drew in my breath: for my de-light was in thy commandments. 132. O look thou upon me, and be merciful un-to me: as thou usest to do un-to those that love thy Name. 133. Order my steps in thy word: and so shall no wickedness have do-min-ion o-ver me. 134. O deliver me from the wrongful deal-ings of men: and so shall I keep thy com-mand-ments. 135. Shew the light of thy countenance up-on thy ser-vant: and teach me thy stat-utes. 136. Mine eyes gush out with wa-ter: be-cause men keep not thy law. Glory be to the Father, and to the Son: and to the Ho-ly Ghost; As it was in the beginning, is now, and ev er shall be: world with-out end. A-men.

(222)

MORNING PRAYER.

Justus es, Domine.

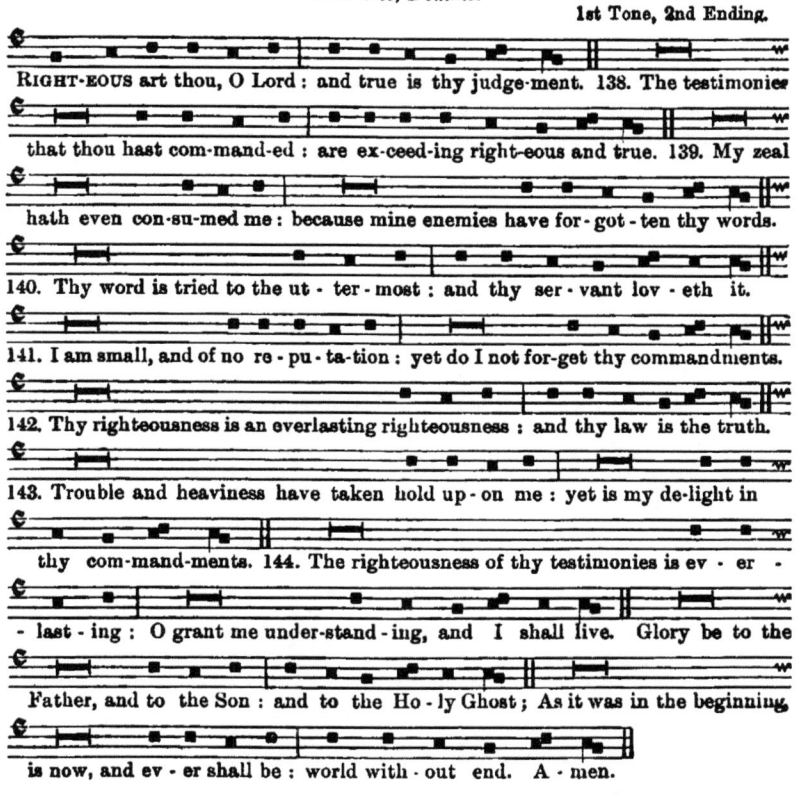

1st Tone, 2nd Ending.

RIGHT-EOUS art thou, O Lord : and true is thy judge-ment. 138. The testimonies that thou hast com-mand-ed : are ex-ceed-ing right-eous and true. 139. My zeal hath even con-su-med me : because mine enemies have for-got-ten thy words. 140. Thy word is tried to the ut-ter-most : and thy ser-vant lov-eth it. 141. I am small, and of no re-pu-ta-tion : yet do I not for-get thy commandments. 142. Thy righteousness is an everlasting righteousness : and thy law is the truth. 143. Trouble and heaviness have taken hold up-on me : yet is my de-light in thy com-mand-ments. 144. The righteousness of thy testimonies is ev-er-last-ing : O grant me under-stand-ing, and I shall live. Glory be to the Father, and to the Son : and to the Ho-ly Ghost ; As it was in the beginning, is now, and ev-er shall be : world with-out end. A-men.

EVENING PRAYER.

Clamavi in toto corde meo.

1st Tone, 4th Ending.

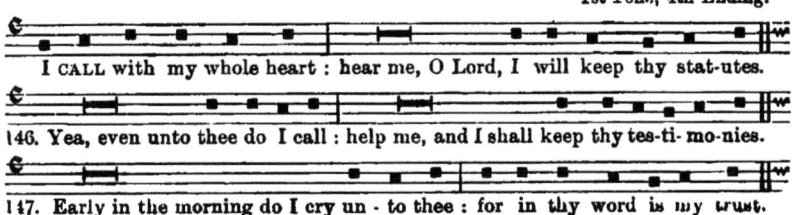

I CALL with my whole heart : hear me, O Lord, I will keep thy stat-utes. 146. Yea, even unto thee do I call : help me, and I shall keep thy tes-ti-mo-nies. 147. Early in the morning do I cry un-to thee : for in thy word is my trust.

DAY 26.   EVENING PRAYER.

148. Mine eyes prevent the night-watch-es : that I might be occu-pi-ed in thy words. 149. Hear my voice, O Lord, according unto thy lov-ing-kind-ness : quicken me, ac-cord-ing as thou art wont. 150. They draw nigh that of malice per-se-cute me : and are far from thy law. 151. Be thou nigh at hand, O Lord : for all thy com-mand-ments are true. 152. As concerning thy testimonies, I have known long since : that thou hast ground-ed them for ev-er. Glory be to the Father, and to the Son : and to the Ho-ly Ghost ; As it was in the beginning, is now, and ev-er shall be : world with-out end. A-men.

Vide humilitatem.

1st Tone, 4th Ending.

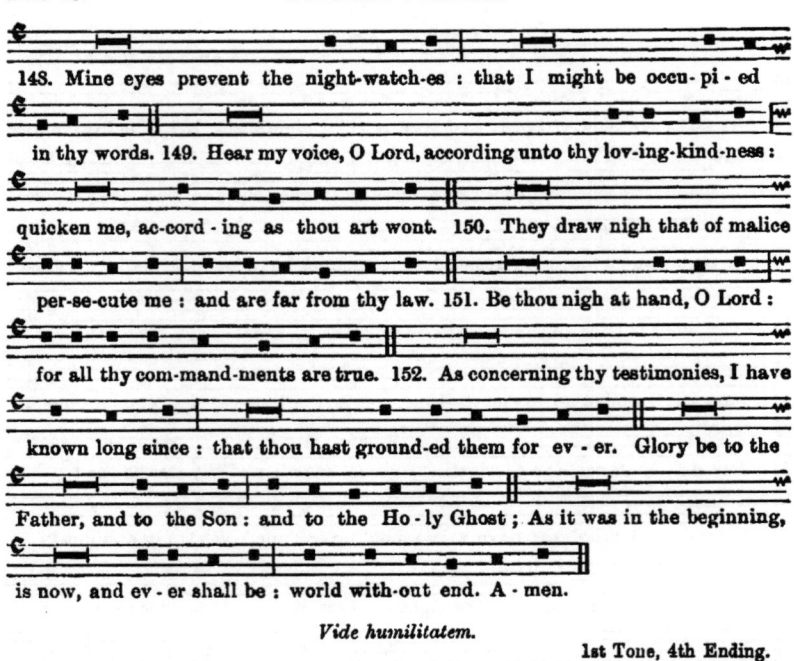

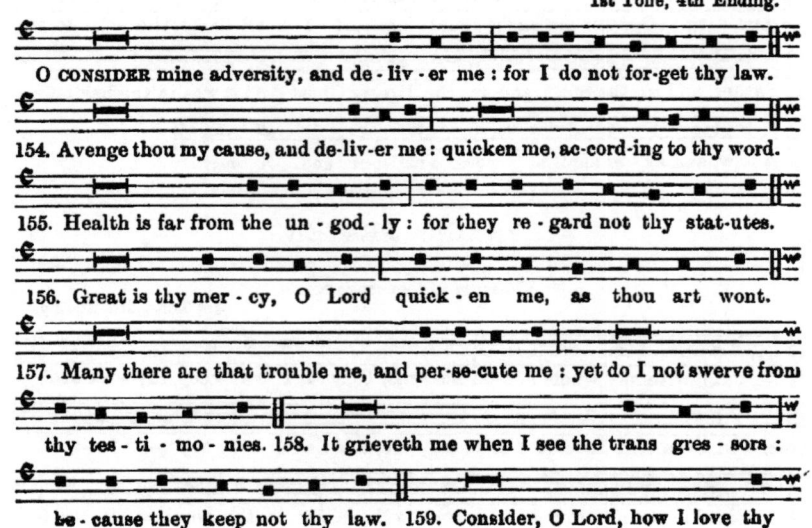

O CONSIDER mine adversity, and de-liv-er me : for I do not for-get thy law. 154. Avenge thou my cause, and de-liv-er me : quicken me, ac-cord-ing to thy word. 155. Health is far from the un-god-ly : for they re-gard not thy stat-utes. 156. Great is thy mer-cy, O Lord quick-en me, as thou art wont. 157. Many there are that trouble me, and per-se-cute me : yet do I not swerve from thy tes-ti-mo-nies. 158. It grieveth me when I see the trans gres-sors : be-cause they keep not thy law. 159. Consider, O Lord, how I love thy

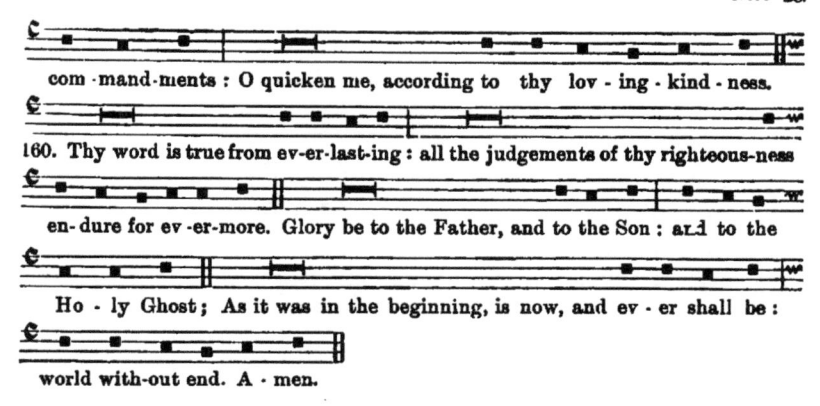

EVENING PRAYER.

com-mand-ments : O quicken me, according to thy lov-ing-kind-ness.

160. Thy word is true from ev-er-last-ing : all the judgements of thy righteous-ness en-dure for ev-er-more. Glory be to the Father, and to the Son : and to the Ho-ly Ghost; As it was in the beginning, is now, and ev-er shall be : world with-out end. A-men.

Principes persecuti sunt.

3rd Tone, 4th Ending.

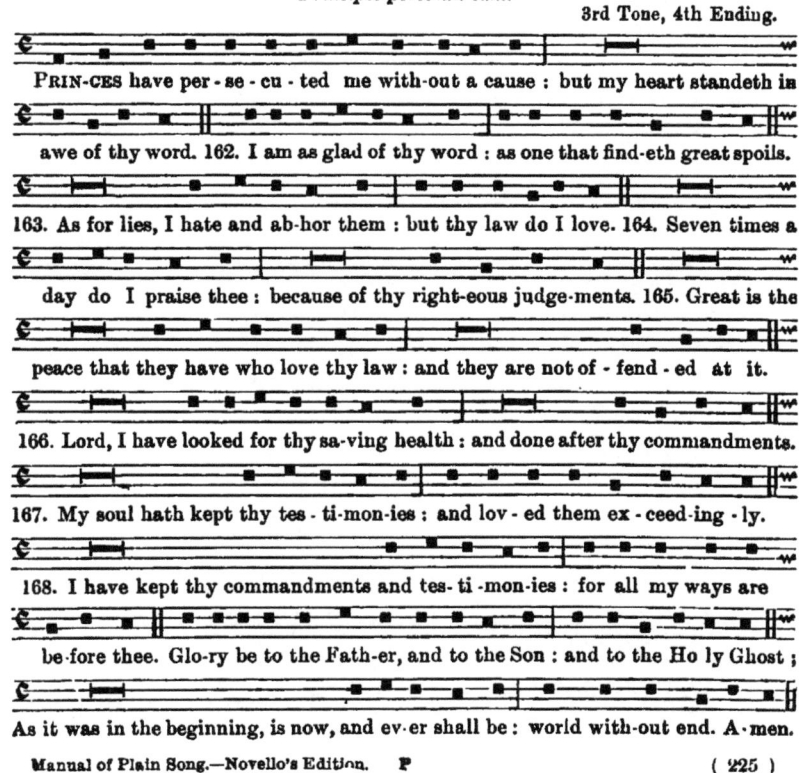

PRIN-CES have per-se-cu-ted me with-out a cause : but my heart standeth in awe of thy word. 162. I am as glad of thy word : as one that find-eth great spoils. 163. As for lies, I hate and ab-hor them : but thy law do I love. 164. Seven times a day do I praise thee : because of thy right-eous judge-ments. 165. Great is the peace that they have who love thy law : and they are not of-fend-ed at it. 166. Lord, I have looked for thy sa-ving health : and done after thy commandments. 167. My soul hath kept thy tes-ti-mon-ies : and lov-ed them ex-ceed-ing-ly. 168. I have kept thy commandments and tes-ti-mon-ies : for all my ways are be-fore thee. Glo-ry be to the Fath-er, and to the Son : and to the Ho-ly Ghost ; As it was in the beginning, is now, and ev-er shall be : world with-out end. A-men.

DAY 26. EVENING PRAYER.

Appropinquet deprecatio.

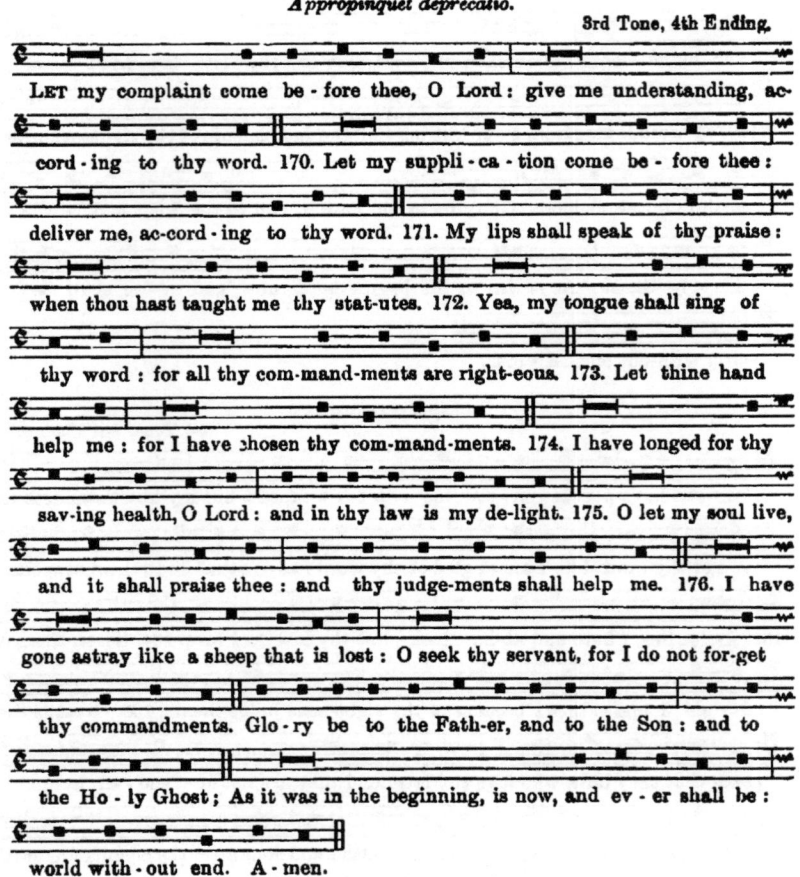

3rd Tone, 4th Ending.

LET my complaint come be-fore thee, O Lord: give me understanding, according to thy word. 170. Let my suppli-ca-tion come be-fore thee: deliver me, ac-cord-ing to thy word. 171. My lips shall speak of thy praise: when thou hast taught me thy stat-utes. 172. Yea, my tongue shall sing of thy word: for all thy com-mand-ments are right-eous. 173. Let thine hand help me: for I have chosen thy com-mand-ments. 174. I have longed for thy sav-ing health, O Lord: and in thy law is my de-light. 175. O let my soul live, and it shall praise thee: and thy judge-ments shall help me. 176. I have gone astray like a sheep that is lost: O seek thy servant, for I do not for-get thy commandments. Glo-ry be to the Fath-er, and to the Son: and to the Ho-ly Ghost; As it was in the beginning, is now, and ev-er shall be: world with-out end. A-men.

DAY 27. MORNING PRAYER.

PSALM CXX.—*Ad Dominum.*

7th Tone, 6th Ending.

WHEN I was in trou-ble I call-ed up-on the Lord: and he heard me.

2. Deliver my soul, O Lord, from ly-ing lips: and from a de-ceit-ful tongue.

(226)

MORNING PRAYER. DAY 27.

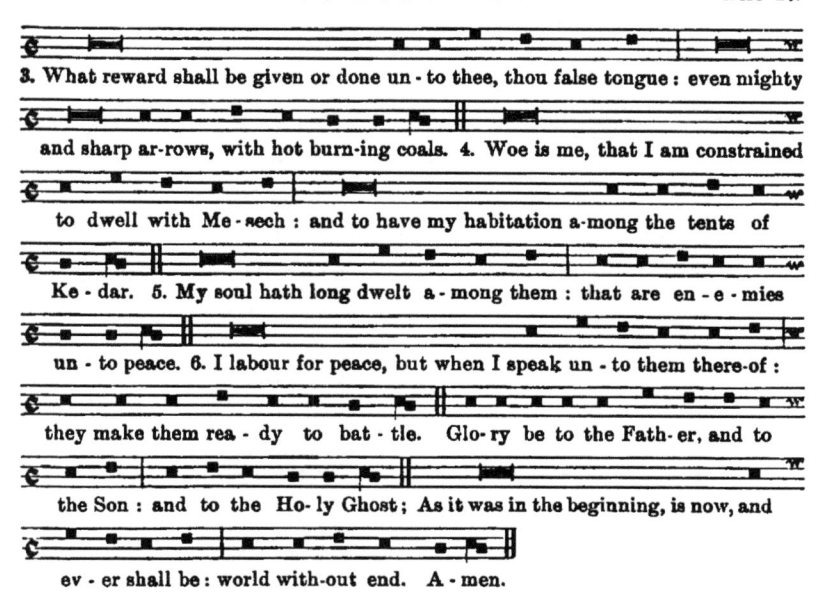

3. What reward shall be given or done un-to thee, thou false tongue : even mighty and sharp ar-rows, with hot burn-ing coals. 4. Woe is me, that I am constrained to dwell with Me-sech : and to have my habitation a-mong the tents of Ke-dar. 5. My soul hath long dwelt a-mong them : that are en-e-mies un-to peace. 6. I labour for peace, but when I speak un-to them there-of : they make them rea-dy to bat-tle. Glo-ry be to the Fath-er, and to the Son : and to the Ho-ly Ghost; As it was in the beginning, is now, and ev-er shall be : world with-out end. A-men.

PSALM CXXI.—*Levavi oculos.*

7th Tone, 6th Ending.

I will lift up mine eyes un-to the hills : from whence com-eth my help. 2. My help com-eth e-ven from the Lord : who hath made heav-en and earth. 3. He will not suffer thy foot to be mov-ed : and he that keep-eth thee will not sleep. 4. Be-hold, he that keep-eth Is-ra-el : shall neith-er slum-ber nor sleep. 5. The Lord him-self is thy keep-er : the Lord is thy de-fence up-on thy right hand ; 6. So that the sun shall not burn thee by day : neith-er the moon by night. 7. The Lord shall preserve thee from all e-vil :

DAY 27. MORNING PRAYER.

yea, it is even he that shall keep thy soul. 8. The Lord shall preserve thy going out, and thy com-ing in : from this time forth for ev - er-more. Glo - ry be to the Fath- er, and to the Son : and to the Ho - ly Ghost ; As it was in the beginning, is now, and ev - er shall be : world with-out end. A - men.

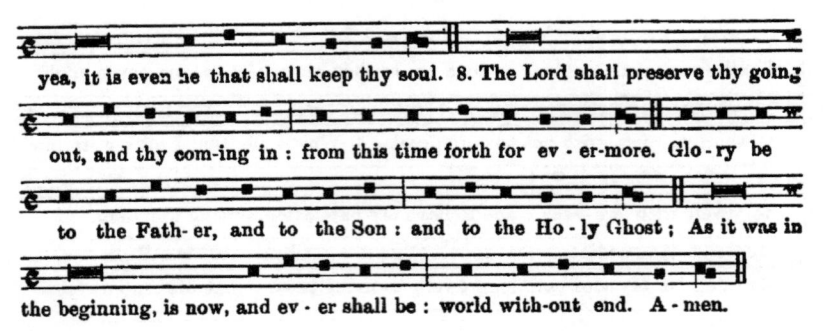

PSALM CXXII.—*Lœtatus sum.*

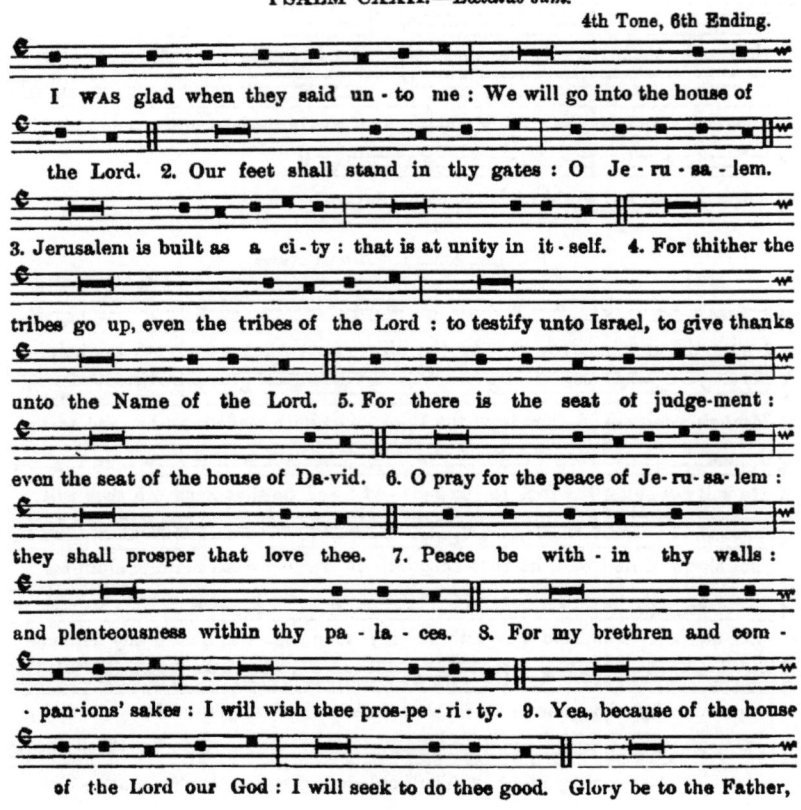

4th Tone, 6th Ending.

I WAS glad when they said un - to me : We will go into the house of the Lord. 2. Our feet shall stand in thy gates : O Je - ru - sa - lem. 3. Jerusalem is built as a ci - ty : that is at unity in it - self. 4. For thither the tribes go up, even the tribes of the Lord : to testify unto Israel, to give thanks unto the Name of the Lord. 5. For there is the seat of judge-ment : even the seat of the house of Da-vid. 6. O pray for the peace of Je - ru - sa - lem : they shall prosper that love thee. 7. Peace be with - in thy walls : and plenteousness within thy pa - la - ces. 8. For my brethren and com - pan-ions' sakes : I will wish thee pros-pe - ri - ty. 9. Yea, because of the house of the Lord our God : I will seek to do thee good. Glory be to the Father,

MORNING PRAYER. DAY 27.

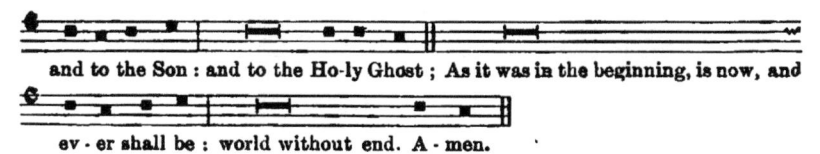

and to the Son : and to the Ho-ly Ghost ; As it was in the beginning, is now, and ev-er shall be : world without end. A-men.

PSALM CXXIII.—*Ad te levavi oculos meos.*
2nd Tone, 1st Ending.

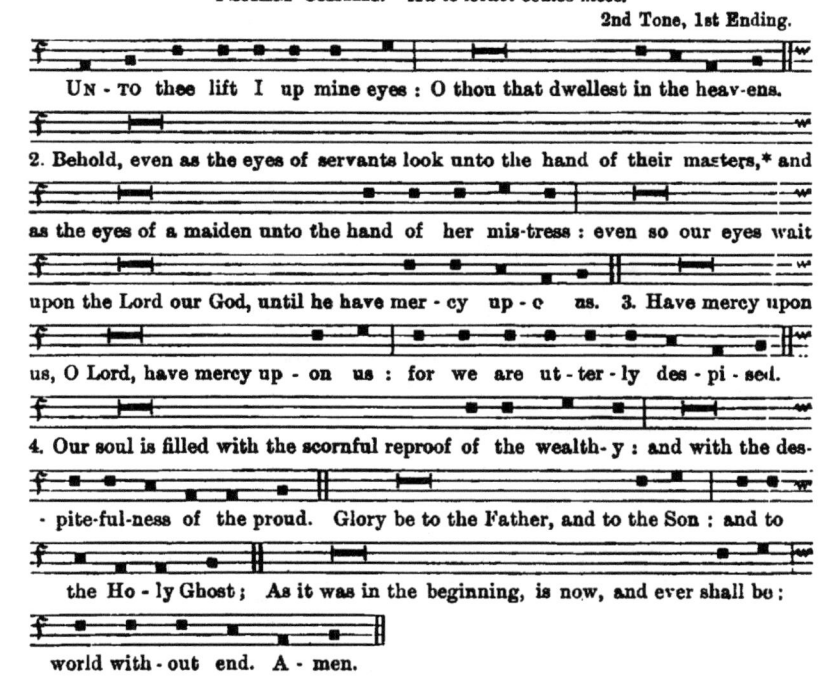

UN-TO thee lift I up mine eyes : O thou that dwellest in the heav-ens.

2. Behold, even as the eyes of servants look unto the hand of their masters,* and as the eyes of a maiden unto the hand of her mis-tress : even so our eyes wait upon the Lord our God, until he have mer-cy up-o as. 3. Have mercy upon us, O Lord, have mercy up-on us : for we are ut-ter-ly des-pi-sed. 4. Our soul is filled with the scornful reproof of the wealth-y : and with the des- -pite-ful-ness of the proud. Glory be to the Father, and to the Son : and to the Ho-ly Ghost; As it was in the beginning, is now, and ever shall be : world with-out end. A-men.

PSALM CXXIV.—*Nisi quia Dominus.*
7th Tone, 2nd Ending.

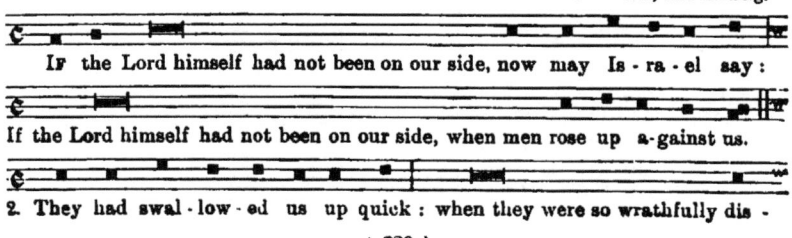

IF the Lord himself had not been on our side, now may Is-ra-el say :

If the Lord himself had not been on our side, when men rose up a-gainst us.

2. They had swal-low-ed us up quick : when they were so wrathfully dis -

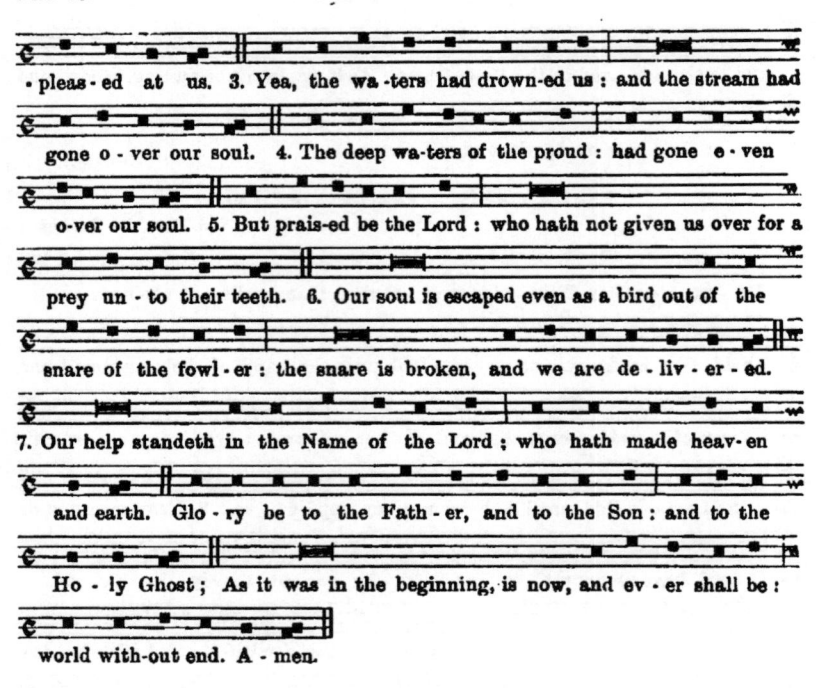

DAY 27. MORNING PRAYER.

pleas-ed at us. 3. Yea, the wa-ters had drown-ed us: and the stream had gone o-ver our soul. 4. The deep wa-ters of the proud: had gone e-ven o-ver our soul. 5. But prais-ed be the Lord: who hath not given us over for a prey un-to their teeth. 6. Our soul is escaped even as a bird out of the snare of the fowl-er: the snare is broken, and we are de-liv-er-ed. 7. Our help standeth in the Name of the Lord: who hath made heav-en and earth. Glo-ry be to the Fath-er, and to the Son: and to the Ho-ly Ghost; As it was in the beginning, is now, and ev-er shall be: world with-out end. A-men.

PSALM CXXV.—*Qui confidunt.*

7th Tone, 2nd Ending.

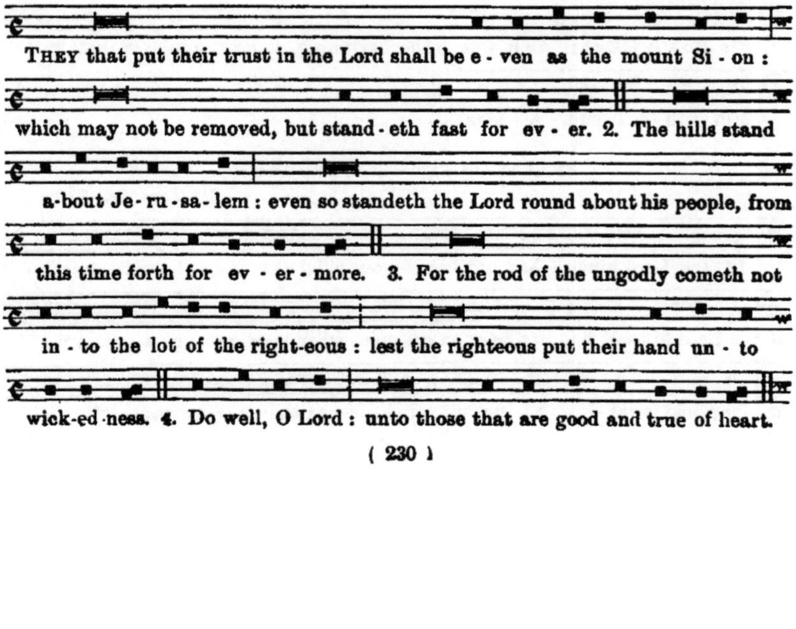

THEY that put their trust in the Lord shall be e-ven as the mount Si-on: which may not be removed, but stand-eth fast for ev-er. 2. The hills stand a-bout Je-ru-sa-lem: even so standeth the Lord round about his people, from this time forth for ev-er-more. 3. For the rod of the ungodly cometh not in-to the lot of the right-eous: lest the righteous put their hand un-to wick-ed-ness. 4. Do well, O Lord: unto those that are good and true of heart.

EVENING PRAYER. DAY 27.

5. As for such as turn back un-to their own wick-ed-ness : the Lord shall lead them forth with the evil-doers ; but peace shall be up-on Is-ra-el.

Glo-ry be to the Fath-er, and to the Son : and to the Ho-ly Ghost ; As it was in the beginning, is now, and ev-er shall be : world with-out end. A-men.

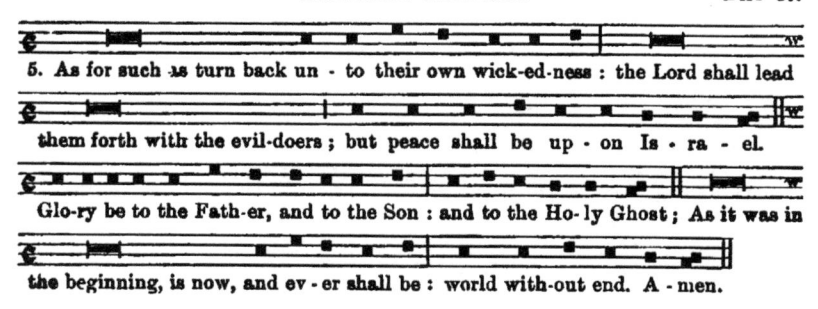

EVENING PRAYER.

PSALM CXXVI.—*In convertendo.*

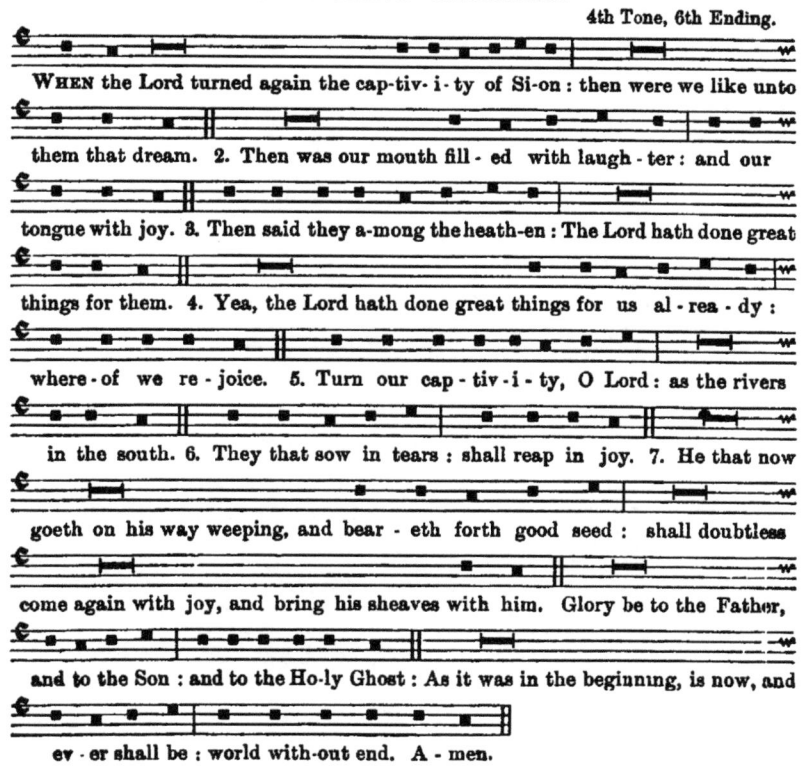

4th Tone, 6th Ending.

When the Lord turned again the cap-tiv-i-ty of Si-on : then were we like unto them that dream. 2. Then was our mouth fill-ed with laugh-ter : and our tongue with joy. 3. Then said they a-mong the heath-en : The Lord hath done great things for them. 4. Yea, the Lord hath done great things for us al-rea-dy : where-of we re-joice. 5. Turn our cap-tiv-i-ty, O Lord : as the rivers in the south. 6. They that sow in tears : shall reap in joy. 7. He that now goeth on his way weeping, and bear-eth forth good seed : shall doubtless come again with joy, and bring his sheaves with him. Glory be to the Father, and to the Son : and to the Ho-ly Ghost : As it was in the beginning, is now, and ev-er shall be : world with-out end. A-men.

DAY 27. EVENING PRAYER.

PSALM CXXVII.—*Nisi Dominus.*

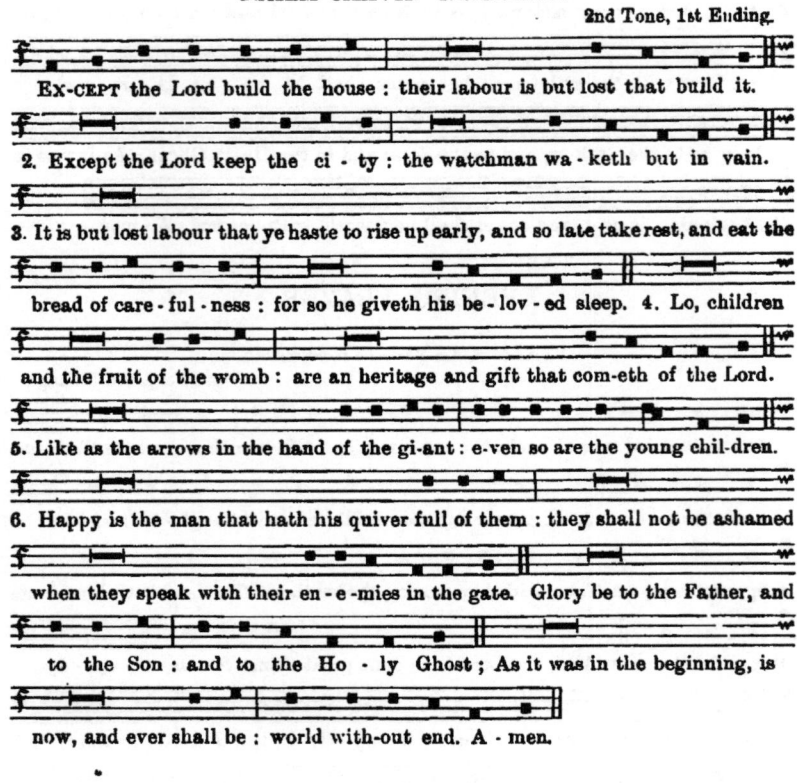

2nd Tone, 1st Ending.

Ex-cept the Lord build the house : their labour is but lost that build it.

2. Except the Lord keep the ci - ty : the watchman wa - keth but in vain.

3. It is but lost labour that ye haste to rise up early, and so late take rest, and eat the bread of care - ful - ness : for so he giveth his be - lov - ed sleep. 4. Lo, children and the fruit of the womb : are an heritage and gift that com-eth of the Lord.

5. Like as the arrows in the hand of the gi-ant : e-ven so are the young chil-dren.

6. Happy is the man that hath his quiver full of them : they shall not be ashamed when they speak with their en - e -mies in the gate. Glory be to the Father, and to the Son : and to the Ho - ly Ghost ; As it was in the beginning, is now, and ever shall be : world with-out end. A - men.

PSALM CXXVIII.—*Beati omnes.*

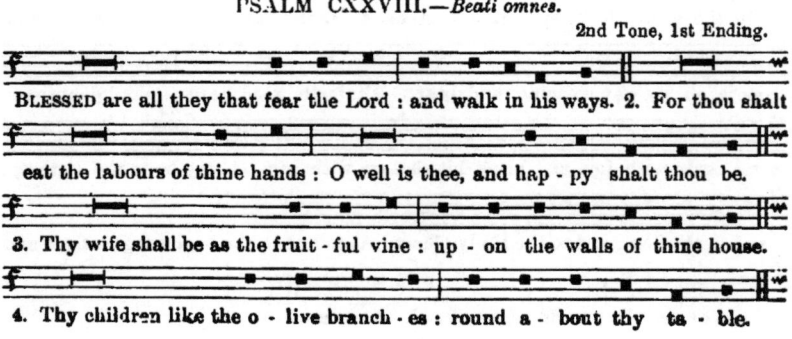

2nd Tone, 1st Ending.

Blessed are all they that fear the Lord : and walk in his ways. 2. For thou shalt eat the labours of thine hands : O well is thee, and hap - py shalt thou be.

3. Thy wife shall be as the fruit - ful vine : up - on the walls of thine house.

4. Thy children like the o - live branch - es : round a - bout thy ta - ble.

(232)

EVENING PRAYER. DAY 27

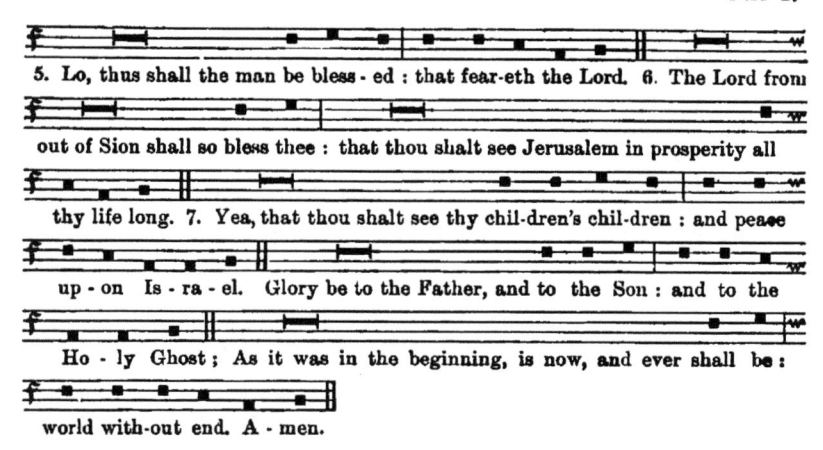

5. Lo, thus shall the man be bless-ed : that fear-eth the Lord. 6. The Lord from out of Sion shall so bless thee : that thou shalt see Jerusalem in prosperity all thy life long. 7. Yea, that thou shalt see thy chil-dren's chil-dren : and peace up-on Is-ra-el. Glory be to the Father, and to the Son : and to the Ho-ly Ghost ; As it was in the beginning, is now, and ever shall be : world with-out end. A-men.

PSALM CXXIX.—*Sœpe expugnaverunt.*

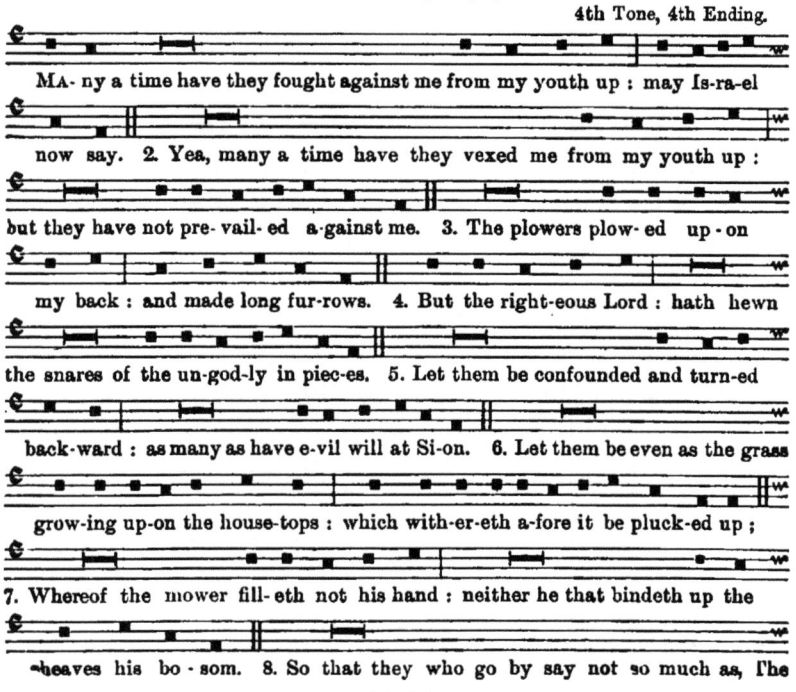

4th Tone, 4th Ending.

MA-ny a time have they fought against me from my youth up : may Is-ra-el now say. 2. Yea, many a time have they vexed me from my youth up : but they have not pre-vail-ed a-gainst me. 3. The plowers plow-ed up-on my back : and made long fur-rows. 4. But the right-eous Lord : hath hewn the snares of the un-god-ly in piec-es. 5. Let them be confounded and turn-ed back-ward : as many as have e-vil will at Si-on. 6. Let them be even as the grass grow-ing up-on the house-tops : which with-er-eth a-fore it be pluck-ed up ; 7. Whereof the mower fill-eth not his hand : neither he that bindeth up the sheaves his bo-som. 8. So that they who go by say not so much as, The

DAY 27. EVENING PRAYER.

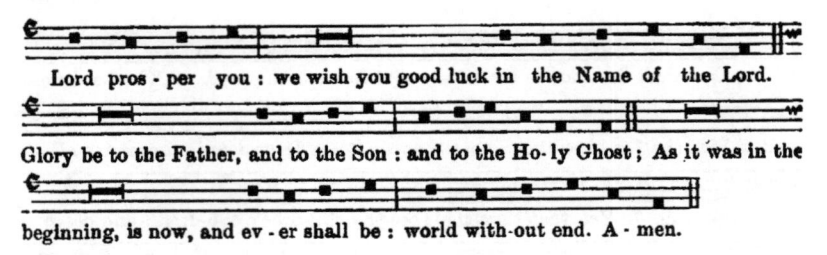

Lord pros-per you : we wish you good luck in the Name of the Lord.

Glory be to the Father, and to the Son : and to the Ho-ly Ghost ; As it was in the beginning, is now, and ev-er shall be : world with-out end. A-men.

PSALM CXXX.—*De profundis.*

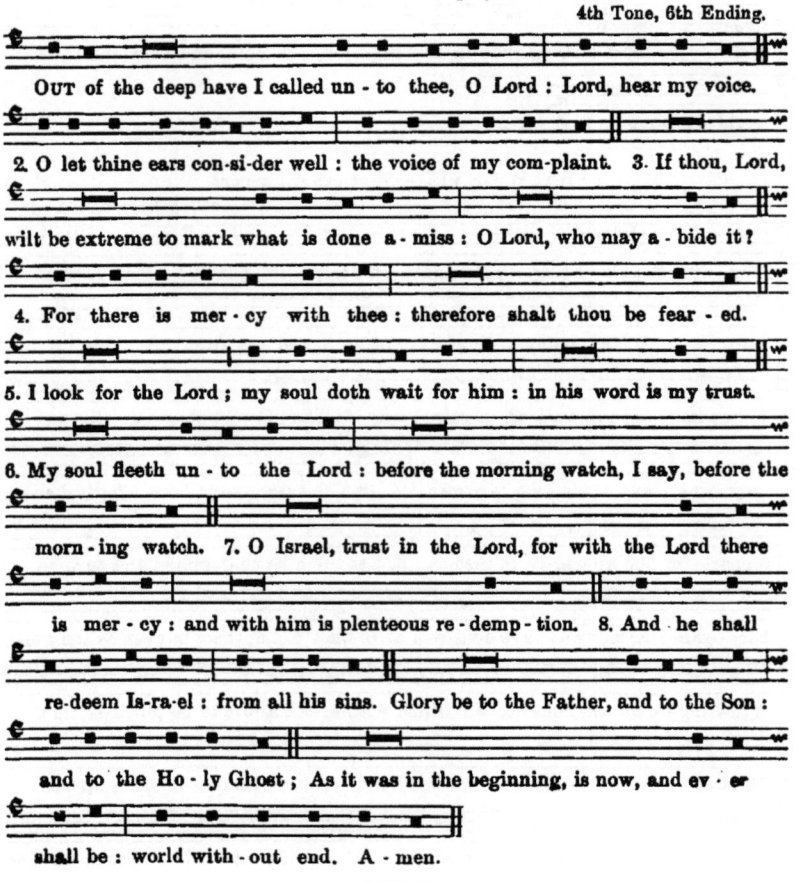

4th Tone, 6th Ending.

OUT of the deep have I called un-to thee, O Lord : Lord, hear my voice.

2. O let thine ears con-si-der well : the voice of my com-plaint. 3. If thou, Lord, wilt be extreme to mark what is done a-miss : O Lord, who may a-bide it?

4. For there is mer-cy with thee : therefore shalt thou be fear-ed.

5. I look for the Lord ; my soul doth wait for him : in his word is my trust.

6. My soul fleeth un-to the Lord : before the morning watch, I say, before the morn-ing watch. 7. O Israel, trust in the Lord, for with the Lord there is mer-cy : and with him is plenteous re-demp-tion. 8. And he shall re-deem Is-ra-el : from all his sins. Glory be to the Father, and to the Son : and to the Ho-ly Ghost ; As it was in the beginning, is now, and ev-er shall be : world with-out end. A-men.

(234)

EVENING PRAYER. DAY 27.

PSALM CXXXI.—*Domine, non est.*

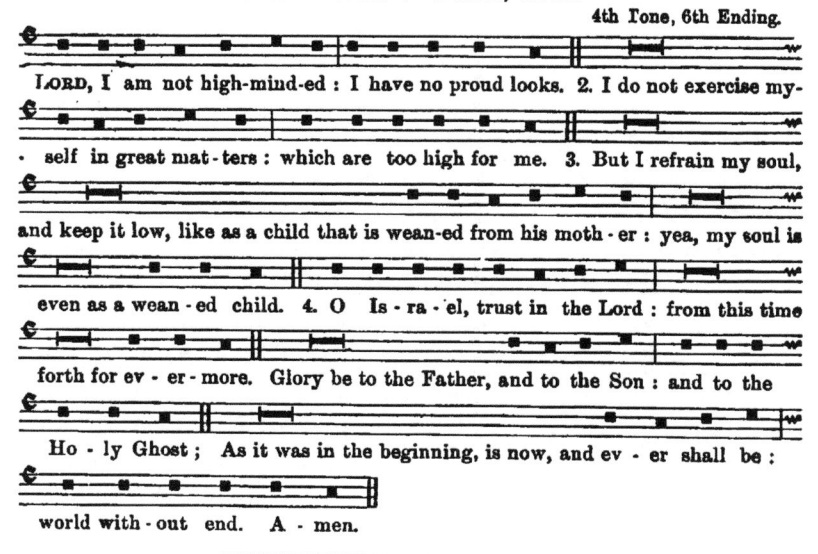

4th Tone, 6th Ending.

LORD, I am not high-mind-ed : I have no proud looks. 2. I do not exercise my-self in great mat-ters : which are too high for me. 3. But I refrain my soul, and keep it low, like as a child that is wean-ed from his moth-er : yea, my soul is even as a wean-ed child. 4. O Is-ra-el, trust in the Lord : from this time forth for ev-er-more. Glory be to the Father, and to the Son : and to the Ho-ly Ghost; As it was in the beginning, is now, and ev-er shall be : world with-out end. A-men.

MORNING PRAYER. DAY 28.

PSALM CXXXII.—*Memento, Domine.*

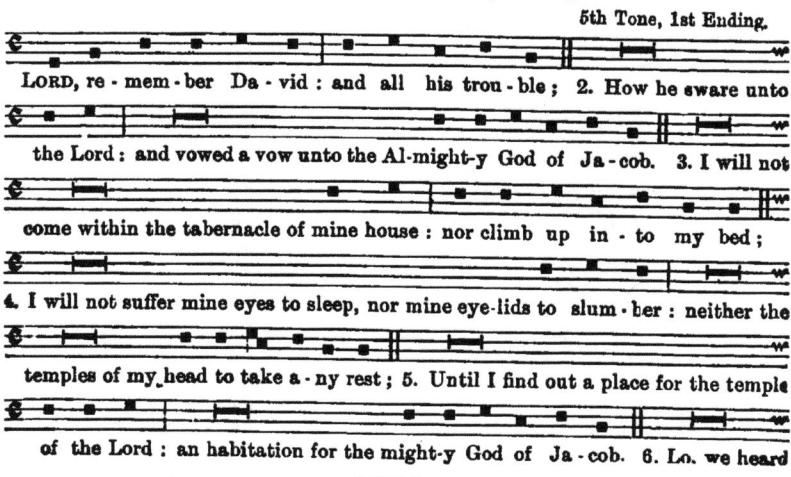

5th Tone, 1st Ending.

LORD, re-mem-ber Da-vid : and all his trou-ble; 2. How he sware unto the Lord : and vowed a vow unto the Al-might-y God of Ja-cob. 3. I will not come within the tabernacle of mine house : nor climb up in-to my bed; 4. I will not suffer mine eyes to sleep, nor mine eye-lids to slum-ber : neither the temples of my head to take a-ny rest; 5. Until I find out a place for the temple of the Lord : an habitation for the might-y God of Ja-cob. 6. Lo, we heard of the same at E-phra-ta : and found it in the wood. 7. We will go into his ta - ber - na - cle : and fall low on our knees be - fore his foot-stool. 8. Arise, O Lord, into thy rest - ing-place : thou, and the ark of thy strength. 9. Let thy priests be clothed with right-eous-ness : and let thy saints sing with joy-ful-ness. 10. For thy servant Da - vid's sake : turn not away the presence of thine An-oint -ed. 11. The Lord hath made a faithful oath un - to Da-vid : and he shall not shrink from it. 12. Of the fruit of thy bo - dy : shall I set up - on thy seat. 13. If thy children will keep my covenant, and my testimonies that I shall learn them : their children also shall sit upon thy seat for ev - er-more. 14. For the Lord hath chosen Sion to be an habitation for him - self : he hath long - ed for her. 15. This shall be my rest for ev - er : here will I dwell, for I have a de - light there - in. 16. I will bless her victuals with in - crease : and will sat-is-fy her poor with bread. 17. I will deck her priests with health : and her saints shall re-joice and sing. 18. There shall I make the horn of David to flou - rish : I have ordained a lantern for mine An - oint - ed. 19. As for his enemies, I shall clothe them with shame : but upon himself shall his

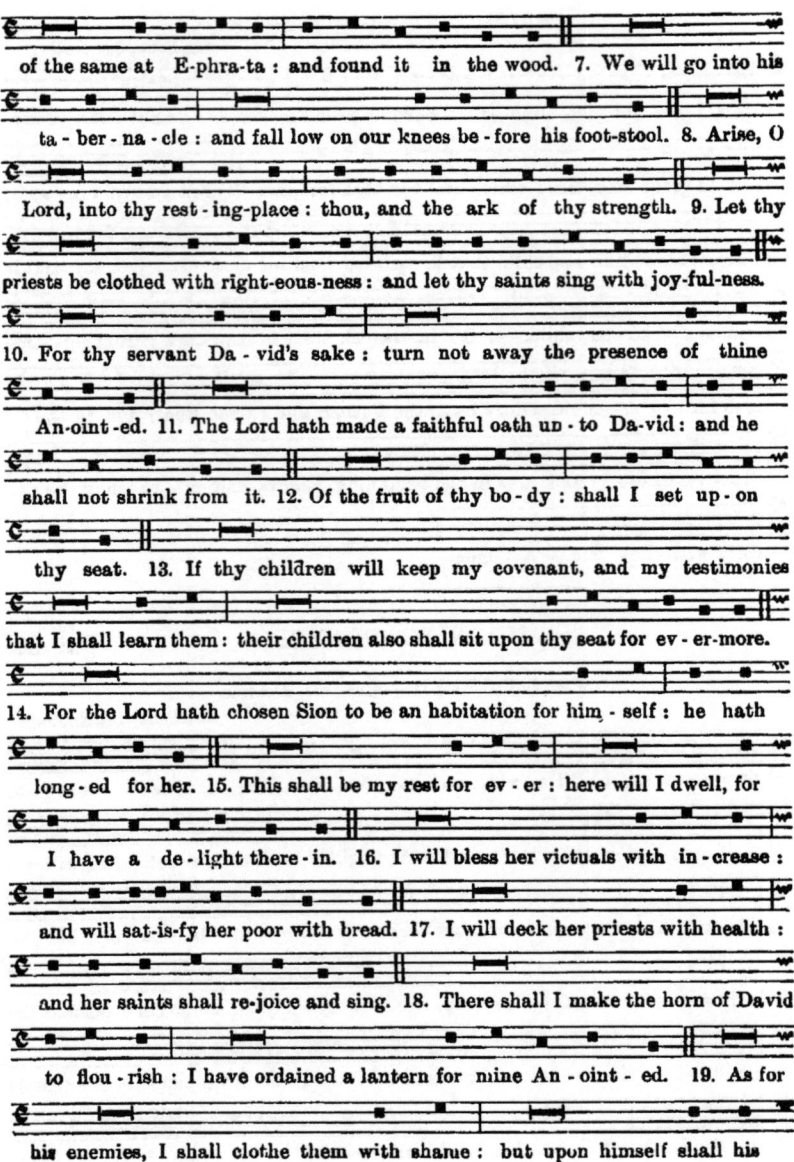

MORNING PRAYER. DAY 28.

crown flou-rish. Glory be to the Father, and to the Son : and to the Ho-ly Ghost : As it was in the beginning, is now, and ever shall be : world with-out end. A-men.

PSALM CXXXIII.—*Ecce, quam bonum!*

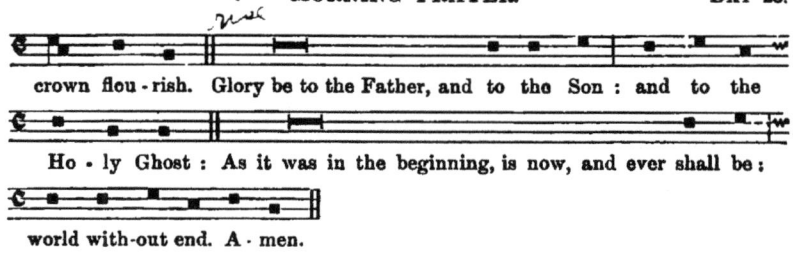

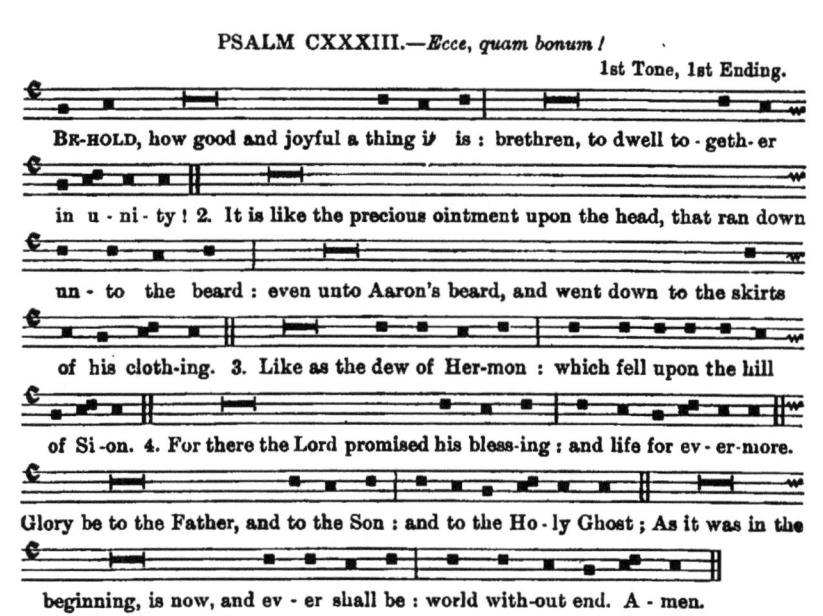

1st Tone, 1st Ending.

Be-hold, how good and joyful a thing it is : brethren, to dwell to-geth-er in u-ni-ty! 2. It is like the precious ointment upon the head, that ran down un-to the beard : even unto Aaron's beard, and went down to the skirts of his cloth-ing. 3. Like as the dew of Her-mon : which fell upon the hill of Si-on. 4. For there the Lord promised his bless-ing : and life for ev-er-more. Glory be to the Father, and to the Son : and to the Ho-ly Ghost ; As it was in the beginning, is now, and ev-er shall be : world with-out end. A-men.

PSALM CXXXIV.—*Ecce nunc.*

1st Tone, 1st Ending.

Behold, now praise the Lord : all ye ser-vants of the Lord ; 2. Ye that by night stand in the house of the Lord : even in the courts of the house of our God. 3. Lift up your hands in the sanc-tu-a-ry : and praise the Lord. 4. The Lord

DAY 28. MORNING PRAYER.

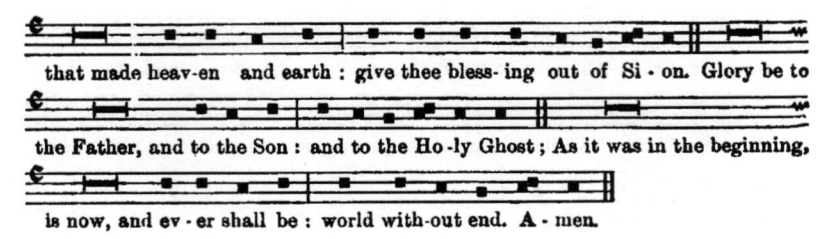

that made heav-en and earth : give thee bless-ing out of Si - on. Glory be to the Father, and to the Son : and to the Ho-ly Ghost ; As it was in the beginning, is now, and ev - er shall be : world with-out end. A - men.

PSALM CXXXV.—*Laudate Nomen*.

7th Tone, 5th Ending.

O praise the Lord, laud ye the Name of the Lord : praise it, O ye ser-vants of the Lord. 2. Ye that stand in the house of the Lord : in the courts of the house of our God. 3. O praise the Lord, for the Lord is gra-cious : O sing praises unto his Name, for it is love-ly. 4. For-wny the Lord hath chosen Ja-cob un-to him-self : and Israel for his own pos-ses-sion. 5. For I know that the Lord is great : and that our Lord is a-bove all gods. 6. Whatsoever the Lord pleased, that did he in heav-en, and in earth : and in the sea, and in all deep pla-ces. 7. He bringeth forth the clouds from the ends of the world : and sendeth forth lightnings with the rain, bringing the winds out of his treas-ures. 8. He smote the first-born of E-gypt : both of man and beast. 9. He hath sent tokens and wonders into the midst of thee, O thou land of E-gypt : upon Pharaoh, and all his ser-vants. 10. He smote di-vers na-tions :

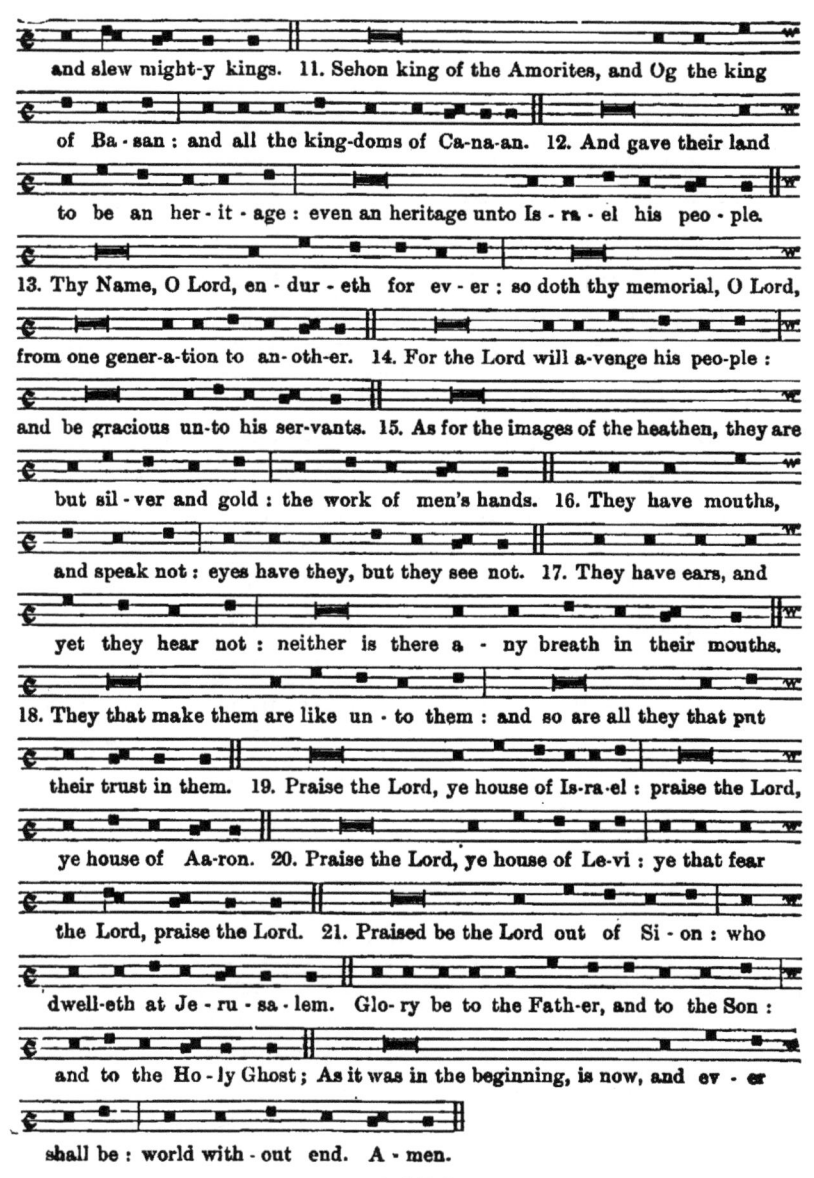

MORNING PRAYER

and slew might-y kings. 11. Sehon king of the Amorites, and Og the king of Ba-san : and all the king-doms of Ca-na-an. 12. And gave their land to be an her-it-age : even an heritage unto Is-ra-el his peo-ple. 13. Thy Name, O Lord, en-dur-eth for ev-er : so doth thy memorial, O Lord, from one gener-a-tion to an-oth-er. 14. For the Lord will a-venge his peo-ple : and be gracious un-to his ser-vants. 15. As for the images of the heathen, they are but sil-ver and gold : the work of men's hands. 16. They have mouths, and speak not : eyes have they, but they see not. 17. They have ears, and yet they hear not : neither is there a-ny breath in their mouths. 18. They that make them are like un-to them : and so are all they that put their trust in them. 19. Praise the Lord, ye house of Is-ra-el : praise the Lord, ye house of Aa-ron. 20. Praise the Lord, ye house of Le-vi : ye that fear the Lord, praise the Lord. 21. Praised be the Lord out of Si-on : who dwell-eth at Je-ru-sa-lem. Glo-ry be to the Fath-er, and to the Son : and to the Ho-ly Ghost ; As it was in the beginning, is now, and ev-er shall be : world with-out end. A-men.

Day 28.   EVENING PRAYER.

PSALM CXXXVI.—*Confitemini.*

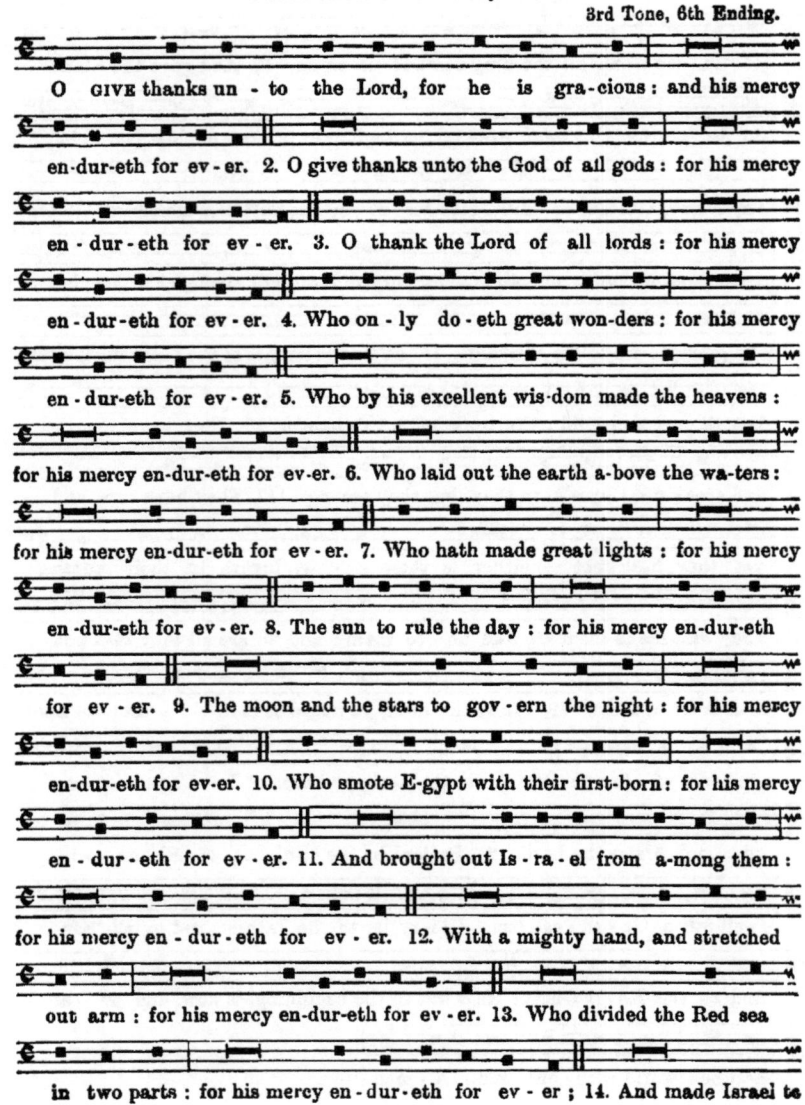

3rd Tone, 6th Ending.

O GIVE thanks un - to the Lord, for he is gra-cious : and his mercy en-dur-eth for ev-er. 2. O give thanks unto the God of all gods : for his mercy en - dur - eth for ev - er. 3. O thank the Lord of all lords : for his mercy en - dur-eth for ev - er. 4. Who on - ly do - eth great won-ders : for his mercy en - dur-eth for ev - er. 5. Who by his excellent wis-dom made the heavens : for his mercy en-dur-eth for ev-er. 6. Who laid out the earth a-bove the wa-ters : for his mercy en-dur-eth for ev - er. 7. Who hath made great lights : for his mercy en -dur-eth for ev - er. 8. The sun to rule the day : for his mercy en-dur-eth for ev - er. 9. The moon and the stars to gov - ern the night : for his mercy en-dur-eth for ev-er. 10. Who smote E-gypt with their first-born : for his mercy en - dur - eth for ev - er. 11. And brought out Is - ra - el from a-mong them : for his mercy en - dur - eth for ev - er. 12. With a mighty hand, and stretched out arm : for his mercy en-dur-eth for ev - er. 13. Who divided the Red sea in two parts : for his mercy en - dur - eth for ev - er ; 14. And made Israel to

EVENING PRAYER DAY 28.

go through the midst of it : for his mercy en-dur-eth for ev-er. 15. But as for Pharaoh and his host, he over-threw them in the Red sea : for his mercy en-dur-eth for ev-er. 16. Who led his peo-ple through the wil-der-ness : for his mercy en-dur-eth for ev-er. 17. Who smote great kings : for his mercy en-dur-eth for ev-er. 18. Yea, and slew might-y kings : for his mercy en-dur-eth for ev-er. 19. Se-hon king of the A-mor-ites : for his mercy en-dur-eth for ev-er. 20. And Og the king of Ba-san : for his mercy en-dur-eth for ev-er. 21. And gave away their land for an her-it-age : for his mercy en-dur-eth for ev-er. 22. Even for an heritage unto Is-ra-el his ser-vant : for his mercy en-dur-eth for ev-er. 23. Who remembered us when we were in trou-ble : for his mercy en-dur-eth for ev-er. 24. And hath delivered us from our en-e-mies : for his mercy en-dur-eth for ev-er. 25. Who giv-eth food to all flesh : for his mercy en-dur-eth for ev-er. 26. O give thanks unto the God of heav-en : for his mercy en-dur-eth for ev-er. 27. O give thanks unto the Lord of lords : for his mercy

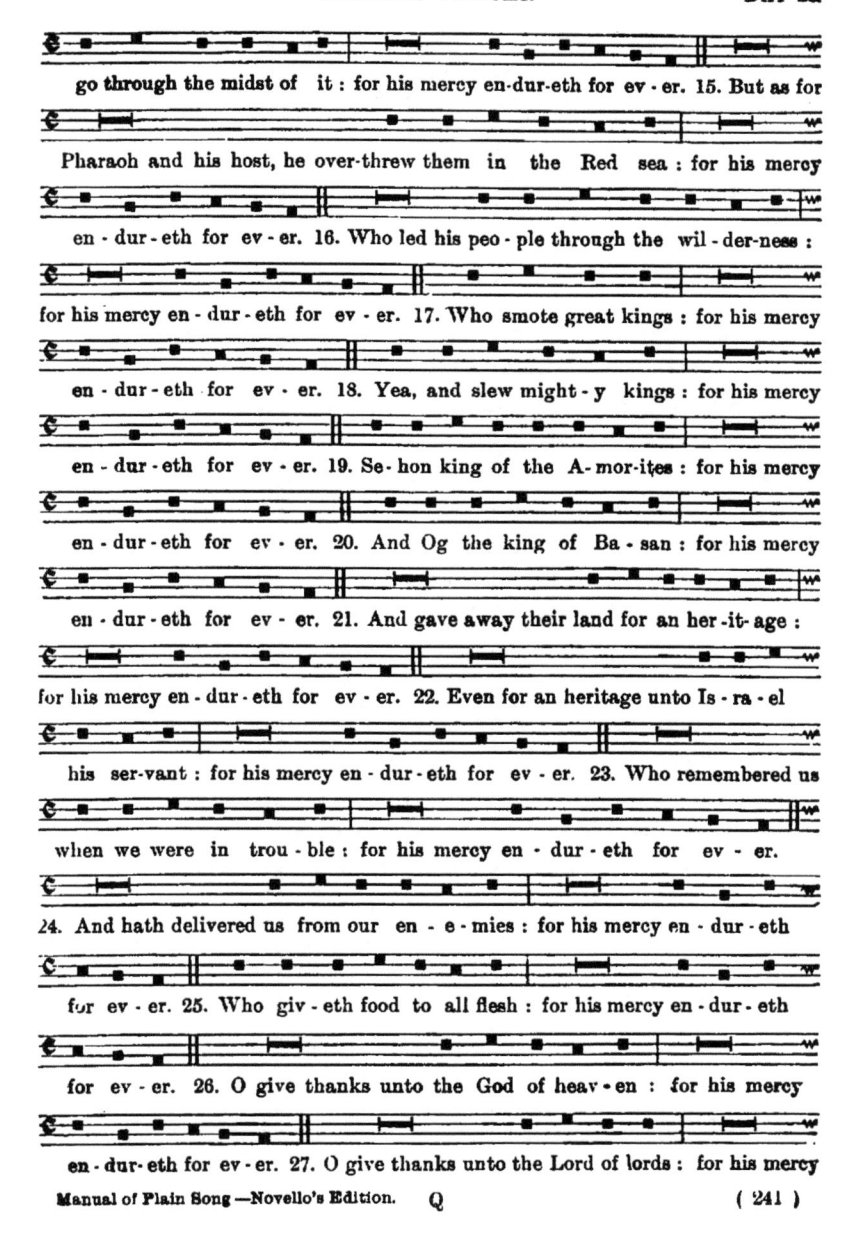

Manual of Plain Song —Novello's Edition.

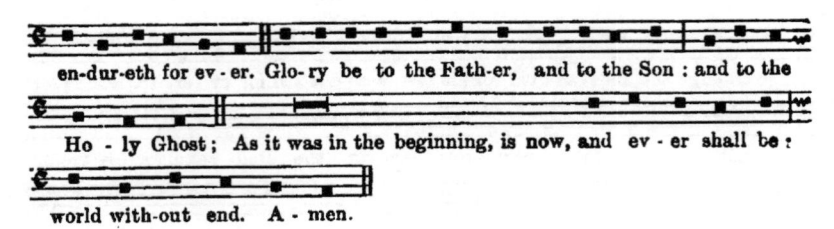

DAY 28.   EVENING PRAYER.

en-dur-eth for ev - er. Glo-ry be to the Fath-er, and to the Son : and to the Ho - ly Ghost; As it was in the beginning, is now, and ev - er shall be : world with-out end. A - men.

PSALM CXXXVII.—*Super flumina.*

2nd Tone, 1st Ending.

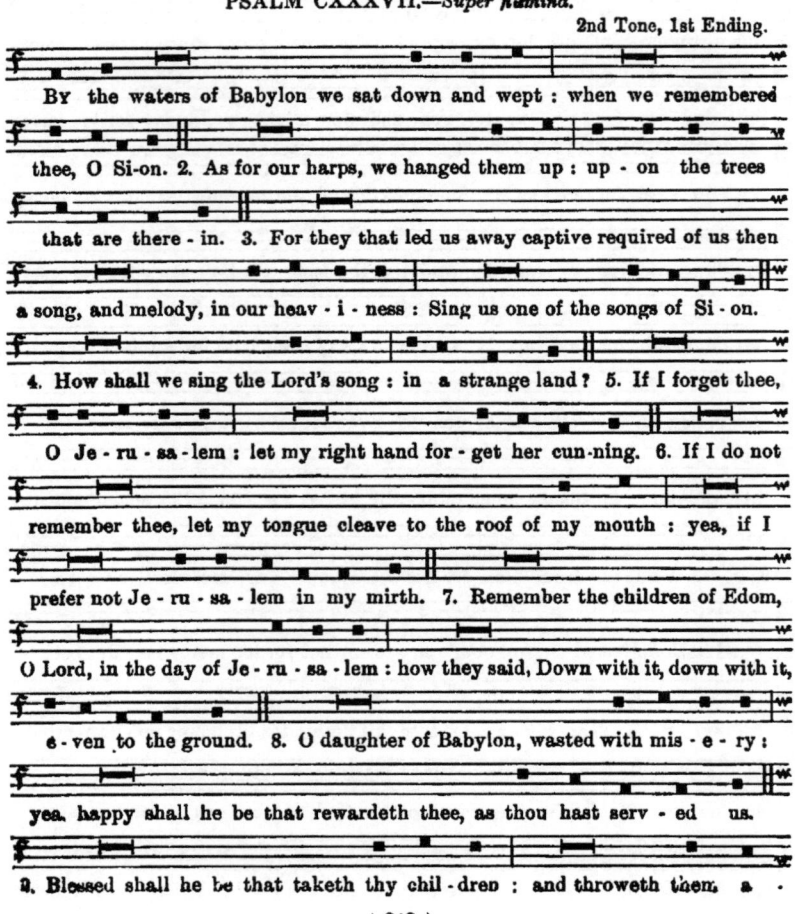

By the waters of Babylon we sat down and wept : when we remembered thee, O Si-on. 2. As for our harps, we hanged them up : up - on the trees that are there - in. 3. For they that led us away captive required of us then a song, and melody, in our heav - i - ness : Sing us one of the songs of Si - on. 4. How shall we sing the Lord's song : in a strange land ? 5. If I forget thee, O Je - ru - sa - lem ; let my right hand for - get her cun -ning. 6. If I do not remember thee, let my tongue cleave to the roof of my mouth : yea, if I prefer not Je - ru - sa - lem in my mirth. 7. Remember the children of Edom, O Lord, in the day of Je - ru - sa - lem : how they said, Down with it, down with it, e - ven to the ground. 8. O daughter of Babylon, wasted with mis - e - ry : yea, happy shall he be that rewardeth thee, as thou hast serv - ed us. 9. Blessed shall he be that taketh thy chil - dren : and throweth them a - -

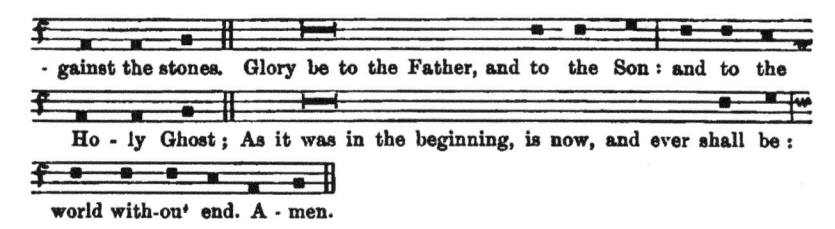

EVENING PRAYER. DAY 28.

- gainst the stones. Glory be to the Father, and to the Son : and to the Ho - ly Ghost ; As it was in the beginning, is now, and ever shall be : world with-ou' end. A - men.

PSALM CXXXVIII.—*Confitebor tibi.*

3rd Tone, 2nd Ending.

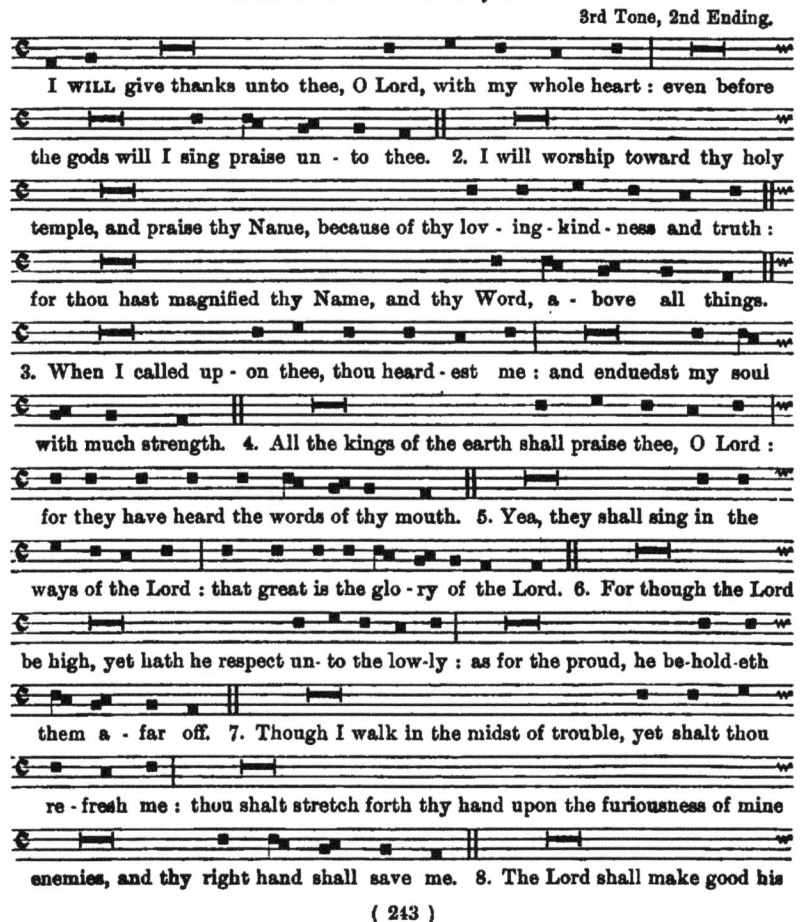

I WILL give thanks unto thee, O Lord, with my whole heart : even before the gods will I sing praise un - to thee. 2. I will worship toward thy holy temple, and praise thy Name, because of thy lov - ing - kind - ness and truth : for thou hast magnified thy Name, and thy Word, a - bove all things. 3. When I called up - on thee, thou heard - est me : and enduedst my soul with much strength. 4. All the kings of the earth shall praise thee, O Lord : for they have heard the words of thy mouth. 5. Yea, they shall sing in the ways of the Lord : that great is the glo - ry of the Lord. 6. For though the Lord be high, yet hath he respect un- to the low-ly : as for the proud, he be-hold-eth them a - far off. 7. Though I walk in the midst of trouble, yet shalt thou re - fresh me : thou shalt stretch forth thy hand upon the furiousness of mine enemies, and thy right hand shall save me. 8. The Lord shall make good his

DAY 29. MORNING PRAYER.

lov ing-kind-ness to-ward me : yea, thy mercy, O Lord, endureth for ever ;

despise not then the works of thine own hands. Glo-ry be to the Fath-er, and

to the Son : and to the Ho-ly Ghost ; As it was in the beginning, is now,

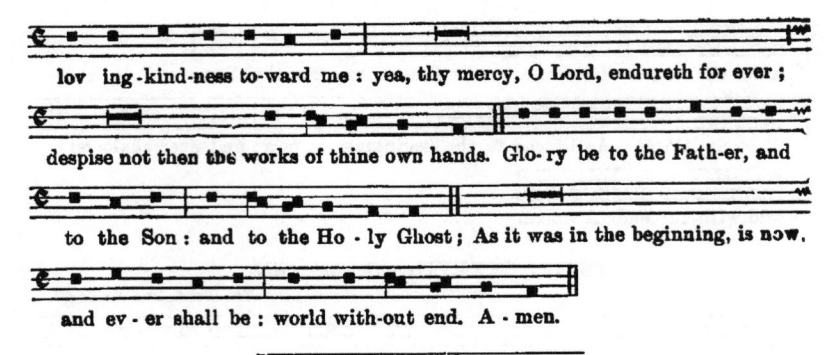

and ev-er shall be : world with-out end. A-men.

DAY 29. MORNING PRAYER.

PSALM CXXXIX.—*Domine, probasti.*

1st Tone, 8th Ending.

O LORD, thou hast searched me out, and known me : thou knowest my down-

-sitting, and mine up-rising ; thou un-der-stand-est my thoughts long be-fore.

2. Thou art about my path, and a-bout my bed : and spi-est out all my ways.

3. For lo there is not a word in my tongue : but thou, O Lord, know-est it

al-to-geth-er. 4. Thou hast fashioned me behind and be-fore : and laid thine

hand up-on me. 5. Such knowledge is too wonderful and ex-cel-lent for me :

I can-not at-tain un-to it. 6. Whither shall I go then from thy spir-it :

or whither shall I go then from thy pres-ence? 7. If I climb up into heaven,

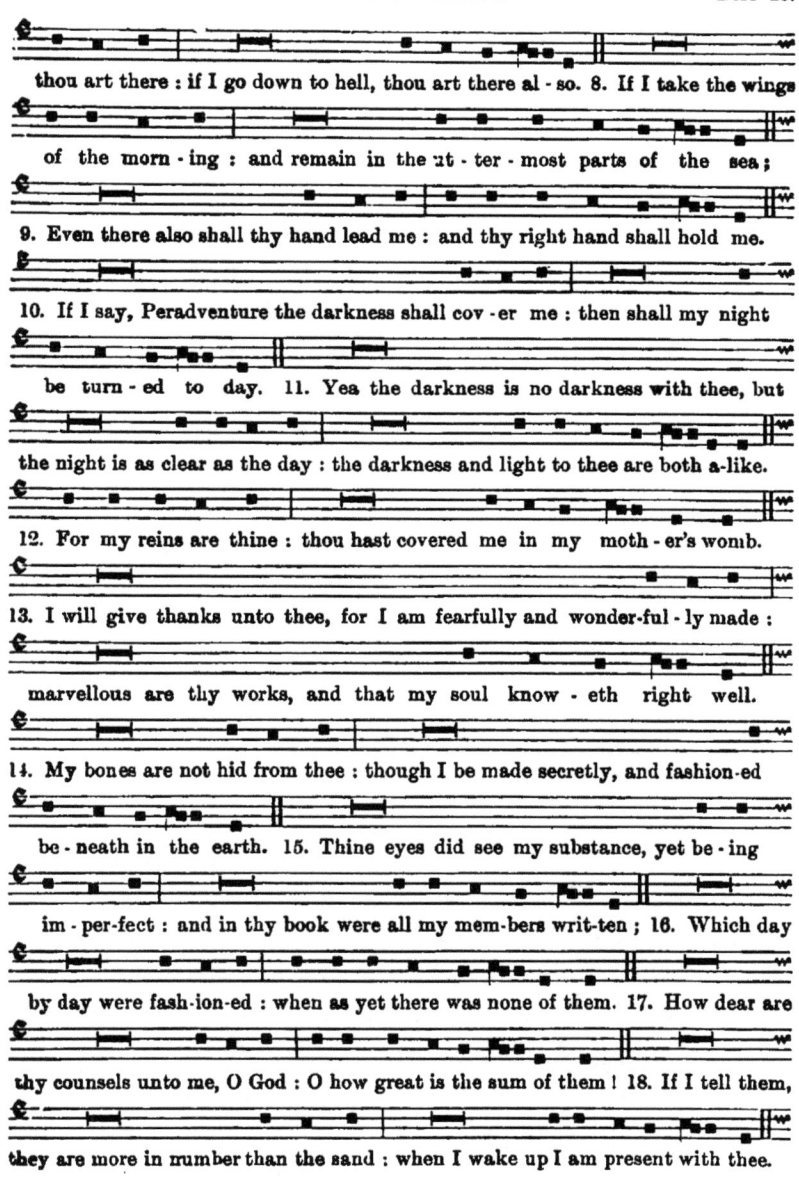

MORNING PRAYER. DAY 29.

thou art there : if I go down to hell, thou art there al-so. 8. If I take the wings of the morn-ing : and remain in the ut-ter-most parts of the sea; 9. Even there also shall thy hand lead me : and thy right hand shall hold me. 10. If I say, Peradventure the darkness shall cov-er me : then shall my night be turn-ed to day. 11. Yea the darkness is no darkness with thee, but the night is as clear as the day : the darkness and light to thee are both a-like. 12. For my reins are thine : thou hast covered me in my moth-er's womb. 13. I will give thanks unto thee, for I am fearfully and wonder-ful-ly made : marvellous are thy works, and that my soul know-eth right well. 14. My bones are not hid from thee : though I be made secretly, and fashion-ed be-neath in the earth. 15. Thine eyes did see my substance, yet be-ing im-per-fect : and in thy book were all my mem-bers writ-ten ; 16. Which day by day were fash-ion-ed : when as yet there was none of them. 17. How dear are thy counsels unto me, O God : O how great is the sum of them ! 18. If I tell them, they are more in number than the sand : when I wake up I am present with thee.

(245)

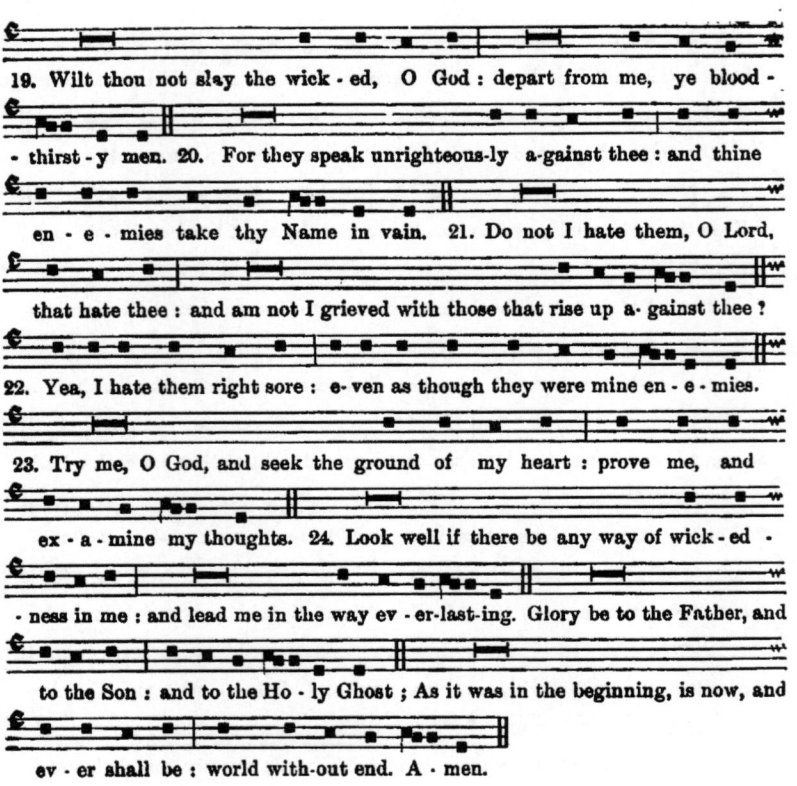

DAY 29.   MORNING PRAYER.

19. Wilt thou not slay the wick-ed, O God : depart from me, ye blood-thirst-y men. 20. For they speak unrighteous-ly a-gainst thee : and thine en-e-mies take thy Name in vain. 21. Do not I hate them, O Lord, that hate thee : and am not I grieved with those that rise up a-gainst thee ? 22. Yea, I hate them right sore : e-ven as though they were mine en-e-mies. 23. Try me, O God, and seek the ground of my heart : prove me, and ex-a-mine my thoughts. 24. Look well if there be any way of wick-ed-ness in me : and lead me in the way ev-er-last-ing. Glory be to the Father, and to the Son : and to the Ho-ly Ghost ; As it was in the beginning, is now, and ev-er shall be : world with-out end. A-men.

PSALM CXL.—*Eripe me, Domine.*

3rd Tone, 5th Ending.

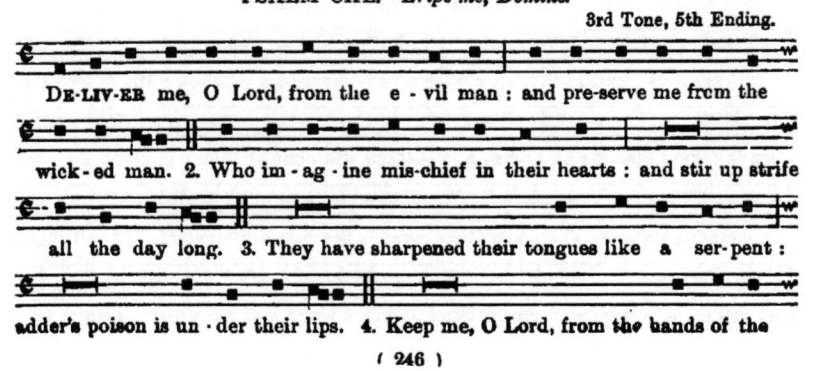

DE-LIV-ER me, O Lord, from the e-vil man : and pre-serve me from the wick-ed man. 2. Who im-ag-ine mis-chief in their hearts : and stir up strife all the day long. 3. They have sharpened their tongues like a ser-pent : adder's poison is un-der their lips. 4. Keep me, O Lord, from the hands of the un - god - ly : preserve me from the wicked men, who are purposed to overthrow my go - ings. 5. The proud have laid a snare for me, and spread a net a-broad with cords : yea and set traps in my way. 6. I said unto the Lord, Thou art my God : hear the voice of my prayers, O Lord. 7. O Lord God, thou strength of my health : thou hast covered my head in the day of bat - tle. 8. Let not the ungodly have his de - sire, O Lord : let not his mischievous imagination prosper, lest they be too proud. 9. Let the mischief of their own lips fall up - on the head of them : that com-pass me a - bout. 10. Let hot burning coals fall up - on them : let them be cast into the fire, and into the pit, that they nev - er rise up a - gain. 11. A man full of words shall not pros-per up-on the earth : evil shall hunt the wicked person to o-ver-throw him. 12. Sure I am that the Lord will a-venge the poor : and maintain the cause of the help - less. 13. The righteous also shall give thanks un - to thy Name : and the just shall con-tin-ue in thy sight. Glo - ry be to the Fath er, and to the Son : and to the Ho - ly Ghost ; As it was in the beginning, is now, and ev - er shall be : world with-out end. A - men.

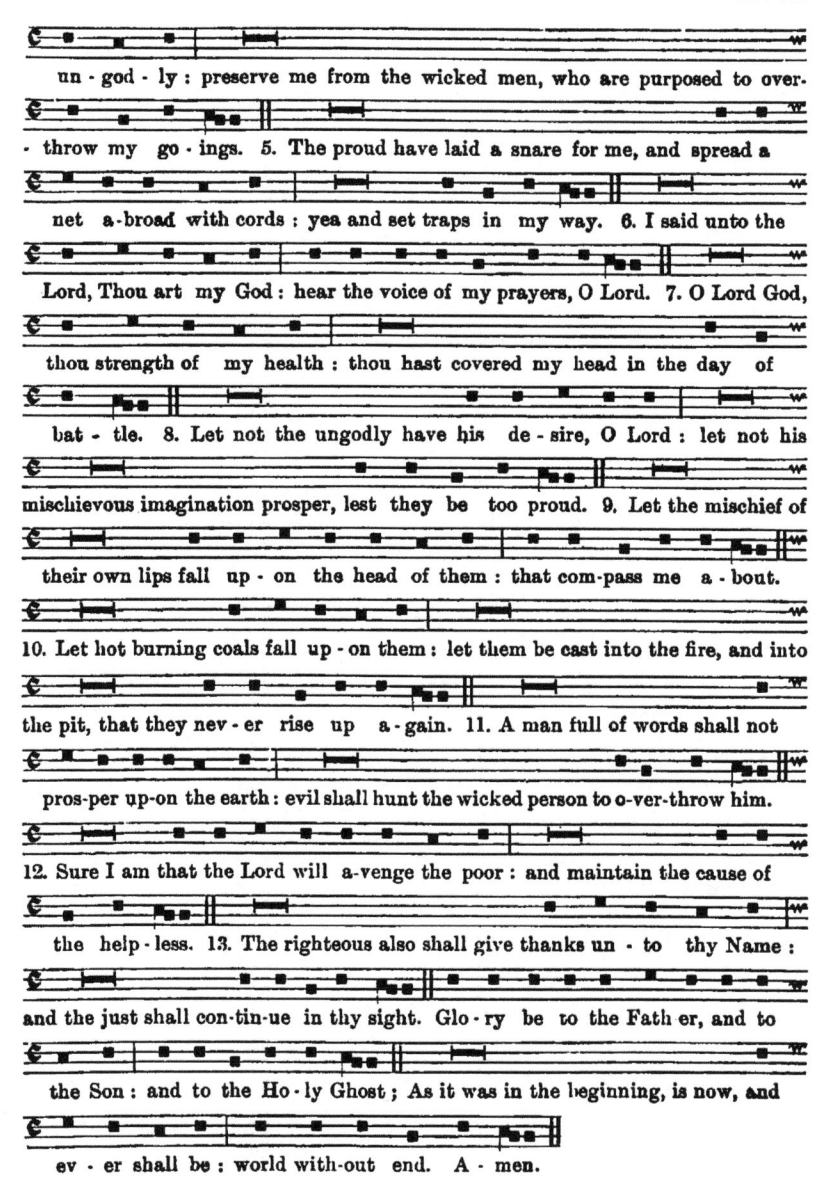

(247)

Day 29. MORNING PRAYER.

PSALM CXLI.—*Domine, clamavi.*

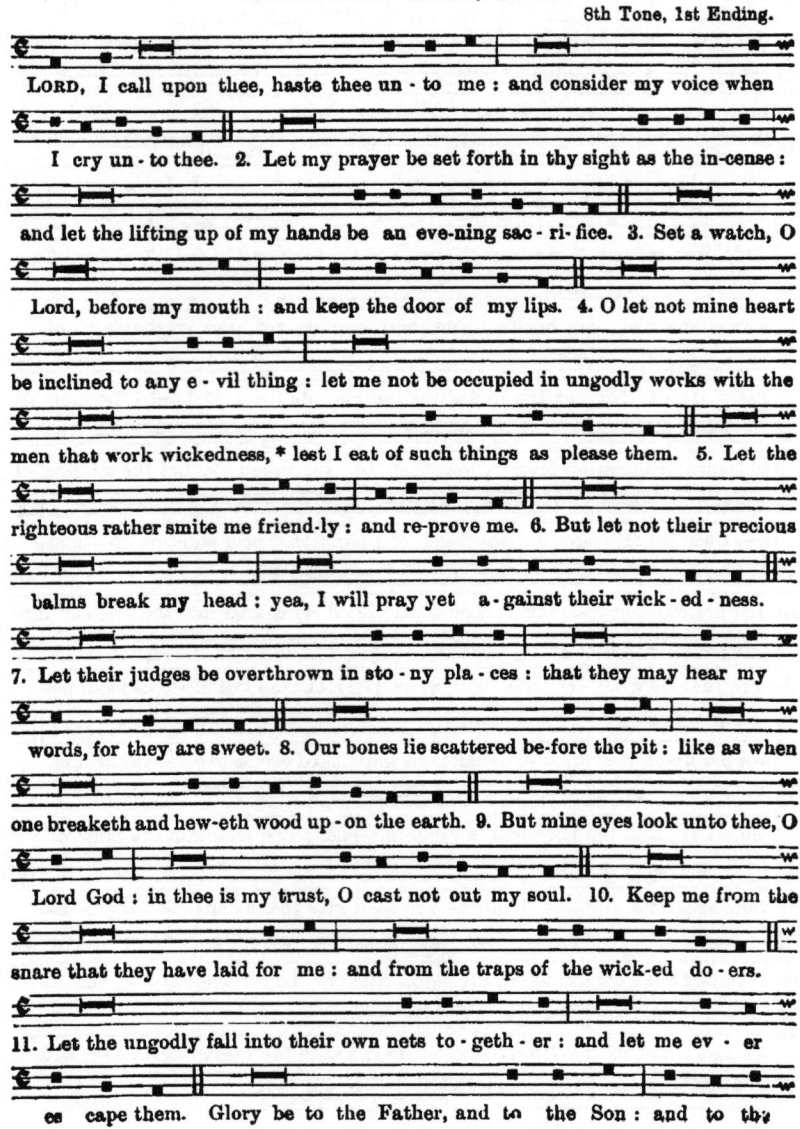

8th Tone, 1st Ending.

LORD, I call upon thee, haste thee un-to me : and consider my voice when I cry un-to thee. 2. Let my prayer be set forth in thy sight as the in-cense : and let the lifting up of my hands be an eve-ning sac-ri-fice. 3. Set a watch, O Lord, before my mouth : and keep the door of my lips. 4. O let not mine heart be inclined to any e-vil thing : let me not be occupied in ungodly works with the men that work wickedness, * lest I eat of such things as please them. 5. Let the righteous rather smite me friend-ly : and re-prove me. 6. But let not their precious balms break my head : yea, I will pray yet a-gainst their wick-ed-ness. 7. Let their judges be overthrown in sto-ny pla-ces : that they may hear my words, for they are sweet. 8. Our bones lie scattered be-fore the pit : like as when one breaketh and hew-eth wood up-on the earth. 9. But mine eyes look unto thee, O Lord God : in thee is my trust, O cast not out my soul. 10. Keep me from the snare that they have laid for me : and from the traps of the wick-ed do-ers. 11. Let the ungodly fall into their own nets to-geth-er : and let me ev-er es-cape them. Glory be to the Father, and to the Son : and to the

(248)

EVENING PRAYER. DAY 29

Ho - ly Ghost; As it was in the beginning, is now, and ever shall be: world with - out end. A - men.

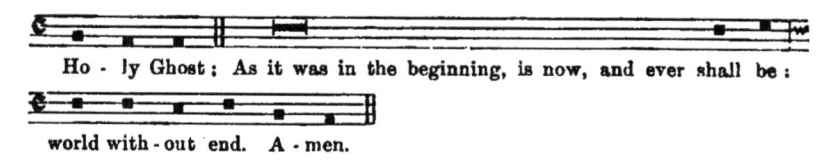

EVENING PRAYER.

PSALM CXLII.—*Voce mea ad Dominum.*

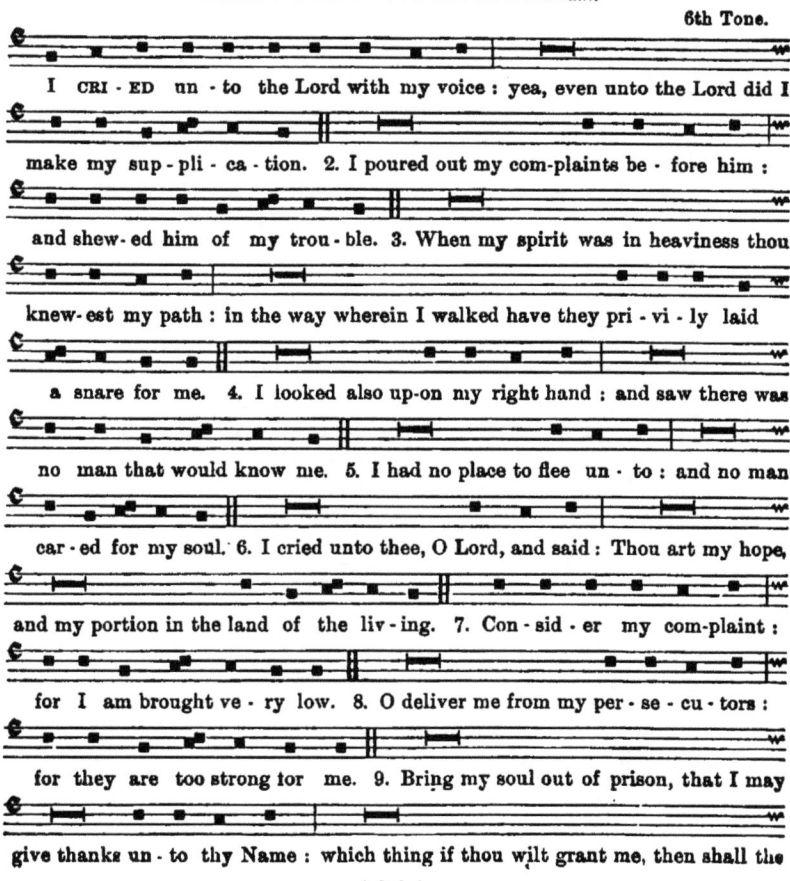

6th Tone.

I CRI - ED un - to the Lord with my voice : yea, even unto the Lord did I make my sup - pli - ca - tion. 2. I poured out my com-plaints be - fore him : and shew- ed him of my trou - ble. 3. When my spirit was in heaviness thou knew- est my path : in the way wherein I walked have they pri - vi - ly laid a snare for me. 4. I looked also up-on my right hand ; and saw there was no man that would know me. 5. I had no place to flee un - to : and no man car - ed for my soul. 6. I cried unto thee, O Lord, and said : Thou art my hope, and my portion in the land of the liv - ing. 7. Con - sid - er my com-plaint : for I am brought ve - ry low. 8. O deliver me from my per - se - cu - tors : for they are too strong for me. 9. Bring my soul out of prison, that I may give thanks un - to thy Name : which thing if thou wilt grant me, then shall the

(249)

DAY 29.   EVENING PRAYER.

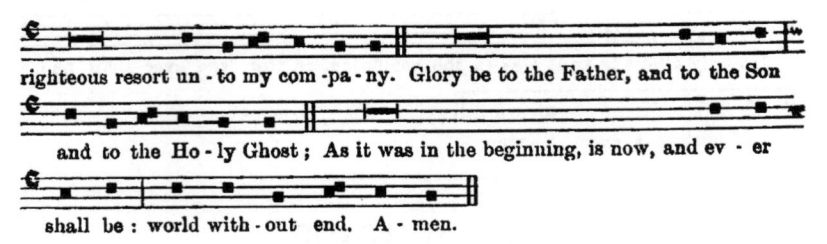

righteous resort un-to my com-pa-ny. Glory be to the Father, and to the Son

and to the Ho-ly Ghost; As it was in the beginning, is now, and ev - er

shall be : world with-out end. A - men.

PSALM CXLIII.—*Domine, exaudi.*

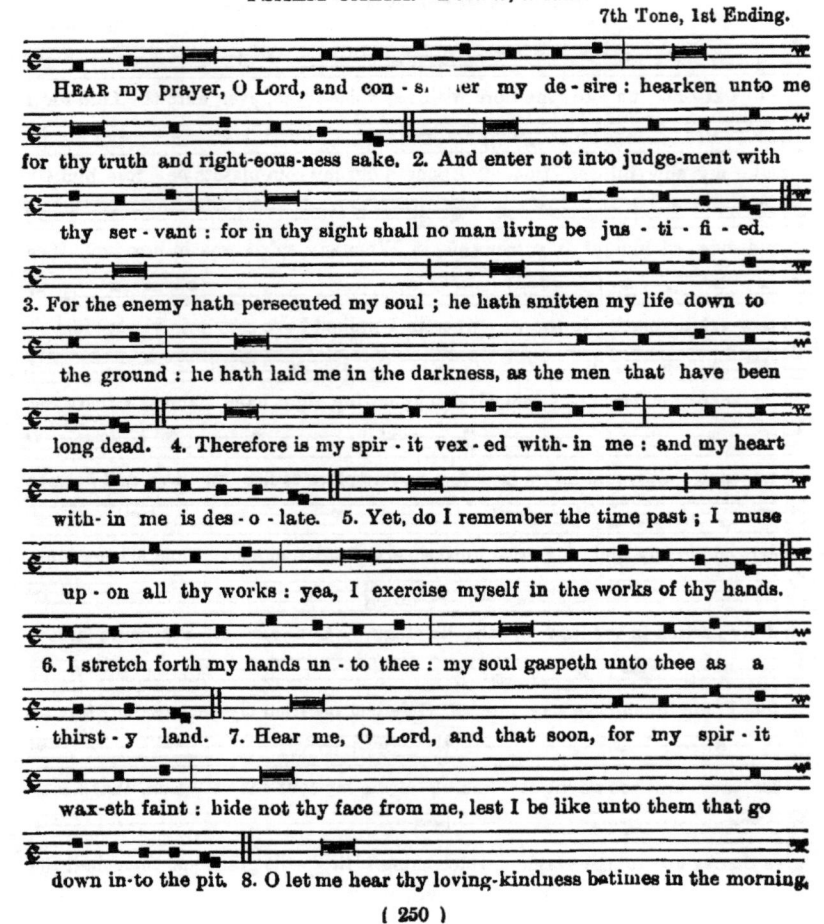

7th Tone, 1st Ending.

HEAR my prayer, O Lord, and con - si der my de-sire: hearken unto me

for thy truth and right-eous-ness sake. 2. And enter not into judge-ment with

thy ser - vant : for in thy sight shall no man living be jus - ti - fi - ed.

3. For the enemy hath persecuted my soul ; he hath smitten my life down to

the ground : he hath laid me in the darkness, as the men that have been

long dead. 4. Therefore is my spir - it vex - ed with-in me : and my heart

with-in me is des-o-late. 5. Yet, do I remember the time past ; I muse

up-on all thy works : yea, I exercise myself in the works of thy hands.

6. I stretch forth my hands un - to thee : my soul gaspeth unto thee as a

thirst - y land. 7. Hear me, O Lord, and that soon, for my spir - it

wax-eth faint : hide not thy face from me, lest I be like unto them that go

down in-to the pit. 8. O let me hear thy loving-kindness betimes in the morning,

(250)

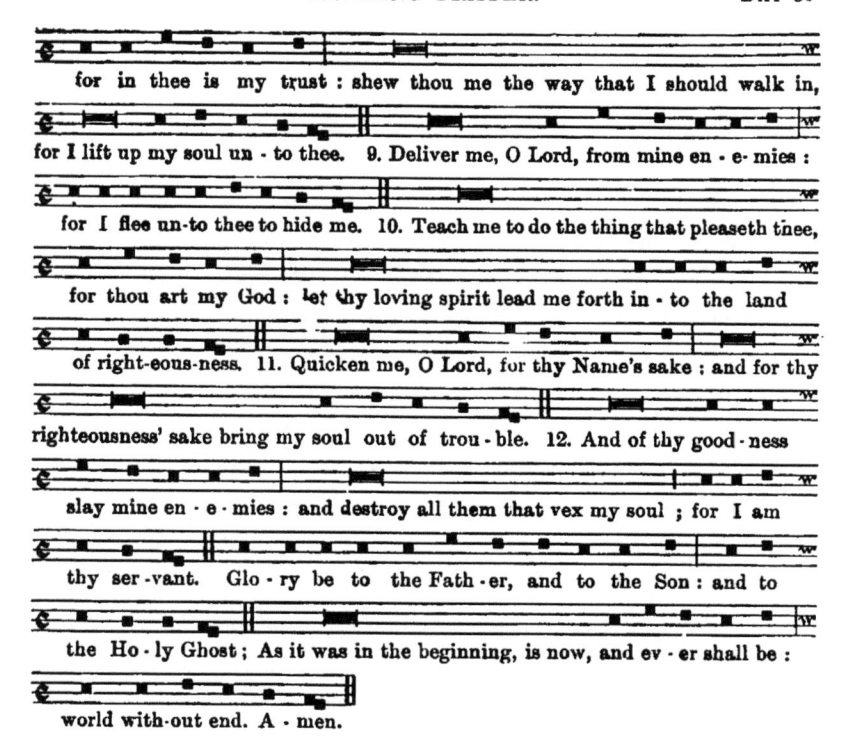

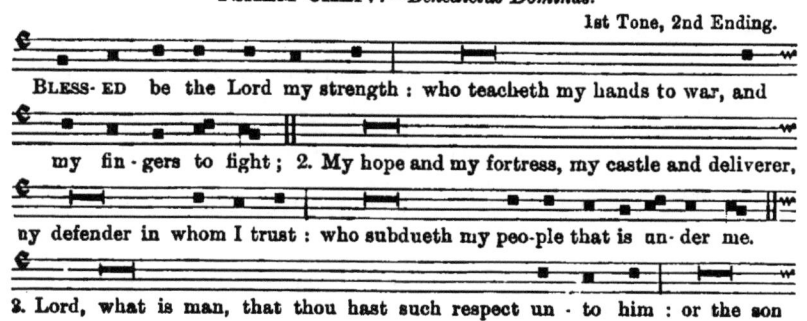

MORNING PRAYER. DAY 30

for in thee is my trust : shew thou me the way that I should walk in, for I lift up my soul un-to thee. 9. Deliver me, O Lord, from mine en-e-mies: for I flee un-to thee to hide me. 10. Teach me to do the thing that pleaseth thee, for thou art my God : let thy loving spirit lead me forth in-to the land of right-eous-ness. 11. Quicken me, O Lord, for thy Name's sake ; and for thy righteousness' sake bring my soul out of trou-ble. 12. And of thy good-ness slay mine en-e-mies : and destroy all them that vex my soul ; for I am thy ser-vant. Glo-ry be to the Fath-er, and to the Son : and to the Ho-ly Ghost ; As it was in the beginning, is now, and ev-er shall be : world with-out end. A-men.

MORNING PRAYER. DAY 30.

PSALM CXLIV.—*Benedictus Dominus.*

1st Tone, 2nd Ending.

BLESS-ED be the Lord my strength : who teacheth my hands to war, and my fin-gers to fight ; 2. My hope and my fortress, my castle and deliverer, my defender in whom I trust : who subdueth my peo-ple that is un-der me. 3. Lord, what is man, that thou hast such respect un-to him : or the son

DAY 30. MORNING PRAYER.

of man, that thou so re-gard-est him? 4. Man is like a thing of nought : his time passeth a-way like a shad-ow. 5. Bow thy heavens, O Lord, and come down : touch the moun-tains, and they shall smoke. 6. Cast forth thy lightning, and tear them : shoot out thine ar-rows, and con-sume them. 7. Send down thine hand from a-bove : deliver me, and take me out of the great waters, from the hand of strange children ; 8. Whose mouth talketh of van-i-ty : and their right hand is a right hand of wickedness. 9. I will sing a new song unto thee, O God : and sing praises unto thee up-on a ten-string-ed lute. 10. Thou hast given victory un-to kings : and hast delivered David thy servant from the per-il of the sword. 11. Save me, and deliver me from the hand of strange children : whose mouth talketh of vanity, and their right hand is a right hand of in-i-qui-ty. 12. That our sons may grow up as the young plants : and that our daughters may be as the polished cor-ners of the tem-ple. 13. That our garners may be full and plenteous with all man-ner of store : that our sheep may bring forth thousands and ten thou-sands in our streets. 14. That our oxen may

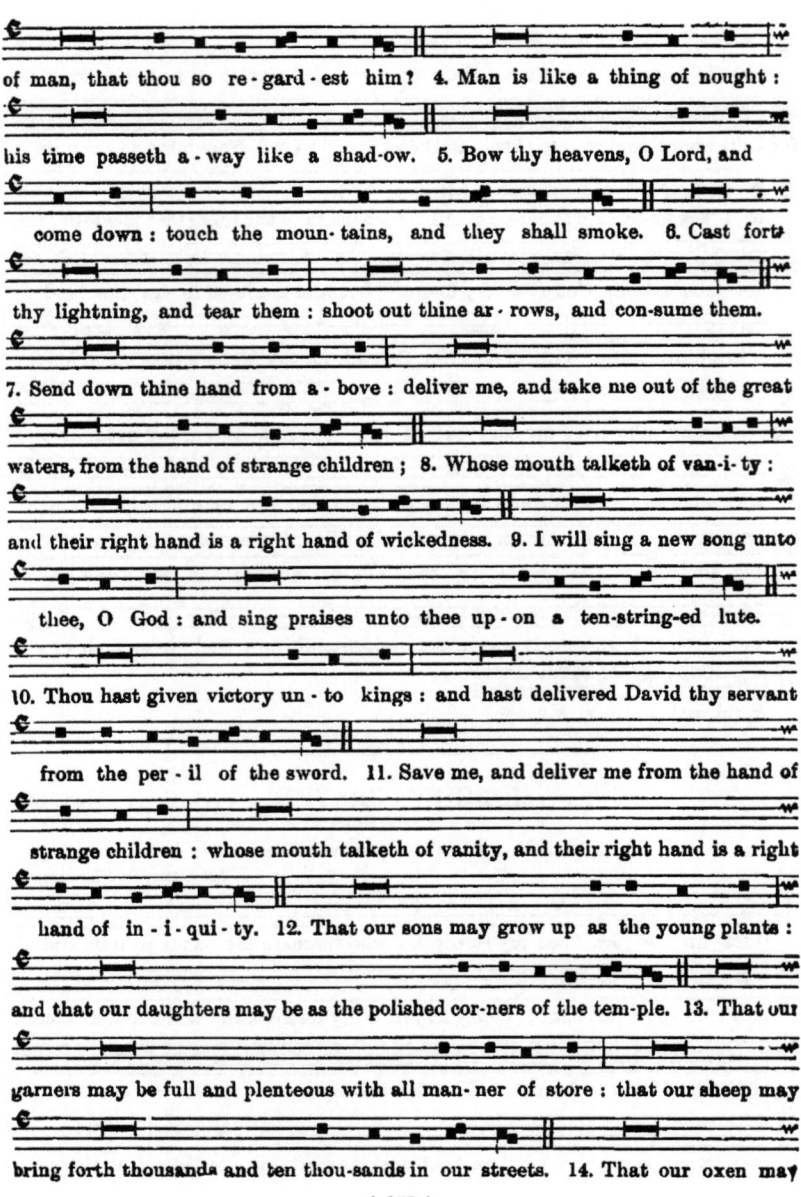

MORNING PRAYER. DAY 30.

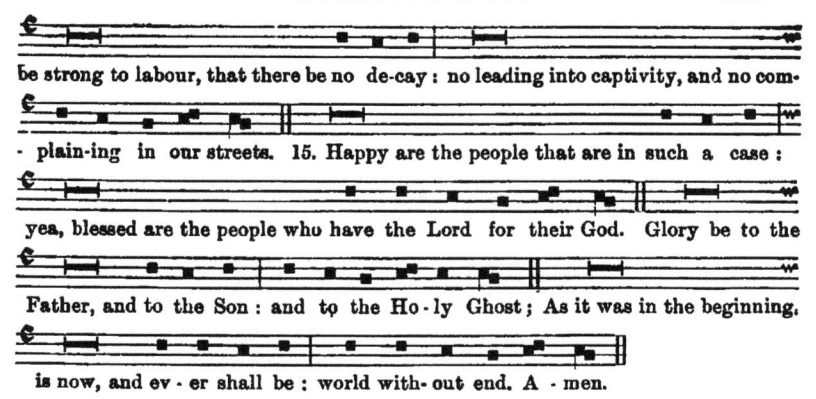

be strong to labour, that there be no de-cay: no leading into captivity, and no com- plain-ing in our streets. 15. Happy are the people that are in such a case: yea, blessed are the people who have the Lord for their God. Glory be to the Father, and to the Son: and to the Ho-ly Ghost; As it was in the beginning, is now, and ev-er shall be: world with-out end. A-men.

PSALM CXLV.—*Exaltabo te, Deus.*

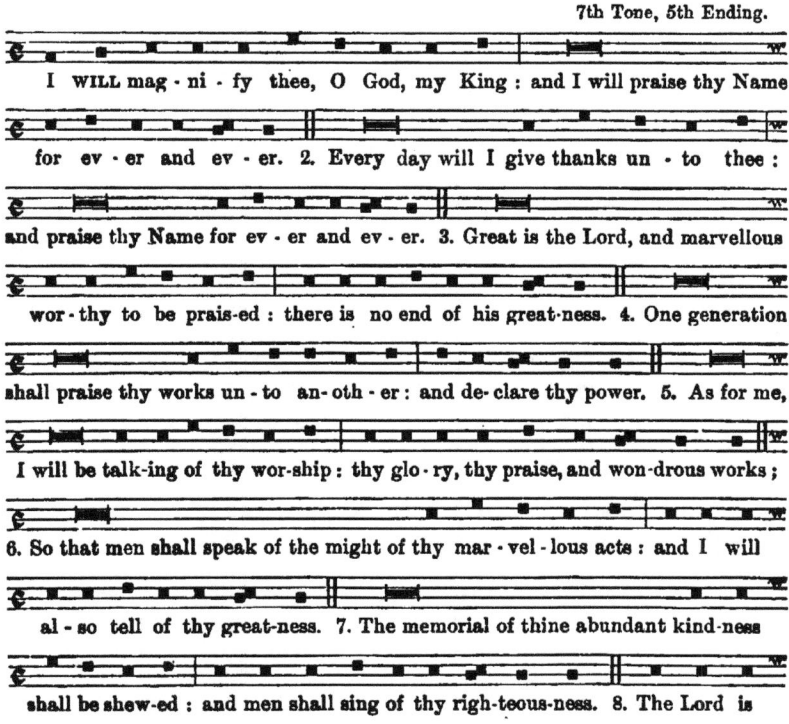

7th Tone, 5th Ending.

I WILL mag-ni-fy thee, O God, my King: and I will praise thy Name for ev-er and ev-er. 2. Every day will I give thanks un-to thee: and praise thy Name for ev-er and ev-er. 3. Great is the Lord, and marvellous wor-thy to be prais-ed: there is no end of his great-ness. 4. One generation shall praise thy works un-to an-oth-er: and de-clare thy power. 5. As for me, I will be talk-ing of thy wor-ship: thy glo-ry, thy praise, and won-drous works; 6. So that men shall speak of the might of thy mar-vel-lous acts: and I will al-so tell of thy great-ness. 7. The memorial of thine abundant kind-ness shall be shew-ed: and men shall sing of thy righ-teous-ness. 8. The Lord is

(253)

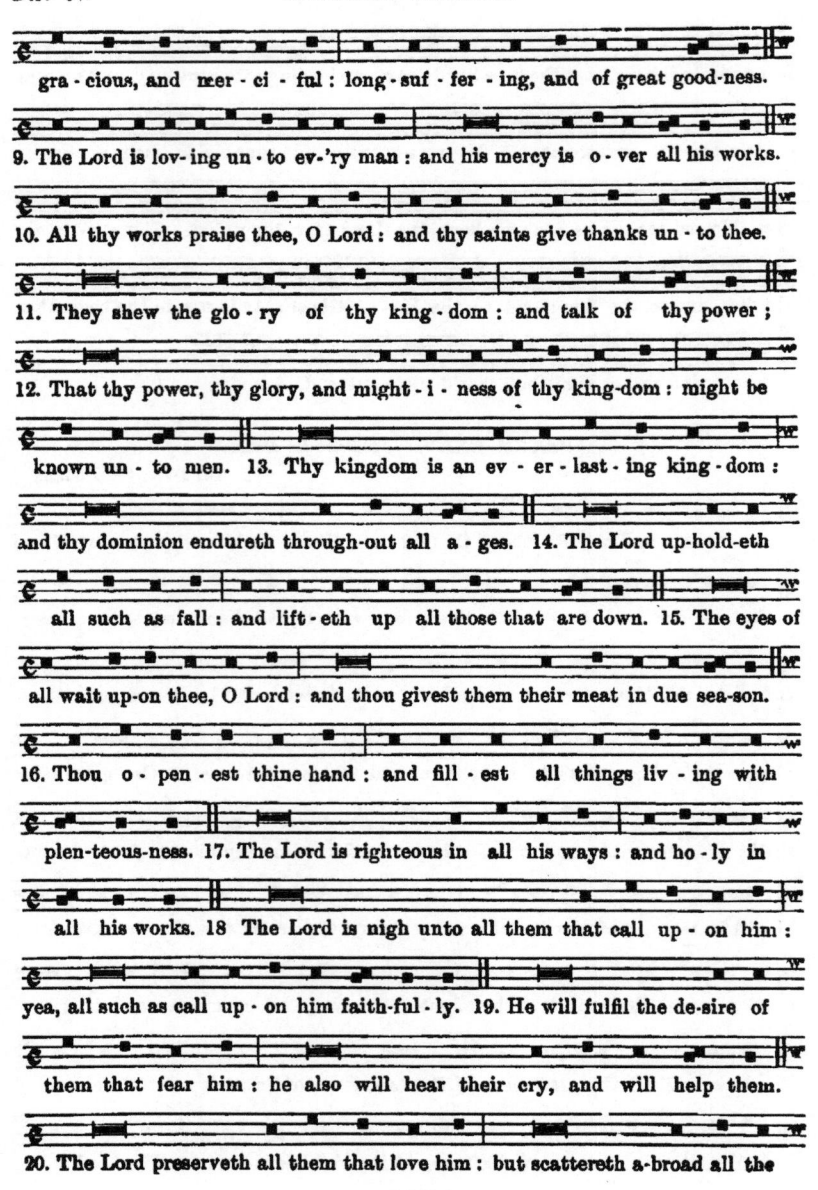

DAY 30. MORNING PRAYER.

gra-cious, and mer-ci-ful: long-suf-fer-ing, and of great good-ness.

9. The Lord is lov-ing un-to ev-'ry man: and his mercy is o-ver all his works.

10. All thy works praise thee, O Lord: and thy saints give thanks un-to thee.

11. They shew the glo-ry of thy king-dom: and talk of thy power;

12. That thy power, thy glory, and might-i-ness of thy king-dom: might be known un-to men. 13. Thy kingdom is an ev-er-last-ing king-dom: and thy dominion endureth through-out all a-ges. 14. The Lord up-hold-eth all such as fall: and lift-eth up all those that are down. 15. The eyes of all wait up-on thee, O Lord: and thou givest them their meat in due sea-son. 16. Thou o-pen-est thine hand: and fill-est all things liv-ing with plen-teous-ness. 17. The Lord is righteous in all his ways: and ho-ly in all his works. 18 The Lord is nigh unto all them that call up-on him: yea, all such as call up-on him faith-ful-ly. 19. He will fulfil the de-sire of them that fear him: he also will hear their cry, and will help them. 20. The Lord preserveth all them that love him: but scattereth a-broad all the

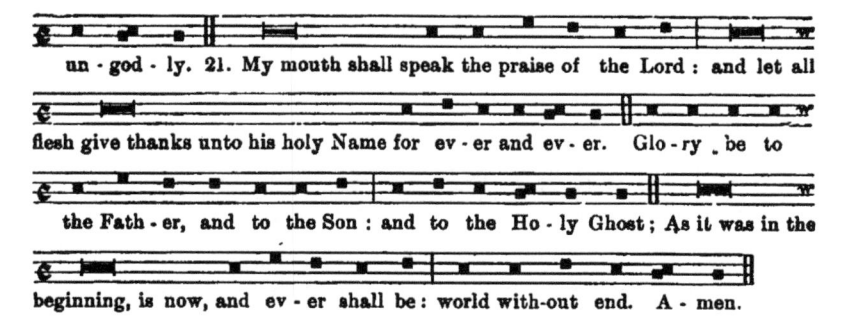

un - god - ly. 21. My mouth shall speak the praise of the Lord : and let all flesh give thanks unto his holy Name for ev - er and ev - er. Glo - ry be to the Fath - er, and to the Son : and to the Ho - ly Ghost ; As it was in the beginning, is now, and ev - er shall be : world with-out end. A - men.

PSALM CXLVI.—*Lauda, anima mea.*

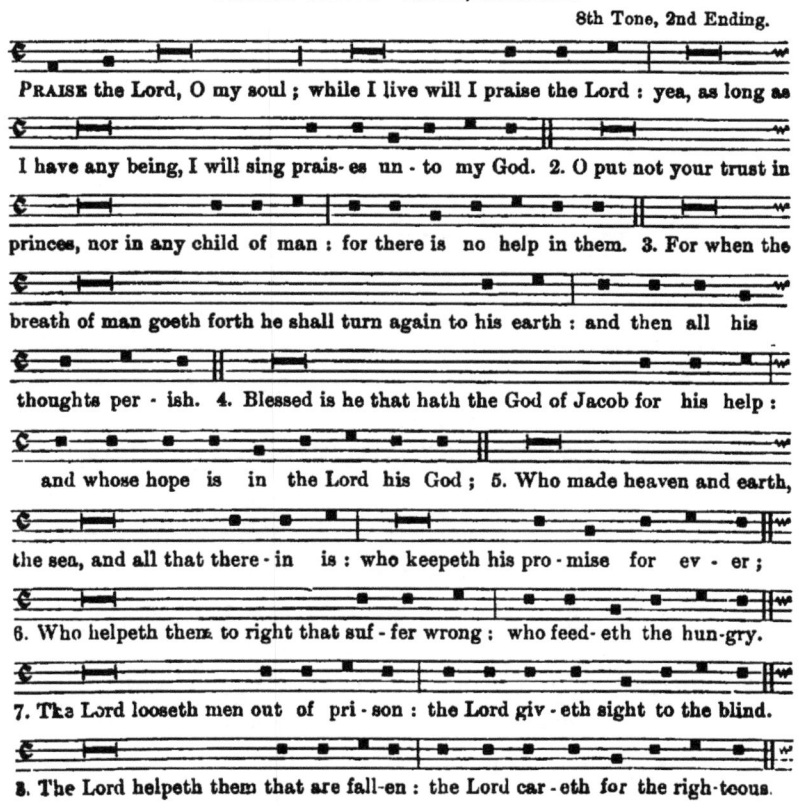

8th Tone, 2nd Ending.

PRAISE the Lord, O my soul ; while I live will I praise the Lord : yea, as long as I have any being, I will sing prais- es un - to my God. 2. O put not your trust in princes, nor in any child of man : for there is no help in them. 3. For when the breath of man goeth forth he shall turn again to his earth : and then all his thoughts per - ish. 4. Blessed is he that hath the God of Jacob for his help : and whose hope is in the Lord his God ; 5. Who made heaven and earth, the sea, and all that there - in is : who keepeth his pro - mise for ev - er ; 6. Who helpeth them to right that suf - fer wrong : who feed- eth the hun-gry. 7. The Lord looseth men out of pri - son : the Lord giv - eth sight to the blind. 8. The Lord helpeth them that are fall-en : the Lord car - eth for the righ-teous.

DAY 30. MORNING PRAYER.

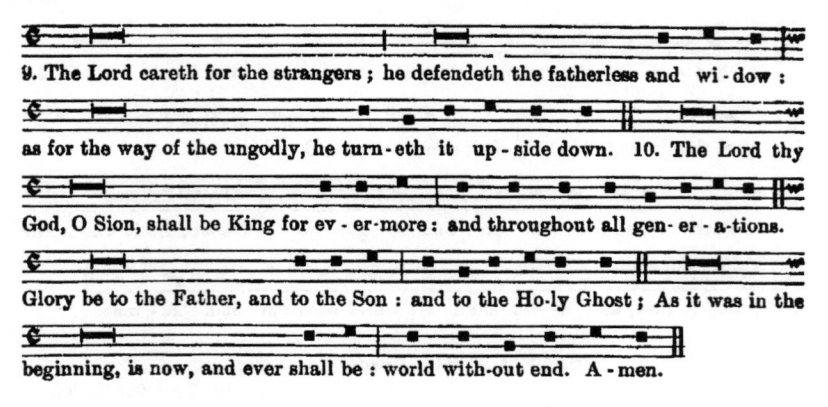

9. The Lord careth for the strangers ; he defendeth the fatherless and wi - dow :

as for the way of the ungodly, he turn-eth it up-side down. 10. The Lord thy

God, O Sion, shall be King for ev - er-more : and throughout all gen- er - a-tions.

Glory be to the Father, and to the Son : and to the Ho-ly Ghost ; As it was in the

beginning, is now, and ever shall be : world with-out end. A - men.

EVENING PRAYER.

PSALM CXLVII.—*Laudate Dominum.*

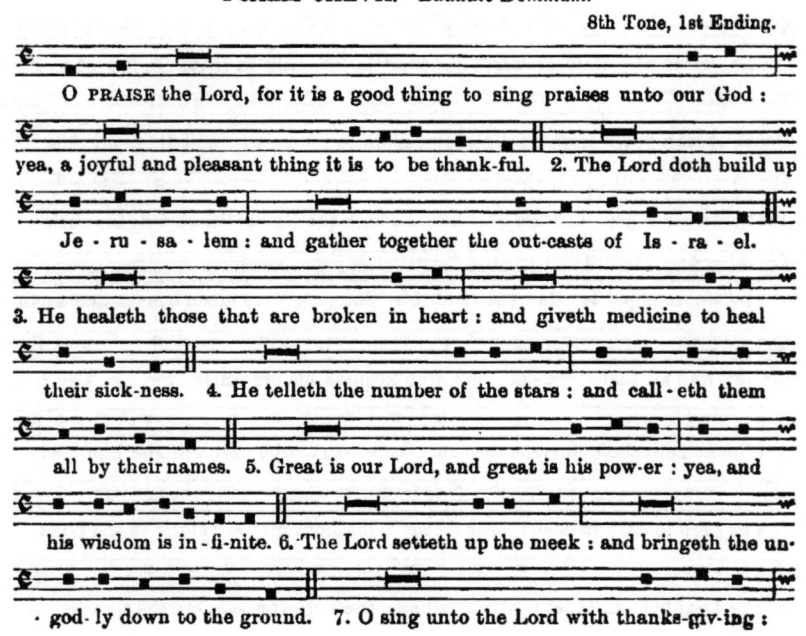

8th Tone, 1st Ending.

O PRAISE the Lord, for it is a good thing to sing praises unto our God :

yea, a joyful and pleasant thing it is to be thank-ful. 2. The Lord doth build up

Je - ru - sa - lem : and gather together the out-casts of Is - ra - el.

3. He healeth those that are broken in heart : and giveth medicine to heal

their sick-ness. 4. He telleth the number of the stars : and call - eth them

all by their names. 5. Great is our Lord, and great is his pow-er : yea, and

his wisdom is in - fi-nite. 6. The Lord setteth up the meek : and bringeth the un-

- god- ly down to the ground. 7. O sing unto the Lord with thanks-giv-ing :

EVENING PRAYER. DAY 30.

sing praises upon the harp un-to our God; 8. Who covereth the heaven with clouds, and prepareth rain for the earth: and maketh the grass to grow upon the mountains, and herb for the use of men; 9. Who giveth fodder un-to the cat-tle: and feedeth the young ravens that call up-on him. 10. He hath no pleasure in the strength of an horse: neither delighteth he in an-y man's legs. 11. But the Lord's delight is in them that fear him: and put their trust in his mer-cy. 12. Praise the Lord, O Je-ru-sa-lem: praise thy God, O Si-on. 13. For he hath made fast the bars of thy gates: and hath blessed thy chil-dren with-in thee. 14. He maketh peace in thy bor-ders: and fill-eth thee with the flour of wheat. 15. He sendeth forth his commandments up-on earth: and his word run-neth ve-ry swift-ly. 16. He giveth snow like wool: and scattereth the hoar-frost like ash-es. 17. He casteth forth his ice like mor-sels: who is a-ble to a-bide his frost? 18. He sendeth out his word, and melt-eth them: he bloweth with his wind, and the wa-ters flow. 19. He sheweth his word un-to Ja-cob: his statutes and ordi-nan-ces un-to Is-ra-el.

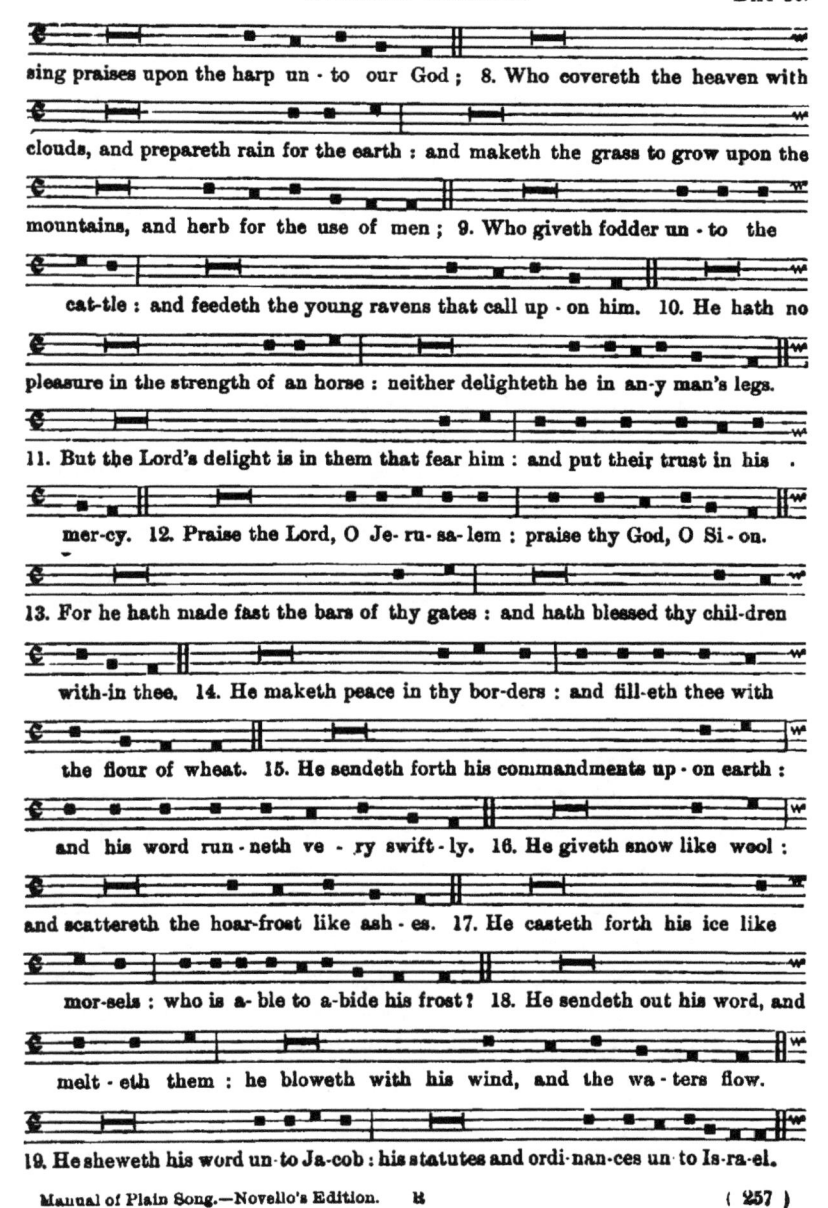

DAY 30 — EVENING PRAYER.

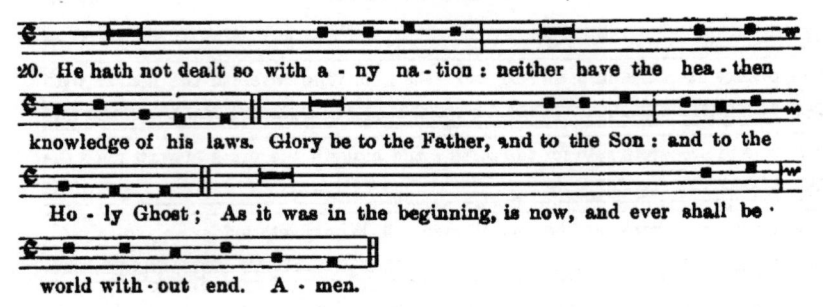

20. He hath not dealt so with a-ny na-tion : neither have the hea-then knowledge of his laws. Glory be to the Father, and to the Son : and to the Ho-ly Ghost; As it was in the beginning, is now, and ever shall be · world with-out end. A-men.

PSALM CXLVIII.—*Laudate Dominum.*

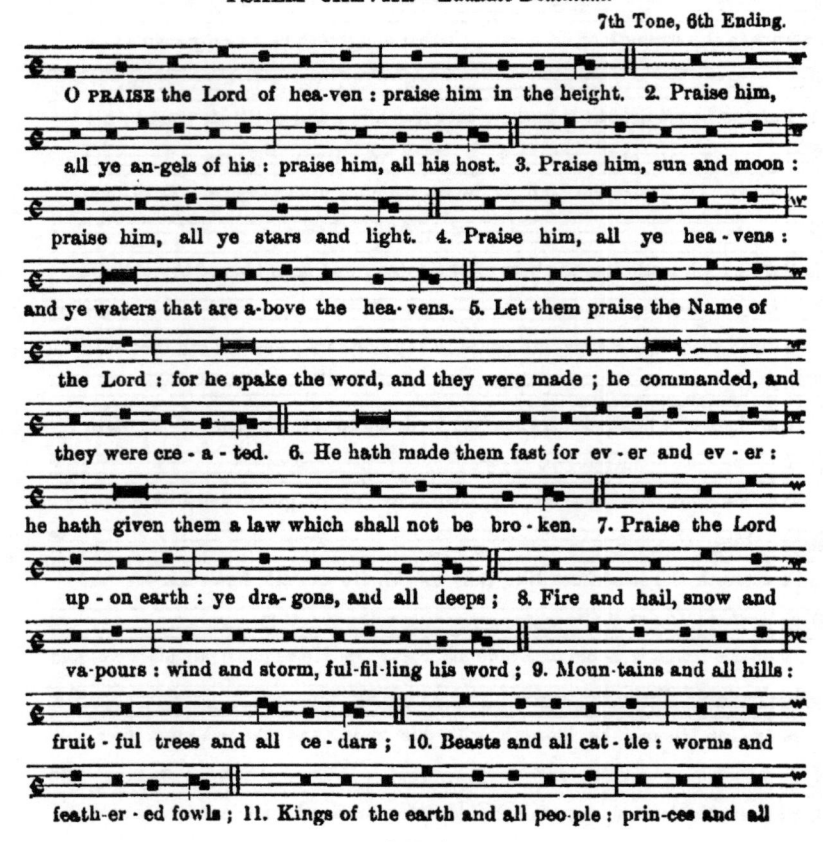

7th Tone, 6th Ending.

O PRAISE the Lord of hea-ven : praise him in the height. 2. Praise him, all ye an-gels of his : praise him, all his host. 3. Praise him, sun and moon : praise him, all ye stars and light. 4. Praise him, all ye hea-vens : and ye waters that are a-bove the hea-vens. 5. Let them praise the Name of the Lord : for he spake the word, and they were made ; he commanded, and they were cre-a-ted. 6. He hath made them fast for ev-er and ev-er : he hath given them a law which shall not be bro-ken. 7. Praise the Lord up-on earth : ye dra-gons, and all deeps ; 8. Fire and hail, snow and va-pours : wind and storm, ful-fil-ling his word ; 9. Moun-tains and all hills : fruit-ful trees and all ce-dars ; 10. Beasts and all cat-tle : worms and feath-er-ed fowls ; 11. Kings of the earth and all peo-ple : prin-ces and all

EVENING PRAYER DAY 30.

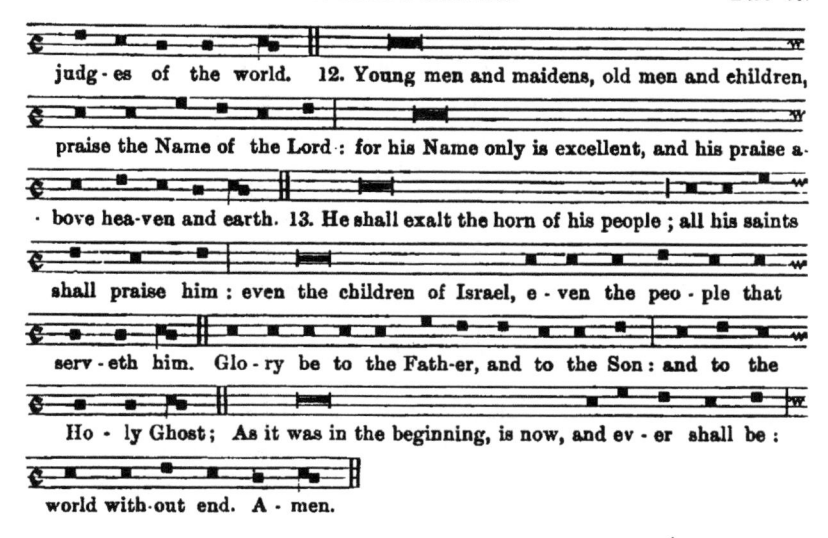

judg-es of the world. 12. Young men and maidens, old men and children, praise the Name of the Lord : for his Name only is excellent, and his praise a- bove hea-ven and earth. 13. He shall exalt the horn of his people ; all his saints shall praise him : even the children of Israel, e-ven the peo-ple that serv-eth him. Glo-ry be to the Fath-er, and to the Son : and to the Ho-ly Ghost ; As it was in the beginning, is now, and ev-er shall be : world with-out end. A-men.

PSALM CXLIX.—*Cantate Domino.*

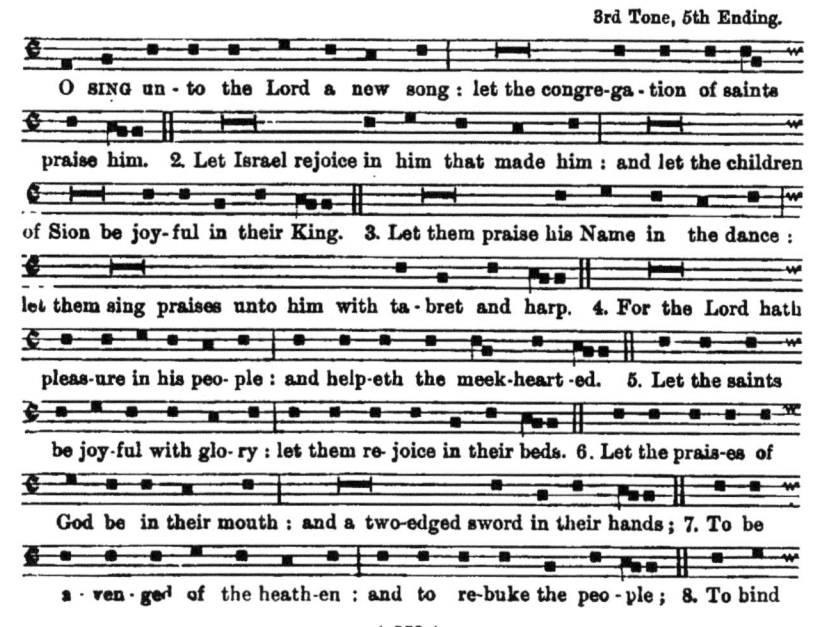

3rd Tone, 5th Ending.

O sing un-to the Lord a new song : let the congre-ga-tion of saints praise him. 2. Let Israel rejoice in him that made him : and let the children of Sion be joy-ful in their King. 3. Let them praise his Name in the dance : let them sing praises unto him with ta-bret and harp. 4. For the Lord hath pleas-ure in his peo-ple : and help-eth the meek-heart-ed. 5. Let the saints be joy-ful with glo-ry : let them re-joice in their beds. 6. Let the prais-es of God be in their mouth : and a two-edged sword in their hands ; 7. To be a-ven-ged of the heath-en : and to re-buke the peo-ple ; 8. To bind

DAY 30.   EVENING PRAYER.

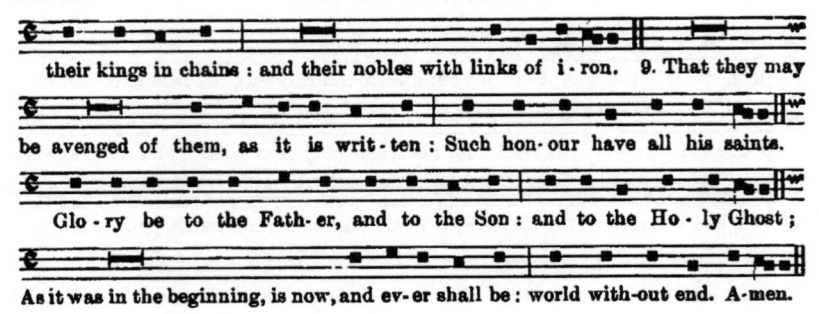

their kings in chains : and their nobles with links of i-ron. 9. That they may

be avenged of them, as it is writ-ten : Such hon-our have all his saints.

Glo-ry be to the Fath-er, and to the Son : and to the Ho-ly Ghost ;

As it was in the beginning, is now, and ev-er shall be : world with-out end. A-men.

PSALM CL.—*Laudate Dominum.*

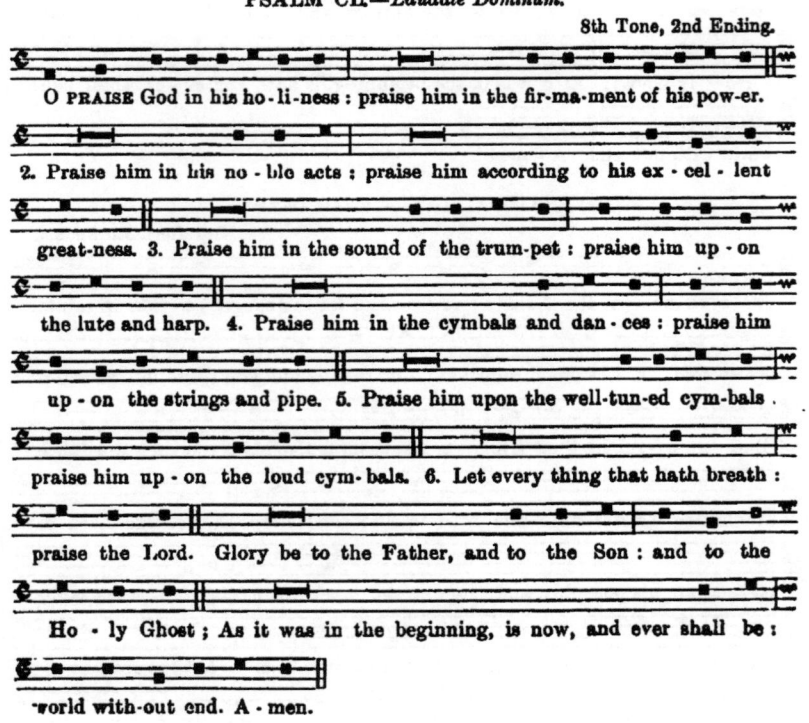

8th Tone, 2nd Ending.

O PRAISE God in his ho-li-ness : praise him in the fir-ma-ment of his pow-er.

2. Praise him in his no-ble acts : praise him according to his ex-cel-lent

great-ness. 3. Praise him in the sound of the trum-pet : praise him up-on

the lute and harp. 4. Praise him in the cymbals and dan-ces : praise him

up-on the strings and pipe. 5. Praise him upon the well-tun-ed cym-bals :

praise him up-on the loud cym-bals. 6. Let every thing that hath breath :

praise the Lord. Glory be to the Father, and to the Son : and to the

Ho-ly Ghost ; As it was in the beginning, is now, and ever shall be :

world with-out end. A-men.

PROPER PSALMS

ON CERTAIN DAYS.

CHRISTMAS DAY.

MORNING PRAYER.

PSALM XIX.—*Cœli enarrant.*

3rd Tone, 5th Ending.

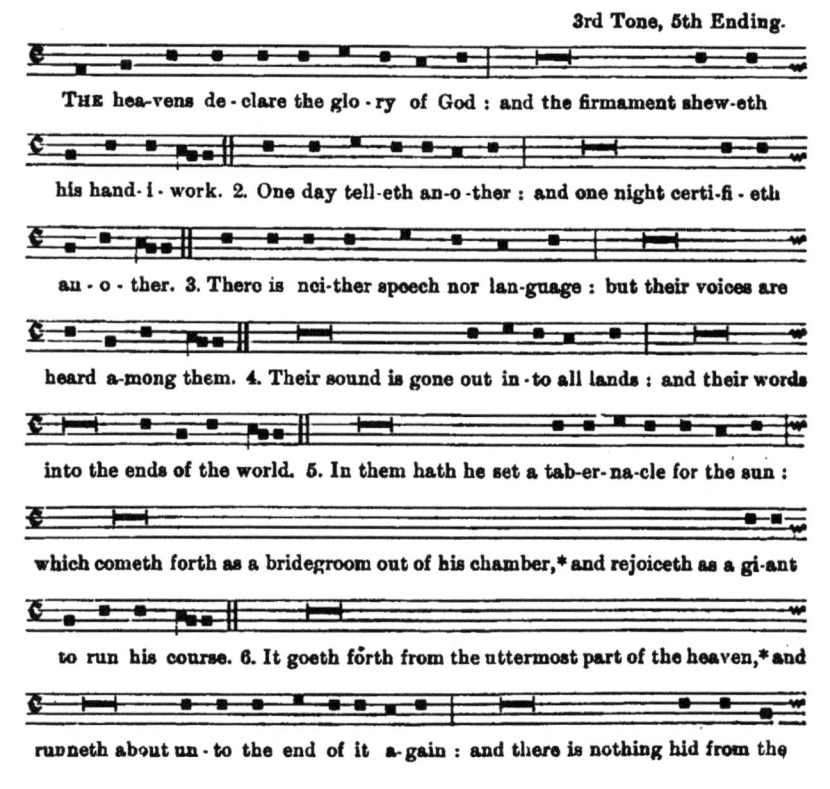

THE hea-vens de - clare the glo - ry of God : and the firmament shew-eth

his hand- i - work. 2. One day tell-eth an-o -ther : and one night certi-fi - eth

an - o - ther. 3. There is nei-ther speech nor lan-guage : but their voices are

heard a-mong them. 4. Their sound is gone out in-to all lands : and their words

into the ends of the world. 5. In them hath he set a tab-er-na-cle for the sun :

which cometh forth as a bridegroom out of his chamber,* and rejoiceth as a gi-ant

to run his course. 6. It goeth forth from the uttermost part of the heaven,* and

runneth about un - to the end of it a-gain : and there is nothing hid from the

PROPER PSALMS.

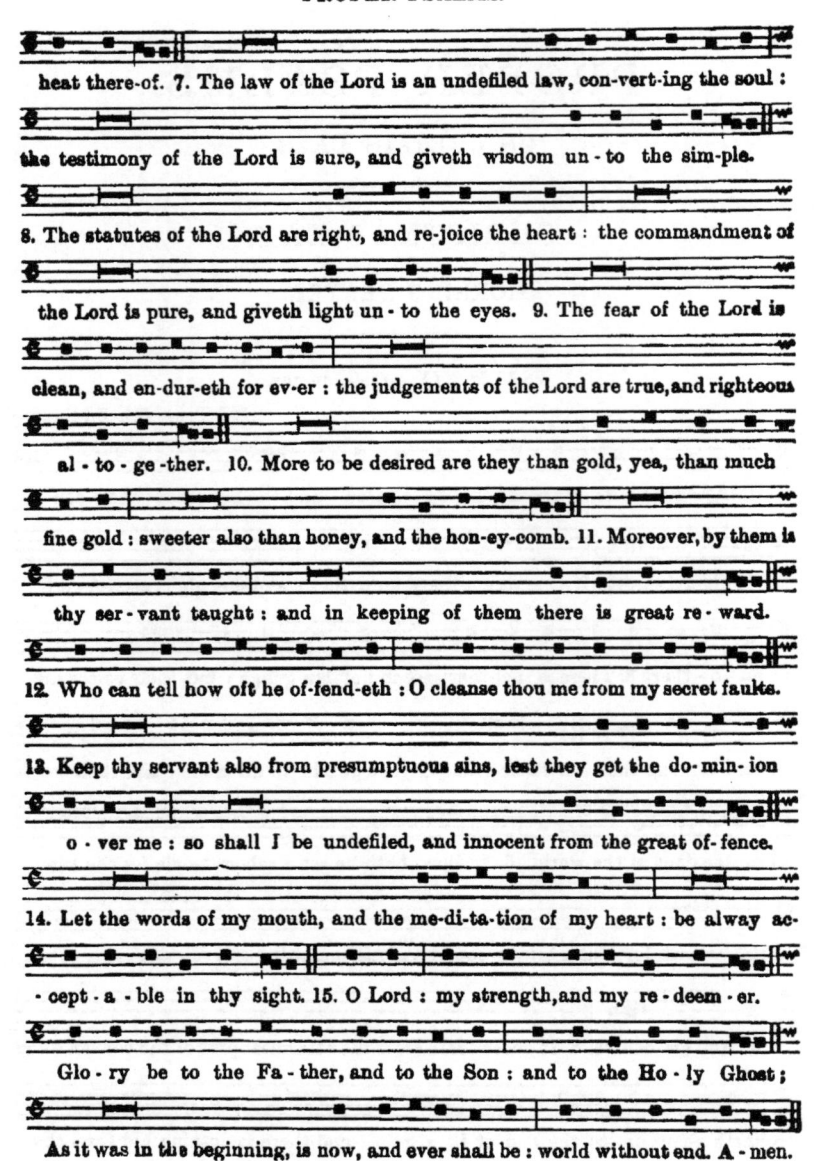

heat there-of. 7. The law of the Lord is an undefiled law, con-vert-ing the soul :

the testimony of the Lord is sure, and giveth wisdom un-to the sim-ple.

8. The statutes of the Lord are right, and re-joice the heart : the commandment of

the Lord is pure, and giveth light un-to the eyes. 9. The fear of the Lord is

clean, and en-dur-eth for ev-er : the judgements of the Lord are true, and righteous

al-to-ge-ther. 10. More to be desired are they than gold, yea, than much

fine gold : sweeter also than honey, and the hon-ey-comb. 11. Moreover, by them is

thy ser-vant taught : and in keeping of them there is great re-ward.

12. Who can tell how oft he of-fend-eth : O cleanse thou me from my secret faults.

13. Keep thy servant also from presumptuous sins, lest they get the do-min-ion

o-ver me : so shall I be undefiled, and innocent from the great of-fence.

14. Let the words of my mouth, and the me-di-ta-tion of my heart : be alway ac-

-cept-a-ble in thy sight. 15. O Lord : my strength, and my re-deem-er.

Glo-ry be to the Fa-ther, and to the Son : and to the Ho-ly Ghost ;

As it was in the beginning, is now, and ever shall be : world without end. A-men.

CHRISTMAS DAY—MORNING.

PSALM XLV.—*Eructavit cor meum.*

8th Tone, 2nd Ending.

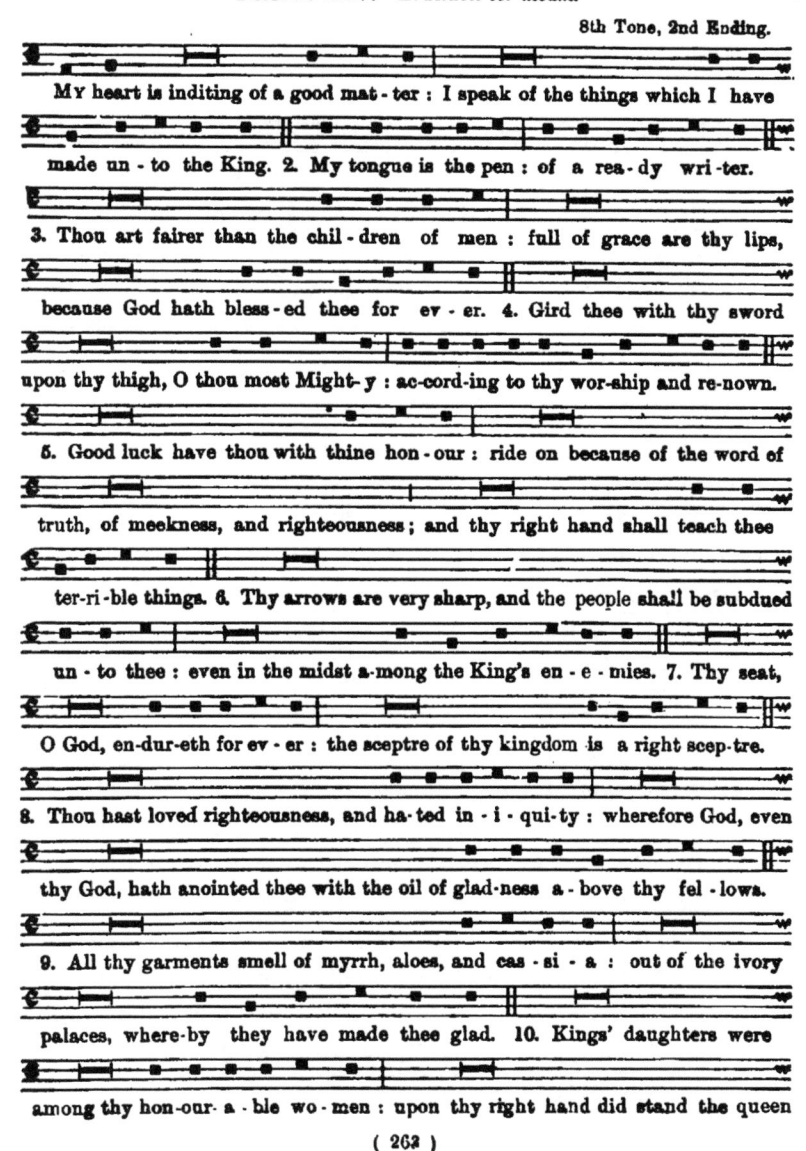

My heart is inditing of a good mat-ter : I speak of the things which I have made un-to the King. 2. My tongue is the pen : of a rea-dy wri-ter.

3. Thou art fairer than the chil-dren of men : full of grace are thy lips, because God hath bless-ed thee for ev-er. 4. Gird thee with thy sword upon thy thigh, O thou most Might-y : ac-cord-ing to thy wor-ship and re-nown.

5. Good luck have thou with thine hon-our : ride on because of the word of truth, of meekness, and righteousness ; and thy right hand shall teach thee ter-ri-ble things. 6. Thy arrows are very sharp, and the people shall be subdued un-to thee : even in the midst a-mong the King's en-e-mies. 7. Thy seat, O God, en-dur-eth for ev-er : the sceptre of thy kingdom is a right scep-tre.

8. Thou hast loved righteousness, and ha-ted in-i-qui-ty : wherefore God, even thy God, hath anointed thee with the oil of glad-ness a-bove thy fel-lows.

9. All thy garments smell of myrrh, aloes, and cas-si-a : out of the ivory palaces, where-by they have made thee glad. 10. Kings' daughters were among thy hon-our-a-ble wo-men : upon thy right hand did stand the queen

PROPER PSALMS.

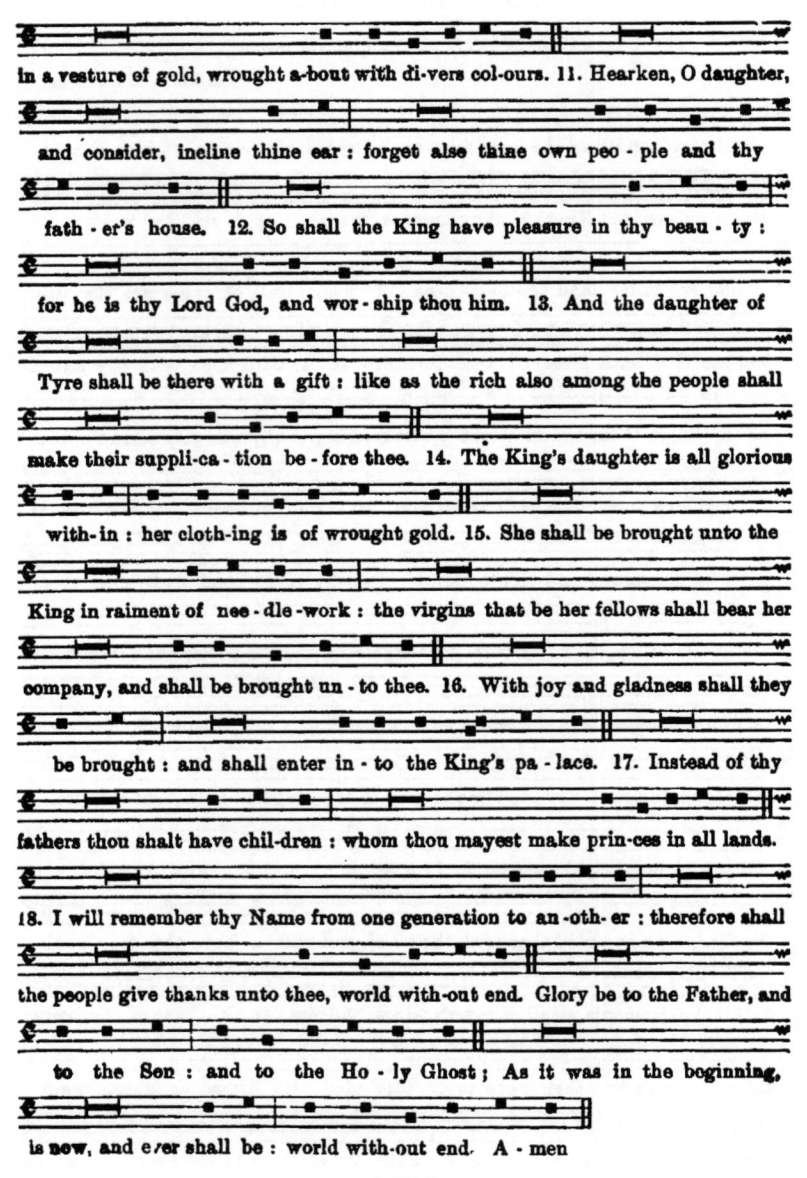

in a vesture of gold, wrought a-bout with di-vers col-ours. 11. Hearken, O daughter, and consider, incline thine ear: forget also thine own peo - ple and thy fath - er's house. 12. So shall the King have pleasure in thy beau - ty: for he is thy Lord God, and wor - ship thou him. 13. And the daughter of Tyre shall be there with a gift: like as the rich also among the people shall make their suppli-ca - tion be - fore thee. 14. The King's daughter is all glorious with-in: her cloth-ing is of wrought gold. 15. She shall be brought unto the King in raiment of nee - dle -work: the virgins that be her fellows shall bear her company, and shall be brought un - to thee. 16. With joy and gladness shall they be brought: and shall enter in - to the King's pa - lace. 17. Instead of thy fathers thou shalt have chil-dren: whom thou mayest make prin-ces in all lands. 18. I will remember thy Name from one generation to an -oth- er: therefore shall the people give thanks unto thee, world with-out end. Glory be to the Father, and to the Son: and to the Ho - ly Ghost; As it was in the beginning, is now, and ever shall be: world with-out end. A - men

CHRISTMAS DAY—MORNING.
PSALM LXXXV.—*Benedixisti, Domine.*

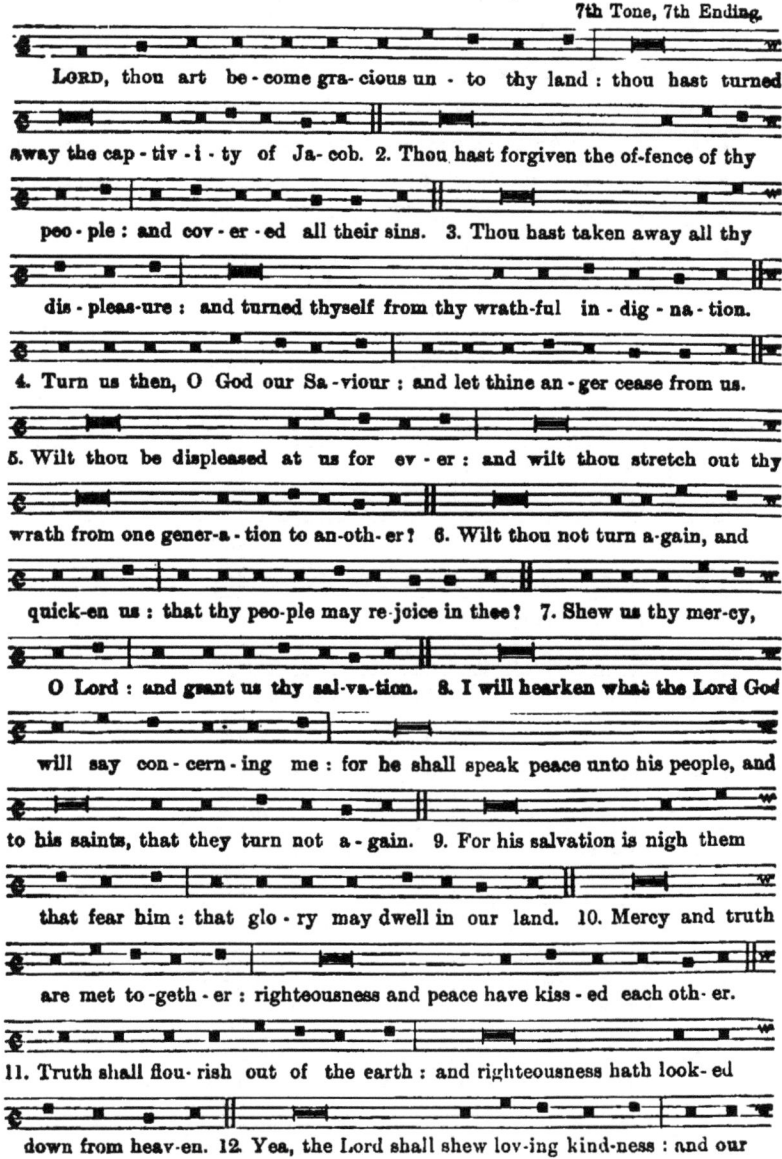

7th Tone, 7th Ending.

LORD, thou art be-come gra-cious un-to thy land : thou hast turned away the cap-tiv-i-ty of Ja-cob. 2. Thou hast forgiven the of-fence of thy peo-ple : and cov-er-ed all their sins. 3. Thou hast taken away all thy dis-pleas-ure : and turned thyself from thy wrath-ful in-dig-na-tion. 4. Turn us then, O God our Sa-viour : and let thine an-ger cease from us. 5. Wilt thou be displeased at us for ev-er : and wilt thou stretch out thy wrath from one gener-a-tion to an-oth-er? 6. Wilt thou not turn a-gain, and quick-en us : that thy peo-ple may re-joice in thee? 7. Shew us thy mer-cy, O Lord : and grant us thy sal-va-tion. 8. I will hearken what the Lord God will say con-cern-ing me : for he shall speak peace unto his people, and to his saints, that they turn not a-gain. 9. For his salvation is nigh them that fear him : that glo-ry may dwell in our land. 10. Mercy and truth are met to-geth-er : righteousness and peace have kiss-ed each oth-er. 11. Truth shall flou-rish out of the earth : and righteousness hath look-ed down from heav-en. 12. Yea, the Lord shall shew lov-ing kind-ness : and our

PROPER PSALMS.

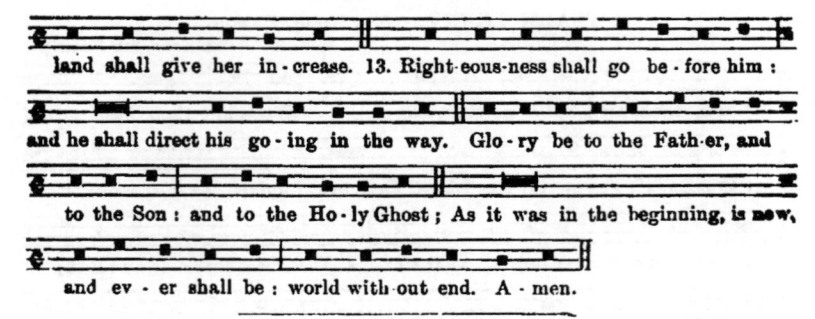

land shall give her in-crease. 13. Right-eous-ness shall go be-fore him:

and he shall direct his go-ing in the way. Glo-ry be to the Fath-er, and

to the Son: and to the Ho-ly Ghost; As it was in the beginning, is now,

and ev-er shall be: world with-out end. A-men.

EVENING PRAYER.

PSALM LXXXIX.—*Misericordias Domini.*

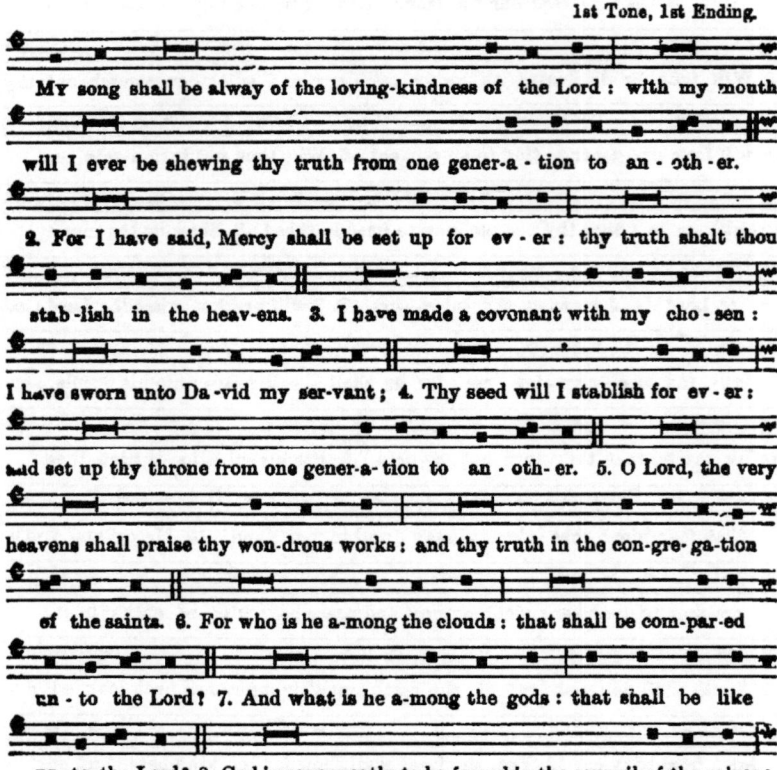

1st Tone, 1st Ending.

My song shall be alway of the loving-kindness of the Lord: with my mouth

will I ever be shewing thy truth from one gener-a-tion to an-oth-er.

2. For I have said, Mercy shall be set up for ev-er: thy truth shalt thou

stab-lish in the heav-ens. 3. I have made a covonant with my cho-sen:

I have sworn unto Da-vid my ser-vant; 4. Thy seed will I stablish for ev-er:

and set up thy throne from one gener-a-tion to an-oth-er. 5. O Lord, the very

heavens shall praise thy won-drous works: and thy truth in the con-gre-ga-tion

of the saints. 6. For who is he a-mong the clouds: that shall be com-par-ed

un-to the Lord? 7. And what is he a-mong the gods: that shall be like

un-to the Lord? 8. God is very greatly to be feared in the council of the saints:

CHRISTMAS DAY—EVENING.

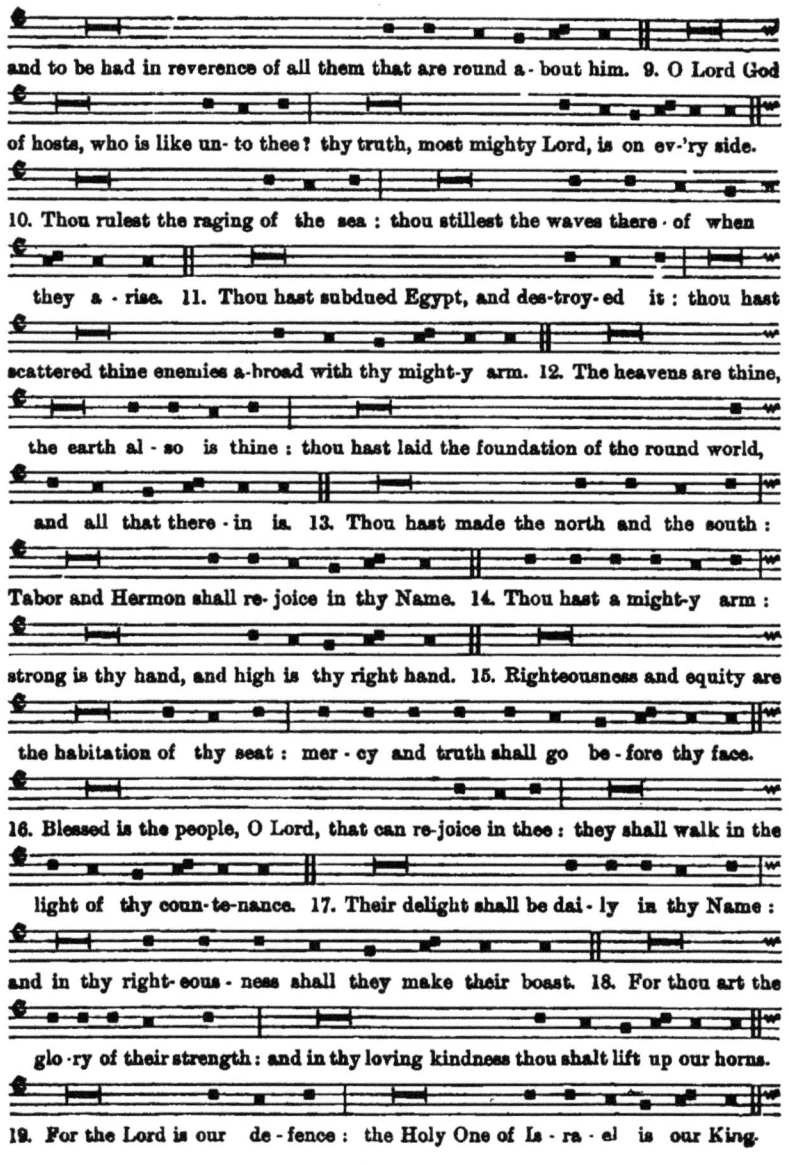

and to be had in reverence of all them that are round a-bout him. 9. O Lord God of hosts, who is like un-to thee? thy truth, most mighty Lord, is on ev-'ry side. 10. Thou rulest the raging of the sea : thou stillest the waves there-of when they a-rise. 11. Thou hast subdued Egypt, and des-troy-ed it : thou hast scattered thine enemies a-broad with thy might-y arm. 12. The heavens are thine, the earth al-so is thine : thou hast laid the foundation of the round world, and all that there-in is. 13. Thou hast made the north and the south : Tabor and Hermon shall re-joice in thy Name. 14. Thou hast a might-y arm : strong is thy hand, and high is thy right hand. 15. Righteousness and equity are the habitation of thy seat : mer-cy and truth shall go be-fore thy face. 16. Blessed is the people, O Lord, that can re-joice in thee : they shall walk in the light of thy coun-te-nance. 17. Their delight shall be dai-ly in thy Name : and in thy right-eous-ness shall they make their boast. 18. For thou art the glo-ry of their strength : and in thy loving kindness thou shalt lift up our horns. 19. For the Lord is our de-fence : the Holy One of Is-ra-el is our King.

PROPER PSALMS.

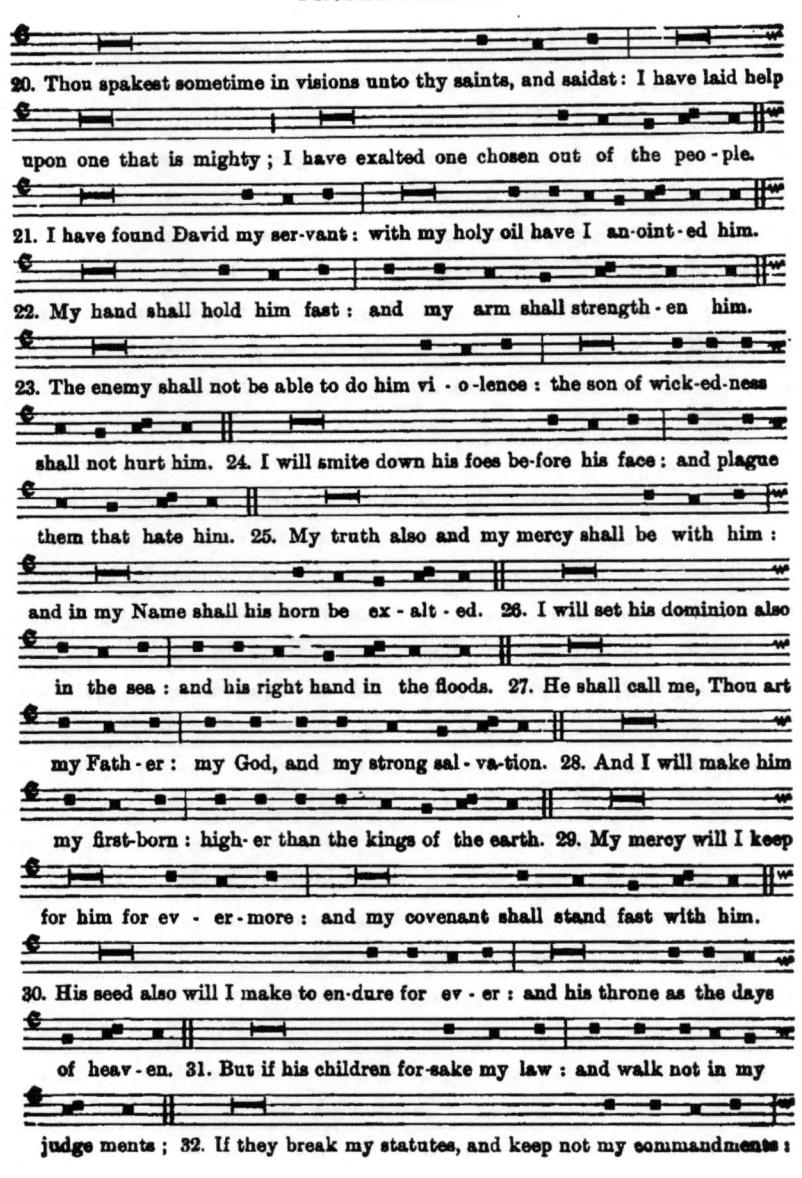

20. Thou spakest sometime in visions unto thy saints, and saidst: I have laid help upon one that is mighty; I have exalted one chosen out of the peo-ple.

21. I have found David my ser-vant: with my holy oil have I an-oint-ed him.

22. My hand shall hold him fast: and my arm shall strength-en him.

23. The enemy shall not be able to do him vi-o-lence: the son of wick-ed-ness shall not hurt him. 24. I will smite down his foes be-fore his face: and plague them that hate him. 25. My truth also and my mercy shall be with him: and in my Name shall his horn be ex-alt-ed. 26. I will set his dominion also in the sea: and his right hand in the floods. 27. He shall call me, Thou art my Fath-er: my God, and my strong sal-va-tion. 28. And I will make him my first-born: high-er than the kings of the earth. 29. My mercy will I keep for him for ev-er-more: and my covenant shall stand fast with him.

30. His seed also will I make to en-dure for ev-er: and his throne as the days of heav-en. 31. But if his children for-sake my law: and walk not in my judge ments; 32. If they break my statutes, and keep not my commandments:

CHRISTMAS DAY—EVENING.

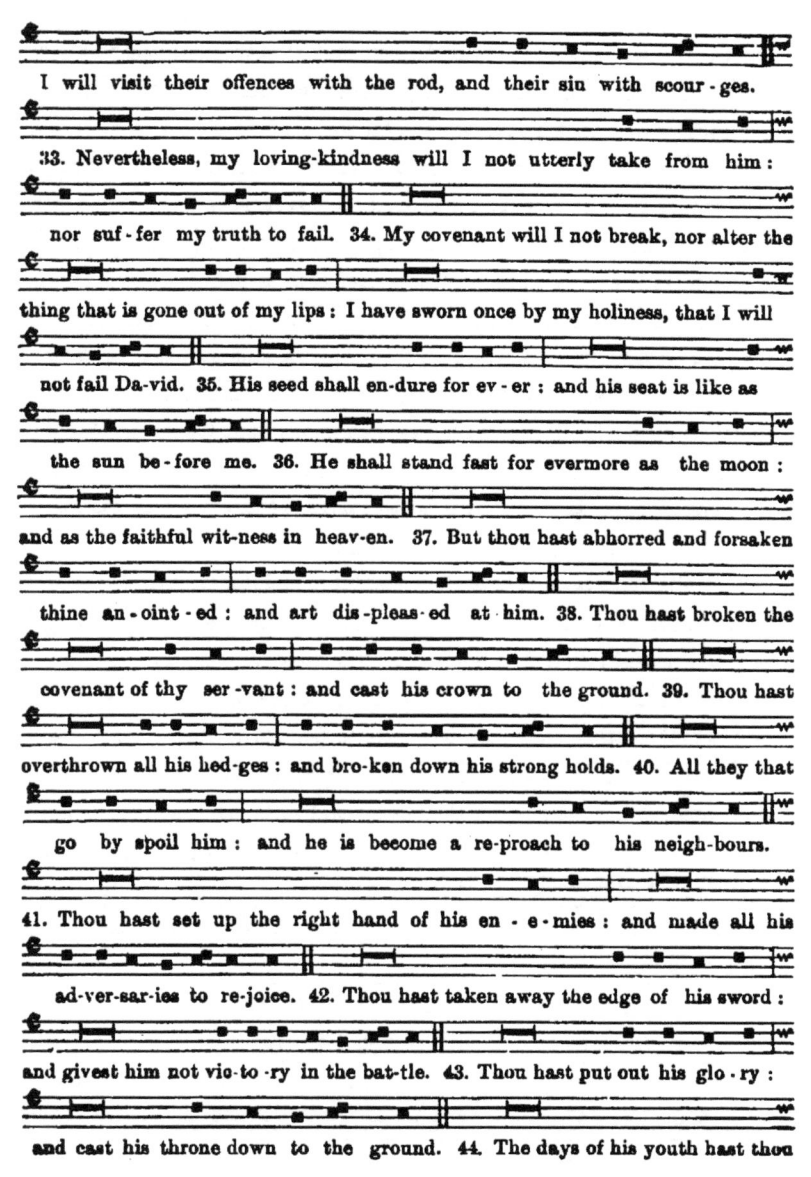

I will visit their offences with the rod, and their sin with scour-ges.

33. Nevertheless, my loving-kindness will I not utterly take from him: nor suf-fer my truth to fail. 34. My covenant will I not break, nor alter the thing that is gone out of my lips: I have sworn once by my holiness, that I will not fail Da-vid. 35. His seed shall en-dure for ev-er: and his seat is like as the sun be-fore me. 36. He shall stand fast for evermore as the moon: and as the faithful wit-ness in heav-en. 37. But thou hast abhorred and forsaken thine an-oint-ed: and art dis-pleas-ed at him. 38. Thou hast broken the covenant of thy ser-vant: and cast his crown to the ground. 39. Thou hast overthrown all his hed-ges: and bro-ken down his strong holds. 40. All they that go by spoil him: and he is become a re-proach to his neigh-bours. 41. Thou hast set up the right hand of his en-e-mies: and made all his ad-ver-sar-ies to re-joice. 42. Thou hast taken away the edge of his sword: and givest him not vic-to-ry in the bat-tle. 43. Thou hast put out his glo-ry: and cast his throne down to the ground. 44. The days of his youth hast thou

PROPER PSALMS.

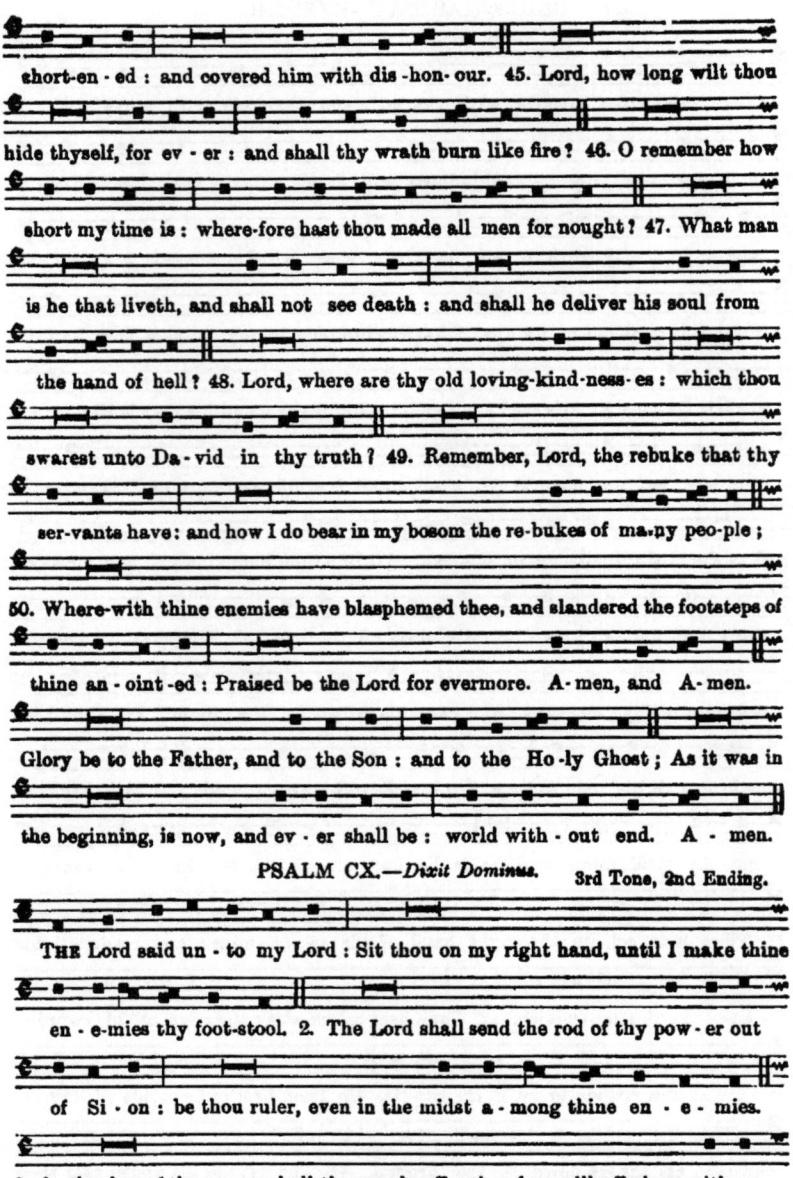

short-en-ed : and covered him with dis-hon-our. 45. Lord, how long wilt thou hide thyself, for ev-er : and shall thy wrath burn like fire? 46. O remember how short my time is : where-fore hast thou made all men for nought? 47. What man is he that liveth, and shall not see death : and shall he deliver his soul from the hand of hell? 48. Lord, where are thy old loving-kind-ness-es : which thou swarest unto Da-vid in thy truth? 49. Remember, Lord, the rebuke that thy ser-vants have: and how I do bear in my bosom the re-bukes of ma-ny peo-ple ; 50. Where-with thine enemies have blasphemed thee, and slandered the footsteps of thine an-oint-ed : Praised be the Lord for evermore. A-men, and A-men.

Glory be to the Father, and to the Son : and to the Ho-ly Ghost ; As it was in the beginning, is now, and ev-er shall be : world with-out end. A-men.

PSALM CX.—*Dixit Dominus.*   3rd Tone, 2nd Ending.

THE Lord said un-to my Lord : Sit thou on my right hand, until I make thine en-e-mies thy foot-stool. 2. The Lord shall send the rod of thy pow-er out of Si-on : be thou ruler, even in the midst a-mong thine en-e-mies.

3. In the day of thy power shall the people offer thee free-will offerings with an

CHRISTMAS DAY—EVENING.

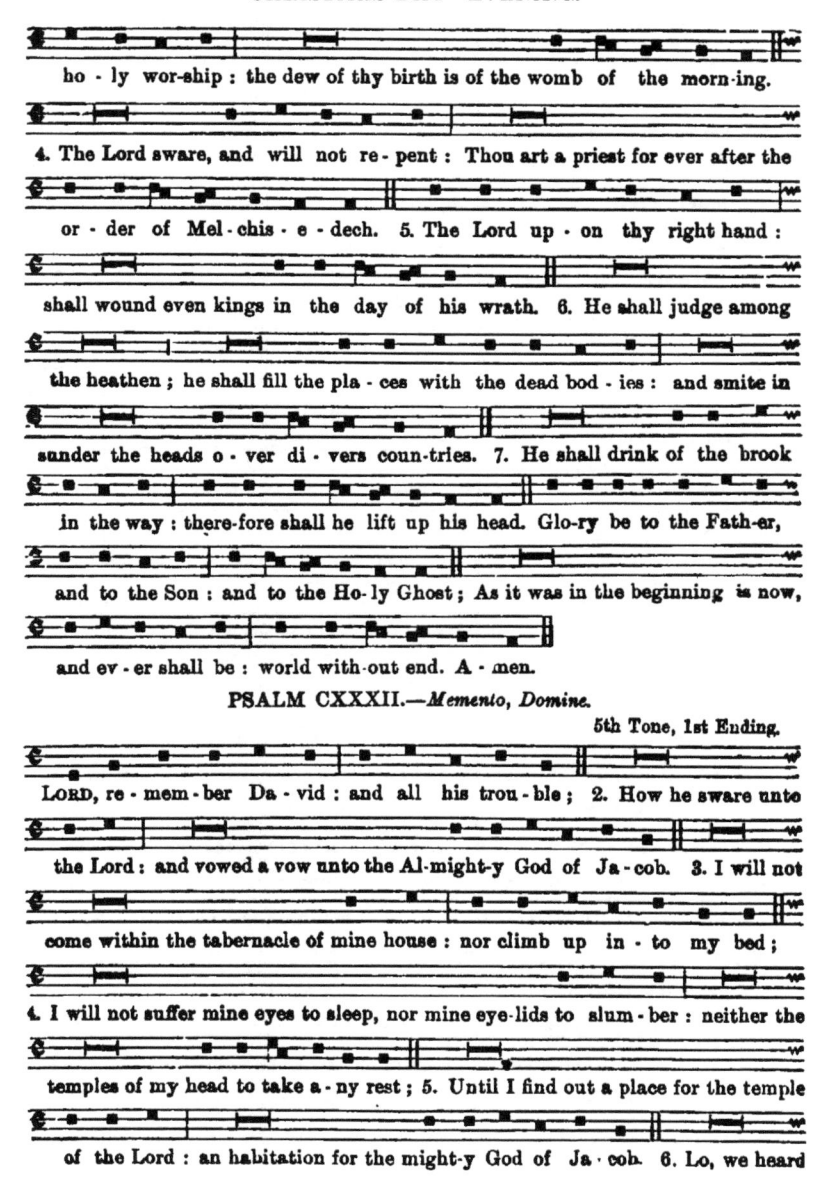

ho - ly wor-ship : the dew of thy birth is of the womb of the morn-ing. 4. The Lord sware, and will not re - pent : Thou art a priest for ever after the or - der of Mel - chis - e - dech. 5. The Lord up - on thy right hand : shall wound even kings in the day of his wrath. 6. He shall judge among the heathen; he shall fill the pla - ces with the dead bod - ies : and smite in sunder the heads o - ver di - vers coun-tries. 7. He shall drink of the brook in the way : there-fore shall he lift up his head. Glo-ry be to the Fath-er, and to the Son : and to the Ho-ly Ghost; As it was in the beginning is now, and ev - er shall be : world with-out end. A - men.

PSALM CXXXII.—*Memento, Domine.*

5th Tone, 1st Ending.

LORD, re - mem - ber Da - vid : and all his trou - ble ; 2. How he sware unto the Lord : and vowed a vow unto the Al-might-y God of Ja - cob. 3. I will not come within the tabernacle of mine house : nor climb up in - to my bed; 4. I will not suffer mine eyes to sleep, nor mine eye-lids to slum - ber : neither the temples of my head to take a - ny rest ; 5. Until I find out a place for the temple of the Lord : an habitation for the might-y God of Ja - cob. 6. Lo, we heard

(271)

PROPER PSALMS.

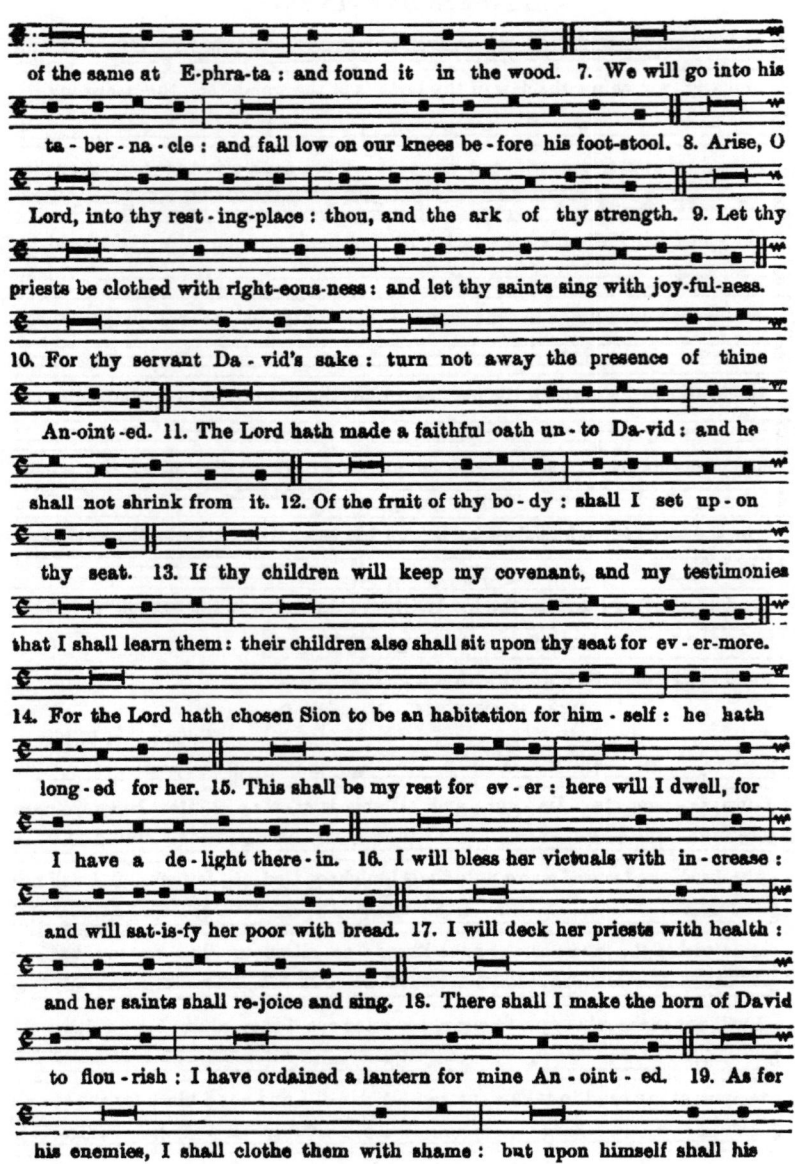

of the same at E-phra-ta : and found it in the wood. 7. We will go into his ta-ber-na-cle : and fall low on our knees be-fore his foot-stool. 8. Arise, O Lord, into thy rest-ing-place : thou, and the ark of thy strength. 9. Let thy priests be clothed with right-eous-ness : and let thy saints sing with joy-ful-ness. 10. For thy servant Da-vid's sake : turn not away the presence of thine An-oint-ed. 11. The Lord hath made a faithful oath un-to Da-vid : and he shall not shrink from it. 12. Of the fruit of thy bo-dy : shall I set up-on thy seat. 13. If thy children will keep my covenant, and my testimonies that I shall learn them : their children also shall sit upon thy seat for ev-er-more. 14. For the Lord hath chosen Sion to be an habitation for him-self : he hath long-ed for her. 15. This shall be my rest for ev-er : here will I dwell, for I have a de-light there-in. 16. I will bless her victuals with in-crease : and will sat-is-fy her poor with bread. 17. I will deck her priests with health : and her saints shall re-joice and sing. 18. There shall I make the horn of David to flou-rish : I have ordained a lantern for mine An-oint-ed. 19. As for his enemies, I shall clothe them with shame : but upon himself shall his

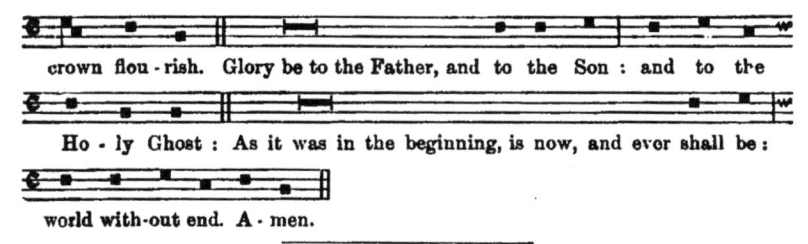

ASH WEDNESDAY—MORNING.

crown flou-rish. Glory be to the Father, and to the Son : and to the Ho-ly Ghost : As it was in the beginning, is now, and ever shall be : world with-out end. A-men.

ASH WEDNESDAY.
MORNING PRAYER.

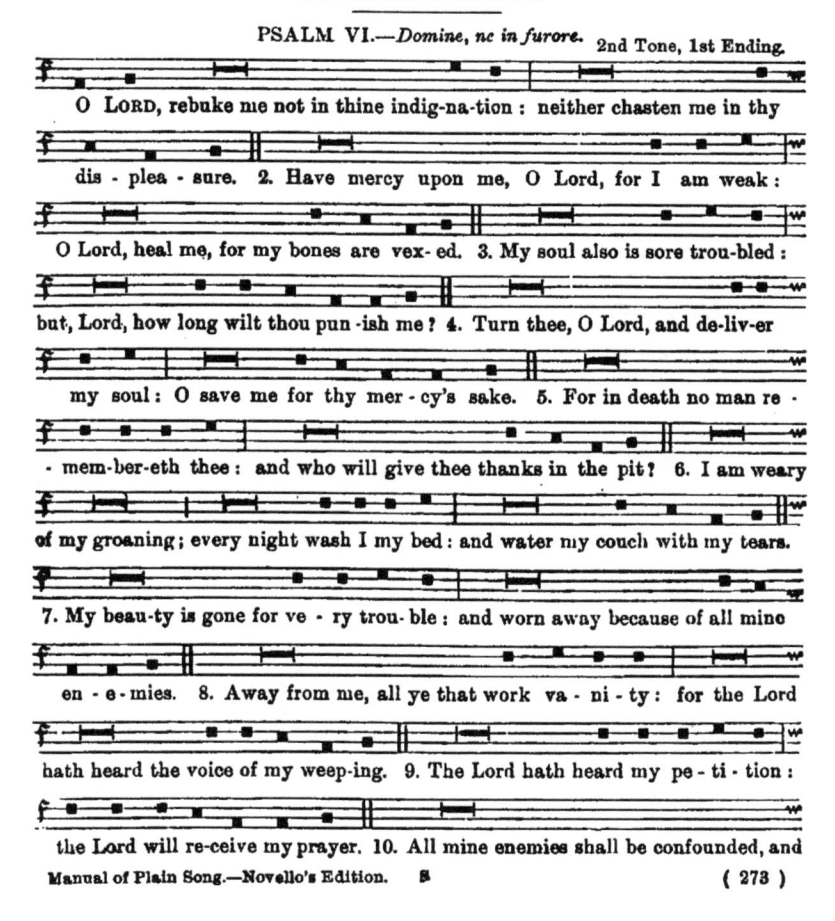

PSALM VI.—*Domine, ne in furore.* 2nd Tone, 1st Ending.

O LORD, rebuke me not in thine indig-na-tion : neither chasten me in thy dis-plea-sure. 2. Have mercy upon me, O Lord, for I am weak : O Lord, heal me, for my bones are vex-ed. 3. My soul also is sore trou-bled : but, Lord, how long wilt thou pun-ish me? 4. Turn thee, O Lord, and de-liv-er my soul : O save me for thy mer-cy's sake. 5. For in death no man re--mem-ber-eth thee : and who will give thee thanks in the pit? 6. I am weary of my groaning; every night wash I my bed : and water my couch with my tears. 7. My beau-ty is gone for ve-ry trou-ble : and worn away because of all mine en-e-mies. 8. Away from me, all ye that work va-ni-ty : for the Lord hath heard the voice of my weep-ing. 9. The Lord hath heard my pe-ti-tion : the Lord will re-ceive my prayer. 10. All mine enemies shall be confounded, and

PROPER PSALMS.

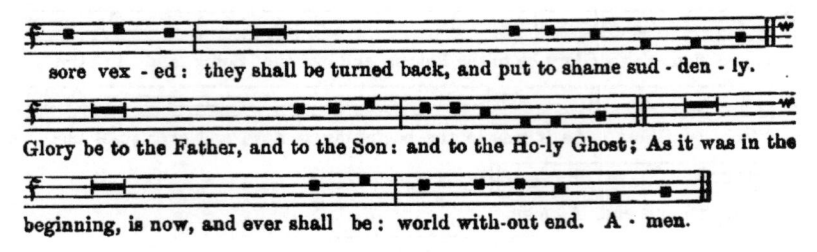

sore vex - ed : they shall be turned back, and put to shame sud - den - ly.

Glory be to the Father, and to the Son : and to the Ho-ly Ghost; As it was in the

beginning, is now, and ever shall be : world with-out end. A - men.

PSALM XXXII.—*Beati, quorum.*

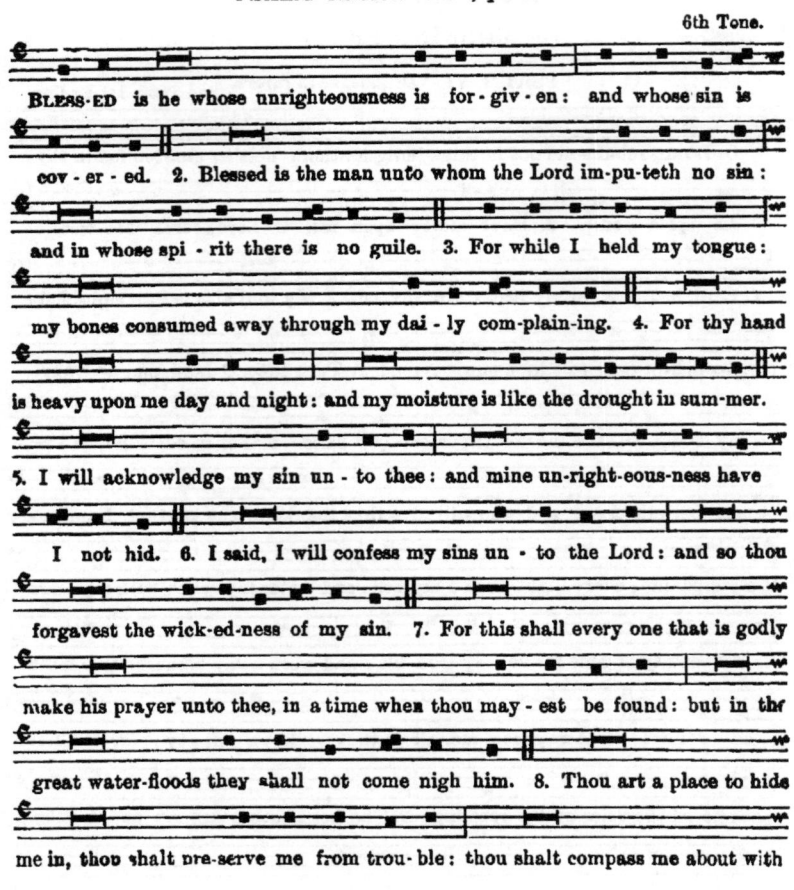

6th Tone.

BLESS-ED is he whose unrighteousness is for - giv - en : and whose sin is

cov - er - ed. 2. Blessed is the man unto whom the Lord im-pu-teth no sin :

and in whose spi - rit there is no guile. 3. For while I held my tongue :

my bones consumed away through my dai - ly com-plain-ing. 4. For thy hand

is heavy upon me day and night : and my moisture is like the drought in sum-mer.

5. I will acknowledge my sin un - to thee : and mine un-right-eous-ness have

I not hid. 6. I said, I will confess my sins un - to the Lord : and so thou

forgavest the wick-ed-ness of my sin. 7. For this shall every one that is godly

make his prayer unto thee, in a time when thou may - est be found : but in the

great water-floods they shall not come nigh him. 8. Thou art a place to hide

me in, thou shalt pre-serve me from trou - ble : thou shalt compass me about with

ASH WEDNESDAY—MORNING.

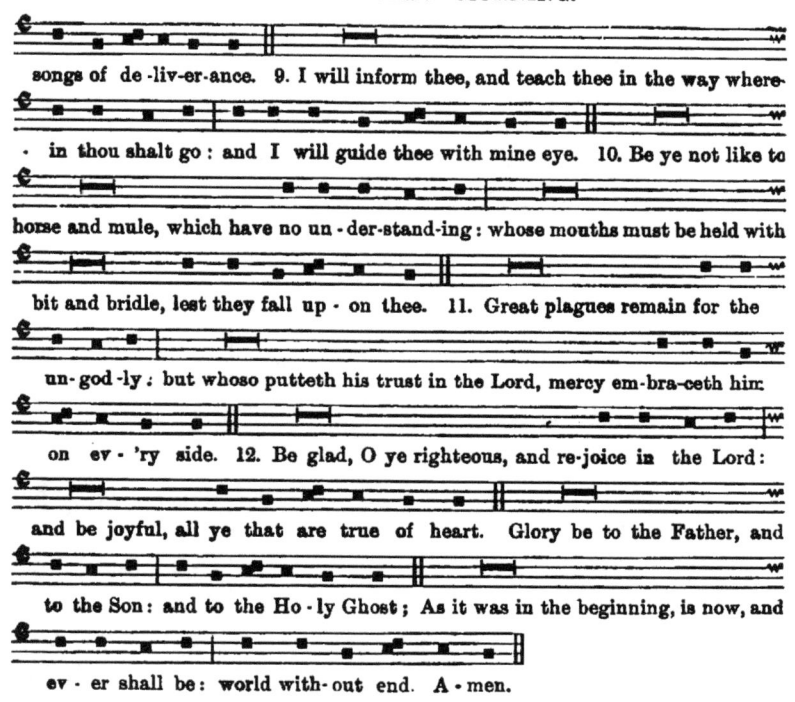

songs of de-liv-er-ance. 9. I will inform thee, and teach thee in the way where- in thou shalt go: and I will guide thee with mine eye. 10. Be ye not like to horse and mule, which have no un-der-stand-ing: whose mouths must be held with bit and bridle, lest they fall up-on thee. 11. Great plagues remain for the un-god-ly; but whoso putteth his trust in the Lord, mercy em-bra-ceth him on ev-'ry side. 12. Be glad, O ye righteous, and re-joice in the Lord: and be joyful, all ye that are true of heart. Glory be to the Father, and to the Son: and to the Ho-ly Ghost; As it was in the beginning, is now, and ev-er shall be: world with-out end. A-men.

PSALM XXXVIII.—*Domine, ne in furore.*

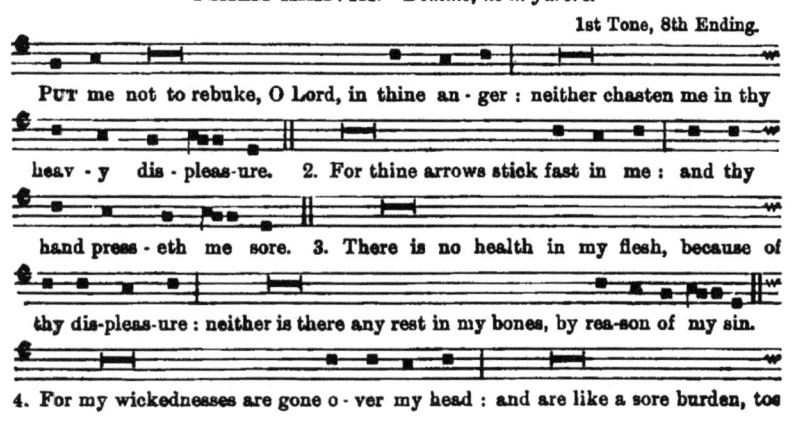

1st Tone, 8th Ending.

PUT me not to rebuke, O Lord, in thine an-ger: neither chasten me in thy heav-y dis-pleas-ure. 2. For thine arrows stick fast in me: and thy hand press-eth me sore. 3. There is no health in my flesh, because of thy dis-pleas-ure: neither is there any rest in my bones, by rea-son of my sin. 4. For my wickednesses are gone o-ver my head: and are like a sore burden, too

PROPER PSALMS.

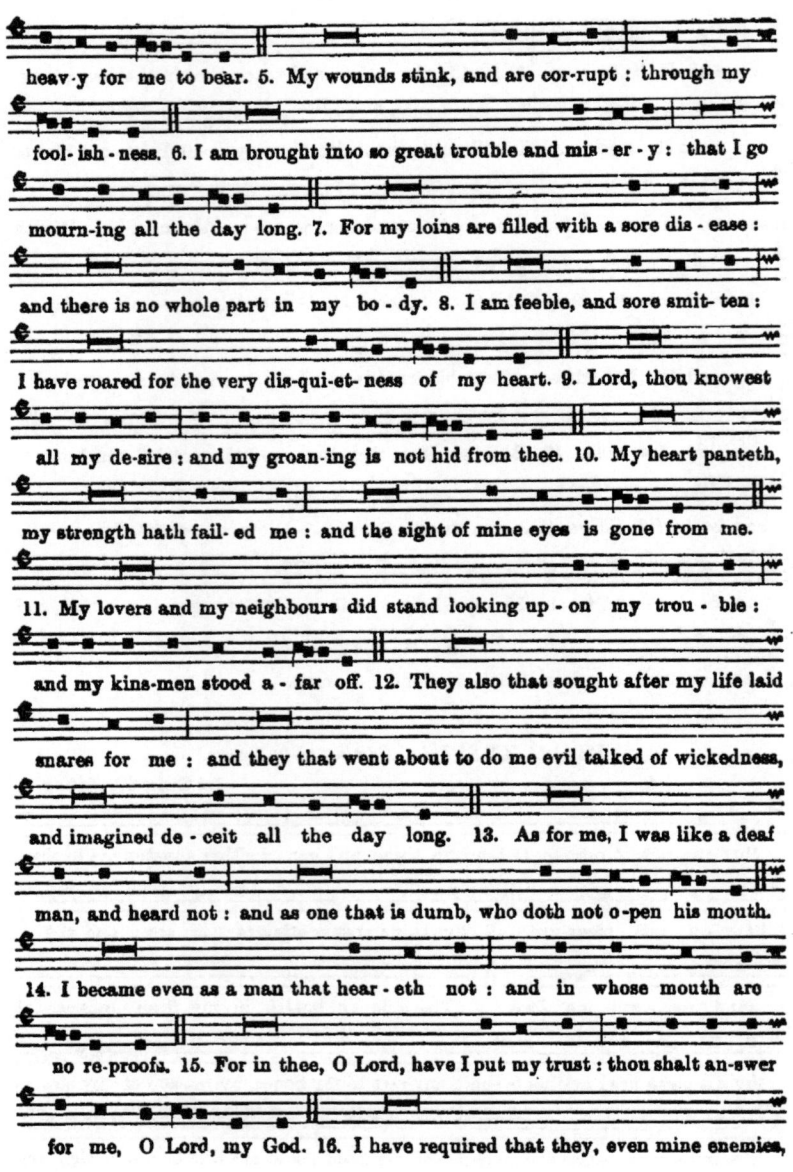

heav-y for me to bear. 5. My wounds stink, and are cor-rupt : through my fool-ish-ness. 6. I am brought into so great trouble and mis-er-y : that I go mourn-ing all the day long. 7. For my loins are filled with a sore dis-ease : and there is no whole part in my bo-dy. 8. I am feeble, and sore smit-ten : I have roared for the very dis-qui-et-ness of my heart. 9. Lord, thou knowest all my de-sire : and my groan-ing is not hid from thee. 10. My heart panteth, my strength hath fail-ed me : and the sight of mine eyes is gone from me. 11. My lovers and my neighbours did stand looking up-on my trou-ble : and my kins-men stood a-far off. 12. They also that sought after my life laid snares for me : and they that went about to do me evil talked of wickedness, and imagined de-ceit all the day long. 13. As for me, I was like a deaf man, and heard not : and as one that is dumb, who doth not o-pen his mouth. 14. I became even as a man that hear-eth not : and in whose mouth are no re-proofs. 15. For in thee, O Lord, have I put my trust : thou shalt an-swer for me, O Lord, my God. 16. I have required that they, even mine enemies,

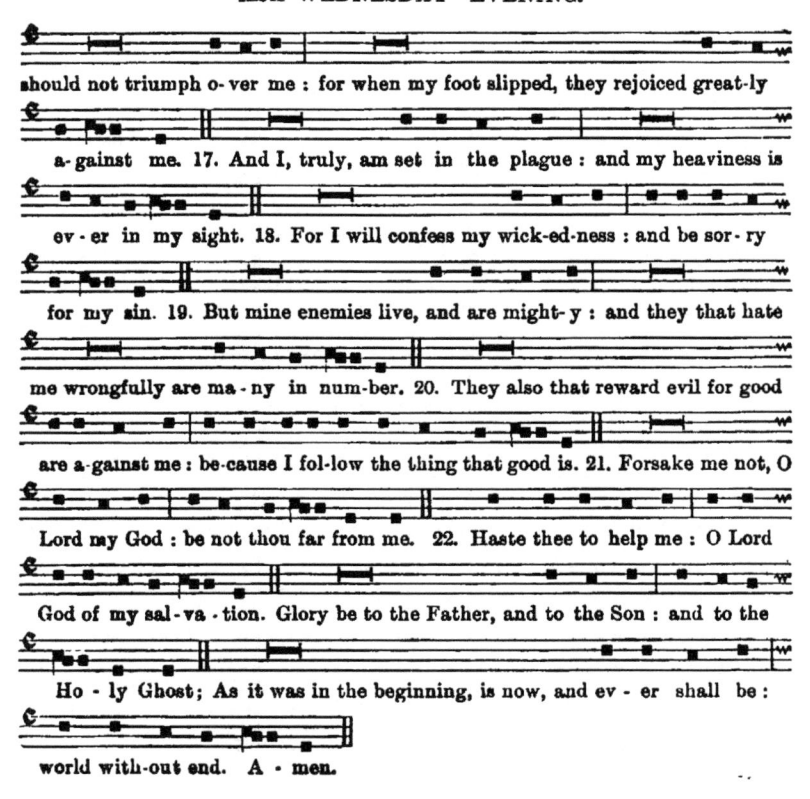

ASH WEDNESDAY—EVENING.

should not triumph o-ver me : for when my foot slipped, they rejoiced great-ly a-gainst me. 17. And I, truly, am set in the plague : and my heaviness is ev-er in my sight. 18. For I will confess my wick-ed-ness : and be sor-ry for my sin. 19. But mine enemies live, and are might-y : and they that hate me wrongfully are ma-ny in num-ber. 20. They also that reward evil for good are a-gainst me : be-cause I fol-low the thing that good is. 21. Forsake me not, O Lord my God : be not thou far from me. 22. Haste thee to help me : O Lord God of my sal-va-tion. Glory be to the Father, and to the Son : and to the Ho-ly Ghost; As it was in the beginning, is now, and ev-er shall be : world with-out end. A-men.

EVENING PRAYER.

PSALM CII.—*Domine, exaudi.*

2nd Tone, 1st Ending.

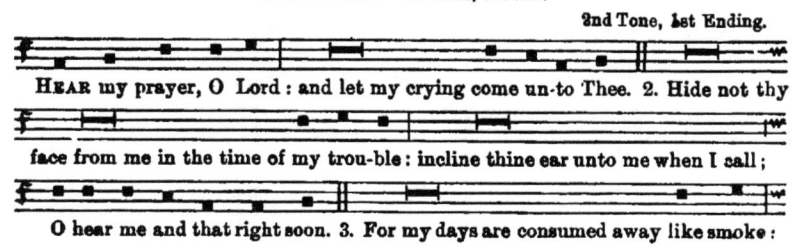

HEAR my prayer, O Lord : and let my crying come un-to Thee. 2. Hide not thy face from me in the time of my trou-ble : incline thine ear unto me when I call; O hear me and that right soon. 3. For my days are consumed away like smoke :

PROPER PSALMS.

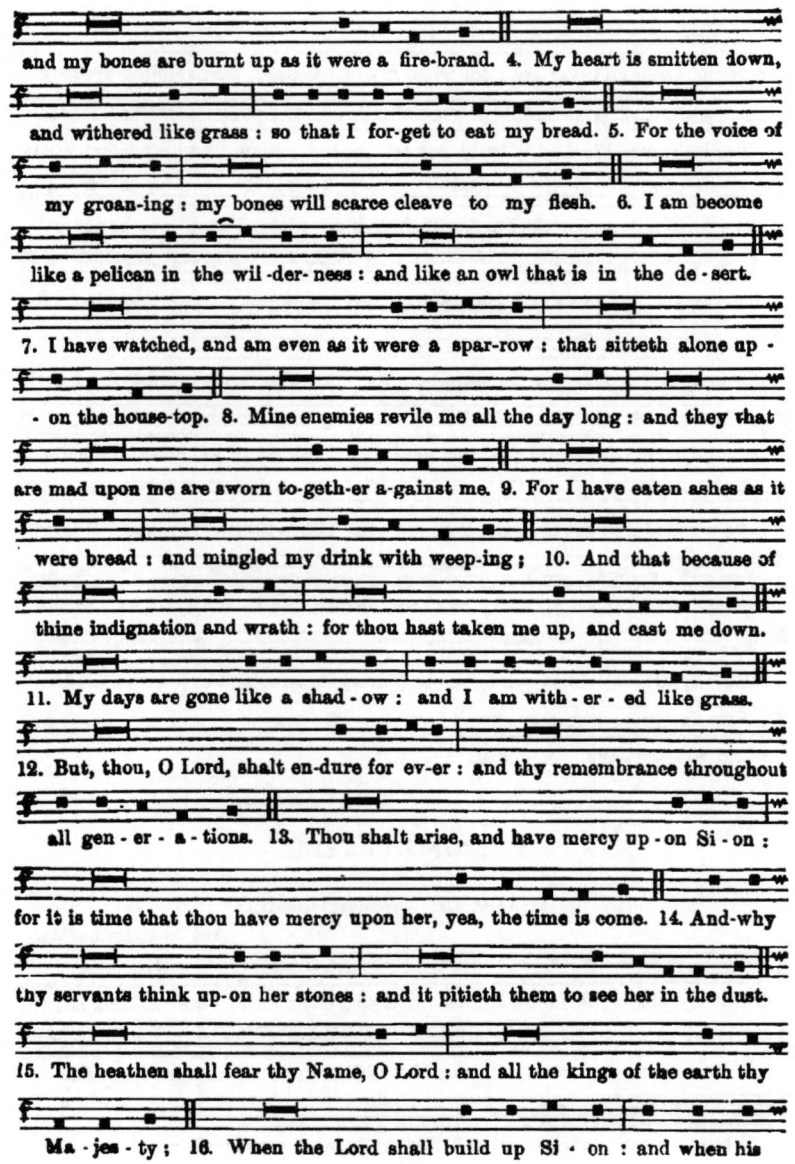

and my bones are burnt up as it were a fire-brand. 4. My heart is smitten down, and withered like grass : so that I for-get to eat my bread. 5. For the voice of my groan-ing : my bones will scarce cleave to my flesh. 6. I am become like a pelican in the wil-der-ness : and like an owl that is in the de-sert. 7. I have watched, and am even as it were a spar-row : that sitteth alone up-on the house-top. 8. Mine enemies revile me all the day long : and they that are mad upon me are sworn to-geth-er a-gainst me. 9. For I have eaten ashes as it were bread : and mingled my drink with weep-ing ; 10. And that because of thine indignation and wrath : for thou hast taken me up, and cast me down. 11. My days are gone like a shad-ow : and I am with-er-ed like grass. 12. But, thou, O Lord, shalt en-dure for ev-er : and thy remembrance throughout all gen-er-a-tions. 13. Thou shalt arise, and have mercy up-on Si-on : for it is time that thou have mercy upon her, yea, the time is come. 14. And-why thy servants think up-on her stones : and it pitieth them to see her in the dust. 15. The heathen shall fear thy Name, O Lord : and all the kings of the earth thy Ma-jes-ty ; 16. When the Lord shall build up Si-on : and when his

ASH WEDNESDAY—EVENING.

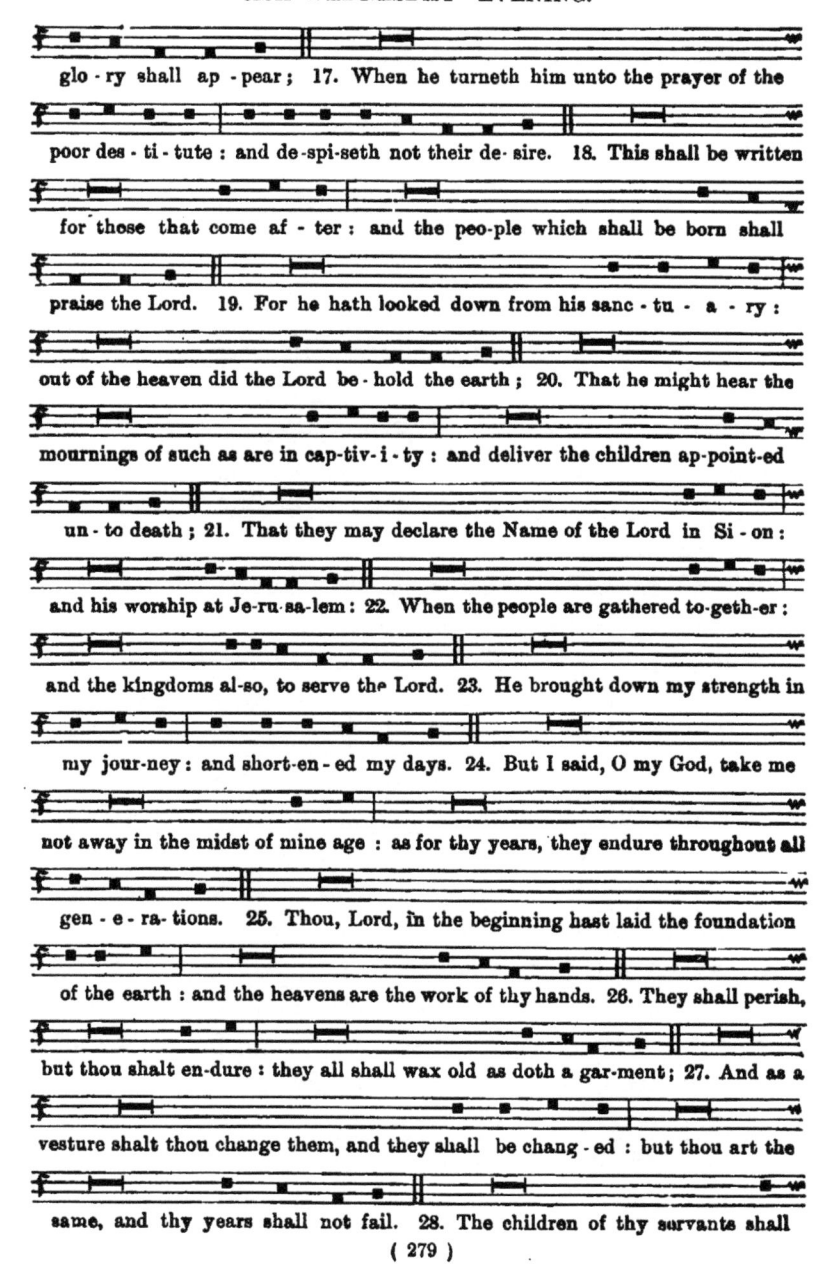

glo - ry shall ap - pear; 17. When he turneth him unto the prayer of the poor des - ti - tute : and de-spi-seth not their de- sire. 18. This shall be written for those that come af - ter : and the peo-ple which shall be born shall praise the Lord. 19. For he hath looked down from his sanc - tu - a - ry : out of the heaven did the Lord be - hold the earth ; 20. That he might hear the mournings of such as are in cap-tiv-i-ty : and deliver the children ap-point-ed un - to death ; 21. That they may declare the Name of the Lord in Si - on : and his worship at Je-ru-sa-lem : 22. When the people are gathered to-geth-er : and the kingdoms al-so, to serve the Lord. 23. He brought down my strength in my jour-ney : and short-en - ed my days. 24. But I said, O my God, take me not away in the midst of mine age : as for thy years, they endure throughout all gen - e - ra- tions. 25. Thou, Lord, in the beginning hast laid the foundation of the earth : and the heavens are the work of thy hands. 26. They shall perish, but thou shalt en-dure : they all shall wax old as doth a gar-ment; 27. And as a vesture shalt thou change them, and they shall be chang - ed : but thou art the same, and thy years shall not fail. 28. The children of thy servants shall

PROPER PSALMS.

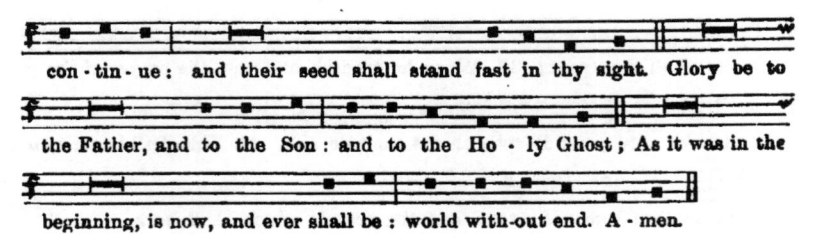

con-tin-ue: and their seed shall stand fast in thy sight. Glory be to the Father, and to the Son: and to the Ho-ly Ghost; As it was in the beginning, is now, and ever shall be: world with-out end. A-men.

PSALM CXXX.—*De profundis.*

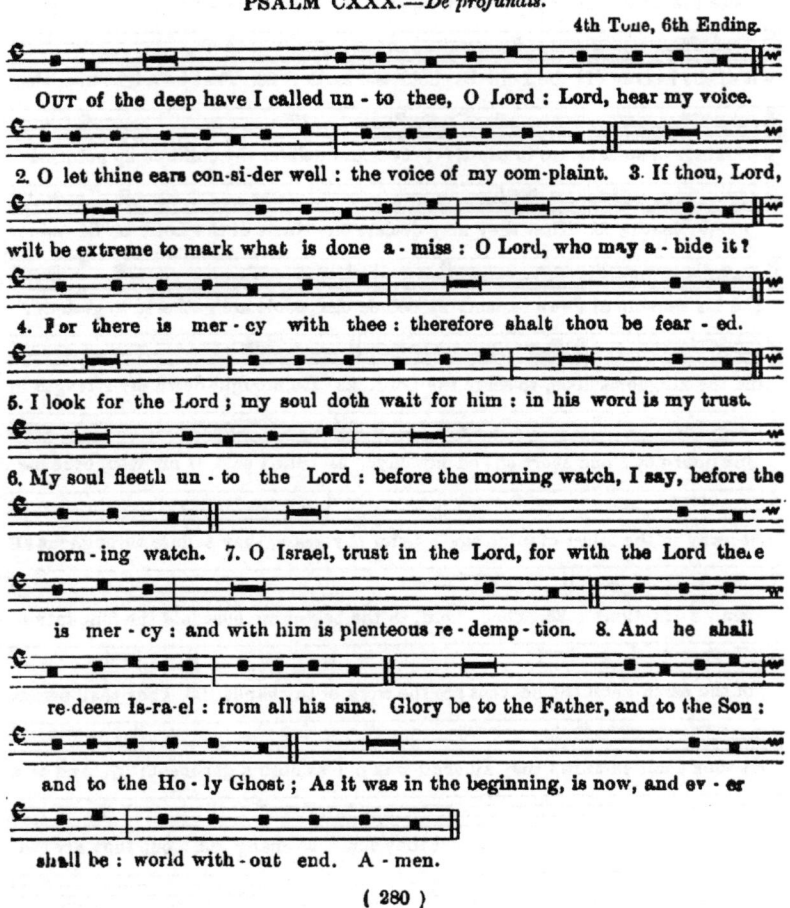

4th Tone, 6th Ending.

Out of the deep have I called un-to thee, O Lord: Lord, hear my voice. 2. O let thine ears con-si-der well: the voice of my com-plaint. 3. If thou, Lord, wilt be extreme to mark what is done a-miss: O Lord, who may a-bide it? 4. For there is mer-cy with thee: therefore shalt thou be fear-ed. 5. I look for the Lord; my soul doth wait for him: in his word is my trust. 6. My soul fleeth un-to the Lord: before the morning watch, I say, before the morn-ing watch. 7. O Israel, trust in the Lord, for with the Lord there is mer-cy: and with him is plenteous re-demp-tion. 8. And he shall re-deem Is-ra-el: from all his sins. Glory be to the Father, and to the Son: and to the Ho-ly Ghost; As it was in the beginning, is now, and ev-er shall be: world with-out end. A-men.

ASH WEDNESDAY—EVENING.

PSALM CXLIII.—*Domine, exaudi.*

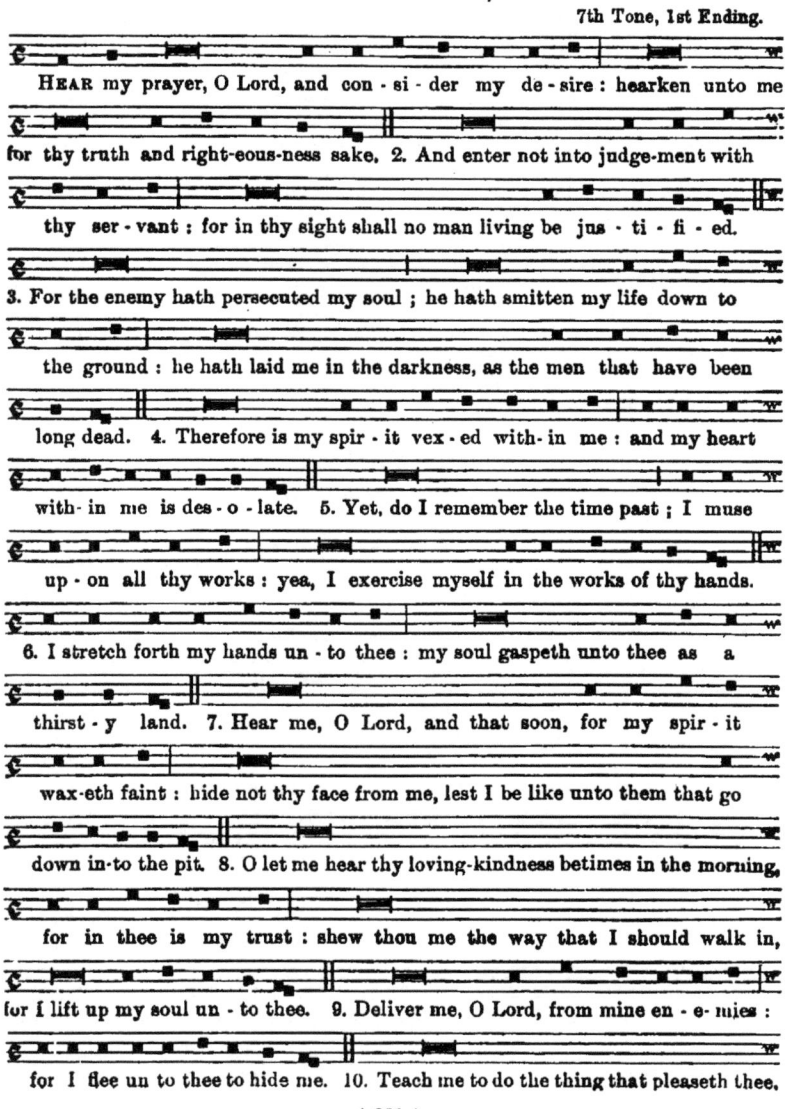

7th Tone, 1st Ending.

HEAR my prayer, O Lord, and con - si - der my de - sire : hearken unto me

for thy truth and right-eous-ness sake. 2. And enter not into judge-ment with

thy ser - vant : for in thy sight shall no man living be jus - ti - fi - ed.

3. For the enemy hath persecuted my soul ; he hath smitten my life down to

the ground : he hath laid me in the darkness, as the men that have been

long dead. 4. Therefore is my spir - it vex - ed with- in me : and my heart

with- in me is des - o - late. 5. Yet, do I remember the time past ; I muse

up - on all thy works : yea, I exercise myself in the works of thy hands.

6. I stretch forth my hands un - to thee : my soul gaspeth unto thee as a

thirst - y land. 7. Hear me, O Lord, and that soon, for my spir - it

wax-eth faint : hide not thy face from me, lest I be like unto them that go

down in-to the pit. 8. O let me hear thy loving-kindness betimes in the morning,

for in thee is my trust : shew thou me the way that I should walk in,

for I lift up my soul un - to thee. 9. Deliver me, O Lord, from mine en - e - mies :

for I flee un to thee to hide me. 10. Teach me to do the thing that pleaseth thee,

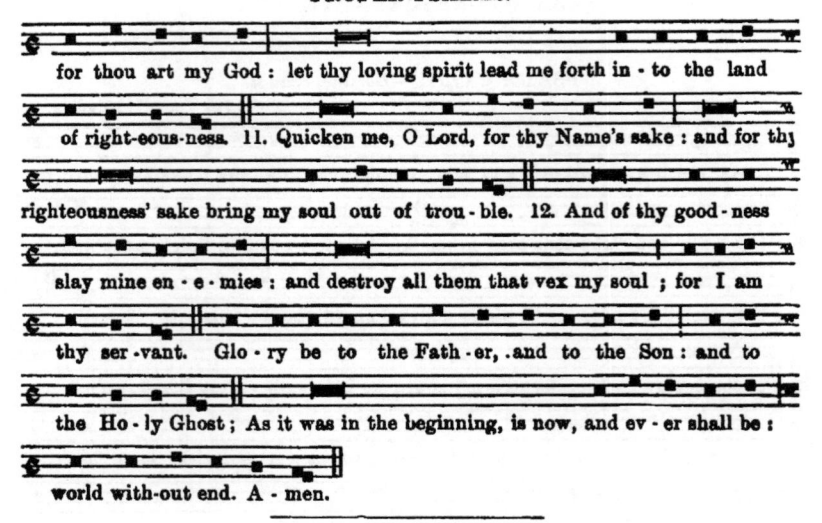

PROPER PSALMS.

for thou art my God : let thy loving spirit lead me forth in-to the land of right-eous-ness. 11. Quicken me, O Lord, for thy Name's sake : and for thy righteousness' sake bring my soul out of trou-ble. 12. And of thy good-ness slay mine en-e-mies : and destroy all them that vex my soul ; for I am thy ser-vant. Glo-ry be to the Fath-er, and to the Son : and to the Ho-ly Ghost ; As it was in the beginning, is now, and ev-er shall be : world with-out end. A-men.

GOOD FRIDAY.
MORNING PRAYER.

PSALM XXII.—*Deus, Deus meus.*

2nd Tone, 1st Ending.

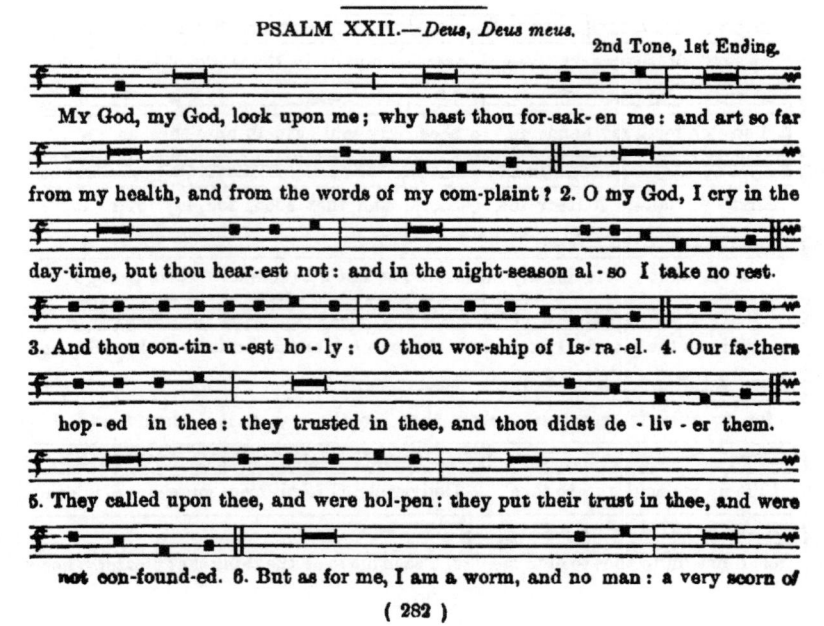

My God, my God, look upon me ; why hast thou for-sak-en me : and art so far from my health, and from the words of my com-plaint? 2. O my God, I cry in the day-time, but thou hear-est not : and in the night-season al-so I take no rest. 3. And thou con-tin-u-est ho-ly : O thou wor-ship of Is-ra-el. 4. Our fa-thers hop-ed in thee : they trusted in thee, and thou didst de-liv-er them. 5. They called upon thee, and were hol-pen : they put their trust in thee, and were not con-found-ed. 6. But as for me, I am a worm, and no man : a very scorn of

GOOD FRIDAY—MORNING.

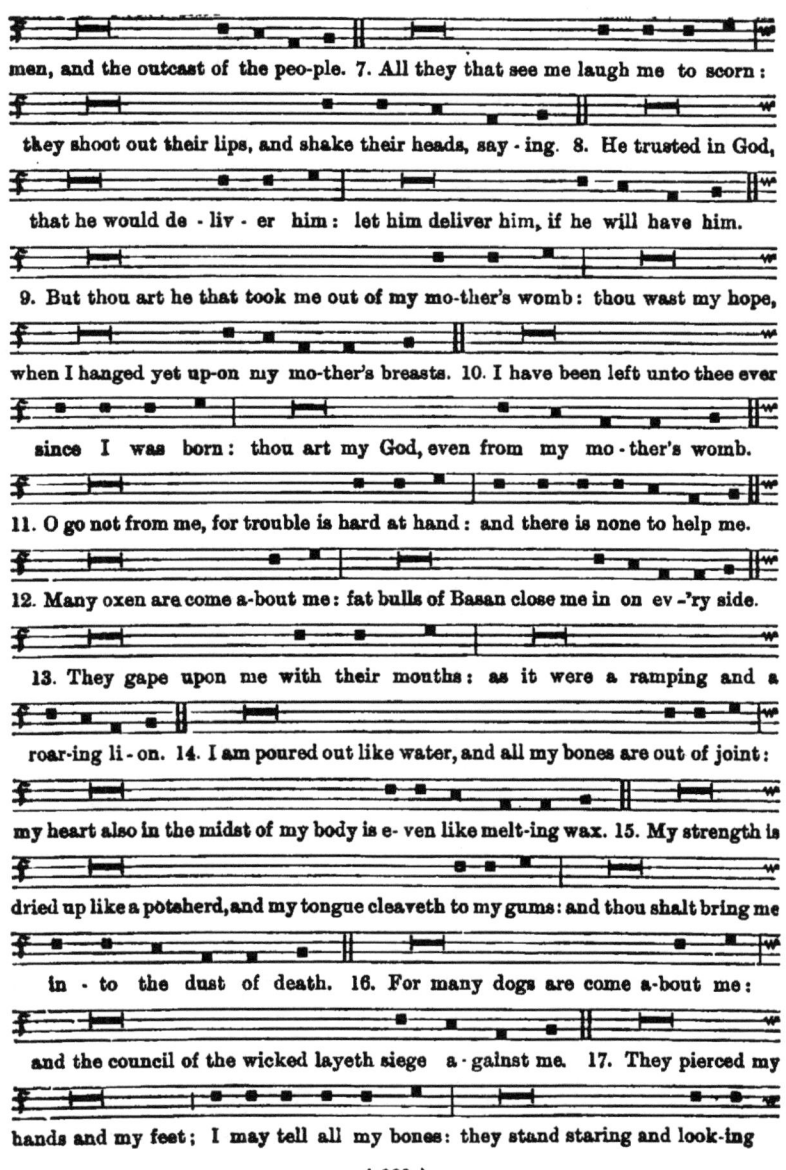

men, and the outcast of the peo-ple. 7. All they that see me laugh me to scorn:

they shoot out their lips, and shake their heads, say-ing. 8. He trusted in God,

that he would de-liv-er him: let him deliver him, if he will have him.

9. But thou art he that took me out of my mo-ther's womb: thou wast my hope,

when I hanged yet up-on my mo-ther's breasts. 10. I have been left unto thee ever

since I was born: thou art my God, even from my mo-ther's womb.

11. O go not from me, for trouble is hard at hand: and there is none to help me.

12. Many oxen are come a-bout me: fat bulls of Basan close me in on ev-'ry side.

13. They gape upon me with their mouths: as it were a ramping and a

roar-ing li-on. 14. I am poured out like water, and all my bones are out of joint:

my heart also in the midst of my body is e-ven like melt-ing wax. 15. My strength is

dried up like a pòtsherd, and my tongue cleaveth to my gums: and thou shalt bring me

in-to the dust of death. 16. For many dogs are come a-bout me:

and the council of the wicked layeth siege a-gainst me. 17. They pierced my

hands and my feet; I may tell all my bones: they stand staring and look-ing

(283)

PROPER PSALMS.

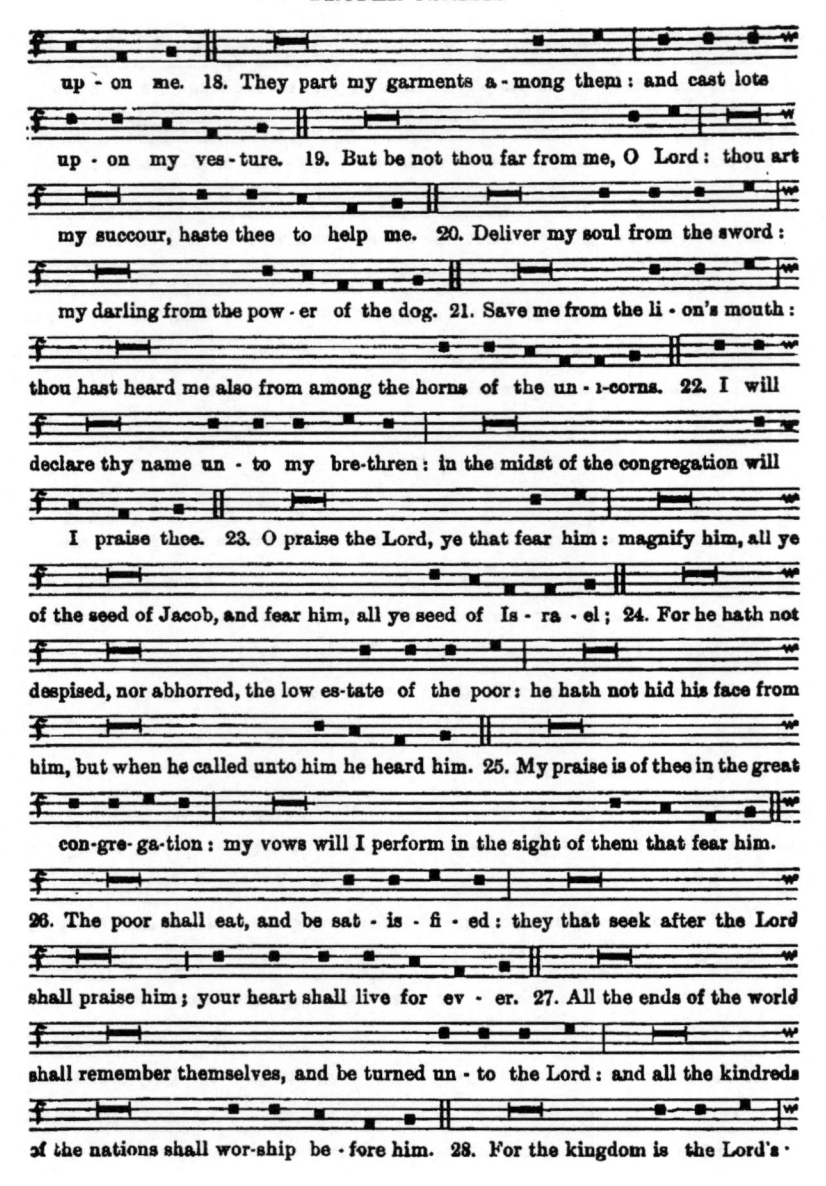

up - on me. 18. They part my garments a - mong them: and cast lots

up - on my ves - ture. 19. But be not thou far from me, O Lord: thou art

my succour, haste thee to help me. 20. Deliver my soul from the sword:

my darling from the pow - er of the dog. 21. Save me from the li - on's mouth:

thou hast heard me also from among the horns of the un - i-corns. 22. I will

declare thy name un - to my bre-thren: in the midst of the congregation will

I praise thee. 23. O praise the Lord, ye that fear him: magnify him, all ye

of the seed of Jacob, and fear him, all ye seed of Is - ra - el; 24. For he hath not

despised, nor abhorred, the low es-tate of the poor: he hath not hid his face from

him, but when he called unto him he heard him. 25. My praise is of thee in the great

con-gre-ga-tion: my vows will I perform in the sight of them that fear him.

26. The poor shall eat, and be sat - is - fi - ed: they that seek after the Lord

shall praise him; your heart shall live for ev - er. 27. All the ends of the world

shall remember themselves, and be turned un - to the Lord: and all the kindreds

of the nations shall wor-ship be - fore him. 28. For the kingdom is the Lord's·

GOOD FRIDAY—MORNING.

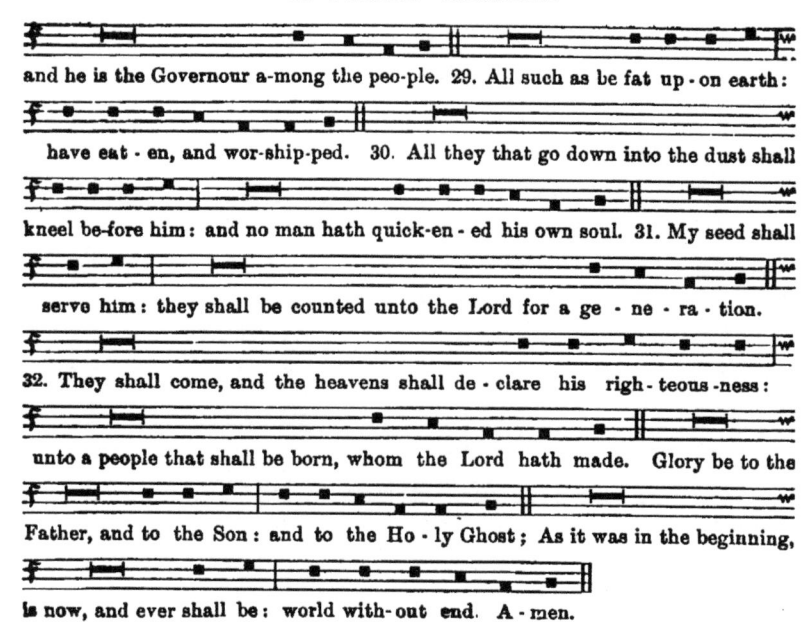

and he is the Governour a-mong the peo-ple. 29. All such as be fat up-on earth:

have eat-en, and wor-ship-ped. 30. All they that go down into the dust shall

kneel be-fore him: and no man hath quick-en-ed his own soul. 31. My seed shall

serve him: they shall be counted unto the Lord for a ge-ne-ra-tion.

32. They shall come, and the heavens shall de-clare his righ-teous-ness:

unto a people that shall be born, whom the Lord hath made. Glory be to the

Father, and to the Son: and to the Ho-ly Ghost; As it was in the beginning,

is now, and ever shall be: world with-out end. A-men.

PSALM XL.—*Expectans expectavi.*

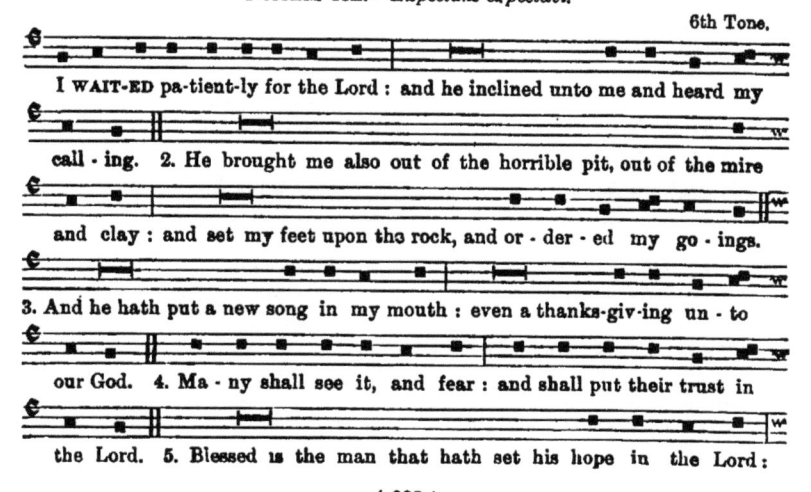

6th Tone.

I WAIT-ED pa-tient-ly for the Lord: and he inclined unto me and heard my

call-ing. 2. He brought me also out of the horrible pit, out of the mire

and clay: and set my feet upon the rock, and or-der-ed my go-ings.

3. And he hath put a new song in my mouth: even a thanks-giv-ing un-to

our God. 4. Ma-ny shall see it, and fear: and shall put their trust in

the Lord. 5. Blessed is the man that hath set his hope in the Lord:

PROPER PSALMS.

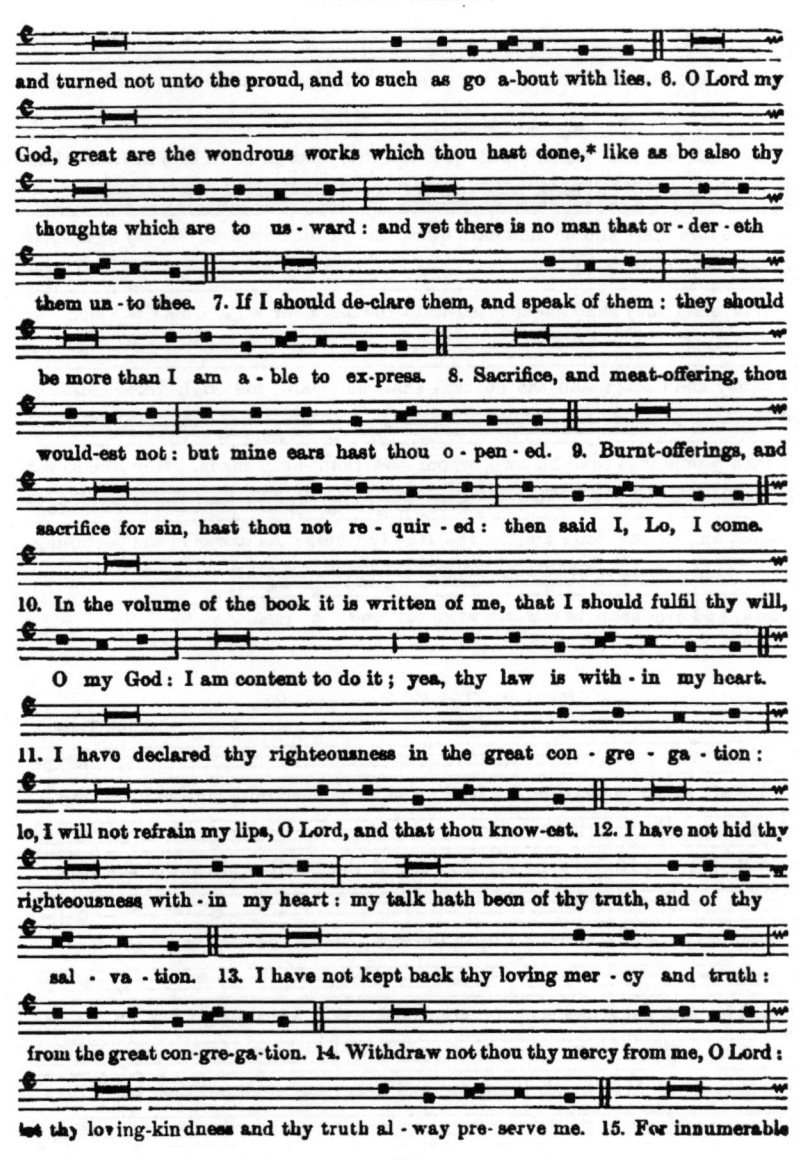

and turned not unto the proud, and to such as go a-bout with lies. 6. O Lord my God, great are the wondrous works which thou hast done,* like as be also thy thoughts which are to us - ward : and yet there is no man that or - der - eth them un - to thee. 7. If I should de-clare them, and speak of them : they should be more than I am a - ble to ex-press. 8. Sacrifice, and meat-offering, thou would-est not : but mine ears hast thou o - pen - ed. 9. Burnt-offerings, and sacrifice for sin, hast thou not re - quir - ed : then said I, Lo, I come. 10. In the volume of the book it is written of me, that I should fulfil thy will, O my God : I am content to do it ; yea, thy law is with - in my heart. 11. I have declared thy righteousness in the great con - gre - ga - tion : lo, I will not refrain my lips, O Lord, and that thou know-est. 12. I have not hid thy righteousness with - in my heart : my talk hath been of thy truth, and of thy sal - va - tion. 13. I have not kept back thy loving mer - cy and truth : from the great con-gre-ga-tion. 14. Withdraw not thou thy mercy from me, O Lord : let thy loving-kindness and thy truth al - way pre- serve me. 15. For innumerable

GOOD FRIDAY—MORNING.

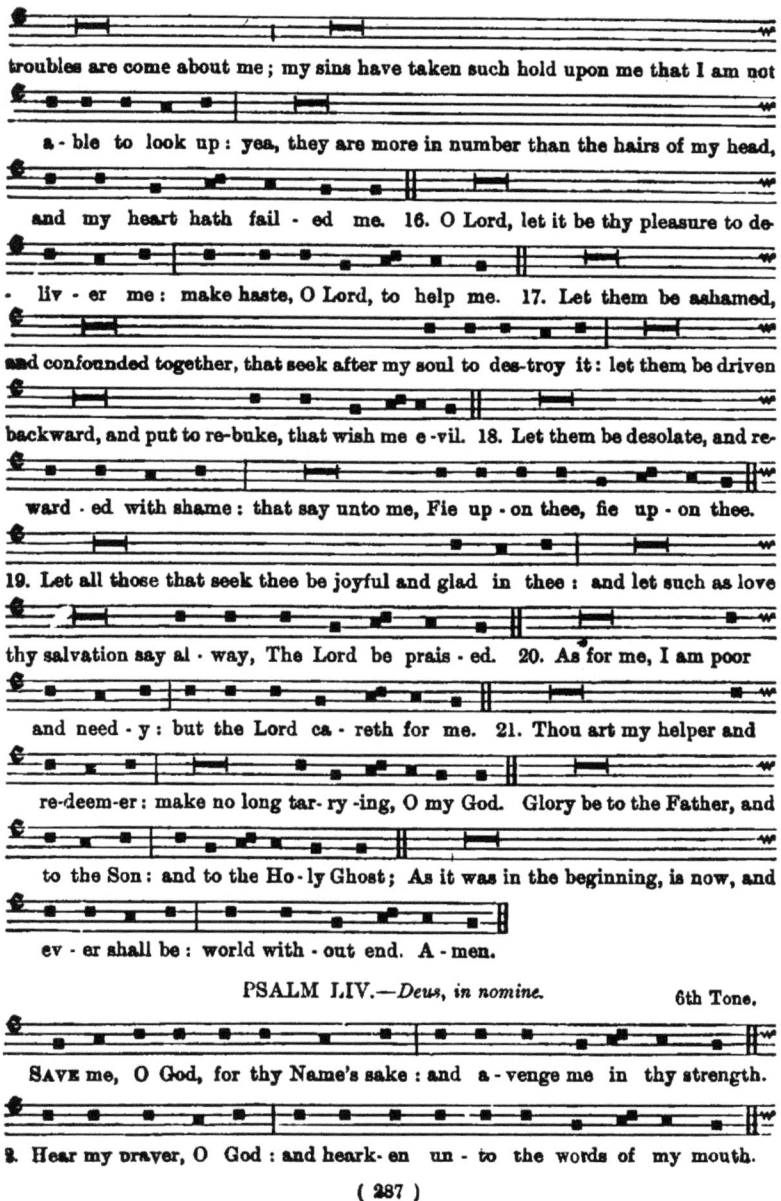

troubles are come about me; my sins have taken such hold upon me that I am not a-ble to look up: yea, they are more in number than the hairs of my head, and my heart hath fail-ed me. 16. O Lord, let it be thy pleasure to de- liv-er me: make haste, O Lord, to help me. 17. Let them be ashamed, and confounded together, that seek after my soul to des-troy it: let them be driven backward, and put to re-buke, that wish me e-vil. 18. Let them be desolate, and re- ward-ed with shame: that say unto me, Fie up-on thee, fie up-on thee. 19. Let all those that seek thee be joyful and glad in thee: and let such as love thy salvation say al-way, The Lord be prais-ed. 20. As for me, I am poor and need-y: but the Lord ca-reth for me. 21. Thou art my helper and re-deem-er: make no long tar-ry-ing, O my God. Glory be to the Father, and to the Son: and to the Ho-ly Ghost; As it was in the beginning, is now, and ev-er shall be: world with-out end. A-men.

PSALM LIV.—*Deus, in nomine.* 6th Tone.

SAVE me, O God, for thy Name's sake: and a-venge me in thy strength.

2. Hear my prayer, O God: and heark-en un-to the words of my mouth.

PROPER PSALMS.

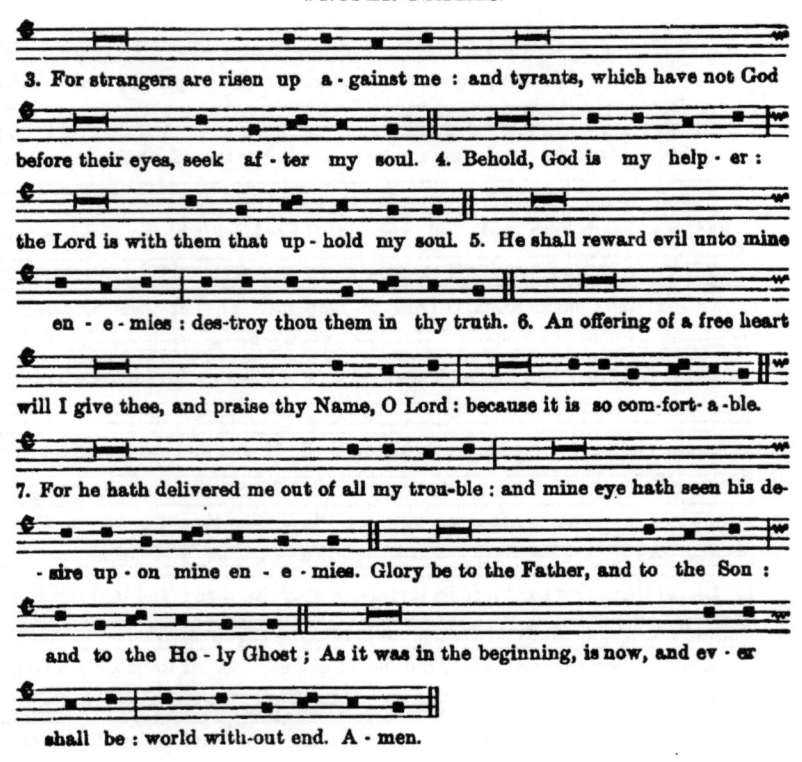

3. For strangers are risen up a-gainst me : and tyrants, which have not God before their eyes, seek af-ter my soul. 4. Behold, God is my help-er : the Lord is with them that up-hold my soul. 5. He shall reward evil unto mine en-e-mies : des-troy thou them in thy truth. 6. An offering of a free heart will I give thee, and praise thy Name, O Lord : because it is so com-fort-a-ble. 7. For he hath delivered me out of all my trou-ble : and mine eye hath seen his de- -sire up-on mine en-e-mies. Glory be to the Father, and to the Son : and to the Ho-ly Ghost ; As it was in the beginning, is now, and ev-er shall be : world with-out end. A-men.

EVENING PRAYER.

PSALM LXIX.—*Salvum me fac.*

4th Tone, 4th Ending.

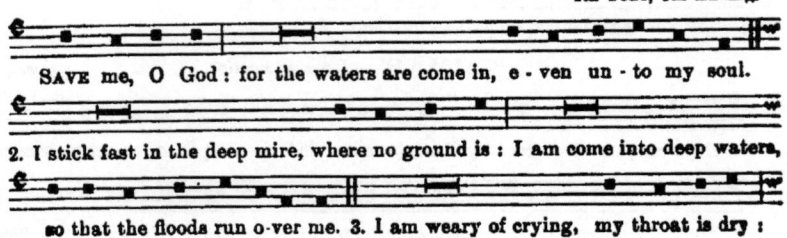

SAVE me, O God : for the waters are come in, e-ven un-to my soul. 2. I stick fast in the deep mire, where no ground is : I am come into deep waters, so that the floods run o-ver me. 3. I am weary of crying, my throat is dry :

GOOD FRIDAY—EVENING.

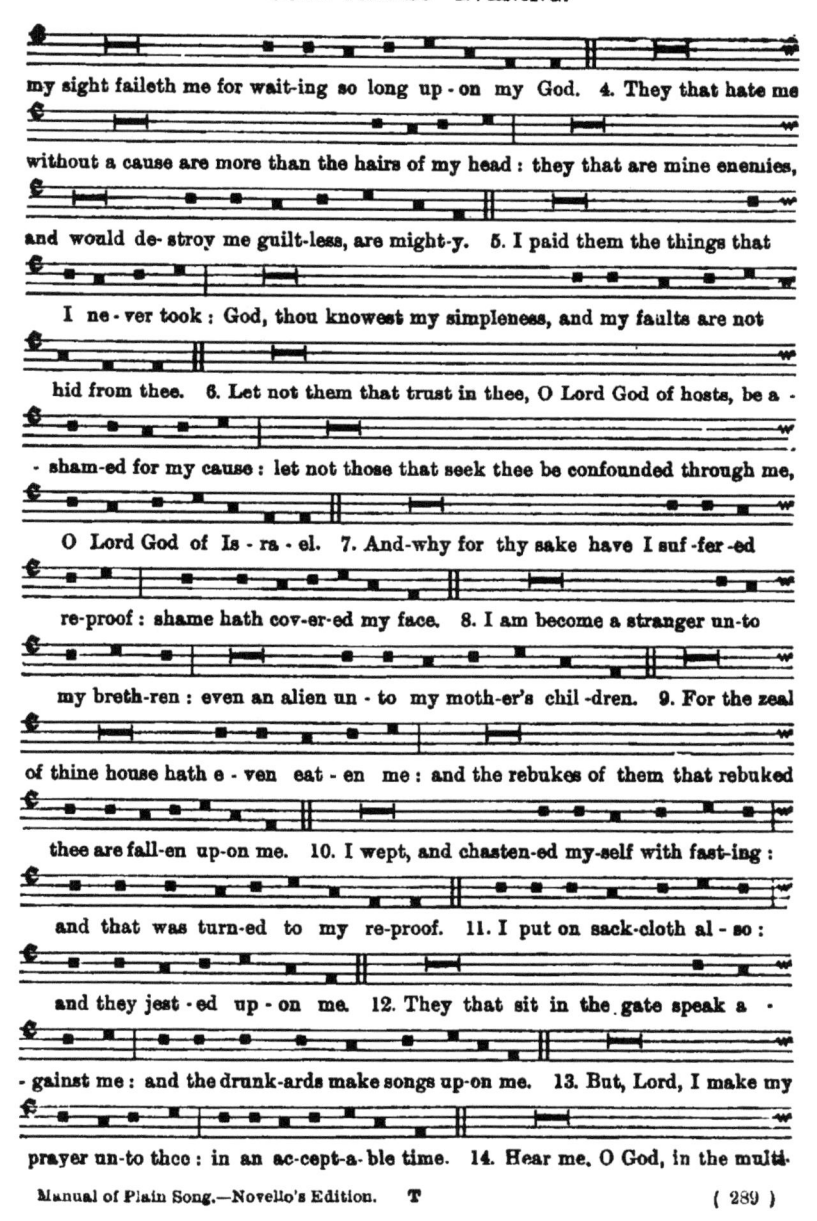

my sight faileth me for wait-ing so long up-on my God. 4. They that hate me without a cause are more than the hairs of my head : they that are mine enemies, and would de-stroy me guilt-less, are might-y. 5. I paid them the things that I ne-ver took : God, thou knowest my simpleness, and my faults are not hid from thee. 6. Let not them that trust in thee, O Lord God of hosts, be a--sham-ed for my cause : let not those that seek thee be confounded through me, O Lord God of Is-ra-el. 7. And-why for thy sake have I suf-fer-ed re-proof : shame hath cov-er-ed my face. 8. I am become a stranger un-to my breth-ren : even an alien un-to my moth-er's chil-dren. 9. For the zeal of thine house hath e-ven eat-en me : and the rebukes of them that rebuked thee are fall-en up-on me. 10. I wept, and chasten-ed my-self with fast-ing : and that was turn-ed to my re-proof. 11. I put on sack-cloth al-so : and they jest-ed up-on me. 12. They that sit in the gate speak a--gainst me : and the drunk-ards make songs up-on me. 13. But, Lord, I make my prayer un-to thee : in an ac-cept-a-ble time. 14. Hear me, O God, in the multi-

Manual of Plain Song.—Novello's Edition.   T   (289)

PROPER PSALMS.

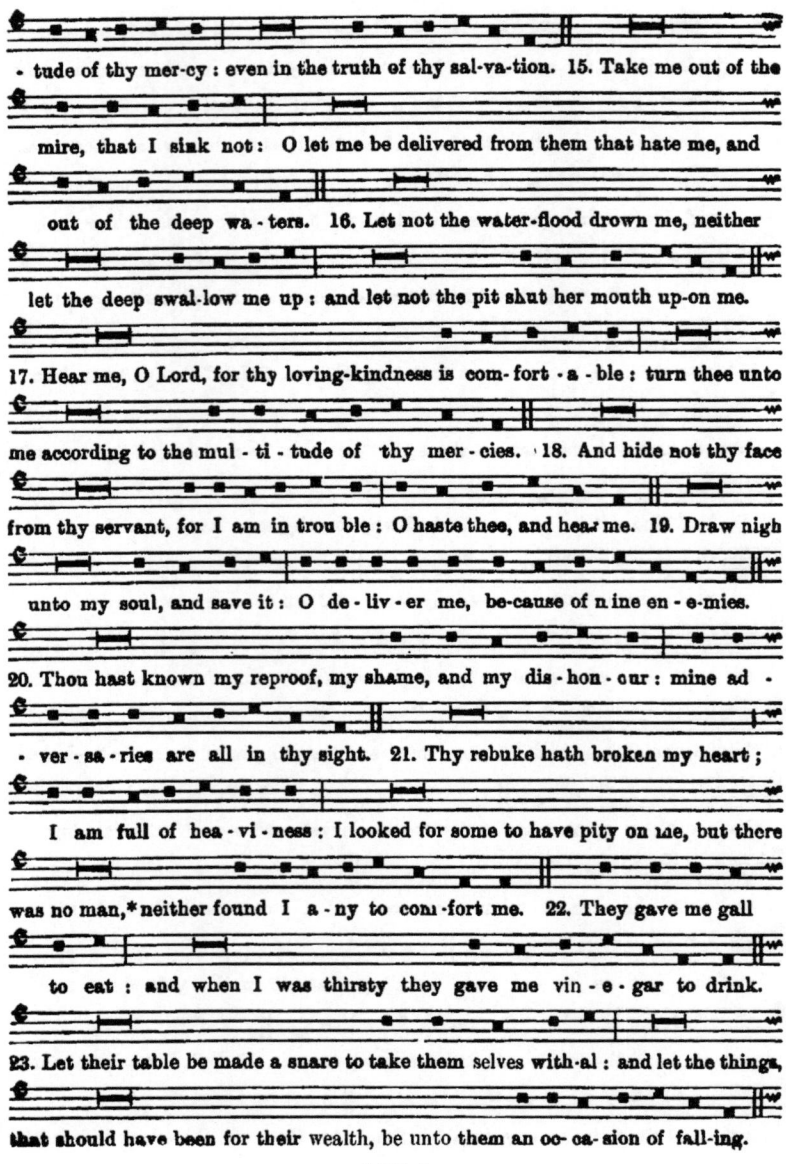

- tude of thy mer-cy : even in the truth of thy sal-va-tion. 15. Take me out of the mire, that I sink not : O let me be delivered from them that hate me, and out of the deep wa-ters. 16. Let not the water-flood drown me, neither let the deep swal-low me up : and let not the pit shut her mouth up-on me. 17. Hear me, O Lord, for thy loving-kindness is com-fort-a-ble : turn thee unto me according to the mul-ti-tude of thy mer-cies. 18. And hide not thy face from thy servant, for I am in trou ble : O haste thee, and hear me. 19. Draw nigh unto my soul, and save it : O de-liv-er me, be-cause of mine en-e-mies. 20. Thou hast known my reproof, my shame, and my dis-hon-our : mine ad-ver-sa-ries are all in thy sight. 21. Thy rebuke hath broken my heart ; I am full of hea-vi-ness : I looked for some to have pity on me, but there was no man,* neither found I a-ny to com-fort me. 22. They gave me gall to eat : and when I was thirsty they gave me vin-e-gar to drink. 23. Let their table be made a snare to take them selves with-al : and let the things, that should have been for their wealth, be unto them an oc-ca-sion of fall-ing.

(290)

GOOD FRIDAY—EVENING.

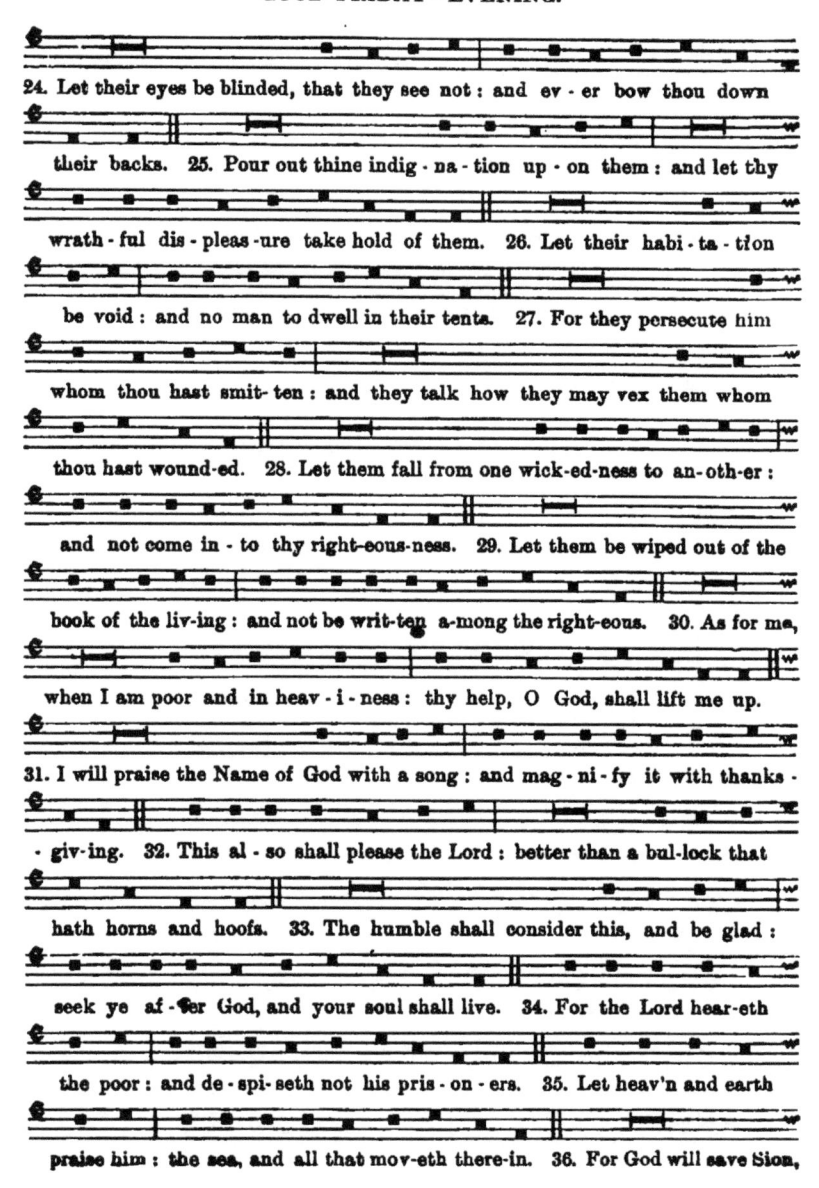

24. Let their eyes be blinded, that they see not : and ev-er bow thou down their backs. 25. Pour out thine indig-na-tion up-on them : and let thy wrath-ful dis-pleas-ure take hold of them. 26. Let their habi-ta-tion be void : and no man to dwell in their tents. 27. For they persecute him whom thou hast smit-ten : and they talk how they may vex them whom thou hast wound-ed. 28. Let them fall from one wick-ed-ness to an-oth-er : and not come in-to thy right-eous-ness. 29. Let them be wiped out of the book of the liv-ing : and not be writ-ten a-mong the right-eous. 30. As for me, when I am poor and in heav-i-ness : thy help, O God, shall lift me up. 31. I will praise the Name of God with a song : and mag-ni-fy it with thanks-giv-ing. 32. This al-so shall please the Lord : better than a bul-lock that hath horns and hoofs. 33. The humble shall consider this, and be glad : seek ye af-ter God, and your soul shall live. 34. For the Lord hear-eth the poor : and de-spi-seth not his pris-on-ers. 35. Let heav'n and earth praise him : the sea, and all that mov-eth there-in. 36. For God will save Sion,

PROPER PSALMS.

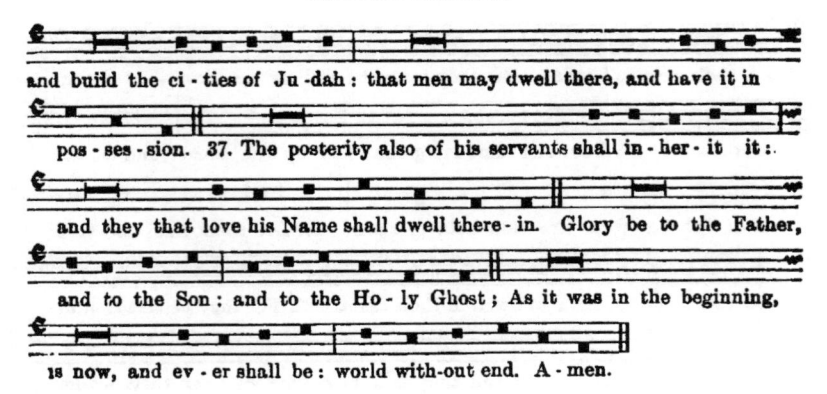

and build the ci-ties of Ju-dah: that men may dwell there, and have it in pos-ses-sion. 37. The posterity also of his servants shall in-her-it it: and they that love his Name shall dwell there-in. Glory be to the Father, and to the Son: and to the Ho-ly Ghost; As it was in the beginning, is now, and ev-er shall be: world with-out end. A-men.

PSALM LXXXVIII.—*Domine Deus.*

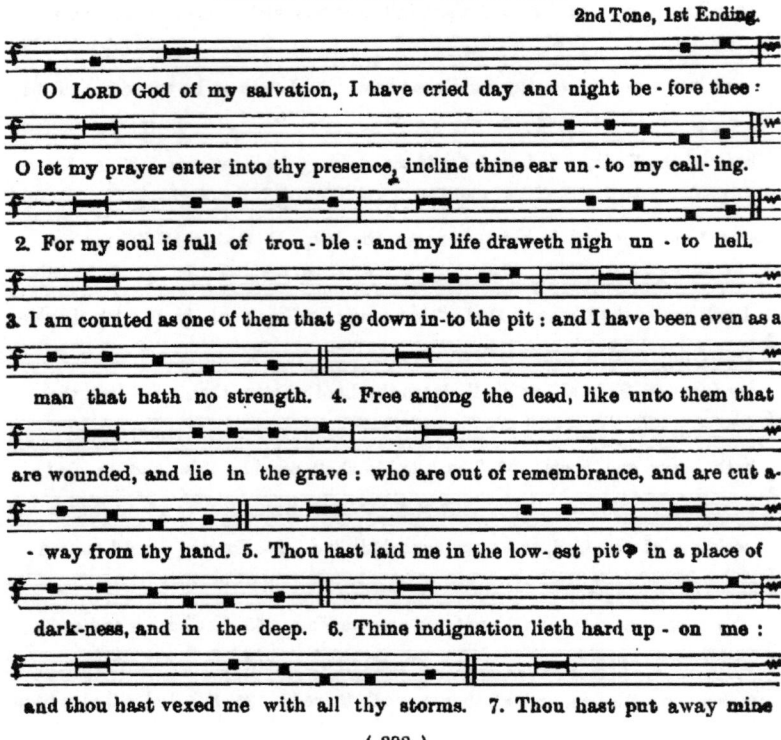

2nd Tone, 1st Ending.

O LORD God of my salvation, I have cried day and night be-fore thee: O let my prayer enter into thy presence, incline thine ear un-to my call-ing. 2. For my soul is full of trou-ble: and my life draweth nigh un-to hell. 3. I am counted as one of them that go down in-to the pit: and I have been even as a man that hath no strength. 4. Free among the dead, like unto them that are wounded, and lie in the grave: who are out of remembrance, and are cut a--way from thy hand. 5. Thou hast laid me in the low-est pit✚ in a place of dark-ness, and in the deep. 6. Thine indignation lieth hard up-on me: and thou hast vexed me with all thy storms. 7. Thou hast put away mine

GOOD FRIDAY—EVENING.

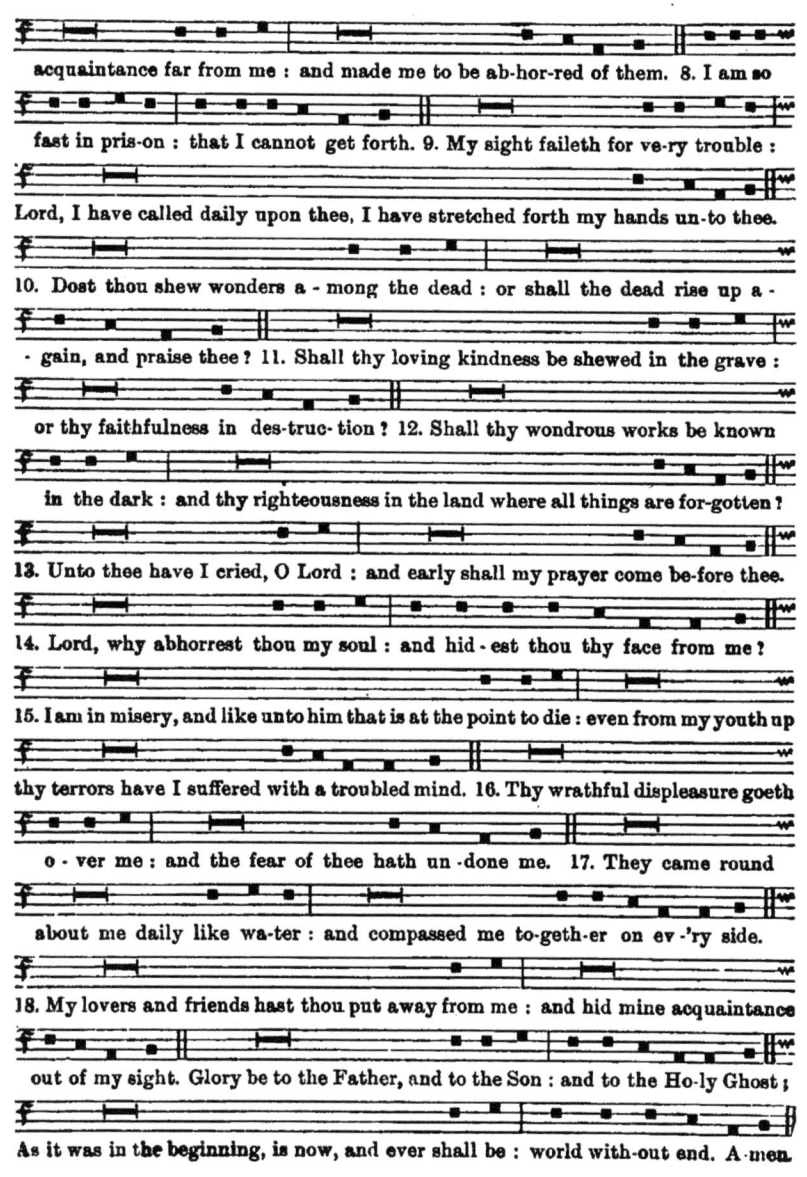

acquaintance far from me : and made me to be ab-hor-red of them. 8. I am so fast in pris-on : that I cannot get forth. 9. My sight faileth for ve-ry trouble : Lord, I have called daily upon thee, I have stretched forth my hands un-to thee.

10. Dost thou shew wonders a-mong the dead : or shall the dead rise up a-gain, and praise thee? 11. Shall thy loving kindness be shewed in the grave : or thy faithfulness in des-truc-tion? 12. Shall thy wondrous works be known in the dark : and thy righteousness in the land where all things are for-gotten?

13. Unto thee have I cried, O Lord : and early shall my prayer come be-fore thee. 14. Lord, why abhorrest thou my soul : and hid-est thou thy face from me?

15. I am in misery, and like unto him that is at the point to die : even from my youth up thy terrors have I suffered with a troubled mind. 16. Thy wrathful displeasure goeth o-ver me : and the fear of thee hath un-done me. 17. They came round about me daily like wa-ter : and compassed me to-geth-er on ev-'ry side.

18. My lovers and friends hast thou put away from me : and hid mine acquaintance out of my sight. Glory be to the Father, and to the Son : and to the Ho-ly Ghost ; As it was in the beginning, is now, and ever shall be : world with-out end. A-men.

EASTER DAY.
MORNING PRAYER.

Instead of the Psalm "O come, let us sing," &c.

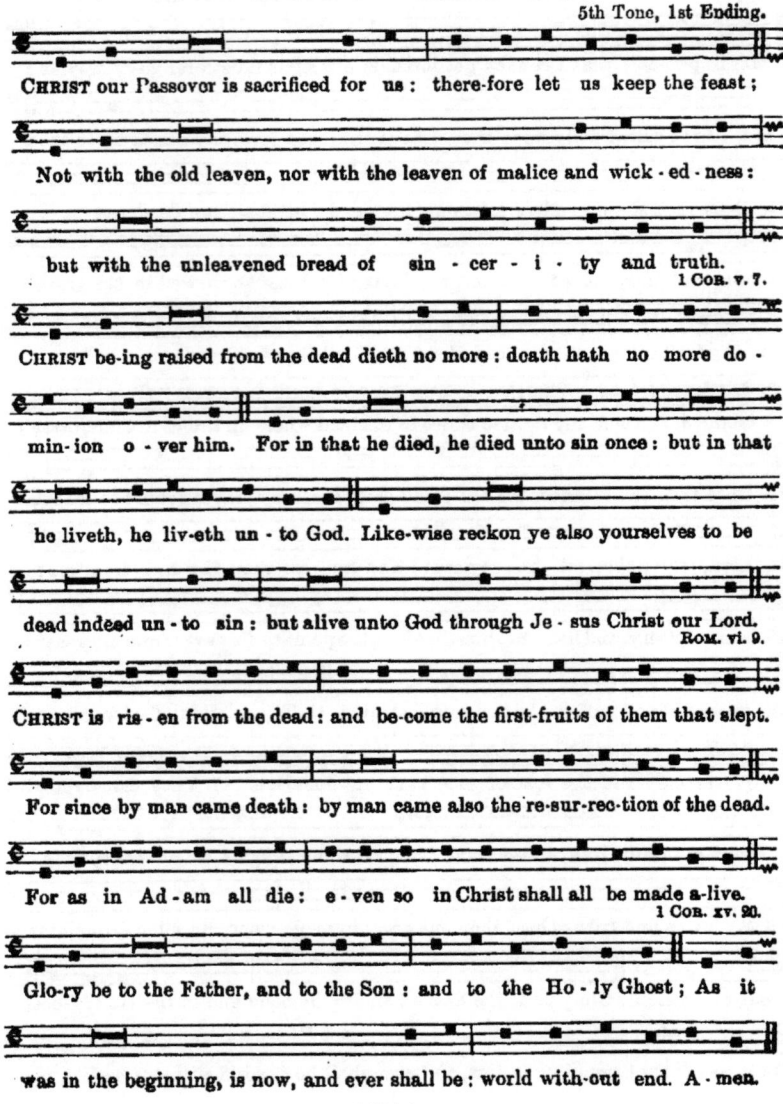

5th Tone, 1st Ending.

Christ our Passover is sacrificed for us: there-fore let us keep the feast;

Not with the old leaven, nor with the leaven of malice and wick-ed-ness:

but with the unleavened bread of sin-cer-i-ty and truth.
1 Cor. v. 7.

Christ be-ing raised from the dead dieth no more: death hath no more do-min-ion o-ver him. For in that he died, he died unto sin once: but in that he liveth, he liv-eth un-to God. Like-wise reckon ye also yourselves to be dead indeed un-to sin: but alive unto God through Je-sus Christ our Lord.
Rom. vi. 9.

Christ is ris-en from the dead: and be-come the first-fruits of them that slept.

For since by man came death: by man came also the re-sur-rec-tion of the dead.

For as in Ad-am all die: e-ven so in Christ shall all be made a-live.
1 Cor. xv. 20.

Glo-ry be to the Father, and to the Son: and to the Ho-ly Ghost; As it was in the beginning, is now, and ever shall be: world with-out end. A-men.

EASTER DAY—MORNING.

PSALM II.—*Quare fremuerunt gentes?*

5th Tone, 1st Ending.

WHY do the heathen so furiously rage to-go-ther: and why do the people i-ma-gine a vain thing? 2. The kings of the earth stand up, and the rulers take counsel to-ge-ther: against the Lord, and a-gainst his A-noint-ed. 3. Let us break their bonds a-sun-der: and cast a-way their cords from us. 4. He that dwelleth in heaven shall laugh them to scorn: the Lord shall have them in de-ri-sion. 5. Then shall he speak unto them in his wrath: and vex them in his sore displeasure. 6. Yet have I set my King: upon my ho-ly hill of Si-on. 7. I will preach the law, whereof the Lord hath said un-to me: Thou art my Son, this day have I be-got-ten thee. 8. Desire of me, and I shall give thee the heathen for thine in-her-i-tance: and the utmost parts of the earth for thy pos-ses-sion. 9. Thou shalt bruise them with a rod of i-ron: and break them in pieces like a pot-ter's ves-sel. 10. Be wise now therefore, O ye kings: be learned, ye that are judg-es of the earth. 11. Serve the Lord in fear: and rejoice un-to him with rev-er-ence. 12. Kiss the Son, lest he be angry, and so ye perish from the right way: if his wrath be kindled, (yea,

PROPER PSALMS.

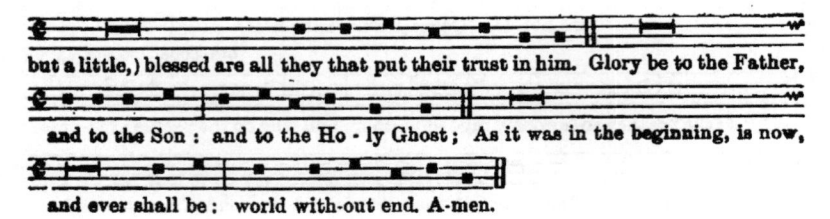

but a little,) blessed are all they that put their trust in him. Glory be to the Father, and to the Son : and to the Ho-ly Ghost; As it was in the beginning, is now, and ever shall be : world with-out end. A-men.

PSALM LVII.—*Miserere mei, Deus.*

8th Tone, 1st Ending.

Be mer-ciful unto me, O God, be merciful unto me, for my soul trust-eth in thee : and under the shadow of thy wings shall be my refuge, until this ty-ran-ny be o-ver-past. 2. I will call unto the most high God : even unto the God that shall perform the cause which I have in hand. 3. He shall send from heav-en : and save me from the reproof of him that would eat me up. 4. God shall send forth his mer-cy and truth : my soul is a-mong li-ons. 5. And I lie even among the children of men, that are set on fire : whose teeth are spears and arrows, and their tongue a sharp sword. 6. Set up thyself, O God, a-bove the heav-ens : and thy glo-ry a-bove all the earth. 7. They have laid a net for my feet, and pressed down my soul : they have digged a pit before me, and are fallen in-to the midst of it them-selves. 8. My heart is fixed,

EASTER DAY—MORNING.

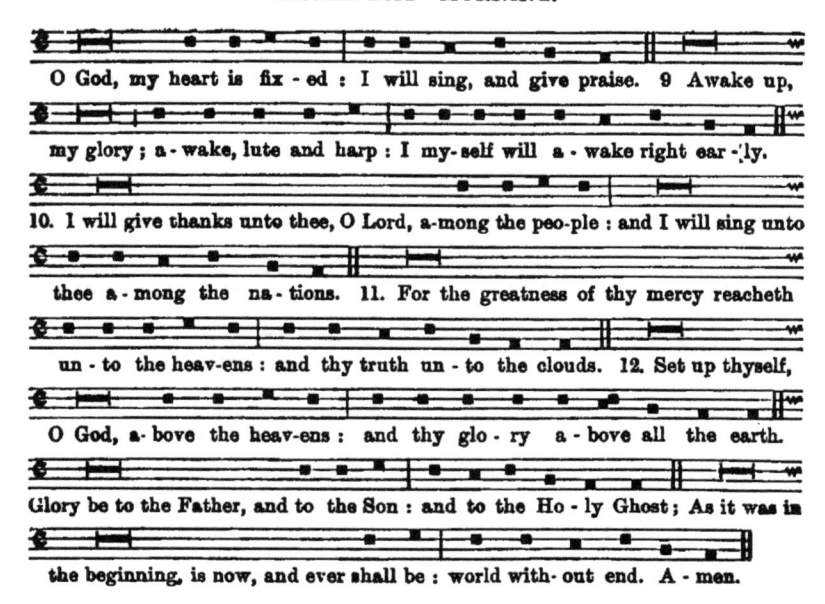

O God, my heart is fix - ed : I will sing, and give praise. 9 Awake up, my glory ; a - wake, lute and harp : I my-self will a - wake right ear -'ly. 10. I will give thanks unto thee, O Lord, a-mong the peo-ple : and I will sing unto thee a - mong the na - tions. 11. For the greatness of thy mercy reacheth un - to the heav-ens : and thy truth un - to the clouds. 12. Set up thyself, O God, a- bove the heav-ens : and thy glo - ry a - bove all the earth. Glory be to the Father, and to the Son : and to the Ho - ly Ghost; As it was in the beginning, is now, and ever shall be : world with- out end. A - men.

PSALM CXI.—*Confitebor tibi.*

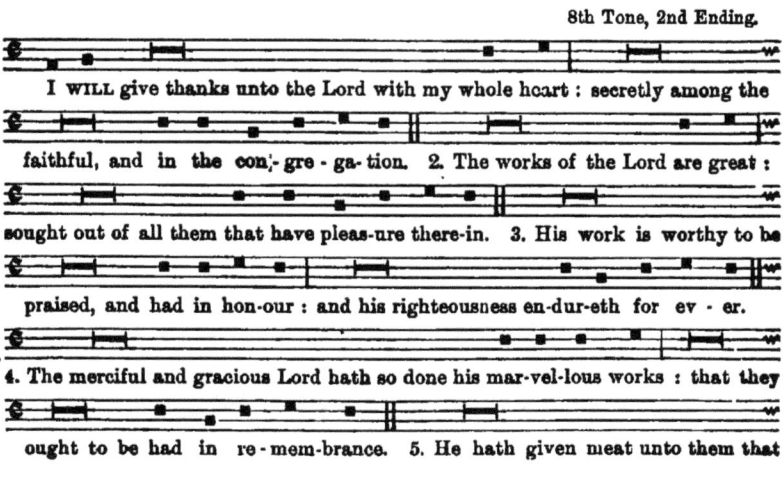

8th Tone, 2nd Ending.

I WILL give thanks unto the Lord with my whole heart : secretly among the faithful, and in the con - gre - ga- tion. 2. The works of the Lord are great : sought out of all them that have pleas-ure there-in. 3. His work is worthy to be praised, and had in hon-our : and his righteousness en-dur-eth for ev - er. 4. The merciful and gracious Lord hath so done his mar-vel-lous works : that they ought to be had in re - mem-brance. 5. He hath given meat unto them that

PROPER PSALMS.

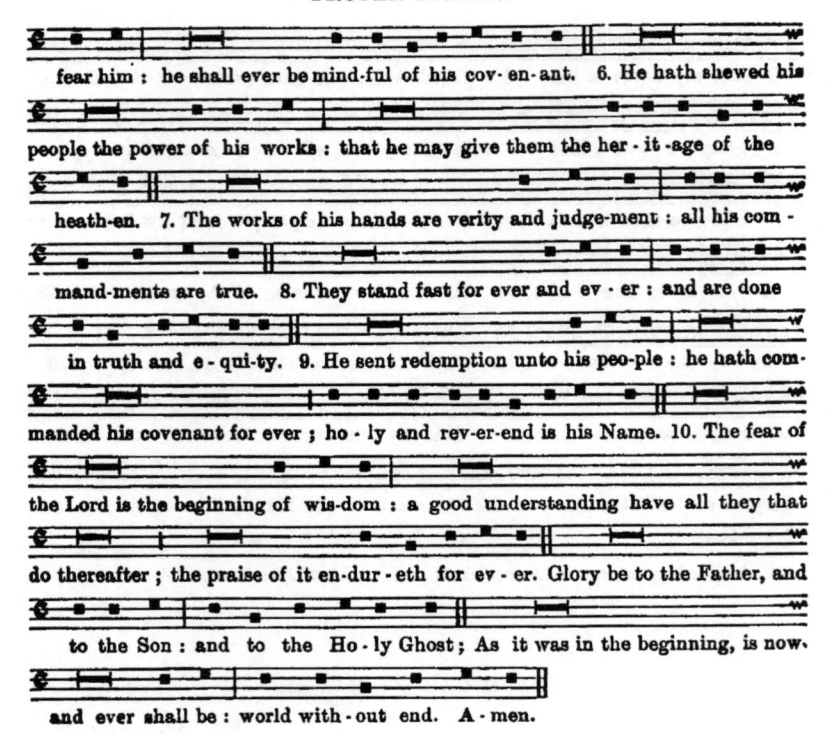

fear him : he shall ever be mind-ful of his cov-en-ant. 6. He hath shewed his people the power of his works : that he may give them the her-it-age of the heath-en. 7. The works of his hands are verity and judge-ment : all his com-mand-ments are true. 8. They stand fast for ever and ev-er : and are done in truth and e-qui-ty. 9. He sent redemption unto his peo-ple : he hath com-manded his covenant for ever ; ho-ly and rev-er-end is his Name. 10. The fear of the Lord is the beginning of wis-dom : a good understanding have all they that do thereafter ; the praise of it en-dur-eth for ev-er. Glory be to the Father, and to the Son : and to the Ho-ly Ghost ; As it was in the beginning, is now, and ever shall be : world with-out end. A-men.

EVENING PRAYER.

PSALM CXIII.—*Laudate, pueri.*

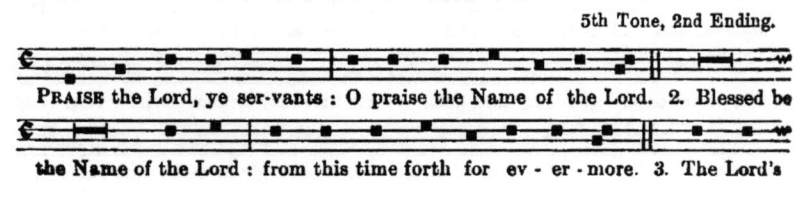

5th Tone, 2nd Ending.

PRAISE the Lord, ye ser-vants : O praise the Name of the Lord. 2. Blessed be the Name of the Lord : from this time forth for ev-er-more. 3. The Lord's

(298)

EASTER DAY—EVENING.

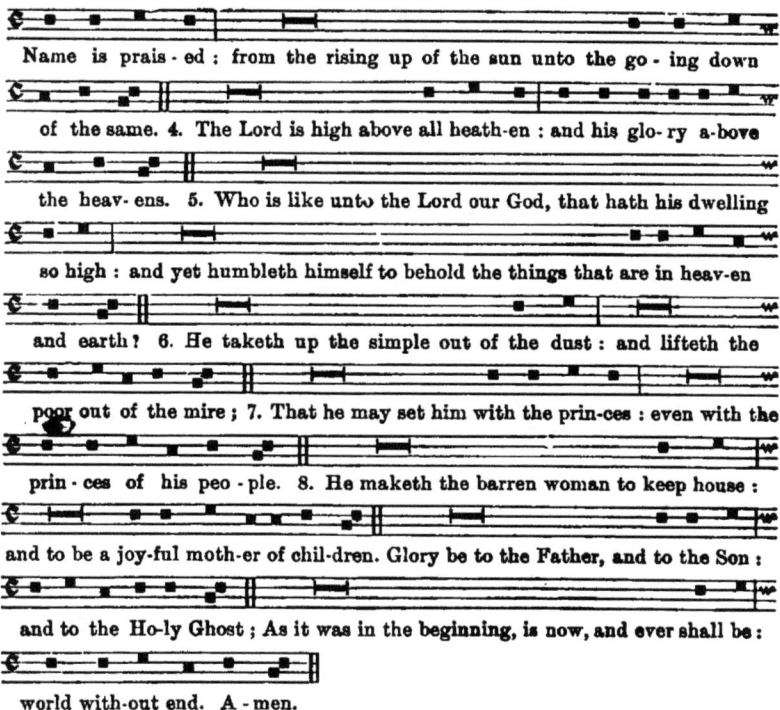

Name is prais-ed : from the rising up of the sun unto the go-ing down of the same. 4. The Lord is high above all heath-en : and his glo-ry a-bove the heav-ens. 5. Who is like unto the Lord our God, that hath his dwelling so high : and yet humbleth himself to behold the things that are in heav-en and earth? 6. He taketh up the simple out of the dust : and lifteth the poor out of the mire ; 7. That he may set him with the prin-ces : even with the prin-ces of his peo-ple. 8. He maketh the barren woman to keep house : and to be a joy-ful moth-er of chil-dren. Glory be to the Father, and to the Son : and to the Ho-ly Ghost ; As it was in the beginning, is now, and ever shall be : world with-out end. A-men.

PSALM CXIV.—*In exitu Israel.*

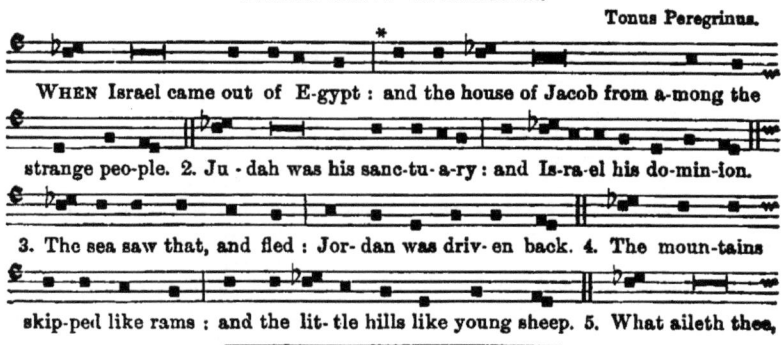

Tonus Peregrinus.

WHEN Israel came out of E-gypt : and the house of Jacob from a-mong the strange peo-ple. 2. Ju-dah was his sanc-tu-a-ry : and Is-ra-el his do-min-ion. 3. The sea saw that, and fled : Jor-dan was driv-en back. 4. The moun-tains skip-ped like rams : and the lit-tle hills like young sheep. 5. What aileth thee,

---

* The notes of the intonation may be omitted in the second half of each verse, and the recitation begin at once on the G.

PROPER PSALMS.

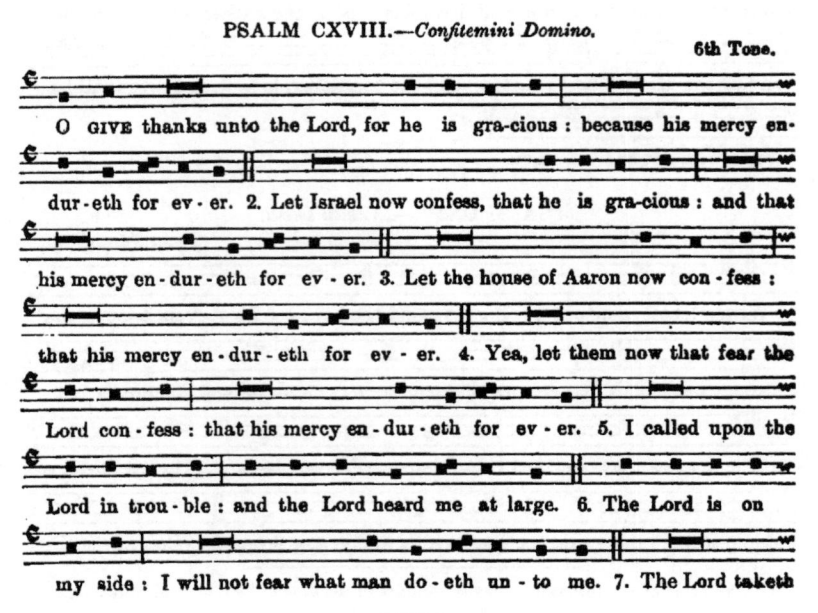

O thou sea, that thou fled-dest : and thou Jor-dan, that thou wast driv-en back?

6. Ye mountains, that ye skip-ped like rams : and ye lit-tle hills, like young sheep?

7. Trem-ble, thou earth, at the presence of the Lord : at the pres-ence of the God of Ja-cob ; 8. Who turned the hard rock into a stand-ing wa-ter : and the flint-stone in-to a spring-ing well. Glo-ry be to the Father, and to the Son : and to the Ho-ly Ghost ; As it was in the beginning, is now, and ev-er shall be : world with-out end. A-men.

PSALM CXVIII.—*Confitemini Domino.*

6th Tone.

O GIVE thanks unto the Lord, for he is gra-cious : because his mercy en-dur-eth for ev-er. 2. Let Israel now confess, that he is gra-cious : and that his mercy en-dur-eth for ev-er. 3. Let the house of Aaron now con-fess : that his mercy en-dur-eth for ev-er. 4. Yea, let them now that fear the Lord con-fess : that his mercy en-dur-eth for ev-er. 5. I called upon the Lord in trou-ble : and the Lord heard me at large. 6. The Lord is on my side : I will not fear what man do-eth un-to me. 7. The Lord taketh

EASTER DAY—EVENING.

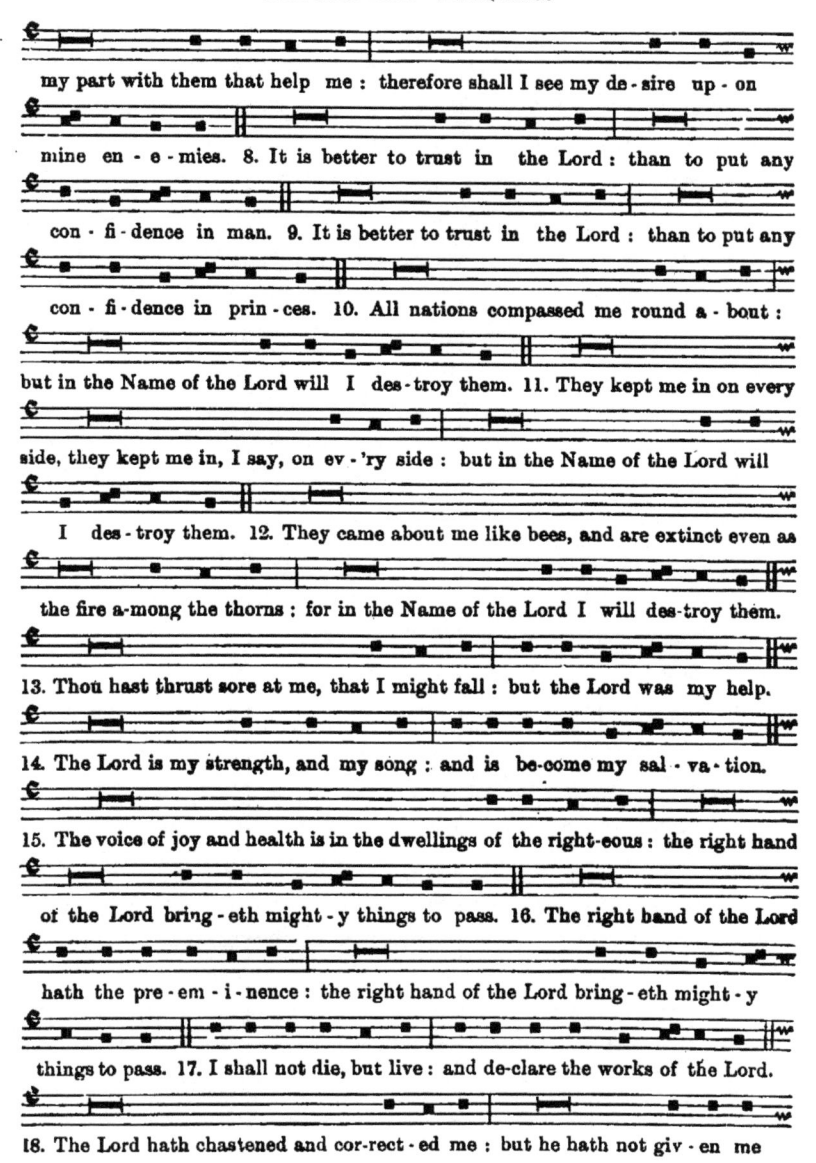

my part with them that help me : therefore shall I see my de-sire up-on mine en-e-mies. 8. It is better to trust in the Lord : than to put any con-fi-dence in man. 9. It is better to trust in the Lord : than to put any con-fi-dence in prin-ces. 10. All nations compassed me a-bout : but in the Name of the Lord will I des-troy them. 11. They kept me in on every side, they kept me in, I say, on ev-'ry side : but in the Name of the Lord will I des-troy them. 12. They came about me like bees, and are extinct even as the fire a-mong the thorns : for in the Name of the Lord I will des-troy them.

13. Thou hast thrust sore at me, that I might fall : but the Lord was my help.

14. The Lord is my strength, and my song : and is be-come my sal-va-tion.

15. The voice of joy and health is in the dwellings of the right-eous : the right hand of the Lord bring-eth might-y things to pass. 16. The right hand of the Lord hath the pre-em-i-nence : the right hand of the Lord bring-eth might-y things to pass. 17. I shall not die, but live : and de-clare the works of the Lord.

18. The Lord hath chastened and cor-rect-ed me : but he hath not giv-en me

PROPER PSALMS.

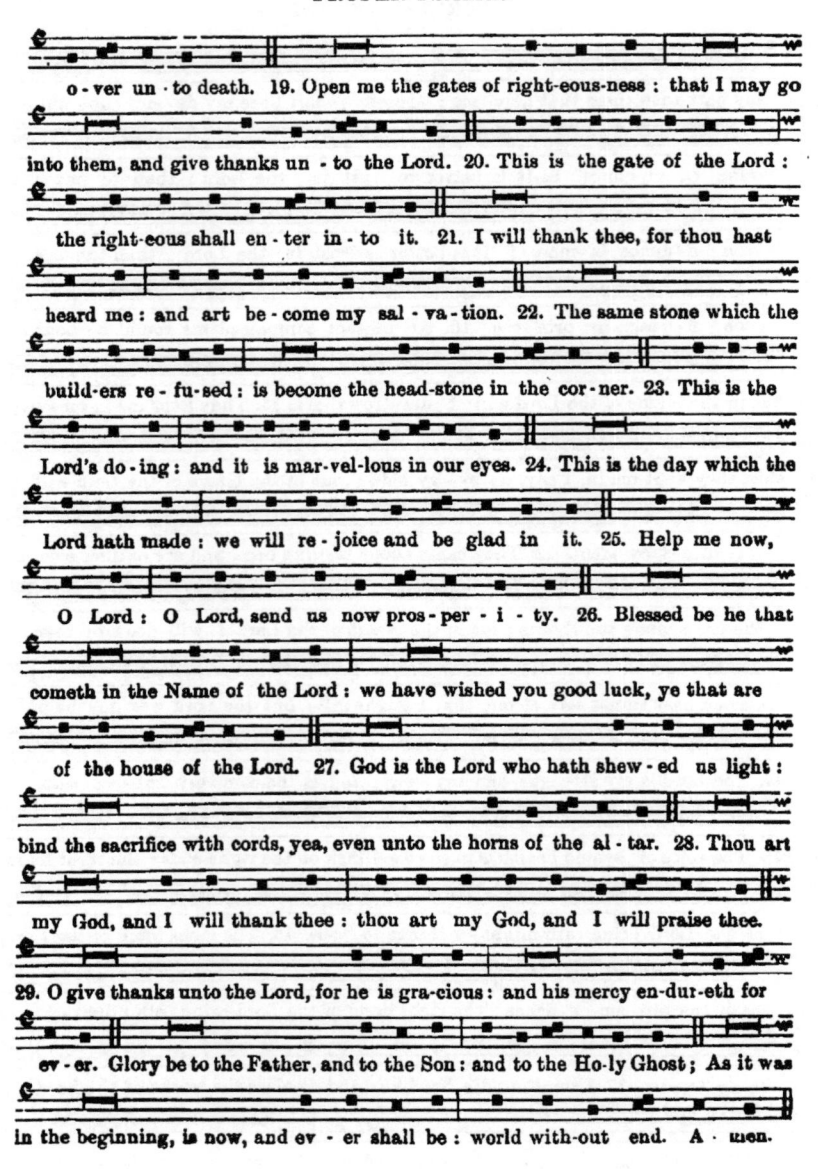

o - ver un - to death. 19. Open me the gates of right-eous-ness : that I may go into them, and give thanks un - to the Lord. 20. This is the gate of the Lord : the right-eous shall en - ter in - to it. 21. I will thank thee, for thou hast heard me : and art be - come my sal - va - tion. 22. The same stone which the build-ers re - fu - sed : is become the head-stone in the cor - ner. 23. This is the Lord's do - ing : and it is mar-vel-lous in our eyes. 24. This is the day which the Lord hath made : we will re - joice and be glad in it. 25. Help me now, O Lord : O Lord, send us now pros - per - i - ty. 26. Blessed be he that cometh in the Name of the Lord : we have wished you good luck, ye that are of the house of the Lord. 27. God is the Lord who hath shew - ed us light : bind the sacrifice with cords, yea, even unto the horns of the al - tar. 28. Thou art my God, and I will thank thee : thou art my God, and I will praise thee. 29. O give thanks unto the Lord, for he is gra-cious : and his mercy en-dur-eth for ev - er. Glory be to the Father, and to the Son : and to the Ho-ly Ghost ; As it was in the beginning, is now, and ev - er shall be : world with-out end. A - men.

ASCENSION DAY.
MORNING PRAYER.

PSALM VIII.—*Domine, Dominus noster.*

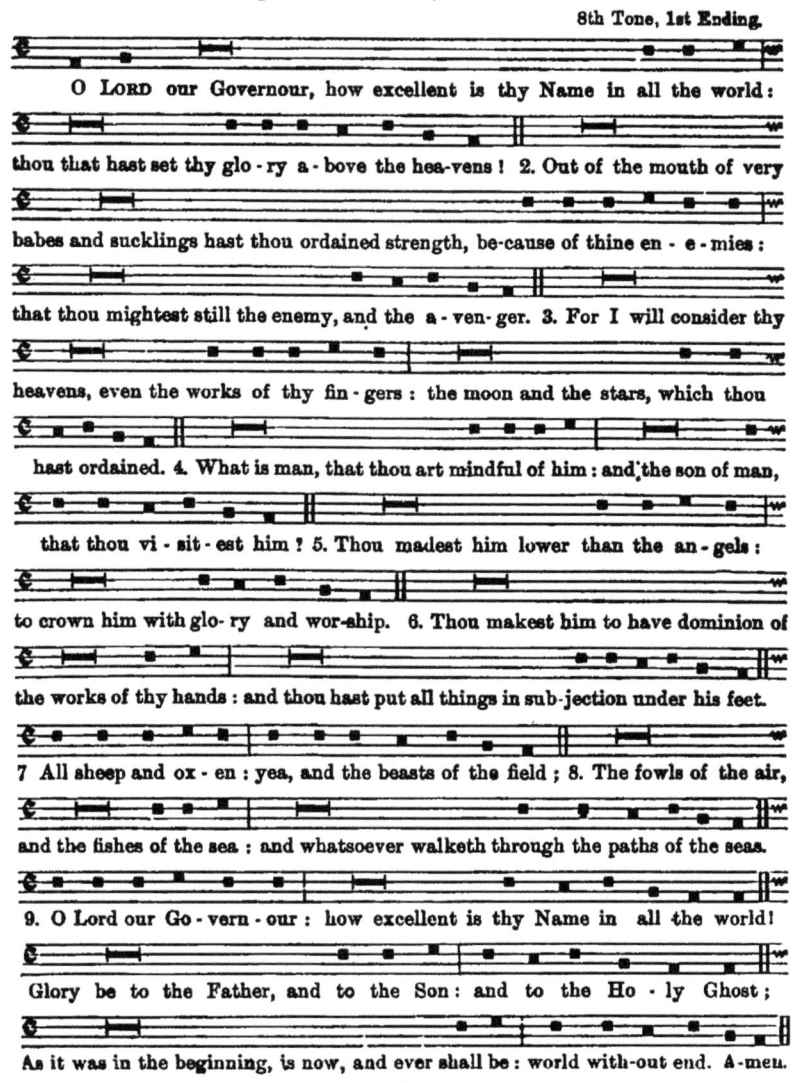

8th Tone, 1st Ending.

O LORD our Governour, how excellent is thy Name in all the world:

thou that hast set thy glo - ry a - bove the hea-vens! 2. Out of the mouth of very

babes and sucklings hast thou ordained strength, be-cause of thine en - e - mies:

that thou mightest still the enemy, and the a - ven- ger. 3. For I will consider thy

heavens, even the works of thy fin - gers: the moon and the stars, which thou

hast ordained. 4. What is man, that thou art mindful of him: and the son of man,

that thou vi - sit - est him? 5. Thou madest him lower than the an - gels:

to crown him with glo - ry and wor-ship. 6. Thou makest him to have dominion of

the works of thy hands: and thou hast put all things in sub-jection under his feet.

7 All sheep and ox - en: yea, and the beasts of the field; 8. The fowls of the air,

and the fishes of the sea: and whatsoever walketh through the paths of the seas.

9. O Lord our Go - vern - our: how excellent is thy Name in all the world!

Glory be to the Father, and to the Son: and to the Ho - ly Ghost;

As it was in the beginning, is now, and ever shall be: world with-out end. A-men.

(303)

PROPER PSALMS.

PSALM XV.—*Domine, quis habitabit?*

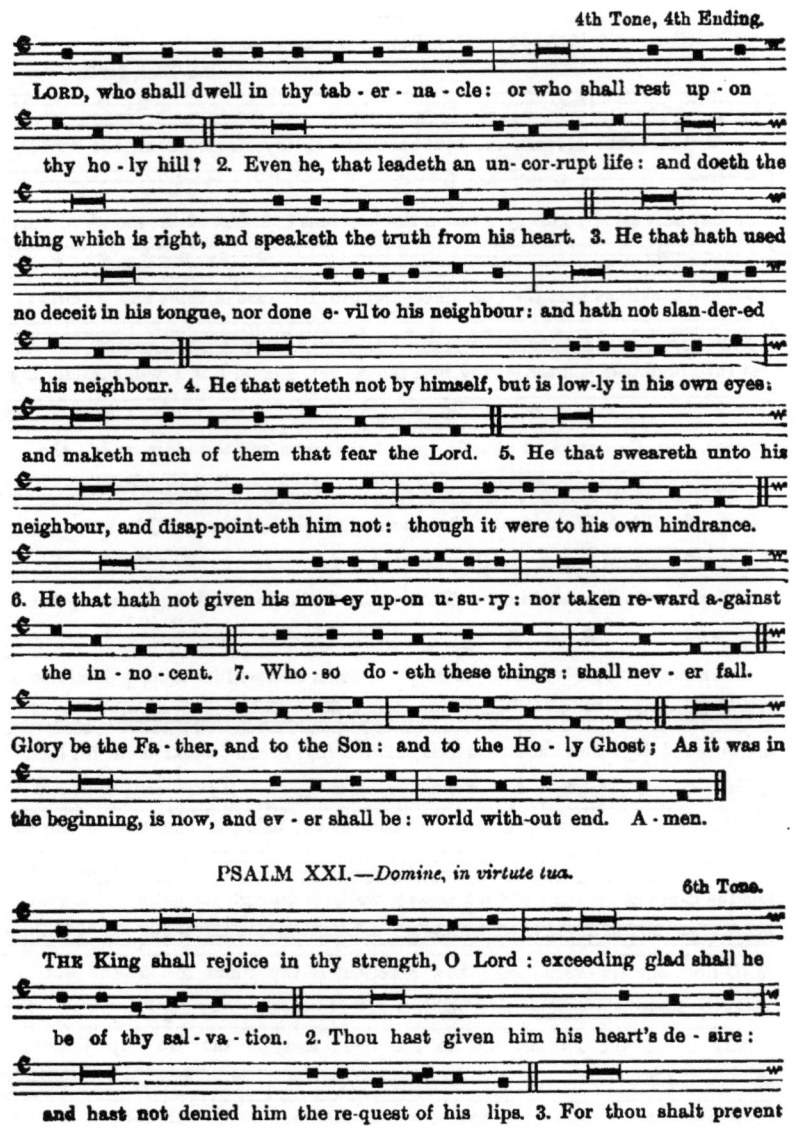

4th Tone, 4th Ending.

LORD, who shall dwell in thy tab-er-na-cle: or who shall rest up-on thy ho-ly hill? 2. Even he, that leadeth an un-cor-rupt life: and doeth the thing which is right, and speaketh the truth from his heart. 3. He that hath used no deceit in his tongue, nor done e-vil to his neighbour: and hath not slan-der-ed his neighbour. 4. He that setteth not by himself, but is low-ly in his own eyes; and maketh much of them that fear the Lord. 5. He that sweareth unto his neighbour, and disap-point-eth him not: though it were to his own hindrance. 6. He that hath not given his mon-ey up-on u-su-ry: nor taken re-ward a-gainst the in-no-cent. 7. Who-so do-eth these things: shall nev-er fall. Glory be the Fa-ther, and to the Son: and to the Ho-ly Ghost; As it was in the beginning, is now, and ev-er shall be: world with-out end. A-men.

PSALM XXI.—*Domine, in virtute tua.*

6th Tone.

THE King shall rejoice in thy strength, O Lord: exceeding glad shall he be of thy sal-va-tion. 2. Thou hast given him his heart's de-sire: and hast not denied him the re-quest of his lips. 3. For thou shalt prevent

ASCENSION DAY—MORNING.

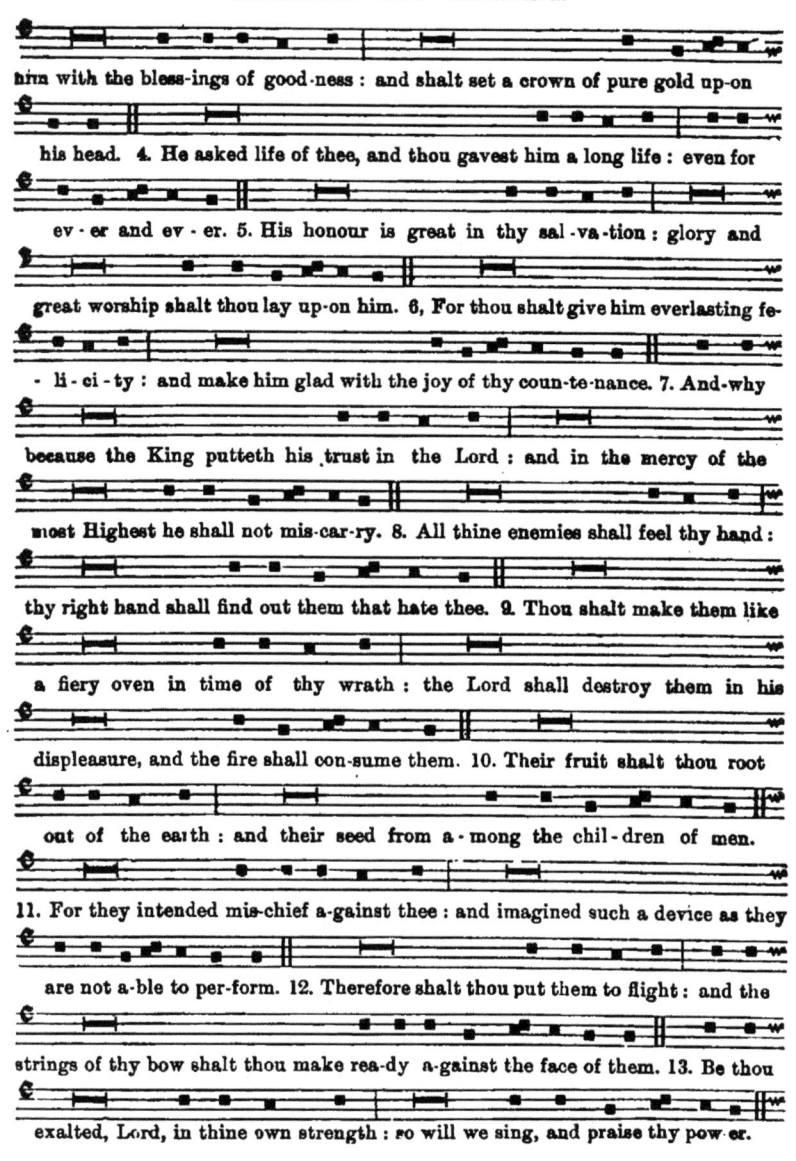

him with the bless-ings of good-ness : and shalt set a crown of pure gold up-on his head. 4. He asked life of thee, and thou gavest him a long life : even for ev-er and ev-er. 5. His honour is great in thy sal-va-tion : glory and great worship shalt thou lay up-on him. 6, For thou shalt give him everlasting fe- li-ci-ty : and make him glad with the joy of thy coun-te-nance. 7. And-why because the King putteth his trust in the Lord : and in the mercy of the most Highest he shall not mis-car-ry. 8. All thine enemies shall feel thy hand : thy right hand shall find out them that hate thee. 9. Thou shalt make them like a fiery oven in time of thy wrath : the Lord shall destroy them in his displeasure, and the fire shall con-sume them. 10. Their fruit shalt thou root out of the earth : and their seed from a-mong the chil-dren of men. 11. For they intended mis-chief a-gainst thee : and imagined such a device as they are not a-ble to per-form. 12. Therefore shalt thou put them to flight : and the strings of thy bow shalt thou make rea-dy a-gainst the face of them. 13. Be thou exalted, Lord, in thine own strength : so will we sing, and praise thy pow-er.

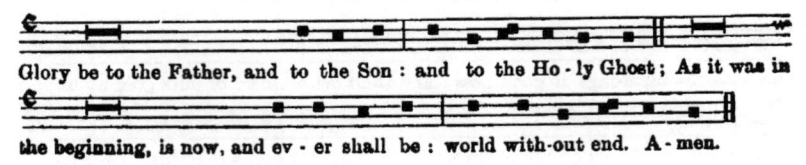

PROPER PSALMS.

Glory be to the Father, and to the Son : and to the Ho - ly Ghost ; As it was in the beginning, is now, and ev - er shall be : world with-out end. A - men.

EVENING PRAYER.

PSALM XXIV.—*Domini est terra.*
7th Tone, 5th Ending.

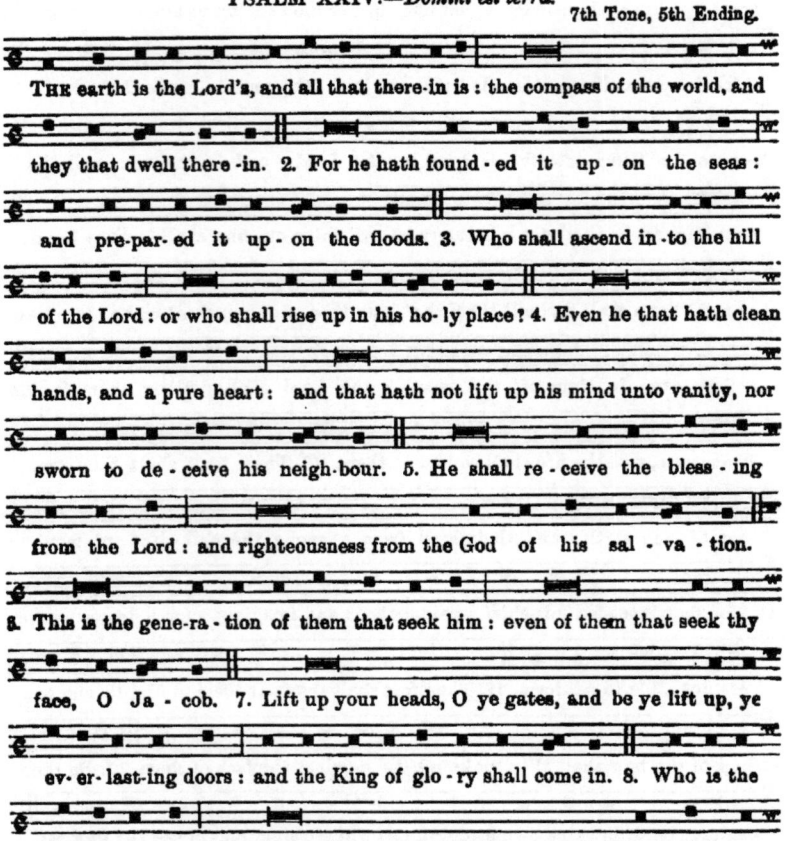

The earth is the Lord's, and all that there-in is : the compass of the world, and they that dwell there -in. 2. For he hath found - ed it up - on the seas : and pre-par- ed it up - on the floods. 3. Who shall ascend in -to the hill of the Lord : or who shall rise up in his ho- ly place ? 4. Even he that hath clean hands, and a pure heart : and that hath not lift up his mind unto vanity, nor sworn to de - ceive his neigh-bour. 5. He shall re - ceive the bless - ing from the Lord : and righteousness from the God of his sal - va - tion. 6. This is the gene-ra - tion of them that seek him : even of them that seek thy face, O Ja - cob. 7. Lift up your heads, O ye gates, and be ye lift up, ye ev- er- last-ing doors : and the King of glo - ry shall come in. 8. Who is the King of glo - ry : it is the Lord strong and mighty, even the Lord might - y

ASCENSION DAY—EVENING.

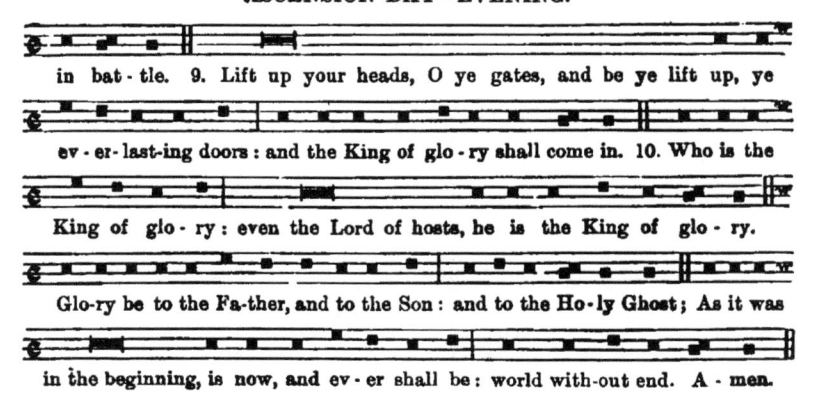

in bat-tle. 9. Lift up your heads, O ye gates, and be ye lift up, ye ev-er-last-ing doors: and the King of glo-ry shall come in. 10. Who is the King of glo-ry: even the Lord of hosts, he is the King of glo-ry.

Glo-ry be to the Fa-ther, and to the Son: and to the Ho-ly Ghost; As it was in the beginning, is now, and ev-er shall be: world with-out end. A-men.

PSALM XLVII.—*Omnes gentes, plaudite.*

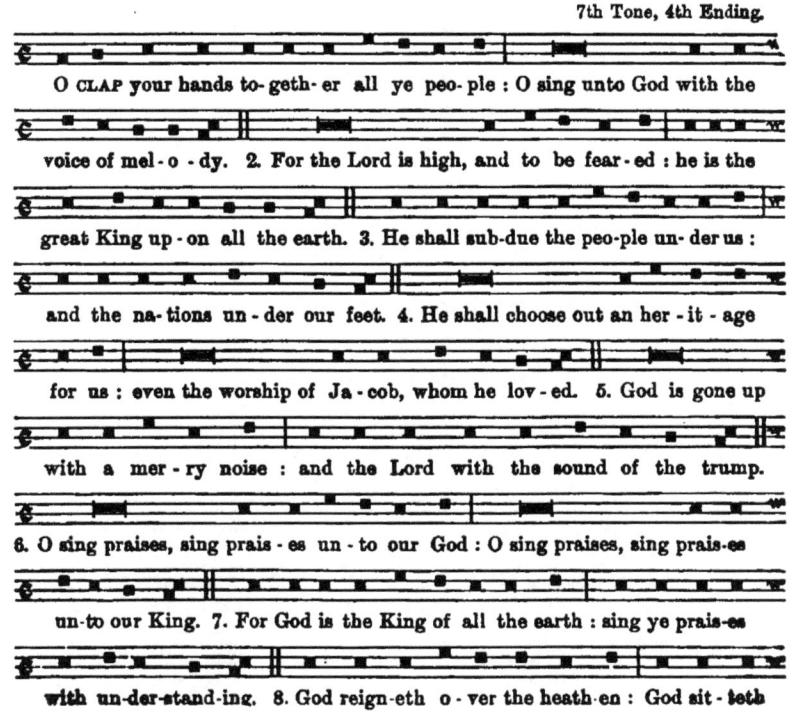

7th Tone, 4th Ending.

O CLAP your hands to-geth-er all ye peo-ple: O sing unto God with the voice of mel-o-dy. 2. For the Lord is high, and to be fear-ed: he is the great King up-on all the earth. 3. He shall sub-due the peo-ple un-der us: and the na-tions un-der our feet. 4. He shall choose out an her-it-age for us: even the worship of Ja-cob, whom he lov-ed. 5. God is gone up with a mer-ry noise: and the Lord with the sound of the trump. 6. O sing praises, sing prais-es un-to our God: O sing praises, sing prais-es un-to our King. 7. For God is the King of all the earth: sing ye prais-es with un-der-stand-ing. 8. God reign-eth o-ver the heath-en: God sit-teth

PROPER PSALMS.

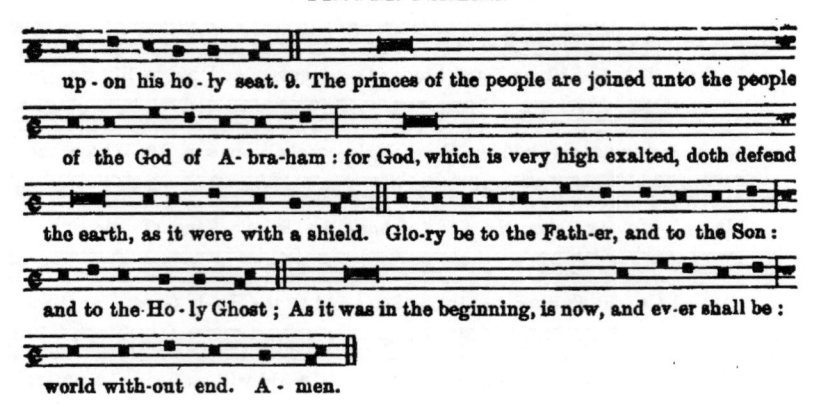

up - on his ho - ly seat. 9. The princes of the people are joined unto the people of the God of A - bra-ham : for God, which is very high exalted, doth defend the earth, as it were with a shield. Glo-ry be to the Fath-er, and to the Son : and to the Ho - ly Ghost ; As it was in the beginning, is now, and ev-er shall be : world with-out end. A - men.

PSALM CVIII.—*Paratum cor meum.*

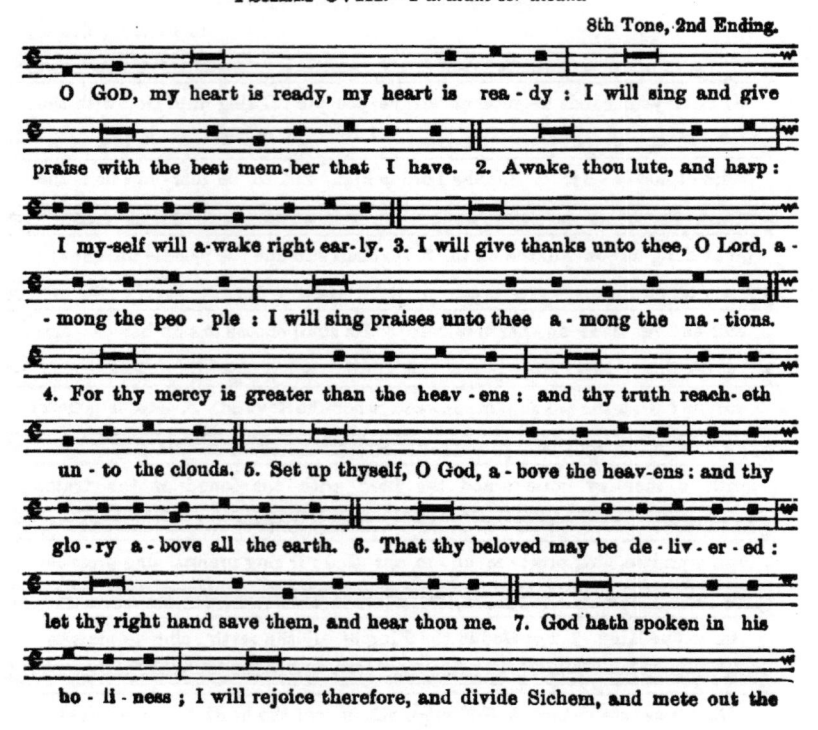

8th Tone, 2nd Ending.

O GOD, my heart is ready, my heart is rea - dy : I will sing and give praise with the best mem-ber that I have. 2. Awake, thou lute, and harp: I my-self will a-wake right ear-ly. 3. I will give thanks unto thee, O Lord, a - mong the peo - ple : I will sing praises unto thee a - mong the na - tions. 4. For thy mercy is greater than the heav - ens : and thy truth reach- eth un - to the clouds. 5. Set up thyself, O God, a - bove the heav-ens : and thy glo - ry a - bove all the earth. 6. That thy beloved may be de - liv - er - ed : let thy right hand save them, and hear thou me. 7. God hath spoken in his ho - li - ness ; I will rejoice therefore, and divide Sichem, and mete out the

(308)

ASCENSION DAY—EVENING.

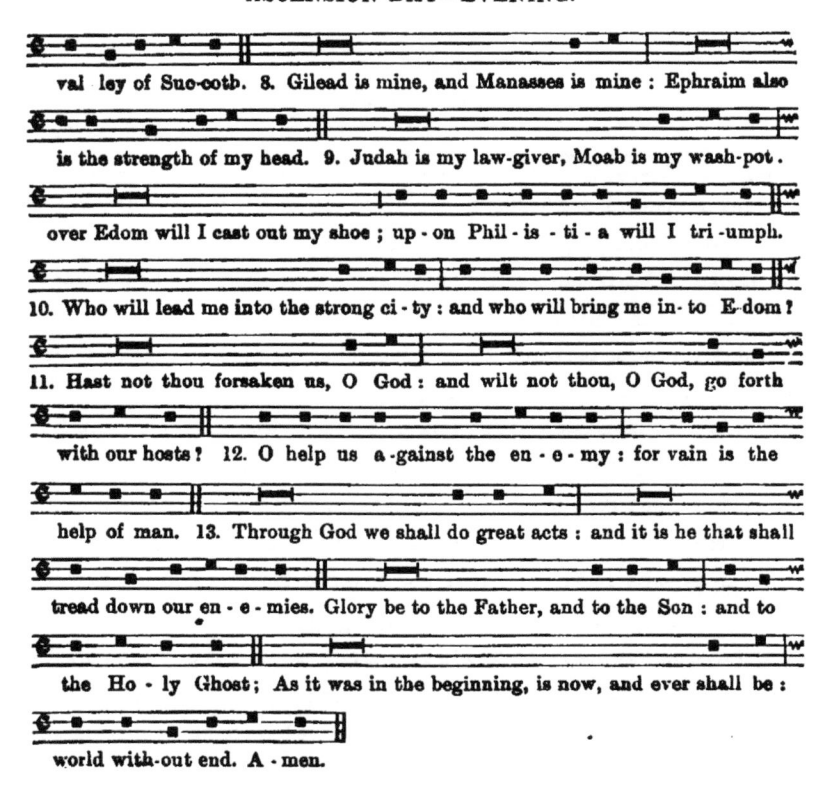

val ley of Suc-coth. 8. Gilead is mine, and Manasses is mine : Ephraim also

is the strength of my head. 9. Judah is my law-giver, Moab is my wash-pot.

over Edom will I cast out my shoe ; up-on Phil-is-ti-a will I tri-umph.

10. Who will lead me into the strong ci-ty : and who will bring me in-to E-dom?

11. Hast not thou forsaken us, O God : and wilt not thou, O God, go forth

with our hosts? 12. O help us a-gainst the en-e-my : for vain is the

help of man. 13. Through God we shall do great acts : and it is he that shall

tread down our en-e-mies. Glory be to the Father, and to the Son : and to

the Ho-ly Ghost; As it was in the beginning, is now, and ever shall be :

world with-out end. A-men.

WHIT-SUNDAY.
MORNING PRAYER.

PSALM XLVIII.—*Magnus Dominus.*

8th Tone, 1st Ending.

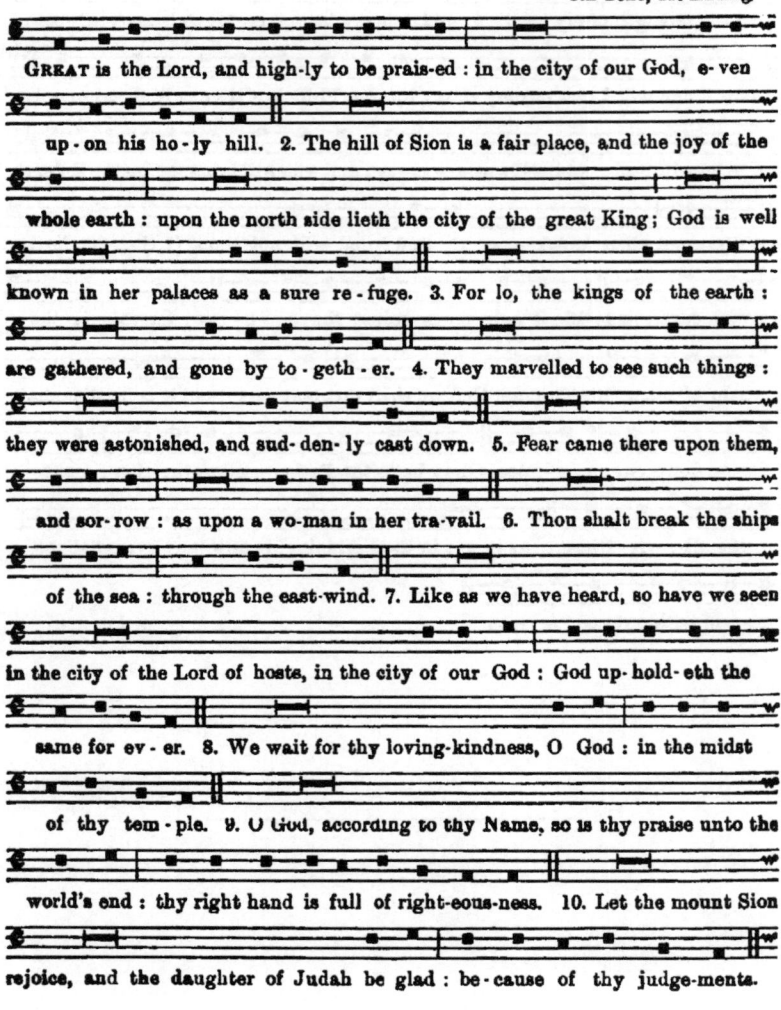

GREAT is the Lord, and high-ly to be prais-ed : in the city of our God, e- ven up - on his ho - ly hill. 2. The hill of Sion is a fair place, and the joy of the whole earth : upon the north side lieth the city of the great King; God is well known in her palaces as a sure re - fuge. 3. For lo, the kings of the earth : are gathered, and gone by to - geth - er. 4. They marvelled to see such things : they were astonished, and sud- den- ly cast down. 5. Fear came there upon them, and sor- row : as upon a wo-man in her tra-vail. 6. Thou shalt break the ships of the sea : through the east-wind. 7. Like as we have heard, so have we seen in the city of the Lord of hosts, in the city of our God : God up- hold- eth the same for ev - er. 8. We wait for thy loving-kindness, O God : in the midst of thy tem - ple. 9. O God, according to thy Name, so is thy praise unto the world's end : thy right hand is full of right-eous-ness. 10. Let the mount Sion rejoice, and the daughter of Judah be glad : be - cause of thy judge-ments.

WHIT-SUNDAY—MORNING.

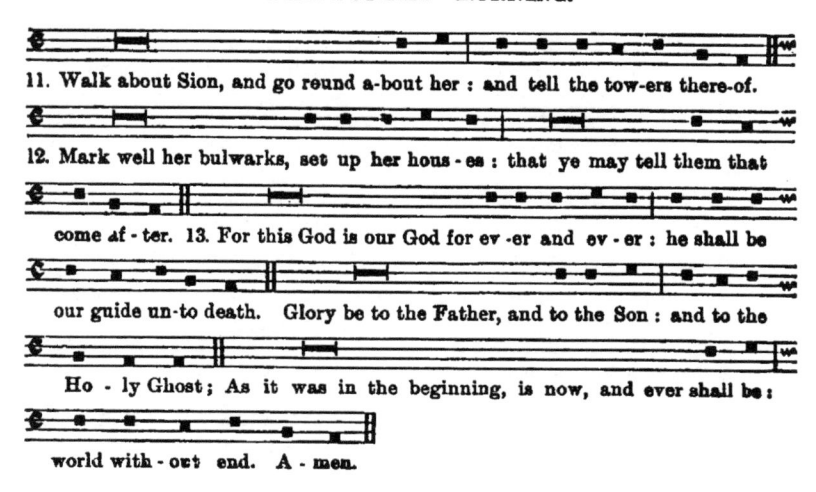

11. Walk about Sion, and go round a-bout her : and tell the tow-ers there-of.

12. Mark well her bulwarks, set up her hous-es : that ye may tell them that come af-ter. 13. For this God is our God for ev-er and ev-er : he shall be our guide un-to death. Glory be to the Father, and to the Son : and to the Ho-ly Ghost; As it was in the beginning, is now, and ever shall be: world with-out end. A-men.

PSALM LXVIII.—*Exurgat Deus.*

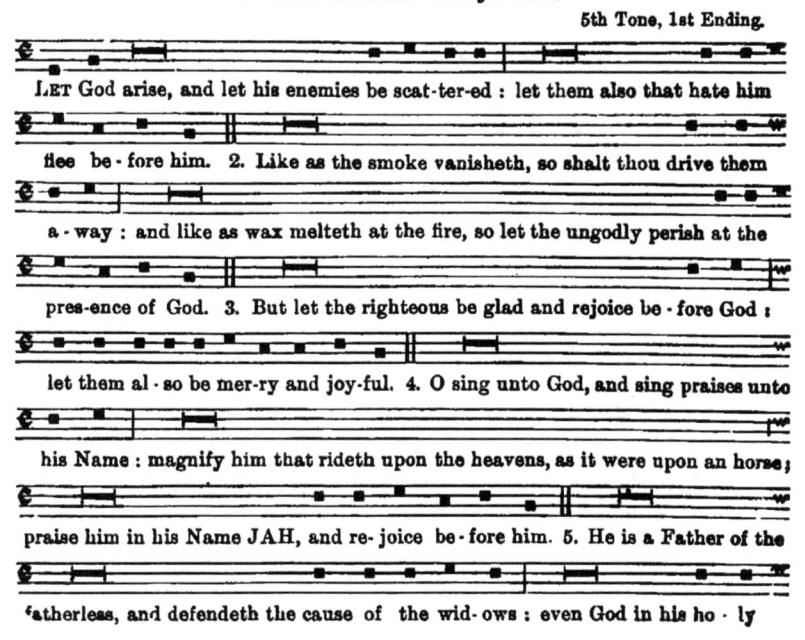

5th Tone, 1st Ending.

LET God arise, and let his enemies be scat-ter-ed : let them also that hate him flee be-fore him. 2. Like as the smoke vanisheth, so shalt thou drive them a-way : and like as wax melteth at the fire, so let the ungodly perish at the pres-ence of God. 3. But let the righteous be glad and rejoice be-fore God : let them al-so be mer-ry and joy-ful. 4. O sing unto God, and sing praises unto his Name : magnify him that rideth upon the heavens, as it were upon an horse; praise him in his Name JAH, and re-joice be-fore him. 5. He is a Father of the fatherless, and defendeth the cause of the wid-ows : even God in his ho-ly

PROPER PSALMS.

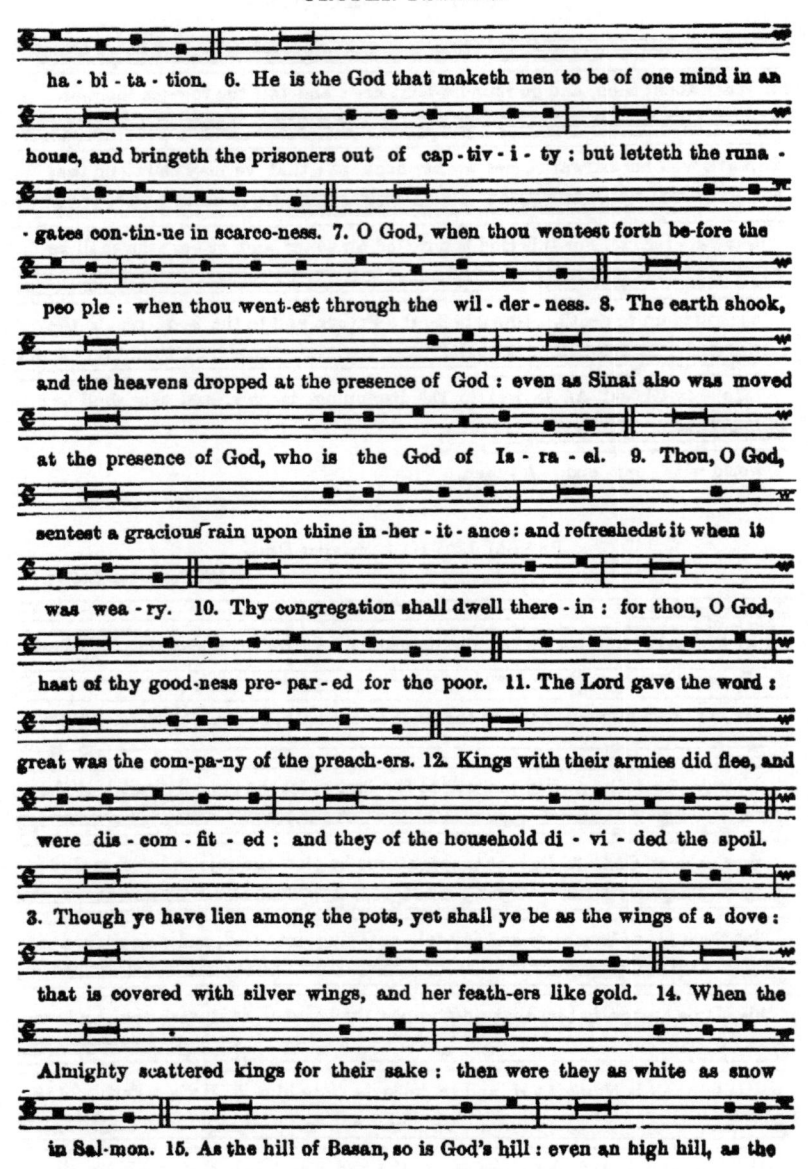

ha - bi - ta - tion. 6. He is the God that maketh men to be of one mind in an house, and bringeth the prisoners out of cap-tiv-i-ty : but letteth the runa - gates con-tin-ue in scarce-ness. 7. O God, when thou wentest forth be-fore the peo ple : when thou went-est through the wil - der - ness. 8. The earth shook, and the heavens dropped at the presence of God : even as Sinai also was moved at the presence of God, who is the God of Is - ra - el. 9. Thou, O God, sentest a gracious rain upon thine in -her - it - ance : and refreshedst it when it was wea - ry. 10. Thy congregation shall dwell there - in : for thou, O God, hast of thy good-ness pre-par-ed for the poor. 11. The Lord gave the word : great was the com-pa-ny of the preach-ers. 12. Kings with their armies did flee, and were dis - com - fit - ed : and they of the household di - vi - ded the spoil. 3. Though ye have lien among the pots, yet shall ye be as the wings of a dove : that is covered with silver wings, and her feath-ers like gold. 14. When the Almighty scattered kings for their sake : then were they as white as snow in Sal-mon. 15. As the hill of Basan, so is God's hill : even an high hill, as the

WHIT-SUNDAY—MORNING.

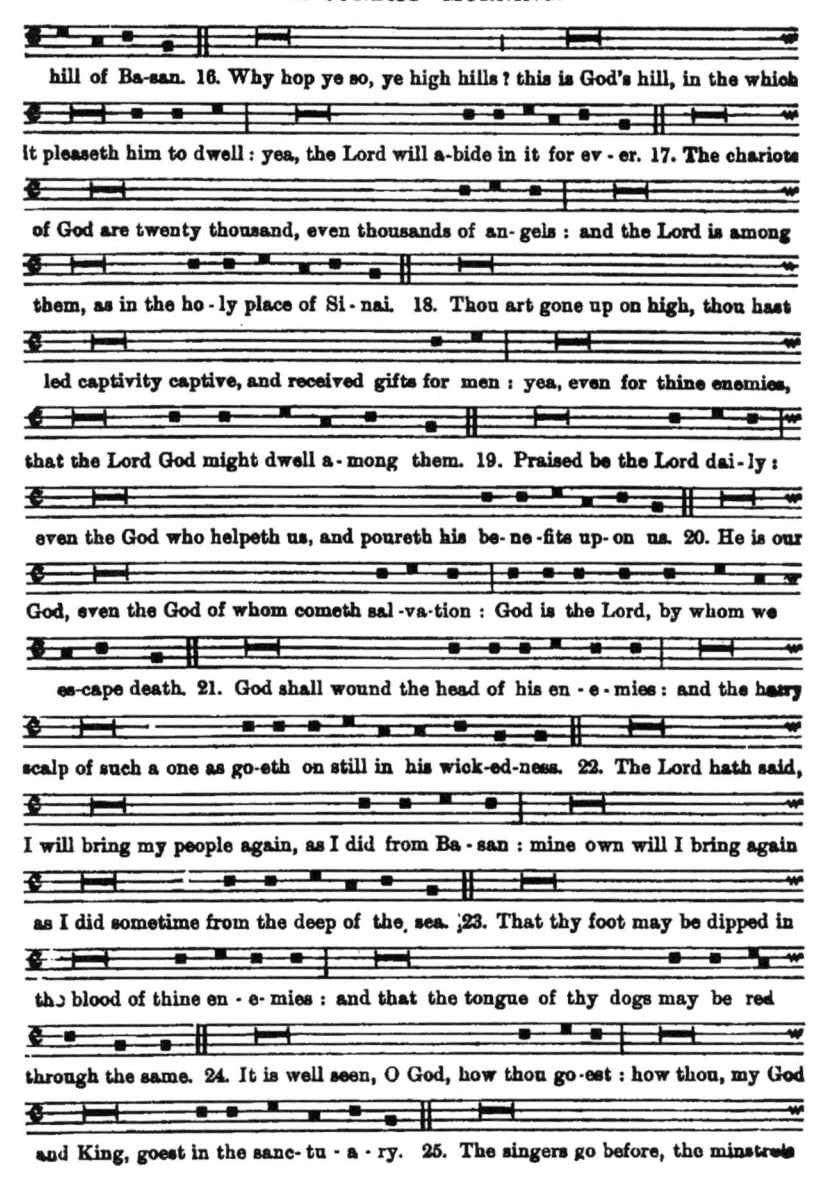

hill of Ba-san. 16. Why hop ye so, ye high hills? this is God's hill, in the which it pleaseth him to dwell: yea, the Lord will a-bide in it for ev-er. 17. The chariots of God are twenty thousand, even thousands of an-gels: and the Lord is among them, as in the ho-ly place of Si-nai. 18. Thou art gone up on high, thou hast led captivity captive, and received gifts for men: yea, even for thine enemies, that the Lord God might dwell a-mong them. 19. Praised be the Lord dai-ly: even the God who helpeth us, and poureth his be-ne-fits up-on us. 20. He is our God, even the God of whom cometh sal-va-tion: God is the Lord, by whom we es-cape death. 21. God shall wound the head of his en-e-mies: and the hairy scalp of such a one as go-eth on still in his wick-ed-ness. 22. The Lord hath said, I will bring my people again, as I did from Ba-san: mine own will I bring again as I did sometime from the deep of the sea. 23. That thy foot may be dipped in the blood of thine en-e-mies: and that the tongue of thy dogs may be red through the same. 24. It is well seen, O God, how thou go-est: how thou, my God and King, goest in the sanc-tu-a-ry. 25. The singers go before, the minstrels

PROPER PSALMS.

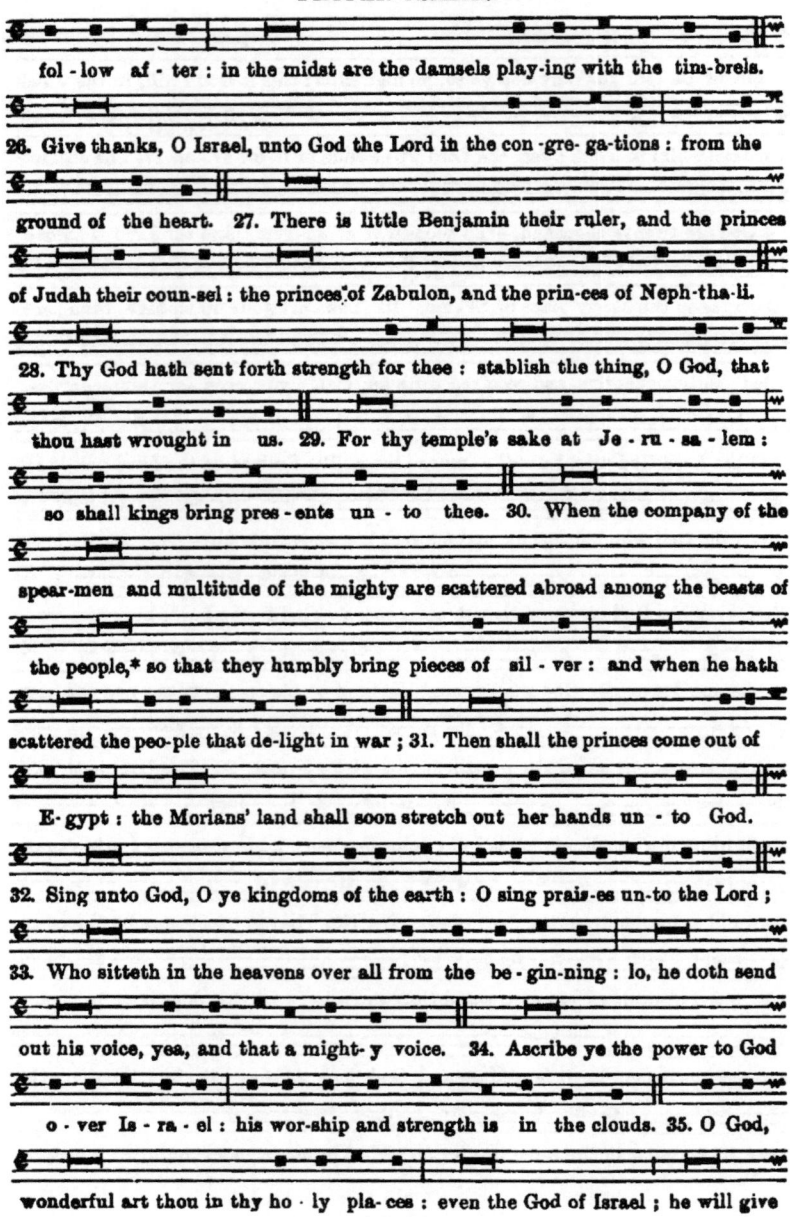

fol-low af-ter : in the midst are the damsels play-ing with the tim-brels.

26. Give thanks, O Israel, unto God the Lord in the con-gre-ga-tions : from the ground of the heart. 27. There is little Benjamin their ruler, and the princes of Judah their coun-sel : the princes of Zabulon, and the prin-ces of Neph-tha-li. 28. Thy God hath sent forth strength for thee : stablish the thing, O God, that thou hast wrought in us. 29. For thy temple's sake at Je-ru-sa-lem : so shall kings bring pres-ents un-to thee. 30. When the company of the spear-men and multitude of the mighty are scattered abroad among the beasts of the people,* so that they humbly bring pieces of sil-ver : and when he hath scattered the peo-ple that de-light in war ; 31. Then shall the princes come out of E-gypt : the Morians' land shall soon stretch out her hands un-to God. 32. Sing unto God, O ye kingdoms of the earth : O sing prais-es un-to the Lord ; 33. Who sitteth in the heavens over all from the be-gin-ning : lo, he doth send out his voice, yea, and that a might-y voice. 34. Ascribe ye the power to God o-ver Is-ra-el : his wor-ship and strength is in the clouds. 35. O God, wonderful art thou in thy ho-ly pla-ces : even the God of Israel ; he will give

WHIT-SUNDAY—EVENING.

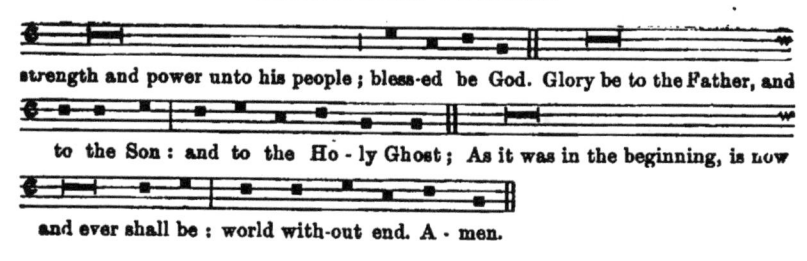

strength and power unto his people ; bless-ed be God. Glory be to the Father, and to the Son : and to the Ho - ly Ghost ; As it was in the beginning, is now and ever shall be : world with-out end. A - men.

EVENING PRAYER.

PSALM CIV.—*Benedic, anima mea.*

3rd Tone, 2nd Ending.

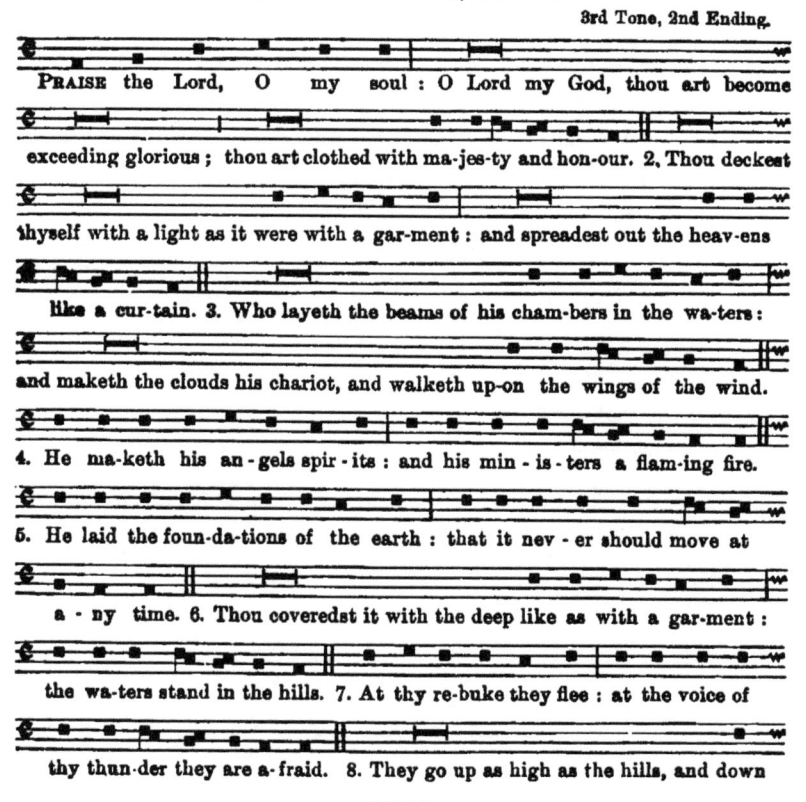

PRAISE the Lord, O my soul : O Lord my God, thou art become exceeding glorious ; thou art clothed with ma-jes-ty and hon-our. 2. Thou deckest thyself with a light as it were with a gar-ment : and spreadest out the heav-ens like a cur-tain. 3. Who layeth the beams of his cham-bers in the wa-ters : and maketh the clouds his chariot, and walketh up-on the wings of the wind. 4. He ma-keth his an-gels spir-its : and his min - is - ters a flam-ing fire. 5. He laid the foun-da-tions of the earth : that it nev - er should move at a - ny time. 6. Thou coveredst it with the deep like as with a gar-ment : the wa-ters stand in the hills. 7. At thy re-buke they flee : at the voice of thy thun-der they are a-fraid. 8. They go up as high as the hills, and down

PROPER PSALMS.

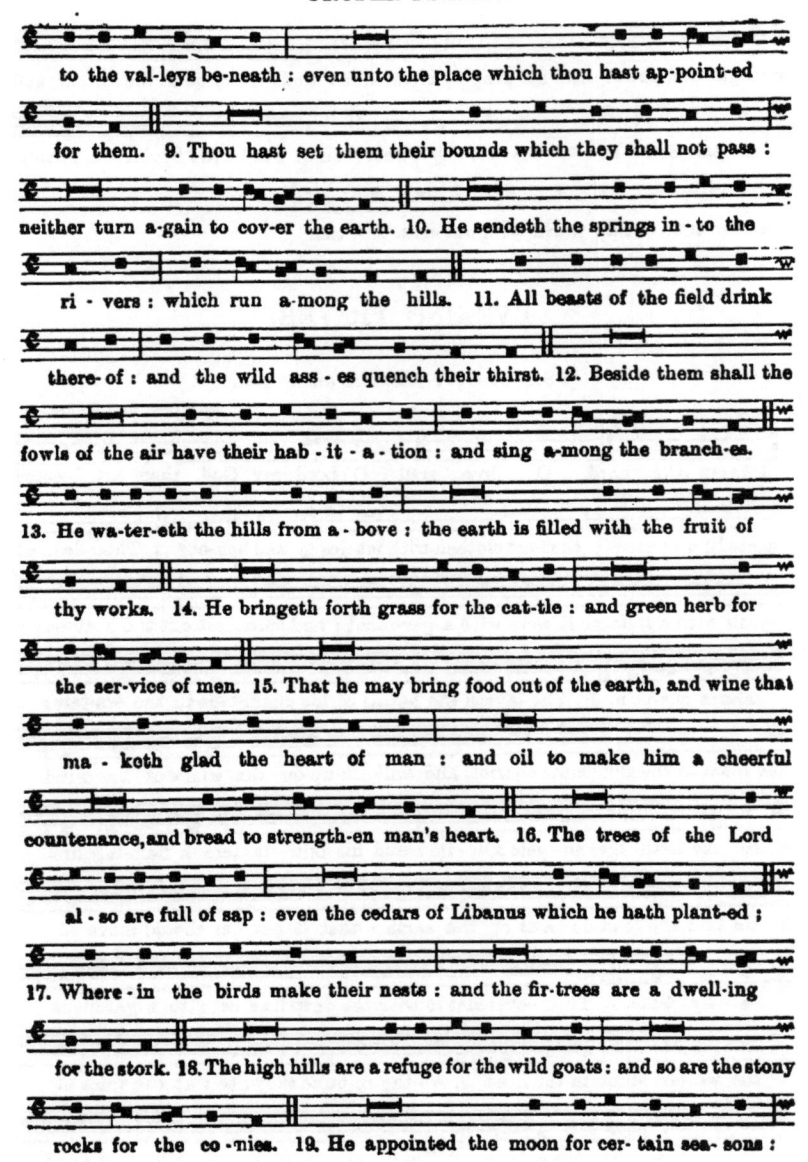

to the val-leys be-neath : even unto the place which thou hast ap-point-ed for them. 9. Thou hast set them their bounds which they shall not pass : neither turn a-gain to cov-er the earth. 10. He sendeth the springs in - to the ri - vers : which run a-mong the hills. 11. All beasts of the field drink there- of : and the wild ass - es quench their thirst. 12. Beside them shall the fowls of the air have their hab - it - a - tion : and sing a-mong the branch-es. 13. He wa-ter-eth the hills from a - bove : the earth is filled with the fruit of thy works. 14. He bringeth forth grass for the cat-tle : and green herb for the ser-vice of men. 15. That he may bring food out of the earth, and wine that ma - keth glad the heart of man : and oil to make him a cheerful countenance, and bread to strength-en man's heart. 16. The trees of the Lord al - so are full of sap : even the cedars of Libanus which he hath plant-ed ; 17. Where - in the birds make their nests : and the fir-trees are a dwell-ing for the stork. 18. The high hills are a refuge for the wild goats : and so are the stony rocks for the co - nies. 19. He appointed the moon for cer- tain sea- sons :

WHIT-SUNDAY—EVENING.

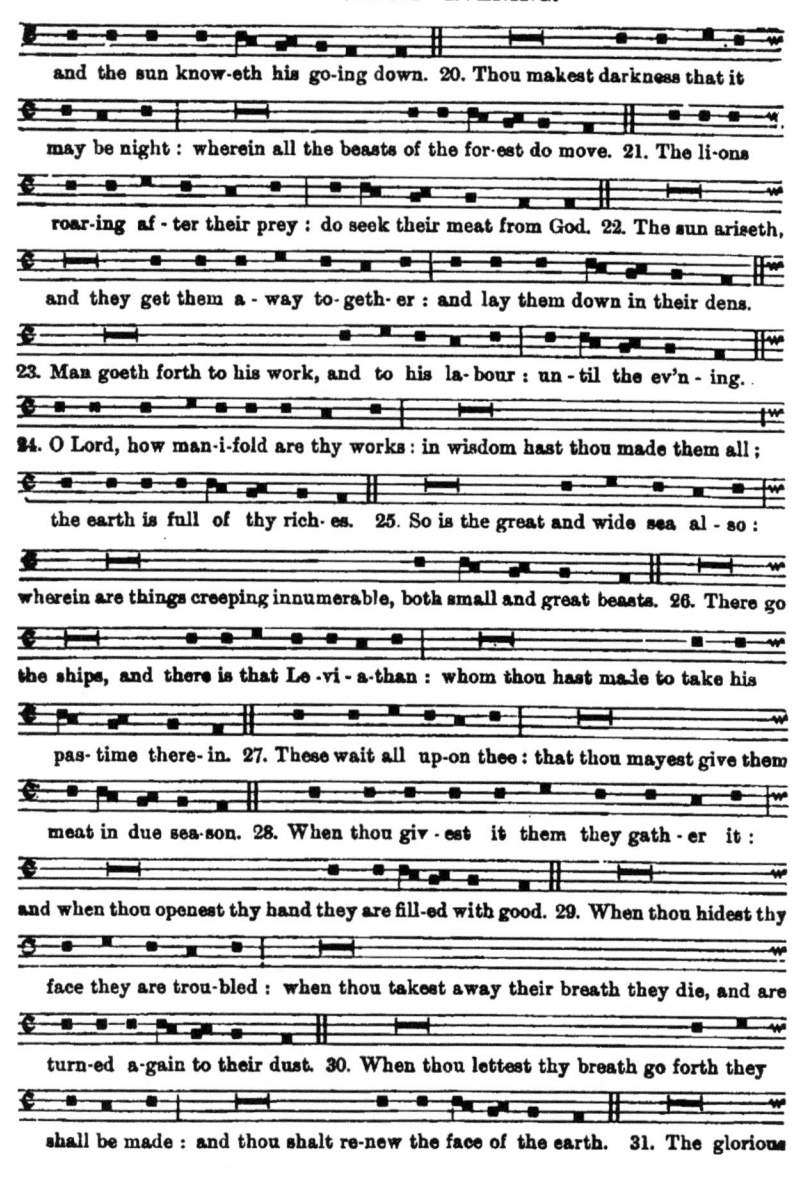

and the sun know-eth his go-ing down. 20. Thou makest darkness that it

may be night : wherein all the beasts of the for-est do move. 21. The li-ons

roar-ing af - ter their prey : do seek their meat from God. 22. The sun ariseth,

and they get them a - way to-geth- er : and lay them down in their dens.

23. Man goeth forth to his work, and to his la- bour : un - til the ev'n - ing.

24. O Lord, how man-i-fold are thy works : in wisdom hast thou made them all ;

the earth is full of thy rich- es. 25. So is the great and wide sea al - so :

wherein are things creeping innumerable, both small and great beasts. 26. There go

the ships, and there is that Le -vi - a-than : whom thou hast made to take his

pas- time there- in. 27. These wait all up-on thee : that thou mayest give them

meat in due sea-son. 28. When thou giv - est it them they gath - er it :

and when thou openest thy hand they are fill-ed with good. 29. When thou hidest thy

face they are trou-bled : when thou takest away their breath they die, and are

turn-ed a-gain to their dust. 30. When thou lettest thy breath go forth they

shall be made : and thou shalt re-new the face of the earth. 31. The glorious

PROPER PSALMS.

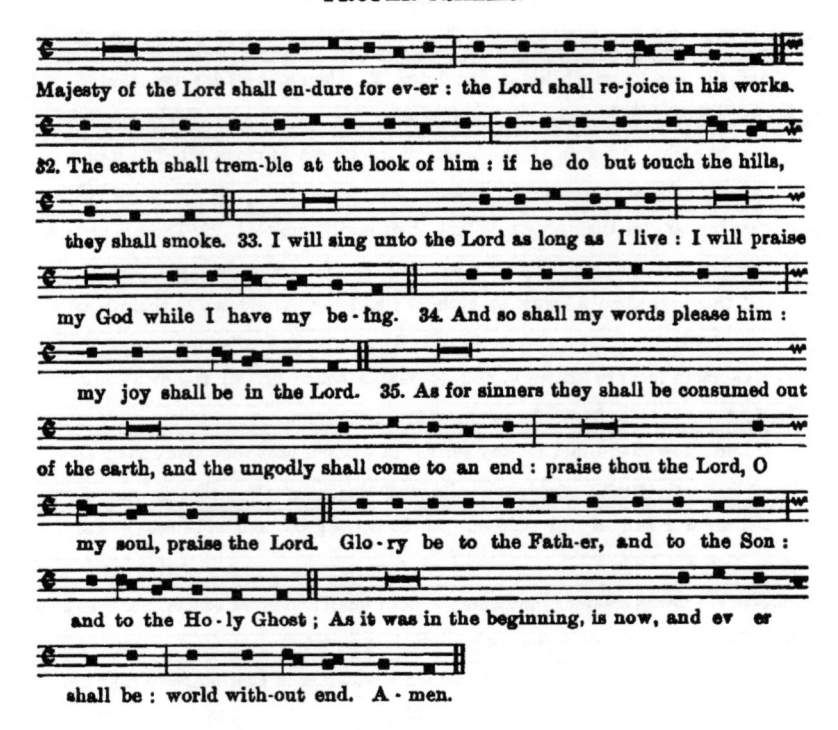

Majesty of the Lord shall en-dure for ev-er : the Lord shall re-joice in his works.

32. The earth shall trem-ble at the look of him : if he do but touch the hills,

they shall smoke. 33. I will sing unto the Lord as long as I live : I will praise

my God while I have my be-ing. 34. And so shall my words please him :

my joy shall be in the Lord. 35. As for sinners they shall be consumed out

of the earth, and the ungodly shall come to an end : praise thou the Lord, O

my soul, praise the Lord. Glo-ry be to the Fath-er, and to the Son :

and to the Ho-ly Ghost ; As it was in the beginning, is now, and ev er

shall be : world with-out end. A-men.

PSALM CXLV.—*Exaltabo te, Deus.*

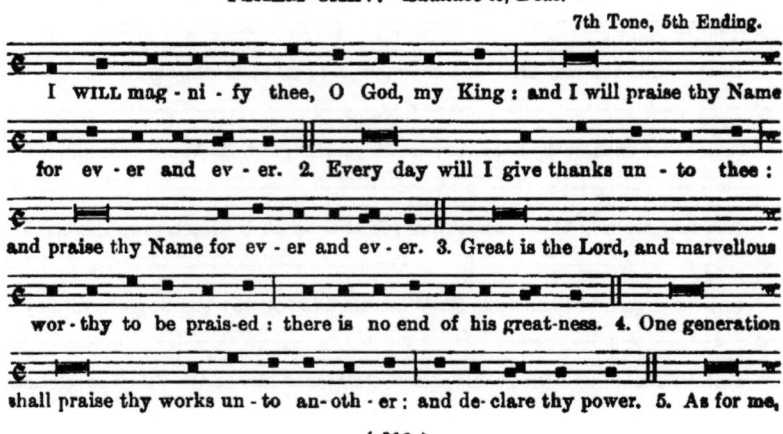

7th Tone, 5th Ending.

I WILL mag-ni-fy thee, O God, my King : and I will praise thy Name

for ev-er and ev-er. 2. Every day will I give thanks un-to thee :

and praise thy Name for ev-er and ev-er. 3. Great is the Lord, and marvellous

wor-thy to be prais-ed : there is no end of his great-ness. 4. One generation

shall praise thy works un-to an-oth-er : and de-clare thy power. 5. As for me,

WHIT-SUNDAY—EVENING.

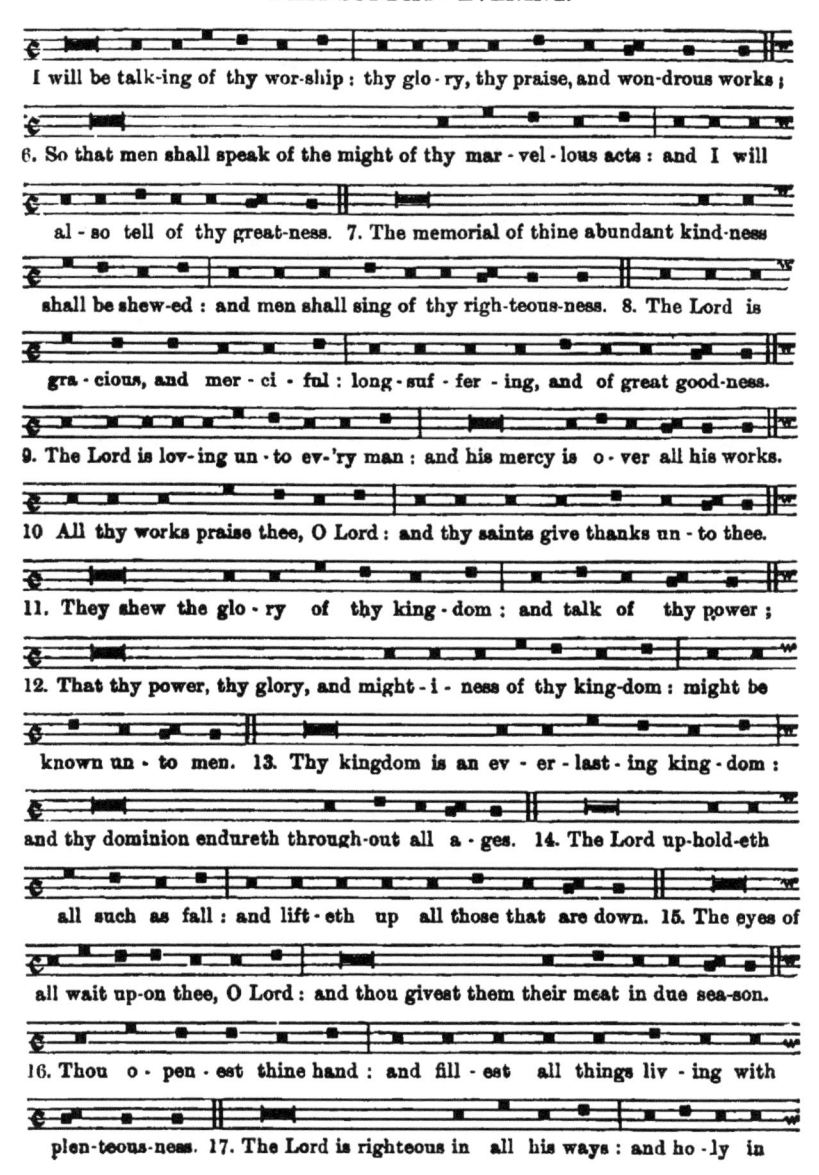

I will be talk-ing of thy wor-ship : thy glo - ry, thy praise, and won-drous works ;

6. So that men shall speak of the might of thy mar - vel - lous acts : and I will

al - so tell of thy great-ness. 7. The memorial of thine abundant kind-ness

shall be shew-ed : and men shall sing of thy righ-teous-ness. 8. The Lord is

gra - cious, and mer - ci - ful : long - suf - fer - ing, and of great good-ness.

9. The Lord is lov-ing un - to ev-'ry man ; and his mercy is o - ver all his works.

10 All thy works praise thee, O Lord : and thy saints give thanks un - to thee.

11. They shew the glo - ry of thy king - dom : and talk of thy power ;

12. That thy power, thy glory, and might - i - ness of thy king-dom : might be

known un - to men. 13. Thy kingdom is an ev - er - last - ing king - dom :

and thy dominion endureth through-out all a - ges. 14. The Lord up-hold-eth

all such as fall : and lift - eth up all those that are down. 15. The eyes of

all wait up-on thee, O Lord : and thou givest them their meat in due sea-son.

16. Thou o - pen - est thine hand : and fill - est all things liv - ing with

plen-teous-ness. 17. The Lord is righteous in all his ways : and ho - ly in

PROPER PSALMS.

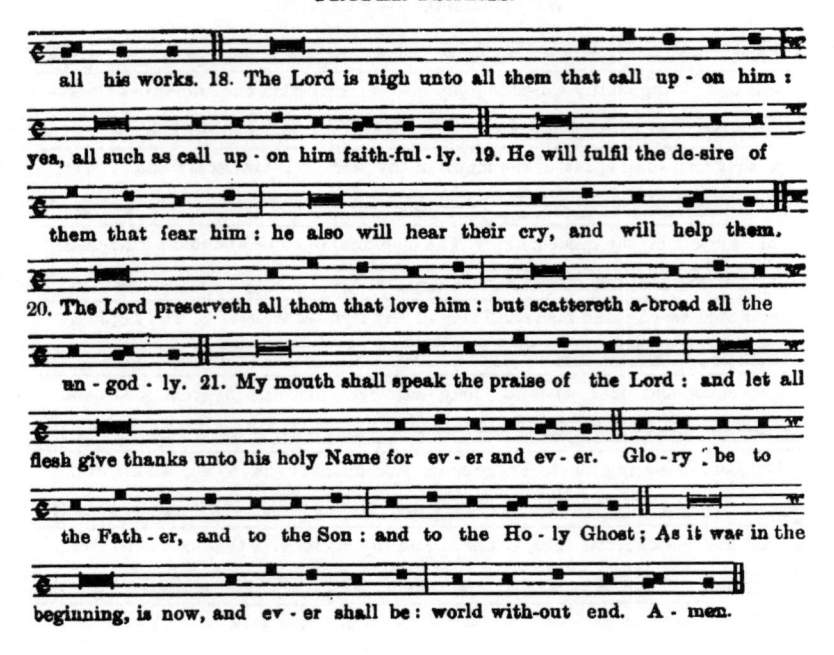

all his works. 18. The Lord is nigh unto all them that call up-on him:
yea, all such as call up-on him faith-ful-ly. 19. He will fulfil the de-sire of
them that fear him: he also will hear their cry, and will help them.
20. The Lord preserveth all them that love him: but scattereth a-broad all the
un-god-ly. 21. My mouth shall speak the praise of the Lord: and let all
flesh give thanks unto his holy Name for ev-er and ev-er. Glo-ry be to
the Fath-er, and to the Son: and to the Ho-ly Ghost; As it was in the
beginning, is now, and ev-er shall be: world with-out end. A-men.

Lightning Source UK Ltd.
Milton Keynes UK
UKHW021250020320
359621UK00008B/2253